PENGUIN BO

REVOLUT

GW00363527

Tim Harris has spent much of his
re-imagining late Stuart Britain. His fascination with the growth of
popular politics, mass journalism and crowds has been expressed in a
number of groundbreaking books, including *London Crowds in the
Reign of Charles II* and *Politics under the Late Stuarts*. He taught
for some years at Emmanuel College, Cambridge, but has since 1986
taught at Brown University, Rhode Island, where he is now Munro-
Goodwin-Wilkinson Professor in European History.

In 2005 he published the widely praised *Restoration: Charles II and
His Kingdoms, 1660–1685*, which is a prelude to the current book.
Restoration won the 2006 John Ben Snow Prize.

James II, by an unknown artist, c. 1690

TIM HARRIS

Revolution

The Great Crisis of the British Monarchy,
1685–1720

PENGUIN BOOKS

PENGUIN BOOKS

Published by the Penguin Group
Penguin Books Ltd, 80 Strand, London WC2R ORL, England
Penguin Group (USA) Inc., 375 Hudson Street, New York, New York 10014, USA
Penguin Group (Canada), 90 Eglinton Avenue East, Suite 700, Toronto, Ontario, Canada M4P 2Y3
(a division of Pearson Penguin Canada Inc.)
Penguin Ireland, 25 St Stephen's Green, Dublin 2, Ireland (a division of Penguin Books Ltd)
Penguin Group (Australia), 250 Camberwell Road,
Camberwell, Victoria 3124, Australia (a division of Pearson Australia Group Pty Ltd)
Penguin Books India Pvt Ltd, 11 Community Centre, Panchsheel Park, New Delhi – 110 017, India
Penguin Group (NZ), 67 Apollo Drive, Mairangi Bay, Auckland 1310, New Zealand
(a division of Pearson New Zealand Ltd)
Penguin Books (South Africa) (Pty) Ltd, 24 Sturdee Avenue,
Rosebank, Johannesburg 2196, South Africa

Penguin Books Ltd, Registered Offices: 80 Strand, London WC2R ORL, England

www.penguin.com

First published by Allen Lane 2006
Published in Penguin Books 2007
1

Copyright © Tim Harris, 2006
All rights reserved

The moral right of the author has been asserted

Set in Adobe Sabon
by Palimpsest Book Production Limited, Grangemouth, Stirlingshire
Printed in England by Clays Ltd, St Ives plc

Except in the United States of America, this book is sold subject
to the condition that it shall not, by way of trade or otherwise, be lent,
re-sold, hired out, or otherwise circulated without the publisher's
prior consent in any form of binding or cover other than that in
which it is published and without a similar condition including this
condition being imposed on the subsequent purchaser

ISBN: 978-1-410-16523-7

For Mark and John

Contents

List of Illustrations

N

Berwick-upon-Tweed

NORTHUMB
Newcastle upon Tyne
• Durham
CUMB   DURHAM

WESTMLD

NORTH SEA

YORKS

IRISH SEA

• York
• Leeds   • Hull

LANCS
Manchester •
Prescot •   • Sheffield
CHESHIRE   LINCS
FLINT   • Chester   DERBYS   • Lincoln
ANGLESEY
CAERN   DENB   NOTTS
DENB
MERION   Derby • • Nottingham
STAFFS   King's Lynn   Great Yarmouth
MONT   SALOP Shrewsbury • Stafford • LEICS RUT-   NORFOLK   • Norwich
CARD   RADNOR   Wolverhampton • LAND
Birmingham •   Leicester •
WARKS   • Coventry   NORTHANTS   HUNTS
PEMB   CARM   HEREFS WORCS • Worcester   Newmarket   SUFFOLK
BRECON   • Hereford WORCS   Northampton • CAMBS • Bury St Edmunds
GLAM   MON   GLOUCS OXON • Banbury   BEDS Cambridge •   • Ipswich
Gloucester •   Sudbury •
• Bristol   Oxford • BUCKS HERTS   Newport • • Colchester
Bath •   Aylesbury •   ESSEX
SOM   WILTS   BERKS • Reading   London • MDX
• Wells   Southwark • • Rochester
Bridgwater • ×Sedgemoor Salisbury •   SURREY   Chatham • • Canterbury
Taunton •   HANTS   KENT   • Dover
• Winchester   SUSSEX
DEVON   DORSET   • Chichester • Lewes
Exeter • Lyme • Dorchester   Portsmouth •
Regis Weymouth
CORNWALL
Saltash •   ENGLISH CHANNEL
• Brixham
Plymouth •

0   50   100 miles

0   50   100   150 km

N

ORKNEY

SUTHERLAND

CAITHNESS

ROSS

CROMARTY

ELGIN

NAIRN

BANFF

Cromdale ✕

ABERDEEN

● Aberdeen

INVERNESS

KINCARDINE

ANGUS

Killiecrankie ✕

✕ Glencoe

Dunkeld ✕

● Dundee

NORTH SEA

PERTH

Crieff ● Perth

● St Andrews

CLACKMANNAN

FIFE

KINROSS

Stirling ●

Dunfermline ●

DUNBARTON

STIRLING

Dumbarton ●

● Edinburgh

HADDINGTON

RENFREW

● Glasgow

LINLITHGOW

MIDLOTHIAN

BUTE

BERWICKS

Peebles ●

Gordon ●

Berwick-upon-Tweed ●

Irvine ●

LANARK

PEEBLES

Campbeltown ●

Lesmahagow ●

SELKIRK

Ayr ●

ROXBURGH

Cumnock ●

● Sanquhar

IRISH SEA

Ballantrae ●

AYR

DUMFRIES

CROMARTY

KIRCUDBRIGHT

● Dumfries

WIGTOWN

0   50 miles

0   80 km

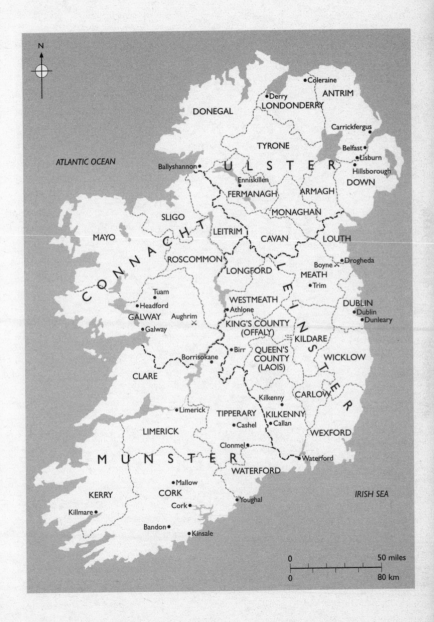

N

ATLANTIC OCEAN

DONEGAL

●Coleraine

●Derry
LONDONDERRY

ANTRIM

Carrickfergus●

TYRONE

Belfast●
●Lisburn

U L S T E R

●Hillsborough

Ballyshannon●

●Enniskillen

DOWN

FERMANAGH

ARMAGH

SLIGO

MONAGHAN

MAYO

C O N N A C H T

LEITRIM

CAVAN

LOUTH

ROSCOMMON

LONGFORD

Boyne ✕ ●Drogheda

MEATH

●Trim

Tuam●

WESTMEATH

●Headford

●Athlone

DUBLIN

GALWAY

Aughrim
✕

●Dublin
●Dunleary

●Galway

KING'S COUNTY
(OFFALY)

KILDARE

Borrisokane●

●Birr

QUEEN'S
COUNTY
(LAOIS)

L E I N S T E R

WICKLOW

CLARE

●Kilkenny

CARLOW

●Limerick

TIPPERARY

KILKENNY

●Cashel

●Callan

WEXFORD

LIMERICK

Clonmel●

M U N S T E R

●Waterford

WATERFORD

●Mallow

KERRY

CORK

●Youghal

Killmare●

Cork●

Bandon●

●Kinsale

IRISH SEA

0   50 miles

0   80 km

Preface

This book is a sequel to my *Restoration: Charles II and His Kingdoms, 1660–1685* (Allen Lane, 2005). It was written first. My study of the Glorious Revolutions in the three kingdoms was initially conceived as one book, and when I first put fingertips to computer keyboard I began with what is here Chapter 1, working my way forward in time, before going back and drafting the earlier sections. When it became apparent that the study was too long to be published as one, the decision was taken to produce two stand-alone books. This study of the Revolutions has therefore been recast with that objective in mind. It does not require a knowledge of *Restoration* to be understood or enjoyed, and every effort has been made to ensure that this book is entirely self-sufficient in that sense. Having said that, the two studies are intended to be complementary, and those who have both the inclination and the time will find that there is much to be gained from reading them together.

Earlier discussions of some of the ideas and arguments developed in this book can be found in 'The People, the Law and the Constitution in Scotland and England: A Comparative Approach to the Glorious Revolution', *Journal of British Studies*, 38 (1999), 28–58; 'Reluctant Revolutionaries? The Scots and the Revolution of 1688–9', in Howard Nenner, ed., *Politics and the Political Imagination in Later Stuart Britain: Essays Presented to Lois Green Schwoerer* (University of Rochester Press, 1997), pp. 97–117; and 'Incompatible Revolutions? The Established Church and the Revolutions of 1688–89 in Ireland, England and Scotland', in Allan I. Macinnes and Jane Ohlmeyer, eds., *The Stuart Kingdoms in the Seventeenth Century* (Four Courts Press, Dublin, 2002), pp. 204–25.

Any previously published material has been reworked and recast when being incorporated into this book. However, I should like to thank the University of Chicago Press (which holds the copyright of my *Journal of British Studies* article), the University of Rochester Press, the Four Courts Press, and the editors of the two respective volumes, for permission to reproduce any material that happens to overlap.

In a project of this size, one inevitably accumulates numerous debts over the years. I benefited enormously from discussions with Lionel Glassey over the significance of the Scottish Claim of Right. Both Allan Macinnes and Jane Ohlmeyer gave me valuable feedback on some of the Scottish and Irish material. Steven Pincus, who is working on his own study of the Glorious Revolution (though in its European context), has been a constant source of inspiration throughout: we came to an agreement whereby I would leave the European context to Steve, and he would leave Scotland and Ireland to me – and if I have learned anything from my work on James II, it is about the importance of not betraying one's friends and of honouring one's own side of the contract. Two of my graduate students – Leigh Yetter and Matt Kadane – gave me the benefit of their expertise on certain specific issues; all of my students (both graduate and undergraduate) have studied this material with me in various ways in classroom situations over the years, and I am deeply indebted to their input and insights.

In addition to the above, I should like to thank Charles Carlton, Tom Cogswell, Brian Cowan, Adam Fox, Mark Goldie, Mark Kishlansky, Peter Lake, Jason McElligott, John Morrill, Kalev Peekna, Lois Schwoerer, Ethan Shagan, Bill Speck, Stephen Taylor and David Underdown, for guidance on sources or discussions about interpretation and approach over the years. I have presented discrete sections of my work at conferences and colloquia across Britain and North America over the last decade or so, and I should like to thank everyone who has attended for their invaluable input; they have had a much greater influence on shaping the final outcome than they would ever have realized. I am particularly grateful to the warm welcome given to me by new friends in Edinburgh and Dublin, people whom I got to meet only after this project was in an advanced stage, but who were incredibly supportive of what I was trying to do. I only hope I have done justice to the integrity of the Irish and Scottish pasts for their own sakes. As with *Restoration*, I need to express my immense gratitude to the publishing team at Penguin, particularly my editor, Simon Winder, his production assistant, Alison Hennessey, my copy-editor, Charlotte Ridings, and my indexer, Caroline Wilding. Simon remains the perfect editor: inspirational and supportive, but with a great critical eye. He certainly made this work much better than it would otherwise have been and brought the best out of me. If only Simon had been able to work with James II, think how different the course of history might have been! However, if Simon had sounded out the views of Charles II or the Duke of Lauderdale beforehand – for which see the Introduction – I suspect he would never have offered James a contract. I certainly doubt whether my agent Clare Alexander would have taken him on with references like those, but I am delighted that she agreed to take me on and I can only hope that the end result repays in some small way all her efforts on my behalf.

My wife, Beth, and my children, Victoria and James, have been of tremendous support to me throughout the years – a necessary distraction to maintain my sanity during the lengthy time it took me to research and write this book (these books). My parents, Audrey and Ron, made much of the research possible by providing a home away from home during my trips to England. Other people who hosted my stays in the 'old country' (as we non-natives say where I live) include my brother and sister-in-law, Kevin and Tina; my sister and brother-in-law, Sarah and Matt; my parents-in-law, John and Grace; Adam Fox and his wife Carolyn; Chris Macleod; and Mark Goldie.

Research for this project would not have been possible without the financial support of a number of institutions. In particular, I should like to record my gratitude for the receipt of fellowships from the National Endowment of the Humanities, the Huntington Library, and the John Simon Guggenheim Memorial Foundation, as well as research support and leave time from Brown University.

I dedicate this book to two inspirational scholars and mentors. The first is Mark Goldie, who taught me when I was an undergraduate in the late 1970s, supervised my Ph.D. in the early 1980s, and has been a valued friend and collaborator ever since. I had always intended to dedicate my big study of the 1680s and the Revolutions to him, as a testimony to my appreciation for all he has done for me over the years; the big study became two, so clearly I must appreciate what he has done an awful lot. The second is John Morrill, who never actually taught me when I was an undergraduate or as a graduate student, but who was the internal examiner for my Ph.D. thesis and who has been a great supporter of all my professional and intellectual endeavours. It was John who first pushed me to explore the three-kingdoms dimension when I announced that I wanted to do a big study of the Glorious Revolution, and it is largely thanks to him that I have developed my fascination for Irish and Scottish history. There is, I appreciate, a certain irony behind an atheistical Protestant dedicating a book on the Glorious Revolution to two Catholics (albeit one lapsed). If I had been around in the late seventeenth century I suspect I would have leaned towards radical Protestant dissent, and perhaps even have been a Monmouth rebel (apart from the cowardice factor, and my reluctance to disobey authority, as my loved ones have been quick to point out). Indeed, a family historian claims that some of my remote ancestors were involved in the Monmouth rebellion (the Selwood branch of the family, for those interested in tracing what happened to them). But then, even the Duke of Monmouth was prepared to extend toleration to Catholics, provided they 'be not found Guilty of Conspiring our destruction'.

In quoting from original sources, I have extended contemporary contractions but otherwise have adhered to the original spelling and capitalization, though I have very occasionally provided modern punctuation to assist in readability. Dates are in old style, although with the new year taken as having started on 1 January (rather than 25 March, as it did at the time).

Introduction

The birth of one's child is supposed to be a joyous occasion – a time to celebrate. So it was for James II. When his second wife, Maria Beatrice Anna Margherita Isabella d'Este (daughter of the Duke of Modena), gave birth to a son on 10 June 1688, James immediately issued proclamations in his three kingdoms of England, Scotland and Ireland announcing the new arrival, urging local magistrates to encourage bonfire celebrations, and setting aside formal days of public thanksgiving.[1] London saw a stunning official pyrotechnic display on 17 July on the River Thames opposite Whitehall, with numerous state-of-the-art devices thought to be the height of ingenuity at the time. Thousands of balloons were launched up into the sky over the Thames, for them to transform themselves magically into various 'figures' as they fell back to earth. Twelve mortars fired grenade shells into the air, which when they exploded revealed 'odd mixtures and shapes', while a figure of Bacchus, representing plenty, discharged eight or nine barrels of combustibles out of its belly. There were also two huge female figures representing 'Fecundity and Loyalty' – somewhat ironically, we can appreciate with hindsight, since events were soon to show that there were reasons to doubt whether the Queen's fecundity and the people's loyalty could go hand in hand. The display cost the court a staggering £25,000.[2]

James himself had particular cause to rejoice. Although he had been married to Mary of Modena since 1673, his consort had struggled to produce the longed-for male heir. There was no doubt that Mary was fertile; indeed, she had numerous pregnancies in the first eleven years of her marriage, but they had all ended either in miscarriage or in children who were short-lived. A son born on 7 November

1677, christened Charles and granted the dukedom of Cambridge, died on 12 December that year. A daughter born in August 1676 who lived until 1681 had been to date Mary's longest-living progeny. She was still childless when she became queen in February 1685, having suffered her latest miscarriage the previous May; although only 26, she was getting on by Stuart child-bearing standards and, given her track record, the signs did not seem encouraging. By now, like many childless couples, the King and Queen were prepared to try anything that might increase their chances of conceiving. A pilgrimage by James to the holy shrine at Holywell in the summer of 1687 while his wife took the waters of Bath seemed to do the trick; rumours of the pregnancy were already circulating by late November, and the following month an official announcement was made.[3]

What is more, the couple got their desired son. The infant, christened James Francis Edward, would take precedence in the succession over James's two daughters – Mary and Anne – from his first marriage, to Anne Hyde. Although women could succeed to the throne in the British kingdoms, in an age of personal monarchy a male ruler was still preferable. However, the importance of the birth went deeper. James was England's first Catholic ruler since Queen Mary (r. 1553–8), and since coming to the throne in February 1685 he had pursued an ambitious policy of trying to increase the religious and civil liberties of his co-religionists across his three kingdoms. James had begun by using his royal prerogative to grant Catholics dispensations from the various laws designed to uphold the Anglican monopoly of office, education and worship, before opting with his Indulgence of 1687 to suspend the entire operation of those laws. He had failed as of yet, however, to persuade parliament in any of his kingdoms to agree to a permanent repeal of the penal legislation against Catholics. Thus whatever benefits Catholics enjoyed, they did so by the grace of the King. James's two daughters (born, as they were, before his own conversion to Catholicism) had been raised Protestants; indeed, his eldest daughter, Mary, was married to the Protestant champion of Europe, the Dutch stadtholder, William of Orange-Nassau. It seemed likely, then, that everything James had achieved for his co-religionists would be undone at Mary's accession. The birth of the Prince of Wales in June 1688 changed matters entirely. The Prince would be raised a Catholic and could be expected to continue his father's policies when he eventually acceded to the throne. Everything James had been working towards now stood the chance of having some long-lasting success.

James Francis Edward was never to inherit the throne. Indeed, his birth was to be the beginning of the end for James II. The Catholic King's policies had been highly controversial and seemed to pose a threat not only to the Anglican ascendancy in England (and the ascendancy of the Episcopalians in Scotland and the Church of Ireland in Ireland) but also to the rule of law. What safeguards were there for subjects' legal liberties if a reigning monarch could decide at will to dispense with or suspend laws that had been passed by parliament? Protestant dissenters, who had benefited just as much as the Catholics from James's efforts to promote greater religious freedom, were equally uneasy about the attempts to set royal prerogative above the law. Unsurprisingly, therefore, James's Protestant subjects, who comprised some 98 per cent of the population of England and Scotland, were far from enthusiastic about the birth of a Catholic male heir; only in Ireland, where three-quarters of the population were Catholic, was there any genuine rejoicing. As the Jacobite *Life of James II* – a retrospective account based in part on James's memoirs and papers – was to put it, 'The birth of the Prince', which gave 'the greatest joy to the King and Queen, and to all those who wished them well', at the same time 'gave the greatest agonys immaginable to the generality of the Kingdom'.[4]

Twenty days after the birth of the Prince of Wales, seven individuals representing discontented elements among the landed aristocracy, the Church, the army and the navy in England – the earls of Devonshire, Danby and Shrewsbury, Bishop Henry Compton of London, Lord Lumley, Edward Russell and Henry Sidney – sent a letter to William of Orange explaining that the vast majority of people were 'dissatisfied with the present conduct of the government' under James II and would join with William, if he were to invade England with sufficient military force.[5] It was an incredible letter – an invitation to a foreign power from high-ranking political and religious figures to invade their own country. It was to set in motion an incredible series of events, which would result in what has come to be known to English history as not 'the Dutch Conquest' but 'the Glorious Revolution' – a revolution seen as glorious, that is, because it rescued England from a popish despot and secured Protestant liberties through a Declaration of Rights (February 1689), subsequently enacted with a few additional safeguards as the Bill of Rights (December 1689). It was also to be a revolution that would have far-reaching consequences – though far from obviously glorious ones – for Scotland and Ireland.

William invaded that autumn with a large, professional army of some 15,000 men. He was taking a huge risk launching a military campaign so late in the season. The sea journey from Holland across to England was likely to be rough at that time of the year, and when William landed he might have to face difficult conditions on the ground. It was undoubtedly a 'perilous and unprecedented venture', and William was prepared for the worst: in advance of his departure he drew up his 'last will and testament' and advised his wife that should he be killed in action she should marry again.[6] William's armada first attempted to set sail on 19 October, but a storm drove it back into the Dutch ports; hemmed in by westerly winds, it was not finally to embark upon its mission until 1 November. The initial plan had been to head for the north-east coast of England, to join up with the northern resistance movement against James spearheaded by Devonshire and Danby, but on the afternoon of the 2nd a ferocious east wind drove the fleet south-west and in sight of the Thames estuary. A hastily convened council of war therefore took the decision to abandon the east coast and head through the straits of Dover into the English Channel; the same 'Protestant wind' that had forced the change of direction also prevented the English fleet from sailing out to cut off the Dutch. After slackening sail on Sunday the 4th, in order to observe not just the Sabbath but also William's thirty-eighth birthday, the Dutch armada was finally to reach Tor Bay (off the south coast of Devon) at about 5 o'clock on the afternoon of 5 November. It being the anniversary of the Gunpowder Plot, the bells were ringing as the Dutch fleet approached land, which William's men 'judged to be a good Omen'; the people of Devon 'came flocking in droves to the side or brow of the Hill to view' the ships, wondering at first whether they might be French, until they saw 'the Standard of the

4

Prince, the Motto of which was, For the Protestant Religion and Liberty', which 'soon undeceived them'.[7] Disembarking at Brixham (on the west side of the bay and one of the three towns, along with Paignton and Torquay, which collectively constitute the area known as Torbay), William made haste for Exeter, the 'capital' of the West, which he entered with little resistance on the 9th. By 18 December he was in London and effectively in control of the government. By 13 February, with James having fled the country, William and his wife Mary were being proclaimed King and Queen.

As far as regime changes go, this one was achieved with remarkable dispatch and, in England at least, remarkably little bloodshed. James had mustered his army on Salisbury Plain to stop William's advance, but facing rebellions in the north of England and desertions within his own military, James panicked. He ordered a retreat from Salisbury on 23 November and returned to London on the 26th. Even William must have been surprised, especially given that James, when Duke of York, had earned himself a reputation as a brave military commander. 'Yet', as one verse satirist rhymed:

> when he [James] went to meet the brave Nassau,
> And all his troops to Salisbury did draw,
> Swearing he'd conquer, or in battle die:
> He basely fled, ere any foe was nigh.[8]

With William continuing to make steady progress on his march eastwards, James began to contemplate fleeing the country. He packed his wife and son off to France on 10 December and decided to follow suit himself in the early hours of the 11th. Even in this last act of cowardice, James was to be unsuccessful. As his boat was taking on ballast at Faversham in Kent for the cross-Channel trip, he was stopped by seamen who recognized the man James was with but not the King himself. Unaware of who they had in their hands (quite literally), they proceeded to strip-search the King to see if he had any treasure secreted about his person. It was only later that they discovered their captive's true identity. Failing at his first attempted flight, James was brought back to London on 16 December, but was deliberately allowed to make a second – and this time successful – escape to France on the 23rd.

It was a truly humiliating experience. James had been brought down without a fight. Not only had he failed to run away but he had been prevented from doing so by people who did not even realize he was their king. Moreover, he had been toppled by his eldest daughter's husband, who was in any case his own nephew, William being the son of the King's older sister, Mary. Indeed, James had been abandoned by his very own children, who seemed decidedly unconcerned by their father's fate. The diarist John Evelyn tells us that it was widely thought Mary 'would have showed some (seeming) reluctancy at least, of assuming her Father's Crowne and made some Apologie, testifying her regret, that he should by his misgovernment necessitate the Nation to so extraordinary a proceeding'. But instead, when the Princess eventually arrived from Holland on 12 February, 'she came into White-hall as to a Wedding, riant and jolly'. When William's chaplain, Gilbert Burnet, asked her 'how it came that what she saw in so sad a revolution, as to her father's person, made not a greater impression on her', she explained that her husband had impressed upon her 'that it was necessary that she should appear at first so cheerful, that nobody might be discouraged by her looks, or be led to apprehend that she was uneasy, by reason of what had been done'. Yet even Burnet, who was also William's chief propagandist at the time, confessed that he 'thought a little more seriousness had done as well, when she came to her father's palace'. James's younger daughter, Anne, had actually fled London in late November to join the rebels in the north of England. As the constitutional crisis unfolded in the early months of 1689, she could be found passing her time playing cards and 'as merry as she used to be'. When the second Earl of Clarendon – a brother of James's first wife, Anne Hyde, who himself was to become a Jacobite – informed her that people 'were extremely troubled to find she seemed no more concerned for her father's misfortune', Anne replied that 'she never loved to do any thing that looked like an affected constraint'. Asked whether 'she thought her father could be justly deposed', she said 'that she was very sorry the King had brought things to the pass they were at, but she was afraid it would not be safe for him ever to return again'.[9]

James's plight in late 1688 contrasts starkly with the enthusiastic reception he had received when he became king less than four years

before. Admittedly, James's very popularity at the time of his accession in February 1685 testified to a recent change in fortune for a man
who had hardly been the darling of the people for much of the reign
of his brother, Charles II (r. 1660–85). As Duke of York, and next-in-
line to the throne by dint of the fact that Charles had failed to produce any legitimate offspring, James had encountered considerable
opposition to his right of succession on the grounds of his religion.
During the Exclusion Crisis of 1679–81, the Whig parliamentary
opposition – the champions of limited monarchy and the rights of
Protestant dissenters – had pushed for legislation to divert the succession in favour of a Protestant heir, claiming that the safety of the
people (*salus populi*) had to come first, and that a Catholic ruler
would mean not just popery but also tyranny and arbitrary government. It was a position which – initially at least – had attracted considerable support among the population at large. However Charles
and his Tory allies had managed to defeat the challenge of the Whigs,
and in the final years of the reign had built up considerable public
support for the Catholic heir – mainly by playing on fears of renewed
civil war (such as England had experienced in the 1640s) should anything be done to tamper with the hereditary succession. When James
was proclaimed king in February 1685, there was extensive rejoicing
in numerous places across England, Wales, Scotland and Ireland, as
large crowds gathered around bonfires to celebrate the news. The
bonfires were followed over the next few weeks by hundreds of loyal
addresses from inhabitants across all of James's dominions, pledging
support for the new monarch. The parliaments which James called to
meet in England and Scotland that spring proved overwhelmingly
loyal bodies, seemingly willing to grant the King whatever he needed
in order to consolidate his position on the throne. And although the
Earl of Argyll and the Duke of Monmouth (the latter being the eldest
illegitimate son of Charles II, and a Protestant) did launch rebellions
in Scotland and England, respectively, in the late spring and early
summer of 1685 in an attempt to topple the new regime, these generated limited support, further confirming the extent to which the
radical Whig challenge had been contained by 1685.

In short, James appeared to be in a strong position at the time of his
accession. His brother had done much to bolster the authority of the

monarchy in his final years – using the law to defeat the political and religious enemies of the crown, enhancing royal control over the judiciary and local government through a series of purges, and making the crown more independent of parliament thanks to a combination of improved royal finances and subsidies from the French king, Louis XIV. People seemed to prefer to have strong monarchy, even if their monarch was Catholic, rather than risk a repeat of the mid-century crisis by tampering with the succession. More than this, people appear to have accepted the Tory-Anglican vision that the monarchy in Britain was divinely ordained and absolute – absolute, that is, in the sense that the king did not share his sovereignty with parliament and could not be resisted by his subjects. In other words, James not only inherited a powerful position but also a considerable amount of goodwill towards him from those who inhabited the dominions over which he was to rule. The fact that his position was to collapse so completely within less than four years, to the extent that he could be forced to flee in the face of a foreign invasion without even being able to engage the enemy in battle, is thus all the more astonishing.

Why, then, did James fall from power so quickly? This is the first main question that this book will seek to address. Was James just a disastrously incompetent ruler, who pursued unpopular and unrealistic policies? What, indeed, was he trying to achieve: a Catholic-style despotism or merely liberty of conscience for religious minorities? Did his position become so untenable that he was essentially brought down by his subjects, with a little help from outside? Or was his position as an absolute monarch in fact so strong that it took a huge invading army from abroad to topple his regime? The second aim of this book is to explore the nature and significance of the Glorious Revolution and the settlement that followed in the wake of James's downfall. Was it a genuine revolution, one that fundamentally changed the nature of the monarchy? Or was it a conservative affair, which merely sought to restore the constitution to what it had been before James II set about trying to extend his prerogative and overturn the rule of law? Did it establish modern-day liberties and give birth to our present system of constitutional monarchy, or did it do nothing of the sort? Did it mark a victory for a particular political interest group, and if so, which one – the Whigs or the Tories – or was it genuinely a bi-partisan affair, one in which the whole nation united to overthrow popery and arbitrary government? And how would our answers to these questions be different if, instead of focusing solely on England, we brought Scotland and Ireland into consideration as well?

James II, it has to be conceded, was not the brightest individual ever to sit on the throne of England (or that of Scotland or Ireland, for that matter). Contemporaries certainly recognized that he had intellectual shortcomings. The Duke of Buckingham once observed to Burnet during Charles II's reign, 'the king could see things if he would; the duke would see things if he could' – a verdict which, Burnet reported, 'was the more severe, because it was true', he himself agreeing that James 'had no true judgment'.[10] Catherine Sedley, one of James's mistresses, when articulating her bemusement at what James saw in any of the women he had sexual relationships with, famously quipped, 'We are none of us handsome, and if we had wit, he has not enough to discover it.'[11] Not that lack of intelligence by itself inevitably dooms a ruler to failure; history affords us plenty of counter-examples, in both hereditary monarchies and modern-day democracies. James's intellectual shortcomings, however, were combined with a stubborn attachment to the Catholic faith and a desire to help his co-religionists at all costs – not in-and-of themselves evil characteristics, but unfortunate ones in a monarch who ruled over an overwhelmingly Protestant (and aggressively anti-Catholic) people who expected their king to protect the Protestant religious establishment. When Charles had sent James to Brussels in the spring of 1679 (essentially to get him out of the way as the crisis over the succession began to unfold in England), James had written that if the occasion presented itself, he hoped God would give him 'his grace to suffer death for the true Catholike religion, as well as Banishment'.[12] It is a remark that encapsulates James's mindset, even if, when push came to shove in 1688, he chose to run away rather than risk death on the battlefield.

Although Charles II did all he could to protect his younger brother's right to the throne, he was under no illusion himself as to whether or not James had the personality to be a successful king: 'My brother will lose his kingdom by his bigotry and his soul for a lot of ugly trollops', he was reputed to have predicted.[13] The Duke of

9

Lauderdale, Secretary of State for Scotland for much of Charles II's reign, observed in the late 1670s that James had 'all that weakness of his father [Charles I] without his strength'. (Given that Charles I had not only brought civil war upon himself in 1642 but suffered execution at the hands of the parliamentary radicals in January 1649, one might wonder what his strengths as king had been.) James loved 'to be serv'd in his own way', Lauderdale continued, and was 'as very a Papist as the Pope himself'. The Scottish Duke had no doubt that this would be James's ruin, predicting that if James 'had the Empire of the whole world he would venture the loss of it, for his ambition is to shine in a red letter [i.e., achieve Catholic sainthood] after he is dead'.[14]

Not surprisingly, James has received a bad press over the generations. The earlier Whig historians, who championed the achievements of the Glorious Revolution, saw James as an evil Catholic despot. Thus the great mid-nineteenth-century historian Thomas Babington Macaulay condemned James as a 'tyrant' in pursuit of an 'insane policy', which was 'to promote the interest of his Church by violating the fundamental laws of his kingdom'.[15] Similarly Macaulay's great-nephew, G. M. Trevelyan, writing on the eve of World War II, argued that 'in his desire to restore Romanism in England' James 'found it necessary to become an absolute monarch like the other Princes of Europe'; he established 'a large army, such as neither the Tudors nor his father or brother had ever commanded in time of peace'; and he 'proceeded to break law on law'.[16] So irrational did James's policies seem that historians not bent on seeing sinister motives behind his actions assumed the King was afflicted by some sort of mental illness. Thus F. C. Turner, in his classic biography published in 1948, suggested that by the time of his accession James 'was suffering from premature mental decline', possibly the result of an infection incurred 'in the sexual excesses of his youth . . . which had resulted in a fairly common mental disease'.[17]

Modern scholars have tried to give a more balanced picture of the man. An important study of the Glorious Revolution that appeared in 1972 maintained that James was pursuing a realistic policy that could have succeeded: no madman in pursuit of an insane policy here. James might have been trying 'to emulate most European sovereigns, using

the contemporarily fashionable and effective methods of absolutism',
but given the way that Restoration politics worked, there was little his
opponents could do to obstruct him; 'it needed William's invasion to
wreck' James's policies.[18] The fullest and most scholarly modern biography of James II, which has enjoyed several reprintings since its first
publication in 1978, not only insists that 'James was not a wicked
man' but also, in fact, that James did not wish to 'establish an absolutism like that of Louis XIV' in France. James did not 'set out to
undermine the English constitution', 'destroy the laws', or impose 'his
religious views on others by force'; his aim, rather, was merely to put
'Catholics on an equal footing with Protestants, by allowing them to
worship freely and to hold public office'.[19] There are signs, however,
that historians are beginning to react against too indulgent a view.
Although James might not have been the popish despot of Whig legend, he was certainly seen by his contemporaries as 'a bigoted Papist',
a recent study of James II reminds us, and one moreover who 'did
increase the powers of the Crown independently of using them to promote toleration'.[20]

Whatever James's personal qualities as king, most scholars seem to
agree that he might well have got away with what he was trying to
achieve were it not for the intervention of William of Orange. As
Trevelyan maintained all those years ago, James was so powerful 'that
his subjects only got the better of him by calling in foreign arms to
their aid'.[21] One modern-day historian, who has examined the
Glorious Revolution from the Dutch perspective, has asserted that
there could not 'have been a Revolution, or anything remotely like
one, without the armed intervention of the Prince of Orange. It was
the Prince who . . . shattered James' power and destroyed his previously considerable military might.'[22] It is true that historians have recognized that William's success was dependent upon obtaining a
modicum of support among James's disillusioned subjects, particularly those of the upper classes. Nevertheless, received wisdom has
tended to regard the Revolution of 1688 – that is, the overthrow of
James II, as distinct from the settlement reached afterwards – as
having been brought about essentially by external forces, rather than
internal ones. To quote the leading modern scholar of British foreign
relations in this period, 'James's fall occurred as the result of an

external invasion of England'; it should be seen not as an 'episode of domestic political turmoil', like the Great Rebellion against Charles I, but more 'as an instance of what had last been seriously attempted a century earlier', by the Spanish Armada of 1588.[23] As the author of one recent influential textbook has put it, it was William of Orange, 'and he alone, who made possible one of the few great revolutions between the seventeenth and the twentieth centuries which was first and foremost an invasion and only very secondarily a rebellion'.[24] If it was William alone who made the Revolution possible, and if the Revolution was not the product of domestic political turmoil, then the conclusion is obvious: there is little need to examine domestic politics, whether in turmoil or not, in order to understand why the Revolution happened.

If there is disagreement over how to understand James, there is even more controversy over the significance of the Glorious Revolution. One contemporary described it as 'the greatest revolution that was ever known'.[25] Few would agree with that today. It was, after all, an event fuelled by anti-Catholic bigotry, one that was to lead to a bloody war in Ireland and the setting up of a severe penal code against the majority Catholic population (the implications of which are still with us), and, ultimately, to the loss of political sovereignty for Scotland. To modern scholars it hardly looks like a proper revolution at all, and certainly nothing like the revolutionary upheavals of the mid-seventeenth century, which have more readily attracted the imagination of historians over the last several decades. There might still be some who believe that the Glorious Revolution laid the foundations for Britain's modern system of parliamentary democracy and constitutional monarchy, and for the eventual emergence of Britain as a great power in the eighteenth century and beyond.[26] To many, however, it fell far short of achieving any meaningful political reform and, instead of having a modernizing effect, essentially left England as an *ancien régime* well into the eighteenth (and perhaps even the early nineteenth) century.[27]

The predominant tendency over the generations has been to cast the actual Revolution settlement of 1689 in a conservative light. Both Macaulay and Trevelyan, for example, saw the Revolution as 'defensive', a 'preserving revolution' that sought to vindicate 'ancient rights', the 'spirit' of which 'was the opposite of revolutionary'.[28] Although Macaulay and Trevelyan nevertheless continued to insist that the settlement vindicated Whig principles of limited government, modern scholars have come to see the settlement, and particularly the Declaration of Rights, as more of a compromise between the two parties, designed to appease the concerns of the Tories as much as the Williamite Whigs, and which failed to address the concerns of the more radical Whigs who wanted more far-reaching constitutional change.[29] It is true that there has been some reaction against the conservative take on the Revolution, with some scholars seeking to reinvest the Declaration of Rights with more radical credentials and to see it at least as a qualified victory for Whig principles.[30] Far from all have been convinced, however, and the image of the Glorious Revolution as one of the least revolutionary revolutions in history continues to persist.

The picture would look different, one might think, if Scotland and Ireland were brought into it. The trouble is, modern scholars working on the later seventeenth-century period have largely studied the three kingdoms in isolation from each other, while the Glorious Revolution itself has been treated by historians primarily as an event in English history. Little work has been done on the Revolution in Scotland – we as yet, for example, possess no detailed study of the Claim of Right of 1689, the Scottish equivalent to the Declaration of Rights – and virtually none on the actual reign of James VII (to give James II his Scottish title). In the absence of much in-depth scholarship, Scottish historians have tended to see the Scots as reluctant revolutionaries who simply imported a ready-made revolution from England, even if ultimately the Scots did forge a settlement that was decidedly Whig and Presbyterian.[31] The reign of James II and the subsequent revolution in Ireland has been somewhat better covered, but there has been an understandable tendency to focus on the war between the two kings – James and William – that ensued in the aftermath of James's overthrow in England.[32] As a result, we have been left with a historiography of the Glorious Revolution that has centred predominantly on England, and which by omitting more radical and more bloody developments in James II's other two kingdoms has helped to perpetuate an image of the Glorious Revolution as a rather tame affair. It is hardly surprising that historians see the events of the

1640s and 1650s (which saw civil war, regicide and the setting up of a republic) as the only genuine revolution in English history.[33]

This book will challenge some of our basic assumptions about the reasons for James's fall and the nature of the revolution that ensued. It will show that external factors alone cannot explain why James's regime toppled but that, on the contrary, it was domestic political turmoil that in the main was responsible for bringing James down. It will also argue that it is wrong to see the Glorious Revolution as unrevolutionary in spirit and in outcome. It has been written as a sequel to my *Restoration: Charles II and His Kingdoms*, which explored political developments in England, Scotland and Ireland in the period from 1660 to 1685.[34] Although the two books are intended to stand alone, they are nevertheless complementary, and between them tell the larger story of the fortunes of the Stuart monarchy between the Restoration and the Glorious Revolution. They are also informed by a shared conceptual approach, designed to redress certain limitations in the existing historiography and to afford us fresh insights into the causes, nature and significance of what transpired in 1688–9.

There are three notable respects in which existing historical writing on the reign of James II and the Glorious Revolution remains deficient. First, most studies have been written from the top down, focusing on the political elite and concentrating on events either at court or at Westminster. Although historians have always been aware that there was some popular political agitation in England at the time of the Glorious Revolution, they have remained unsure how to integrate high and low politics into their analyses. Key political agency, in most historical accounts, is afforded to the aristocracy and gentry; if the Glorious Revolution was more than a foreign invasion, it was at most a revolt of the nobility.[35] The present volume argues for the need to set politics in a broader social context – to develop a social history of politics, one which looks at the nature of governance at the local level, pays attention to the importance of public opinion, and recognizes the crucial agency of those below the level of the traditional ruling classes. *Restoration* demonstrated how courting those 'out-of-doors' was a vital factor in Charles II's success in defeating the Whigs and bolstering the authority of the crown in his final years; its findings naturally suggest the need to explore in turn the extent to which

James's ability or inability to carry public opinion with him contributed to the success or failure of what he sought to achieve.

Second, there exists no major modern study of the reign of James II and the Glorious Revolution that offers an integrated analysis of developments in all three kingdoms. Yet the toppling of James II from the throne of England had the inevitable consequence of toppling him from the thrones of Scotland and Ireland; indeed, when William of Orange invaded he came with the explicit intention of rescuing Protestant liberties in Scotland and Ireland as well as in England. The Glorious Revolution was, by definition, a three-kingdoms event, and needs to be studied as such; as we shall see, incorporating Scotland and Ireland into our account provides a markedly different perspective on the significance of the Revolution from that which obtains when we focus on England alone. Moreover, *Restoration* showed how both the government's actions and public reactions to political developments were shaped by an awareness of the fact that the Stuart kings ruled over three kingdoms and not just one. We thus need to explore the extent to which what James sought to achieve, how he sought to achieve it, and how people reacted to what he was trying to achieve, were conditioned by the fact that the King made policy for Scotland and Ireland as well, not just for England.

Third, scholars have, in the main, failed to appreciate the revolutionary significance of 1688–9, largely as a result of their failure to set political developments at this time in their broader social context and three-kingdoms' perspective. This book will show that 1688–9 was genuinely revolutionary, both in the making and in the outcome.

Before proceeding with our account of the reign of James II and the Revolution which brought him down, however, it would be helpful to say a little more about the particular approach adopted and provide some additional context on the precise nature of James II's inheritance.

A SOCIAL HISTORY OF POLITICS

Let us begin by asking why we need a social history of politics. At first glance it might seem logical to assume that in an age of personal monarchy, where rulers laid claim to possessing an absolute authority and where the parliamentary franchise was limited to men of property, a focus on high politics is appropriate. Thus is it not right that we should be looking at the king and his immediate circle of advisers, on the peers and MPs who sat in parliament, and the landed and mercantile elite who held sway at the local level? At most, perhaps, we might need to extend our horizons to include those who had the right to vote in parliamentary elections – the forty-shilling freeholders in the counties and the more well-to-do in the towns, depending upon the particular type of borough franchise.[36] Surely it was these who comprised the political nation; were not the rest of the people, the vast majority of the population, politically excluded?

The seeming logic here quickly falters, however, once we take a closer look at the way in which politics operated in the early modern period. To start with an obvious point, politics is not just about how those with greatest political authority determine policy; it is also about how those responsible for determining policy manage to get their initiatives enforced at the local level. In the seventeenth-century context, this meant in practice relying on a wide range of unpaid agents in the localities, from peers, gentry and wealthy merchants at the top level who served as Lord Lieutenants, deputy Lieutenants, grand jurors, JPs, mayors and common councilmen, down to the men of lesser social standing who served as petty jurors, militiamen, tax-assessors, churchwardens, overseers, vestrymen, constables and other parish and ward officers. Most who served in these lowlier positions would have been men of middling status. However, the middling sort often had no desire to assume the less prestigious or more burdensome local offices – such as that of parish constable – and some of these could, as a result, come to fall on fairly humble types. Recent research has concluded that 'an astonishingly high proportion of early modern people held office'. In much-governed London, one in ten householders held office in any one year in the mid-seventeenth century. Across England and Wales as a whole, about one-twentieth of the adult male population would have held parish office at any one time. Given that many parish offices worked by a system of rotation, with officers serving for a period of one or two years, the proportion of the population who held office over any given decade would have been much higher.[37]

The implications of these findings for the nature of early modern governance are worth contemplating. If the government wanted to enforce the laws against Protestant nonconformists, to take the example of one of the more controversial aspects of government policy in the Restoration period, it needed the cooperation of men below the level of the political elite to arrest and convict offenders. Without the support of parish constables and trial jurors, government policy towards religious dissent could easily become non-effectual – as indeed it did in England during the late 1670s and the beginning of the 1680s.[38]

Furthermore, those who determine policy never work from a blank slate; they have to deal with issues that emerge out of the society they are responsible for governing. Rulers – to state the obvious – rule people, and they have to address problems that are created for them by the people over whom they rule. At the very basic level, all societies need to be policed. In the aftermath of civil war and a period of republican experimentation in government, the restored monarchy was naturally highly concerned about the issue of how a population which had shown itself to be prone to rebellion and a society which had thrown up both political and religious dissidents was to be policed. If this society needed careful policing, who was going to do it: the traditional unpaid agents of law-enforcement in the localities, or a professional force, such as an army? If the latter, where would the money to fund it come from? Would higher taxes be required? How would the army itself be policed? Where would it be garrisoned? Then we have to consider how the people might react to the government's initiatives. Would they accept them and perhaps even welcome them, to the point of actively cooperating in the enforcement of the government's policies? Or would they resent them and do their best to obstruct what the government was trying to do, either passively, through non-compliance, or actively, through open resistance? In other words, would the government's attempt to address the problems of how society was to be policed create more of the very problems it was trying to solve? The point has been made in the abstract. Nevertheless, the issue was a concrete one that needed to be addressed by the governments of both Charles II (as *Restoration* showed) and James II (as the present study will make clear).

Viewed like this, we can see that many more people were drawn into the political process than might at first have been suspected. The views of ordinary people counted to a much greater extent than typically recognized and could be ignored only at the ruler's peril. It was not just that if people were upset by the government's policies they might rise in rebellion, although groups of disaffected people across England, Scotland and Ireland did in fact do this (or else threatened to do this) on a number of occasions during the seventeenth century – not least, of course, during the reign of James II himself! It was also that if the government failed to carry with it the support of enough of the right sort of people – particularly those who were responsible for governance at the local level – then it could find it very difficult to rule effectively. Hence why, in order to understand fully how politics operated in late-seventeenth-century England, Scotland and Ireland, we need to look at much more than the activities and designs of a narrow political elite. We need to appreciate the nature of a particular ruler's inheritance and the problems of governance that the people over which he came to rule presented him with. We have to explore the extent to which the ruler was dependent upon the active cooperation or tacit compliance of ordinary people at the local level to make his policies effective, as well as the extent to which he might be vulnerable to – or able to make himself immune from – public opinion. And we need to understand the strategies he chose to pursue in order to make his will effective, whether they be coercive mechanisms, such as tougher policing or purging from office those who refused to co-operate, or ideological forms of control, such as propaganda designed to convince local office-holders of the wisdom of supporting and carrying out the government's policy.

THE POLITICAL INHERITANCE

If we are going to come to terms with why James II came unstuck so quickly, we need a firm understanding of the nature of his political inheritance. This in turn necessitates reminding ourselves of the particular problems Charles II faced and how he chose to deal with them, so that we can appreciate the precise nature of the situation he bequeathed to his successor and how James II might need to structure his rule if he was to contain those self-same problems that had threatened to destabilize his brother's reign.

The political inheritance of the Restoration monarchy was far from an easy one. Although the vast majority of people across the British Isles welcomed the return of monarchy in 1660, all three kingdoms had been left bitterly scarred by the experiences of civil war and Cromwellian rule in the 1640s and 1650s and it proved difficult to rebuild consensus. In England, there were overlapping political and religious sources of contention. On the political front, some believed that the king shared his sovereignty with parliament (and thus that England was a mixed monarchy, a view seemingly confirmed by the fact that it had been parliament that had called back Charles II), and others that he did not and was in that sense absolute (a view which required attributing the Restoration to God's providence). Both groups acknowledged that the king should, in normal circumstances, rule according to law (though the latter tended to afford the king more licence to abrogate certain laws in times of necessity); they disagreed over the extent to which the king could be held accountable if he did violate the law: for absolutists, the king was accountable to none but God. On the religious front there were three main interest groups: separatists (a smallish minority), who objected to a Church governed by bishops and to many aspects of Anglican worship, who held that the only true Church was a Church of true believers, and thus who naturally favoured liberty of conscience; Presbyterians or old-style Puritans (a much more sizeable group), who would have been prepared to accept a restored Church run by bishops if agreement over certain desired reforms (especially in the Book of Common Prayer) could have been reached that would have allowed them to be accepted within a more broadly defined established Church of England (though they themselves had little desire to see the separatist sects tolerated); and hard-line Anglicans, who believed in strict conformity to a Church of bishops and Prayer Book and were unwilling to grant concessions to either separatists or Presbyterians. Hard-line Anglicans also tended to be the strongest supporters of the royal prerogative, with the Presbyterians and separatists more prone to advocate various styles of limited monarchy.

With regard to the religious settlement, hard-line Anglicans won the day with the passage of the Act of Uniformity in 1662 and the establishment of a fierce penal code designed to punish those who worshipped outside the restored Church of England and to prevent non-Anglicans from holding office. Hence began the dissenting schism in the Church, with those forced out and vulnerable to persecution forming a significant minority – much more than the official government calculation of 5 per cent of the population in 1676, and in some communities as much as 20, 33 or even 40 per cent. (Those of the Roman Catholic faith, by contrast, who remained vulnerable to penal laws passed since the time of the Reformation, by now comprised about 1.2 per cent of the population.)[39] The situation was less clear cut on the political front. Charles II was certainly not as limited a monarch as some might have wished; indeed limitations were ultimately eschewed in 1660 and the Restoration, in that sense, was unconditional. Yet in reality there proved to be both practical and legal limitations to Charles's authority, and when he did try to push the boundaries too far – such as when he issued Declarations of Indulgence in 1662 and 1672 to grant liberty of conscience to both Protestant nonconformists and Catholics by dint of his royal prerogative – he invariably had to back down, not least because of his need to appease parliament in order to obtain grants of taxation. It was only in the 1680s, when the crown found itself freed from dependence upon parliament for ordinary revenue, that Charles II came anywhere close to living up to the rhetoric of Tory-Anglican champions of royal absolutism, and even then he still professed that he was determined to rule by law and to see that the rule of law should run its course. The Restoration monarchy was, however – at least in theory – irresistible. Various statutes passed in the early years of the Restoration required all office-holders in Church and state not only to take the traditional oaths of allegiance and supremacy but also an oath renouncing armed resistance to the king or those commissioned by him. (Similar non-resistance oaths were required of office-holders in Scotland and Ireland.)[40]

Scotland was bedevilled by a bitter religio-political divide between the Presbyterians (who were particularly strong in the Scottish south and west) and Episcopalians (whose stronghold was the north-east lowlands). The Scottish revolution of the late 1630s and early 1640s had seen the radical restructuring of the ecclesiastical and political establishments north of the border, with the government of the Church by bishops overturned and the crown stripped of many royal prerogatives. Support for this agenda had been cemented by the National Covenant of 1638 and the Solemn League and Covenant of 1643 (the latter of which had sought to export the Scottish revolution to England), although most Scottish covenanters did not wish to overthrow Charles I completely and recoiled from the regicide of 1649: their ideal was a covenanted king. There were many champions of the royal cause in Scotland, however – and not least Charles II himself – who blamed the Scottish Presbyterians for starting the crisis that was to lead to the outbreak of civil war in 1642, the overthrow of episcopacy in all three kingdoms, and, ultimately, the setting up of a republic. For them the best solution was to bring back episcopacy, since a Church run by bishops (who were crown appointees) seemed the only way to ensure the authority of the crown in its northern kingdom. The problem was that there was not the same natural constituency of support for bishops north of the border as there was in England. The Restoration in Scotland offered little compromise with the past and saw the complete overturning of the covenanter revolution, undoing all the religious and political reforms of the late 1630s and early 1640s and putting things back to where they had been when Charles I had come to Scotland to be crowned in 1633. The restoration of episcopacy – first by royal fiat in 1661, and subsequently by act of parliament in 1662 – was followed in 1669 with the passage of the Act of Supremacy, which confirmed the Scottish king as head of the Church (thereby, according to Presbyterians, setting up Charles Stuart in Christ's stead). It was accompanied by the enactment of a particularly brutal penal code intended to deal with the menace of Presbyterian dissent, resulting in a religious persecution much more severe than anything seen in England, and more far-reaching when we realize that Presbyterians in Scotland formed a much higher proportion of the population than did dissenters in England (and by their own estimates even outnumbered the Scottish Episcopalians). Thus in Scotland, Presbyterians not only faced the threat of fines for attending illegal religious meetings, but by the terms of the Conventicle Act of 1670 those who preached at field conventicles could face the death penalty. Moreover, the heavy-handed policing of the Presbyterian south-west – which included the deployment of troops to collect fines, the use of torture (often without official sanction), the imposition of bonds to make landlords and masters liable for the religious behaviour of their tenants and workers, and (most notoriously) the deployment of a Highland Host in 1678 (an army of some 8,000, mainly Highlanders) to try to enforce obedience to the Restoration Church settlement by means of outright intimidation (from the taking of free quarter through to theft, physical violence and, allegedly, much worse) – left a bitter and festering legacy of resentment. Twice the Presbyterians in the south-west rose in rebellion, in 1666 and again in 1679, the latter uprising being preceded by the brutal murder of the Archbishop of St Andrews in his own diocese by Presbyterian extremists. The government, with some justification, saw itself as conducting a war against self-declared enemies of the state, and hence took stern measures. Indeed, there were extremists who had never accepted the legitimacy of the Restoration settlement that had led to the overthrow of Presbyterianism and the denunciation of the covenants, and in the early 1680s the radical covenanting wing of the Presbyterians, the Cameronians or the Society People, as they came to be known, proceeded to declare war on Charles II and engage in what were essentially terrorist acts against the state. Yet most Scottish Presbyterians, even in the south-west, were not diehard political agitators, and perceived themselves as acting defensively in the face of oppression, driven to extremes by the brutality of the government and those who acted in its name. The Scottish Catholics, by comparison – who comprised less than 2 per cent of the population of Scotland in 1681 and were concentrated overwhelmingly in the Highlands and the Islands – had things relatively easy under Charles II.[41]

In Ireland there was a wide range of political, religious and economic sources of tension. Only Protestants of the Established Church were afforded full political and economic rights under the terms of the Restoration settlement, although these comprised about 10 per cent of the total population. Some three-quarters of the population were Catholics; the remainder were Protestant dissenters of some kind (mainly Presbyterians, although there were also a few Quakers and other independents). The confessional divide was further complicated by an ethnic one. The Catholic community comprised both the native or Gaelic Irish (the original inhabitants of Ireland) and the Old English (those descended from the original conquerors of Ireland but who did not change their religion at the Reformation), although inter-marriage and cultural mixing over the generations, coupled with a shared sense of grievance against Anglo-Protestant rule, were bringing these groups closer together. The Protestants of the Established Church were mainly New English, that is descendants of those who had come to Ireland from England in various waves since the Reformation. The Protestant dissenters in the south were predominantly English Presbyterians; Ulster, by contrast, had a heavy concentration of Scottish Presbyterians, who continued to maintain strong ties with their co-religionists back in Scotland. Religious divide in Ireland, however, was not inflamed by religious persecution as it was in England and Scotland, not least because the Anglo-Protestant ascendancy was hardly in a position to persecute some 90 per cent of the population. Thus the laws against Catholics and Protestant dissenters were not that strictly enforced, while under the *regium donum* established in 1672 ministers of the Presbyterian Church were even to receive a grant of £600 per annum from the crown – although certainly those outside the Protestant establishment harboured resentment at their political, economic and religious marginalization.

The most bitter source of contention in Restoration Ireland proved to be the land settlement. During the 1650s, Cromwell had stripped most Catholic landowners of their land, on the grounds that all Catholics shared in the guilt of the Irish Rebellion of October 1641, which had resulted in the massacre of over 3,000 Protestant settlers and the deaths of many more who were driven from their homes in winter time, and of fighting for the royalist cause against the English parliament. By the terms of the Act of Settlement of 1662, Irish Catholics who could prove they had been innocent of any involvement in the Irish Rebellion were, in theory, entitled to recover their lands. However, once the Restoration regime had met all its obligations – which included compensating those who had to relinquish Irish land they had bought in good faith in the 1650s, and rewarding loyal supporters and court favourites with grants of Irish estates as a way of building up political patronage – it soon became apparent that there would not be enough land in Ireland to go around. As a result, many Catholics who felt themselves entitled to be restored to their estates had their expectations disappointed; indeed, the Act of Explanation of 1665, which sought to clarify the mess and put a stop to the endless legal proceedings, meant many dispossessed Catholics were denied even the opportunity to try to prove they were innocent of involvement in the Irish Rebellion. The upshot was that Catholics, who by the late 1650s held only 9 per cent of the profitable land of Ireland, came to hold about 20 per cent under Charles II – just one-third of the pre-Civil War figure of 60 per cent. Even this was too much for many Protestants, however, who felt that all Catholics were by definition rebels and traitors, and who resented having to give back any land at all to their religious adversaries. Ironically, one of the major beneficiaries of the Restoration land settlement in Ireland was the future James II, who was gifted the land taken from those convicted of killing Charles I – an estimated 169,431 acres.[42]

The troublesome legacy bequeathed to all three kingdoms by the 1640s and 1650s and the settlements that followed in the wake of the Restoration were soon to cause problems for Charles II – problems which, although he managed by and large to contain, he was never able to solve. The situation was made worse by Charles's own style of government: his sympathy for Catholics; his pro-French foreign policy (notably his alliance with Catholic France against the Protestant Dutch in the Anglo-Dutch War of 1672–4, at a time when Louis XIV's expansionist ambitions were beginning to threaten not only the balance of power in Europe but also the security of the Protestant interest); his attempts to subvert the independence of parliament by bribing MPs with pensions and office; his efforts to build up a standing army; and his policy towards both Scotland (where the need to meet the Presbyterian threat seemed to push his government into the pursuit of ever-more arbitrary measures) and Ireland (where Charles II's regime did make some efforts to try to alleviate the plight of the Catholic majority). To many Protestants it seemed that the Restoration regime was soft on popery and prone to arbitrary government. Their fears grew deeper when the heir to the throne, the Duke of York, made his conversion to Catholicism public in 1673, raising the prospect of a future Catholic king.

The succession issue came to a head following the revelations by Titus Oates in the summer of 1678 of a supposed Popish Plot to murder the King, burn London (a credible threat given that Catholics were blamed for the Great Fire that had destroyed London in 1666), and massacre hundreds of thousands of English Protestants. If the King were to be killed, the Catholic heir would inherit, and what then would become of cherished Protestant liberties? It was the Popish Plot which gave rise to the Whig movement to try to exclude York from the succession. A Catholic monarch, the Whigs predicted, would persecute Protestants, overturn the rule of law, abandon parliament, rule through a standing army, and be a threat to the lives, liberties and estates of Protestants; the principle of *salus populi* necessitated the exclusion of the popish heir and the example of history, together with the logic of natural law, seemed to suggest to Whigs that the people had both the ability and the right to do this. The Whigs dominated the three English parliaments which met between 1679 and 1681 and introduced Exclusion Bills barring the Catholic heir from inheriting the crown successively into each. They also showed themselves openly hostile to Charles II's own style of government and the Restoration establishment in Church and state. In order to put pressure on Charles to agree to Exclusion, they launched an impressive propaganda campaign designed to convince the public of the dangers of a popish successor and the need to support the Whig agenda; they even encouraged large-scale public demonstrations and petitioning campaigns in support of their cause. There were also signs of a growing alliance between the political opposition in parliament and radical discontented elements across the three kingdoms, many of them Protestant dissenters, prompting government fears of a potential rebellion should Charles decline to accede to Whig demands. The similarities with the tactics pursued by John Pym and the parliamentary opposition to Charles I in 1641 were obvious. By 1679–80 it seemed – as opponents of the Whigs were quick to point out – that '41 was come again. And everyone knew that it had been but a short step from 1641 to the outbreak of civil war in 1642.

By 1679–80 the Restoration regime was in crisis. Charles was finding it difficult to rule his three kingdoms effectively, to formulate policy initiatives of his own, to raise taxes, or to enforce the law against those he regarded as the political enemies of Church and state. In addition, he faced the prospect that if things got too far out of hand, his subjects might rise up against him. Yet Charles recovered from the crisis. He saw off the challenge of the Whigs and successfully rebuilt the authority and prestige of the crown. An understanding of how he was able to do this is vital if we are to appreciate how and why it was that James II came unstuck.

Most accounts relate the royal recovery of the final years of Charles II's reign to the power inherent in the monarchy. Charles had made serious mistakes and blundered into a difficult situation by the late 1670s, one historian has told us, but 'the position of the monarchy was fundamentally so strong that, only providing he did not show consistent folly, Charles's control of his realms was never in doubt'.[43] The King, it seems, held all the trump cards. He never lost control of the House of Lords, and in November 1680 the Lords threw out the only Exclusion Bill that was to make it as far as the upper house. He was able to frustrate the Whigs by picking his moments when to prorogue and dissolve parliament, while after 1681, with his regime buoyed up by increased revenues from customs and excise and subsidies from Louis XIV's France, he simply refused to call another parliament altogether, thereby denying the opposition an effective power base from which to challenge the court. During the years of 'Tory Reaction' that followed, Charles carried out a ruthless persecution of his political and religious opponents through a judicial system that had been purged to guarantee its loyalty, and interfered with urban electoral franchises (through his *quo warranto* proceedings against corporation charters, challenging 'by what warrant' corporations held their charter) so as to ensure that when his brother came to the throne and called a parliament – as he would be obliged to do upon his accession – one dominated by Tories would be elected. By this account, Charles essentially won by suppressing the voice of the people. Indeed, the final years of Charles II's reign are usually seen as marking a drift towards royal absolutism, with the King emerging as 'an unfettered sovereign'.[44] James II consolidated this trend towards absolutism, building up a sizeable standing army, and using his power quite blatantly to promote the interests of his fellow Roman Catholics. On this logic, so strong had the crown's position become by 1688 that there was little the British could do to challenge James's rule. Hence the view that the Glorious Revolution happened only as a result of a successful foreign invasion – that it came from above and outside, not from inside or below.[45]

Restoration argued the need for a different reading of how Charles II managed to escape from the crisis he faced in 1679–80. Charles's strategy during the first two decades of his rule had been to play off the competing political and religious factions against each other and to clamp down on political discussion out-of-doors, in the hope of creating a more autonomous role for the crown. It did not work. From about 1681, he therefore changed tack. He threw himself into alliance with one particular faction, the Tory-Anglican interest, and began in earnest the struggle to win over the hearts and minds of his subjects. There was thus a significant ideological dimension to the royal recovery in the early 1680s. Charles and his Tory allies deliberately set out to appeal to opinion 'out-of-doors', seeking to delegitimize the position of the Whigs and thereby denude them of their extensive support among the population at large. They took their stance in defence of the monarchy, the traditional constitution, the rule of law, and the Anglican Church against what they represented as a radical and subversive threat from an alliance of republicans and nonconformists seeking to undermine the existing legal establishment in Church and state. In addition to launching this ideological onslaught against the Whigs, the Tories also encouraged public manifestations of support for their position in the form of loyal addresses and demonstrations, in an attempt to show that the Whigs could not claim to represent the voice of the people. It was a strategy that met with considerable success. Not everyone was converted to the loyalist platform, but the crown was able to mobilize latent royalist sympathizers and win over moderates and waverers on a sufficient scale to serve its purpose.

The Tories, it should be stressed, were no friends of popery and arbitrary government; in fact, they claimed to be as much against both as any self-respecting British Protestant. Yet they recalled how when Pym and the parliamentary opposition of 1641 had raised the cry of popery and arbitrary government the result had been not only civil war but also the subsequent disestablishment of the Church of

England, the execution of the reigning monarch, and oppressive republican rule backed up by a standing army. The Whigs, by posing a threat to the security of the Protestant monarchy and seeking to undermine the Established Church of England, so the Tories alleged, were seeking the self-same ends as the Pope and thus acting on 'popish' principles. They were also risking the revival of the sort of arbitrary government that had been seen during the 1640s and 1650s. It was but a short step for the Tories to insist that the way to defeat the threat of popery and arbitrary government was to defeat the challenge of the Whigs. England would be safe under a popish successor, they maintained, because the Protestant establishment was secure under the law. There were laws enough, in all three kingdoms, to deal with the challenge posed by religious dissenters (whether Protestant nonconformists or Catholics): the Test Acts of 1673 and 1678 in England and of 1681 in Scotland excluded both Catholics and nonconformists from office or from sitting in parliament, thereby denying all who were not communicating members of the Established Church any access to political power.

In the government's campaign against the Whigs, it would be wrong to emphasize ideological factors alone. Charles also needed to re-establish royal control over the agencies of government at the local level: hence the crown's attempts to purge political opponents from office and give loyalists a monopoly of power in the localities. And it did take a remorseless legal drive against the political and religious enemies of the government to defeat the Whig and nonconformist challenge. Whig activists were hauled before the courts on charges of sedition or treason; others were detained in custody on mere suspicion. Those against whom the government had enough evidence paid with their lives or else heavy fines. In Scotland, torture was used to bring the government's enemies to 'justice'. Many of those accused were undoubtedly guilty of some sort of conspiratorial activity against the state – in 1683 the government unearthed a plot by extremists in England and Scotland (the so-called Rye House Plot) either to assassinate the King and the Duke of York or to raise a rebellion to force the Whig agenda through at sword-point – although the government did have recourse to some bending of the law in order to make sure that it nailed the people it wanted to get. The final years of

Charles II's reign also saw the worst period of religious persecution in British history. In England, thousands of dissenters suffered heavy fines, imprisonment and even the loss of life (since not a few were to die in jail) for failing to conform to the Restoration Church. In Scotland those who adhered to the political tenets of the radical Presbyterians and refused to renounce violence against the state could be summarily executed in the fields.

The point is, however, that in order to carry out this policy of repression the crown needed allies not just at the centre but also at the local levels of government. The King could give loyalists a monopoly of political power in the localities only if he had persuaded enough people (of the right sort) of the need to support what he was trying to do in the first place. The men Charles placed in power during the final years of his reign were those with an ideological commitment to the Tory-Anglican platform of defence of the Church and state as by law established, and who wanted to see the law enforced against the political enemies of the government. The crown could carry many of its subjects with it as long as – but only as long as – it remained committed to that platform. Thus although Charles strengthened the position of the monarchy, he did not emerge as an unfettered sovereign; instead he made the crown the prisoner of a party. It is questionable whether, in England at least, Charles had laid the basis for effective royal absolutism. Royalist propagandists did, to be sure, frequently seek to represent the monarch as absolute, insisting that he did not share sovereignty with parliament and could not be held accountable by his subjects, and that he certainly could not be resisted. Indeed, the pulpits of the Established Church (in all three kingdoms) resounded with sermons preaching divine-right monarchy and condemning resistance. But there was always a strong emphasis within Tory propaganda on Charles's commitment to the rule of law, against those who might seek to undermine it. Charles was left with little freedom of manoeuvre; he was, essentially, trapped within an agenda – the Tory-Anglican one – that was not of his own making and to which, earlier in his reign, he had not shown himself particularly committed.

This book will show that James II came undone because he failed to realize the extent to which the strength of the monarchy was based on this alliance between the crown and the Tory-Anglican interest.

Believing that his powers were unfettered, James immediately embarked on a policy to promote the interests of his Catholic co-religionists in violation of the law. In doing so, he provoked opposition from those very people who had been the chief supporters of the monarchy during the final years of his brother's reign, and he failed to build up a sufficient support base among alternative interest groups who benefited from his policies of religious toleration (the Catholics were simply too few in number; the nonconformists too suspicious of James's broader agenda). James's regime had already begun to disintegrate before the invasion of William of Orange. James did not fall because he was overthrown by the superior military might of a foreign invading power. He fell because he failed to understand the realities of power within the Restoration polity and the (limited) ways in which royal authority could be effectively exercised. The collapse of his regime was, in that sense, due to domestic political turmoil.

THE THREE-KINGDOMS CONTEXT

Let us now turn to a consideration of why it is important to look at Scotland and Ireland as well as England. On one level this is because the man who was toppled in 1688 was king of all three kingdoms. The kings of England had obtained suzerainty over Ireland by the terms of a papal grant of 1155, but it was not until Henry VIII's reign that they assumed the title of king of Ireland: by the terms of an act of 1541, Ireland was established as a separate kingdom in its own right, though one where the 'imperial crown' was 'united and knit to the imperial crown of England'.[46] Constitutionally Ireland's position was somewhat ambiguous: was it an independent kingdom or an English colonial dependency? It remained unclear as to whether or not the English parliament could legislate for Ireland: at times the English parliament certainly did, and it partly depended on the issue and the context. What was clear was that by the terms of Poynings' Law of 1494 the Irish parliament could not enact its own legislation unless it had been first approved by the English king and council. Scotland undoubtedly was an independent kingdom, but one whose ruling Stewart dynasty (to employ the Scottish spelling) had happened to inherit the English throne (and therefore also the Irish throne), when James VI became James I of England by dint of the fact that he was the closest surviving heir to the childless 'Virgin Queen', Elizabeth I (r. 1588–1603). When William of Orange overthrew James II, he claimed his Scottish and Irish crowns as well as his English one; in that sense the Glorious Revolution was intrinsically a three-kingdoms event.

Yet the need to include Scotland and Ireland in our narrative goes deeper than this. The three-kingdoms context is also vital for understanding the problems that both Charles II and James II faced and the strategies they adopted for tackling them. As *Restoration* showed, Whig fears of popery and arbitrary government under Charles II need to be set against the backdrop of developments in Ireland (where there was a threat of popery) and Scotland (where there was the threat of arbitrary government). The Whigs themselves were quite explicit about this. On 25 March 1679, the Earl of Shaftesbury, a leading Whig spokesman in the House of Lords, famously proclaimed: 'Popery and slavery, like two sisters, go hand in hand, and sometimes one goes first, sometimes the other; but wheresoever the one enters, the other is always following close at hand.' 'In England,' he continued, 'popery was to have brought in slavery; in Scotland, slavery went before, and popery was to follow', while Shaftesbury predicted that 'our other sister, Ireland', could not 'long continue in English hands, if some better care be not taken of it'.[47]

The Stuart multiple-kingdom inheritance was a tricky one to manage. The king found it difficult to pursue particular policies in one kingdom without running the risk of upsetting certain groups in either of the others. This was particularly evident on the religious front. In the aftermath of civil war and regicide brought about by Presbyterians and radical Protestant nonconformists, many of whom were far from happy with the nature of the settlement in Church and state that occurred after 1660, domestic security concerns seemed to dictate the necessity of stringent laws to deal with the possible menace posed by Protestant dissent. At the same time, in an age of continued confessional conflict in Europe, a Protestant monarch was expected to uphold the Protestant establishment by enforcing the penal laws against Catholics, not least because the papacy claimed a power to depose heretical rulers and absolve subjects from allegiance. However, it was impractical to enforce too stringent measures against those outside the Established Church in Ireland – Catholics and Protestant dissenters – because they comprised the vast majority of the population and might well pose a genuine threat to the stability of the government if driven to desperate measures. English Protestants, who saw Charles's government persecuting Presbyterians in Scotland but not enforcing the penal laws against Catholics in Ireland, inevitably had cause to worry about what Charles might be up to, especially when their king also seemed softer on popery than on Protestant dissent in England as well as inclined to a pro-French foreign policy. On the other hand, if Charles did not clamp down on Protestant dissent in England and Scotland, the episcopalian interest in both kingdoms grew alarmed, and this was an interest that Charles found he could not afford to alienate. It was a 'damned if you do, damned if you don't' situation; whichever path Charles chose to tread ran the risk of creating problems.

However, the multiple-kingdom inheritance was not necessarily a source of instability. It could work to a king's advantage, providing he knew how to play the different kingdoms off against each other. This is something Charles II did with tremendous success in the early 1680s. One of the most compelling arguments that the government and its Tory allies made against Exclusion was that the Scots would never accept it, so that if the Whigs managed to force an Exclusion Bill through the English parliament, war between England and Scotland would likely follow. The Whigs did not listen, and kept pushing for an Exclusion Bill regardless. Charles therefore decided to play the three-kingdoms card to try to guarantee the succession. After he had dissolved the third and final Exclusion parliament in England in March 1681, he called a parliament in Scotland, where because of the control the crown possessed in managing the legislative agenda through the select steering committee known as the Lords of the Articles, he felt confident about getting his legislative agenda enacted. This Scottish parliament proceeded to pass a Succession Act in August 1681, stipulating that upon the death of the king the Scottish crown passed immediately to the next-in-line to the throne, regardless of his religion. This effectively trumped the English Whigs; if they pushed ahead with Exclusion now, war between Scotland and England could only follow, as the Succession Act itself pointed out. At the end of the same month the Scottish parliament passed a Test Act, which required all office-holders not only to pledge their commitment to the Established Church but also to promise 'faith and true allegiance to the Kings Majestie, his heirs and laufull successors', to defend the king in all his rights and prerogatives, and to renounce resistance. Although an internal inconsistency in the oath – which appeared to ask office-holders to acknowledge in one place that the king was head of the Church and in another that Jesus was – caused some to scruple over taking the oath until the government issued a statement offering further clarification, the Act by and large served its purpose well, ensuring that those who held office under the crown would be Protestants who had pledged their unconditional loyalty to the crown and the hereditary succession.[48] Swarms of loyal addresses that poured in from Ireland in 1682–3, furthermore, suggested that Ireland – even the ruling Protestant ascendancy there – would be far from happy if the English excluded the Catholic heir, raising the possibility of war with that kingdom as well if the Whigs were to succeed.[49] Developments in Scotland and Ireland, in other words, help explain why so many people in England became convinced that the Whigs threatened to engulf the three kingdoms in civil war once more. Tory propagandists further played on fears of the potential threat posed by the English Whigs and their nonconformist allies by comparing them to their Scottish counterparts, the radical Presbyterians north of the border, who had twice risen in rebellion against Charles II, and who in the early 1680s continued to engage in insurrectionary activity against the government.[50] The loyalist reaction in England of the early 1680s therefore was predicated upon a perception of what was going on in Scotland and Ireland. In short, the three-kingdoms context not only explains some of the problems Charles II faced, but it also reveals how he was able to resolve them.

How, then, did the multiple-kingdom inheritance affect the strategies that James II chose to pursue as king? Could he manage that inheritance successfully, and, if not, what sorts of problems did that inheritance create for him? As Duke of York, James had spent two spells in Scotland between 1679 and 1682, where he had headed the government in his brother's name. He did a remarkably good job, in terms of what he set out to achieve, working with the Episcopalian interest to meet the threat of radical Presbyterian dissent and even bringing some degree of peace to the Highlands. He should have understood the realities of Scottish politics well and have known how to handle the Scottish situation. He had no direct experience of governing Ireland, but as a Catholic himself we might expect that his accession would be welcome to the Catholic Irish; the question was, would that help stabilize Ireland, or would it destabilize the situation by causing anxiety for the Protestant ascendancy in Ireland and Protestant interests in England and Scotland? We need to examine, therefore, not only how James chose to manage affairs in Scotland and Ireland, but also what impact this in turn had on his affairs in England. We shall see that, like his brother before him, James self-consciously tried to play the three-kingdoms card, but with much less success. Indeed, this book will demonstrate that the three-kingdoms context is a vital factor in explaining why James failed to achieve what he intended and why he came to fall from power by late 1688.

BRITISH REVOLUTIONS

Finally, this book will argue that the Glorious Revolution was a genuine revolution, and that it played a more significant role in transforming the nature of the polities in England, Scotland and Ireland than the unsuccessful (or successfully undone) revolution of the mid-seventeenth century. The Glorious Revolution was, it should be pointed out, styled a revolution at the time, whereas that of the 1640s and 1650s was not. Yet it is normally argued that this was because in the late seventeenth century the word 'revolution' was used mainly in an astronomical sense, as in the revolutions of the heavenly bodies, and thus carried the connotations of coming full cycle or returning to the *status quo ante*. Thus the contemporary sense of revolution, it has been claimed, was almost the exact opposite of the modern meaning of the word.[51] This is misleading. It is true that revolution was occasionally used in a political context to mean coming full cycle, hence why observers sometimes referred to the Restoration of 1660 as a revolution. But more typically the word, when applied by contemporaries to politics, simply carried the meaning of a sudden and dramatic transformation, without implying a return to the way things had been before. Contemporaries even had the concept of a revolution as marking a fundamental break with the past or the setting up of a radically new order, and some did employ it in this sense to refer to what happened in 1688–9. Thus one English Jacobite complained in 1689 how 'this Revolution' had broken 'the very Constitution' and set up a 'New Fabric'.[52] It is simply wrong to assume that because contemporaries described what happened in 1688–9 as a revolution that they saw the Glorious Revolution as a conservative affair.[53]

The Glorious Revolution is typically seen as a relatively tame revolution in comparison to its mid-century counterpart. There was not the same sort of revolutionary violence, so the argument runs, nor the same degree of popular upheaval and crowd unrest. Again, this needs to be called into question. The Glorious Revolution would not have appeared tame to people who lived through it. This is true even if we focus our attention on England, where there was in fact considerable popular unrest and crowd violence in the final months of 1688. It becomes even more true once we add Scotland and Ireland to the picture. Things did not get out of hand in 1688–9 in quite the same way they did in the 1640s: the crowds were quieted fairly quickly in England, and although Scotland and Ireland remained troublesome for longer, the Jacobite military threat in both kingdoms was essentially contained by the autumn of 1691. Nevertheless, it is far from clear that the crowds that we see in England in late 1688 exhibited a form of behaviour that was that much different from that exhibited in England on the eve of the Civil War. In Scotland, over the winter of 1688/9, there certainly were revolutionary crowds, which had a huge impact in shaping the eventual Revolution settlement north of the border. And in Ireland, of course, the Revolution did spawn a lengthy bloody conflict, in which approaching 25,000 men died in combat and thousands more of disease.[54]

This book will argue that the dynastic shift that occurred in 1688–9 as a result of William of Orange's invasion precipitated three very different revolutions in the three kingdoms. Constitutionally, that in England was the most conservative, but its implications were wide-ranging. That in Scotland set about to overturn much of the Restoration settlement in Church and state, and was thus intrinsically more radical than its English counterpart. In Ireland there was both an attempted Catholic revolution and a Williamite counter-revolution. These revolutions, different as they were, also altered the nature of the relationship between the three kingdoms and, in turn, necessitated a fourth British revolution to readjust the balance between England and its sister kingdoms of Scotland and Ireland. Scotland was to lose its status as an independent kingdom as a result, being merged into a greater British state with the Act of Union of 1707. Ireland was, in effect, to be confirmed as a colonial dependency of England rather than as an independent kingdom in its own right, with the passage of the Declaratory Act of 1720. The political world for people who lived in England, Scotland and Ireland was very different by the 1720s compared to what it had been in the 1680s, and this was due in no small part to what had happened in 1688–9 and the working out of the implications of the dynastic shift that occurred at that time. This was, in short, Britain's age of revolutions.

PART ONE

The Reign of James II and VII, 1685–8

I

The Accession of the True and Lawful Heir

It was on this occasion that the world stood astonished to see the Metamorphoses in a manner of a whole Kingdom; this Prince, who so little a while before had been persecuted, banished, and by the wishes of the people as well as the violent endeavours of the Parliament on the point of being disinherited . . . to see (I say) this same Prince wellcom'd to the Throne with such universal acclamations of joy, such unexpressible testimonys of duty and affection from all ranks of people, was what history has no example of.

Life of James II, II, 2

When Charles II died on 6 February 1685, at the age of 54, the succession passed to his Catholic brother, the 51-year-old James, Duke of York, who succeeded as James II in England and Ireland and as James VII in Scotland. Despite the recovery of the crown's position over the previous four years, the royal administration remained extremely nervous about what might happen when James did eventually succeed his brother. After all the fuss that had been made during the Exclusion Crisis, when the Whigs had portrayed James as a lover of arbitrary power and predicted that a Catholic successor would inevitably be a threat to Protestant political and religious freedoms, how would people actually react when they faced the reality of a Catholic monarch on the throne? The Whig challenge might have been contained, but had it been defeated? What could be expected from those who had suffered during the years of Tory Reaction or who had been forced into political exile? Throughout the autumn of

1684 and early 1685, the government received reports that Scottish and English dissidents in the Low Countries, led by the Earl of Argyll and the Duke of Monmouth respectively, were contemplating launching a rebellion. And if Argyll and Monmouth were to invade, how much support might they be able to win among the British people? In England, the Whigs might have been removed from local office and the dissenters fined until they could no longer afford to attend their conventicles, but their hearts and minds had hardly been won over. In the Scottish south-west the radical Presbyterians, the Cameronian remnant or Society People, continued to hold their field conventicles and engage in acts of open defiance against the government. With regard to Ireland, the government could perhaps feel confident of the loyalty of the Catholic majority and even of the Protestants of the Established Church; they were less sure of the allegiance of the Protestant dissenters, especially the Scottish Presbyterians in Ulster, who maintained close links with their brethren in the Scottish south-west.

Those in authority certainly felt they could take no chances. When Charles II fell seriously ill on 2 February, the government took immediate security precautions, closing the ports, having suspicious persons arrested, and readying troops in various parts of the kingdom to suppress any disorder. A premature report of Charles II's death on 4 February prompted Sir Edward Philips, a deputy Lieutenant in Somerset, to call out the regiments of the county militia under his command to stop 'ill affected persons' from attempting 'to disturb the legall succession of his Royall highnesse'.[1] When the Duke of Ormonde in Ireland learned the news of Charles's actual death, his immediate fear was that 'some endeavours might be used to raise disturbance in opposition to his present Majesty's accession to the Crown'.[2]

As it turned out, James's reign began better than anyone could have expected. There was no immediate challenge to the accession of a Catholic ruler, as had been feared; indeed, there is considerable evidence of popular support for the new monarch across all three of his kingdoms. Moreover, the parliaments that met in Scotland and England that spring proved not only overwhelmingly loyalist bodies but even zealous in their loyalism. There were certainly those who were far from happy at the prospect of living under a Catholic king, but the disaffected were a small minority who, after the Tory Reaction of the final years of Charles II's reign, were in no position to mount an effective challenge to the government. When the rebellions of Argyll and Monmouth came in the late spring and early summer of 1685, they both failed miserably for lack of support.

However, the support James enjoyed at the time of his accession was, in essence, conditional, although loyalists would not have seen it this way themselves at the time. The vast majority of those who backed the new monarch and rallied behind him in the face of the residual challenge by radicals north and south of the border did so because James promised he would observe the rule of law and uphold the existing establishment in the Church. When it began to become clear that he was not going to keep his promises, the enthusiasm of those who had welcomed his accession soon began to cool. Sixteen eighty-five might have started better for the King than he could have expected; it finished with him already having begun to turn the natural supporters of the late-Stuart monarchy against him. This chapter will analyse the climate of opinion in England, Scotland and Ireland at the time of James II's accession in order to assess the extent of popular support for the King when he came to the throne. The following chapter will take the story through 1685, looking at the meetings of the Scottish and English parliaments, the rebellions of Argyll and Monmouth (and the reactions to them), and the beginnings of the growth of loyalist disaffection in England towards the end of 1685.

FAR FROM BEING A MAN FOR ARBITRARY POWER

Immediately upon the death of his brother on 6 February, James delivered an impromptu speech to his privy council in an attempt to reassure those at the centre of power they had nothing to fear from his accession. Deeply upset by his brother's demise and with tears still in his eyes, he resolutely promised that he would 'preserve this Government both in Church and State as it now by Law Establish'd'. Far from being 'a Man for Arbitrary Power', he said, he knew 'the Laws of England' were 'sufficient to make the King as Great a

Monarch' as he could wish, and although he would 'never Depart from the just Rights and Prerogatives of the Crown', he would like-wise never 'invade any man's Property'. The council realized the prop-aganda value of such royal assurances, and insisted that what James had said should immediately be written down and published.[3] James later maintained that the published version of the speech was worded more strongly than he would have liked: it would have expressed his meaning better, he claimed, if it had read that 'he never would endeav-our to *alter* the established religion', rather than that he would 'pre-serve' it, but he had been so busy when asked to approve the wording that he passed it over without reflection. This sounds like *ex post facto* special pleading. One contemporary alleged that James had in fact offered even fuller assurances in his original speech, promising to sacrifice 'the last drop of [his] blood to maintain the Protestant reli-gion', and to follow his 'late Brother's example' as far as it lay within him. Whatever the truth, James was to be forever haunted by words he had uttered in the first few hours of his reign while still in a state of considerable emotional distress following the death of his brother.[4]

The official version of the speech was widely disseminated. It was published separately and printed in the official government news-paper, the *London Gazette*. The leading Tory journalist and Charles II's licenser of the press Roger L'Estrange reported the speech in his bi-weekly *Observator*, and remarked that here was as much of a secu-rity 'as any Good Christian, or Subject' could pray for.[5] The Anglican clergy read it to their congregations. Benjamin Camfield rejoiced from his pulpit at Aylestone, near Leicester, at having a king who chose to begin his reign by emphasizing his concern for his people's 'just Rights, Properties and Liberties' and 'that most excellent, pure, and Reformed Religion which is by Law Established'.[6] The Archbishop of York, John Dolben, visited a number of communities in Yorkshire to 'enlarge upon' the King's declaration 'to preserve the government of the Church and State as it is established by law', which apparently made 'noe small impressions upon the People of all Sorts'.[7] Friends wrote to each other to check if they had 'hard the grate asureance by the word of sow grate a monarch in promising to maintane the now Establisht government both in Church and State as now by Law Established', as one correspondent put it.[8] According to another letter writer, although people were upset at the news of Charles II's death, their sorrows were 'much abated by the great assurances' King James had given 'to govern by the laws to maintain the Protestant Religion and to follow the steps of his worthy brother, as the best pattern'.[9] And if anyone had still chanced to miss what the King had said, James was soon to reiterate his promises to protect the Established Church and the rights of his subjects at the openings of both the Scottish and English parliaments.

Arrangements were quickly made for proclaiming James king, and a proclamation was issued for the continuance in office of all those who held positions at the death of Charles II, in order to ensure that there was 'noe disturbance among his Majesties Subjects' and that 'peace [might] be continued'.[10] There was thus considerable continuity in the personnel of government. In England, James retained all his brother's judges, appointing them at royal pleasure according to the practice firmly established in the previous reign. He took on a strongly Tory judicial bench: Charles II himself had made eleven arbitrary removals since 1676 to ensure its loyalty.[11] There was some reconstruction of the ministry, but those who had been influential under Charles remained in office. James retained the earls of Sunderland and Middleton as Secretaries of State. He appointed his brother-in-law, the Earl of Rochester (the brother of James's first wife, Anne Hyde) Lord Treasurer, choosing to put the treasury into one man's hands, as he put it, so 'That there might be nothing like a Common Wealth in his own Court'.[12] James made Rochester's older brother, the Earl of Clarendon, Lord Privy Seal, in place of the Marquis of Halifax, who replaced Rochester as Lord President of the council. Francis North, Baron Guilford, continued as Lord Chancellor and Keeper of the Great Seal. In Scotland, James retained all existing officers of state, privy counsellors, magistrates and other office-holders. This left the Earl of Perth as Chancellor and his younger brother, John Drummond (soon to be Earl of Melfort), as Secretary of State for Scotland. At this time both were still Protestants, although they were not to remain so for much longer. The Duke of Queensberry remained in charge at the treasury. In Ireland, where Ormonde had been about to be recalled just prior to Charles's death, James chose to entrust the administration to two Protestant lords justices: Michael Boyle, Archbishop of Armagh, and the Earl of Granard.[13]

The coronation was set for 23 April, which did not leave much time for preparations but, according to the French ambassador, James believed that once crowned his title as king could not be disputed.[14] It is also revealing that James started to touch for the King's Evil from the beginning of March, presumably in an attempt to offer confirmation to his new subjects that he was indeed the legitimate, divinely ordained monarch.[15] He did not show any of these concerns with regard to Scotland, however, where he made no arrangements to be crowned. The omission is perhaps understandable. Ever since the Scottish Stewart dynasty had inherited the English crown in 1603, England had become their home and trips to Scotland regarded as luxuries which took the monarch away from the important task of running England. Thus Charles I, who came to the throne in 1625, was not crowned in Scotland until 1633. Charles II, who was declared king by the Scots following the execution of Charles I in 1649, was crowned in Scotland in 1651, but under circumstances that he would later regret – and even resent – having been forced as a condition of Scottish support to take the Covenant. The Scottish Succession Act of 1681, which declared that the succession passed immediately to the next-in-line upon the death of the reigning monarch, seemed to make clear that the actual coronation played no role in conferring legitimacy on the new king (something confirmed by the language used to proclaim James VII king in Scotland in 1685). Indeed, the Succession Act even appeared to obviate the need for a new king to take the coronation oath, which James also failed to do upon his succession. It did not seem a big issue at the time, though it was to become one four years later.[16]

The most immediate concern at the start of the new reign was over finance. The major contributions to government revenue came from customs and excise, but these had been granted to Charles II for life, with no provision for their continuation for a specified number of months under his successor. On 9 February, therefore, James issued a proclamation for continuing the collection of customs and tonnage and poundage, announcing at the same time that parliament would soon meet to settle a sufficient revenue on the crown. Something

Scotland and Ireland – ten more if we include the Channel Islands, the West Indies, the American colonies and Madras. Local sources confirm the official view. The people of Loughborough, which was not even mentioned by the *Gazette*, allegedly 'exceeded all others in theyr zeal at Proclaming the king, sacrificing severall Hogsheads to his Majesties Health'. The sheriff of Northumberland reported that 'noe County in England could proclaime him [James II] with more Acclamation of Joy nor express more intire resolutions to serve him with their lives and fortunes'.[24] Similar scenes occurred in Scotland: in Edinburgh, when Perth proclaimed James VII on 10 February, he was seconded by 'an Universal Acclamation' from a crowd supposedly totalling 'more than 30,000 of all Ranks of people', and by the afternoon 'the Town was full of Bonfires', while Aberdeen similarly saw 'the greatest demonstrations of Joy'. So too did Dublin and several other places in Ireland; at Downpatrick, County Down, James was proclaimed to the 'generall unanimous and chearful consent of all present', which one observer estimated to be 'no lesse than a 1000 persons at least'.[25]

Care is needed in the interpretation of this evidence. The accounts in the *Gazette* should be regarded less as objective reporting than as an official attempt to ascribe a particular meaning to the events purportedly being described: pro-government propaganda, in other words, as much as straightforward 'news'.[26] Moreover, the demonstrations were hardly spontaneous. The proclaiming of a new king was a highly formal occasion, involving all the important local dignitaries – lords, gentry, clergy, magistrates and civic officials – dressed in their official regalia. The local authorities typically provided alcoholic refreshment to put the local inhabitants in a festive mood. The corporation of Lyme Regis, for example, sent twenty-four bottles 'to the towne Hall att the proclamation of the King'.[27] In many towns the public drinking fountains ran with wine.[28] In Dublin, Ormonde caused 'several Hogsheads of Wine to be placed' at the three places where James was proclaimed, 'for any that pleased to drink', and also caused 'Bonfires to be made at Night'.[29] In Edinburgh, the council directive ordering celebrations on the accession of James VII warned that those who did not show the correct 'expressions of loyalty and great joy' would be regarded as disaffected to the government and punished accordingly.[30] Even then,

Fountainhall thought that 'peoples greiff was more then ther joy, having lost ther dearly beloved King'.[31] One Irish diarist similarly alleged that there was 'little joy' in people's countenances when James was proclaimed in Dublin.[32]

Nevertheless, there are reasons to believe that those who helped orchestrate the celebrations of February 1685 were tapping into deeply felt and widespread loyalist sentiments. In addition to officially sponsored bonfires, local residents often built their own. At Lisburn, in County Antrim, Ireland, for example, there were apparently bonfires 'at every house' on the day James was proclaimed. If James's succession had not been generally welcomed, we might expect the huge crowds that gathered to hear him proclaimed to have caused some disturbance. Only in Ulster does there appear to have been any noticeable trouble. At Belfast, with its sizeable population of Scottish Presbyterians, a hostile crowd pulled down the proclamation, a gesture which seemed to displease only the town sheriff. A more minor incident happened at Downpatrick, when a man was arrested for speaking seditious words when James was proclaimed, although the offender later claimed to have been drunk.[33]

There was further public rejoicing on 23 April, the day of James's English coronation. The coronation itself in London was a splendid affair, 'the whole Solemnity being performed with great Order and Magnificence', the *Gazette* tells us, 'and with all the Expressions of an Universal Joy', although the nonconformist London diarist Roger Morrice alleged that 'above one halfe of the Nobillity made excuses for one reason or another and were absent'.[34] The *Gazette* also documented elaborate displays of public feasting and drinking, followed by bonfires, bells and fireworks in Bristol, Manchester, Newcastle upon Tyne, Norwich, Nottingham, Prescot (in Lancashire), Saltash and Shrewsbury, while local records reveal that similar events took place elsewhere.[35] An elaborate ceremony took place at Lyme Regis in Dorset, which involved the procession of 300 virgins through the town pledging 'their Majesties healths', followed by fireworks and innumerable bonfires as the town conduits 'ranne with wine'.[36] The English coronation was also commemorated in Scotland and Ireland.[37] Again, sponsorship from above can be detected, with town authorities or local churchwardens invariably providing money for alcohol and bonfires.[38] Yet it would be wrong to see the celebrating crowds as manipulated mobs. As with the demonstrations in February, what we see here are attempts by local political leaders to encourage local inhabitants publicly to demonstrate their allegiance to the new king and testify their support for the hereditary succession – testing, in the process, how deep-seated those sentiments were, but no doubt being delighted with their findings.

The impression of extensive popular support for James is strongly reinforced by the evidence of loyal addresses congratulating the King on his accession to the throne. The *Gazette* reported a total of 439 such addresses – 346 from England and Wales; 75 from Ireland; 5 from Scotland; and 13 from residents overseas or foreign dominions – from a wide variety of different groups: county leaders, grand juries, town magistrates, diocesan clergy, local inhabitants, loyal societies, merchants, apprentices and various trades. Some had large numbers of signatories. The address from the Cornish tin workers was purportedly signed by more than 12,000 hands; that from the gentry, chief inhabitants and freeholders of Norfolk by about 6,000 people.[39]

Invariably the addressers expressed support for the hereditary succession and relief that Exclusion had failed. The mayor, aldermen, freemen and other inhabitants of Newark-upon-Trent, Nottinghamshire, for example, acknowledged James as 'the most Rightful and Undoubted Heir and Successor', and said it was 'a great blessing of the Divine Providence, that in spight of all Democraticall Spirits, we still live under the best of Governments, Monarchy, wherein the Crowned Head is not determinable by plurality of Votes' and that 'a Bill of Exclusion' could not 'cut off Your Majesties Succession to that Inheritance' to which he was entitled 'by all Law Sacred and Civil'. The inhabitants of Deal in Kent rejoiced that the crown had descended to James, 'notwithstanding the Votes of Exclusion, and the Endeavours of Factious, and unreasonable Men to the contrary'.[40]

Various companies of merchants pledged their willingness to pay the customs tax, because of the need to maintain the navy both for the 'defence of the Nation' and 'the security of Trade', as the general trading merchants of London put it.[41] Even companies that in the past had been 'looked upon as fanatical' were 'as forward as the best' in addressing the crown, because they recognized that 'the necessity of trade' required there be 'no intermission of payments'.[42] The barristers and students of Middle Temple argued that an intermission in the customs would have disastrous consequences for national security, and insisted that the common law allowed the monarch to act by his prerogative in such an emergency to secure 'the Liberty and Property of the Subject'.[43] Beyond these, most of the addresses focused on James's assurances to protect the established government in Church and state. John Sharp, Dean of Norwich and rector of St Giles-in-the-Fields in London, drew up an address from the grand jury for the City of London, thanking the King for 'the gracious assurances' he had given his people 'to maintain and support the government both in Church and State as established by Law'.[44] The gentry and other inhabitants of Anglesey in Wales stated that the King's resolution 'to maintain the present Government by Law Established both in Church and State' rendered them 'the happiest Subjects in the World'. Most addressers were at pains to emphasize James's promise both 'to defend and support the Established Church of England' and 'to preserve the Laws of this Realm', to cite the address of the lords and gentry of the loyal society which met near Gray's Inn.[45]

This is not to say that the addressers saw their support for the new Catholic king as conditional upon his willingness to rule according to law and to protect the Church. Anglicans – as several of the addresses pointed out – believed that their religion taught them unconditional loyalty. Thus the 'Loyal Subjects' of New Malton, Yorkshire, affirmed it 'would be to Contradict the Principles of our Religion' to 'make our obedience Conditional'.[46] Many addressers also happily recognized that James's declaration to his council had included an assertion that he would never depart from the prerogatives of the crown. The corporation of Hereford thanked James for declaring he would 'maintain [his] Prerogatives' as well as 'the present Government in Church and State'; the inhabitants of Rutland acknowledged the King's 'Just Rights and Prerogatives' to be the 'best Security' for their 'Religion and Properties'; while those of Westminster proclaimed they would expose their 'Lives and Fortunes' in defence of the King's person 'and of the Rights and Prerogatives of the Crown'. The address from the corporation of Monmouth acknowledged that it was the King's

'Right to Rule and Govern' and 'Subjects' Duty to Obey'.[47] Never-theless, many of the addresses were intended to remind James that he had publicly pledged to protect the Church of England and that this was a promise he should not break. As the gentry of Cumberland put it: 'it is the Royal Word of a Prince who hath always born the Character of being a strict and inviolable Observer of His Promise'. The Berkshire addressers said they built their confidence 'as on a Rock', because 'the Truth' of James's 'Royal Word' had 'ever been as undoubted' as his 'Courage in the greatest dangers hath been undaunted'. The Canterbury addressers were grateful for the declara-tion, which proceeded 'from so famous a Prince, who by a most Religious observance of his Royal Word both in Adversity and Prosperity', they claimed, had 'attained the Character of James the Just'.[48]

However, these addresses cannot be read as straightforward evi-dence of public opinion. Many came from corporations or judicial benches that had been purged during the years of the Tory Reaction to ensure their loyalty. The corporation of Lyme Regis, for example, under new mayor George Alford, delivered a congratulatory address on James's peaceful accession in March; a few months later Lyme Regis was to be where the Duke of Monmouth was to start his reb-ellion to try to prevent James's accession from being anything but peaceful. We should not, though, put too much weight on the remod-elling of the corporations. Despite Lyme Regis's reputation for radi-calism, there had always been a significant loyalist presence in the town, and Alford had been active (and successful) in promoting loyal addresses in the early 1680s.[49] Berwick-upon-Tweed delivered two loyal addresses: one before and one after the *quo warranto* had come into effect.[50] There may have been a certain amount of fraud in ascribing signatories to an address. The Dean of Salisbury received a complaint that he had affixed the names of several clergy to an address he delivered in the name of his diocese; indeed, the Dean acknowledged that he had taken for granted the consent of some who were too far away to sign the address themselves, although he claimed he had presumed only 'for the *Loyal* Clergy' within his jurisdiction, namely those who had opposed Exclusion.[51]

Having said all this, many of the addresses seem to have been promoted by energetic and apparently sincere loyalists at the local level, who actively assumed the initiative themselves, without any prompting from government agents or those at the centre of power. The corporation of Leicester, for example, agreed to their own address before they received the proposed address sent to them by the Earl of Huntingdon, who had been created recorder of the borough during the years of the Tory Reaction.[52] 'The yong men and apprentices of the citty of Yorke' were keen to 'showe their loyaltie' to the new king on his accession: they had already petitioned the governor of the castle, Sir John Reresby, for permission 'to exercise themselves in arms some days in every year', so that they could 'gain experience to serve the King', before handing him an address signed by 440 of their number 'to present to the King as ther congratulation for his happy accession to the Crown'.[53] Indeed, initially some of the addressers were unsure as to whether their initiatives would be regarded as appropriate. As early as 9 February officials in Southampton were inquiring whether it would be proper for them to show their 'duty to his Majestie in an humble and early Address', and asked for advice.[54] On 26 February Ormonde's servant, Sir Christopher Wyche, waited on Lord Treasurer Rochester with an address from Trinity College Dublin, in order to find out 'whether he conceived addresses of that kind from several parts of Ireland, after the example of England, would be acceptable to the King'. Rochester replied 'that since addresses were now in fashion, if they were drawn with due prudence and modesty, he believed his Majesty would receive them with the same grace' as those from England.[55]

Although the addresses point to the extensiveness of loyalist sentiment at the time of James's accession, we should not necessarily conclude that there was a Tory-Anglican consensus in 1685, or that the Whigs had all but disappeared. Several of the addresses express concern about a residual Whig presence in the localities. The Cinque Ports promised that they would 'not Elect or admit into any Office . . . any Persons that abetted or voted that diabolical and unjust Bill of Exclusion, designed to involve us in Blood, and destroy the Constitution of the antient Monarchy of your Majesties Kingdoms'. The address from Evesham, Worcestershire, expressed a hope that

James's declaration would 'charm those Seditious Spirits into a peaceable acquiescence'. The grand jury for the county of Essex stated that they hoped 'the most Republick and Phanatick Spirits may be convinced that the Law of Heaven is never to be violated by an Exclusion Bill upon Earth', and that the King's declaration would 'oblige the worst of Men to repent of their former Mistakes'.[56] Those addresses delivered during the parliamentary elections that spring often gave assurances that the signatories would do their utmost to secure the return of MPs who would be loyal to the crown, implying that there were still potential candidates, with local support, who might not be so loyal. The corporation and 'other inhabitants' of Scarborough on the East Yorkshire coast promised the King that they would do their best to ensure that the 'Imprudent Promoters of the Bill of Exclusion' would 'for ever be excluded your Majesties great Council of Parliament'. The 'Truly Loyal Inhabitants' of Poole, Dorset, stated that they were aware 'of that Odium this Corporation Labours under through the Malevolent Influence of some few disaffected Persons', but promised to endeavour to return to parliament members who would 'readily concur and comply with whatsoever shall be offered for better settling the Revenues on the Crown'.[57] The 'Loyal Subjects' of Aylesbury, Buckinghamshire, who claimed to be 'the principal and major part of the inhabitants', admitted that their town 'hath lain under the unhappy Character of Phanaticism', though alleged this was because of 'the Irreclaimable Tempers and Spirits of Persons of the Inferior Rank only' who had been encouraged in their disaffection by their former MPs. The 'Loyal Subjects' had now, however, secured the election of two new men – both Tories – and they therefore implored the King 'to distinguish us from the said Disaffected Persons'.[58] The corporation of Kingston upon Hull promised James they would choose as MPs men who were 'truly Loyal and Cordial Lovers of Your royal Person and Government, and Abhorrers of the late Votes for Exclusion', assuring him that those who had signed the address were 'much the greater number' of those who had the right to vote in parliamentary elections.[59]

The Scottish and Irish addresses were broadly similar to those from England, though with their own local coloration. The royal burghs of Scotland stated that they acknowledged James enjoyed his right to the crown 'by the unalterable Laws' of his 'ancient Kingdom', and that he held 'the same immediately from God Almighty alone' (language which echoed that of the Scottish Succession Act of 1681). Edinburgh's address recalled 'the joyful Acclamations with which the news' of James's accession had been received in the Scottish capital and how James, during his stint as head of the government in Scotland, had managed 'to overcome all these desperate Designs which tend to make us Atheists under the pretence of Religion, and Slaves under the pretext of Liberty'. Glasgow's magistrates recorded not only their joy at James's succession but also their optimism that under his rule Scotland would 'be again reduced to Quiet and Happiness'.[60] The corporation of Dublin blessed God for James's 'accession to the imperiall crownes of these your kingdomes', promising to 'obey and serve' their 'true and . . . lawfull sovereign' with their 'lives and fortunes', although they pointedly added that they also thanked James for his 'gratious expressions at [his] first sitting in councill'. Waterford rejoiced at James's 'quiet and peaceable possessing' of his 'lawful and hereditary throne', beseeched God that both James and his 'rightfull heires' might 'long reign over us', and thanked the King for his promise to protect them 'in the injoyment of those things that are most dear unto us'. The members of Trim corporation not only pledged their 'lives and fortunes' in the defence of James's 'person, prerogative, and government' but also offered their 'hartie thanks for the gratious assurances' the new king had been pleased to give them 'of Maintaining the government as by law Established in Church and State'.[61] The Protestant clergy of Ireland sent in addresses thanking James for his promise to protect the Church of England, although according to a retrospective account by the Protestant clergyman William King, they were soon told by the Roman Catholics, 'that his Majesty did not intend to include Ireland in that Declaration', which was to 'be a Catholick Kingdom'.[62] The Catholic clergy of Ireland certainly had cause to be optimistic: when they sent in their own congratulatory letters, James replied by assuring them that he would continue to give them his 'royall protection and favour . . . upon all occasions'.[63]

The acid test of the extent to which the Whig threat had been contained would be the parliamentary elections in England that spring.

(In Scotland, the electorate was small and largely under the patronage of the nobility and merchants; in Ireland there was to be no parliament called in 1685.) From the government's point of view, the results could not have been much better. An overwhelmingly Tory-Anglican House of Commons was returned, with a mere 57 of the 513 seats going to known Whigs.[64] How had this been achieved?

Government management provides part of the answer. Contemporaries noted the 'greate industry' that was used to 'promote the Courte Interest': 'all possible Intrigues, and Closetings' were 'made use of, to elect such Persons as would comply with the King's designs', while letters were written from court 'to a great many Counties, and Corporations . . . with downright Insinuations that their not compliance herein, would be looked upon by the King, as dissatisfaction to the Government'.[65] The Earl of Sunderland, as Secretary of State, wrote to several constituencies advising them whom the King would like to see elected. Other privy counsellors and the Lord Lieutenants were also active on behalf of the crown.[66]

The *quo warranto* proceedings against the borough corporations of Charles II's last years – which had led to many corporations being forced to surrender their old charters in return for new ones which gave the crown greater control over the composition of local town councils – had certainly had a beneficial electoral effect, helping to create safe seats for the government where the corporation controlled the franchise. At St Albans, for example, only the freemen created by the mayor and aldermen under the new charter were allowed to vote, which reduced the electorate from about 600 to less than 100, one half of whom were non-residents. As a result, the two Whigs who had been returned in 1679 and 1681 were ousted in 1685.[67] Perhaps the most significant impact of the purges of both town and county government carried out towards the end of Charles II's reign, however, was to put Tories in a position of strength from which they could best manage the elections to their advantage. Electoral malpractice was rampant. The contemporary diarist Narcissus Luttrell recalled how 'great tricks and practices were used . . . to keep out all those they call whiggs or trimmers', such as holding the poll secretly, at night, with no publicity; adjourning the poll from place to place, 'to weary the freeholders', and refusing 'to take the votes of excommunicate persons and other dissenters'.[68] At St Albans, to return to our earlier example, Whig canvassers were threatened with prosecution, and innkeepers with the dragooning of troops or the loss of their licences if they provided hospitality for Whig voters.[69] At Leicester, the Whig Sir Edward Abney intended to contest one of the seats and was said to have had numerous committed supporters; he was outmanoeuvred, however, being informed that the election was to take place on Monday 16 March only to discover, too late, that it had been held the Friday before.[70] In Derbyshire, the Whig candidate, William Sacheverell, was shut out of the poll by the Tory sheriff, on the grounds that he was not resident in the county when the election writs were sent out, even though Sacheverell could claim 'Custome to the Contrary'.[71] A riot ensued at the Cheshire elections when the Tory sheriff, after first having polled the Tory voters, decided to shut up shop early before he had counted all the Whig voters, thereby manufacturing a Tory victory. Angry crowds of Whig supporters and dissenters broke the windows of the houses of local loyalists, shouting 'Down with the clergy, down with the bishops'; the local Tories celebrated, in turn, at a huge bonfire where they burnt the Bill of Exclusion.[72]

Yet Tory success at the polls in 1685 also reflected the shift in public opinion that had occurred since the Whig-dominated parliaments of 1679–81. As L'Estrange recorded in his *Observator*, it became 'the Common Out-cry at All Elections; No Excluders! No Excluders!'[73] At the Nottinghamshire election, held at Newark on 23 March, for example, a party of electors paraded a banner bearing the words 'No Black Box, No Bill of Exclusion, No Association', which they subsequently burnt at a bonfire in the market place, while there was a similar anti-Whig ritual at a public bonfire at Newcastle under Lyme on 1 April, sponsored by the mayor.[74] (The 'Black Box' referred to the box which the Whigs of the Exclusion Crisis claimed carried the marriage certificate of Charles II and Lucy Walter, thus proving Monmouth was legitimate; the Association was a reference to Shaftesbury's alleged plan in 1681 to form an association of Protestants to protect against the advent of a Catholic successor.[75]) The Tories did well not only in the smaller borough constituencies (where they won 86 per cent of the seats compared to only 50 per cent in 1681), but also in the larger boroughs and the counties (where they won over 90 per cent of the seats, compared to about 25 per cent in 1681). Whereas the Whigs had held between two-thirds and three-quarters of the ninety-two county seats in England and Wales after the elections to both the second and third Exclusion Parliaments, after the 1685 elections they held on to less than one tenth (just eight county seats). Nevertheless, although the Whig position had been seriously weakened and their public support eroded, we should not conclude that Whiggism was all but dead or that, with the exception of a few hardliners, most of those who had supported the Whigs during the Exclusion Crisis had now turned Tory. Some 72 constituencies saw electoral contests in 1685, compared to just 54 in 1681 and 79 in the second general election of 1679; and even in some of those seats that did not go to the polls, there were Whig challenges to the 'selection' of two Tories.[76]

Preaching Loyalism:
The Protestant Clergy and their Catholic King

Further insight into the nature of the loyalist position at this time can be gained by looking at the sermons delivered by the Anglican clergy during the first few months of the reign. These tended to stress divine right and non-resistance, themes that had been heard time and time again during the Exclusion Crisis and Tory Reaction. For example, in a sermon delivered on the first Sunday following James's accession (8 February), Erasmus Warren, rector of Worlington, Suffolk, reminded his congregation that kings were 'Gods upon Earth' who derived their authority from 'God alone', and 'Not at all from his Subjects': 'Elect him they cannot; Confirm him they need not; Depose him they may not.' Subjects, Warren claimed, were under an obligation to obey their king and the 'wholesom Laws' made by 'rightful Legislators'. He did insist that one should not obey the king's laws if they were impious; 'Yet in this case,' he continued, there was 'not the least resistance to be made upon any terms', beyond 'Holy Prayers and Tears'. 'If the rightful King . . . should strein the Government', 'loosen our Laws' and 'lay most heavy burdens upon us,' Warren concluded, 'we must stand under them couragiously . . . till Providence is pleas'd to alleviate or remove them; though they be so ponderous as to crush us to Death.'[77] John Curtois, rector of Branston, Lincolnshire, took as his text that day Romans 13, v.1, 'The Powers that be are ordained of God' – St Paul's classic injunction against resistance – in order to emphasize that all kings were 'to be Obeyed' (as the subtitle of the printed version of his sermon put it). Curtois did allow for passive obedience: 'The Commands of a King,' he said, were 'obligatory to every Subject except where they contradict the Commands of God; and then the Subject may lawfully deny the performance of them.' Nevertheless, treason and rebellion were out of the question and were 'punishable both in this and the next World'. In the process, Curtois articulated what was in essence a defence of royal absolutism. 'The King is not subject to the Coercive Power of the Law,' he insisted. 'There is no Law made but with His Royal Assent: And when the Law is in force it can have no power over him, because the Authority it hath, it receiveth from him both as to the Being and Execution of it.' Although it was true, he went on, that the king, at his coronation, took 'an Oath before the People to govern by the Law', this did not mean that the king was 'Coordinate with or inferiour to the people or the Law, because it giveth him no Right or Title to the Government': his 'Right and title' were 'Antecedent', and both 'the Crowning and Proclamation of him' were 'onely Publick Declarations that he is by Birth-Right in Lawfull Possession of it'.[78] Similar principles were articulated by clergy of the Established Church in Scotland and Ireland.[79]

It is significant to note, however, that despite preaching obedience to the Catholic king, many of these loyalist sermons employed the rhetoric of anti-popery to make an attack on their political and religious opponents. Curtois, for example, reminded his audience that under the terms of the royal supremacy, the Church was subject to the king: 'upon this principle our Reformation from all the other Popish corruptions was founded'. It therefore followed that 'the Presbyterians, Independents, Anabaptists, Quakers', and other Protestant sects who denied the royal supremacy, were 'not to be accounted of our Church', but were 'Retainers still to the Church of Rome, being not yet reform'd from this Romish corruption, of subjecting the King to the Church'.[80] The Scottish Episcopalian minister James Canaries, preaching at Selkirk on 29 May, at the time of Argyll's rebellion, insisted that no justification could be found in scripture for taking up arms 'to resist the Supream Authority', and argued that this doctrine came to Scotland from Rome via Calvin's Geneva, concluding that although 'our Rebels and Fanaticks' made 'such a clutter upon pretence of keeping out Popery', they were in fact 'as great Papists themselves, and sure as dangerous too, as those whom they are so eager against'.[81]

Furthermore, the Anglican clergy's support for the King was never totally unqualified. Many of the loyalist sermons combined a championship of royal authority with a defence of the rule of law. In this respect, a sermon on *The Doctrine of Passive Obedience* by James Ellesby, vicar of Chiswick, is revealing. It was delivered on 30 January 1685 but published shortly after James's accession, to justify 'the Principles of Subjection' to the new king. Ellesby was explicit in stating that the king was absolute. By king, he said, 'we are to understand a Sovereign Prince, one invested with the Supream Power of a Nation', 'one who is acknowledged Sovereign in his Kingdoms', and who has 'no Equal, much less Superiour upon Earth'. 'Such a one as this,' he continued, the laws affirm to be 'Legibus Solutus, free from the Coercive Power of the Law.' Yet in his preface Ellesby insisted that the intent of his sermon was 'not to flatter Princes into an Abuse of their Power, or make them more Absolute than the Law hath done (a Calumny, which some are apt to fasten on the Doctrine of Passive Obedience;) but to teach Subjects their Duty to Governours'. Such things did not vary with the times, hence why his sermon was equally appropriate under James II as it had been under Charles II, especially since James had promised to govern and continue things as now settled and established by law. In the text of his sermon, Ellesby confirmed that people might 'endeavour the Security and Preservation' of their 'Liberties and Estates by all Lawful means, in a Legal Way, and after a Modest, Humble, and Peaceable Manner', as was consistent with 'the Laws of the Land' and 'that Duty and Respect, which by the Law of God we owe our Prince'.[82]

When Francis Turner, Bishop of Ely, delivered the coronation sermon on 23 April, he did not tell James that he could take his subjects' obedience for granted as their divinely ordained ruler. Rather, he implied the need to cultivate their support. 'We have a King who understands,' he claimed, 'that in an Hereditary Monarchy, 'tis the great peculiar advantage of the Prince as well as People, that their Interest is one and the same, their Happiness so closely united.' At this juncture, Turner chose to assure those present that James was 'the Sharer of his Royal Brother's Cares', someone who could be expected to practise 'Justice with Equity' and govern 'according to Law'; Turner naturally did not stop to consider what the situation would be should the people become unhappy because the King chose not to govern according to law.[83] Canaries, preaching at Selkirk in late May, went somewhat over the top in heaping praise upon James, whom (if anything) he thought was better than the great Charles II. Yet his praise for James was linked to the promise the Catholic king had made 'to defend and protect our Religion as established by Law, and all our Rights and Properties', and he was at great pains to emphasize that all the world knew that James was a man who adhered to his word.[84]

One of the most revealing sermons is that delivered by Dr William Sherlock, Master of the Temple and a royal chaplain, before the Commons on 29 May, the anniversary of the Restoration. When asking whether the Church of England was in danger from the Catholic King, Sherlock insisted that 'next to having our King of the Communion of the Church of England', we could 'desire no more, than to have a King, who will defend it', referring to 'those solemn and repeated assurances' that James had 'given us of this Matter'. Although Sherlock urged loyalty, he also said that 'Loyalty and Obedience' were 'a powerful Obligation on Princes to rule well'. He even seemed to imply that the King would endanger his throne should he be rash enough to upset his subjects by failing to protect the Established Church:

for Princes must value Obedience and Subjection as they do their Crowns. To this we owe the present Security and Protection of the Church of England; for if there were nothing else to be liked in it, yet a generous Prince cannot but like and reward its Loyalty; and it would seem very harsh for any Prince to desire that Religion should be turned out of the Church, which secures him in a quiet possession of his Throne.

Sherlock therefore urged the assembled MPs to 'a Church of England-Loyalty'. To be 'true to our Prince', he insisted, 'we must be true to our Church and to our Religion'; it would be 'no Act of Loyalty to accommodate or complement away our Religion and its legal Securities', since 'if we change our Religion, we must change the Principles of our Loyalty too, and I am sure the King and the Crown will gain nothing by that'. Although Sherlock defended the Catholic King, he nevertheless attacked Roman Catholics, on the ground that they did not profess the same principles of loyalty as did members of the Established Church: some papists 'in some Junctures of Affairs, may have been very Loyal', but 'the Popish Religion is not', since, he said, 'it teaches them to rebel'.[85]

The evidence of sermons preached by the clergy of the Established Church (in all three kingdoms) seems to confirm the picture presented by the loyal addresses: many of those who welcomed James's accession in 1685 did so in the belief that the new king would uphold the rule of law and protect the existing Protestant establishment in the Church. After all, James had promised that he would do both, and he was reputed to be a man of his word. At the time, Protestants of the Established Church would not have seen their loyalty as conditional, since they expected that James would indeed keep his word. Nevertheless, it is important to recognize that most of those who championed James II in 1685 adhered to what Sherlock had styled 'a Church of England-loyalty'; it was not quite the unconditional loyalty which James II himself took it to be.

Manifesting Disloyalty: Seditious Rhymes and Treasonous Words

Not everyone welcomed James's accession. Isolated murmurings of discontent can be detected in the early months of the new reign. A seditious rhyme found by a carver's apprentice affixed to the gate of a merchant's house in Deal, Kent, just four days after the accession of the Catholic monarch, asked: 'O Ingland will thow sitt still and see thy neck put in a yoke'?

Thow may remember quene Mary promisde fair
before she the crowne did weare
But when she the crowne she had poscest
she never did let the prodistants rest
From place to place she maid them fly
like birds which dow mount up into the skey
What a dreadful sight it was to behold and see
how poor prodistants lay burning by twos and thres
All thous who would not popish turne
must go to the stake and thear burne.[86]

In Leicester, shortly after James's accession, a 'most hellish damnable treasonable paper against his sacred Majestie' was delivered to the town mayor, suspected to have been written by local buttonmaker John Broadhurst.[87] At about the same time, a woollendraper from Lewes, East Sussex, allegedly expressed his belief 'That every good Protestant or good Christian would be for the Bill of Exclusion'.[88] At the beginning of March the government learned of a seditious paper doing the rounds in Barking, Essex, on the main road into London, which asserted that although the council had declared James 'England's Lawfull King' this was 'not by the Consent of the nation Esembled in parliament and tharfore noe waise binding upon the people to looke upon him as realley sutch'. Indeed, the paper continued, his 'Virtuses' no man knew, but his 'Vices' were 'vary publick and unumerable', including the 'Burning of London' (the Great Fire of London of 1666 had been blamed on Catholics and James was later suspected of complicity himself), 'Murdaring of Justis Godfrey' (the Middlesex JP found dead in mysterious circumstances after taking depositions relating to the Popish Plot in 1678) and 'Grate Essex' (the Rye House plotter who had allegedly committed suicide in jail in 1683), and 'Poisning his Brothar to come to the Crowne'.[89]

Some quickly became anxious about what it might mean to have a Catholic monarch. A man from Charing in Kent was ordered to be fined, pilloried and whipped for repeating a 'report' he had heard in London shortly after James's accession that 'the King would govern by a Standing Army'.[90] One correspondent reported from London that when the King and Queen heard mass at their private chapel in

Whitehall on Sunday 15 February, it gave 'great dissatisfaction to all', 'the great Tories as well as the Whigs', so that 'one could almost believe that they are United'.[91] Thomas Smith, a labourer from Billingsgate, was convicted of having said in March that 'The King of England is a knowne papist, And hee hath forfeited the Kingdome . . . And he ought not to inherit the Crowne.'[92] From Tower Hill in the east of London it was reported in mid-April that 'many ordinary people' were 'secured for dangerous words, and all meanes . . . underhand used by the disaffected to distemper the rabble'.[93] That same month, Londoner Christopher Smitten was found guilty of saying that 'The Catholickes are as liable to be punished as any other Dissenter, And God blesse his Majestie, Hee is as liable to be punished as any other person'.[94] In June, Katherine Hall, the wife of a London malt factor, was accused by her servant, Thomas Tothall, of saying that 'the late King was a blacke bastard and that the Duke of Yorke his present Majestie was a duke of Devills'.[95] Concern about the King's Catholicism led some two to three hundred inhabitants of Portsmouth to stage a pope-burning procession on 1 May.[96] Others had a distaste for the exalting of royal authority by the Anglican clergy. John Curtois encountered some opposition when he preached his sermon vaunting the powers of the crown at Lincoln Cathedral; though it was kindly received 'by many Loyal persons', Curtois said, 'there were a few Heterogeneous men crept in among them that were as much disgusted at it'.[97]

Quite a few people expressed their support for Monmouth's pretensions to the crown, even before there was any inkling that the Protestant duke might attempt to launch a rebellion. The day after Charles II's death, Londoner John Payne (or Paine) was charged with having greeted the news of James's accession by saying 'God blesse the Duke of Monmouth', 'the Duke of Monmouth shall be King for all this' and 'in spight of their hearts'. Payne was subsequently found guilty, fined, and condemned to stand in the pillory.[98] In mid-February, Secretary of State Sunderland received a report from the mayor of Chichester of a rumour spreading through the south-coast town 'that the Duke of Monmouth was proclaimed King in Scotland'; the source, apparently, was a shoemaker's wife named Anne Warnett, who pleaded ignorance and claimed 'she heard it from some persons walking in the street . . . who were strangers to her'.[99] A few days later Sunderland learned how 'the phanatique party' in the north were talking of 'a great moore beyond York where . . . two dukes shall fight for the Crowne of England' – meaning York and Monmouth – and that 'In this battle the Duke of Yorke shall be slain, and the Crown party totally routed'.[100] Towards the end of February, a Yorkshireman lamented the fact that 'Wee have a King but he is uncrown'd, for the Crowne belongs to the Duke of Monmouth'.[101] In early March, Deborah Hawkins, from Holborn, London, told a female acquaintance that there was 'noe King but an Elective King, and if there were Warrs', as she believed there would be, she would 'put on breeches . . . to fight for the Duke of Monmouth'.[102] In mid-March, Dr Benjamin Carr (or Care), from Storrington, Sussex, confronted a drinking companion with the words: 'you are always drinking the King's health but if Monmouth had been King Then wee had had a brave Kingdome indeed'.[103] The following month a man was found guilty of treason for saying that he thought 'the Duke of Monmouth was righteous King'.[104] On 23 April (Coronation day), Edward Apps of Broadwater, Sussex, reported how he had been told 'that the Duke of Monmouth had sent to the Officers that were about Chichester to Aid and Assist him at the Sound of a Trumpet and beate of a Drum'.[105]

Although talking through the examples in this manner might give the impression of a groundswell of popular discontent, it is difficult to get a measure from isolated reported cases of treasonous words or seditious rumour of how extensive popular disaffection might have been. All we can do is set this evidence in the balance against that of the numerous loyal addresses and demonstrations and the tremendous success of the Tories at the polls discussed earlier. There certainly was discontent, and there certainly were seditious grumblings (in various parts of the country) that were enough to give a jittery government cause for concern. But the overall impression left is that the openly disaffected were an isolated minority who were out-of-tune with the general drift of public opinion, even in London where opposition to the popish succession had been so intense at the time of the Exclusion Crisis. When Titus Oates, the Popish Plot informer, was sentenced to stand in the pillory on two occasions in different parts of London in May 1685, we have accounts of huge crowds pelting him with eggs and crying out 'cutt off his ears' and 'hanging's too good for him!' It was only after Oates had left the pillory on the second occasion that a small group of sympathizers turned up and broke the pillory to pieces.[106] In Scotland, there continued to be some rumblings in the south-west, where the fanatics were reported to be 'very insolent, especially against the Ministers'.[107] The Episcopalian minister of Irongray, Dumfriesshire, was violently assaulted and 'left for dead' by some local Presbyterians 'for prayeing for the King'; in the eyes of the assailants, both the King and the loyal clergyman were 'papist dogs'. Although obliged by law to protect their minister from such assaults, the heritors (landowners and householders) of the parish made no attempt to pursue the rioters and were duly fined for their negligence.[108] Outside the south-west, however, things seemed relatively calm. The government, it should be said, was concerned about the potential for unrest in the Highlands, either from 'Rebels within the country, or Argyle, landing with forces from abroad', and therefore issued an order for the demolition of nine forts, castles or fortified houses belonging to the Earl in his ancestral lands, because garrisoning the area would be too expensive.[109] Against this, as we have seen, there is evidence of enthusiastic support for James's accession in the eastern lowlands, from Aberdeen down to Edinburgh, and not just amongst the political and clerical elite, but also amongst the masses. Likewise, in Ireland, there was little sign of disaffection, right at the beginning of the reign, outside Ulster.

2

Meeting the Radical Challenge:
The Scottish and English
Parliaments and the Rebellions of
Argyll and Monmouth

*We are now ready with a considerable stoke of armes and
ammonitions to goe to Scotland, and if God bliss us wee shall
goe abroad the morrow. In a fiwe days the Deuke of
Monmouth goes for Ingland, that both keingdoms may
oppose this apostate papist, who haith murthered his brother
to pave his waiy to the crowne, and as is apparent to all
thinkin men, intends to destroy the nations in all her concerns,
religious and civill. But God who has hitherto helped us, will
yet helpe to pull down that bloddy tyrante . . . All protestaints
in both keingdoms ar longing for us, and will as one man
joyne in with us.*

Sir John Cochrane, Amsterdam, 23 April 1685[1]

In Lime began a Rebellion,
For there the Rebells came in,
Rebells almost a Million,
Came there to Proclaim M. King.

The Glory of the West (1685)

The previous chapter sought to assess the climate of opinion at the
time of James's accession and found that there was a considerable
degree of public support for the new king across England, Scotland
and Ireland, as manifested in loyalist demonstrations and addresses.
Not all were happy with the accession of a Catholic king, to be sure,
and there was smouldering discontent among certain groups across

all three kingdoms. Yet for the time being, at least, the radical Whig challenge appeared to have been contained. What remains to be seen is how this apparent loyalist ascendancy at the time of James's accession would convert into political practice. Its limits had yet to be tested. What would the mood of the political classes be once they were called to assemble in parliament and invited to establish the necessary financial underpinnings for the new king's reign? How would the people at large react if presented with a chance – as they soon were to be – to back a rival Protestant claimant to James's throne? And if most of the Protestants who had welcomed James's accession did so because James had promised he would protect the Established Church and observe the rule of law, what limitations – if any – lay behind this Church-of-England loyalty?

This chapter will focus on political developments in England and Scotland from the spring of 1685 until the end of the year. (Ireland during this time period will be treated in the following chapter.) It will begin by looking at the Scottish and English parliaments, which met in April and May respectively that year, and the quite remarkable degree of goodwill that existed within both towards the Catholic monarch (which nevertheless contained some limits, something that James himself was unable fully to grasp). It will then proceed to examine the challenge posed by the rebellions of Argyll and Monmouth in the late spring and early summer, and show that one of the main reasons why these rebellions failed was because the platforms of Argyll and Monmouth were simply not popular enough at this time: the cause of radical Whiggism in 1685, whether of the Scottish or English variety, was out of tune with the mood of the country. The chapter will conclude by looking at the aftermath of the rebellions and developments during James's second session of his English parliament in November 1685. It will show that already, towards the end of 1685, James had begun to alienate those very people who had welcomed his accession at the beginning of the year, precisely because he had begun to deviate from his promise to protect the Protestant establishment and uphold the rule of law. The key to understanding James's ultimate downfall lies not in the fact that there were radical Whigs and nonconformists who never wanted him to become king in the first place; they made their move in 1685 and

James easily survived their challenge. Instead, it lies in the fact that James proceeded to alienate precisely the people who had supported his succession in the first place and had done their utmost to see that the challenge posed by the radical Whigs was defeated.

THE MEETINGS OF THE SCOTTISH AND ENGLISH PARLIAMENTS

James decided that the Scottish parliament should meet before that in England, in the expectation that its loyalty would serve as 'a good example' for English MPs to emulate when they came to take their seats.[2] As he explained in his letter to the Scottish parliament, to be read on the opening day of the session, and which was printed in the *London Gazette* to make sure the message reached an English audience, the experiences he had had of the Scots' loyalty under Charles II made him decide to call them at this time to give them an opportunity to show their 'duty to Us in the same manner' and 'of being exemplary to others' in the 'demonstrations of affection to our person and compliance with our desires'.[3]

Like his brother before him, James was self-consciously playing the British card. He had every reason to feel optimistic. Not only had the Scottish political elite demonstrated their loyalty to the succession in the parliament of 1681, but the passage of the Test Act in that year – which required office-holders and MPs not only to be Protestants but also to swear an oath of loyalty to the king and his lawful successors, renounce resistance, disown the Covenants, and acknowledge the Scottish king as supreme governor in both Church and state – ensured that most of those who had opposed the policies of Charles II in his last years would be barred from standing for election. James also knew that he could control the legislative agenda through the Lords of the Articles, the select steering committee designed to balance the interests of the various estates (bishops, nobles and shire and burgh commissioners) in Scotland's unicameral parliament, the composition of which was effectively determined by the crown.[4] In a further effort to promote a public climate of loyalty, the formal opening of the Scottish parliament, with all its ritualized pageantry, was timed to coincide with the day of the royal coronation in England, 23 April, which the Scottish council ordered should be commemorated with bonfires.[5] The result was a public relations success. Reporting on the celebrations in Edinburgh, the *London Gazette* boasted of 'the great and universal satisfaction of the whole People, who were gathered together in great Crowds from all parts of the Countrey upon this solemn Occasion'.[6]

In his letter to the Scottish parliament, James explained that he was determined to maintain his royal power 'in its greatest Luster', but 'to the end' that he might 'be the more enabled to defend and protect' the 'Religion as established by Law' and people's 'Rights and Propertys' against the contrivances of the radical Presbyterians.[7] Queensberry, as high commissioner, offered further reassurances of the King's resolve to protect the Established Church and people's 'just Rights and Properties according to the Established Laws of this Kingdom', and asked that parliament in return 'assert the Rights and Prerogatives of the Crown', settle an ample revenue on the crown, and find effective means 'for destroying that desperate Phanatical and irreclaimable Party who have brought us to the brink of Ruine and Disgrace'.[8]

Parliament proved true to its trust. On 28 April it passed an Excise Act, permanently annexing the excise to the crown for 'all time coming', not just for the life of the king as had been the case under Charles II. More remarkable, however, was the Act's preamble. This asserted that the Scottish people had lived for 2,000 years under a continuous line of hereditary monarchs and owed their security and tranquillity 'to the solid, absolute authority wherewith' the 'Sacred Race' of Scotland's glorious kings 'were invested by the first and fundamentall Law of our Monarchy', and expressed abhorrence of all who advocated 'principles and positions' that were 'contrary or derogatory to the King's sacred, supreme, absolute Power and authority'.[9] Parliament, in other words, was confirming by statute that Scotland's monarchy was an absolute one. More money was forthcoming on 13 May, when parliament made an additional gift of Scots £216,000 (£18,000 sterling) per year in order to meet the threat posed by Argyll's rebellion.[10]

Parliament also passed a series of measures designed to protect the Church establishment. It began on 28 April by enacting a bill ratifying all previous laws in favour of the established religion, perhaps revealing its priorities and hinting at a continued concern about the possible threat of popery. Henceforward, however, it turned its attention to dealing with the Presbyterian menace. On 6 May it made it a treasonable offence either to talk or write in defence of the Covenants of 1638 and 1643. This act further stated that husbands should be liable for any fines imposed on their wives, thereby confirming a practice that the government had followed since 1684 in dealing with Protestant recusants which at the time had seemed like a questionable extension of law. It also passed a measure that day stipulating that witnesses who refused to give evidence in cases of treason or pertaining to violations of the laws against field and house conventicles should be punished as if guilty of those crimes themselves. Two days later, parliament made preaching at house conventicles or mere presence at a field conventicle a capital offence. As one Presbyterian author pointed out after the Revolution, together the two pieces of legislation meant that 'the Wife or Child must either contribute to take away the Life of her Husband or Father, or lay down their own Life'.[11] On 13 May parliament extended the Test Act, to make it a requirement of all burgesses and even masters of ships, while on 13 June it made assaults on the Episcopalian clergy a capital offence.[12]

To Presbyterian apologists, the actions of the 1685 Scottish parliament provided the worst example of Stuart tyranny yet. As one later put it, there were 'more Cruel Acts of Parliament enacted in this Tyrant's time, than the former [Charles II] made all his reign'.[13] Yet the actions taken by this parliament in its first few weeks need to be set in the context of the deep insecurity felt by the Scottish government. We should not underestimate the extent to which both James and those who exercised power on his behalf north of the border felt vulnerable to a potential resurgence of Presbyterian radicalism. There were reports that conventiclers were going to their meetings armed,[14] while it was also clear by the time this parliament met that Argyll was going to attempt an invasion from the Low Countries. According to the Jacobite *Life of James II*, 'an apprehension of new troubles' explains 'the King's earnestness to have the field conventicles suppress'd'.[15] The Lord Advocate, Sir George Mackenzie of Rosehaugh, later sought to vindicate the parliament of 1685 by insisting that it was reacting to Argyll's challenge. By its preamble to the Excise Act, for example, Mackenzie explained, parliament did not intend 'to introduce a blind Slavery' but rather 'meerly to exclude these Rebellious Limitations of Obedience invented by the Covenanters'. For staunch Scottish Episcopalians, like Mackenzie, bolstering royal authority was the only way to protect the Established Church in what appeared to be a crisis situation. But there was a *quid pro quo*: the legislation of 1685 was passed in response to the King's promise to protect the Church and his subjects' rights and properties as established by law.[16]

The English parliament, which met on 19 May, was going to require more careful management. It was, however, a staunchly Tory-Anglican body; as seen in the previous chapter, the general election that spring had seen the Whigs capture just 57 of the 513 seats in the Commons. James's approach was to combine a no-nonsense toughness with a few conciliatory gestures. In his opening speech, delivered on the 22nd, he renewed the promise he had made upon his accession to 'Defend and Support' the Church of England and 'Preserve this Government both in Church and State, as it is now by Law Established'. In return, he said, he expected parliament to vote him his revenues for life, as had been the case under Charles II. Indeed, he warned MPs not to attempt to use the power of the purse – 'Feeding Me from Time to Time by such Proportions as they shall think convenient', as he put it – in order to secure frequent parliaments. 'The best Way to Engage Me to Meet you Often', he advised, was 'Always to Use Me Well'. The Commons resolved unanimously to settle on James for life the same ordinary revenues that had been granted to Charles at the Restoration, though remained silent on the unauthorized collection of customs and excise since February. It also made three additional grants of customs and excise duties – two for eight years, the third for five – to meet the cost of the extra forces raised to deal with the threat of rebellion, but these were temporary revenue enhancements designed to address short-term needs. It can hardly be claimed, therefore, as was once argued, that a servile and loyal House recklessly oversupplied the crown, enabling James in effect to be free from parliamentary restraint. What proved to be to James's advantage, however, was that the Commons failed to make a proper assessment of the current value of the ordinary revenue and chose to grant additional supplies through indirect taxation. The expansion of trade meant that the yield from customs and excise went up, with the result that the annual revenues of the crown increased from about £1.3 million in 1683-4 to £2 million for the greater part of James's reign.[17]

James was undoubtedly pleased with the results of this first parliamentary session. As an added bonus, in July parliament revived the Licensing Act of 1662, the lapsing of which in 1679 had allowed for the flood of pamphleteering critical of the court during the Exclusion Crisis. The job of regulating the press fell once more to Roger L'Estrange, knighted in April for his services to the crown, who received a warrant to 'exercise all such power as he formerly did'.[18] James not only got the revenue he wanted; he also, it seems, had the political classes on his side and control over the media.

Undoubtedly the loyalism of this parliament provides a stark contrast with the Whig-dominated parliaments of the Exclusion Crisis. One member even suggested that parliament 'should call to mind the Loyall Example of Scotland that had made it death to goe to Conventicles' and 'not be behind them in Loyalty, and good affection to the King and Church'.[19] Yet the loyalism which the overwhelming majority of MPs professed was a Church-of-England loyalty, and there were already hints that this might create tensions with the Catholic king. On 22 May, Sir Edward Seymour, an Anglican stalwart who had opposed Exclusion under Charles II in the belief that there were laws enough on the statue book to keep the Protestant establishment safe under a popish successor, launched a bitter attack on the way the general election had been run: there had been so many irregularities, he claimed, that many doubt 'whether this is a true representative of the nation or not', and he proceeded to point out that if the government were able to pack parliament, it might also be able to undermine those legal safeguards that had made people conclude that Exclusion was unnecessary. 'The people of England', he intoned, 'were strong in their aversion to the Catholic religion and were attached to their laws', and while it was true that 'these laws could not be altered except by Parliament . . . alterations could easily be made,' he warned, 'when there was a Parliament dependent on those who had that end in view'.[20] The following day a committee of the whole House, comprising some 330 members, sat 'to consider the best meanes to secure religion', and voted unanimously that the House should address the King, asking him to put 'the laws in execution against all Dissenters whatsoever from the Church of England'. James took great offence, and instructed various court members to do what they could to frustrate the measure. The Commons got cold feet and on 27 May instead agreed a resolution that they were 'wholly satisfied in his majesty's gracious Word, and repeated Declaration, to support and defend the Religion of the Church of England, as by law established'.[21]

THE REBELLIONS OF ARGYLL AND MONMOUTH

It was during the first session of the English parliament that the exiles in the Low Countries finally made their move. The two leading actors were Archibald Campbell, ninth Earl of Argyll, and James Scott, Duke of Monmouth, the eldest illegitimate son of Charles II. Argyll was the son and heir of the Covenanter leader, the eighth Earl and first Marquis, who had been executed in May 1661 for treasonous compliance with the Cromwellian regime. The ninth Earl, however, despite initially being imprisoned and sentenced to death by the Restoration regime, managed to get his sentence rescinded and be restored to his family's estates and title in 1663. This opened up a door to service under the crown. He was appointed to the Scottish privy council in June 1664 and for the next decade and a half seemingly remained loyal to the Stuart regime, even when the Whigs in England were pushing for the Exclusion of the Duke of York in 1679–81. Indeed, he joined with the Scottish council in praising York's achievements during the heir to the throne's first stint in Scotland in 1679–80, and went so far as to support the Scottish Succession Act of 1681, which affirmed York's title to the crown of Scotland upon the death of Charles II. However, Argyll fell out with the regime over the Scottish Test of 1681, to which he would swear only a conditional compliance on the grounds that it was contradictory (the Act had been poorly framed and seemingly invited office-holders to swear both that Jesus and the reigning monarch were head of the Church). What made matters worse was that Argyll opted to put his objections to the Test in writing, and as a result he found himself charged with treason, convicted, and sentenced to death. It was a harsh judgment, to say the least; however, the government did not particularly want to see Argyll die, it merely wanted to destroy his power base in the western Highlands which the forfeiture of his estates upon a conviction for treason would achieve. Hence it was not especially alarmed when Argyll managed to escape from Edinburgh Castle in late December 1681 and flee into exile; Argyll's estates were confiscated and his hereditary jurisdictions conferred upon the Marquis of Atholl. However, Argyll was to remain a thorn in the government's side. The radical Whigs courted him in 1683, as they conspired to launch coordinated rebellions across England and in Scotland to bring down the government of Charles II. It was only natural that discontented radicals would look to him again upon the death of Charles II in 1685.[22]

The Duke of Monmouth was born at Rotterdam in April 1649, the product of a casual liaison between Charles and a certain Lucy Walter when the heir to Charles I's inheritance was in exile in the Low Countries. Not the smartest of men, Monmouth was nevertheless stunningly handsome (enjoying some notoriety in his youth as a playboy at the Restoration court), and was doted upon by his father, who made him a privy counsellor, Captain of the Life Guards, and finally (in April 1678) Captain-General of all the land forces in England, Wales and Berwick. Brought up a Protestant, Monmouth seemed the natural alternative to his Catholic uncle, if only his father could be persuaded to declare him legitimate or switch the succession in his favour. Never the Whigs' first choice to supplant York in the succession (the Exclusion Bills of 1679–81 would have favoured James's Protestant daughter, Mary), the Whigs nevertheless realized that Monmouth's popularity with the masses and his following in the army could make him a valuable ally, especially if peaceful means of altering the succession failed. Monmouth's involvement with the Whigs led to his removal from office in 1679, whereupon Monmouth seemed to throw himself more and more wholeheartedly into radical intrigues. His ultimate disgrace came in 1683 following his implication in the Rye House Plot of that year, after which he was forced into exile. Convinced of his own entitlement to succeed his father, motivated by a deep hatred of his Catholic uncle, and surrounded by discontented radicals in the Low Countries who knew he was the man to lead them when the time was right to strike, it seemed all but inevitable that he would make some sort of challenge for the throne upon the death of his father.[23]

The plan was for a coordinated uprising. Argyll was to make a diversionary attack in Scotland, with the intent of reaching Edinburgh; Monmouth was then to start his rebellion in the West Country, which in turn was to be the cue for similar uprisings in London and Cheshire. Writing on the day of James II's coronation, one of Argyll's leading associates, Sir John Cochrane, expressed his conviction that 'All protestaints in both keingdoms' were 'longing for us' and would 'as one man joyne in with us'.[24] Argyll set sail from Amsterdam on 2 May, landing first at Orkney. He sailed round the Western Isles gathering recruits until finally reaching Campbeltown in Kintyre on 20 May, from where he began his campaign. Monmouth was eventually ready to set sail by 24 May, but, delayed by bad weather, did not land at Lyme Regis until 11 June. Cochrane's optimism, however, proved unfounded. Both rebellions were fairly quickly put down: Argyll was captured at Inchinnan (on the banks of the Clyde to the north-west of Glasgow) on 18 June; Monmouth's rebel army was decisively defeated at Sedgemoor (near Bridgwater in Somerset) on 6 July.

Since a little over three years later an invasion from the Low Countries would eventually topple James's regime, it is worth spending time considering why Argyll and Monmouth failed. Some historians have suggested that disaffection in both Scotland and England was sufficiently widespread in 1685 that the rebellions could have succeeded, and that they failed mainly due to poor organization and some crucial tactical mistakes by their leaders.[25] There is no doubt that military weaknesses and tactical errors played a large role in the lack of success of both rebellions (and no doubt whatsoever that William of Orange's invasion of 1688 was much better organized and backed up with considerably more military force). Perhaps the biggest failing was the inability to coordinate the timing of the respective risings. Argyll was ready long before Monmouth's preparations were complete, and could not delay departure partly because his recruits needed paying and partly because his men could not be trusted to keep quiet.[26] As a result, there were essentially two separate rebellions; by the time Monmouth eventually landed at Lyme Regis, Argyll's effort was almost over.

Militarily, Argyll never posed much of a threat to the Scottish government. He arrived with fewer than 300 men, hoping to recruit first in the western Highlands, the area of his ancestral lands, before marching down to Glasgow and eventually on to Edinburgh. Whether strategically the western Highlands was the best place to launch the rebellion is debatable. On the plus side was the fact that the government had always found the Highlands notoriously difficult to police, while Argyll hoped to be able to draw on clan loyalty and the support of his former tenants. He therefore expected he would be able to build up a sizeable army before he would have to engage government troops in battle. The downside was that he had to negotiate difficult terrain on his way south, which inevitably made his progress slow. Moreover, Argyll had not been a popular landlord, and thus found it difficult to raise recruits. He tried to win people over by promises to release them from their debts. However, many of those who joined him did so only under threat of losing their homes or cattle.[27] To judge from the amount of weaponry he brought with him, Argyll was hoping to recruit somewhere in the region of 20,000 horse and foot. At its peak, his rebel army may have numbered 2,500 men, but it dwindled to about 1,500 by early June as a result of desertions or his men simply losing their way.[28] The figures were a desperate disappointment; the last rebellion in Scotland, that of 1679, had generated some 8,000 recruits, 6,000 of whom were still there to take the field against government forces (ironically under the command of the Duke of Monmouth) at Bothwell Bridge.[29] Argyll might have done better to have landed in the south-west, the stronghold of radical Presbyterianism and where both the rebellions of 1666 and 1679 had begun, although it should be pointed out that the government had posted troops all over the area to prevent any outbreak of disorder.[30] The government took prompt and extreme measures to put down the rebellion, calling on not just the militia and the standing forces, but ordering all heritors and all men in the Highlands between the ages of

16 and 60 to be armed in readiness to assist the authorities against Argyll. Even though control of the army was given to the Earl of Dumbarton, a strict Catholic, who was granted a special commission by the King without taking the Test, most people stood by the government.[31]

If Argyll failed miserably because he failed to muster enough recruits, it has to be recognized that this was in large part because his cause was not attractive enough to win the sort of support that was necessary. According to the motto engraved on his standard, Argyll came to fight 'For God and Religion against Poperie, Tyrrany, Arbitrary Government, and Erastianisme', worthy catchphrases, perhaps.[32] The precise agenda of the rebels, however, was set forth in two declarations issued at Campbeltown on 20 May, one intended to appeal to the Presbyterians, the other to members of his own clan. The second, the shorter of the two, was a self-vindication by Argyll, in which he demanded the restoration of his confiscated property and condemned the Duke of York for his 'Usurpation and Tyranny'. The first was a lengthy statement of grievances explaining why the 'Protestant People . . . of Scotland' had risen in arms. It began by claiming that everything done by Charles II since his restoration had been 'Illegal, Arbitrary and Tyrannical'. It condemned both the English and Scottish parliaments of the early 1660s for rescinding laws made during the civil wars and Interregnum, and the Scottish parliament in particular for turning out nonconformist ministers and enacting laws by which Protestant blood was shed. It further accused the government of putting 'innocent and faithful men' to death contrary to law, of 'the desolating of the Churches and changing of the ordinances of God', of 'conniving at Papists' and their 'Idolatrous masses' while 'all Protestant Nonconformists' were 'persecuted with endless severities', and of 'the raising of standing forces', 'the very bane of all civil and Lawful Government'. The rebels next denounced the royal supremacy; the wars against the Dutch (of 1664–7 and 1672–4); and the actions taken against political and religious dissidents in the 1670s and early 1680s (particularly the execution of the murderers of the Archbishop of St Andrews and the proceedings against the Bothwell Bridge rebels; the use of judicial torture against the Scottish Rye House plotters William Spence and William

Carstares; and, naturally, the forfeiture of Argyll's estates). Such actions, all committed during the reign of Charles II, they condemned as 'Tyranny and Popery twisted together'.

They then declared against the Duke of York (as they styled James VII), insisting that he had been excluded from the succession by the English House of Commons (despite the fact that the Scottish parliament in 1681 had passed a measure – which Argyll at the time had supported – stating that the Duke could not be excluded from the Scottish succession), and also against the present English House of Commons, which they said was 'Packed and Caballed and returned by Fraud and Injustice'. Their aims, they proclaimed, were threefold: to restore and settle the Protestant religion; to suppress and exclude popery; and to restore all those who had suffered upon account of their adherence to their party. No attempt was made to appeal to moderate opinion, or to try to win over those who had been loyal during the last years of Charles II's reign but who might have had qualms about the accession of a Catholic monarch.[33] In other words, such a manifesto stood a chance of attracting support only from those who were already disaffected under Charles II; it was likely to confirm the loyalty of those who had rallied to the crown in the years following the Exclusion Crisis because they feared the subversive threat posed by the radical Presbyterians.

Ironically, Argyll failed to win over many of those whom we might have expected to share the political and religious grievances against Charles and James outlined in the manifesto. The Cameronian radicals refused to join the rebellion because it was not undertaken on a covenanting platform and because it included among its leaders malignants – such as Argyll himself and Sir John Cochrane – who had been untrue to the covenants. Instead, the Cameronian leader, James Renwick, and about 200 of his followers posted their own declaration to the market cross at Sanquhar in Dumfriesshire, protesting against James II's succession to the crowns of England, Scotland and Ireland, accusing him of being an 'idolater' and 'murderer of saints', and condemning the present parliament of Scotland.[34] The moderate Presbyterians distanced themselves totally from the rebellion.[35]

Monmouth's rebellion proved more troublesome to the government than Argyll's. In fact Monmouth came over with just eighty-three men – far fewer than Argyll – the main cohort being former Rye House plotters, such as Lord Ford Grey of Warke, Nathaniel Wade, Robert Ferguson and Richard and Francis Goodenough. Among them were a few with military experience, such as Major Abraham Holmes and Captain Edward Matthews, while some English mercenaries serving abroad also joined with Monmouth.[36] Yet Monmouth's aim was to enlist and train an army once in England and he expected the West Country – an area where both Whiggery and dissent had been strong and which had given him a warm reception during his quasi-royal progress of 1680 – to prove a fertile recruiting ground. There undoubtedly remained considerable latent support for Monmouth in the west of England in 1685. The Duke received enthusiastic welcomes on his landing at Lyme Regis and on his subsequent march through Dorset and Somerset, and volunteers were soon flocking to join his cause. Exactly how many joined is a matter of some dispute. Monmouth himself claimed that he mustered an army of some 7–8,000 men. The government believed there were 6,000 rebels in arms.[37] Both estimates seem on the high side. Modern historians would suggest that Monmouth's army at Sedgemoor was certainly less than 4,000 and perhaps little more than 3,000, although by then the number of rebels was certainly below its peak.[38] To put this figure in perspective, some 30,000 armed men had joined the rebellion in the north of England of 1536, known as the Pilgrimage of Grace, to protest against the religious innovations of Henry VIII.[39] In his relation of the battle given after his capture, Monmouth did claim that 'he could have had 20,000 or 30,000 men more but he had no arms for them and thought he needed no more [men than he had] to fight with the king's forces',[40] although this sounds like mere bravado in the aftermath of defeat. The simple fact is that Monmouth came nowhere close to raising that many men. The Monmouth rebellion may have been England's last popular rebellion, but as early modern rebellions go, it was not particularly popular.

James II initially hoped that the local militias would be able to put down the rising, but they proved woefully inadequate: they were not only poorly trained and ill-equipped, but they also showed a general reluctance to march against their neighbours who had joined the rebel force. The King therefore had to call on the army, which he placed under the command of Louis Duras, Earl of Feversham. Even then, the Monmouth men gave the government a run for its money. Feversham was not a great tactician and made a number of errors during the campaign; it was the talented commander Brigadier John Churchill who was really responsible for winning the day at Sedgemoor. Monmouth, by contrast, showed himself to be a commander of considerable tactical skill – perhaps not surprising for the man who had once been Charles II's Captain-General. At one point Monmouth was in reach of Bristol, and might have been able to make an effective strike on the city had he not been delayed by heavy rainfall. Even his plan of attack at Sedgemoor appears to have been an ingenious one, which might have given his troops success, had he not suffered from a certain amount of bad luck. Having said that, however, the military odds were clearly stacked against Monmouth. His inexperienced men made mistakes and ultimately proved no match for trained professionals, especially once Churchill assumed control of the battle.

Monmouth's plan at Sedgemoor had been to surprise Feversham's troops at night with a full-frontal attack. Feversham's army was said to have numbered a mere 700 horse and 1,900 foot (although it was supplemented by the Wiltshire militia quartered nearby), and Monmouth felt confident that if his men kept their discipline he could win the day. He rallied his men at their base at Bridgwater at 11 o'clock on the night of Sunday 5 July, telling them that

the King's forces were incamped upon a common that was very even, large and placed about 3 miles off etc. That they were generally laid down in their tents and many of them asleep . . . and that now it was probable they might take them in their tents without fighting if they would observe these two directions, First to make no noise in their march neither by talking nor otherwise 2: nor to [shoot] till he ordered them.

Unfortunately, the long march in the pitch dark across uneven terrain took its toll of Monmouth's inexperienced men, inducing tiredness and increasing stress. They encountered difficulty crossing Langmoor Rhine: the path they had been following had already become very narrow while the ground mist made it difficult to see even the next man in line, and tension mounted as the guide searched for the appropriate place to cross. One trooper, seeing a shadow moving, panicked and fired his pistol. In an instance, the element of surprise was gone. One of the King's dragoons quickly raised the alarm, shouting 'the enemy had come . . . beat your drums, to arms'. Even then all was not lost, although Monmouth was forced to make a last-minute change of plan, sending his cavalry commander Lord Grey quickly forward with his horse while the royalist soldiers were still emerging from their tents. Things soon began to go wrong for Monmouth's army, however. Grey failed to make the necessary breakthrough, and as Monmouth's foot soldiers began to engage the enemy in battle they showed their lack of experience, shooting repeatedly but wildly at where they thought the royalists troops were, wasting their ammunition as the King's men in turn held their fire. The royalists had by now recovered from their surprise, and although Feversham himself was late on to the battlefield because he had mislaid his wig, Churchill was well in control. As dawn approached, Monmouth's men started to lose their discipline; some sensed the battle was already lost and began to retreat. The King's troops held back from pursuing the rebels until daylight had actually broken, but then the pursuit of the enemy in retreat began in earnest. One estimate suggests that less than 200 Monmouth men were killed in battle, but that 1,000 more were killed in flight.[41]

Before concluding that the rebellion failed essentially for military reasons, it should be pointed out that Monmouth initially had hoped that it would not be necessary to engage in battle. He thought that the soldiers, if they would not join their former commander, would at least remain neutral, and expected not only the common people but also the Whig gentry to rally behind him. Faced with a withdrawal of political support and a loss of control over his army, the rebels felt James would have to give way. Yet the support Monmouth anticipated never materialized. The army remained loyal: not only were there no desertions but it soon showed its willingness to engage the rebels in battle. The gentry remained aloof. Local landowners refused to join the rebels, and the anticipated rising by the Cheshire gentry never happened. Nor did London show any signs of rising in support. The rebellion remained, therefore, a local and predominantly plebeian affair. Monmouth drew support from the lower classes and the young, and the more radical of the dissenters.[42] It was not the sort of troop to bring down a government.

There were a number of reasons why the sociological base of support for the rebellion was so limited. As a result of the revelations of the Rye House Plot, the government was now wise to the intrigues of the radical Whigs. Many were marked men, and in no position to act. At the first sign of trouble, the government rounded up anyone it had cause to suspect and could get its hands on, from prominent Whig magnates such as the influential Cheshire noble Lord Delamere, to smaller-time Whig-leaning political activists in the metropolis or the provinces. To keep such potential troublemakers safely locked up for as long as possible, huge sums were demanded as bail: a Westminster cheesemonger named Gerard had his bail set at £40,000; for Delamere himself the figure was £60,000.[43] Other Whig radicals, including the Rye House plotters John Trenchard and John Wildman, fled to avoid arrest. Trenchard, it was thought, had 'gon into Ireland, with designe from thence to passe over into Scotland' to join with the rebels there – which was substanceless speculation (Trenchard fled to Holland), but indicative of the way the authorities thought of the threat in three-kingdoms terms.[44] Years of persecution had taken its toll on the nonconformists. Many of their leaders were in prison, or had fled abroad; others were heavily in debt. Only those with nothing to lose, the young and the poor, could gamble on joining Monmouth; for most the venture was just too risky, especially given the ostensibly loyalist mood of the country in the early months of the new reign.

There were clearly some who sympathized with the aims of the rebellion who simply lived too far away for them to contemplate joining it. From Newcastle upon Tyne came reports in early June of local people expressing support for Argyll and Monmouth, and a month later even of them raising money to help finance Monmouth's efforts, though this may have been no more than idle gossip.[45] A Portsmouth man, William Reynolds, when drinking with a soldier that June, professed that 'the Duke of Monmouth had a great force and would have a bigger and that he was a true Protestant'.[46] In early July a tailor from East Sussex said that he wondered why the King should set forth a declaration condemning Monmouth when Charles II had issued a proclamation stating that 'the said Duke of Monmouth was his lawful borne sonn'.[47] There was certainly latent support for Monmouth in the capital, and if the Duke had got anywhere near London then there might have been more people willing to join with him. On 1 July, for example, one Thomas Ley was arrested for publicly declaring in the streets of Westminster that Monmouth was 'the true and lawful King of this realm'.[48] A few days later another Londoner, Alexander White, was accused of saying 'that he was for Monmouth and would drinck Monmouth's health'.[49] Yet despite these expressions of sympathy, the simple fact remains that Monmouth failed to generate enough support for his cause, and the major reason for this was because, like Argyll ahead of him, the platform on which he stood lacked a broad enough appeal. Monmouth made no attempt to attract the support of the moderate middle ground or of people who had previously been well-disposed to the crown. Instead, his Declaration, which was penned by the Scottish Independent divine Robert Ferguson, and issued at Lyme Regis on 11 June, espoused a radical Whig ideology.[50]

Monmouth's Declaration was split into two halves. The first offered a justification for taking up arms. It started by asserting that governments existed 'for the peace, happiness and security of the Governed', not 'the private Interest, and personall greatness of those that Rule' and that the 'supreme Magistrates' should 'preserve the people from violence and oppression' and 'promote their prosperity', not 'injure and oppress them'. However, the government of England, it alleged, had been 'wrested from what it was in the first setlement and Institution' and turned from a 'limited Monarchy into an absolute Tyranny'. The Declaration then proceeded to attack the Duke of York, as the rebels styled the King, accusing him of 'contriving the burning of London', 'Instigating a confederacy with France, and a Warr with Holland' (a reference to the Anglo-Dutch War of 1672–4), 'fomenting the popish Plot', and 'advising and procuring the Prorogation and Dissolution of Parliaments'. Since snatching 'the Crown from his Brother's head', it claimed, York had acted against all the laws made for the security of the Protestant religion, by 'avowing himself of the Romish Religion' and calling in 'multitudes of Priests and Jesuits', for whom it was treasonous to enter the kingdom, and had trampled 'upon the Laws which Concerne our Properties', by continuing the collection of customs and excise after Charles II's death. York was thus 'a Traytor to the Nation, and a Tyrant over the

People'. Yet because the course of justice had been perverted by the packing of juries and the judicial bench, there was 'no means left for our reliefe, but by force and Armes'. Significantly, the Declaration spoke of resistance not as a right but as a duty, proclaiming 'Wee are bound as Men and Christians . . . in discharge of our duty to God, and our country, and for satisfaction of the expectations of the Protestant Nations about us, to betake ourselves to Armes.'[51]

The second half of the Declaration outlined the aims of the rebels. They were resolved, it said, to restore the proper balance 'of the old English Government', so that future rulers could only do good and not have the power 'to invade the Rights, and infringe the Liberties of the People'. This meant making sure the Protestant religion was secure 'beyond all probability of being supplanted, and overthrown' and establishing a complete religious toleration for Protestant dissenters. (Interestingly, the rebels were prepared to extend this toleration to Roman Catholics, provided they 'be not found Guilty of Conspiring our destruction'.) But it also involved a series of far-reaching constitutional and legal reforms. Parliaments, the rebels demanded, should be 'annually chosen and held, and not prorogued, dissolved, or discontinued within the yeare' before grievances had been redressed. To stop the various abuses of the law that had occurred during the years of the Tory Reaction, parliament, and not the king, should appoint judges, who should hold their commissions on good behaviour, not at the pleasure of those who appointed them. The rebels further proclaimed that corporations should have their old charters restored; that the Corporation Act of 1661, which debarred Protestant nonconformists from corporate office, should be repealed; as too should the Militia Acts of 1661–2, which gave the king sole command of all armed forces within the country; that the outlawries declared against supposed Rye House plotters should be reversed; that all judgments against any Protestant dissenters 'upon any of the penall statutes . . . made null and void'; and that various laws should be enacted 'for placing the Election of Sheriffes in the Freeholders', for reforming the county militias, and 'for preventing all military standing Forces, except what shall be raised and kept up by Authority and consent of Parliament'. Finally, the Declaration accused the Duke of York of having poisoned Charles II in order to secure the throne, and stated that Monmouth would endeavour 'to have justice executed upon him'. For the moment, however, Monmouth did not 'insist upon his Title' to the throne, but stated that he would leave that to the determination of a legally chosen parliament, 'acting with freedom'.[52]

The manifesto served only to confirm what Tory propagandists had been arguing since the Exclusion Crisis, and what the evidence of loyal addresses and demonstrations suggests many people had come to believe by 1685 – namely, that those who opposed James's title to the throne were nonconformist and republican king-killers, who would foment civil war, and who sought radical reforms to the existing establishment in both Church and state. This was a group of 'traitorous and bloody Associates . . . assisted by the whole body of the Malcontent, dissenting and Phanaticall Party', as an address by the grand jury for East Sussex put it on 16 July.[53] Monmouth's position was probably too radical for many Exclusionists, those more moderate Whigs who had simply wanted to replace the Catholic heir with a Protestant one. Fearing the republican overtones were costing them support, especially that of the landed elite, Ferguson persuaded Monmouth to issue a proclamation at Taunton on 20 June, assuming the title of king.[54] Such a move, however, failed to win over moderate opinion, and only served to alienate some of those who already supported Monmouth. Some appeared to fear that if Monmouth could change his position on the crown in order to appeal to the Anglican gentry, he might go back on his promises of religious toleration. The Sussex gentleman John Ashburnham, when travelling through Dorset two years later, was told by local men that when Monmouth was proclaimed king at Taunton 'the Rabble asked him what Religion he would maintain'. When he replied 'the Church of England as his Father had done . . . they were disgusted, and forsook him in great numbers', expecting 'he should have declared for liberty of conscience'.[55] Richard Rumbold, a Rye House plotter who had joined with Argyll, thought that Monmouth had made a mistake in assuming the title of king, 'seeing his best men ware Republicans'.[56]

Although we cannot question the genuine attachment to Monmouth's cause of many in the West Country (or elsewhere, for that matter) – particularly among the lower orders and religious nonconformists – it is clear that on the whole support for the rebellion in the nation at large was limited. Indeed, there were celebrations in several parts of the country when the rebellion was eventually put down. Often these were encouraged by local Tories in an effort to rally people once more behind the regime, although local organizers in turn were tapping into the groundswell of loyalist sentiment that we have already seen existed at the time of James's accession. On receiving the news that the rebels had been routed, the Lord Mayor of York, for example, ordered bells and bonfires, 'which was forth-with done through out this Cittie with all other Demonstrations of Joy'.[57] Some celebrations were disrupted by disgruntled Monmouth supporters. In London on the night of 9 July, the day after Mon-mouth's capture, a 'Loyal Gentleman' who was 'Drinking the King's Health, at a Bonfire of his Own Making' outside his house, was set upon by 'Six Brutal Ruffians', though he was shortly rescued 'by some honest gentlemen'.[58] The bonfire celebrations at Hitchin, Hertford-shire, on the 10th, which were sponsored by the town authorities, were disrupted by a group of men who had been enlisted by one of Monmouth's recruiting agents. Even so, the crowd of loyalists was so great that the Monmouth men had to wait until the chief inhabitants had gone home to bed, whereupon 'they set upon the best men's sons of Our Town and knock[ed] them down as they was A drinkinge of his Majesties health in the Markett Place'.[59] The official day of thanksgiving for deliverance from the rebellion, Sunday 26 July, pre-dictably witnessed a flood of sermons stressing the obligation of non-resistance.[60] The next day saw the celebrations. The inhabitants of Ashby de la Zouch, Leicestershire, celebrated Monmouth's defeat with 'Bells and Boonfires' where 'His Majesties Royall Families . . . good health were often drunk'. The corporation of Leicester itself held a lavish venison feast, the deer being provided by the Earl of Huntingdon.[61] In Scotland the King's proclamation announcing offi-cial days of thanksgiving for deliverance from Monmouth's and Argyll's rebellions on 23 July (in the diocese of Edinburgh) and 30 July (elsewhere) urged people to feel free 'to use all laufall demon-strations of joy and gladness'. In Edinburgh the day was accordingly observed with 'preaching in the forenoon, and bells, cannons, and bonfires . . . in the afternoon'.[62]

The failure of Argyll and Monmouth confirmed that by 1685 the Whigs were not in a position to offer an effective challenge to the security of the regime. Following the defeat of the rebel armies, the government took speedy measures to ensure that no similar threat could come from that quarter in the future. Argyll was executed in Edinburgh on 30 June, under the sentence of death pronounced against him in 1681. He remained unrepentant on the scaffold, praying, as he did, that God would 'send peace and truth to these king-domes . . . incurage the glorious light of the gospell and restraine the spirite of profanitie, atheisme, superstition, poprey and persicution', and 'that ther should never want one of the royall familie to be a defender of the trew, ancient, apostolicall, catholicall Protestant fath'.[63] A scuffle that developed as his body was being carried away from the scaffold hints at some level of latent sympathy for the Earl among the lower orders in the Scottish capital. Thus when a Catholic woman started railing that she 'wished shee could wash hir hands in his [Argyll's] heart's blood', several other women grabbed her and dragged her to a quiet place, where they 'beat hir soundly', 'tore hir cloaths', and 'robbed hir of hir crucifix and beids.'[64] Two Rye House conspirators who had joined with Argyll were also executed: Richard Rumbold in Edinburgh on 26 June, and John Ayloffe in London on 30 October. Rumbold, who had sustained terrible wounds in his efforts to evade arrest, was 'so weak' by the day of his execution that he had to be helped to the scaffold by two officers of the law, who then continued to prop him up as he delivered his final words. He went to his death defending a contract theory of government. Denying that he was 'Antimonarchial', he protested that he had always thought 'That Kingly Government was the best of all, Justly Executed', by which he meant 'such as by our Ancient Laws, that is, a King and a Legal Free Parliament'. But the king and the people 'were contracted to one another', with the king having 'Power enough to make him Great' and 'the People also as much Property to make them Happy'. It was 'absurd', he therefore thought, 'for Men of Sence to maintain, That tho' one Party of this Contract breaketh all Conditions, the other should be obliged to perform their Part'. He concluded by condemning the present generation as 'Deluded' and 'vail'd with Ignorance', because 'Popery and Slavery' were 'riding in upon them' and they did 'not perceive it'.[65] Of 292 suspected Scottish rebels brought before the Scottish council at the end of July, 177 were sentenced to transportation to New Jersey, 49 of whom were to be 'cut in the eare'; a further 26 were retained in prison or remitted to the justices, and 40 set at liberty.[66] There were some atrocities committed in Argyllshire against the Clan Campbell by government forces under the command of the Duke of Gordon and the Marquis of Atholl: some twenty-two or -three who had surrendered under promise of protection were put to death, while the countryside around Inveraray was laid waste, with parties sent out to pull down houses, destroy fruit trees and burn fishing nets, in an effort to ruin the local economy. Such action did not meet with official approval, however, and Atholl was deprived of his lieutenancy for his pains.[67]

The fiercest retribution took place in England.[68] About a hundred Monmouth rebels were summarily executed by royalist soldiers following the battle of Sedgemoor. Another 1,300 were taken prisoner. Monmouth himself, who had fled the scene of battle and been found three days later hiding in a ditch, was taken to London and beheaded on 15 July. Despite paying his executioner well, Monmouth was literally butchered on the scaffold. It took the executioner five strokes of the axe to sever the head from Monmouth's body; after the first stroke, Monmouth was purportedly seen to lift his head in anguish, and, according to Evelyn, the crowd of onlookers was so incensed that 'they would have torne' the executioner 'in pieces' if he had not been protected by a heavy guard.[69] Immediately after Sedgemoor, a special commission of oyer and terminer (literally 'to hear and determine') was issued to Lord Chief Justice Jeffreys and four other judges to clear the West Country jails of all prisoners, although the commission did not begin its work until 26 August due to the fact that Jeffreys was afflicted by a painful attack of kidney stones. A number of the rebels, crammed as they were into tiny West Country prisons in appalling conditions in the heat of the summer, succumbed to jail fever or their battle wounds before Jeffreys' infamous 'Bloody Assizes' even got under way. The vast majority of those brought to trial were found guilty and sentenced to death, although in the end only about 250 were executed, while 850 had their sentences commuted to transportation – ten years' obligatory labour in the West Indies. The rest either died in jail or received pardons. A few score of the Monmouth rebels escaped to the Continent, mainly the Low Countries, among them Robert Ferguson. Although the execution-rate might seem low, the sight of so many people being butchered in such a short space of time, with their quartered remains set up for public viewing, left a deep scar on the West Country. Some twenty-nine were appointed to die at Dorchester on 7 September, until the two executioners sent down from London – Jack Ketch and Pascha Rose – protested that they could not hang, draw and quarter that many in one day; in the end they managed to get through thirteen. Jeffreys justified his actions by stating that it was important that the 'Whiggs' had 'the utmost vengance of the Law taken upon them'. Lord Chief Justice Sir Edward Herbert, however, felt there was a class bias in the recriminations, observing that 'the poor and the miserable were hanged, but the more substantiall escaped'.[70]

The government also took the opportunity to pursue a number of alleged Rye House plotters, on the basis of new information provided by seized Monmouth rebels eager to turn King's evidence in order to save their lives. Both Henry Cornish, the London sheriff responsible for impanelling the Whig-packed juries of 1680–1, which saved so many of the government's religious and political enemies from feeling the lash of the law during the Exclusion Crisis, and Charles Bateman, the late Earl of Shaftesbury's surgeon, were executed for conspiring the death of Charles II in 1683. Another Rye House conspirator, John Hampden, was convicted for a similar offence after pleading guilty and confessing, although he had his death sentence commuted to a fine of £6,000. The retributions, in addition, threw up two noted female martyrs – Lady Alice Lisle and Elizabeth Gaunt – for harbouring and assisting supposed Monmouth rebels. Lisle was beheaded at Winchester on 2 September; Gaunt was burned at the stake in London on 23 October. As she was brought to her execution, Mrs Gaunt reportedly picked up one of the faggots 'and kissed it', saying 'it was of little consideration to her, whether she dyed in the fire' or 'in her bed'. All the while, she protested her innocence of treason, claiming that she had merely given charity to the wife and children of the rebel she was deemed guilty of helping, who had come to her 'ready to perrish for want of bread and cloathing'. Gaunt holds the dubious honour of being the last woman to be executed for treason in England; she was not strangled first, as was often done out of mercy, but instead left to be consumed alive by the flames.[71]

A certain amount of residual support for Monmouth can be detected in England following the defeat of the rebellion. Shortly before Monmouth's execution, one Yorkshire man defended Monmouth's right to fight against his uncle to claim an estate left to him by his father, and added that it was 'a pittie that the Duke should loose his right'.[72] Shortly after the execution, rumours began circulating that Monmouth was not really dead. The earliest such report can be traced to August 1685.[73] In February of the next year a husbandman from Lyme Regis confessed to having said that 'Munmouth was noe more dead then he was' and that 'an old man with a Beard' had been executed 'in his place', and to having predicted 'that wee should see other manner of doeings here'.[74] Nor was it just in the West Country that such sentiment was to be found. For example, a local innkeeper allegedly declared at Ely market on 24 October 1685 that Monmouth was still alive.[75] There also appear to have been pockets of support for Monmouth up in Yorkshire. In October 1686 a man named Alexander Cranston from near Scarborough affirmed 'that the Duke of Munmoth was alive, and that he could goe to him before night', and that one Colonel White was beheaded in his stead – adding that 'he hoped that Monmouth would weare the crowne of England on his head in two yeares time';[76] at the York Assizes in March 1687, a Scotsman was fined £500 and ordered to stand in the pillory for making the same claim;[77] and in April 1687 a blacksmith from the North Riding allegedly pledged a health to the Duke and claimed that he 'had sown oats . . . for Monmouth's horses to eat'.[78] The dissenters in Derbyshire were disabused of the notion that Monmouth might still be alive only in August 1687, when a visitor to the area confirmed that he had witnessed the execution.[79] In early 1688 a Bristol surgeon reported that Monmouth would land at Cornwall on 15 May 1689 with 40,000 Irish men, that 40,000 more would join from Plymouth, 7,000 from Holland would land in Wales, 5,000 more would sign up at Weymouth, and 40,000 Swedes and Bohemians would land at Dover – information which he claimed he had been told by someone who had fought under Monmouth.[80] The figures are astronomical, but their inflated size perhaps reveals how desperate some people had come to feel under James II by early 1688. In July of that year a person was convicted in Lincolnshire for reporting that Monmouth was alive, 'and would shortly be in England'. The authorities were alarmed enough to sentence the deluded individual to a public whipping through the town of Spalding.[81] By July 1688, of course, the prediction that one of King James's nephews would shortly be in England was right on the money; the nephew concerned (James's sister's son, rather than his brother's) was very much alive.

The English government feared that diehard extremists might attempt a further rebellion, with an impostor acting in Monmouth's name. In the spring of 1686 government spies learnt of reports that a young gentleman, posing as Monmouth's eldest son, was intriguing with exiled political dissidents in the Low Countries.[82] In May an informant revealed that a woman in Ilchester prison in Somerset, a sister of two Monmouth rebels, was boasting that there would be a second rebellion before midsummer, and that Monmouth was going about 'in woman's Cloaths in Bristol and Summersettsheer', and that his friends and agents in those parts were 'bisy a getting person's hands to subscribe to assist him'. In July information was received that a Taunton woman, by the name of Mary Mead, had turned up at a house in Southwark, where she believed Monmouth was hiding, carrying 'a banner or warlike colour of red and blue silk' which she wanted to show the Duke. The following February more information linked Mary's name with an Oxford woman called Tabitha Smith, a glover by trade, in a nationwide conspiracy to raise money for a second rebellion from places as far afield as London, Bristol, Worcester and Lancashire. Tabitha allegedly predicted that Monmouth would launch another rebellion the next summer, and be at Hounslow Heath with 40,000 men.[83] A man claiming to be Monmouth was indeed found concealed in a house some ten miles outside London (a little beyond Hampstead) in October 1686, although 'no person of Condition or Estate' was drawn to him, only 'Apple women, Higglers, etc.'. The government was not too concerned with him, since it proceeded against the imposter not for high treason but for high misdemeanours, though even then conviction was enough to earn a whipping from Newgate to Tyburn and a stint in the pillory.[84]

Although the rumours of renewed plots may be treated with

scepticism, some of Monmouth's supporters continued to cause problems for the authorities, especially in the West Country. In the first place, there were the fugitive rebels. In early December 1685 came reports of some two or three hundred West-Country rebels (who had been hiding out in the woods since Monmouth's defeat) descending upon the town of Chard, near Lyme Regis; two companies of horse were sent to deal with them, and the Monmouth-men quickly disappeared back into the woods. Reports continued in the early months of the new year of 'small parties' of armed rebels in the West robbing the gentry of their cattle and engaging in the occasional conflict with locally stationed troops, before disappearing back to their caves and woods. These Monmouthites were in reality no more than desperate men who feared legal retribution if they returned to civil life – 'vagabond people' or 'a sort of Banditi' on the search for food, as contemporaries described them – rather than unrepentant insurrectionists trying to sustain the cause for which Monmouth had given his life (though at the end of December 1685 there was a report that they had killed the hangman responsible for the executions of the rebels at Taunton in an act of revenge). It was a problem that was largely resolved by James's decision to grant a royal pardon on 10 March 1686.[85] However, tensions clearly remained between communities that had taken different sides during the rebellion. In the late spring of 1687 two riots occurred in northern Somerset between Monmouth supporters from Burnham and the inhabitants of the neighbouring parish of Huntspill, who had been loyal during the rebellion and assisted in the capture of several of the Burnham rebels. The first happened on 23 May, a revel day at Burnham, when a local victualler called Stephen Wride, a former Monmouth rebel himself, confronted a Huntspill man for 'riding in the King's army'. Wride declared 'that he was for the Duke of Monmouth', and drew up the Burnham men and a few from the surrounding area 'into a distinct body' in opposition to the Huntspill men, challenging them to fight and calling them 'popish rogues'. The more serious incident happened at Huntspill fair on 29 June. About a hundred Burnham men descended upon Huntspill, marching behind a bloody handkerchief, which they said was Monmouth's colours, singing pro-Monmouth songs and claiming that 'there would shortly be an alteration of the times and that

Monmouth was daily expected amongst them'. Falling upon the Huntspill men, they said they 'would see what those Papist Rogues that were for the King could doe now', and boasted that 'Now Holland had conquered France'.[86]

This last remark contained a double irony. Within a year and a half, Holland would indeed conquer France, metaphorically speaking, in that a successful invasion by William of Orange would topple James II's Catholic regime and bring England into a European coalition against the French king, Louis XIV. The reason why James's regime proved unable to withstand William's challenge, however, had little to do with the activities of the radical Whigs. Rather, it was in large part due to the fact that James managed to alienate those who supported him in 1685, the very people who had championed his accession and defended him against the Monmouth threat.

In order to appreciate the reasons for this alienation, we need to return to the language in which defenders of James at this time chose to couch their loyalty. As this and the preceding chapter have made clear, loyalists expected the new Catholic king to protect their Church against the double threat of popery and nonconformity. James was given a clear reminder of this fact when he visited the corporation of Windsor in August 1685. The recorder made a forthright speech in which he gave 'his Majestie all possible assurance' that the members of the corporation 'would stand by him with their lives and fortunes in the defence of his Majestie's Supremacy against all Papists and Presbyterians'.[87] Valuable insight into the loyalist mindset is provided by a sermon preached at Oxford by Charles Allestree on the day of thanksgiving for the defeat of the Monmouth rebellion. The rebels, Allestree said, claimed that it was their aim to defend the true religion, but in fact 'our Religion' was not 'in the least danger of being invaded or snatch'd from us'. Not only did English subjects have 'the free use of the Sacraments, and all the Ordinances of God uncorrupted for the assistance of our Devotion', but they also had 'the promise of our King for the continuance of these spiritual enjoyments to us', a king, indeed, 'that never had the imputation and scandal of breaking his Word'. The first half-year of James's government, Allestree moreover thought, made it clear that the Catholic king intended to remain faithful to the promise he made at his accession 'to preserve this government both in Church and State, as it is now by law establish'd'. For 'all the Vacancies, that belong to the disposal of the Crown', had been 'carefully fill'd . . . with Men of Great learning and Abilities to support our Religion, of Great zeal and inclination towards it, whose secular Interest is inseperably bound up in the preservation of it'.[88]

The problem was that in the remaining months of the first year of the King's reign, it began to become apparent that James was not going to remain faithful to his promise to preserve the government in Church and state as by law established, and that he was willing to promote to positions of authority men who were not committed to the Established Church. As a result, the limits to loyalty soon began to reveal themselves. Because the context was different in each of the King's three kingdoms, they need to be treated in turn. The remainder of this chapter will focus on the situation in England in the second half of 1685. Subsequent chapters will deal with developments in Ireland and Scotland.

THE LIMITS TO LOYALTY IN ENGLAND

Appropriately staged royal events continued to offer public manifestations of support for the King. A royal visit to Winchester on 18 September, for example, not only provided an occasion for a display of respect and loyalty from the civic authorities, but the local inhabitants reportedly followed James's coach through the city 'with continued Acclamations of God save the King'.[89] Court festivities for the queen's birthday on 25 September caused 'great rejoicing at Windsor' and bonfire celebrations in London,[90] while James's own birthday on 14 October saw 'publick demonstrations of joy' in the capital and several provincial centres. In particular, there was 'a great bonfire' in Drury Lane, London, where locals had made effigies of the nonconformist divines Richard Baxter, Robert Ferguson and Stephen Lobb, and also of the Popish Plot informer, Titus Oates, which stood in the pillory with the words 'Perjury and Forgery' affixed to its shoulder. There is no doubt that James's birthday celebrations were encouraged from above. The Lord Mayor of London had issued an order for bonfires to be lit, while churchwardens' accounts reveal that some parishes paid for bonfires 'under direction'. Similarly, the magistrates of Norwich ordered 'bonefires to be made through the whole City at night', while at Newcastle upon Tyne the mayor arranged for a high pyramid of tar barrels to be erected in the market place, with a gibbet fixed on the top hung with 'the Association' and 'Bill of Exclusion', to be burnt at the hands of the common hangman. Nevertheless, there were also more spontaneous celebrations. In London we hear of 'divers Youths makeing bonefires in or near Smithfield', although there was a violent scuffle at one as a hostile group tried to 'take away the Wood . . . gotten for that purpose', which resulted in one of the loyalists receiving a fatal blow to the head. At Newcastle upon Tyne, in addition to the great display at the market place, the streets, we are told, 'were full of particular Bonfires'.[91]

At the same time, the government did its best to prevent the public expression of opinion hostile to the regime. In London, precepts were issued forbidding bonfires on 5 November, Gunpowder Treason Day. The ban was not totally successful. Roger Morrice noted four fires or more in Holborn, six or seven in Bread Street, and a number in Cripplegate and various other places, while a Westminster tailor got into trouble for provoking a tumult by making a bonfire in Shrugg Lane. In some parts, instead of bonfires several great barrels were piled up on top of each other, with lighted candles fixed upon them. In the main, however, Londoners restricted themselves to illuminating their windows with candles.[92] Although not widespread, there were certainly similar displays in other parts of the country. Prestbury in Gloucestershire commemorated 5 November with a gigantic bonfire sponsored by the local churchwardens.[93] In response, the privy council issued an order on 6 November forbidding bonfires upon any solemnity whatsoever, without the King's special licence or allowance.[94] This led one London woman to curse 'the King and his Popish religion', complaining that 'Wee never lived well since such Popish Doggs ruled the Land',[95] yet the prohibition proved effective in keeping things quiet on the 17th, the anniversary of Queen Elizabeth's accession to the throne in 1558 (following the death of England's last Catholic ruler, Mary Tudor).

Nevertheless, signs of increasing disaffection were beginning to show themselves. The main source of grievance was the army. James had responded to Monmouth's challenge by dramatically increasing the size of his standing army, from the 8,565 troops he inherited from his brother to 19,778 by the end of December, while concern about the ineffectualness of the militia in dealing with the rebellion made him determined to keep this army in being.[96] Different regiments were stationed in various parts of the country, much to the disgruntlement of the local population. To one Berkshire man, 'all the Kings Soldiers' were 'Rogues'.[97] The inhabitants of Aylesbury in Buckinghamshire were deeply upset about having troops quartered in their town and petitioned the King to have them removed, though the worst atrocity that appears to have happened was a soldier killing poultry that belonged to the country people.[98] When the Duke of Norfolk's regiment was billetted in the east of the city in mid-August there were reports not only that they 'stoll all . . . they could lay their hands on' but also that they were 'very abussiffe' to the local householders and threatened to rape their wives. At Great Yarmouth, Norfolk, towards the end of the year, when one Harry Flemin and his brother were arrested for hurling abuse at the soldiers stationed there, calling them 'treacherous villains' and 'rogues', a crowd in excess of 200 people gathered to try to rescue them; they were dispersed only when the guard threatened to open fire – a measure that was effective but hardly likely to endear the soldiers to the local inhabitants.[99] Indeed, the government received so many complaints against soldiers stationed in various parts of the country that James had to publish a declaration on 25 August commanding that all troops should duly pay for their quarters, use no violence, and that none should be quartered in any private houses.[100]

In addition to increasing the size of the army, James had given a number of commissions to Roman Catholics, in direct violation of the Test Act of 1673, which had required all office-holders under the crown to take the Anglican sacrament. Halifax, the peer who had spoken out most forcefully against the Exclusion Bill in the Lords in November 1680, challenged the royal initiative in council; James responded by dismissing Halifax from his position as Lord President and appointing the Earl of Sunderland as his replacement. Four of Halifax's supporters – the Duke of Ormonde, the Earl of Bridgwater, Viscount Falconbridge and Bishop Compton of London – stopped attending council meetings, sensing their presence would not be welcomed by the King. The Duke of Albemarle and the earls of Devonshire, Dover and Thanet resigned their army commissions – Albemarle in protest against the continuation of Feversham (who was nominally a Protestant) as commander-in-chief, the others in protest against the commissions given to Catholics.[101]

A serious confrontation over the army broke out in parliament when it reconvened on 9 November. In a mood of brash and aggressive self-confidence, James was quite forthright in his opening speech. The Monmouth rebellion, he said, had revealed the inadequacy of the militia, and that 'nothing but a good Force of well-disciplined Troops, in constant Pay' could defend the country from such enemies either at home or abroad. He therefore asked parliament to grant him a supply for the support of this army, which had doubled in size, and calmly announced that he had given commissions to Catholics in violation of the Test Act, something which he said no one should take exception to.[102] It was a speech that provoked a furore in the predominantly Tory parliament. There were heated debates in the Lords as to whether the House should vote an address of thanks; supporters of the court were only able to win the day as a result of an intervention by Halifax, who sarcastically said that 'They had now more reason than ever to give Thanks to his majesty, since he had dealt so plainly with them, and discovered what he would be at'.[103]

The King's speech came to be debated in the Commons on the 12th. Although some MPs were prepared to defend the King, many Tories were deeply alarmed about the threat to the rule of law posed by James's granting of dispensations from the Test. Sir Thomas Clarges, a Tory-Anglican stalwart who had served in the Exclusion parliaments, recalled that the Whigs had predicted that a popish successor would 'have a Popish Army' and explained that his own opposition to Exclusion had been grounded on the belief that the existence of the Test Act would ensure that no papists could 'possibly creep into any employment'. Edward Seymour, another outspoken opponent of Exclusion in Charles II's reign, acknowledged the problems with the militia, but said he would rather pay double to see it improved than half on a standing army, of which he 'must ever be afraid', pointing to the recent abuses committed by the army since the suppression of

Monmouth's rebellion. As for employing officers who had not taken the Test, it was 'dispensing with all the laws at once', Seymour said, while granting the supply asked for would be equivalent to 'establishing an army by act of parliament'. On 16 November the Commons presented an address to the King, insisting that those officers in the army who did not qualify under the Test Act could not 'by law be capable of their Employments' and that their incapacities could not 'be taken off but by an act of parliament'. James was outraged, stating in his official answer on the 18th that he 'did not expect such an Address from the house of commons'. Thomas Lord Wharton immediately moved that the Commons set aside the following Friday (the 20th) to consider its reply to the King's answer. John Coke, Tory MP for Derby, seconded the motion, adding 'I hope we are all Englishmen, and are not frighted out of our duty by a few high words'. It was an outburst that was sufficiently offensive to see Coke dispatched to the Tower, following the protestations of Viscount Preston, despite the fact that Coke tried to deny the words and other MPs testified to his loyalty. Nevertheless, Coke's words were to prove prophetic; as the course of James II's reign was to show, many committed Tory Anglicans were not to allow the Catholic king to frighten them out of what they took to be their duty.[104]

Fierce debate resumed when the Commons came to consider the grant of supply on the 17th. Sir John Ernly, the Chancellor of the Exchequer, suggested the sum of £1,200,000. Others, however, were for voting much less: Viscount Campden, MP for Hampshire (who was to become a Nonjuror after the Revolution – that is, one who would not swear allegiance to the new regime) moved for as little as £200,000. Clarges was for giving 'little now, to have opportunity to give more another time', intimating the need to keep the King financially dependent upon parliament. John Wyndham, MP for Salisbury and a staunch High Churchman, said he was 'for the least sum', because it was 'for an army', which he wanted to be rid of as soon as he could, 'being satisfied that the country is weary of the soldiers, weary of free quarters, plunder, and some felons'. Thomas Christie, MP for Bedford and another Tory Anglican, feared the threat to liberty posed by a standing army: 'We owe . . . a duty to our country', he affirmed, 'to leave our posterity as free in our liberties and properties as we can', while the fact that there were officers in the army that had not taken the Test, he continued, 'greatly flats my zeal for it'. After a series of close votes, the Commons agreed on the compromise sum of £700,000.[105]

James was also to face opposition in the Lords, when, following the lead given by the Commons, the Earl of Devonshire moved on 19 November that the peers should reconsider the King's speech. Clarendon and Jeffreys tried to forestall the attack, on the grounds that it would be inappropriate to discuss the King's speech when they had already voted their thanks for it, but in the end the motion was carried without division. Although Devonshire was a Whig who had voted for Exclusion, and was joined by other peers with Whiggish leanings, such as Anglesey and Mordaunt, what is notable about the debate that ensued is the criticism that came from representatives of the Tory-Anglican interest. Bishop Compton of London, who had spoken against Exclusion in the Lords in 1680, gave a lengthy speech warning of the threat to the civil and religious constitution of the realm if the laws against Catholicism were broken, and he claimed to represent the views of the entire episcopal bench. The Earl of Nottingham, a staunch Tory Anglican, and Halifax also spoke out in condemnation of the King's speech. From the accounts of the debate that survive, it is not always possible to attribute specific remarks to particular peers. What is apparent, however, is the emphasis that was placed on the need to adhere to the law even in defiance of the King's wishes. Thus it was insisted that 'the Test was now the best fense they had for their religion', and that 'if the king, might by his authority, supersede such a law . . . it was vain to think of law any more. The government would become arbitrary and absolute.' It had become obvious, as one peer put it, that 'The King's promise for their religion was not sufficient to rely on'. The Lords were also concerned about the international situation, and the threat to the security of Protestants in western Europe more generally, now that there were Catholic kings on both sides of the Channel. One suggested that the 'French king would not have ventured to use his Protestant subjects so ill' – an allusion to Louis XIV's recent rescinding of the toleration granted to the French Protestants (or Huguenots) under the terms of the Edict of Nantes of 1598 – 'had he not seen that the English had a popish King, who would not resent it'.[106]

James, who was present to hear the debate in the Lords, had by now had enough. He prorogued Parliament on 20 November, thereby losing even the grant of £700,000 that the Commons had agreed to give. He was never to call a parliament in England again. He then proceeded to dismiss those who had displeased him, including all the Protestant officers in the army who had voted against his interest, and Bishop Compton of London, whom he removed from the council.[107] It revealed a deeply ingrained arbitrary streak to his personality, an inability to tolerate anyone who would not support what he wanted to get done. Politically it was naïve. The rich men in the City of London were said to be 'very discontented', so much so that trade had become 'very dead, for the men of most wealth and money ther, being il affectioned to the present government, keep up ther money, and will not let it circulate in trade, and care not for a while to lose ther interest and profite'.[108] Even more significant, perhaps, are the early signs of a rapprochement between the dissenters and the Church. Thus in London by December 1685, we are told, the terms Whig and Tory were 'quite laid by, and now nothing talked of but whether a Protestant or a Papist', and that 'the fanatics' complied 'more than before with the Church of England for having upon this trial appeared to make a stand' – indeed, so pleased were the Presbyterians with 'this honesty of the Bishops . . . that many of them went and communicated with them'. 'The wise Catholics', it was said, were 'troubled to see those united who were formerly tearing of each other.'[109]

The wise Catholics were right to sense trouble. James was to embark upon an ambitious reform programme across England, Scotland and Ireland that was to cause nothing but trouble – initially for the Protestants, but ultimately for the Stuart monarchy and the Catholic interest. Exactly how James set about helping his co-religionists in his three kingdoms – and the effect his initiatives had – will be the subject of the next three chapters. Because of the impact that Irish and Scottish developments had on opinion in England, we shall start with Ireland, then turn to Scotland, before finally looking at affairs in England.

3

'That unhappy Island of Ireland'

> *It was chiefly upon their Account, by shewing Favour to them*
> *[the Irish Catholics], that K.J. brought upon himself all his*
> *Misfortunes. Putting them into Power, and displacing*
> *Protestants to make Room for them, made more Noise, and*
> *rais'd K.J. more Enemies, than all the other Male-administra-*
> *tions, charg'd upon his Government put together.*
> [Charles Leslie], *An Answer to a Book Intituled, The State of*
> *the Protestants* (1692), pp. 125–6

> *Get out of our country!*
> Irishman Henry O'Hagan to Scotsman Andrew Johnston,
> 10 June 1685[1]

Of the three kingdoms that comprised the British Isles, Ireland had
proven the least trouble to Charles II. This is not to say that it had
been trouble free. The restored monarch's Irish inheritance had been
far from propitious and there remained deep-seated religious and economic tensions, with the most divisive issue being the land settlement,
which had left many Catholics who felt they had been wrongfully dispossessed during the 1640s and 1650s unable to recover their estates.
Yet during Charles II's reign a workable, if somewhat fragile equilibrium had been achieved: the Protestant ascendancy was maintained,
but the penal laws against Catholics were not too strictly enforced;
the population of Ireland recovered from the ravages caused by civil
war, pestilence and famine; and the economy began to pick up.[2] In
Scotland, religious tensions, combined with a policy of persecution,

had prompted two rebellions, in 1666 and 1679. England had seen a serious challenge to the Restoration monarchy in the late 1670s, a threatened rebellion (in conjunction with malcontent Scots) in the early 1680s, and an actual rising against the Catholic succession in 1685 (again, in coordination with a synchronous rebellion north of the border). Yet despite the impact that the *perception* of what was going on in Ireland had had in England during the Exclusion Crisis, there was little sign of significant opposition to the government of Charles II from within Ireland itself. Similarly, although there was an Irish dimension of sorts to the Rye House Plot, malcontents in Scotland and England found it difficult in practice, at this time, to stir up active resistance in Ireland to the Stuart monarchy. Furthermore, there was no rebellion in Ireland in 1685.

Ireland, however, was to become rapidly and dramatically destabilized under James II. One Protestant author, writing in 1690, argued that this was because as soon as James became king, 'he fixed his whole study upon the Establishment of his darling Twins, Popery and Slavery' and determined that 'Ireland should be the first unhappy Scene of the ensuing Tragedy'.[3] Yet in truth, Ireland was a lower priority for James than England or Scotland. He certainly wanted to help his co-religionists in his western kingdom, but he was well aware that doing too much, too quickly, would alarm the English and undermine his chances of establishing religious and political freedom for Catholics in England. Any attack on the Protestant ascendancy in Ireland, moreover, would hit trade and reduce the revenues of the crown, since two-thirds of the Irish revenue came from customs and excise.

However, James did allow himself to be swayed by Irish interests at court, particularly his friend of thirty years' standing, Richard Talbot, a native Catholic of Old English stock. Born in 1630, as a teenager Talbot had been with the royalist garrison at Drogheda in 1649 when Oliver Cromwell laid siege to the town and ordered his troops to give no quarter; Talbot himself 'received so many wounds that . . . he was left for dead and spent three days lying amongst the slain' before eventually managing to escape. An embittered enemy of the man who came to head the Republic in the 1650s, he joined in a conspiracy to assassinate Cromwell in 1655; arrested by the English authorities and threatened with torture, he again managed to escape. He went to the Spanish Netherlands, where he met the future James II in the autumn of 1656 and rose to be a groom of the then Duke of York's bedchamber. The pair soon developed what proved to be a life-long friendship, with Talbot, three years older than the Duke, apparently the dominant partner in the relationship. Returning to England with the Duke in 1660, Talbot took on the responsibility of assisting James in managing his various sexual intrigues at the rakish Restoration court, which led Macaulay to style Talbot the Duke's 'chief pandar'. The contemporary Whig historian Gilbert Burnet, who had spells as a royal chaplain under both Charles II and William III, described Talbot as a man 'who had much cunning, and had the secret both of his master's pleasures and of his religion'. A fierce critic of the Restoration land settlement in Ireland and of Charles II's Lord Lieutenant of Ireland, the first Duke of Ormonde (whom he blamed for the bad deal the Irish Catholics had received under the Acts of Settlement and Explanation of 1662 and 1665), Talbot became a spokesman of the dispossessed Catholic landed interest, though he also made himself a personal fortune by accepting payments from former Irish landholders for helping them secure the restoration of their confiscated estates. Accused by Titus Oates in 1678 of being part of the Popish Plot against Charles II, Talbot spent a brief period in jail before being released on bail on the grounds of ill-health in July 1679 and allowed to leave for Paris to convalesce. He was back in Ireland by 1683, by which time the political climate had changed dramatically following the defeat of Exclusion and the subsequent Tory Reaction. It was perhaps inevitable that James, upon his accession, would turn to Talbot for help in running Irish affairs. Talbot must have felt the sweetness of revenge when James recalled Ormonde in February 1685 and gave Talbot Ormonde's old regiment. Then in June 1685 Talbot acquired the requisite social status to go with the political influence he craved, being promoted to the peerage with the titles Baron of Talbotstown, Viscount Baltinglass and Earl of Tyrconnell in June 1685. Under James II, Tyrconnell became the dominant voice in Iri h policy formation, immediately taking over responsibility for military affairs and eventually rising to the position of Lord Deputy in January 1687. His ambition was to restore the wealth and political and military power of the Old English Catholics, with the eventual aim of breaking, or at least seriously modifying, the Restoration land settlement. Since James was only three years younger than Charles II at the time of his accession, and did not as yet have a Catholic heir, Tyrconnell saw the need to act quickly, so that when James died the Catholics in Ireland would be in a position to defend their interests, and, if necessary, overthrow English domination.[4] It was a plan that almost came to fruition in 1689, and was only defeated by William of Orange's victory at the Battle of the Boyne in July 1690.

Tyrconnell must bear considerable responsibility for the way the situation developed in Ireland under James II, and likewise James himself for allowing Tyrconnell to pursue the courses of action that he did. Yet in accounting for the rapid destabilization of Irish politics after 1685 it would be wrong to place too much emphasis on the role of individuals. There were major structural problems in Ireland, pent-up resentments, fears and insecurities that came to a head with the accession of a Catholic king. James II's reign, therefore, did not so much destabilize Ireland as reveal, with a clarity and forcefulness not seen during Charles II's time, what the destabilizing forces in Ireland were. Tensions between Protestants and Catholics were obviously a fundamental cause of conflict, but it is important to recognize that opinion in Ireland never divided simply along Protestant versus Catholic lines. Divisions existed within both Protestant and Catholic groupings: there were tensions between those of the Established Church of Ireland and various Protestant nonconformists, such as the Presbyterians and Quakers; the Catholics were divided between the Old English and Gaelic Irish; while not even all Catholics of Old English stock responded to developments under Tyrconnell in similar ways. There were other sources of tensions besides religion. One concerned the nature of the relationship between England and Ireland and whether Ireland was a conquered colony or an independent kingdom ruled by the king of England, which was a source of division amongst Protestants as well as an issue which Old English Catholics typically saw differently from the native Irish. Legal and constitutional issues were also at stake, which raised questions about the power of the crown in Ireland and the extent to which policies pursued under James II were in violation of the rule of law. Last, though by no means least, there were fundamental economic tensions, relating to both trade and land, which tended to coincide with the Catholic/Protestant divide, but not invariably so: those Catholics who had managed to regain their land at the Restoration or purchased land from the Cromwellian settlers, or who had achieved a healthy living through trade under Charles II, might be just as alarmed about developments under James and Tyrconnell as Protestants.

EARLY SIGNS OF DESTABILIZATION

In late 1684 the Earl of Sunderland, in an attempt to neutralize the influence of his main political rival at court, Lord Treasurer Rochester, persuaded Charles II to send Rochester to Ireland as Lord Lieutenant to replace the ageing Ormonde. Rochester was a staunch Anglican royalist and Charles, on making the appointment, was himself determined that his new man should uphold the Protestant interest in Ireland. He thus instructed Rochester to fill any vacant livings 'with pious and Orthodox persons', and to ensure that the oaths of allegiance and supremacy were administered to all officers and soldiers in the army and all governors of towns, forts and castles.[5] At his accession James, angry at Sunderland's attempt to dispatch his brother-in-law and loyal ally into the political wilderness, cancelled Rochester's appointment and instead ordered Ormonde to hand over the government of Ireland to two lords justices – Archbishop Boyle of Armagh, the Lord Chancellor, and Arthur Forbes, Earl of Granard, marshall of the army – until a new Lord Lieutenant was chosen.[6] James also appointed a new, Protestant, privy council, although he did instruct the lords justices to consult Tyrconnell on matters regarding the army. Tyrconnell had hoped to be put in charge of the government of Ireland himself – Sunderland, who was busy trying to cement his own position at the English court by building alliances with Catholics, having allegedly promised him as much. At this stage, however, James was unwilling to risk alienating Protestant opinion in England by entrusting Ireland to a Catholic native, and in August decided to make Rochester's elder brother, the staunchly Anglican-royalist Earl of Clarendon, Lord Lieutenant. The Catholics were bitterly disappointed to see the government lodged in the hands of a person from whom they could expect little favour. Clarendon eventually took up his position in Ireland in January 1686.[7]

This change in personnel immediately introduced a degree of instability into Irish politics. Under Ormonde, Ireland had been in the hands of an experienced politician who knew the Irish situation well: Ormonde was an Irish peer and landowner whose interests were based predominantly in Ireland, and although a Protestant himself, headed an Old English family that was predominantly Catholic. Clarendon knew nothing about Ireland, and frequently confessed his ignorance to the King during the early months of his administration. Clarendon's position was further undermined by the fact that for advice about Irish affairs James chose to rely extensively on Tyrconnell, who for much of the period between December 1685 and December 1686 was based at court in London. Clarendon felt, with much justification, that he was continually being undermined by decisions taken at Whitehall as a result of Tyrconnell's influence, and on at least one occasion was to protest that he thought 'the Chief-Governor should be a little consulted with'.[8] When Clarendon was recalled from the government of Ireland in January 1687, Ormonde quipped that it was questionable whether 'in truth and reallity hee was ever in it'.[9]

The mere fact that a new monarch had succeeded to the throne raised hopes that the time might at last have come when the existing state of affairs in Ireland could be challenged. At the broadest level of generality, there were two main sources of resentment within Ireland: English imperial domination (i.e., undue control by a foreign power), and the privileged position (politically, religiously and economically) enjoyed by Protestants of the Established Church. Although these tended to overlap, since the Catholics of Ireland were the biggest losers in the imperial relationship, they did not invariably do so. Protestant merchants, in particular, resented the way the Irish economy was subordinated to that of England. One of the first acts of James's English parliament was to revive those laws that had lapsed with the death of Charles II. Thus in June 1685 it revived the Navigation Act, which prevented Ireland from trading directly with the North American plantations, and other acts forbidding the importation of certain Irish products, such as tallow and hide, into England, leaving 'the merchants of this country . . . much dejected', as one Protestant correspondent reported.[10] Some commercial interests simply found the domestic market too small to sustain their economic prosperity. It was for this reason, for example, that the Dublin clothiers and stuff-weavers petitioned Clarendon in 1686 'to intercede with the King to suspend the act prohibiting Irish manufactures from export to his foreign plantations', although to no avail.[11]

The fact that the new king was a Catholic, however, inevitably raised expectations (or conversely created anxieties) that the balance of power in Ireland might shift in favour of the Catholics. According to Charles O'Kelly, a Catholic landowner of Old Irish stock writing after the Revolution, the Catholics had great hopes that the King 'would forthwith restore to the heavenly powers their temples and altars, and also to the natives their properties and estates, of which they had been, for so many years, so unjustly despoiled'.[12] The Protestant clergyman Dr William King, in another retrospective account, alleged that on the accession of James II the Irish Catholics 'affirmed, both publickly and privately' that they would soon get back their estates and churches, 'that Ireland must be a Catholick Country whatever it cost', and that they would make the English 'as poor devils as when they came first into Ireland'.[13] Some Protestant landowners were certainly apprehensive right from the beginning of the reign. In August 1685 Sir William Petty, who had acquired substantial landholdings in County Kerry for his services to the Protectorate, recorded his fears that something might be done 'to the danger of the Settlement'.[14] In early October Ormonde, who had by now returned to England, learned that 'the Irish Roman Catholics' from the area around his estates in Kilkenny had been encouraged to believe that but for him 'they should long since have obtained an act of indemnity and restitution to all their estates', and that 'the rabble', egged on by the clergy, were threatening to vent their spleen by setting fire to his house and 'all in it'.[15]

Such accounts are perhaps more testimony to the paranoia (mixed, no doubt, with a sense of guilt) of Protestant landlords than to the reality of any violent challenge they faced at this stage from dispossessed Catholics. Some Catholics in Ireland, however, did begin to organize to bring peaceful pressure to bear for change. During the autumn of 1685, the Catholic lords and gentry of the province of Leinster, with the backing of Tyrconnell, drafted a circular letter to fellow Catholics in other parts of Ireland to solicit contributions to cover the cost of sending agents to England to represent their grievances to the crown. After first complaining about the unjustifiable separation of the Church of England from the Catholic Church, the Leinster Catholics stated they intended to ask the King to remove 'all marks of distinction' from his subjects in Ireland 'by rendering them and their posterity capable of employments, civil and military, and freedom of corporations'. In this way, it was hoped, 'animosities will be forgot' and 'discord and division removed'.[16] Efforts to organize an effective Catholic pressure group to lobby the King continued through the winter of 1685/6. On 11 January, a group of dispossessed Catholic landlords held a meeting at the Dublin home of Thomas Nugent, a Catholic lawyer from an Old English family, where they decided to send agents to England to explain to James (or, rather, remind him) 'how there were several lands vested in the King by law, whereby he might relieve them in a great measure, without shaking the acts of settlement'. Clarendon insisted that they should address any grievances through him, while on 20 February James himself sent orders stating that he did not want any agents representing the old proprietors coming over to England. The irony was that one of the major beneficiaries of the Restoration land settlement in Ireland had been the King himself, who as Duke of York had been granted 169,431 acres taken from the regicides in the early 1660s, thereby diminishing the stock available to compensate the dispossessed.[17] Moreover, there were clearly divisions within the ranks of the Irish Catholics. Some doubted whether sending Catholics was the best way to proceed and refused to contribute anything towards the cost, while those who had been restored to their old estates by the Acts of Settlement and Explanation or acquired new land since the Restoration were naturally reluctant to rock the boat. There was even a report at one stage that 'the natives' who had gained 'by the present settlement' were to join 'in an address to his Majesty not to alter it'.[18]

The campaign against the land settlement was also fought out in the press. In September 1685, Nicholas French's *Narrative of the Settlement and Sale of Ireland*, a bitter attack on the Restoration settlement and on how the Irish nation had been betrayed by a corrupt English administration, which had first appeared in 1668, was republished. At the same time appeared *Twelve Quaeries relating to the Interest of Ireland*, attacking Ormonde and everyone else involved in the Irish settlement, and complaining 'that no people upon the Face of the Earth' had been so 'unchristianly and inhumanely' dealt with as the Irish.[19] In March 1686, Dublin customs officials seized various books that had been smuggled in from France, including a tract entitled 'A Ponderation upon Certain Branches and Parts of the Act of Indemnity and Oblivion, passed Anno 1660' and French's *Bleeding Iphigenia* of 1675, which went beyond his earlier *Narrative* by offering a justification of the Irish rebellion of 1641 as a defensive war.[20]

The English (both in England and Ireland), by contrast, saw the land settlement as 'the Magna Carta of Ir[eland]', which 'like the banks of Holland' kept out 'an ocean of barbarisme and poverty', as one manuscript reply to French's *Narrative* put it in November 1685. The Irish, this tract continued, had forfeited their land 'by the most barbarous rebellion that ever was', and although the natives might outnumber the English by ten to one, 'their rebellions have been 100 for one'. The land settlement, to this author's mind, had brought nothing but benefit; in less than twenty years it had transformed Ireland, which had been made desolate by war and plague, into 'a fruitful, populous and pleasant country', 'drained the bogs', and 'improved the whole Kingdom to double the revenue to the K[ing] and rent to the Subject it yeelded before the rebellion'.[21] In fact, the various Protestant landowning groups in Ireland were so alarmed by the Catholic challenge to the land settlement that they drafted petitions to the King and the English parliament, responding to the claims made in French's *Narrative* and the *Twelve Quaeries* and asking to be confirmed in the possession of their estates, although the prorogation of 20 November 1685 meant that they were never presented. A petition from the 'Old Protestants' claimed that in 1641 the Church and the English Protestants had possessed about one-third of the land in Ireland, worth £450,000 p.a., but that by 1653, as a result of the depredations caused by civil war, their lands were not worth one-thirtieth of what they had been in 1641 and that, still, in 1685, despite the recoveries since the Restoration, their lands were worth only £220,000 p.a. Another petition, from 'the '49 Men' (those Protestants who had served in the royal forces in Ireland prior to June 1649), claimed that they had not yet received four shillings in the pound for their investiments in the estates of Irish rebels, nor had they been compensated for the land restored to the Catholics at the Restoration. A third, from adventurers and Cromwellian soldiers (those who had acquired lands in Ireland as a result of parliament's victory in the Civil War), claimed that the parliament which made the Act of Settlement had been illegal and had wrongly turned them out of their estates, adding that they thought the Catholics of Ireland were in a better position in 1685 than they had been for the past 500 years.[22]

James assured Clarendon, when he appointed him Lord Lieutenant, that he would not touch the settlement of Ireland but rather leave 'all things as they were'.[23] His immediate worry was over security, and whether discontented Protestants in Ireland might choose to rise in sympathy with Monmouth or Argyll. In fact, there does not appear to have been a significant Irish dimension to the rebellions of 1685; indeed, many in Ireland rejoiced when they were finally put down. One Dubliner recorded that there was 'great joy' on the news of Monmouth's defeat, 'especially amongst the Irish papists', who burned an effigy of the Duke in Francis Street.[24] Yet most Protestants too, contemporary accounts agree, were pleased to see the rebellions fail. The official day of thanksgiving, 23 August, saw public bonfires in a number of towns, including Dublin, Waterford and Youghal; Waterford even sent a loyal address to the King.[25]

It is true that there were hints of disaffection amongst Protestants in Ireland in 1685. The government feared that the Ulster Protestants might join with the Scottish covenanters, or even that Argyll might land in the north of Ireland, but it speedily dispatched troops to the area and Ulster remained loyal.[26] Rumours of disaffection in certain quarters circulated both at the time and in the immediate aftermath of the rebellions, but it is unclear how much truth lay behind them. Most appear to have been of little substance; indeed, the government had to issue a proclamation on 10 July against the spreading of false reports to try to put a stop to the 'many stories about Monmouth's followers'.[27] In the summer of 1685 one Isaiah Amos gave a series of depositions in which he alleged that the mayor of Clonmel, John Hanbury, and the former mayor, Stephen Moore (who, when mayor in 1682, had opposed the town's loyal address), were conspiring to raise men to 'arise and join with Argyll and the Duke of Monmouth', to ensure that 'no Popish King should reign'. Subsequent investigations, however, revealed that Amos was pursuing a personal vendetta against Moore and had conspired to persuade others to give false evidence.[28] Some time after the failure of the Monmouth rebellion, a Kinsale merchant by the name of Robert Clarke wrote to the commander of the troops stationed in the town admitting that he had been involved in a Monmouthite conspiracy involving some thirty-five local men, including the town sovereign (the head of the town government). According to Clarke, when they learned of Monmouth's landing in England, they held a number of meetings 'where they dranke to Monmouth's good successe, wishing he had Landed there instead of England', and drew up lists of those who were ready to serve, some of whom were to go to England 'to represent the friendship of the County to Monmouth'. Whatever the truth of the matter, the plans came to nothing. Clarke later refused to confirm what he had initially written and was said by some to be mad; the justices who examined him 'thought him more knave than mad'.[29]

Malicious prosecution became something of a craze in Ireland in the autumn and winter of 1685/6. 'If a man be angry with his neighbour upon any private account', Clarendon reported to Sunderland, 'he is threatened to be accused of having said ill things of the King, when Duke, four or more years ago.' Clarendon received many such frivolous accusations 'from most parts of the kingdom', which he dutifully investigated, even though 'multitudes of people' were 'thereby harassed to very little purpose'. For example, he uncovered a conspiracy to swear treason against John Chetwood, vicar of Ardbracan in County Meath, alleging that Chetwood had said the previous June that 'the Duke of Monmouth has as good a title to the crown as the Duke of York' and that he 'hoped in God that the King's head would be cut off as his father's was'. Apparently the conspirators had raised a 'common purse' to pay 'twenty pounds and half-a-crown a day . . . unto every man that would give any information of treason'. A number of outlawed Tories (that is, Irish bandits who made their living by stealing cattle) also came before Clarendon, offering to make 'great discoveries of the Duke of Monmouth's plot' if they could receive pardons.[30]

The rebellions in Scotland and England nevertheless had a powerful impact in Ireland, even though there was no rising in Ireland itself. According to one Irish-based correspondent, the news of the rebellion, and the fear of what might happen in Ireland if Monmouth were to succeed, generated 'a great deal of ill blood . . . between the English and Irish'. The Irish, who had for so long been castigated as rebels by the English, were now able to turn the charge on the English. The English tried to defend themselves by saying that although this was a rebellion in England, it was 'only by the worst of the King's subjects there'; the Irish, however, alleged that 'all the English universally', both in England and Ireland, were 'devoted to Monmouth'. The spread of such 'hot discourses' promoted a climate of increased distrust between the English and the Irish, leading to reciprocal accusations that the others were about to rise against them. Reports spread among the English that a number of friars, in various parts of the country, had preached sermons on Ezekiel 9, vv. 5–9, a text which contains the exhortation to 'slay utterly old and young, both maids, and little children, and women', although it does not appear that any such sermon was ever preached.[31] On 21 June 1685 the town of Borrisokane in County Tipperary was alarmed by a rumour that there was to be 'a rising . . . of the Irish' and that all the Protestants 'should have their throats cut by them'. In self-defence, the Protestants decided to keep watch that night, parading through the streets armed with swords, staves, or guns. The government, on the other hand, was concerned about what appeared to be 'disorderly and suspicious meetings of the disaffected', and ordered the judges to prosecute the Protestants for 'a riotous and seditious unlawful assembly'. Ten were found guilty, while over fifty people were convicted for spreading the report.[32] Many Catholics were convinced that if Monmouth and Argyll had been victorious, the Cromwellians in Ireland would all have joined with the rebels 'and cut our throats'.[33]

Tensions ran particularly high in County Londonderry, in the area known as the Glen or Society of London Woods, between the local

Scottish Presbyterians and the Irish Catholics. The Irish started 'Braging over their Ale' that 'the British and Protestants had [had] their tyme and they Expected theires', and 'if the Duke of Monmouth gave the Kinge ane defeate . . . the Irish would all Rise and Kill and Murder'. Lists were drawn up of those Irish fit to bear arms, and many Irish were seen carrying swords who had never previously worn them. Fearful that the Irish might 'fall upon them and Cutt theire throts', the Scots decided to keep armed watches at night. These 'Tumultuous watches' in turn 'soe terrifyed the Irish', it was said, 'that they durst not sleepe in their beds for that they were told they designed to fall upon them'. The depth of national antagonisms is revealed by an incident that happened on the night of 10 June 1685, when an Irishman called Henry O'Hagan, somewhat the worse for drink, accosted a Scottish alehousekeeper, asking 'what had . . . the Scotch to doe in their country' and bidding him 'Get out of their Country'. The proprietor could only protest that he had been born in Ireland. A local JP tried to allay fears by telling the Scots that 'the Irish Idle discourse over theire drinke was little to be regarded', and assuring the Irish that 'the Brittish', as he called the Scottish Presbyterians, had no option but to 'be peaceable' lest 'the protestants and papists should take parte together against them'. Nevertheless, the incident, like that at Borrisokane, highlights the extent of the distrust and hatred between the different religious and national communities within Ireland.[34]

Concerns about security at the time of these rebellions, coupled with rumours questioning the loyalty of the militia, led the English government in June to order the lords justices to disarm all disaffected and suspected persons – first in the north of Ireland, then in the rest of the country – and to have all the arms currently in the hands of the militia delivered into the government stores. Militiamen even had to give up their personal guns or pistols that they kept for hunting or protection, while many Protestant gentry who were not in the militia also found they had their weapons seized, although this was certainly not authorized. Catholics, given that they could not serve in the militia, were not subject to the recall.[35] The Protestants resented the implication that they were 'not fit to be trusted with arms', as if they were 'persons disaffected to [the King's] service', when they had all taken the oaths of allegiance and supremacy, and many tried to defy the order. The Irish gentry, by contrast, taunted the Protestants by spreading reports that their arms were 'thus called in to be given to them [the Irish] as the King's best subjects'.[36] Disarming was not at heart a Catholic versus Protestant issue. Archbishop Boyle thought that 'several of the Militia' were 'faulty enough, at least in their inclinations, and deserved to be proceeded against', and agreed that James had the right to disband any part of his armed forces when he no longer required their services. But Boyle, who claimed it had always been the intention to give back the weapons to those 'believed to be honest and fit to be intrusted with their arms', thought the disarming was carried too far, and left the English (especially those in more remote places) vulnerable to attack from Irish Tories.[37] Reports flooded in of various robberies and other acts of violence committed against the English by Tories over the winter of 1685/6: houses were broken into; livestock stolen or killed; and English farmers physically assaulted in broad daylight. In English eyes, all the Irish came to be tarnished by association. When Clarendon took up his position as Lord Lieutenant, he agreed that 'the English could not but think themselves in great danger, when they were left exposed without any one weapon in their houses, and the Irish were all well armed'. His suggestion that some of the English be given their weapons back, however, came to nothing.[38]

THE FIRST STEPS TOWARDS CATHOLICIZATION, 1685–6

It soon became apparent that James, despite his promises, was not going to continue 'all things as they were'. Although he wanted to preserve the Act of Settlement, of which he himself had been a major beneficiary, he was determined to restructure the military and civil establishments. The army was to be remodelled, to ensure its loyalty, while he wanted Catholics to be admitted to the privy council, to serve as sheriffs, judges and JPs, and to be given 'the same freedom and privileges in all corporations as his other subjects' – seemingly in the belief (wildly mistaken, as it turned out) that there were 'great numbers of wealthy Irish merchants abroad' who would bring their wealth home 'upon this encouragement'.[39]

James had already convinced Charles II, shortly before the latter's death, of the need to reform the army in Ireland by bringing in Catholics 'and making it a security for the King to trust against his other subjects'.[40] James proceeded to appoint a handful of Catholic officers upon his accession, among them the soon-to-be Earl of Tyrconnell, whom he sent over to Ireland with a list of sixty officers that were to be replaced. When Tyrconnell returned to England at the end of 1685 he convinced James that most Protestants in Ireland were Cromwellians and republican sympathizers and that the King could never be secure unless the army were 'purged of that dross'. James responded by appointing Tyrconnell Lieutenant General of the army and sending him back to Ireland in May 1686 with a commission to inspect all the Irish regiments and replace all 'unfit persons'. By the end of the summer about two-thirds of the army had been remodelled. Ostensibly, Tyrconnell's objective was to remove those who were disloyal or else unfit for military service (because too old or too short). In actuality, he set about dismissing Protestants and replacing them with Catholics. Whereas in 1685 the entirety of the Irish officer corps and the overwhelming majority of the rank and file had been Protestants of the Established Church, by 30 September 1686, 5,043 of the 7,485 privates (67 per cent) were Catholic; 166 out of 414 (40 per cent) of the officers; and 251 out of 765 (33 per cent) of the non-commissioned officers. At the same time, the Protestant chaplains were replaced by Catholic priests. James told Clarendon that he did not see that 'employing some of the Catholic natives of the country' did 'any prejudice to what is the true English interest there, so long as the Act of Settlement is kept untouched', which, the King affirmed, 'it must always be'; nevertheless, since that settlement secured 'many ill and disaffected people . . . in their possessions', James continued, it was 'the more necessary for me to secure myself and the Government against such . . . so that I must be sure of my troops'. However, many of the officers to whom Tyrconnell took exception were Cavaliers, experienced commanders with a long history of loyal service to the crown; there were, in fact, very few ex-Cromwellians left in the Irish army by 1685. Likewise Tyrconnell removed numerous 'brave, lusty, young fellows'. The chief beneficiaries were the Old English, who were given the highest positions in the army; Tyrconnell had little time for the 'O's and the Macs', as he called the native Irish, although he did of necessity admit them into the lower ranks. The officers dismissed, who had often made large investments to secure their positions, naturally felt bitterly aggrieved; left with no means of support, a number found themselves 'reduced with their families to beggary or extreme want'. Troopers found themselves being sent away without compensation for the horses or uniforms they themselves had paid for, or even the month's pay they were supposed to receive. Many of those discharged left the country. Most went to England, though a significant number went to Holland, where they joined with the Prince of Orange.[41]

The purge of the army was accompanied by changes in the civil administration. In April 1686 James replaced Lord Chancellor Archbishop Boyle with a creature of his own from England, Sir Charles Porter, albeit a Protestant, and removed three of the nine judges (one each from King's Bench, Common Pleas and the Exchequer) and replaced them with three Catholics – one from England, one of Old English stock in Ireland, the other of old Irish stock.[42] In May he made twenty additions to the privy council, eleven of whom were Catholics, including Tyrconnell, the new judges and some other Catholic peers.[43] James also wanted Clarendon to appoint some Catholic sheriffs, but in fact Clarendon had already nominated sheriffs for the ensuing year that February, choosing in the main zealous Protestant loyalists – though there were a couple who, he said, came from Catholic or Irish backgrounds and were thought to be Catholic. Tyrconnell was furious and accused Clarendon of selecting Whigs and fanatics.[44] The King was able to insist, however, that Clarendon allow Catholics to be admitted to the corporations and even to hold office if duly elected. By the autumn, many Catholics had taken up their freedoms and some had been appointed magistrates, displacing Protestants removed to make way for them.[45] Catholic gentry were also put into the commissions of the peace: three of the McGorees were made JPs in County Fermanagh, four of the McMahons in County Monaghan, while nine Protestant JPs were superseded in County Limerick, ten in County Clare, and twenty-one in County Cork.[46]

The legal impediment to the employment of Catholics within the military and civil administrations in Ireland was somewhat different from what it was in England. There was no equivalent in Ireland of the Test Act of 1673, requiring office-holders to be communicating members of the Established Church. The Elizabethan Act of Supremacy of 1560, however, which was still in force, did require all office-holders to take the oaths of supremacy and allegiance. With regard to the army, there had been numerous exemptions from the Elizabethan statute in the past, so the appointment of Catholics was hardly unprecedented, though the numbers were now of a different order from anything that had happened previously. In May 1685 the King simply instructed the lords justices to dispense the Catholic officers he had appointed from taking the oaths, and followed this in July by ordering that a general oath of fidelity should be the only oath administered to any of the officers or soldiers in the army or governors of forts and towns.[47]

The appointment of Catholics to civil offices, however, proved much less straightforward. Clarendon, while a loyal servant of the crown, scrupled to do anything of dubious legal propriety. When Sunderland solicited his opinion in March 1686 about appointing Catholic sheriffs and JPs, Clarendon replied that he thought it would be a violation of the Act of Supremacy. He accepted that some Catholics had served as sheriffs or JPs before 1641, but they were generally from the English Pale; moreover, all the commissions he had seen had required the oath to be administered, so he was unclear how such appointments had been connived at.[48] Clarendon also raised objections to the King's dispensations to the three newly appointed Catholic judges, maintaining that this was the first time the oath of supremacy had 'been dispensed with in a judicial place' and was in breach of the law. He also thought it totally inappropriate that someone 'of old Irish race' should be a judge; his own research revealed 'that none of the natives' had ever been 'allowed to be upon any of the benches, even before the difference in religion'.[49] With regard to the corporations, James informed Clarendon that he had been told that there was no law in Ireland excluding Catholics from being admitted freemen.[50] Yet the legal situation was not quite as clear cut as James had been led to believe. Although there was no equivalent of the English Corporation Act, many corporations had by-laws that required new freemen to take oaths of allegiance and supremacy and had regularly insisted on this requirement under Charles II.[51] In the late spring of 1686 the Lord Mayor and aldermen of Dublin actually removed their recorder because he refused to take the oaths; Clarendon backed the corporation, but the recorder complained to Tyrconnell in London, who got him reinstated.[52] Under pressure from London, Clarendon complied with the King's wishes and on 22 June sent a circular letter to the corporate towns instructing them to admit Catholics to their freedoms 'without tendering the Oath of Supremacy', adding that if any of these Catholics were subsequently elected to office their names should be forwarded to him so that he might dispense them from the oath.[53]

It is undeniable that the king did possess a power to dispense with the law in certain circumstances. Yet he was only supposed to do so in cases of necessity, or when enforcing a law would create a blatant injustice. William King, writing after the Revolution, denied that any such necessity had existed under James II to justify dispensing with the oaths of supremacy and allegiance for office-holders, since 'Protestants were numerous enough, and willing enough to serve him in every thing that was for the Interest of the Kingdom'. Although James had issued similar dispensations to Catholics 'without any apparent Necessity' in England, he went on, there things had been done 'in some colour or form of Law, and many of them at least passed the Offices and Seals'. In Ireland, 'they did not trouble themselves with these Formalities. A verbal Command from the King was a sufficient Dispensation to all Laws made in favour of a Protestant.'[54] On the other side, it could be argued that excluding the vast majority of the population from the opportunity of serving their king was inequitable. Supporters of Tyrconnell's purge of the army maintained it was only fair to give some 'poor Irish gentlemen . . . a share of the King's bread and bounty', which had for so long been monopolized by English Protestants.[55] One tract argued that 'it was both Politick and Reasonable, to give every Subject a possibility of sharing in the King's Favour, as he might deserve'.[56] James justified admitting Catholics to the corporations on the grounds that this would encourage trade and unite the affections of his subjects, whereas it was concerns about security that led him to Catholicize the army in Ireland, since he wanted to be sure of the loyalty of his own armed forces.[57]

On the ecclesiastical front, James made a number of efforts to improve the position of the Catholic Church in Ireland. In March 1686 he instructed the sheriffs, JPs and the Protestant bishops 'not to molest the Roman Catholic clergy in the exercise of their ecclesiastical functions amongst those of their own communion'; set up pensions for the titular Archbishop of Armagh and the rest of the Catholic bishops; and gave permission for the clergy to wear their clerical dress in public, with the exception of the pectoral cross. He also encouraged the regular clergy, particularly the Capuchins, 'to settle and reside peaceably in all cities, towns and places'.[58] The Catholics jumped at the opportunities now afforded them. In mid-May, the Catholic clergy held a week-long convention in Dublin and decided, amongst other things, that they would 'openly own and exercise their Episcopall Ecclesiasticall Jurisdiction' within Ireland.[59] Old mass houses began to be repaired and new ones erected.[60] Meanwhile, the Protestant Church was allowed to run down. James decided not to appoint successors to bishoprics and the lesser livings that fell vacant, instead keeping the revenues for the crown; ultimately, if only indirectly, the funds thus accrued went towards the payment of the Catholic clergy, 'directly against the Laws and Constitution of the Kingdom', as William King later protested.[61] To silence potential criticism from the Protestant clergy, James issued directives in February 1686 forbidding them from meddling with matters of controversy or preaching against popery. On a number of occasions Clarendon found it necessary to rebuke indiscreet clergymen, among them the Bishop of Meath, and he even had to suspend two preachers for 'impertinent' sermons delivered before him in Dublin on Hallowe'en and Gunpowder Treason Day in 1686.[62]

To many Catholics, who had been economically and politically marginalized for so long, the changes introduced in the first two years of James II's reign must have appeared welcome but modest. Service in the army could provide prestige for the Catholic gentry who acquired commissions and valuable new career opportunities for lower-class Irishmen who served in the rank and file, although

Catholics still remained proportionately under-represented, given their percentage of the population as a whole. James's reforms had also resulted in Catholic merchants being placed on a more equal footing with Protestants, some degree of Catholic representation within the legal system, and the Catholic Church in Ireland achieving a quasi-official status. The biggest grievance, however, namely the land settlement, had remained unaddressed.

We need to recognize, however, that there were tensions within the Catholic community in Ireland. Many Irish Catholics looked forward to the day when they would regain control of their own country, be restored to their estates, and achieve the political, economic and religious rights so long denied them. As Clarendon's secretary, Sir Paul Rycaut, put it in July 1686: 'the Irish talk of nothing now but recovering their land and bringing the English under their subjection'.[63] It was natural, therefore, that the Catholics in Ireland should look to the Catholic King as their ally. In August 1686, Dr Patrick Tyrrell, the Roman Catholic Bishop of Clogher and Kilmore, implored the King that 'now that a needful Alteration [had] begun in Ireland, it should be carried on speedily', assuring him that God would spare his 'precious Life' until he had accomplished 'the glorious work' of replanting the Catholic religion in his dominions.[64] At the same time, however, many Irish realized that their priorities were not the same as those of the King of England. Clarendon believed that there were many in Ireland who refused to accept the sovereignty of the English crown over their country. In December 1686 he informed his brother Rochester that 'the generality' of 'the natives' had been encouraged by their priests to believe 'that this kingdom is the Pope's, and ... that the King has no right, further than the Pope gives him authority', and that it was therefore 'lawful for them to call in any foreign power to help them against those who oppose the jurisdiction of the church'. The account written after the Revolution by Charles O'Kelly confirms that there were many Irish Catholics who wanted to promote their religion and their country's interests who found themselves at odds with James, believing him to be a weak prince who was too subservient to the interests of the English. However, there were more 'sober' Roman Catholics, particularly those who had purchased lands from the Cromwellian soldiers,

Clarendon recognized, who had a vested interest in defending the status quo, and protested against 'the violent proceedings here', claiming to be as afraid as anyone else 'of their countreymen's getting too much power'.[65]

To Protestants, the negative implications of these initiatives were all that were visible. They were alarmed to see 'the sword and administration of justice' put into the hands not just 'of a conquered people' but even 'the bloody Murtherers of Forty-one, and their Offspring', and this despite the existence of laws incapacitating these men from bearing arms or holding office.[66] Fear about what the future might bring created a crisis of confidence for Protestant landlords and merchants, with serious knock-on effects for the economy.[67] There were repeated reports of the scarcity of money and the deadness of trade. In July 1686 the Earl of Longford informed Ormonde that the unexpected changes in the civil administration and the army had caused such a general alarm, 'that every man who has money pockets it up', so that there was 'no trading . . . in the country' and 'no possibility of receiving rents'.[68] Another correspondent reported in January 1687 that 'the British off the wholle Easterne shoare of Ireland' were sending their gold, silver and jewels to England, Scotland and Wales, because 'they see the Cities, forts and the sword put into the hands of the Brothers, Cusins or Children of those that Murthered ther predecessors in '41'.[69] Some Protestant families decided to cut their losses and withdraw to England; Scots in the north – 'many thousands' according to one report – began to remove 'with their whole families into Scotland'.[70] The emigration, at this stage, was in fact relatively small-scale, but even just a few leaving could have serious economic consequences. In May 1686, Clarendon told his brother about a wealthy Cork merchant who, until recently, 'had forty looms at work', and of a large landowner from Munster, who kept '500 families at work', both of whom had now decided to sell up and go to England.[71] The value of land fell. In September 1686 Petty calculated that rents had fallen by about one-third and that the lands of Ireland were worth about £8 million less than they had been three years earlier.[72] Clarendon was worried about the adverse effect such developments were having on the Irish revenue. In fact, total receipts into the Irish treasury were higher in 1686 than they had been in any of the previous three years.[73] Nevertheless, when the receipts from customs and excise were analysed more closely, there appeared cause for concern. Customs received an artificial boost as a result of merchants calling in their effects from abroad. Thus, in the second quarter of 1686 they were up nearly £4,500 against the same quarter of 1685. However, that had been a time of rebellion in England and of temporary dislocation to trade, so the increase was nothing to boast about; the customs for the second quarter of 1686 were down by over £7,000 from what they had been in the comparable quarter of 1684. The excise experienced a straightforward drop; it fell by over £1,000 in the first quarter of 1686, and by the second quarter was nearly £2,300 down on what it had been in the same quarter the previous year.[74]

If James's policy towards Ireland was intended to unite the interests of his subjects there, as he claimed, it was not succeeding. The moves towards Catholicization under Clarendon merely served to heighten tensions between the Catholic and Protestant, Irish and British (English and Scottish) populations. The Protestant inhabitants of Athlone, a garrison town on the frontier between the Pale and the Gaelic hinterland, staged several bonfires on 23 October 1685 to commemorate the anniversary of the Irish Rebellion, including a particularly impressive one at the Tholsell (or market house). There was plenty of ale for the assembled crowd and all the locals brought what fuel they could for the bonfire. A local shoemaker, Stephen Smith, donated a wooden block which he usually used for beating leather on and which he had long jokingly referred to as 'the Fryer'. Some of the young men present decided to set a pair of beast's horns upon it (the symbol of a cuckold), as a joke, they later claimed, on 'some younge marryed men then present': the horns, it appears, were first turned towards one George West's door, because he 'had been longe marryed and had noe Child'; West turned them towards Stephen Smith the younger, 'merryly telling him that they would become him for a Coate of Armes'; Smith junior then turned them towards one Edward Proctor's house, saying 'they would as well become him . . . as himselfe'. However, one William Ellis, known locally as 'Wicked Will', chimed in, saying that 'the hornes then on the said block lookt like one of the Pope's Bulls', and proceeded to fire at the block, saying 'he would shoote the Pope to the heart'; a number of others also fired shots, saying 'they would Shute the Pope out of the Fryer's Gutts'. One of the active participants was a corporal in the local garrison. The precise truth behind the incident, however, is difficult to unravel. A couple of the key witnesses who gave evidence about the episode were men with Irish surnames, and the town sovereign, Peter Stern, reported that some of their evidence was shown to be false. Some of the participants denied that anyone had uttered 'any reflecting words . . . of the Pope or any of his clergy', claiming instead that they had fired shots into the air after toasting the King's health, although the examinations clearly reveal that some sort of anti-Catholic ritual had been staged. Stern could only conclude 'what dangerous people this Place affords'.[75]

The purges of the army, in particular, brought latent resentments to the surface. There were some skirmishes between new recruits and dismissed soldiers, and increasing reports of conflicts between Catholic troops and Protestant civilians. The people of Derry were said to be 'strangely dejected and sad at the appearance' of the new officers and troops sent to quarter in their town, who in turn were 'so jealous of the inhabitants', that they would not eat or drink anything they were given, 'until their hosts taste[d] before them'.[76] The native Irish who flocked into Dublin to take up positions in the army – 'strange wretches', in the eyes of Clarendon, who could speak not a word of English – found themselves teased and heckled by the local youths. A violent clash occurred on 1 July 1686, allegedly at the instigation of 'the Popish Officers' who 'bid the men beat any that jeered them'; one or two were reportedly killed in the scuffle.[77] Back in London, Roger Morrice heard rumours towards the end of the same month that animosities in Dublin were 'so great' that 'two, or foure, or six a night' were 'frequently killed'.[78] In May of that year, a troop of Catholic dragoons quartered at Callan, County Kilkenny, broke into the house of a local minister, spoiling his goods and treating his children 'barbarously', while in Kilkenny itself there was trouble in early October, when Irish troops insulted a local nonconformist at his meeting-house. There was further unrest at Kilkenny on 23 October, as Catholic soldiers tried to disrupt the Protestant commemoration of the Irish Rebellion. One soldier took it upon himself to extinguish the bonfire that was burning outside the mayor's door, breaking the mayor's windows, and calling the mayor 'a fanatic dog, and other very ill names'. A townsman who had constructed a bonfire outside his own house was similarly abused by a group of Irish troopers, who called him 'fanatic rogue and dog' and dragged him out of the house; in the scuffle, one of the soldier's guns accidentally went off, killing a fellow soldier. There were also reports of Irish soldiers trying to extinguish bonfires on 5 November.[79]

Conflicts over quarters frequently erupted. William King later complained that the Catholic troops never paid a farthing for meat and drink, and that they extorted 'vast Sums of Mony' from Protestant innkeepers.[80] In January 1687 Morrice recorded that the 'Soldiery in Ireland' was 'not only very burdensome, but grown terrible', causing people to fear for their safety when travelling by road and 'quitt their habitations' in places where soldiers were quartered, since with the exception of Dublin, they were quartered in private as well as public houses.[81] Even Tyrconnell recognized there were problems, and on 24 February 1687, shortly after having been installed as Lord Deputy, issued a proclamation insisting the army maintain proper discipline and pay for their quarters at the agreed rates.[82] It had little effect. In April 1687, the soldiers in the Earl of Clancarty's regiment refused to pay a local innkeeper in Mallow, County Cork, for a horse seized for the use of one of the troopers; when he confronted them about what he was owed, they called him 'a whigg' and tossed him 'soe long in a Blanket' that he died the next day.[83]

The degree of mutual enmity between Catholics and Protestants was reflected in various rumours of intended uprisings that began to spread in the autumn of 1686. They started in the counties of Waterford and Cork: 'sometimes it was pretended, that the English would cut the throats of the Irish; and, sometimes, that the Irish would do the same to the English'. Clarendon had information brought to him 'of great meetings in the night of armed men', which caused such 'great fears amongst the poor people' that many left their homes and camped out in the fields. Army officers stationed in the area confirmed that no such meetings had ever taken place, and government directives to the local JPs to prosecute those people who maliciously spread such rumours helped quieten things down. Similar alarms soon began to be raised in other parts of the kingdom, however, particularly in the counties of Longford and Westmeath. Reports started circulating at the end of October of night meetings by the 'Scotch and English', who 'had resolved to destroy all that came their way', causing panic among both the 'gentry and rabble', who fled to the woods at night for fear of being massacred in their beds. The mobilization of local forces, to prevent any possible uprising, merely added to the tension. JPs ordered local constables to call out the watch, 'for fear of Scots and disbanded soldiers, and others that were coming to destroy the Irish', while army troops were also dispatched to keep the peace at night. One informant said that on the night of 29 October he saw 100 horsemen march in rank and file through the town of Mullingar, whom he and others believed were Presbyterians, 'for honest men did not use to march in that manner, nor at that time in the night'. Another eyewitness concluded that these men must be Whigs, because 'in Monmouth's time they did use to meet and march by night'. When one impatient army officer asked a third informant whether these horsemen had done any harm and was told 'no', he sarcastically replied: 'Then they must be fairies.' 'That cannot be,' retorted the Irishman, 'for fairies are not seen by more than one man at a time.' In Athlone, on the night of 10 November, the inhabitants were awoken from their sleep by the watch, who raised the alarm that a body of 100 horse and 300 men had been seen entering the town and that 'they were all undone'. Clarendon concluded from his examination of the evidence that the troops reported to have been seen marching at night were none other than local troops dispatched to protect against any possibility of an uprising.[84]

'UNDER THE INFLUENCE OF A NATIVE-GOVERNOUR', 1687–8

James had decided to replace Clarendon as head of the government in Ireland with Tyrconnell in the summer of 1686. It was not until January 1687, however, that Clarendon received official notification that he was to be recalled to England. Tyrconnell arrived to take up his post in early February, with the lesser title of Lord Deputy, though with all the powers of a Lord Lieutenant.[85] The *London Gazette* did its best to promote Tyrconnell's appointment as popular within Ireland. His arrival in Dublin on 6 February, which coincided with the anniversary of the King's accession, was greeted, we are told, with great enthusiasm by 'most of the Nobility and Persons of Quality' and other inhabitants who expressed 'their general Satisfaction by loud Acclamations as he passed through the Streets, by Ringing of Bells, and by Bonfires at Night throughout the City'. Pressure had been brought to bear, however, to ensure Tyrconnell was given an appropriate reception. The Lord Mayor had ordered the constables several days in advance to advise 'the people' that they 'should make bonfires'; in fact, a number of constables took it upon themselves to warn people 'to make none', but Tyrconnell found out and complained to the Lord Mayor, who had them put in the stocks.[86] Clarendon handed over the sword of state to Tyrconnell on 12 February, in an official ceremony 'attended by all the Nobility and Persons of Quality in Town', the day concluding, according to the *Gazette*, 'with all possible Demonstrations of Joy'.[87]

Undoubtedly many amongst the Catholic community in Ireland did welcome Tyrconnell's appointment. One Catholic poet wrote of James's inspiration '. . . in giving Power / To brave Tirconnell in a happy hour', adding they were '. . . blest with one in this auspicious day, / Who knows as well to Govern as Obey'.[88] Protestant opinion, however, was generally hostile. 'Few or none of the Protestant gentry', one account states, went to meet the new Lord Deputy when he landed at Dunleary on 6 February. The clergy of the Established Church were particularly alarmed, and began to talk 'as if . . . they should be immediately turned out', though the rumours that some of the students of Trinity College were plotting to murder Tyrconnell when he arrived appear to have been without substance.[89] Tyrconnell was sufficiently worried by reports that he intended to govern 'otherwise than by the known law of this land' – apparently spread by 'several disaffected persons' and 'some few fiery Spirits in the Pulpits' – to issue a proclamation on 21 February promising to protect 'all His Majesties Subjects . . . of what Perswasion in Religion or Degree . . . in their just Rights and Properties due to them by Law, and in the free Exercise of their Religion', so long as they remained loyal to the King.

The proclamation was intended not just for those in Ireland, but also to calm the fears of Protestants in England and Scotland, where it was also published.[90] Such gestures did not prove particularly reassuring. On that same day, a Protestant from Cork wrote, 'our great man is Arrived but god knows what he will doe with us', and reported how the Protestants were 'dayly threatned by the ordinary people [that is, the local Catholics] that theay will have all'. As a result, he said, there was no money to be got for anything, people were beginning to stop trading, and many had sent what plate or gold they had to England, predicting that before spring many tenants would give up their land.[91]

It was following Tyrconnell's appointment as Lord Deputy that the English Whig Thomas Wharton (whose family owned land in counties Carlow and Westmeath) composed his famous verse satire 'Lilliburlero'. Written to imitate the way the Irish sounded (at least to English ears), and sung to a catchy traditional melody (similar to 'Rock-a-bye Baby'), it opened with the lines:

> Ho, brother Teague, dost hear de decree,
> Lilli burlero bullen a-la;
> Dat we shall have a new debittie.
> Lilli burlero bullen a-la.

Subsequent stanzas warned ominously 'Ho, by my shoul, it is a Talbot/ And he will cut de Englishman's troat' and 'Now, now, de heretics all go down, / By Chreist and St Patrick, the nation's our own!' Finally published in London in October 1688, it was to play an important role in swaying public opinion in England at the time of William of Orange's invasion.[92]

Upon assuming the reins of government, Tyrconnell told the privy council the King had ordered him to maintain the laws regarding civil and ecclesiastical matters and promised he would see they were put into execution.[93] Nevertheless, under his lord deputyship the policy of Catholicization picked up speed. Most of the remaining Protestants were removed from the army; by the autumn of 1688 90 per cent of the army was Catholic.[94] The most dramatic changes came in the civil administration. Only the revenue commission remained relatively unscathed. The Catholic convert Thomas Sheridan was appointed First Commissioner of the Revenue, but the need to keep experienced men in office, coupled with concern about the adverse effects that rumours of possible displacements might have on the revenue, led Sheridan to issue a circular letter confirming that no one would be put either in or out on account of his religion. The judiciary was another matter. The Protestant Porter was replaced as Lord Chancellor by the Catholic Alexander Fitton, and three more Catholic judges appointed in the place of Protestant ones, so that the Catholics now outnumbered Protestants by two to one on each bench. The Gaelic poet David Ó Bruadair rejoiced that the Irish Catholics on the bench could now give justice to the natives, and 'listen to the plea of the man who can't speak / The lip-dry and simpering English tongue'.[95] More Catholics were added to the privy council, while in all counties except one the Protestant sheriffs were turned out and Catholics appointed in their stead. Even the survival of the single Protestant – Charles Hamilton of Cavan – was a mistake, the man being confused with a Catholic of the same last name. Since sheriffs were responsible for impanelling juries, they could ensure that juries would now also be composed of Catholics.[96]

The Catholic domination of the legal system led Protestants to complain that it was impossible for them to get justice at law.[97] (Now they knew how the Catholics had felt, when the legal system had been dominated by Protestants.) Protestant landlords found the courts were unlikely to support their attempts to sue for arrears of rent, while Catholic tenants, egged on by the clergy, increasingly began to withhold payment, knowing they could get away with it.[98] One Dublin Protestant wrote in December 1687 that it was 'ill for any that have controversys at Law, the Courts and Innes favouring one side now, as much as heretofore they did the other'.[99] William King later protested that 'for Two Years before the Revolution in England, very few received any profit out of their Estates'.[100] Under Tyrconnell, 'if the least flaw could be found in a Protestant's Title to an Estate', one Protestant pamphleteer complained, Catholics would dispute the claim at court and invariably get a decision in their favour.[101] The bias of juries towards fellow Catholics or native Irish allegedly extended to even the most barbaric of crimes. In the summer of 1687, a jury in Antrim acquitted 'three great Rogues' accused of burglary and of cutting out the tongue of their victim to stop him from talking, 'against full evidence and the positive direction of both the judges'.[102]

Tyrconnell also gave further encouragement to the practice of the Catholic faith. He made a clear statement of his own position on 13 February, the first Sunday after his being sworn into office, when he arranged for a French Catholic priest to preach a sermon, in French, before him and the rest of his government at the Jesuits' church in Dublin. To Protestants, this was a sign of Tyrconnell's 'inclinations for the interest of France'.[103] Two days later, according to a local Protestant diarist, he heard a sermon which took for its text Numbers 33, v. 55, God's speech to Moses in the plains of Moab as the Children of Israel were about to enter the Holy Land: 'if ye will not drive out the inhabitants of the land from before you; then it shall come to pass, that those which ye let remain of them shall be pricks in your eyes, and thorns in your sides, and shall vex you in the land wherein ye dwell'.[104] Tyrconnell took over the chapel in Dublin castle for Catholic worship, and also that in the new hospital at Kilmainham on the outskirts of Dublin, despite the fact that Clarendon had hastily arranged for the latter to be consecrated before his departure, in an attempt to prevent it from falling into Catholic hands. Henceforth, the retired soldiers, for whom the hospital had been built, were forced to hold their religious services in the dining hall. Protestants in Dublin began to fear that all their churches would be taken away from them. Some local wit affixed a notice to the door of Christ Church Cathedral in Dublin announcing banns of matrimony between that church and the see of Rome, 'bidding any that could, forthwith to shew cause why they should not be joined together'.[105]

Although James did not issue his English Declaration of Indulgence of April 1687 in Ireland, he nevertheless extended liberty of conscience to his western kingdom that spring; the only restriction was that he forbade large numbers of people from meeting at night and anyone preaching 'against his person or government'.[106] With full liberty now established, Catholic religious orders openly flourished. According to William King, the priests and friars built about fourteen chapels and convents in Dublin, and set up two nunneries.[107] Within the diocese of Cashel, Dominicans, Franciscans and Jesuits all kept their own schools and public chapels. More controversially, when the

Dean of Derry, Peter Manby, announced his conversion to Catholicism in 1687, James issued a dispensation allowing him to continue to hold his deanship. There was also an attack on Protestant educational institutions. Trinity College successfully resisted an attempt to force it to admit a Catholic convert to a fellowship, though more by luck than anything else. The College statutes did, in fact, contain a clause granting the king the power to dispense with the said statutes, and the man in question – Bernard Doyle – was given a royal dispensation. Someone had not done their homework, however, since the dispensation still required Doyle to take the oath of a fellow, which included the oath of supremacy, and even the Catholic judges recognized 'the insufficiency of his Dispensation'. The government was rather more successful in undermining Protestant schools. Under the terms of an Elizabethan statute of 1570, the chief governor of Ireland was responsible for appointing qualified schoolmasters in all but four dioceses. In direct contravention of this act, Tyrconnell failed to supply positions as they fell vacant. Jesuits were allowed to set up Catholic schools in opposition to Protestant ones, and finally in June 1688, in a bold initiative that was certainly against existing law, James gave orders for vacancies in government-sponsored schools to be filled by Jesuits.[108]

The Catholic religious revival generated increasing tensions between Catholics and the Protestant minority. The Irish-language literati praised James II and Tyrconnell for their efforts in bringing relief to the suffering Catholics of Ireland and rejoiced at the reversal of Protestant fortunes.[109] Ó Bruadair championed James II as the 'Light of our Church ... The first King of England who gave rank and dignity ... / To Irishmen after the risk they encountered / Conduct that freed them from tyranny', and concluded that James 'hath changed our despondent hopes'.[110] In a mood of rising Catholic triumphalism, the Catholic clergy began to forbid their congregations to pay tithes and other dues to Protestant ministers, under pain of excommunication. Following a petition from the Protestant bishops, Tyrconnell and the Irish council did issue orders to the judges in June 1687, instructing them to command people to pay all church dues as formerly.[111] In practice, however, Protestant ministers found it very difficult to secure redress through a legal system that was now dominated by Catholics; if writs were obtained against those who refused to pay tithes, Protestants complained, the Catholic sheriffs would simply refuse to execute them.[112] There were growing signs of conflict within the parishes. At Barrettstown, County Kildare, in early October 1687, seven men armed with poles and pitchforks tried to prevent the burial of a corpse on the south side of the chapel yard on the grounds that the dead man 'was an Englishman'.[113] In Drogheda, on 30 January 1688, the Catholic clergy were bold enough to hold a funeral for the late Catholic mayor in the Protestant church of St Peter's. The ceremony started with a 'Solemne Procession' of the regular clergy 'in their Respective habitts, together with severall Jesuitts, and the Titular primate . . . through the publique streets' who carried a large cross before them, 'singing as they went, and Guarded on each side with a Considerable party of Musquetiers'. The muske-teers then kept guard at the great west door to keep out unwanted intruders, while the clergy held the service in the church before the assembled congregation. The local vicar was outraged at such 'a publique Violation of the lawes of this Kingdom' and 'an open Invasion' of his right and freehold.[114]

Tyrconnell's main ambition was to modify the land settlement. Some action certainly needed to be taken. All but the most uncom-promising of Protestants could appreciate that there had been injus-tices, while repeated speculation that the settlement was to be altered had created a destabilized environment and produced an adverse knock-on effect on the Irish economy. Clarendon, when Lord Lieutenant, had wanted to issue a commission of grace, whereby those currently in possession of land could, for a fee, confirm their titles, allowing the King to use the money thereby raised to relieve those Catholics whose cases he thought worthy of his compassion. However, Clarendon had also warned that any attempt to undo the settlement would alienate not only Protestant opinion but also those Catholic proprietors in Ireland who had either regained their lands at the Restoration or else purchased new lands from Cromwellian adventurers since then.[115] James recognized that it was necessary to do something 'to settle the minds of people in Ireland, by freeing them from any apprehensions they may have of a design to break the Acts of Settlement and Explanation', but thought that more money could be raised to compensate dissatisfied Catholic claimants through a parliament than a commission of grace.[116] Tyrconnell also did not like Clarendon's scheme, and was already putting his own plans in place long before he was officially to take over as Lord Deputy himself. Thus in August 1686 he brought over to England the Catholic barrister Sir Richard Nagle, with the aim of convincing James to call a parliament to modify the settlement, restore the ancient proprietors, and raise money to compensate those English landowners who would thereby be dispossessed.[117] James agreed that preparations should be made for the calling of a parliament in Ireland, but decided that it should not meet until after he had met with his parliament in England.

In a conversation with Nagle in October 1686, Sunderland suggested it would be a good idea to issue a proclamation when the change of governors in Ireland took place confirming that the King had no intention of breaking the Act of Settlement, in order to settle the minds of the people and prevent a potential depopulation of the country. Nagle disagreed, and decided to express his disagreement in a letter, ostensibly addressed to Tyrconnell in London, which he penned from Coventry on 26 October as he was making his way back to Ireland. Sunderland's argument that fears and jealousies would occasion a depopulation of the country if such a proclamation were not issued was fallacious, Nagle insisted: those with estates were not selling up and leaving, whereas the Protestant traders did not possess land, so confirming the settlement would not affect them. On the other hand, a proclamation confirming the land settlement would, Nagle continued, dishearten the dispossessed Catholics, who would see no hope of getting their lands restored, and even the Catholic merchants, who recognized that the only hope Catholics could have of achieving security for their religion and property under an eventual Protestant successor was 'to make the Catholics there considerable in their fortunes'. Thus, it would be the issuing of such a proclamation that would 'tend to the dispeopling of the country, to the discouragement of trade, and to the disheartening of the Catholics of that country', who were, after all, 'the greatest part of that kingdom'. Whoever confirmed that present settlement, Nagle continued, would take 'upon himself the guilt of what was already transacted'. It was inconceivable that James, 'a Prince of great piety', would allow 'all Innocents that never were heard' to 'be condemned, and their estates taken away from them, contrary to . . . Magna Charta', or so order matters that those who had spilt their blood fighting for the crown against Cromwell, and who had been promised their estates by Charles II, 'should for ever be barred of their ancient rights', and 'their estates . . . confirmed to those who served the Usurper'.[118]

The 'Coventry Letter' was clearly intended for public consumption; Clarendon received his copy on 4 January, and recorded in his diary that it showed 'plainly what is designed to be done in this country'.[119] In April 1687 Petty learned how 'The "Coventry Letter" runns now about in every hand' in Ireland, 'and gives terrour'.[120] The Protestant community in Ireland were understandably alarmed. Petty himself, who held estates in County Kerry, penned a reply defending the land settlement as just, since the king had the right to dispose of lands forfeited by rebels and the Act of Settlement had been passed by an Irish parliament 'out of which no man was Excluded for being a Roman Catholique' – Catholics had also been allowed to vote in the general election – and that the proprietors who proved their innocence were for the most part restored to their lands without suit at law, and found them in a much better condition than when they lost them. Besides, 'the Irish Nation . . . had no reason to complaine', Petty said, since they were 'equally protected by the Lawes'; had 'the free exercise of their religion . . . connived att' while dissenting Protestants, especially in Ulster, were 'severely prosecuted'; and had been allowed to trade in corporations and sit on juries.[121] Another reply, dated 15 November 1686 and supposedly penned by an English Catholic, warned that since in the three kingdoms as a whole Protestants greatly outnumbered Catholics, it was important not to provoke them while the Catholics in England were trying to procure relief from the penal laws and secure a better position for themselves – especially given that it was likely (as it still seemed at the time) that James would be succeeded by a Protestant. Many of the forfeited lands, this author pointed out, had ended up in the possession not of parliamentarians or Cromwellians but of 'the best of his Majestie's protestant subjects' of the Established Church, and quite a few had gone to James II himself, while it was believed in England that the restored Catholics had got more by the settlement 'than was formerly their own'. 'What allarme will it make in this Kingdome [England]', the author asked, 'when laws of property are overthrown in that?'; 'it is beginning at the wrong end to resolve things on that side without first haveing made sure work on this and even the noyse and all rumours from thence might blast and prejudice things here of much higher value and importance'.[122]

James next set about trying to ensure that, should he decide to call a parliament in Ireland, it would be one inclined to his interest. This was part of what turned out to be a three-pronged strategy across all his kingdoms to secure a pliant legislature. Only in Ireland, however, was the success of the strategy eventually put to the test: in England and Scotland, James's efforts were foiled by William's invasion; Ireland, which became James's base for his attempts to regain his lost crowns from William after the Glorious Revolution, was, by contrast, to see the calling of a parliament in 1689 along the lines that James had envisaged. In the first half of 1687 James reversed the outlawries against eleven Irish lords, in order to increase Catholic representation in the upper House.[123] To guarantee control over the composition of the Commons, he instructed Tyrconnell, on taking up the lord deputyship, to remodel the corporations.[124] Tyrconnell dutifully summoned all corporate towns and incorporated bodies to surrender their charters, ostensibly so that their privileges could be enlarged, though he made no secret of the fact that the real reason was because too many corporations had sought to frustrate the King's design of admitting Catholics as freemen or to corporate office.[125] The Lord Deputy did his best to convince the Protestant Irish that admitting Catholics to the corporations would offer 'no damage to their Religion', which 'he would in no manner intrench upon', but only be of 'advantage . . . to their temporal concerns', since by uniting people in 'their affections' it would prove 'a mighty encouragement to trade'.[126] A few corporations voluntarily surrendered, such as the town of Drogheda and the surgeons of Dublin, while the natives of the town of Galway took pride in 'being the most forward of the whole Kingdom' in having 'the first Popish Mayor and Sheriffs, and Common-Councilmen, and other Officers'.[127] Most decided to put up a fight. The government retaliated with writs of *quo warranto*: by

June 1687 it had initiated *quo warranto* proceedings against Dublin and 104 other corporations in Ireland.[128] On 1 April, the Lord Mayor, sheriffs and citizens of Dublin petitioned the King, insisting that they had made concessions to Catholics, maintaining they had always been loyal to the crown, and protesting that 'the public good' would suffer if their charter and liberties were either surrendered or evicted. Three days later the city assembly formally repealed all their acts which entailed disqualifications on Catholics. It was all to no avail. The case went to trial, where it was determined that the city had forfeited its charter, and a new one was granted at the end of November. Derry similarly put up a great battle, but it too was at last forced to forfeit its charter.[129]

The *quo warranto*s did not result in the removal of all Protestants from the corporations; the general pattern was to leave about 'one third Protestants and two thirds Papists'.[130] In Dublin, for example, the new Lord Mayor and sheriffs were Catholics, but fifteen of the forty-eight burgesses were Protestants, as were ten of the twenty-four aldermen. Some of the Protestants who were allowed to serve on the remodelled corporations, however, were nonconformists. In Belfast, the Presbyterian merchant Thomas Pottinger was named town sovereign. In Dublin, the Quakers Samuel Claridge and Anthony Sharp became aldermen, together with two other nonconformists. Quakers were also named as masters of the corporation of weavers and of the new corporation of hosiers. Quakers were particularly resented, because they were happy to take advantage of the benefits of the corporation but refused to serve 'in any office' that admitted 'the least trouble or charge', as the corporation of Youghall had complained back in July 1686. 'The peaceable Quakers, who before would not under a Protestant Government take upon them so much as the Office of a Constable', one Protestant tract quipped, 'now under a Popish every where readily conform.' Another Protestant pamphleteer protested in 1689 that some of the Protestant nonconformists intruded into the corporations 'were as irreconcileable Enemies to the Protestant Church, as they were Friends to, and Confederates with the Romish', especially the Quakers who, this author claimed, derived their 'ridiculous Profession . . . from the Jesuits'. Under such circumstances, not all conformist Protestants who survived the purge agreed to serve. In Dublin, for example, eleven of the Protestant burgesses refused to take their seats.[131]

The battle over the corporations, however, reveals that Tyrconnell's agenda for Ireland was somewhat at odds with the imperial pretensions of the English crown. James wanted not just to help his co-religionists but also to enhance the authority of the crown, and he therefore insisted that a clause be put into the new charters giving the king's chief governor the power to remove or appoint whom he pleased.[132] Tyrconnell objected, and tried to persuade James to make the new charters unalterable, though with no success. Tyrconnell wanted to give the Irish corporations more control over their own affairs and free them from interference by the government in England; since there was at this time (spring 1687) still no prospect of a Catholic successor to James, James's clause would enable a future Protestant king of England to undo all the changes that had been introduced during James's reign.[133] Tyrconnell also sought to promote the economic interests of the trading communities in Ireland by issuing an order to repeal the duty on iron, which he knew would bring Spanish coin into the country. The government in England, however, had no desire to allow the Irish to set themselves up in competition with English commercial interests and forced him to back down, on the grounds that his proposal was contrary to statues passed in England, which took precedence under Poynings' Law.[134] Frustrated in these efforts, Tyrconnell allegedly declared to the Irish council that he would get the forthcoming Irish parliament 'to expunge' the clause inserted in the new charters to which he had objected, repeal Poynings' Law, and allow the export of wool into France and the importation of tobacco and other plantation commodities into Ireland, 'without unlading first in England', as required by the Navigation Act. He continued with a threat that 'unless the King would consent to all these things, as well as to an alteration of the Irish Act of Settlement, they should not pass no money bills'.[135]

With the corporations in safe hands, the election of a parliament sympathetic to Catholic interests could be guaranteed. Now all Tyrconnell needed to do was to persuade James to reopen the question of the land settlement. His chance came in August 1687, when the King, who was then on his own electoral tour through England, summoned him to Chester for a general discussion of English and Irish affairs. Tyrconnell managed to convince James that some alteration of the Act of Settlement was necessary; Sheridan, who accompanied Tyrconnell on the trip, went further and suggested that the Act needed to be broken entirely and a new one set up. James ordered them to draw up two draft bills for his consideration. Two Catholic judges, Thomas Nugent and Thomas Rice, came to England in February 1688 with the proposals. One involved opening up the whole question of the settlement again, by allowing those claims for innocency that had never been heard to be granted a hearing. The other simply proposed that the estates of the Cromwellians should be equally divided between the new owners and the old. The schemes were rejected by the English privy council, and met staunch opposition from English Catholics, who were worried about the implications for their own position in England if such radical measures were pursued in Ireland. Lord Belasyse said that if such designs were encouraged, the English Catholics would have to look for another country. Lord Powis similarly maintained 'that the King had better use to make of his Catholick Subjects in England, than to Sacrifice them for reprize to the Protestants of Ireland in lieu of their Estates there'. Londoners also let the judges know how they felt about the proposals. Whenever Nugent and Rice travelled through the streets of the capital, crowds of youths would run after their coach, 'with Potatoes stuck on sticks', shouting 'Make room for the Irish Embassadors'. The crowds appear to have been stirred up by Catholics within the English government, who were desperate to make the King realize to 'what mischief' the proposals would lead.[136]

Tyrconnell's administration inevitably had the effect of alienating Protestant opinion in Ireland even further. More Protestants decided it was time to leave when Tyrconnell was appointed Lord Deputy. According to one account, some 1,500 families deserted Dublin when Clarendon was removed from office, 'to avoid the Tyranny of him that was to follow'.[137] Sheridan alleged that Tyrconnell's 'over hasty making all Catholic sheriffs and issuing out *quo warranto*s against the Corporation Charters', coupled with the fact that 'the Catholic natives indiscreetly' began 'giving out they were soon to be restored . . . to their ancient possessions' and were 'to engross all the civil as well as military employments', so alarmed the Protestants that 'vast numbers of all sorts, gentlemen, artificers, tradesmen and merchants as well as the disbanded officers of the army quit the kingdom, apprehending a bloody persecution and the breaking of the Act of Settlement'.[138] Sources hostile to Tyrconnell, it has to be said, give a somewhat exaggerated impression of how many Protestants fled the country. Some Protestants found it difficult to sell up and leave, with land prices being driven down, while there were also 'great multitudes' with little or no money who had no option but to stay put.[139] In fact, probably no more than 5 per cent of the Protestant population left Ireland during James II's reign. Certain areas, however, were affected much more than others: Dublin lost 25 per cent of its Protestant population; Cork 16 per cent. Moreover, it was the economically most important classes who left, namely the landlords and merchants.[140] Those who stayed were clearly not happy. Trouble seemed to be brewing in the north, where radical Presbyterians who had come over from the Scottish south-west were supposedly trying to foment discontent. In the summer of 1687, Tyrconnell received a report that 'above 4,000 Scotch fanatics, many of them besides the preacher come from Scotland, had a meeting for several days in Ulster, and discoursed many things tending to sedition and rebellion'; the preacher was arrested and sent back to Scotland, though he subsequently escaped to Holland.[141]

The economic consequences of an unsettled Ireland were worrying. Sheridan, no friend to the Lord Deputy, alleged that the sudden change of affairs in Ireland during Tyrconnell's period of office 'proved a great stop and discouragement to the trade and improvement of the kingdom, both in cities, towns and country'.[142] Hostile accounts written in 1689 tended to express their criticisms in hyperbolic terms. One pamphleteer asserted that 'the infinite numbers of people deserting the Kingdom from all parts of it upon Tyrconnell's coming to the Government made the Towns and Cities almost waste; discouraged all manner of Trade, and sunk the Revenue to an incredible Ebb, and deduction from its former Value'.[143] The economic downturn was real enough. Petty calculated that the value of lands in Ireland in 1687 was little more than one half of what they had been in 1683, and the value of cattle and stock only about three-quarters.

The price of butter, cheese, milk, eggs and meat all began to fall. Urban trade was also hit. Among other things, the flight to England of so many from Dublin led to a significant downturn in the consumption of beer. As a result, by August 1687 the Dublin excise was down one-seventh from what it had been the previous quarter, which was already below normal; the customs of Dublin fell even further, by one-quarter.[144] The Irish revenue as a whole fell by almost £30,000, from £334,576 in 1686 to £305,985 in 1687.[145] Protestants complained that Catholics refused to do business with them, or purchase things in Protestants' shops.[146] Yet it was not only the Protestants who suffered; 'the Trading part of the Papists' also felt the effects of this 'general Consumption of Trade', while 'the Countrey-man, tho pleas'd with the restoration of his holy father', nevertheless complained that 'the times [were] worse' and that he would 'bee undone'.[147]

Other factors affected the Irish economy. Bad weather, coupled with French duties on wool and butter, led to a near collapse of Ireland's two staples, leading one Cork Protestant to predict in June 1688, 'this Country will Infallibly be Begard'.[148] Economic dislocation brought with it increased crime, more theft, and more rural violence, much of it directed against Protestants, if only because they were the ones with more wealth.[149] Several sources attest to a rise in sectarian violence. At the beginning of 1687 there were reports of 'Several Murthers . . . Comited upon the brittish in many places', including a brutal incident that had allegedly happened at a house about eight miles outside Dublin, where a family of seven was killed, the father and son having 'ther bellyes ript upp' and the mother and four daughters 'Burnt in there beds'.[150] In Dublin on 23 October that year, Protestant celebrations on the anniversary of the Irish Rebellion were disrupted by 'a rabble of Popish soldiers with drawn swords and crowd of other rabble' who ran about the town trying to extinguish the bonfires. Violent scuffles ensued, which led to several people being wounded and two Protestant tradesmen being killed; one of them was killed outside his own door by a Catholic who allegedly boasted that 'he was sorry he did not kill twenty more'. Some accounts allege that as many as five Protestants and two or three Catholics were killed.[151] To prevent similar trouble on

5 November, Tyrconnell issued a proclamation forbidding unauthorized public bonfires on festival days.[152] In the face of such violence from certain sections of the Catholic community, and with control of the agencies of law enforcement and the army firmly in Catholic hands, rumours began to spread in some communities that 'a general Massacre [was] to be suddainly put in Execution' on the Protestants.[153] A Dublin Protestant recorded the dire situation in April 1688: 'The Country here is very poor; so many families being removed with their effects, and dayly going, because of the Irish army; from whence we can expect nothing but a massacre in case the King should dye.' 'The uncertainty of the titles of land', he continued, made men 'keep all the money by them they can get' and send all their plate to England, while 'Our Church here stands totteringly . . . there being great expectations that a Parliament here will transfer all, or a good part, to their own clergy'. Ominously, he concluded that 'The Irish have many prophecies of this year 1688, and are in great expectations of the fulfilling them.'[154]

CONCLUSION

The policy of Catholicization pursued by James and Tyrconnell in Ireland destroyed the fragile equilibrium that had been established during the reign of Charles II. Yet the problems that developed during the period 1685–8 reveal not just the errors or misguided initiatives of the men in charge; they also highlight the inherent instabilities in the Restoration Irish polity and the fundamental structural problems that made a long-lasting, working solution to the governance of Ireland so difficult to achieve. Merely the accession of a new king, and the expectations or anxieties this created, destabilized the situation and revealed the deep-seated tensions and mutual antagonisms that existed within Ireland. Because it was James's and Tyrconnell's decision to promote the interests of the Catholics in Ireland that was the apparent cause of the rapid destabilization of Irish affairs, it might seem that the Irish problem at this time was essentially religious in nature. Certainly religious factors were highly important. But the Irish problem was always about much more than simply religion. It was also about access to political and economic power, to trading privileges or land, to justice at law; it was about the nature of the relationship between England and Ireland, and the extent to which the latter should be treated as a colonial dependency of the former; it was about whose country it was and who should be in charge. It is true that these issues tended to reinforce the confessional divide, since by and large the Protestants were the ones with the power and the Catholics the ones who were dispossessed. But they did not invariably so do. Thus we have seen that there were divisions within Protestant ranks, and that some nonconformists even served on some of the purged corporations with Catholics following the *quo warranto* proceedings. In addition, there were divisions within the Catholic interest in Ireland, between the Old English and the Gaelic Irish, and also between those Catholics who had been restored to their estates at the Restoration and those who had not (a division, that is, mainly within the Old English community itself).

There was a tendency among those engaged in the struggle against English hegemony to perceive the conflict in national terms – as a struggle to throw off English colonial domination and achieve autonomy and self-determination for the Irish nation. As we have noted, there was frequent bragging by the Irish during James II's reign that they were soon to have their day, recover their lands, and bring 'the English under their subjection'.[155] According to O'Kelly, writing after the Revolution, Tyrconnell's reforms had made him 'the Darling of the Nation'.[156] The concept of the Irish 'us', however, tended by now to be used to refer to all those who had lost out at the hands of the English or British 'them' – that is, not just the Gaelic Irish themselves, but also the Catholics of Old English stock. The author of another retrospective history, written in the early eighteenth century from the perspective of the Old English, conceived of 'the nation of Ireland' as equivalent to the Catholics of Ireland, whether of Old English or Gaelic Irish stock.[157] The sense that there was a basic conflict between Ireland and England, the Irish 'us' and the English or British 'them', is brought out in a contemporary vindication of Tyrconnell's government of Ireland that appeared during the course of 1688. The pamphlet began with a bold assertion of the author's opinion that Ireland was more likely to thrive 'under the Influence of a Native-Governour, than under any Stranger to us and our Country'. By contrast, 'a Man altogether of English Interest, never did, and likely never will . . . project any thing for us, which may tend to our Advantage, that may be the least bar or prejudice to the Trade of England; which is the only Nation in the World that impedes our Trade'. 'Former Governours' had 'brought over as many Strangers to us, as lick'd up all the Imployments in Church and State . . . to the Grief of the whole Nation'. The author conceded that Ireland consisted of 'divers Interests', but then went on to posit the existence of a basic dichotomy between 'The Irish', who were pleased that they were 'under the Government of a Native' who had removed 'all Jealousies of Inequality from them', and 'the British', who had no reason to feel insecure, given Tyrconnell's 'Education', the 'stake he has in England', and the fact that he had an English wife and was himself 'descended from a Famous Ancient Stock of English Nobility'. The fact that Tyrconnell was a native and Irish (albeit of Old English stock) was more important than the fact that he was Catholic, 'because a Stranger may have that Qualification'. As far as this author was concerned, the issue was at heart about the Irish having control over their own affairs, so that their interests would not be continually sacrificed to those of England.[158]

The ripostes to the *Vindication* show that the English saw the Irish situation in similar 'us' versus 'them' terms. Thus one pamphleteer wrote that ever since the original conquest of Ireland, it had always been a maxim that an Englishman should be chief governor of Ireland; if this was so before the Reformation, how much more necessary it was now that there was a religious divide. Ireland was 'a conquer'd Country', and 'the Conquerors have a right to establish Laws . . . as shall seem fitting and convenient towards the keeping of it in their hands'. The British in Ireland wanted Ireland to be ruled by an Englishman, and 'the ill effects the contrary method' had had 'on their Persons and Estates' were 'but too visible'. The author tried to claim that it was better for the natives to be under English government, arguing that they were 'beholding to us for reducing them from a state of Barbarity, which left but little difference between them and Brutes', since 'We taught them to Live, to Eat, Drink, and Lodge like humane Creatures', and they also had the benefit of 'the gentleness of the English Government' and 'the equal Protection of the Laws'. The author of the *Vindication* of Tyrconnell, he continued, in reality wanted Ireland to be 'an independent Kingdom, and in the hands of its own Natives: he longs till the day, when the English Yoak of Bondage shall be thrown off'.[159]

A manuscript reply to the *Vindication* made the similar point that the English conquerors should not be under the government of the Irish conquered, and warned that history demonstrated that the Irish were 'the veterane and Irreconcilable Enimies of the English'. The attempt to construct a rational argument about the loyalty of the British, the rebelliousness of the Irish, and the fact the Irish had little to complain about under English rule (since they were always allowed liberty of conscience) was mixed with recourse to crude anti-Irish prejudice. Thus, the author castigated the alleged contradictory arguments of the *Vindication* as 'Excellent Irish Logick'. Similarly, in explaining the economic misfortunes that he saw as having befallen Ireland since the English had been disarmed and subjected to rule by the Irish, he asserted that 'the Irish' were 'knowne generally' to be 'a slothfull and Idle people haveing as little Industry or ingenuity to improve their labour to an advantage of themselves and families', and consequently, now Ireland had been deprived of English improvements, the countryside and cities were swarming with beggars.[160] Mutual antagonisms clearly ran deep; the situation in Ireland by 1688 was already highly volatile.

4

Scotland Under James VII

> *When two brothers we shall see*
> *Quite the northern heresie . . .*
> *Then shall a Lord espouse our cause*
> *Whose Grandsire framed the penal laws . . .*
> *When Toleration we shall see*
> *Joined with Indemnity*
> *When a Kind letter at one puff*
> *Shall blow the bloody statutes off*
> *The Declaration and the Test*
> *Shall for a small oath be supprest . . .*
> *When all these things shall come to passe*
> *Then shall we freely go to Masse*
> *And ne're a penal law transgress*
> *Then let us Catholicks sing and say*
> *Te Deum on that happy day.*
>
> 'A Catholic Prophecy' [April, 1687]
> (though clearly a Protestant satire)[1]

From the monarchy's point of view, the situation in Scotland in the aftermath of Argyll's rebellion appeared healthier than it had been for a long time. Scotland had been the most troublesome of the British kingdoms for the crown during the seventeenth century. A rebellion there had already helped bring down James's father, Charles I, while James's brother, Charles II, had faced insurrections in his northern kingdom in 1666 and 1679. When English Tories during the Exclusion Crisis expressed their fear that '41 was come again, their concern was that the British monarchy might once again be threatened by an alliance of English dissidents and radical Presbyterians north of the border. Yet by 1685 – due in part to James's own efforts as head of the Scottish government in the early 1680s – Scotland had been reduced to a loyal and manageable kingdom. There were enthusiastic demonstrations of support for James at the time of his accession, and loyal addresses from the political and religious elite, while the parliament, which met in the spring, had not only supported the crown's entire legislative programme but had even gone on to proclaim that the Scottish monarchy was absolute. Admittedly, significant pockets of disaffection remained, especially in the Presbyterian heartland of the south-west. However, politico-religious extremists no longer posed a serious threat to the government, as the debacle of Argyll's rebellion proved.

James's own confidence in the strength of the monarchy's position in Scotland can be seen in the way he pressed forward with measures designed to help his co-religionists. It was not that his Catholic subjects in Scotland needed much help. A small minority, they had been largely free from persecution during Charles II's reign, and before the passage of the Test Act of 1681 they had even found it possible to enjoy political office. Prior to his accession, James was reputed to have observed that the Scottish Catholics had 'so much privat liberty of their religion' they 'had no reason to complain'.[2] We cannot be certain why he changed his mind once king. The evidence suggests, however, that he decided to use Scotland as a testing ground: if he could establish Catholics with a right to toleration in Scotland – and he clearly expected that it would be easiest to achieve this in Scotland, given the powers of the monarchy north of the border – this would set a powerful precedent for the English to follow. Most of the measures James was to adopt to promote the interests of his co-religionists in England were tried first in Scotland. As his own daughter, the Princess Anne, observed in June 1688: what 'has been done there [in Scotland], has been but a fore-runner of what in a short time has been done here [in England]'.[3] Right from the beginning of his reign, James gave Scottish Catholics positions of authority in the service of the crown, using his prerogative powers to dispense them from the provisions of the Test. He sanctioned the construction of public Catholic chapels and encouraged Catholics to worship openly. In 1686, he tried to force the Scottish parliament to pass legislation in favour of liberty of conscience, and when that failed he proceeded to grant it anyway through the use of his prerogative. He followed this with a general edict of toleration in 1687, in the hope of winning over the support of Protestant nonconformists, prior to issuing a similar Indulgence in England. Thus, in Scotland – as he was to do in England – he launched an attack on the dominant position of the Episcopalian establishment, using his prerogative to undermine the laws that upheld and defended the religious monopoly of the Church in Scotland.

All of these initiatives were justified in terms of an appeal to the absolute authority of the crown. Scotland during the reign of James VII, therefore, provides us with a test-case of later-Stuart absolutism in action. What were the realities of royal power at this time, and what did absolutism mean in practice? How far was James able to go in promoting the cause of Catholicism on the basis of his own authority, in opposition to the established laws of the land? What obstacles stood in his way? Who opposed him, on what grounds, and to what effect?

The reign of James VII has been a largely neglected area of Scottish historiography, and thus the precise extent of James's relative success or failure in Scotland remains under-explored.[4] Historians looking back on James's reign from the perspective of the Glorious Revolution, however, seem to agree that the opposition to James in Scotland was muted and ineffectual. 'The antecedents to the Glorious Revolution in England found few if any parallels in Scotland despite the similarity of the policies pursued by James VII in his northern kingdom', one scholar has argued; 'in political terms James appeared to be impregnable'.[5] Similarly, the author of an influential survey of Scottish history has written that 'the crisis which suddenly befell [James VII] in late 1688 . . . was an English crisis, with its roots there, and it is hard to find any trace of the same in Scotland'.[6] Such assumptions require critical re-evaluation. As this chapter will show, there were many of the same antecedents to the Revolution in Scotland as in England, precisely because the policies pursued by James in the two kingdoms were so similar. There was thus extensive opposition in his northern kingdom to his attempts to promote the interests of Catholics through the use of his royal prerogative, both in parliament and out-of-doors, among sections of the political and religious elite, as well as among the lower orders. Moreover, despite the fact that the Scottish parliament of 1685 had recognized the king as absolute, we see in Scotland, as in England, a legalist opposition to the initiatives of the crown, taking its stance in defence of the rule of law against the illegal actions of the King. Indeed, it is far from clear whether James's position in his northern kingdom by the summer of 1688 was any less fragile than it was in England. James VII, by his actions as king, contributed to the development of a genuinely revolutionary situation in Scotland. He broke the alliance between the Church and king and alienated the traditional Scottish ruling elite; and by granting religious toleration, he allowed the Presbyterians to organize and develop a more united front, without achieving any significant, new political support. In short, James managed to destroy the very system whereby effective royal control had been established over this difficult-to-rule kingdom under Charles II.

THE GROWTH OF DISCONTENT

The radical Presbyterians continued to be a minor irritant for the authorities after the defeat of Argyll's rebellion, but by now their threat had been effectively contained. In August 1685, a group of 'phanatique Whigs' from Lesmahagow in Lanarkshire brutally murdered a local official who had helped in the capture of the plotter Richard Rumbold, ripping open his belly and tearing out his heart, in imitation of the punishment inflicted upon Rumbold.[7] The Scottish council continued to receive the occasional report of armed meetings of field conventiclers, especially in the south-west, where the Cameronian remnant remained active under James Renwick's leadership.[8] Yet after a quarter of a century of persecution, the Presbyterian interest in Scotland had been significantly weakened,[9] and the diehard opponents of the crown were a small minority. The loyalty of 'the moderate and judicious people'[10] seemed confirmed by the celebrations for the King's birthday on 14 October 1685, ordained by royal proclamation also to commemorate the defeat of the Monmouth and Argyll rebellions. The council in Edinburgh sponsored bonfires at Holyroodhouse and on Arthur's Seat, arranged for the drinking fountains to run with wine, and 'caused Sweat-meats to be distributed among the People'. The promotion worked. There were so many bonfires and other 'demonstrations of joy among the Ranks of the people' that night, one observer commented, that 'the Streets were hardly passable'.[11] By contrast, 5 November was quietly ignored, with neither bells nor bonfires in the nation's capital.[12]

However, the goodwill that seemed to exist towards the monarchy in Scotland was soon put to the test. There was a sudden rise to prominence of Catholics in the administration within Scotland. As seen already, Argyll's rebellion gave James the excuse to appoint the Catholic Earl of Dumbarton commander of all the forces in Scotland in May 1685, justifying the appointment by appeal to his royal prerogative. He shortly thereafter appointed the Duke of Gordon, another Catholic, Lord Lieutenant of the north, in command of the Highland forces.[13] Then, in the autumn of 1685, Lord Chancellor Perth announced his own conversion to Catholicism. The conversion appears to have been sincere, and Perth even offered to resign his offices, though James refused to accept. Some months later Perth's brother, the Earl of Melfort, James's Secretary of State for Scotland in London, also converted.[14] There were a few other high profile conversions to Catholicism, the most notable being that of Dr Robert Sibbald, Professor of Medicine at the University of Edinburgh and the King's physician (though Sibbald was later to regret his decision and rejoin the Protestant Church).[15]

As yet, James saw no need to restructure his central administration. Queensberry remained as Treasurer (though he was to fall in the spring of 1686); the Marquis of Atholl was Lord Privy Seal; the Duke of Hamilton, Viscount Tarbat and the Earl of Mar (the last being Governor of Stirling Castle) remained influential figures on the privy council; while the scrupulous Protestant lawyer Sir George Lockhart was appointed president of the court of session in January 1686.[16] But Catholics were brought in at the level of local government. In November 1685, James granted dispensations to twenty-six Catholic landlords to serve as commissioners to collect the revenues voted by parliament the previous spring, directly contrary, in Fountainhall's view, to the act of 1685 ratifying the existing laws for the established religion.[17] The threat of popery became even more readily apparent when, upon his return to Edinburgh in late December, Perth began to celebrate mass openly in the Scottish capital and encouraged others to do the same. Soon the London-based diarist Roger Morrice was reporting that the King had ordered a Catholic chapel to be built in Edinburgh's royal palace, and had sent twelve priests to Scotland 'to say mass in it'. Acts of 1560 and 1567 had declared the mass idolatrous, and made attendance punishable by death at the third offence. Yet Perth confidently assured James that Scotland was 'not as England': 'Measures need not be too nicely keept with this people', he opined, 'nor are wee to be suffered to imagine that your Majesty is not so far above your laws as that you cannot dispence with them.' Perth himself, with all the zeal of a convert, had no desire to keep things 'nicely'. One contemporary Catholic observed that the Chancellor 'would jade the Masse, he caused say it so oft'. On Christmas day that year, Perth not only celebrated the mass, but 'rocked a child in the cradle, in memoire of our saviour', Fountainhall informs us. An astonished Fountainhall could only add: 'this ceremony is not used by the French Romanists'.[18]

The prominence of Catholics in central and local office, however, provoked a storm of anti-popish sermonizing by the local clergy. Twice in October 1685 Bishop Paterson of Edinburgh had to warn his clergy to desist, reminding them that they had 'the King's promise and assurance to protect our religion' and 'strong laws in favour of our reformed religion', though to limited effect.[19] Nervous about the prospect of anti-Catholic invective finding its way into print, Perth issued orders at the beginning of 1686 forbidding printers, stationers and booksellers from printing or selling 'any books reflecting on Popery'.[20] The government's attempts to silence the media were far from a complete success. In April, George Shiell, minister of Prestonhaugh (now Prestonkirk, Haddingtonshire), was heard to proclaim from the pulpit of St Giles, Edinburgh, that 'he would believe the moon to be made of green cheese as soon believe Transubstantion'; when rebuked by his bishop, Shiell defiantly replied that he thought 'a ridiculous religion might be treated in ridicule'.[21] One of the most virulent anti-Catholic sermons, however, was delivered by James Canaries at the East-Church of St Giles, Edinburgh, on 14 February 1686, which also found its way into print. Its arguments are worth examining in some detail.

Canaries was far from being an inevitable opponent of the later Stuart monarchy. Indeed, he had preached a strongly loyalist sermon on 29 May 1685, the published version of which he had dedicated to Perth. By the new year, however, he had turned against the Lord Chancellor. As he made clear when he published his 1686 sermon, he was concerned not because he feared 'that Popery will ever be impos'd upon us by our King', but because there had been some eminent defections.[22] Canaries, who when a younger man had flirted with Catholicism himself, thought popery a nonsensical religion, and claimed that no rational man could believe in papal infallibility or transubstantiation. Yet it was the political dangers of popery that Canaries emphasized. Since the Pope claimed a deposing power, how could any ruler then be assured of the loyalty of his nation, unless he had an army of 200,000, as in France? The conclusion was clear: 'a King in a Popish Countrey, must either live at his Holiness's Beck, or else . . . upon the confidence of an Army'. Canaries was careful to distance himself from the radical Presbyterians, claiming that he looked upon them 'as the scandal of Christianity, and plague of humane Society'. He was also keen to profess his loyalty to the monarchy, arguing that it was in James's best interests to support the religion of the Established Church in Scotland, since this was 'the most loyal Religion in the World; so that the more closely we stick to it, the more ground we give our King to trust us'.[23] In the preface to the published version he insisted he was 'dissatisfied with Popery' because 'it is of disloyal Principles, and vastly prejudicial to the Rights of Princes', and sought to defend the authority of the crown while at the same time appealing to the safeguards offered to the King's subjects by the law. Protestants had nothing to fear from King James, because he had assured the Scottish parliament in 1685 that he wanted the crown powerful for no other reason than to be able 'to defend and protect our Religion as established by Law, and all our Rights and Properties'. Rather, it was the monarchy that was threatened by the recent conversions to Catholicism. Pointing out that Britain might well have a Protestant ruler again one day, Canaries sarcastically asked 'what if Britain were as much Popish' then 'as now it is the contrary', would not a Protestant king 'have a pretty Tenure for his Crown?'[24] Despite such protestations of loyalty, James remained unconvinced, and had Canaries suspended from his ministry for preaching and publishing a seditious sermon.[25]

The inhabitants of Edinburgh did not suffer the public celebration of the mass in their city quietly. On the afternoon of Sunday 31 January, a huge crowd of tradesmen, apprentices and college students attacked a house in the Canongate, where Lady Perth was attending mass, destroying the altar, crucifixes and everything else in the chapel, smashing the windows, and throwing dirt and stones at the worshippers. Continuing in the streets with 'great cries and outrageous speeches, threattenings and menaceings', they 'assaulted and set upon severall off his majestie's good subjects', we are told, 'beatt and wounded them, robbed and ruffled the cloaks, hatts, perivicks, and other abulziaments', and even 'draged some of them through the streets'. They forced one of the priests they caught to 'swear the oath of the Test, and renunce Poperie' on his knees. Crowds also attacked the houses of several Catholics in the city, including that of Dr Robert Sibbald (which induced Sibbald to resign his presidency of the Royal College of Physicians of Edinburgh and flee to London), breaking open their doors with iron bars. The English diarist Narcissus Luttrell recorded the news matter-of-factly in his journal: 'Letters out of Scotland speak of some tumult or stir . . . there in the citty of Edenburgh, occasioned, as is said, by the chancellor's goeing or endeavouring to sett up masse, which putt the common people into a tumult.' It was, of course, a major breach of the civic peace in Scotland's seat of government and an outrageous affront directed against the man who ruled Scotland in the King's name. Perth himself, in fact, proved more elusive than his wife. One gang stopped a coach, which they thought was bearing Perth through the streets of the capital, and pulled out the passenger, only to find it was the (Protestant) Duke of Hamilton: 'so they let him goe saying that if it had been the Earle of Pirth they would have pulled him into as many pieces as they had broken the windows of the house.'[26]

Crowds also threw stones at the city guards sent in to suppress the disturbances, causing injury to several soldiers, though eventually the troops were able to restore order and make several arrests.[27] That night, however, a fencing master by the name of Alexander Keith met in the cellar of a house off the High Street with about eighteen other tradesmen and apprentices to plan the rescue of apprentices taken in the tumult. Each conspirator undertook to raise a certain number of men from their respective trades and to obtain as many arms as they could. Although their priority was to rescue the prisoners, the conspirators also proposed that they should 'gett assistance from the countrey, and . . . pull downe the papist's houses and stop ther meetings', and drank several healths 'to the confusione off the Papists'.[28] The following morning, as the magistrates ordered a baxter's (baker's) apprentice named Robert Grieve to be whipped in the Canongate for his participation in the rioting on the day before, a crowd of youths led by a shoemaker named David Mowbray, who had allegedly also been involved in the previous day's disturbances, rescued the young man and carried him down the streets, again 'with great cryes, outragious speeches, and menaces'. They then went in search of local papists, storming their houses, rifling their goods, and smashing their windows. The soldiers again were called in; this time they fired at the crowd, killing three people, one of whom at least being a totally innocent bystander.[29]

The council decided that Mowbray should be prosecuted for his part in the both the riot and the rescue, although there was some dissent. One counsellor wondered what the Lord Advocate would say if the accused argued in his defence that he was only dissipating 'a meeting declared treasonable by Law', and suggested that 'if it had been a fanatical conventicle' he 'would have got thanks'. Nevertheless, Mowbray was tried on 8 February and, having confessed to his role in the rescue, was found guilty and sentenced to hang two days later. The council granted a short reprieve, to allow for the chance of a royal pardon, and Mowbray was eventually released from prison at the end of May. However Keith, the fencing master, found guilty at his trial on 26 February for his role in the disturbances, was hanged on 5 March. There were other victims too. One soldier, who had taken the rioters' side saying 'he would not fight in that quarrel against the Protestants, for he was sworn to that religion', was remitted to a council of war. A drummer was accused by two Catholics of drawing his sword and saying 'he could find it in his heart to run that through them'; the drummer claimed that he meant the rioting apprentices, but his accusers insisted he was referring to those attending the mass, and the drummer was executed under martial law on 23 February, even though Scottish law prohibited Catholics from serving as witnesses.[30]

The King did write to Perth suggesting that he had been too open in celebrating mass, and warning him 'to be more cautious and private' in the future.[31] But, if anything, the policy of promoting the interests of Catholics proceeded with greater pace after the disturbances. The riots were used by Perth to secure the removal of the Treasurer, Queensberry, who was accused not only of fiscal mismanagement but also of failing, in his capacity as Constable of Edinburgh Castle, to keep order in the capital. Queensberry was a staunch Protestant who was going to be an obstacle in the way of any attempts to promote Catholicism. Yet faction also played a part in Queensberry's downfall; on this occasion the Duke of Hamilton, another Protestant who was to frustrate efforts to promote toleration of Catholics under James VII, sided with Perth and Melfort in pressing for Queensberry's dismissal. The treasury was placed under the authority of a commission, with Perth as first commissioner, and Queensberry was replaced as Constable of Edinburgh Castle by the Catholic Duke of Gordon.[32] The Catholics seemed more firmly entrenched in the government of Scotland than ever. James's next aim was to secure legal recognition for the position of the Catholics by getting parliament to agree to the repeal of the Test.

THE 'BLACK RAINY PARLIAMENT' OF 1686

Given his frustrations in dealing with the English parliament in November 1685, James decided to push for Catholic toleration in Scotland before he attempted any such measure in England. In doing so, he was again self-consciously trying to play the British card, hoping that the Scottish parliament would 'cast England a good copie and example', as they 'had done in 1681, in declaring the right of succession'.[33] He therefore extended the prorogation of the English parliament, which had been set to reconvene on 10 February,[34] to allow the Scottish parliament to meet first, on 29 April. James had reason to feel confident, given the ultra-royalism the Scottish parliament had demonstrated in 1685 – this was, after all, not a new parliament, but the same body of men who had met the previous year – and the fact that the government could normally guarantee the success of its legislative initiatives through the Lords of the Articles. Tarbat visited James in London in February to assure him that parliament would agree to rescind the penal laws against Catholics, even showing him the roll of MPs and pointing out who would be for and who against.[35] To try to ensure the support of the burgh representatives, James let it be known he was intending to promote free trade with England as a *quid pro quo*.[36]

On 4 March James wrote to the secret committee of the Scottish council informing them of his desire to procure 'the entire abrogation of the sanguinary laws against the Papists' and 'the taking away of the test' (this to be replaced by a short oath of allegiance 'against defensive arms and covenants'), so that Catholics could be admitted to office. 'All laws against phanaticisme' would continue in force, however. The first hints of potential opposition were already becoming apparent. The committee insisted that they would have to consult with the bishops before they could give their opinion on the matter. When the King summoned Hamilton, Lockhart and Major-General William Drummond to London for further instructions, they argued that parliament would grant freedom of worship to Catholics only if the same were allowed to dissenters, and that if the Test were to be removed alternative safeguards for the security of the Protestant religion would be needed. James reluctantly agreed to make some concessions to moderate Presbyterians, without allowing them the full liberty he was intending for his co-religionists. He refused, however, to promise not to attempt anything to the prejudice of the Protestant religion, apparently saying he would not guarantee not to use his power against what he regarded as a false religion.[37]

Defenders of the crown's position tended to take the line that James had the power to pursue such a policy even without parliamentary approval, and that therefore parliament should acquiesce in the King's demand. Melfort tried to convince Hamilton that the King's desire to help the Catholics arose from 'the fatherly care' he had 'of all the concerns of the people' and his inclination to be 'mercyfull . . . to all', but he also stressed that he (Hamilton) was one of the 'guardians of the King's prerogatives' and that it was important to take care that 'none should be lost'.[38] Bishop Paterson of Edinburgh, in a speech delivered before the synod of Edinburgh on 13 April, maintained that James still intended to defend the Protestant religion and only craved that Catholics might be allowed to exercise their own in private; however, Paterson went on to insist that the King's desire 'could not be denied him', since James 'might take it by his prerogative of the church supremacy', as settled by the Scottish Supremacy Act of 1669.[39] James himself informed the secret committee that he conceived it his 'unquestionable prerogative . . . to employ in our Royal service any of our subjects' and 'that by the same prerogative' he had power 'to suspend all penal laws, and all oaths relating to government'.[40]

A number of pamphlets appeared in the spring of 1686 supporting James's plans for toleration, which were 'carefully spread . . . about' in an attempt to influence parliamentary opinion.[41] Thomas Burnet, professor of philosophy at the Marischal College of Aberdeen, produced a short Latin work arguing that the king of Scotland was absolute and could abrogate and annul laws, and that the three estates could not question his pleasure.[42] Another pamphlet, said to be written by Sir Roger L'Estrange, with the aid of 'the Jesuits and Popish Priests, in and about Edinburgh', and which was circulated among members during the parliamentary session, maintained that since 'Kings in Scotland were before Parliaments . . . all the legislative, as well as executive Power, did reside sovereignly in them', and therefore the King could grant relief to his co-religionists without parliament's consent. The author then proceeded to ask whether it was necessary, or even politically desirable, to keep the laws in place. The laws against papists had been passed, he pointed out, in the early years of the Scottish Reformation, when Catholics were plotting against the king and government; given that Scottish Catholics were now quiet and peaceable, such laws were no longer needed.

Moreover, how could the Scots condemn 'the Persecution in France, or the French King's Method in forcing Men's Consciences', when they were doing the same themselves? In a curious turn of argument, the author then warned that if James were 'irritated and provoked', he might 'without violating of any Law, at one stroke, remove all Protestant Officers and Judges', since they held their offices during his pleasure, and that by dint of the Supremacy Act he could even dismiss 'all Protestant Bishops and Ministers from the Government of the Church'. 'The whole Government both of Church and State' might then become lodged 'in the Hands of such as' were not 'so friendly to the Protestant Interest'; and we, as Protestants, would be powerless to do anything about it, since Protestants' religious principles did not allow for resistance.[43] Various pamphlets that had been published in England as part of the English debate over the dispensing power, and which set out to champion the royal prerogative and defend Catholics from the charges of idolatry and disloyalty, were also circulated in Scotland with the intent of influencing opinion there.[44]

If James could act by his prerogative alone, we may wonder why he decided to act through parliament. The publicly proclaimed reason was that James was 'a gentle and moderate Father and Governor'.[45] The real reason can be gleaned from the explanation James gave as to why he was reluctant to allow parliament to extend toleration to the moderate Presbyterians. Any concessions granted to the Presbyterians, he told Melfort, should be by his own act, 'because ane act of parliament . . . Givs some shadow of Right to the Partys Concerned'.[46] In other words, James was determined to keep the Presbyterians in line by making them dependent upon the goodwill of the monarch. By contrast, he wanted to establish the Catholics with a right to toleration, which they would continue to enjoy if he were to be succeeded, as seemed likely at the time, by a Protestant ruler.

In response to this pro-government propaganda, a number of manuscript works appeared criticizing the plans for Catholic relief – in manuscript, because the government had taken 'great Care . . . of the printing Presses that nothing might be published against the King's favourite Design, or in Defence of the present standing Laws'.[47] Several scurrilous handwritten verses circulated attacking the Archbishop of St Andrews and the Bishop of Edinburgh for their support of the King's proposals.[48] In addition, three manuscript pamphlets were produced urging MPs not to agree to a repeal of the penal laws and Test. Despite adopting a fiercely anti-Catholic position, the authors were careful not to be critical of the King or to question his prerogative. Instead, they insisted that MPs were legally prevented from giving their consent to a repeal. Thus 'Reasons why a Consent to abolish the penal Statutes against Papists, cannot be given', which appeared at the end of April 1686 and was distributed among all MPs and many courtiers, accepted that James was 'our supreme Ruler' and not tied to the laws; nevertheless, the author continued, his subjects were so tied, and to support any measure for Catholic relief would be 'most contrary to the Oath of the Test', which required MPs to swear never to consent to any change or alteration to the true Protestant religion. Besides, a repeal would remove 'all the Security we have in Law for our Religion', a foolish thing to do right now, with 'Popery having so prevailed abroad, and being so cruel and raging, and the Court and these Lands being filled with the Emissaries of Rome' and Catholic converts. As for the argument that the repeal of the anti-Catholic legislation was 'His Majesty's Pleasure', the tract continued, James had publicly declared that his pleasure was 'to secure the Protestant Religion in this Nation'; the proposal for Catholic relief could thus only be construed as 'a Temptation from the Enemies of our Religion, who will incessantly labour to induce him to alter his royal Resolution and Promise'.[49]

The second manuscript tract agreed that, despite 'whatever his Majesty may legally do by virtue of his Prerogative', the Test prevented MPs from consenting 'to a suspending of the Execution of penal Statutes against Papists'. Moreover, in this instance James had limited his own prerogative at the beginning of his reign 'by ratifying and confirming all Laws for the Protestant Religion'; and, furthermore, James did not have the authority to 'dispense with an unrepealed Law of God', such as 'the Law for punishing Idolaters'.[50] The third pamphlet, while likewise insisting that MPs were tied by the Test, recalled that Scottish law stated that popish worship was idolatry and the pope and his clergy Antichrist, and asked what Christian could, 'without Horror, think of consenting to a Liberty for Antichrist?' Papists were obliged to extirpate heresy and propagate the Catholic faith not by gentle ways of Christian persuasion, 'but by the infernal Methods of lying, dissembling, plotting, massacring, torturing, and imbruing their Hands in the Blood of all who stand in their Way', as both history and the present-day example of France showed. Why was this Act being sought, the author asked, 'at a Time when the Protestant Religion, all Europe over, is so low? when the Papacy hath gained and doth daily gain such Ground upon the Reformation . . . whilst other Popish Countries are endeavouring to transcribe the French example, and this Island remains . . . the only considerable Part of Christendom, wherein the Reformed Religion stands yet free from the cruel Attacks of Romish Rage'.[51]

Other forms of pressure were brought to bear to influence opinion in parliament. Towards the end of April the clergy of the diocese of Aberdeen petitioned their bishop against supporting any measures of relief for Catholics, maintaining that all persons in any public office were obliged by the Test 'not only to adhere to the Protestant Religion' for the rest of their lives, 'but never to consent to the Alteration thereof'.[52] The bishop was, indeed, to follow this advice in parliament.

It was in this climate of fierce public debate that the proposed measure for Catholic relief came before parliament in the late spring. James appointed as his high commissioner the Earl of Moray, a man already widely suspected of having converted to Catholicism (though he was not formally to go public about his conversion until 1687),[53] and in his letter to parliament asked simply that Catholics be given 'the Protection of Our Laws and that Security under Our government' which other subjects enjoyed; in return, he offered free trade with England and a full indemnity for all crimes committed against 'our Royal Persone or authority'.[54] The omens were not good, however. The opening day of the session, 29 April, saw a torrential downpour, and the weather continued foul all summer, earning the assembly the nickname 'the black rainy Parliament'.[55] Indeed, parliament proved not to be in a compliant mood. Right at the start, one member moved that no one should be allowed to take his seat if he had not taken the Test; Moray (against whom the motion was clearly intended) only managed to prevent a vote on the matter by threatening to commit anyone who supported it to the Tolbooth (Edinburgh's chief prison).[56] In reply to the King's letter, parliament promised to go to 'as great lengths' in helping the Catholics 'as our Conscience will allow', 'Not doubting that Your Majesty will be carefull to secure the Protestant Religion established by Law', though some members were heard to observe in private that 'they had fully examined the case, and found they could goe no lenth at all'. In the debates that followed, the question 'whether the Laws against Roman Cath[olics] should be repealed' was rejected by a sizeable majority, some said by 'above 10 to one'.[57] Eventually, the Lords of the Articles agreed, by a majority of eighteen to fourteen, to a draft bill granting Catholics immunity from prosecution under the penal laws if they met certain conditions, which they presented to parliament for approval. Among those prepared to back the measure were the Archbishop of St Andrews, the Bishop of Edinburgh, Tarbat and Atholl, whose support had never been in doubt, and also more moderate figures like the Marquis of Tweeddale, and even Hamilton, Lockhart and Major-General Drummond, who had expressed their concerns about Catholic relief to the King the previous March. Ranged against them were the Archbishop of Glasgow, the bishops of Galloway, Brechin and Aberdeen, staunch Episcopalians like Lord Advocate Mackenzie of Rosehaugh (said to be 'one of the chief opposers'), the Earl of Mar and Sir William Bruce, and six burgh provosts, including Alexander Milne of Linlithgow, who was expected to manage the burgh interest for the court but who deserted to the other side. The resultant bill nevertheless contained so many restrictions that Moray refused to accept it, and when the King suggested modifications, Hamilton made it clear that these would be unacceptable.[58] A frustrated James prorogued parliament on 15 June, astonished 'that considering the former good disposition of the Scotch Nobility and Gentry, they should demur to so modest a request'.[59] It had generally been regarded in England that things would work out in Scotland 'to the King's satisfaction'.[60] What had gone wrong?

There was a spectrum of opinions in parliament over the repeal of the penal statutes. At the poles were those who were either in favour or against, but in between there were many who, for varying reasons, were prepared to agree to repeal if certain conditions were met. Some who sought a compromise on a conditional repeal were just as hostile to the crown's policy and played as big a part in defeating the proposed toleration as those who were obstinate in their refusal to allow any concession to Roman Catholics. Let us examine the various positions in turn.

Some maintained that parliament should simply acquiesce in whatever James demanded. The Bishop of Edinburgh preached before parliament on its opening day 'against resisting in any Case whatsoever', telling members it was 'their duty' to comply.[61] There were those, however, who 'were for pleasing the Court' but who were far from endorsing the logic of the crown's position. These proposed that the indulgence should last only during the King's life and requested certain minimal safeguards, namely that any Catholics who took the benefit of the toleration should first abjure the pope's deposing power and declare that 'they were not obliged by the principles of their religion to persecute and extirpate Hereticks'. They believed that parliament could safely yield to the King's demands because 'a Protestant successor would rescind all' and that, besides, it was pointless to oppose James's plans since if this parliament proved obstinate he would simply dissolve it and get another to do his business.[62] Here, then, we see no identification with the King's belief that Catholics had a right to toleration, which should continue beyond his death.

There were yet others, however, who were prepared to agree to some measure of relief for Catholics only if there were firm safeguards for the Protestant religion. The job of determining what form the proposed legislation should take was entrusted to a special twelve-man committee appointed out of the Lords of the Articles. Here, Hamilton put forward the provocative proposal that parliament should grant toleration not just to Catholics but to Protestant nonconformists as well, predictably (and doubtless intentionally) drawing the alarm of 'the Church and Cavalier party'. Lockhart moved that Catholics should be given liberty to worship only in their private houses, and that they should continue to be barred from all public offices; any Catholics who took office would be guilty of treason, 'irremissable even by the King, except with the consent of Parliament'.[63] The bill which the Lords of the Articles presented to parliament on 1 June was, in the end, not much different from Lockhart's proposal. Thus it provided that Catholics would not 'incur the Danger of sanguinary or other Punishments contained in any Laws or Acts of Parliament' made against them 'for the Exercise of their Religion in their private Houses, (all publick Worship being hereby excluded)'. However, it concluded by affirming that 'this Immunity' should not be taken as an approbation of the Catholic religion or any ways 'infringe or prejudge the Laws and Acts of Parliament made against Popery, or in favour of the Protestant Religion', in particular the Test Act or any other laws enjoining the oaths of allegiance or the Test oath, which it declared should continue in full force 'to the Ends and Intents for which they were made'.[64] The proposed measure, in other words, explicitly confirmed that all Catholics who had been given public office by James – who included those in the highest level of the Scottish government – were in violation of the law. It is hardly suprising that Moray refused to let the bill be enacted. As one court-based newsletter writer put it: 'how short this is come of the mighty hopes we formed of their plenary complynace with all his Majesties desires in favour of those of the R. C. persuasion I need not tell you'.[65]

Some opposed any measure of relief for Catholics, even with the limitations which the bill provided, believing that to support Catholic toleration would put them in violation of the Test oath and thus render them guilty of perjury. The campaign against compliance was led by the Earl of Mar, Governor of Stirling Castle, and the Laird of Gosford. There was also considerable hostility from the representatives of the burghs. Most alarming from the government's point of view was the vehement opposition from the Church establishment. Eleven of the fourteen bishops objected to parliament's reply to the King's letter intimating that they might be prepared to go to some lengths to help the Catholics. Four of the bishops on the Lords of the Articles, as we have seen, voted against the proposed bill. Bishop Bruce of Dunkeld and Bishop Ramsey of Ross were also outspoken in their criticism in parliament, the latter delivering such an inflammatory sermon before parliament that other bishops had to be stopped from preaching to the assembly because they refused to give assurances not to preach against popery.[66]

Catholic toleration failed despite efforts by the government to secure a compliant assembly. Three deaths among the Lords of the Articles prior to the opening of the parliamentary session had allowed

Moray to appoint his own men as replacements, even though there was a protest that they should have been appointed by the nobility and bishops.[67] Moray was also active in closeting MPs, using both threats and promises.[68] Attempts were made to intrude some new members. James had suspended burgh elections in Edinburgh the previous autumn, so that he could nominate his own man as provost, and at the beginning of the parliamentary session the court interest tried to persuade the old provost to relinquish his seat in favour of the new man, though he declined.[69] The Earl of Balcarres brought in Lord Newark, who had not sat in the previous parliamentary session, to fortify the court side, though in the end Newark declared against Catholic toleration.[70] There were others whom the court managers tried to make stay away. Objections were raised against several burgh members that they were not actually burgesses and were therefore incapable of sitting, though in the end they kept their seats. Military commanders such as Mar, Lord Ross, William Livingston of Kilsyth and Sir John Dalzeell were instructed to return to their charges, but instead they offered to resign their commissions rather than not be able to attend the session; Hamilton of Orbiston was ordered to the Highland commission of justiciary, but he refused on the grounds that the King's writ to attend parliament was more important. Others were simply told 'to stay away or goe home'. The meeting of the parliament was deliberately prolonged, and the proposal for Catholic toleration left until other legislation had been enacted, in the hope that 'the poorer sort, who had exhausted both money and credit', would be forced to retire and the measure could be forced through a depleted house.[71] Those who criticized the proposed toleration were removed from office. In mid-May James sacked his Lord Advocate, Mackenzie of Rosehaugh, removed the Earl of Glencairn and Sir William Bruce from the privy council and Lord Pitmedden from the court of sessions, and revoked Glencairn's and the Bishop of Dunkeld's pensions, as 'warning shots' intended 'to terrify and divert other members of Parliament from their opposition'. When that did not do the trick, James sacked the Laird of Gosford from the council, turned Gosford, Mar and Ross out of the army, and deprived the Bishop of Dunkeld of his see, even though Dunkeld's appointment had been 'for life'.[72] In June, Hamilton of Orbiston and the Provost of Glasgow, John Johnston, were imprisoned on trumped-up charges – in reality because of their stance against Catholic toleration; Milne of Linlithgow lost his position as assistant-receiver of the customs; and Queensberry was finally removed from all his remaining offices.[73]

The significance of James's failure to persuade the Scottish parliament to agree to the repeal of the penal laws cannot be overestimated. It foiled his entire strategy. As we have seen, James was self-consciously playing the British card, hoping the Scottish parliament would set a good model for the English to follow. It was a tactic that he had seen his brother, Charles II, play with great success in 1681, when James himself had been high commissioner to the Scottish parliament, and it was one that James had pursued in 1685, again achieving the desired result. Yet in 1686 it was a tactic that was to fail, being frustrated by the Scottish parliament itself – and what is perhaps more remarkable, by a Scottish parliament that had done so much to vaunt the powers of the Scottish monarchy only a year earlier. There was no logic now in reconvening the English parliament until James had achieved what he wanted in Scotland through other means. (In fact, James's English parliament was not to meet again.) In short, the events in Scotland dictated the way James subsequently chose to proceed in England.

Having failed to achieve what he wanted through parliament, James decided to act by his prerogative. As he told the French ambassador, 'the affairs of Scotland had not taken the turn he at first expected', but 'by the authority which the laws give him, he could establish in Scotland that liberty in favour of the Catholics which the parliament refused to grant'.[74] On 21 August, therefore, James wrote to his Scottish council announcing that he had decided to grant Catholics the freedom to exercise their religion in private, indemnifying them against all the penal laws, and to establish a chapel in Holyroodhouse, with a number of chaplains and others whom 'We are resolved to maintaine in their just Rights and Privileges', so that 'Catholick Worshipp may with the more Decency and Security be exercised' in the Scottish capital. The penal laws, he explained, had been passed on the supposition that loyalty was inconsistent with the Catholic religion, but on the contrary, during all the 'unnatural Rebellions' raised by Protestants 'against Our Royal Father, Brother, and Us', the Catholics had 'still adhered to the Royal Interest'. The Catholics therefore deserved relief. Moreover, James was sure that parliament would have granted relief had not 'Our Enemies' misled 'well-meaning Men' that it would have been a violation of the Test, which did not preclude people from consenting to changes or alterations in the Church 'not contrary to the express Tenets of the Protestant Religion'. The people could nevertheless rest assured, James's letter said, that he did not intend to make 'any violent Alteration', since he was resolved to maintain the bishops and the inferior clergy 'in their just Rights and Privileges, and the Professors of the Protestant Religion, in the free Exercise of it in their Churches, and to hinder all Fanatical Encroachments upon them'. The letter concluded with James promising to ensure the impartial administration of justice and to keep the army disciplined.[75]

James undertook a further purge of the council to ensure that it would agree to his request, displacing the earls of Mar, Dumfries, Lothian and Kintore, and Lord Ross, and bringing in the Presbyterian Earl of Dundonald (mainly to help make way for the future appointment of Catholics) and the Catholic Earl of Traquair, both of whom took their seats without taking the Test.[76] Nevertheless, there was still some dissent when the council came to consider its reply to the King's letter in mid-September. Some wondered what the 'rights and privileges' of the Catholic clergy at Holyroodhouse were that the King was so determined to maintain. Hamilton and Lockhart successfully opposed a suggestion by Tarbat that the council recognize that the King's prerogative gave the Catholics a 'legal security', Hamilton insisting that although he did not question the prerogative, he failed to see why the council needed to 'declare it to be law'. The council structured its reply to emphasize the assurances James had given to protect the rule of law. It began by thanking the King for his promise 'to have Justice Impartially administered' and his troops 'well regulated', and then for his renewed assurance 'to maintain the Bishops and the inferior Clergy as they are Established by Law in their Just rights and privileges, together with all the Professors of the Protestant Religion'. In return, the council promised to stand by the King and 'the inviolable prerogatives' of his 'Imperial Crown, for the exercise whereof' he was 'accomptable to God only', and agreed to 'humbly acquiesce' in his desire to grant immunity to his Catholic subjects. Fountainhall concluded that the council had 'granted what the Parliament had refused'.[77] This is misleading, however. James had sought to obtain a *legal* security for his Catholic subjects, yet this was something which not only parliament but also his council had refused to concede.

PREROGATIVE, INDULGENCE AND THE RAPPROCHEMENT WITH DISSENT

By the autumn of 1686 James's Scottish policy seemed to be failing. It is true that Catholics had been appointed to positions of high authority within the Scottish government, the mass was being celebrated openly in the Scottish capital, and the council had acknowledged the King's power to grant his co-religionists immunity from the penal laws. Yet in the pursuit of such gains, James had met opposition all the way: from the Edinburgh crowd, from many of the clergy of the Established Church, and from significant sections of the political elite. Even his own privy counsellors and the Lords of the Articles had obstructed his proposals, and as a result James had failed to get the Scottish parliament, which had in the past proven such a pliable body, to pass a suitable measure for Catholic toleration. Moreover, the basic strategy of pushing reforms through in Scotland first so it could be used as an example for England was backfiring. The worrying thing was that the problems were not being caused by those who had been the traditional enemies of royal policy under Charles II, the Presbyterians or radical Covenanters, although pockets of Presbyterian resistance certainly did survive. Rather, the crown was losing the support of those who had been its traditional allies in Scotland since the Restoration, namely the Episcopalian nobility, gentry and clergy. Nor did there seem much chance of recapturing support from this quarter. In the summer of 1686 Secretary Melfort summoned Archbishop Cairncross of Glasgow to London to try to persuade him to drop his opposition to Catholic toleration. At the same time Melfort was looking for suitable candidates to fill the sees left vacant by the deprivation of the Bishop of Dunkeld and the recent death of the Bishop of Galloway, and offered a choice of either one to John Birnie, minister of Broomhill, if he would agree to support the repeal of the penal laws. Both Cairncross and Birnie refused. The following January, James deprived Cairncross of his see, without a trial or hearing or even stating cause; he was later to appoint Bishop Paterson of Edinburgh as his replacement.[78]

James needed to rethink his strategy. His priority remained the promotion of the interests of his co-religionists and the encouragement of the Catholic faith. Since this could only be done through the royal prerogative, he needed to consolidate the authority of the crown north of the border. All forms of opposition were to be silenced, and everything made subordinate to royal authority. He further sought to achieve an explicit recognition not only of the ability but also of the right of the king to act by his prerogative alone – a recognition, that is, that the king's will was law and carried the same force and provided the same security as parliamentary statutes. In short, James set out to establish royal absolutism in Scotland, in practice as much as in theory. At the same time he recognized the need to try to broaden the base of his support. To this end he began to make concessions to Protestant dissenters, by granting an Indulgence to moderate Presbyterians and Quakers, although the aim here was primarily to get more groups to acknowledge their dependency upon the absolute authority of the crown. In all these respects, however, James proved largely unsuccessful: the crown's authority in Scotland was not effectively enhanced; the policy of indulgence proved to be poorly thought through and had to be recast to such a degree that it failed to have the desired effect; and even the efforts to help Catholics had disappointing results, since the faith made little headway in Scotland.

James started by appointing more Catholics to his council: the Duke of Gordon and the Earl of Seaforth in November, and the Laird of Niddry in December.[79] All, of course, required dispensations from the Test. James was determined not to let his dispensing power be seen to work exclusively in favour of his co-religionists, however, and began to experiment with ways of co-opting conformist Protestants by making their positions dependent upon the dispensing power. As a ploy to get the ecclesiastical establishment to recognize the legitimacy of his dispensing power, in October 1686 James authorized the

Archbishop of St Andrews and the Bishop of Edinburgh to allow conformist ministers who had relinquished their cures for refusing to take the Test – some had done so on the grounds that the Test was internally inconsistent – to take up vacant livings without having to take the Test. The results were mixed: some accepted the 'door opened them by Providence', though others 'thought they should not embrace it, because it was a strengthening the prerogative on which the toleration of Popery and dispensing with our laws were founded'.[80] When the King appointed the Catholic Gordon and the Protestant Balcarres as commissioners to the treasury on 19 November, he dispensed both from the requirement to take the Test, even though Balcarres, who had been a privy counsellor since 1682, had previously taken it.[81] Some Protestants who had scrupled to take the Test in 1681 and had resigned their offices as a result, were restored to their positions. In January 1687 Alexander Swinton of Mersington and James Daes of Cowdenknowes were reinstated as advocates, the King declaring that he dispensed them from the requirement to take the Test 'by his prerogative royall'.[82] The following month James installed Sir John Dalrymple (the son of the Presbyterian lawyer Sir James Dalrymple of Stair who had been driven into exile after 1681 for his refusal to take the Test), as Lord Advocate with a dispensation from the Test.[83]

James also took further steps to promote Catholic worship in Scotland. On 30 November 1686, St Andrew's Day, the Catholics consecrated their chapel at Holyroodhouse, and the following March James granted a pension of £50 sterling per year to four of the priests who served as chaplains there. Then, in July 1687, James gave the abbey church at Holyroodhouse to the newly recreated Order of the Thistle, which James had established as a statutory foundation under new rules on 29 May of that year, to reward Scottish peers who supported his political and religious agenda. As Fountainhall ominously recorded, 'so . . . is the first Protestant church taken away from us'. The first to be installed as Knights of the Thistle were Perth, Gordon and the Protestant Atholl, though the requirement to give their oaths on the popish missal proved difficult even for Atholl's flexible conscience, and he 'stumbled a while' as he was sworn in. In August 1687 the apartments in Holyroodhouse that had traditionally been set aside as the residence for the Lord Chancellor were turned into a college for the Jesuits. When the rules of the college were printed the following March, it promised that all children could be educated there free of charge.[84] In order to encourage conversions to Rome, in the first half of 1687 James gave £600 to the Scots mission.[85]

The inhabitants of Edinburgh were far from happy with these developments. Perth had to post a troop of Catholic soldiers from Dumbarton's regiment at the chapel at Holyroodhouse on Christmas Day 1686 to prevent the possibility of any disturbances during the saying of mass. The guards were out in force in the capital again at the beginning of January 'on a suspition that the prentises and other boyes intended to make a procession of the Devill's effigies and the Pope's'. In the middle of April 1687, an Edinburgh tailor who went to visit the Catholic chapel 'out of curiosity' revealed his distaste for what he saw by urinating upon Lady Blairhall and a number of other worshippers there, although he claimed that this had not been a deliberate affront but that he had merely been caught short. On Sunday 6 November a paper listing five queries about the Catholic faith was posted up at the chapel, asking, amongst other things, whether 'the Popish custom of serving God in ane unknown tongue' was not contrary to the doctrine taught by the apostle Paul, and therefore as much of a sin as adultery, and criticizing the Catholic priests for being dumb dogs who mumbled the mass because they did not want people to hear what they said. Outside the capital, the only Protestant church to be turned over to Catholic worship was Trinity chapel in Aberdeen in the spring of 1688, although it was a move that prompted resistance from the local trades, to whom it belonged.[86]

As he continued with his efforts to help the Catholics, James did his utmost to suppress the expression of any critical opinion. A particular concern was with the pulpit, since many of the clergy had been so outspoken in raising the alarm about popery. On 16 June 1686 the council, on the King's orders, issued a proclamation forbidding ministers from reflecting 'on the King, his person, principles, designs, or Government' in their sermons, in accord with an Act of 1584. The clergy were upset, partly because the 1584 Act had been made against Presbyterians, and partly because it accused the clergy of the Established Church of promoting 'seditious Designs . . . to alarm the People'. Three months later the proclamation was reissued, with the additional requirement that the clergy themselves read it four times a year, 'to keep them in mind of it'.[87] Some ministers refused to comply.[88] At the end of July 1687 the King wrote to his Scottish primate, the loyally dependent Archbishop Rose of St Andrews, requiring him to instruct the bishops to suspend or deprive any minister who preached that the established religion was in danger, or reflected upon 'our royall inclinations or authority'; any bishops who refused would themselves be regarded as disaffected.[89]

The government also took further measures against the press. Although Perth had issued orders at the beginning of 1686 prohibiting printers or stationers from printing or selling books reflecting on popery, there remained the problem of anti-Catholic works being imported from England. As the press campaign against popery picked up south of the border, many of these works found their way north into Scotland. In August 1687 the Scottish council called upon the printers and booksellers of Edinburgh to declare on oath what books they had imported, printed or sold over the past twelve months: some booksellers were imprisoned or fined; all were in future prohibited from printing or selling any books without special license. Efforts were even made to prevent the reproduction of manuscript works. The government took no measures against Catholic literature. Indeed, the King allowed James Watson to set up a Catholic press at Holyroodhouse and to print, import and sell books against the Protestant religion. This was in breach of the monopoly of Scottish printing granted to Andrew Anderson in 1671, and required a special dispensation from the King; it was also in violation of long-standing Scottish laws against the publication of heretical literature, which had been reconfirmed by the Scottish council in 1661. Upon Watson's death towards the end of 1687, the press was taken over by the German Catholic, Peter Bruce.[90]

On 12 February 1687 James issued his Declaration of Indulgence for Scotland, establishing toleration by royal fiat. The Declaration began by lamenting the fact that religious animosities in Scotland had led to the 'decay of Trade, wasting of Lands, [and] extinguishing of Charity', as well as the 'contempt of the Royal Power'. Claiming to be resolved 'to Unite the Hearts and Affections of Our Subjects to God in Religion, to Us in Loyalty, and to their Neighbours in Love and Charity', James therefore declared that he had decided to grant by his 'Soveraign Authority, Prerogative Royal, and absolute Power', which all subjects were 'to obey without Reserve', his 'Royal Tolleration' to 'several professors of the Christian Religion'. 'Moderate Presbyterians' were to be allowed to meet in their private houses, provided they did not say or do anything seditious or treasonable, though they were not allowed to build special meeting-houses or meet in out-houses or barns, and field conventicles were to continue to be prosecuted with 'the utmost severity'. Quakers, by contrast, were to be allowed to hold their meetings 'in any place or Places appointed for their Worship'. But the main benefits were intended for the Catholics. Since they had shown themselves to be loyal subjects, James said he had decided to 'Suspend, Stop, and Disable all Laws and Acts of Parliament' against them, so they might enjoy the same freedoms as Protestants 'not only to Exercise their Religion, but to enjoy all Offices, Benefices and others' which he might 'think fit to bestow upon them' in the future. They were therefore to be allowed to worship in private houses or in chapels, though they were forbidden to preach in open fields, invade Protestant churches by force, or make public processions in the high streets of any of the royal burghs. James further declared that he had decided to 'Cass, Annul and discharge all Oaths whatsoever' incapacitating his subjects from holding office, including the Test oath of 1681; instead, office-holders would be required to take an oath of non-resistance, acknowledging James VII as 'rightful King and Supream Governour' and promising never to 'rise in Arms against Him, or any Commissionaned by him' or to oppose his 'Power or Authority', but to 'Assist, Defend and Maintain Him, His Heirs and lawful Successours, in the Exercise of Their absolute Power and Authority'. James also indemnified all religious groups for past infractions of the penal laws, again by virtue of the king's 'absolute Power and Prerogative-Royal', except those Presbyterians who had been guilty of uttering treasonable speeches at conventicles. The Declaration concluded with promises to protect the clergy of the Established Church 'in their Functions, Rights and Properties, and all . . . Protestant Subjects in the free exercise of their Protestant Religion in the Churches', and to maintain 'the Possessors of Church-Lands' for-

merly belonging to the Catholic Church 'in their full and free possession', though James warned that he intended to 'employ indifferently
all . . . Subjects', regardless of their religious persuasion.[91]

The logic behind this policy was straightforward: James wanted to
establish complete toleration for the Catholics; broaden the base of
his support in Scotland by extending toleration to Quakers and, in a
more limited sense, to the moderate Presbyterians, while maintaining
the full force of the laws against field conventiclers and others who
were likely to prove seditious or politically subversive; and to achieve
a recognition that he could do this by virtue of his absolute power. In
a subsequent letter to the council, dated 1 March, he insisted that no
Presbyterians should be allowed to preach unless they first took the
oath requiring them to defend the king's 'Absolute Power and
Authority'.[92] James also hoped that if he could establish an Indulgence by means of his prerogative in Scotland, the path would be
clear for him to pursue a similar policy in England. Gilbert Burnet,
writing from exile in the Low Countries, published a tract condemning the 'new designation of his Majestie's Authority here set forth of
his Absolute Power', the true meaning of which seemed to be 'that
there is an Inherent Power in the King, which can neither be
restrained by Lawes, Promises, nor Oaths'. Burnet, however, was
writing more for the English than the Scots; he concluded his tract by
warning that 'we here in England see what we must look for'.[93] This
designation of the king's absolute power was, in fact, not new in
Scotland: the Excise Act of 1685 had affirmed that the king of
Scotland was absolute, while the Scottish council had acknowledged
that James could grant a toleration to Roman Catholics by virtue of
his 'inviolable prerogatives'. Yet champions of royal authority had
invariably linked a defence of absolutism with the doctrine that
although the king could do no wrong, those who acted in his name
could and were therefore obliged to uphold the law (and could be
held accountable if they did not). The Scottish Indulgence, however,
by insisting that James's subjects were obliged to obey him 'without
reserve', seemingly removed any possible checks upon the abuse of
power by the crown.[94] The Rye House plotter and Monmouth rebel
Robert Ferguson – like Burnet, writing from exile – condemned the
Indulgence as 'an unpresidented exercise of Despoticalness, as hardly

any of the Oriental Tyrants or even the French Leviathan would have ventured upon', for its attempt to bind subjects to maintain and defend the King and his successors in the exercise of their absolute power. In effect, Ferguson proclaimed, the Indulgence required the people 'to swear themselves his Majestie's most obedient Slaves and Vassals', and was 'an encouragement to his Catholic Subjects . . . Authorised with his Majestie's Commission . . . to set upon the cutting Protestants throats, when by this Oath their [Protestants'] hands are tied from hindring them'.[95]

The council gave its response to the royal declaration in a formal letter to the King on 24 February, in which they essentially endorsed the Indulgence, though in somewhat guarded language. They stated that they hoped that no one would abuse such extraordinary acts of mercy and promised they would 'mentaine and assert' the King's 'royal prerogative and authoritie' if anyone were 'to make any wrong use' of James's 'goodness'. Protesting their willingness to see the King's peaceable and loyal subjects 'at ease and securitie', regardless of their religion, they acknowledged that any who should 'be employed by your Majestie in offices of trust civill or militarie' were 'sufficiently secured by your Majestie's authoritie and commissione for ther exerceing the same'; they did, however, omit to mention ecclesiastical offices, even though the Indulgence had specifically mentioned that Catholics should be free to enjoy any benefices bestowed upon them. The letter concluded by thanking James for promising to maintain 'the church and our religione as it is now established by law'.[96] Even after all the purges, there was still some opposition. Hamilton and his two sons-in-law, the earls of Dundonald and Panmure, withdrew from the council when they saw the letter, to avoid having to sign it; the last two were subsequently dismissed. The Marquis of Tweeddale, his son Lord Yester and William Hay of Drummelzier absented themselves. Henceforth, they opted for semi-retirement rather than associate themselves further with James's policies.[97]

The Presbyterians refused the benefit of the Indulgence, objecting to the limitations placed on their freedom to worship, the fact that the Indulgence was quite explicitly designed to help mainly the Catholics, and to the oath recognizing the King's claim to 'absolute obedience, without reserve', which, according to the contemporary historian of the Society People, Alexander Shields, far surmounted 'all the lust, impudence, and insolence of all the Roman, Sicilian, Turkish, Tartarian, or Indian Tyrants that ever trampled upon the Liberties of Mankind'. Many of the moderate Presbyterians continued to attend the services of the Established Church; the radical Covenanters persisted in meeting in field conventicles, for which they were prosecuted 'with the greatest severity', some being transported, and a few even sentenced to death.[98] On 31 March James sent a letter to his council granting Presbyterians the benefits of the Indulgence without being required to take the oath. This seems to have made little difference.[99] Therefore James decided to issue another Indulgence on 28 June (published in Edinburgh on 5 July), declaring that by his 'sovereaigne authority, prerogative royall and absolute power' he had decided to 'suspend, stop and disable all penall and sanguinary laws made against any for non-conformity to the religion established by law', thereby giving the Presbyterians the same liberties as the Catholics, and allowing them to meet in chapels or purpose-built places of worship as well as private houses, although retaining the prohibition against field conventicles.[100]

Most Presbyterians accepted the revised Indulgence, with the exception of the radical Convenanters, the followers of the field preacher James Renwick.[101] The benefits were felt most in the southwest, the area that had suffered the most during the years of persecution. Meeting-houses were speedily erected, and large numbers of parishioners deserted their parish churches, often leaving the Episcopal clergy with none to hear them, 'save their own Families'.[102] One hostile account, written after the Revolution, claimed that the Presbyterians used intimidation to force people to join their meetings.[103] While some scepticism is needed here, undoubtedly James's Indulgence had the effect of exacerbating tensions between Presbyterians and Episcopalians in what was already a highly volatile area. By contrast, there were very few meeting-houses erected north of the Tay.[104] Field conventiclers, on the other hand, who also tended to be concentrated in the south-west, continued to be pursued in the second half of 1687 and throughout 1688, and a reward of £100 sterling each was offered for the capture of James Renwick, Alexander Shields and others who preached at field conventicles.[105] Renwick himself was finally captured in Edinburgh at the beginning of February 1688. At his trial he disowned James VII's authority, and stated that 'to give him the absolute power he assumed, was to put a creature in place of the Creator'. Renwick was executed on 17 February.[106]

Presbyterian ministers from different parts of the kingdom gathered in Edinburgh on 20 July 1687 to discuss whether to offer the King thanks for the Indulgence. Although some were averse to the idea, they agreed the next day to a cautiously worded address, acknowledging the King's 'gracious and surprizing Favour in . . . putting a Stop to our long sad Sufferings' and professing their resolution 'to preserve an entire Loyalty in our Doctrine and Practice, (consonant to our known Principles . . .)'. The 'Inhabitants of the Presbyterian Perswasion in Edinburgh and Canongate' drew up a 'more florrid' address, in which they said they could not 'find suitable Expressions' to show their 'most humble and grateful Acknowledgments' for the Indulgence, and expressed the hope that their sincerity would make it clear that there was 'no Inconsistency betwixt true Loyalty and Presbyterian Principles'. There was a third address, 'from the Pastors and People of God in the West of Scotland in and about Glasgow', which according to a hostile source, far out-did the first two 'for high Strains of Flattery and vast Promises of Duty and Compliance'.[107] Some Episcopalians found the Presbyterians' apparent change of heart difficult to swallow. One satirical address, which circulated in manuscript, had the Presbyterians give their 'most humble and hearty Thanks' and proceeded to mock the whole logic of giving such people religious toleration: 'whereas our predicessors By whose principalls we are led', it had the Presbyterians say, 'did molest and trouble the happie Reign of . . . your Grandfather [James VI and I]' and also 'most Industriously did disturb, shake and alter the Government under the reigne of your pious father [Charles I] till we brought him to the block', so they too 'shall never want good will to show your majestie the lyke Kydnes whenever a fairr opportunity shall present'.[108] As we shall see in Chapter 9, the remarks contained more irony than the satirist could have foreseen.

The radical Covenanters, who refused to accept the toleration because it was based on the pretension to 'absolute power' and was intended 'to make way for the introduction of Popery',[109] were bitterly critical of those who did. Prior to his capture and execution, Renwick complained that never before in Scotland had a favour been 'obtained to Papists to practise their Idolatries, without a resolute Protestation against it, much less was it ever heard that the open Profession of it' should be 'applauded in the congratulatory Addresses of some called Protestants and Presbyterians'.[110] Similarly, the Episcopalian namesakes, George Mackenzie of Tarbat and Sir George Mackenzie of Rosehaugh, writing in early 1689, charged the Presbyterians with 'compliance with the Papists', and alleged that while those of the Established Church 'hazarded all rather than comply', the Presbyterians 'magnified the dispensing Power'.[111] Presbyterian apologists, writing after the Revolution, naturally put a different slant on their actions. As the historian of the Presbyterian sufferings, Robert Wodrow, pointed out, the Presbyterians did not play an active part in seeking this liberty, and they refused to accept the Indulgence 'as long as it was connected with a Liberty to Papists in its Promulgation, and untill all the former Restrictions were taken off'.[112] Gilbert Rule, a Presbyterian divine who had suffered imprisonment himself at the hands of the Restoration regime, insisted that accepting 'the Liberty granted them, after it had been unjustly withheld from them', did not imply an acknowledgement of the dispensing power, because this was 'their Due by a Grant from Christ in the Gospel'; the Presbyterians merely 'gave Thanks for restoring them to their just Right'. As for being complicit in the design to bring in popery, the Presbyterians thought 'the best way to keep it out', Rule added, 'was to make use of the Liberty, for setting people in the right way'; nevertheless they expressed their 'dislike of the Tolleration given to the Papists for their Heresies and Idolatries'.[113] A few Presbyterians certainly did this. In a sermon delivered at Gordon, Berwickshire, on 18 October 1687, John Hardy 'thanked his Majesty for his toleration', but added 'if they behoved to take away the laws against Popery, it were better to want it: And any that consented to it, Zachariah's flying roll of curses would enter the house'. Summoned before the council, Hardy refused to retract, and at his trial on 1 December he not only boldly admitted what he had said, but added, 'it is the Presbyterian principle, that idolatry . . . is punishable by death' and that 'they can never think but laws against Popery are both just, lawful and necessary'. Hardy persisted in maintaining, however, that he had said nothing seditious, and the judges eventually agreed, and set him free.[114] In April 1688 Alexander Orrock, a Presbyterian minister from Dundee, was summoned before the council for allegedly 'having called the King an idolator in his sermon'. Orrock was forbidden to preach any more at Dundee, and so he simply moved elsewhere. He was, seemingly, a man with some following. When the Archbishop of St Andrews had him arrested for trying to preach there, a riot ensued, and some of Orrock's supporters attacked the town officers who had come to make the arrest.[115]

The Indulgence afforded the Presbyterians a chance to rebuild after years of persecution had severely weakened their movement. Ministers who had been imprisoned or else forced into exile, returned to lead their flocks; indeed, parishioners were actively encouraged to call home their pastors who had fled the country. A basic Presbyterian structure was re-established, with monthly meetings of presbyteries; cooperation was sought over the building of meeting-houses; and provisions were set up for the encouragement of young students, so that they could be licensed and ordained to new congregations. Ironically, James's actions were to mean that when the Revolution came the Presbyterians were in a position to challenge for control of the Church.[116]

By contrast, James's policy of Indulgence undermined the unity of the Protestants of the Established Church. James sought to make his Protestant subjects complicit in his design to remove the Test for office-holders. In June 1687 he issued new commissions for the Lords of Session and the privy council, nominating the same men, but discharging them from taking the Test.[117] The final adjustment to James's Indulgence policy came on 7 May 1688, when the King issued a proclamation reaffirming the Indulgence of 12 February 1687, as explained and enlarged by that of 28 June, and reporting that he had dissolved all 'judicatures of privy Councell, Session, Exchequer, Justiciary, and magistracy of our burroughs royall, that by their acceptations of new commissions' without the requirement to take the Test, 'wee might convince the world of the justice of our proce-dures'.[118] Even the loyalist Episcopalian Earl of Balcarres conceded that this was a serious mistake, which 'occasion'd a great Consternation'. It was made worse by an additional order that all crown employees purchase remissions for breaking the laws, even though done at the King's command.[119]

James could count upon the loyalty of his two archbishops, Rose of St Andrews and Paterson of Glasgow. Both, as privy counsellors, had signed the letter in support of the Indulgence in February 1687. But there were many disturbing signs of hostility from the Epsicopalian establishment. In March 1688, when Archbishop Rose prevailed upon the University of St Andrews to send an address to James acknowledging that the King 'may, by his prerogative, take away the penal laws without a Parliament', five of the fourteen masters refused to sign.[120] Few ministers of the Established Church appear to have welcomed the Indulgence. Balcarres, writing after the Revolution, claimed the Episcopal clergy condemned the Indulgence in their private discourses and sermons, being fearful that 'by giving a general Liberty of Conscience' the King designed 'to ruin the Religion then established'.[121] A contemporary correspondent reported that not just bishops but even some privy counsellors were upset by the June Indulgence, believing it 'too large'; this correspondent later observed how it was 'above all the episcopal party' who were 'most opposite to this liberty and its establishment'.[122] Some Episcopalians simply refused to recognize the Indulgence. Roger Morrice learned in December 1687 that 'divers of the Legall Ministers in Scotland' had 'revived the old national Scotch Covenant against Popery' (presumably the Negative Confession of Faith of 1581 condemning Catholicism), and got their congregations to signify 'their resolution to stand by it'.[123] In the summer of 1688 the masters of the University of Aberdeen were in trouble 'for presuming to take an oath from the Students' upon graduation, 'to profess the Protestant religion', when the King 'had discharged the exacting of any oaths'. The masters protested that they were required to do so by the University statutes, which they had sworn to uphold, and so they could not omit this oath without committing perjury.[124] In some areas Episcopalian magistrates sought to ensure the Presbyterians would not have a quiet toleration: by arresting ministers under the pretext that their names were not on the list of approved preachers given to the magistrates;

harassing people who did not come to church or who hired out their barns or other buildings as places of worship; or denying burgh freedom to those who frequented meeting-houses. One particular trouble spot was Dundee, where the town's provost was the fanatical anti-Presbyterian crusader the Earl of Claverhouse, who busied himself investigating Presbyterian preachers suspected of going beyond the terms of the Indulgence by endeavouring to alienate the people from the royal government.[125]

James still seems to have hoped to secure a more permanent toleration in Scotland by getting parliament to turn his Indulgence into law. To achieve this goal he would need to procure the return of a compliant parliament, and this was most readily achievable by securing control over the election of burgh representatives, who were normally chosen and also paid for by the town councils. In September 1686, James suspended local elections in all the royal burghs, and then proceeded to nominate his own men as provosts, magistrates and town councillors. This was a direct invasion of the burghs' legal right under their old charters to elect their own magistrates. Nor was there any pretence to a legal process of *quo warranto*; the King simply acted by virtue of his prerogative. In some burghs, the crown appointed members of the nobility and gentry, in violation of an act of 1609 barring them from serving as town magistrates.[126] The King repeated the policy of suspending elections and nominating his own officials in 1687 and 1688.[127] In July 1687, James tried to get the Convention of Royal Burghs to suspend the residential qualification for burgh representatives, to make way for some of the gentry he had nominated. Although he failed in this particular regard, he did succeed in getting the Convention to remove the restriction against the election of Catholics.[128] By February 1688 it was being rumoured in London that James was not only about to call a parliament in Scotland, but that he was 'resolved to be present at it himself', which it was thought would make it easier to enact 'the gracious designs his Majesty has formed and remove all obstacles that have hitherto hindred the effecting of them'.[129]

James did not call another parliament in Scotland and it is unclear how far he got with his plans to do so. In late 1687 and early 1688 he did begin canvassing the opinions of the parliamentary classes about the possibility of repealing the penal legislation, even approaching some of the more powerful figures in Scottish politics directly himself. Thus in February 1688, for example, he wrote to Hamilton asking if he would agree to a repeal of the penal laws and the Test and be in favour of 'settling an entire liberty of conscience'. Hamilton wrote back saying he had been ill and had not had the chance to discuss the issue with any lawyers or clergymen, protesting that he was still of the opinion that no one 'should suffer for conscience-sake' and 'every peaceable subject should be allowed the exercise of their own religion', but adding that how this might 'be done with security to the Protestant religion, our laws, and oaths' was something he was unable to make up his mind about just yet. James also commissioned Perth, Tarbat and Balcarres to get officers of state, judges and army officers to give a written pledge of their support for a repeal. Although Balcarres claimed that most were prepared to subscribe, albeit grudgingly, the process left 'such a cruel Apprehension of other things farther to be press'd upon them, that it made them extremely uneasie'. Others were far from convinced whether the tactic had produced the desired results. In March 1688, the Earl of Shrewsbury informed the Prince of Orange that James's attempts to solicit the support of the parliamentary classes for a repeal of the penal laws had met with not 'much better success' in Scotland than they had in England – where, as we shall see in the following chapter, the policy was a noticeable failure.[130]

ASSESSING THE COST

The policy of indulgence had been pursued with the main aim of helping promote the cause of Catholicism. To what extent had this been successful? Professed Catholics formed a tiny minority of the population in Scotland, probably less than 2 per cent. Moreover, the penal laws had never been comprehensively enforced. Few recusants had suffered persecution since the Restoration; the major inconvenience was the ban on holding public office, and even this had not been applied absolutely under Charles II, prior to the Test Act of 1681.[131] It is difficult to see that there were any major gains for the Catholic faith in Scotland under James VII. There had been some notable converts to Catholicism, early in the reign, and Catholics had been given prominent positions in the service of the crown. Beyond that, the results were extremely disappointing. As Chancellor Perth bemoaned in a letter to Cardinal Norfolk of 3 February 1688: 'one might have hoped a considerable progress would have been made in the advancement of the Catholic interest, but we have advanced little or nothing'. There were two public Catholic chapels, one at Holyroodhouse, another in Aberdeen; there was a Jesuit College at what used to be the Lord Chancellors' residence at Holyroodhouse; and there were six or seven monks from Germany active as missionaries. Yet there had been very few conversions of late; 'the ministers and University men' were 'wild and furious'; and not one man in a hundred in the army was a Catholic.[132] A few days later Thomas Nicholson, a Scottish Catholic returning to his country after several years' absence, wrote how he 'found things as to the advancement of the Catholic faith far short of my expectations . . . there were but few converts . . . and a greater aversion in the people than there was five or six years ago'.[133]

Yet the efforts to help the Catholics had been pursued at immense political cost. In 1685 James had inherited a strong position in Scotland: the Scottish political elite were resolutely behind him, and even prepared to recognize his absolute authority; the political challenge of the radical Presbyterians had been effectively controlled; and Presbyterianism as a religious movement had been so seriously undermined as a result of years of persecution that many Presbyterians had been driven into at least a nominal conformity to the Established Church. There even appears to have been genuine popular support for James at the time of his accession. However, as a result of his policies, James had managed to destroy this favourable state of affairs. He had broken the unity of the political elite; provoked an ultra-loyalist parliament into opposition and failed to get passed his desired legislation, despite the existence of the Lords of the Articles; and alienated many members of his privy council. While there were some compliant types who were prepared to support the King in whatever he did, there were others who by instinct were royalists and prone to support the authority of the crown but who were nevertheless driven from office, such as Mar and Mackenzie of Rosehaugh. There were yet others, such as Hamilton and (to a lesser degree) Lockhart, whom James felt unable to force out of office, but who obstructed royal policy in significant respects. Moreover, James was inconsistent in the way he dealt with people. Having appointed Sir John Dalrymple as Lord Advocate to replace Mackenzie, he subsequently reappointed Mackenzie in February 1688, a move which helped lose Dalrymple's support without succeeding in winning back Mackenzie's full commitment.[134] James also destroyed the unity of the Episcopalian Church. While he retained the support of Rose of St Andrews and Paterson of Edinburgh (and later Glasgow), many churchmen became disaffected. In short, by alienating the traditional ruling elite and the Episcopalian interest, James destroyed the very foundation on which a strong Scottish monarchy had been reconstructed after the Restoration. At the same time, he enabled the Presbyterians to recoup their strength and begin to reorganize. All this, in order to achieve what were rather insignificant gains for Scottish Catholicism. Indeed, if anything, anti-popery had increased in Scotland: there was serious rioting against the celebration of the mass in Edinburgh in early 1686; the Episcopalian clergy did all they could from the pulpit to enflame their congregations against Catholicism; and from July 1687 they were joined in their efforts by the newly indulged Presbyterian ministers. In short, James had created a revolutionary situation in Scotland.

5

Catholic Absolutism in England

*If ever a Popish Successor comes among you, let his promises
of keeping your Religion and Laws . . . be never so plausible,
credit 'em not; for if you do, you will be infallibly deceiv'd.*
[Charles Blount], *Appeal from the Country to the City*, p. 4

*He [King James] . . . was far from meriteing the reproach of
having receded from his engagement in reference to Religion
and the liberties of the people; he made not one single step in
that affair without being assured by men learned in Law and
antiquity that he might do it, without any breach either of his
word or the Laws themselves.*   *Life of James II*, II, 612

During the Exclusion Crisis, Whig polemicists had painted a graphic
and gruesome picture of what English Protestants could expect
should a Catholic come to the English throne: brutal religious persecution; rule by a standing army; high taxes; the demise of parliament;
and subjection to the power of France. However, the nightmare of
exclusionist propagandists' imagination never materialized. Not only
were there no Marian-style persecutions, but James II turned out to
be the most religiously tolerant English monarch since the Reformation. Indeed, it is possible to put a fairly favourable gloss on what
James tried to achieve in England. He did not make England subservient to the French, but sought to maintain a studied neutrality and
keep England out of war. Trade prospered thanks to peace and toleration, and England consequently enjoyed a period of relative prosperity and low taxation. James's desire to allow his co-religionists to

hold office under the crown can be represented as perfectly understandable: why should he not seek the advice and support of those he trusted? Besides, Catholics were such a small proportion of the population that it can scarcely be said that they posed a significant threat to the Protestant establishment in Church and state. Moreover, James's legal experts assured him that in his efforts to help his fellow Catholics, he was technically acting within his legal powers. These are all arguments found in the Jacobite *Life of James II*, a retrospective history that makes extensive use of James's own papers and memoirs,[1] but echoes of them can be found – with varying degrees of refinement and modification – in the writings of modern scholars, who have rightly sought to develop a more nuanced and sophisticated understanding of James's reign and free us from the preconceptions and biases of Whig mythology.[2]

In many respects, however, it seemed to most of James's Protestant subjects that the worst predictions of the Exclusionists had come to pass. True, there were no Smithfield fires – no burnings of Protestant 'martyrs' at the stake – as there had been under England's last Catholic ruler, Mary Tudor (r. 1553–8). But there was to be no further meeting of parliament in England after the prorogation of November 1685, and when James did begin to make plans for calling a parliament again in 1688 his efforts to pack it were so blatant that it was clear to all that it would not be a free assembly. James kept a standing army, in peacetime, that was much larger than had been seen in England before. He also broke the Anglican monopoly of worship, education and office-holding, and he did so by setting his prerogative above the law, through the use of the dispensing and suspending powers. He even erected an Ecclesiastical Commission to discipline recalcitrant Protestant clergymen.

The purpose of this chapter, then, is to explore what James set out to achieve in England, the extent to which he acted in violation of the law, and how his English subjects responded. We shall see that in his efforts to help Catholics, James undoubtedly did exceed his legal powers. In the process, he managed to alienate broad cross-sections of the population: clerical and lay; upper, middling and lower sorts in both town and countryside; those at the centre of power and those remote from it. Most significantly, James succeeded in alienating the

Tory-Anglican interest, which had backed the crown so wholeheartedly during the final years of his brother's reign but which now proved determined to uphold the rule of law against what they perceived to be the illegal actions of an arbitrary monarch.

THE BRITISH AND INTERNATIONAL CONTEXTS

The reaction to James's policies in England was conditioned, in part, by what English people perceived to be going on in his two other kingdoms. Contemporary diarists and newsletter writers traced developments in Scotland and Ireland with alarm. So too did pamphleteers. What the King could do in one kingdom he might well attempt in another. Gilbert Burnet, we have already noted, insisted that the Scottish Indulgence of February 1687 was but a prelude for what could be expected in England. As we shall see, he was right. Elsewhere, Burnet pointed to the fact that papists 'in the Metropolitan City of the neighbouring Kingdom' (i.e. Dublin) had been allowed 'to usurp the publick Churches and Cathedrals'; here Burnet made no claim about the King's intent for England, but the warning was there for all to see.[3] The Earl of Tyrconnell soon emerged as the bogeyman of popular imagination, whose desire to help his co-religionists in Ireland was seen as indicative of a larger design to take England, too, back to Rome. For example, when Tyrconnell visited a family tomb on the outskirts of Chester, in the latter part of 1685, it was said that he criticized how the church had been allowed to decay since the Reformation and warned that the Catholics would 'have it shortly again'.[4] When Lord Spencer saw a Punch and Judy show at Bartholomew Fair in London in August 1687, he thought the figure of Punch so resembled Tyrconnell that he drew his sword and cut off Punch's head, proclaiming to the crowd of spectators that he did this 'that he might deliver the poore Kingdom of Ireland out of slavery'.[5] Even Catholic apologists for James II believed that what was intended for England could be gleaned from royal initiatives pursued in Scotland and Ireland, and that James should come clean about this. Thus one manuscript tract of

November 1686, suggesting various ways of protecting the Catholic interest in England, acknowledged that it was now 'the Generall Opinion of the Nation, that his Majesty Intends to Introduce the Catholick Religion into all his Dominions', and it was 'labour in Vaine' to try to deny it, especially with 'the things that have been done in Scotland and Ireland seeming to tend to that purpose'.[6]

Public anxieties over James's domestic policies were also affected by the international context, and especially the growing threat of Louis XIV in France, whose aggressive, expansionist foreign policy seemed to threaten the balance of power in Europe generally and the Protestant interest in particular. James, to be fair, was not the French puppet of Whig legend. He sought to adopt a middle position in his foreign policy between the French and the Dutch interests so as to avoid dragging England into an expensive war, not least because he did not want to be forced by a foreign crisis into having to recall parliament. He did, it is true, take regular subsidies from the French king. Yet at the same time he was far from approving of Louis XIV's policies of aggression in western Europe, which hit at Catholic powers as well as Protestant; he renewed existing treaties with the Dutch upon his accession; he tried to get Louis to recognize William of Orange's rights to the Principality of Orange, which the French had annexed in 1672; and he stood up to Louis in North America.[7]

Nevertheless, there was widespread suspicion in England that James was in cahoots with the French king. Already by June 1685 there was a report going around of the English having entered 'into a new alliance with France', while the contemporary diarists Narcissus Luttrell and Roger Morrice carried similar reports of an Anglo-French concord in the spring of 1686, supposedly for a naval campaign against the Dutch.[8] Moreover, James's accession to the English throne coincided with Louis XIV's intensification of the persecution of the Huguenots in France, culminating in the revocation of the Edict of Nantes in October 1685, which formally rescinded Henry IV's edict of toleration of 1598. In mid-October Morrice recorded how the persecution in France was 'far more cruell' than previously reported or believed: great numbers of Huguenots had been kept without meat and sleep until they became distracted, and then forced to go to mass; others had been 'hung up by their toes and hands and fingers, and other tender parts', or else 'had their Noses and lips slit'. Further French edicts issued in 1686 ordered Huguenot ministers to leave the kingdom upon pain of death; those who helped or harboured them were to be condemned to the galleys forever (or to the cloisters, if female) and have their goods confiscated. In November, Morrice learned how two Huguenot ministers had had 'their hands first cutt off and then sewed on again, and after that fires were kindled round them . . . so they were in tract of time broiled or roasted to death'.[9] The sense of alarm was further intensified when in the spring of 1686, the Duke of Savoy (a client of Louis XIV) invaded Piedmont and, together with his French allies, massacred some eight to ten thousand Protestants (the vast majority women, children and old people), selling into slavery those who managed to escape with their lives.[10]

Although James ordered collections of aid to be made for those Huguenots who fled to England, many doubted whether he was truly concerned about their plight. Indeed, the French ambassador, Barillon, claimed that James spoke of Louis XIV's attempts to extirpate heresy in France 'as a thing that gave him great pleasure', although of course we should not take what James chose to say to please the French ambassador as necessarily indicative of his true sentiments.[11] Tellingly, before James allowed the charity brief for the French Protestants of March 1686 to pass the great seal, he had the preamble changed to omit a passage that had referred to the Huguenots as suffering a 'cruell persecution'.[12] When Barillon complained about the 'scandalous Reflections' upon Louis XIV in a French account of the sufferings of the Huguenots that was circulating in England in translation, James had the printer and translator arrested and ordered the book to be burnt by the common hangman – a provocative public gesture that must have made James's Protestant subjects wonder where his true sympathies lay.[13] In June 1686 one newsletter carried an account of how James's privy council had proposed issuing *quo warranto* proceedings against the Huguenot church in London and other parts of England that did not conform to the ceremony of the Anglican Church, so that he could rid the kingdom of the French Protestants.[14] In fact, James almost certainly did not approve of the violent persecution of the Huguenots in France. Nevertheless he was suspicious of the Huguenots, believing they were all at heart republicans, and had no genuine desire to welcome them into England; any efforts he undertook to help them were grudging and done mainly to placate English public opinion.[15]

DOMESTIC DANGERS

To Englishmen and women, looking at the international situation and developments in the two other Stuart kingdoms, the portents were not encouraging. The threat of popery and arbitrary government appeared a frightening reality. Worse still, there were signs that England was becoming a victim too. There was a series of concerns: James's expansion of the army, his intrusion of Catholics into the military and civil establishments, his encouragement of Catholic worship, and his use of the royal prerogative to remove the legal disabilities on his co-religionists.

The Standing Army

In the aftermath of the Monmouth rebellion, James expanded his army to just under 20,000, around which number it stabilized until the eve of the Revolution, when there was a further build-up of forces. Whether James had the legal right to keep such an army in being during a time of peace is a complicated issue. The Militia Act of 1661, which confirmed the crown's control over all forces by land and sea, dealt with the militia and soldiers who might be recruited for a foreign war; it made no mention of a standing army in times of peace. There was nothing technically to prevent the English king from hiring soldiers if he had the resources to pay for them, but normally such funding would have to come from parliament. Charles II had kept a small military establishment for his own personal security, and those occasions when he did seek to build up his standing forces were purportedly to fight a foreign war, with the troops funded through parliamentary subsidies; when peace was secured or if war never materialized, parliament called for the disbanding of such troops. James's parliament of 1685 had discussed the issue of the standing army and had been prepared to vote funds for its support (if not as much as the King had wanted), though James prorogued this parliament before the necessary legislation had been passed. Yet thanks to the improvement in the yield from customs and excise, James found he could afford to fund the army without parliamentary assistance. The legal situation was thus unclear, though it appears to have been the assumption among those who framed and voted legislation that the king would rely on the militia in times of peace, only recruit soldiers when needed for foreign war (on which occasions he would go to parliament for financial backing), and disband such troops again in peacetime.

Yet if the king did have the resources to hire his own forces without parliamentary funding, he faced the problem of how to discipline and where to quarter them. The Petition of Right of 1628 had declared against both the imposition of martial law in times of peace and the billeting of troops on private householders, while the Disbanding Act of 1679 had categorically stated that no private householders could be compelled to receive soldiers into their houses without their consent. James did declare martial law in Berwick-upon-Tweed in February 1685, when there were fears of possible unrest at the border at the time of his accession; he also appointed a general court martial in July 1685 to deal with deserters or other crimes and misdemeanours committed by soldiers, though this was revoked after the suppression of the Monmouth rebellion. In June 1686, a council-of-war set up a court martial to enforce martial law within the bounds of the military encampment on Hounslow Heath, because James believed that the civil magistrates were too lenient towards deserters. Yet James realized he could not declare martial law generally across England without being in flagrant violation of the Petition of Right, and so he tried to get desertion accounted a felony at common law. The recorder of London, Sir John Holt, steadfastly refused to give judgment against deserters on the grounds that no one could be put to death for running away from their colours unless there had been a proclamation of war. In September 1686, however, Jeffreys (who had been appointed Lord Chancellor the previous September, following Baron Guilford's death) canvassed the opinion of nine of the judges, who all determined that desertion in peacetime was a capital felony. Holt was subsequently dismissed. In March

1688 James established a standing court martial in London to hear all cases concerning those in the armed forces and to handle civilian complaints against the military, and in August of that year he issued orders that deserters could be tried before a regimental or general court martial, without even issuing a formal declaration of martial law. Increasingly, the armed forces seemed to be beyond the control of the common law.[16]

Lacking sufficient barracks, James had no option but to quarter many of his troops in public and even private houses, and although he insisted they should pay their way, there were frequent reports of abuses and of soldiers not paying for food and lodging. James even stationed troops within the City of London, without seeking the permission of the corporation (which was an overwhelmingly Tory body after the purges of Charles II's final years): some of the troops were quartered in taverns and alehouses in Fleet Street and Salisbury Court, others in converted nonconformist meeting-houses in the Broad Street area, which had been seized on the grounds of their owners' alleged disaffection to the government.[17] It was a tactless move that could only serve to antagonize both ends of the political spectrum within the metropolis. When the civic authorities tried to resolve a dispute that flared up over the quartering of troops in Aldgate in April 1687 – the soldiers had a warrant from a Middlesex JP for quarters in Middlesex, but not for within the City of London itself – the soldiers responded by telling the city magistrates 'that they were Cuckolds and should be so made by them, That they would Quarter in their houses, and turne them out of Guild Hall . . . that they were not worthy to kiss their Arses, And that not the Civill Officers but the Soldiers were the Keepers of the Peace of the Kingdome'. It was an affront that Londoners were not prepared to take lying down. A crowd of local butchers and seamen assembled, armed with cleavers and other weapons, determined to teach the troops a lesson, and it took considerable effort on the Lord Mayor's part to defuse the situation and prevent a potential bloodbath. On this occasion, upon complaint by the City, James was quick to reassure the Lord Mayor 'that itt was never his designe that the Military power should oversway the Civil but they should allwayes behave themselves orderly', and he immediately suspended the troops' captain from duty.[18] James was doubtless sincere. The question was, could he realistically control the soldiery? Only a couple of months later a few soldiers forced entry into the garden of a man who lived in the village of Teddington in Middlesex; the man and some of his neighbours tried to stop them, and in the ensuing fight two of the villagers were killed.[19]

Problems with troops were reported from all over the country. A number of complaints reached the privy council in early 1686 of soldiers stationed in the West 'beating' men, 'prostituting' women and 'wasting' people's provisions.[20] Towards the end of the year soldiers in the East Midlands killed a barrowman at Loughborough and another man at Leicester.[21] When, in December 1686, a Maidstone innkeeper dared to suggest that the captain of the troops he was quartering should settle his account speedily, because the captain was losing so much money gambling, the captain and his men took their revenge by shaving one side of the innkeeper's head and leading him through the streets in a halter, first to the whipping-post, then to the pillory. Only a timely intervention by the mayor managed to prevent a riot between the troops and the townsmen, although the captain subsequently threatened to kill the mayor if he reported the incident to the King.[22]

The sorts of tensions that could develop between soldiers and civilians are well illustrated by what happened at the funeral of the Countess of Strafford (the wife of the second Earl) at York on 13 January 1686. Trouble erupted because troops from the Castle were appointed to march with the hearse as it was transported through the city to the Minster. A crowd of over 500 'Prentices and lusty young fellows' attacked the soldiers as they marched through Stonegate, crying 'letts knock the Black Guards braines out', throwing stones and brickbats at them and beating them with clubs. The rioting continued into the Minster itself and a number of soldiers were badly hurt before eventually the troops opened fire in an attempt to drive the crowd away. After the commotion had died down, the lieutenant of the company attacked sent the Lord Mayor the names of the ringleaders, demanding warrants for their arrest. The mayor refused, however, protesting that he 'would know by what Order the Souldiers Guarded the Herse', claiming that the governor of the Castle had no right to give such an order since the city of York itself was 'noe

Garrison'. For some time after the riot, soldiers found they could not walk the streets without being called 'Red Coate Rogue' or 'black Guard dog'. Informers were reluctant to come forward against the rioters, and although a few of the ringleaders were eventually tried and convicted, they were too poor to pay their fines, and at the intercession of the Lord Mayor and aldermen the judges decided to issue a reprieve and release them from prison.[23]

The Issue of the Dispensing Power

Public anxiety stemmed not just from the fact that James had established a standing army, but that it was a standing army into which he had begun to intrude Catholics. This anxiety was further fuelled by a couple of powerful broadsides written by the Whig cleric Samuel 'Julian' Johnson (nicknamed Julian for his stinging attack on the doctrine of passive obedience in 1682, entitled *Julian the Apostate*). In March 1686 a trenchant satire of his literally hit the streets of London (apparently being left lying around for passers-by to pick up), advertising 'Several Reasons for the Establishment of a Standing Army, and Dissolving the Militia'. Among them were the supposed facts that 'the Lords, Gentlemen, and Free-holders of England' were 'not fit to be trusted with their own Laws, Lives, Liberties, and Estates'; that there were 'no Irish Papists in the Militia', who were 'certainly the best Souldiers in the World', because they had 'slain Men, Women, and Children, by Hundreds of Thousands at once'; and that 'the Dragooners' had made 'more Converts than all the Bishops and Clergy of France'. Later that spring, Johnson produced his 'Humble and Hearty Address to all English Protestants in this Present Army' (some 20,000 copies of which were distributed among the army at Hounslow Heath, and a further 20,000 across the country at large), in which he pleaded with the Protestants in the army to consider why they had joined with the papists, who would 'fight for the Mass . . . burn the Bible, and who seeke to extirpate the Protestant Religion with your Sword because they cannot do it with their own'. It was a bold, confrontational tract, which earned its author a fine of 500 marks, degradation from the ministry, and a severe whipping at the hands of the common hangman.[24]

Although James appears to have been keen to intrude Catholics into the English army, there were limits to what he could do, given the small size of the English Catholic population. By the end of 1685 about 10 per cent of the commissioned officers were Catholic, a figure that fell to less than 9 per cent by November 1687 before rising to about 11 per cent by October 1688. Among the rank and file of the soldiery, Catholics probably constituted considerably less than 10 per cent of the whole.[25] Nevertheless, these percentages were much higher than the proportion of Catholics in the English population as a whole, and by the terms of the Test Act of 1673 officers were required to swear the oaths of allegiance and supremacy and sign a declaration against transubstantiation within three months of taking up their commission, or face dismissal. James had granted Catholic officers dispensations from these requirements in November 1685, and did so again in January 1686, but to do this every three months (or else dismiss and reappoint his Catholic officers) would be costly, cumbersome and time-consuming. A more satisfactory, longer-term solution was necessary. It was provided by the test case of Godden v. Hales, which came before King's Bench in June 1686.

Sir Edward Hales was a Catholic who had taken up a commission as colonel without meeting the requirements of the Test Act, an offence which carried with it a fine of £500; the action against him was brought by his own coachman, Arthur Godden, who, under the terms of the Test Act, was entitled to recover the fine for himself. Hales pleaded a royal dispensation; the prosecution accepted the plea as true but denied it was a sufficient answer. It was a collusive action, purposefully brought in order to provide an opportunity for a judicial ruling on whether or not the dispensing power was legal. The judges concluded by a majority of eleven to one that it was. In giving his judgment, the presiding judge Lord Chief Justice Herbert asserted that because kings of England were 'sovereign princes' and the laws 'the king's laws', it was 'an inseparable prerogative in the kings of England, to dispense with penal laws in particular cases, and upon particular necessary reasons', and that 'of those reasons and those necessaries, the king himself is sole judge'. During the trial the judges heard arguments from both sides concerning the various legal precedents. The case for the dispensing power, made by the Solicitor

General Sir Thomas Powis, rested upon a distinction between an offence that was *malum in se* (wrong in itself) and one that was *malum prohibitum* (illegal merely because prohibited by statute). The king could not dispense with the former – he could not dispense with the law of God. But he could dispense someone from a statute which prohibited something that had once been lawful, provided he did not violate the private interest of any of his subjects. Powis then proceeded to draw a distinction between acts of parliament concerning property, which could not be dispensed with, and those concerning government, which could. Although citing various precedents, the most telling was a judicial decision from the second year of Henry VII's reign (1486) as reported by the early Stuart jurist Sir Edward Coke, which had confirmed that the king could dispense with an Act of 23 Henry VI, c. 8 (1445), forbidding any man from serving as sheriff of one county for a period of more than one year. It was this which clinched the argument for Herbert, since the original statute of Henry VI's reign had stated that if a sheriff were appointed for a period longer than one year, 'the patent shall be void, notwithstanding any Non Obstante [dispensation] to the contrary', and yet 'by the opinion of all the judges of England', Herbert said, the king could still dispense with that statute.[26]

Legal historians, following such reasoning, have tended to conclude that James was well within his rights when issuing dispensations from the Test Act.[27] Most contemporaries would have disagreed, however. The case was not only a feigned action, but the King had rigged the bench to ensure a favourable verdict. He had sounded out the views of his twelve judges in advance, and removed six who had said that he could not dispense Catholics from the Test. Six more pliable individuals were found as replacements, one of whom, Christopher Milton, was a suspected Catholic. When the King told Lord Chief Justice Jones of Common Pleas of his determination to find twelve lawyers who would stand by him 'in this matter of the Dispensation', Jones replied that he might 'find 12 Gownmen, but not 12 Lawyers'.[28] A stanza affixed to the gate of Westminster Hall compared the judges' decision to Judas's betrayal of Christ:

When nature's God for our offenses di'd
Amongst the twelve one Judas did reside.
Here's twelve assembled for the nation's peace
Amongst which twelve, eleven are Judases.
One's true to's trust, but all the rest accord
With Jews and pagans to betray their Lord.
What madness, slaves! What is't could ye provoke
To stoop again unto the Romish yoke?
May ye be curs'd and all your hopes demolish'd–
And perish by those laws ye have abolish'd![29]

Local JPs were upset with the verdict, praising the 'one honest Church of England judge amongst the twelve that was against the Dispensation' and refusing to wait on the other judges when they went on their circuits that summer, as a sign of their disgust.[30] Morrice relates that many legal experts questioned the reasoning behind Herbert's verdict. Some held that the statutes about the sheriffs were not of the same nature as the Test Act, so that the dispensing of the former could not serve as a precedent. Others insisted that even though many sheriffs had served for terms of longer than a year, in all cases their commissions had run only for one year, and they were renewed every year, so there had never been any dispensation from the Act of 23 Henry VI. Besides, Coke had been wrong, many observed, in claiming that in Henry VII's time a judgment had been given 'by all the Judges that the King might dispense in this case', since the year books recorded that the judges specifically stated that anything they had said about this matter should 'be looked upon as not said'. Justice Street, the sole judge who opposed the ruling, later claimed that although outnumbered eleven to one on the judicial bench, 'there were more then eleaven of the people' that took his side 'for one of the people that were of the eleaven Judges side'.[31]

James's desire to give commissions to Catholics in the army, then, had led him to assault the independence of the judiciary and, as far as many contemporaries were concerned, to subvert the rule of law. He had upset the magisterial classes of England in the process, while the mere existence of such a large standing army had caused serious tensions with the civilian population. And for what end? The King had an army that was still overwhelmingly Protestant, though one which now had more internal divisions thanks to the intrusion of Catholics. James had created a climate of distrust with seemingly little, if any, political gain for himself.

Catholic Toleration

James not only wanted to ensure that his co-religionists had the ability to practise their religion peaceably but also to create an environment that would encourage his Protestant subjects to convert. He appears to have believed that by providing toleration for Catholics and allowing them to promote the faith through the general arts of persuasion, conversions would inevitably follow.[32] As a strategy it was naïve, if not in and of itself particularly sinister. The way in which he pursued it, however, involved a vaunting of the powers of the monarchy and further violations of the rule of law.

At first, James proceeded cautiously. Shortly after his accession, he set up an official council of Catholics to advise him on religious affairs, and towards the end of the year he removed a few MPs from office who had opposed him in the Commons in November, but otherwise he continued to rely on those who had served his brother at the end of his reign, with Rochester as Lord Treasurer, Jeffreys as Lord Chancellor, and the flexible Sunderland as Secretary of State (as yet still Protestant, though beginning to set himself up as the head of the Catholic interest). James appointed perhaps one Catholic judge and possibly no more than one Catholic JP prior to the winter of 1686/7. The decision in Godden v. Hales, however, allowed him to admit Catholics to his privy council and five Catholic peers – Lords Powis, Arundell of Wardour, Belasyse, Dover and the Earl of Tyrconnell – were sworn in over the summer and autumn of 1686. Then in November 1687 James admitted the Jesuit priest and his trusted confidant, Edward Petre, to the council. Described by Burnet as 'a man of no learning, nor any way famed for his virtue, but who made all up in boldness and zeal', Petre's influence with the King was such that he soon came to be 'considered as the first minister of state'.

In September 1685 James had reopened diplomatic relations with Rome, sending the Earl of Castlemaine there as ambassador and receiving (in November) Ferdinando d'Adda as a papal envoy (and from the spring of 1687, papal nuncio). However, James never intended to make the British monarchy subservient to the papacy. Thus he maintained his position as head of the Church and insisted on his right to nominate all ecclesiastical dignitaries within his kingdoms – not just Protestant bishops in England and Scotland (as we would reasonably expect) but also Catholic bishops and deans in Ireland, where his legal right to do so was highly questionable.[33] With regard to the Church of England, James recognized that his most realistic option was to try to work with its leadership, since he was unable to sack the Anglican bishops, whose appointments were for life. The only time he could affect the complexion of the episcopal bench was when a particular bishop died. He kept the archiepiscopal see of York vacant following the death of its incumbent, John Dolben, in April 1686, so that the revenues could revert to the crown; it was not until November 1688, at the time of William of Orange's invasion, that he finally appointed a replacement, the Bishop of Exeter, Thomas Lamplugh. In the autumn of 1686, he found two pliant individuals, Thomas Cartwright and Samuel Parker, to appoint to the vacant sees of Chester and Oxford. Both were to prove their worth to the crown over the next couple of years, in supporting James's more controversial policies.

There had been talk from the very beginning of the reign that James was going to declare a general religious toleration, but the King was unwilling to take such a bold initiative so soon.[34] He did, however, devise a scheme of helping his co-religionists while at the same time continuing to allow for the enforcement of the penal laws against Protestant nonconformists. Thus on 11 May 1685, James ordered the stay of all processes against recusants who came from families that had suffered for their loyalty during the Civil War or who could otherwise prove their loyalty; given that most Catholics had been loyal, whereas most Protestant nonconformists came from parliamentary backgrounds and had sided with the Whigs under Charles II, it is clear which religious group such an order favoured. James followed this on 2 June by ordering that monies collected from recusants that had not yet been paid into the Exchequer be restored to the persons fined. The procedure needed to be repeated to ensure continued relief, and so on 24 February 1686 James issued a more general warrant, discharging all fines and staying all proceedings against loyal recusants until his pleasure 'be further known'.[35]

James encouraged his Catholic subjects to follow his example and celebrate the mass openly. He opened his own chapels to the public, encouraged foreign ambassadors in and around London to do the same, and provided money to the secular and regular Catholic clergy to advance their missionary efforts. Catholic laymen and women, both rich and poor, also provided money for the establishing of chapels, while Catholic chapels were set up in garrison towns to serve those Catholics in the armed forces. By the spring of 1686 there were Catholic chapels 'in many of the great Cityes in England', including London, Worcester and Bristol, and by 1688 in most provincial towns of any size. London itself had eighteen Catholic chapels by the autumn of 1688. James also promoted Catholic schools, including two Jesuit schools in the capital.[36] A couple of disused Anglican chapels were made over for Catholic use, but on the whole the Catholics either erected new buildings or rented halls or rooms for their purposes. There was no attempt, as in Ireland and Scotland, to convert buildings in use by the Established Church into places of Catholic worship. In January 1686 reports spread that James was about to issue *quo warranto* proceedings against cathedral churches, though this was something the King was quick to deny.[37] The government did, however, launch enquiries into the titles to former monastic lands, with the ultimate aim not of restoring such lands to the see of Rome but to the English crown. Many of the grants made by Henry VIII had been for long leases, and the proprietors had often not bought the reversion of the lease when it expired, so the land technically had reverted to the crown. In April 1686 James issued a commission to seize the temporalities of the Archbishopric of York into the King's hands. He also challenged the rights of the proprietors of Bermondsey Abbey, St Thomas's Hospital in Southwark, St Katharine's Hospital near the Tower, and other parts of London, on the grounds that their leases were no longer valid, as well as those of some provincial landowners, such as Sir Ralph Dutton in Gloucestershire (the greatest part of whose estate was in abbey lands).[38]

In the campaign to win converts, James believed the press could play a crucial role. He therefore sanctioned the publication of numerous books, pamphlets, broadsheets and devotional manuals, with large print runs to make sure there were enough to reach the intended target audience. Most of them were produced by the King's official printer, Henry Hills; many of them ended up being given away free of charge. Instead of fulminating against Protestant heresies, the strategy pursued was to offer a plain and clear exposition of what the Catholic Church actually stood for, in the hope that by freeing people's minds from prejudices inculcated by years of misrepresentation, they would become more receptive to the possibility of conversion.[39] Yet James's missionary effort produced very few conversions. A handful in the higher echelons of government became Catholics, among them the earls of Salisbury and Peterborough and, eventually, also the Earl of Sunderland (though not until after the birth of the Prince of Wales in June 1688, and Sunderland was to convert back after the Revolution). So too did a few JPs and a handful of Oxbridge dons. In the navy, Rear-Admiral Sir Roger Strickland converted in the winter of 1686/7, followed by a number of his clients; James was subsequently to reward this pool of converts with rapid promotion (Strickland himself rose to vice-admiral and then admiral), which obviously alienated those Protestant seamen who saw their own advancement thwarted. The visibility of these converts certainly caused alarm, but they hardly constituted a numerically significant trend. Very few amongst the mass of the population were won over to the Catholic faith. In Worcestershire, one of the more Catholic counties in England, there were just 12 reconciliations in 1685, 11 the next year, and only 6 more in the next two years – a mere 29 in four years, compared to 30 in the four years 1660–63 and 46 in 1693–6. In Birmingham there were more: 147 in 1685–8, compared to 121 in 1660–62.[40] However, nationwide, the figures were extremely low. As a result, with the exception of a few areas, there simply were not enough Catholics to fill all the new chapels. Some 300 Catholics heard mass in Worcester on Candlemas Day (2 February) in 1687, but this was an exception. In York, the Catholics took over five rooms for the public celebration of mass, but there were only about fifty or sixty Catholics in the city, and just three converts. A small congregation gathered at Oxford, but it included no more than four scholars, the rest being local residents (among them, two of the most infamous city prostitutes). Even the Jacobite *Life* was later to concede that James proceeded with 'an imprudent zeal in erecting more Chappels, than there were faithful sufficient to fill, or Priests to be found well qualify'd to officiate in', thereby exposing 'the holy misteries to the mockery and dirision of the people'.[41]

The Anglican Response and the Ecclesiastical Commission

James's attempts to promote the Catholic faith provoked widespread opposition from his Protestant subjects, and particularly from Tory-Anglican interests. The Anglican clergy orchestrated a press and pulpit campaign to defend their version of true faith against the efforts of Catholic polemicists. The lead was taken by a group of London-based divines, among them John Tillotson, Edward Stilling-fleet, Thomas Tenison, Simon Patrick, William Sherlock and William Wake, who formed an agreement both to preach against the errors of the Roman Church and to publish 'a great variety of small books, that were easily purchased and soon read'. The nonconformist clergy were not totally silent: the Presbyterians and Independents in and around Oxford, for example, held morning meetings during the week when they preached against popery. Most dissenters, however, aware of the vulnerability of their position after years of persecution, were prepared to leave the job of defending the Protestant religion 'to the Pastors and Gentlemen of the Church of England'. According to one contemporary calculation, nonconformists published just three books against popery in James II's reign, compared to 228 by members of the Church of England.[42]

James and his supporters were horrified by the apparent rapid change of allegiance of the clerical establishment. It appeared that 'the very same men' who had helped place James on his throne by preaching up non-resistance now 'had a mind to Preach him out again', as one pamphleteer put it, 'Arbitrary Power, Popery, Protestant Religion' being made 'more the Theme of the Pulpit, than before it had been of the Fanaticks Pa)ers and Pamphlets'.[43] On 5 March 1686, therefore, James issued his Directions to Preachers (it was, in fact, a reissue of Charles II's Directions of 1662), ordering the clergy to avoid religious controversy and concentrate on practical and moral divinity.[44] Anti-Catholic sermonizing nevertheless continued. Some did at least pay lip-service to the prohibition. One witty Oxford cleric, instructed by his vice-chancellor not to preach against popery, gave his audience 'a brief Scheame' of what he would have said, had he not been forbidden.[45]

James's efforts to promote Catholic worship provoked unrest in several communities when Catholic chapels first began to be opened. Although James had issued dispensations from the Tests and stopped loyal Catholics being prosecuted for recusancy, Catholic worship remained, for the time being, illegal. There was one exception, however: foreign ambassadors and diplomats were allowed to erect their own chapels where they and their servants could worship in private. In early 1686, James encouraged James Stamford, the Elector Palatine's envoy, to take up a residence in Lime Street in the heart of London and convert it into a Catholic chapel; the money came in part from the King, and in part from Catholic merchants in the City and the secular clergy. The chapel was clearly much too big for the needs of Stamford's household, and it was unprecedented for foreign ministers, who typically resided around the court in Westminster, to erect places of Catholic worship within the City of London itself. Moreover, Stamford was an Englishman, not a foreigner merely seeking to continue to practise the official religion of his home country while temporarily resident abroad, while the Elector himself did not even know about the chapel and was later to deny that he had wanted it built. The whole scheme was a transparent sham, an attempt by James to establish Catholic worship in the City under a cloak of legality, and in late March the Tory Lord Mayor of London, Sir Robert Geffrey – perhaps at the instigation of Bishop Compton of London – tried to stop the construction work on the grounds that the chapel was illegal. The King intervened, rebuked the Lord Mayor, and ordered the work to continue.

When the chapel opened on Sunday 18 April, a crowd of people, many of them apprentices, followed the priests to mass, threatening to 'break their crosses and juggling-boxes down'. The local constables and trained bands came to suppress the disturbances, but on the whole their sympathies were with the crowd. They let one of the ringleaders they had apprehended 'slip away' and rejoin the fracas; he was later seen pulling one of the priests out of the chapel and dragging him through the gutter. Crowds gathered again the following Sunday, saying 'they would have no wooden gods worshipped there'. When the Lord Mayor tried to restore order, back came the cry: 'What! Is the Lord Mayor of our city come to preach up Popery?' The trained bands were again reluctant to act, feeling that if the crowd intended 'Only pulling down Popery' they could not 'in conscience hinder'. The King threatened to send in his own troops if the Lord Mayor did not take better care to preserve the peace, but the attempts of the trained bands the following week to protect the celebrants as they made their way to mass merely provoked further conflicts with Protestant protesters. Although over the course of the disturbances the authorities did succeed in making about twenty arrests, some of those taken into custody turned out to be Catholics – presumably the innocent victims rather than the perpetrators of the unrest, but guilty by dint of their religion in the eyes of the Protestant arresting officers – who were later released by special warrant.[46]

There were similar riots against Catholic worship in Worcester and Coventry that spring.[47] At Bristol in late April, the mayor, at the instigation of a local Tory zealot, Sir John Knight, not only put a stop to the celebration of the mass at a hastily constructed chapel near the Custom House, but had the priest and his entire congregation arrested and thrown into prison. When those arrested threatened to report his actions to the King, the mayor defiantly replied that he would save them the trouble and do it himself. Knight was subsequently indicted at King's Bench for going armed with a blunderbuss through the streets and disrupting a public church service 'to the terrour of his Majesties' Liege people', but a jury composed of Bristol men acquitted him.[48] Towards the end of May the 'lower orders' of Bristol staged a public procession 'in Scoff of Popery . . . carrying before them a piece of Bread with much ceremony'; as part of the parade, a couple dressed as the Virgin Mary and a monk were seen fondling each other 'very rudely and immoderately'.[49]

Believing such attacks had been fuelled by anti-Catholic preaching, James determined he needed to keep the Anglican clergy in line. Many clergy, however, felt that they could not properly fulfil their pastoral role if they were not allowed to address the concerns of their parishioners about the right path to salvation. It was an anonymous letter from one of his parishioners in spiritual doubt that provoked John Sharp, Dean of Norwich and rector of St Giles-in-the-Fields, London, to speak on a forbidden subject from the pulpit of St Giles in May.[50] James ordered Bishop Compton of London to suspend Sharp, but Compton (who had already taken a public stance against James in the parliamentary session of November 1685) refused, insisting that due legal process had to be followed and that Sharp was entitled to a fair hearing.[51] This brought the issue of control of the Anglican clergy to a head. Since the bishops could not be trusted to police the Church, James decided in July to set up a commission 'for the inspecting of Ecclesiastical Affairs'. There were to be seven commissioners – Archbishop Sancroft of Canterbury, Lord Chancellor Jeffreys, Lord Treasurer Rochester, Lord President Sunderland, the bishops of Durham and Rochester, and Lord Chief Justice Herbert – though only three were required for a quorum, of whom the Lord Chancellor had to be one. Sancroft refused to sit; he was later replaced by Cartwright of Chester. The main purpose behind the establishment of this Ecclesiastical Commission was 'for the prevention of Indiscreet Preaching', though the commissioners were authorized to execute and exercise all ecclesiastical jurisdiction, punish offences against the ecclesiastical laws and impose Church censures as they thought fit, and visit and discipline ecclesiastical institutions (including the universities). The Ecclesiastical Commission's first act was to suspend Compton from his duties as bishop for his refusal to suspend Sharp.[52]

Since the Ecclesiastical Commission was to be declared illegal in 1689, let us consider its status at law more fully. The crown's powers of governance over the Church in England were based upon the royal supremacy established by the Henrician Reformation of the 1530s and confirmed under Queen Elizabeth. Article 17 of the Elizabethan Act of Supremacy of 1559 vested in the crown visitorial power over all ecclesiastical bodies, including colleges and universities, while article 18 permitted the crown 'by Letters Patentes under the Greate Seale' to appoint commissioners to 'execute all manner of Jurisdictions, Privileges, and Preheminences in any wise touching or concerning any Spiritual or Ecclesiastical Jurisdiction' within England and Ireland.[53] Elizabeth had set up a Court of High Commission to keep discipline in the Church, but during her reign its scope was limited to imposing ecclesiastical censures on those in clerical orders. Charles I, however, had allowed the Court to fine and imprison lay people and to tender oaths *ex officio*. In 1641, on the eve of the Civil War, the Long Parliament determined that Charles had misinterpreted article 18 of the Elizabethan Act of Supremacy and repealed that article in its entirety. This repeal was confirmed by legislation enacted in 1661 following the Restoration.[54]

Despite the repealing legislation, however, historians have tended to the view that James was technically within his rights when he established his Ecclesiastical Commission in 1686.[55] This is supposedly because Charles I's Court of High Commission and James II's Ecclesiastical Commission were two very different bodies: the latter, it has been said, was not a court, did not call itself such, and limited itself to imposing ecclesiastical censures on ecclesiastical persons. Moreover, the repealing legislation of 1641 had not touched article 17 of the Elizabethan Act of Supremacy, while the act of 1661 had reaffirmed the crown's supremacy in ecclesiastical affairs, and how could the royal supremacy be exercised, unless the king was allowed to appoint commissioners to act on his behalf? When James consulted his judges they told him that the Elizabethan Act of Supremacy had, in fact, given the crown no new power, but had only declared what power was originally in the crown; therefore, the King might set up an ecclesiastical commission 'by Vertue of the Supream Power originally Vested in him in all Ecclesiastical matters', which had been confirmed by the act of 1661.[56] According to the Jacobite *Life*, James believed that his Ecclesiastical Commission was sanctioned by the act of 1661 so long as the commissioners kept within the bounds of ecclesiastical censures and did none of those things proscribed by the act of 1641 (such as fining, imprisoning, or tendering oaths *ex officio*). James also, apparently, had an honourable motive: 'it seem'd incongruous to him', given that he was a Roman Catholic, that 'he should exercise in person that Jurisdiction over the Church of England, which the Law vests in the Sovereign'. Was he not, therefore, not only acting within the letter of the law but also with due scrupulousness in setting up a commission of Anglican clerics and laymen to inspect ecclesiastical affairs?[57]

With regard to James's scruples, one must both recognize the positive retrospective gloss put on James's intentions by the Jacobite *Life*, and also ask why he found it necessary to inspect ecclesiastical affairs at this juncture in the first place. As to the law, it was certainly open to interpretation. A number of points need to be made, however. Contemporaries unquestionably thought of James's Ecclesiastical Commission as a 'court' from its inception, 'for so properly it is', as one newsletter writer sympathetic to the court put it. When Compton asked at his trial to see 'a copy of their Lordships Commission', the commissioners replied that 'no Courts granted copies of their commission'; Jeffreys, who presided over the Commission, referred to it as a court, and the erstwhile Whig publicist turned government propagandist, Henry Care, subsequently wrote a tract vindicating 'the Legality of the Court Held by His Majesties Ecclesiastical Commissioners'.[58] Furthermore, although the act of 1641 had not specifically repealed article 17 of the Elizabethan Supremacy Act, when repealing article 18 it had explicitly repealed and voided 'for ever' the crown's right to appoint commissioners to exercise any manner of spiritual or ecclesiastical jurisdiction, 'Any thing in the said Act to the contrary in any wise notwithstanding' – clearly implying that article 17 could not be used to legitimize the setting up of an ecclesiastical commission at a future date.[59]

After consulting with a number of lawyers, Compton decided 'to demur to the jurisdiction of the Court', protesting to the commissioners that although he did 'not intend any thing . . . Derogatory to the King's Supremacy' or 'undutifull to his Majesty', his counsel had told him that their 'proceedings in this Court [were] directly Contrary to the Statute Law'.[60] The belief that the Ecclesiastical Commission was illegal appears to have been fairly widespread. When a group of Sussex gentlemen met for dinner at the residence of Sir John Ashburnham, MP for Hastings and a JP and deputy Lieutenant, there was 'a great deale of discourse concerning the Legallity of High Commissions', which all 'considered to be unlawfull'.[61] On 16 August an anonymous correspondent wrote to the Lord Mayor of London, inviting him to petition the King to review or recall his

Ecclesiastical Commission and enclosing a letter for James, informing the King of 'the dreadful apprehensions' many of his 'truest Subjects' had 'of the tendency of your Late Commission' and urging him to reconsider whether 'it bee noe way Injurious, to the established Laws in Church and State'.[62] A number of manuscript treatises were prepared that sought to demonstrate beyond doubt that the Ecclesiastical Commission was illegal. Sir Robert Atkyns considered the argument that the King might set up an Ecclesiastical Commission, notwithstanding the act of repeal, by virtue of the ecclesiastical supremacy vested in the crown by the Henrician Reformation, to be fallacious. Even if the Elizabethan Act of Supremacy had merely declared what power was originally in the crown, an examination of the Henrician Reformation statutes made it clear that the crown's ecclesiastical jurisdiction was to be exercised in the appropriate ecclesiastical courts: the archidiaconal, diocesan, or metropolitan courts, or else convocation. On the other hand, if Elizabeth 'by her meer prerogative and supreme power' could already have granted an ecclesiastical commission, then there was no need of article 18 in the Elizabethan Act of Supremacy. It was clear, then, 'that it needed an act of parliament to give such authority to Elizabeth to grant such letters patents, or commission; and that without an act of parliament such commission could not have been granted'. Since article 18 had been repealed in 1641, and the repeal confirmed in 1661, Atkyns concluded that 'no such commission nor letters patents' could 'now be granted, but the repealing act . . . stands in force against it'.[63]

BUILDING NEW ALLIANCES AND THE POLITICS OF INDULGENCE

By the summer of 1686 James, now approaching 53 years of age, had managed to establish a sizeable peacetime standing army, won a vitally important test case upholding his right to dispense Catholics from the Test, broken the Anglican monopoly of worship and established effective toleration for loyal recusants, and had erected an Ecclesiastical Commission that could be used to discipline the Church. All this had been achieved at enormous political cost, however. James had alienated his parliament, an overwhelmingly Tory-Anglican body that had shown itself deeply supportive of his succession. He had upset the Anglican divines, including key figures on the episcopal bench, such as Bishop Compton of London, provoked the opposition of Tory magistrates in key corporations, such as London and Bristol, and had managed to generate considerable opposition out-of-doors, with his policies causing outbursts of rioting in several parts of the kingdom.

Nor had he, as yet, secured any lasting benefits for his co-religionists. Granting individual Catholics dispensations from the penal laws not only took time and involved expensive legal fees for the beneficiary, but they could only be expected from a Catholic monarch; James still had no Catholic heir and looked set to be succeeded by his Protestant daughter Mary and her husband William of Orange. To establish a permanent toleration for the Catholic population in England would require a repeal of the penal laws, and this could only be achieved through parliament. However, given the opposition there had been to the limited relief granted Catholics to date, it seemed unlikely that the traditional allies of the crown would show much support for such an initiative. In the end, James decided to abandon the Tory-Anglican interest and forge an alliance with Protestant nonconformists, the crucial shift occurring in the winter and spring of 1686–7. It is more accurate to think in terms of a phased transition, however, since James began courting dissenters long before he had any thoughts of abandoning the Church party, and he tried for as long as possible to carry the Tory-Anglican interest with him.

James's policy of wooing the dissenters began piecemeal over the course of 1686. On 10 March he issued a general pardon embracing a wide range of offences, including attending unlawful conventicles and not coming to church and excluding only desperate moral deviants and certain categories of rebels.[64] Over the next month some 1,200 Quakers were freed.[65] Later that spring he informed the Quakers that they were free to hold their religious meetings, and when the Baptists delivered an address of thanks for the royal pardon he told them, too, that they could expect his protection, so long as they remained loyal. In several parts of the country Anglican zealots responded by stepping up their drive against dissent – disturbing meetings 'with as great fierceness as ever' and hauling conventiclers before the local authorities, 'notwithstanding what verball immunity they said they had' – insisting that if they did not enforce the penal laws strictly against nonconformists, it would be impossible to protect the Church against popery. James started granting Quakers dispensations, for a fee, to protect them from persecution (it cost 50 shillings to secure a dispensation for a whole family), but soon showed himself ready to extend protection to other dissenting groups who petitioned for relief. Those who refused to petition – mainly Presbyterians and Independents – continued to suffer.[66]

Dispensing dissenters from the Conventicle Act, however, raised the issue of whether the king could deny informers one-third of the fine levied on convicted conventiclers that they were entitled to under the terms of the 1670 Conventicle Act. Both the defence counsel and the presiding judge in Godden v. Hales had acknowledged that the king could not issue dispensations even for *mala prohibita* if doing so violated a third party's property rights. Although Hales had, in fact, been forgiven the fine due the plaintiff, the dispensation had been ruled valid on the grounds that the case was analogous to that of dispensations given to sheriffs to serve for more than one year. Could the ruling be extended to conventicling? Besides, Godden had been acting in collusion with the defendant and never had any intention of collecting the fine; the case would be different when there were parties who were determined to do so. In Leicester in October 1686, a local informer named Smith continued to spy on Quaker meetings, insisting that the King did not have the power to remit his part of the fine. The Leicester magistrates agreed, and told the Quakers 'that if the Informer doe Still proceed, they must fine as before'.[67] When a nonconformist preacher in Exeter presented the magistrates who came to disturb his meeting in January 1687 with 'a Protection from the King', they replied that 'the King could not protect them, nor dispense with them against Law', and proceeded to break up the meeting.[68] Nevertheless, James was ready to take on the informers. On the petition of the Quaker George Whitehead he appointed two treasury solicitors in June 1686 to investigate the activities of an infamous gang of London informers led by John and George Hilton. The inquiry resulted in the gang leaders being prosecuted for perjury at the

Middlesex sessions and prompted further inquiries into the activities of informers operating in other parts of the country.[69]

Towards the end of the summer, James decided to make a progress through the West Country, the area that had shown itself to be most disaffected at the time of his accession and which had benefited most from his royal pardon, in order to test the level of support for him. He set off from Windsor on 23 August, passing through Reading, Marlborough, Badminton, Bristol, Winchester, Salisbury, Southampton, Portsmouth and Farnham, before heading back to Windsor on 31 August. The *London Gazette* represented the progress as a great public relations success, claiming that both the magistrates and inhabitants of the several places he passed through gave 'all possible demonstrations of their Duty and Loyalty'. James was certainly received in style by the various members of the nobility with whom he stayed – the Duke of Somerset at Marlborough, the Duke of Beaufort at Badminton, and the Earl of Pembroke at Winchester – and by the leaders of the corporations through which he passed, while the fact that progresses had been 'very rare of late' meant that huge crowds gathered 'in cityes, towns, villages and lanes' in the hopes of catching a glimpse of royalty. Everywhere he went, James touched for the King's Evil; at Winchester, for example, he touched 250, and gave out the traditional gold coins.[70] However, the well-informed Roger Morrice, albeit a man who had little time for James II, was sceptical of the success of the progress. He did 'not heare', he wrote, 'that any considerable number of Noblemen or Gentlemen came to wait upon' the King; the reception at Bristol had been a little frosty, the town having failed to present the expected gift of gold, and in general it seemed that James 'was not received with that honour and Respect' afforded other princes.[71]

Nevertheless, James's birthday on 14 October seemed to offer confirmation of the continued support of many of his subjects. Bonfires were forbidden in the City of London as a precautionary measure against possible disorder, but in Westminster there were bells and bonfires and 'the greatest demonstrations of joy', which, the *Gazette* claimed, 'never appeared more general than on this occasion'. At Lincoln's Inn Fields, where 'two very good Church of England Magistrates' had arranged with the local churchwardens and constables to set up 'a common purse' to fund a bonfire celebration, Titus Oates was burnt in effigy. Another Popish Plot informer, William Bedloe, met the same fate in Drury Lane. There were similar displays in a number of provincial cities and towns, as at Bath, where Charles II's widow kept her court and gave 'several Hogsheads of Wine . . . to the People', Newcastle upon Tyne, where the mayor and aldermen ensured the public fountains ran continuously with wine, Norwich and Oxford.[72]

Whatever comfort James derived from such displays of public support, however, events on 5 November (the anniversary of England's deliverance from the Catholic Gunpowder Plot of 1605) were soon to remind him that anti-Catholic sentiment across the country continued to run high. In Cambridge a number of clergymen preached so zealously against popery that the University Senate later forced them to make a public recantation.[73] In several provincial towns local inhabitants circumvented a royal order against fireworks and bonfires by placing candles in their windows to testify their opposition to popery.[74] At Gloucester, the mayor agreed to allow just two bonfires in the city, but the bishop insisted that the mayor had no jurisdiction within the precincts of the Cathedral, and so ordered another two bonfires to be made there.[75] London observed the day with sermons in most churches, the ringing of bells, and – despite the prohibition – bonfires and candlelight illuminations in many parts of the city. In Fleet Street a crowd paraded a man on their shoulders 'with hornes on his head stuck with candles', presumably to satirize the way people worshipped 'the Whore of Babylon', as Protestants styled the Pope (the horns being the symbol of a cuckold). In another part of the capital locals took a goose, the symbol of a simpleton, and stuck a big piece of paper on its breast with the word 'Torey' written on it in large letters; the goose, 'much out of Countenance', rushed about aimlessly, crying out what sounded like 'Torey', the moral being 'that the Papists Counts [sic] the Toreys' geese'. A group in Warwick Lane reportedly carried an effigy of the Pope in procession, though the locals later claimed they were processing a real corpse and there was certainly no tumult. A stern rebuke from the King ensured that the City authorities took greater care not to allow similar tumults on 17 November (the anniversary of Queen

Elizabeth's accession in 1558), though it was reported that 'the bells rung very much that day'.[76]

By late 1686 it was becoming clear to James that he would not be able to work with the Tory-Anglican interest. One Catholic tract of November 1686 suggested that 'the Mallice, and Industry of most of the leading Members of the Church of England, must needs att last have Convinct his Majesty how little he can trust their principles, for the Repose, Much lesse Grandure of his Reigne', and that 'Liberty of Conscience' was now 'the onely thing left' on which James could hope to 'build Either his Glory or Safety for the future'.[77] Symbolically, the most significant indication of James's intention to break with the traditional allies of the crown came when he dismissed the Hyde brothers (his own brothers-in-law) from office in December, replacing Clarendon in Ireland (as we have seen) with the Catholic Tyrconnell, and Rochester at the treasury with a commission presided over by the Catholic Belasyse. James had hoped that Rochester would convert, and admitted in a conference with the Earl on the night of Sunday 19 December that putting him out of his employment came very 'uneasy to him', apparently weeping 'almost all the time' as he spoke. But, James declared, 'he found it absolutely necessary for the good of his affairs, that no man must be at the head of his affairs that was not of his own opinion'. Over the autumn and winter of 1686/7 James also set out to reform the county magistracy, an overwhelmingly Tory-Anglican body of men following the purges of Charles II's final years.[78] In October 1686 he established a special privy council committee to review the commissions of the peace, and by March of the following year it had ordered 498 new appointments (two-thirds of whom were Catholics) and 245 dismissals (the great majority of whom were Anglicans and members of the leading families in their respective shires). Those removed included some former Whigs who had survived the earlier purges of Charles but also many whose loyalty to the crown had never been called into question in the previous reign, including notorious anti-Whig campaigners who had promoted loyal addresses in the early 1680s.[79]

Although James had kept parliament prorogued since November 1685, he had not given up all hope of working with that body. In December 1686 he started interviewing members of both houses to see if they would be willing to support the repeal of the penal laws and the Test Acts; the judges and a few trusted peers put similar questions to those members who remained in the country. The answers received were far from reassuring: most either asked for more time to consider or else replied that they could not possibly decide until they had heard the debates in parliament. A frustrated James dismissed the obstinate peers and MPs from office. Danby, who had no office to lose, told the King emphatically that he would not support a repeal of the penal laws or the Test, stating that he looked upon those laws as 'the Security of our Religion'.[80]

The Declaration of Indulgence of April 1687

In the spring of 1687 James took the next logical step: instead of granting individual dispensations from the penal laws, he would suspend their operation in their entirety until he could persuade a parliament to repeal them. Exactly when James decided upon this policy is difficult to say, though it may have been as early as September 1686 and it was certainly before the end of that year.[81] It was not until 18 March 1687 that James made the official announcement to his privy council that he was going to issue a general liberty of conscience, claiming that the attempts to enforce religious uniformity had not worked and that toleration would promote domestic peace and increase trade.[82] The first step, however, had been taken with the issuance of an Indulgence for Scotland on 12 February; the speed with which the English Indulgence followed makes it clear that James was not waiting for reaction in his northern kingdom before deciding upon how to act in England, but rather that the two Indulgences were phased aspects of the same policy (see pp. 169–71).

The English Declaration of Indulgence appeared on 4 April. It opened with the King proclaiming that although he wished all his subjects 'were members of the Catholic Church', it had long been his opinion 'that conscience ought not to be constrained, nor people forced in matters of mere religion', and that religious persecution ruined the interest of government 'by spoiling trade' and 'depopulating countries'. He therefore thought fit to grant indulgence by virtue of his 'royal prerogative'. He promised he would continue to 'protect and maintain' both the clergy and laity of the Church of England 'in the free exercise of their religion as by law established, and in the quiet and full enjoyment of all their possessions', including any church or abbey lands they might happen to possess. But it was his 'royal will' that 'the execution of . . . all manner of penal laws in matters ecclesiastical' should 'be immediately suspended', so that his 'loving subjects' might have 'leave to meet and serve God after their own way and manner, be it in private houses or places purposely hired or built for that use'. The Declaration further stipulated that no tests would henceforth be required of office-holders and that the King would grant dispensations to those he wished to employ who would not take the required oaths. It concluded by saying that the King expected parliament to give legal sanction to this toleration when he thought it convenient for it to meet.[83]

In 1689 the Declaration of Rights unequivocally declared that the suspending power was illegal. Modern historians, however, have claimed that James's Indulgence was technically within the law. There are two strands to the argument. The first is that the English monarch, by dint of the royal supremacy, did have the power to suspend penal laws in matters of religion; it is true that the Commons had issued a resolution against the suspending power in 1673, when it had forced Charles II to withdraw his Declaration of Indulgence of 1672, but resolutions of the Commons, it has rightly been pointed out, do not make law. The second is that James did not strictly speaking claim a suspending power, but instead saw his Indulgence as resting on the dispensing power, for which he had legal sanction by dint of the verdict in Godden v. Hales.[84] The second point can be easily dealt with. While contemporaries often did speak of the Indulgence as resting upon the 'dispensing power', they certainly understood the difference between dispensing individuals from the penalties of particular laws and dispensing with (that is, suspending) the operation of an entire statute. The Indulgence itself clearly distinguished between suspending the penal laws and granting individuals dispensations from the Test, even if it did not speak explicitly about a 'suspending power'. In a tract published in 1688, Lord Chief Justice Herbert, the judge who had given the ruling in Godden v. Hales, forthrightly asserted that the Declaration of Indulgence was based on the suspending power, which was entirely different from the dispensing power.[85] The first point is a little more complicated, and hinges upon the legal significance of Charles II's withdrawing his Indulgence of 1673. The important thing to recognize, however, is that the Commons in 1673 did not declare the suspending power to be illegal; rather, the lower house insisted that Charles withdraw his Indulgence because, they claimed, the King was mistaken in his belief that he enjoyed the power to suspend penal statutes in matters ecclesiastical. Charles's withdrawal, in other words, seemed a tacit acknowledgement by the King that the English sovereign had never possessed such a power.[86]

A number of contemporaries explicitly condemned James's attempt to suspend the penal laws in 1687. One pamphleteer acknowledged that the king did possess a dispensing power, but only to correct faults in the law: 'If any thing happen[ed] after the making of a Law, which was not foreseen when it was made' or was 'contrary to the original intention of the Law-makers', and rendered 'the execution of the Law manifestly and notoriously oppressive to the Public', then the sovereign might 'certainly suspend the Execution' of such a law until it was 'alter'd or repealed by the Power which made them' (namely parliament). But this 'must be for the publick good', this author insisted, 'or else it is the abuse, not the natural Right of Soveraign Power'.[87] Similarly, Robert Ferguson wrote that although everyone acknowledged that there was 'a Royal prerogative setled on the Crown', to apply it beyond 'the received Customes' of the nation 'and the universal good, preservation and safety of the People in general' was 'an Usurpation and Tyranny in the Ruler'. Only parliament, Ferguson claimed, could determine the extent of the prerogative: one could not accept the opinion of the king's advisers, 'Mercinary lawyers', or 'Sycophantic Clergy-men', since they were hardly likely to be unbiased. So 'a Power arising from Royal prerogative to suspend and disable a great number of Laws at once' – laws, moreover, designed for 'the great security of the people . . . which the whole Community represented in Parliaments have often made void Princes medling with' – was 'a changing of the Government', Ferguson alleged, 'and an overthrowing of the Constitution'.[88] Burnet similarly agreed that 'the King's suspending of Laws' struck 'at the root of this whole Government' and quite subverted it. Even 'the most obsequious and servile Parliament to the Court that ever England knew' (i.e. Charles II's Cavalier Parliament of 1661–79), he wrote elsewhere, 'not only denied this Prerogative to the late King, but made him renounce it by revoking his Declaration of Indulgence' of 1672.[89]

James was aware that his policy was controversial and that the benefits of the Indulgence would have to be sold to the English public. He had also seen how his brother's regime, in response to the Exclusionist challenge, had successfully used the press to defend its record and to convince people to stop supporting the Whigs and to rally behind the crown. The people could, in other words, be won over to a cause they might not instinctively support; James's own present occupancy of the throne was proof of that. The secret was knowing how to go about it. One could follow the logic of high Tory-Anglican ideology as espoused during the years of the Tory Reaction: if the king was indeed an absolute monarch who was above the law, then of course he had the power to suspend the penal laws, especially when he thought that doing so was in the best interests of his people. Several anonymous tracts appeared defending the Indulgence along precisely those lines. James also had the services of that diehard Anglican-Royalist and genius of Charles II's propaganda campaign Sir Roger L'Estrange, who was still producing his bi-weekly pro-government periodical the *Observator*, and who, from late 1686, began churning out defences of the monarch's right not only to dispense with the law but even to suspend the entire operation of certain laws. Yet James also needed to try to win over the dissenters. To this end he recruited the services of the erstwhile Whig publicist Henry Care, and the Quaker William Penn to produce defences of the royal pursuit of religious toleration, in an effort to appeal to Whig and non-conformist sensibilities.[90]

In trying to sell James's Indulgence, propagandists sought to make the case both that the King had the power to issue a general edict of toleration and that it was in the best interests of the nation for him to do so. Although the English Declaration, unlike the Scottish Declaration, had not explicitly justified the crown's ability to suspend the laws by claiming that the king of England was an absolute monarch, a number of defenders of the Indulgence were quick to make that assertion. For L'Estrange, 'Imperial Princes' were 'Absolute . . . and

Immediately under God' and 'To him Alone . . . Accountable'; the laws were 'the Kings Laws', and although there were 'Many Political Laws', which a prince could not depart from, 'without being Manifestly Guilty before God', there were 'Other Cases . . . that would make him Culpable before God, if he did not Break them'.[91] Yet L'Estrange, who had spent much of his career in journalism calling for the strict enforcement of the penal laws against religious nonconformists, was finding it a strain to sustain public credibility and, with his health beginning to fail, he ceased writing the *Observator* in March 1687. He later denied that this was because things had not gone his way: everything he had written about toleration, he insisted, had 'not been made a Question of Religion, but of Government', the main point of debate being 'Whether Liberty of Conscience be a . . . Right of the People, or an Act of Grace, and Indulgence, Issuing from the Prerogative of the Supreme Magistrate'.[92] One anonymous author insisted that 'by the antient Laws of this Realm', England was 'an absolute Empire, and Monarchy', where the king was 'furnished with plenary and Entire Power, Prerogative and Jurisdiction', and tried to show that generations of Anglican divines, from Archbishops Bancroft and Laud through to Dr William Sherlock, had accepted that the king had the power to dispense with the penal laws. Curiously, however, this author concluded by insisting that 'Liberty of Conscience' was 'a Natural Right', not an 'Act of Grace' from the crown.[93] Similarly, William Penn argued that the most venerable of the Church of England's own clergy had acknowledged that power in ecclesiastical affairs rested wholly and absolutely in the crown.[94]

Authors also emphasized the positive benefits of toleration. One poem, licensed for publication two weeks before the Indulgence was issued, predicted:

> Holland no longer shall our people drain,
> No more our wealthy manufactures gain;
> Henceforth rebellion can have no pretense
> To arm the rabble for their faith's defense.
> Since each mode of religion now is free,
> They'll all, I hope, conspire in loyalty.[95]

A tract, purportedly written by a minister of the Church of England, insisted that persecution did not work, since men could 'not be frighted or aw'd out of their Opinions', and that the experience of other states, such as Holland and Poland, proved that toleration promoted peace at home and encouraged trade.[96] Penn made similar points concerning trade and domestic peace, and went so far as to suggest that if the King had declared for liberty of conscience earlier there would have been no Monmouth rebellion. He also wondered why any man's religious affiliation should 'hinder him from serving the Country of his Birth'.[97] Most writers, in addition, pointed out that members of the Established Church should have nothing to fear from the Indulgence, because of the King's promise to maintain and protect the Church of England.[98]

Finding it in their Hearts to Thank the King

James believed all religious groups would see that they benefited from the Indulgence and expected his subjects to respond with addresses of thanks – although the rumour that he had ordered the payment of large sums of money to those who were willing to make such addresses was probably not true.[99] Eventually 200 addresses came in from various groups throughout the kingdom: Catholics, dissenters, the clergy, local authorities and various trading interests. The total fell well short of the 346 addresses from England and Wales congratulating him on his accession. Moreover, many were slow to come in: only seventy-nine had been received by mid-August (prior to James setting out on a progress to the West Midlands on 16 August to drum up support for his policies); thirty-three in fact were not to be announced until the New Year, although many of the later ones were also able to promise to support the return of MPs who favoured the repeal of the penal laws (following the dissolution of parliament in July 1687) and to congratulate James on his wife's pregnancy (announced in December). A closer exploration of the history of these addresses – both of how they were drawn up and how they were worded – however, reveals considerable opposition to the Indulgence in many parts of the country, especially from Anglican interests.

The Catholics were naturally delighted with the Indulgence. At the end of May Lord Arundell presented an address of thanks to the King on behalf of the Roman Catholics of the kingdom, signed by several lords and many gentlemen of quality, while in August the Catholics of Lancashire, headed by Lord Molyneux, presented their own address to James while he was on his tour of the West Midlands.[100] These were the only two addresses, however, to be delivered in the name of English Catholics; there were not, after all, that many English Catholics who could have addressed.

The response of the nonconformists to the Indulgence was complex. After years of suffering under the weight of the law, most were happy to avail themselves of the relief the Indulgence afforded. Many, nevertheless, remained suspicious of James's motives and concerned by the fact that the toleration was dependent upon the King's arbitrary will and lacked any legal basis. The Presbyterians were the most hesitant. The Governor of York Sir John Reresby observed that in York, Leeds and Sheffield, the 'Geneva Party' chose to stick by the Church of England and continued to go to church; only the Quakers and Independents, who were not particularly numerous in this area, showed any sign that they were pleased with the toleration.[101] In London, one observer noted that, the week before the Indulgence was issued, the churches were more crowded than ever, the conventiclers saying they would rather 'now stay there then return'.[102] The Presbyterian preacher Daniel Williams told a meeting of London dissenting ministers that 'it was better for them to be reduced to their former hardships, than declare for measures destructive of the liberties of their country' and convinced them not to present an address of thanks. Likewise, the Baptist minister William Kiffin persuaded his followers not to address.[103] However, some dissenters, in different parts of the country, did welcome the Indulgence. One correspondent from the diocese of Norwich informed Archbishop Sancroft in late April how 'our dissenters have greedily swallowed the bayt and every where expressed their Joy with bells and bonfiers'. In Norwich itself, Dr John Collins immediately opened up a meeting of Presbyterians and Independents, and began boasting to the city's clergy that he now stood 'upon a levell with them' and would rather have 'the kindnesse of the Indulgence' than submit to the unreasonable terms of the Church of England, although the Bishop of Norwich believed that

Collins was 'not much to be regarded', since many of his erstwhile followers had deserted him and rejoined the Established Church.[104] In the west of England, meetings were soon 'very many and full', while elsewhere we learn how dissenters rushed to 'repair, beautify and adorn their meeting-houses with great diligence'.[105] One Welsh Baptist praised James as 'an instrument in God's hand to give us a lovely, likeable freedom by a strong unshakable declaration'.[106]

A total of 78 addresses came in from various nonconformist groups throughout England and Wales: 4 from Quakers; 8 from Baptists (or Anabaptists); 10 from Congregationalists; 11 from Presbyterians; 1 jointly from the Independents, Baptists and others of Gloucestershire; 43 from people who simply identified themselves as dissenters or nonconformists; and 1 from those who had been 'in Arms against your Majesty' (presumably Monmouth rebels).[107] The first to come in was in the name of the Anabaptists in and about London.[108] William Penn, by now a government agent, presented an address signed by about 800 London Quakers towards the end of April, and another a month later in the name of all 'Quakers in this Kingdom' agreed to by their yearly meeting, before then embarking on a preaching tour through England to promote the King's Indulgence.[109] James also secured the services of the Presbyterian divines Vincent Alsop and Thomas Rosewell, and the Independent Stephen Lobb, to act as agents to solicit addresses from dissenters in London by offering pardons for their previous offences. On Thursday 28 April, Rosewell presented an address in the name of the Presbyterian ministers of London, but only nine ministers subscribed. Two days later, Lobb presented an address from the Independents, signed again by just 9 ministers and about 140 laymen.[110] Employing a looseness in his use of rhetoric, which revealed that he did not quite get some of the basic points of English constitutionalism, James told the Presbyterian ministers who delivered their address 'that he hoped they now had a Magna Charta for the exercise of their religion, the same as there was for the preservation of every one's estate'.[111] Legal rights wrought from the crown and enshrined in a charter that was subsequently confirmed by parliament, it should go without saying, were clearly somewhat different from a liberty based on a declaration founded upon the royal prerogative!

Some of the addresses were a long time coming. Only forty-three had come in by mid-August; the dissenting ministers of Leicestershire did not present theirs until mid-December.[112] A few addresses were fulsome in their praise for what James had done. The dissenting ministers of west Somerset thanked James 'for the Liberty we enjoy by that Soveraign Act of Grace', and prayed that his reign might 'be long and prosperous' and 'the Glory of it' remembered 'to all Generations'.[113] The Norwich congregationalists claimed that, contrary to popular belief, they had always been in favour of monarchy, which they thought was 'the only ancient, legal, and rightful Government of this Nation' and also 'the best Government', adding – in an echo of the patriarchalist language deployed by Cavalier Anglicans under Charles II – that a king was the 'common Father of all his People' who cares 'for the good of all'.[114] The Presbyterians of both Norwich and Macclesfield embraced the idea of the divine right of kings by stating in their addresses that they also owed thanks to God, 'By Whom Kings Reign'.[115] Yet most nonconformist addresses were cautiously worded, and James was reportedly disappointed that the dissenters in general merely thanked him for granting them liberty, without declaring in favour of 'the Dispensing power'.[116]

It was the response of the Anglican clergy that proved most disappointing to the crown. On 20 April Sunderland informed the bishops of Durham, Rochester, Peterborough, Oxford and Chester 'it would be acceptable to the Court' if they made 'a Congratulatory Address' of thanks for the declaration, and particularly for the King's 'renewed assurance' to 'protect them in their Religion and Liberties', and produced a text to this effect for them to sign. The bishops of Durham, Oxford and Chester immediately agreed. Thomas Sprat of Rochester at first begged to be excused, though eventually he concurred. Thomas White of Peterborough openly condemned the Declaration, saying 'that he did not thinke the Church of England had received any advantage but a great prejudice by it' and predicted that none of the London clergy would sign. Indeed, most of the London clergy, 'both the Hierarchists, and the moderator sort', did refuse. The Bishop of Lincoln wanted to support the address, but the clergy of London wrote to his archdeacons and urged them not to concur. Cartwright of Chester, who owed his elevation to James and who was fully behind the King's policy, had problems getting his own clergy to fall in line. One protested that rather than protecting the Church, the King had 'let loose all our enemies upon us'; another 'that he would never thank the King for breaking the Lawes'. Even when the four bishops redrafted the address, so that it gave thanks only for the promise to protect the Church, the London clergy still refused to sign.[117]

With it being impossible to secure the support of the Church as a whole, the bishops in favour of addressing had no option but to go their separate ways. When Parker of Oxford tried to promote his own address, all but one of his clergy refused to sign. They spelled out their reasons in a detailed paper, which circulated in manuscript. Thanking the King for continuing them in their possessions, they insisted, was 'but our Thanks for his Majestie's continuing our Legal Rights: which either equally concerns all States of Men in the Kingdom, and ought properly be considered in parliament; or else it supposeth our possessions less Legal, and more arbitrary, than other Subjects'. As for the King's promise to maintain them in 'the free Exercise of our Religion', they continued, this 'necessarily heards us among the various Sects under Toleration . . . depending for protection upon no legal Establishment, but entirely upon soverain pleasure and Indulgence, which at pleasure is revocable'. And why should the clergy give thanks to the King for abrogating the laws for the dissenters' sake, laws which, they opined, 'perhaps cannot be repealed'.[118]

Of the five bishops Sunderland had initially approached, only two – Durham and Chester – presented addresses from their diocesan clergy. The King received that from Durham at the end of May, but was clearly disappointed, saying he expected it 'sooner' and to be 'much fuller'.[119] The dioceses of Coventry and Lichfield, Lincoln and St David's also produced addresses of thanks, as did the dean and chapter of the collegiate church of Ripon, making a grand total of six from the Anglican clergy (or seven if we include an address from the magistrates and clergy of the Isle of Guernsey, delivered in February 1688).[120] As one pamphleteer later complained, 'scarce any' of the Church of England men 'could find in [their] hearts to thank the King at all', and 'those Few' that did, 'proceeded so Awkwardly in their Acknowledgements', as to thank the King not 'for the Main Scope of

His Healing Declaration', but only for that part relating to the Church, so as to render the addresses 'of very little value'.[121]

Eighty-eight addresses were presented in the name of counties, grand juries, towns, corporations or local inhabitants. Certainly some groups were willing to offer the sort of fulsome thanks that must have pleased the government. The lawyers of the Middle Temple thought they had particular reason to thank the King for the honour he had done them in asserting his royal prerogatives, which were 'the very life of the Law, and our own Profession' and 'must always remain entire', since they 'were given by God himself'.[122] L'Estrange was a notable enthusiast, proclaiming at a specially convened meeting at Sam's coffee house in London on 7 May that 'we Loyall men of the Church of England did alwayes acknowledge and aver the King to be above the Laws' and exhorting those present to sign a congratulatory address.[123] A closer examination of this category of addresses, however, reveals deep divisions in many communities over the Indulgence. In Devon, a JP by the name of Bear, 'a most fervent man for delivering up of Charters and encourageing Informers' under Charles II, proposed at the county sessions that 'the high loyall Church of England-men' should deliver a congratulatory address, but the local JPs were divided in their response; those that opposed the idea withdrew, leaving those who remained to draw up an address.[124] At Bath, the high steward, mayor, aldermen and capital citizens drew up a cautiously worded address, which started by reminding James that they had given him thanks at his accession for his promise to protect their religion, rights and properties and had defended the city against the Monmouth rebellion, before going on to thank the King again not only for his 'Gracious Favour to us for the enjoying our Religion', but also for his 'Mercy, Clemency and Goodness in pardoning [his] greatest Enemies', in the hope that this might 'cure their distracted Minds'. At the same time, several members of the corporation and other freemen and inhabitants presented a more fulsome address, in which they expressed a desire to cast themselves at the King's sacred feet 'with all the Dutifull and Loyal deference unto Your Royal Pleasure, and undoubted Prerogative in publishing Your late Gracious Declaration'.[125] In a number of towns and boroughs, local inhabitants drew up their own addresses because the corporation itself failed to do so. Thus the Gloucester address was delivered in the name of several of the aldermen, common councilmen, gentlemen and burgesses, on behalf on themselves and several hundred freemen of the city, while that from Coventry came from the citizens and inhabitants.[126]

Some local leaders tried to avoid subscribing without appearing to be against the idea of addressing. When asked by the high sheriff of Yorkshire if he would help frame and present an address from the 'Church of England Gentlemen' of the county, Reresby claimed that he was so tied up with the King's business that he would be late getting to the York assizes, where the matter was being discussed. As it turned out, very few of the local gentry made it to the assizes, and those who did were not inclined to comply with the sheriff. Some Catholics and a few Protestants who had special reasons to give thanks (presumably nonconformists) did suggest framing an address from the grand jury, but they could not agree on the wording. In the end, no address came from Yorkshire at this time, and Reresby, who finally did make it to the assizes, managed to emerge blameless.[127] Others had the courage of their convictions. The sub-recorder of Exeter, a man who under Charles II had been very active in promoting anti-Whig addresses, was removed from office for speaking 'very unmannerly and scandalously of his Majesties Declaration and Addresses'.[128] Exeter, for the time being, declined to address. The mayor and the recorder led the opposition to addressing in Totnes; the former was discharged, the latter suspended.[129] The corporation of Leicester decided by a vote of thirty-five to nineteen to reject a proposed address, even after the mayor had modified the wording suggested by the town's absentee recorder, the Earl of Huntingdon, in the hope of making it more acceptable. The sticking point was over the inclusion of any reference to the Indulgence: a majority would have been willing to support an address 'with Relation only to the Church of England', but Huntingdon's man on the ground feared that this would 'not find a good acceptance from the King'.[130]

The Lord Mayor and aldermen of London did send in an address of thanks in October, but only because the government had removed seven Tory aldermen that summer for opposing an address, replacing them with Whigs, and appointed a nonconformist lord mayor, Sir

John Shorter.[131] Indeed, it was not until after James had conducted a further purge of local office-holders in late 1687 and early 1688 that some communities could be induced to thank the crown for the Indulgence. The corporation of Gloucester finally delivered an address in January 1688, following a purge the previous November.[132] The grand inquest for Staffordshire did not draw up their address until 3 April 1688, but insisted that such 'lateness' should 'not be attributed to want of Loyalty', since this was 'the first opportunity the Body of the County could be prevailed on, having hitherto been detained from Paying its Duty by an over-ruling Party among us'. The address went on to thank the King for his 'Indulgent Distribution of [his] Dispensing Power'.[133] The mayor, aldermen, bailiffs and citizens of Carlisle drew up their address in April 1688, 'being now at Liberty, by the late Regulation made here', to offer their 'late, but unfeigned Thanks'. Thanks to the late regulation, it should be pointed out, the mayor of Carlisle was now a Catholic.[134] It took two purges – in November 1687 and February 1688 – before the corporation of Banbury agreed to address on 22 February 1688; there had been an address from Banbury the previous September, but without official backing, having been delivered simply in the name of the freemen of the borough.[135] Similarly, it took a series of purges from the summer of 1687 to the spring of 1688 to induce Scarborough and Totnes to address, which they eventually agreed to do in late April 1688.[136] The mayor, aldermen, bailiffs and burgesses of Newcastle under Lyme addressed twice: the first in June 1687, giving thanks for James's promise to protect the Church of England and expressing the hope that the King would find as 'much Faith and Sincerity' from those whom the toleration benefited; the second in January 1688, following a purge the previous month, proclaiming that the Indulgence had 'fully answered us in the desires of our Heart' and promising to endeavour to return MPs who would support a parliamentary repeal of the penal laws.[137]

A further twenty-six addresses were presented in the names of particular trading interests across the kingdom – nineteen from London livery companies,[138] plus others from the master builders and related traders and craftsmen in and about London, the clothiers of Stroud-Water (Gloucestershire) and Worcester, the goldsmiths of Hull, the seamen of Hull, the merchants of Exeter, and the serge manufacturers of Taunton. The last rejoiced that James had freed them 'from the rapacious Hands of those that made a Prey of our very Labour, and raised their own private Fortunes on that which should have fed our Wives and Children', and predicted that now the interest of parties had been 'laid aside, the Common Interest, Trade and Safety of the Nation may be advanc'd and promoted by All'.[139] The numbers were hardly overwhelming; indeed, those from the London livery companies came only as a result of government-orchestrated purges.

THE ATTACK ON THE ANGLICAN MONOPOLY OF EDUCATION

In order to provide more Catholic priests and encourage further conversions, James needed to break the Anglican monopoly of education. He thought it unfair, as a matter of principle, that Catholics should be denied access to public schools and universities, but he also appeared to believe that the mere presence of Catholics would encourage secret sympathizers at such institutions openly to acknowledge their preference for Catholicism and that the open debate that would ensue between Protestants and Catholics would convince others of the merits of converting.[140] At every step of the way, however, he met opposition from Tory-Anglican interests who believed that the King was acting in violation of the law and that they were bound not to assist the King in his illegal acts.

In January 1687 James recommended to the governors of Charterhouse that they elect a Catholic to a scholarship, and Lord Chancellor Jeffreys produced a royal dispensation on the young man's behalf. However, most of the governors, spearheaded by the Earl of Danby, and backed by Ormonde, Halifax and Archbishop Sancroft, refused to countenance the election; Danby even stated that he thought 'the power of Dispenceing . . . to be illegal', and that he found the judges' opinion in Godden v. Hales 'to be thought unwarrantable by the Lawes of England, and by the generallity of the best Lawyers'.[141] In this case, the school governors successfully stood their ground.

James proved more determined with regard to the universities, though he ran into the same kind of difficulties. In March 1686 he granted dispensations to four Oxford academics who had converted to Catholicism (Dr Obadiah Walker and two other fellows of University College and a fellow of Brasenose) so that they would not have to resign their fellowships.[142] James made a bolder move the following October, when he appointed the 'popishly-affected' John Massey, a client of Walker's, to the vacant position of Dean of Christ Church, Oxford, and dispensed him from coming to prayers, receiving the sacrament, taking all oaths, and performing the religious duties normally required of the dean. Nevertheless, the right to appoint the dean was in the gift of the crown, and Massey might not have been a declared Catholic at the time of his appointment (though he was certainly regarded as one by early 1687).[143]

James was on more controversial ground when he decided to appoint Joshua Bassett, a Catholic convert, master of Sidney Sussex College, Cambridge, in January 1687. The Duke of Albemarle, as chancellor of the university, wrote to the King and asked him to allow the college to choose their own master, as his royal predecessors had done, informing him that the fellows were obliged by their statutes, upon oath, to choose a Protestant of the Established Church. James replied that he had already given his mandate to Bassett and could not revoke it. When Bassett came to be admitted at the end of the month, the fellows accepted his mandate and dispensation, but another impediment soon emerged. Sidney Sussex had been an Elizabethan foundation, and by the terms of its statues the fellows were sworn to admit no one as master unless he took an oath promising to uphold the true religion against papistry. Since Bassett had no dispensation from this oath, the fellows decided they could not admit him. The case dragged on, and in March some of the fellows presented a petition to the King asking him 'to withdraw his commands because they were against the Colledge statutes'. The fellows were summoned before the Ecclesiastical Commission and they eventually backed down.[144]

In February 1687 James sent a mandate to the vice-chancellor of Cambridge, Dr John Peachell, to admit Father Alban Francis, a Benedictine monk, to an MA, and another Catholic to the degree of

Doctor of Physic, without administering any oaths. Peachell called a special congregation of the heads of house, where all but three agreed it would be 'utterly inconsistent with their oaths and with the statutes of the University' to comply with the King's request. James reissued his mandate; the vice-chancellor again refused to admit the pair, having been informed by two prominent jurists, Sir Francis Pemberton and Heneage Finch, that the King's mandate could have no effect and that the admitter could be fined for breach of trust if he violated the acts of parliament stipulating the oaths. The vice-chancellor and eight specially elected deputies of the University were therefore summoned to appear before the Ecclesiastical Commission that spring, where they protested that they were bound by their oaths, under penalty of law, to administer the oaths of allegiance and supremacy and the Test to all graduates, and challenged the right of the Ecclesiastical Commission to hear their case on the grounds that all such courts had been abolished in 1641. The commissioners decided to make an example of Peachell and deprived him of all his offices and benefices, though James let the deputies off the hook, for fear of turning them into martyrs.[145]

James's most controversial step was his attack on Magdalen College, the richest college in Oxford. On the death of its president at the end of March 1687, James decided to seek the election of a crypto-Catholic, Anthony Farmer. However, the right of election lay in the College and by the terms of the College statues the fellows were obliged to chose a Protestant of good character who had at one time held a fellowship either at Magdalen or at New College. Although he had yet to declare himself a Catholic, Farmer associated himself with known Catholics in the university (such as Dr Obadiah Walker) and the fellows suspected he was no longer an Anglican. Nor did he meet the fellowship requirement. He was also a notorious drunkard and womanizer, having been known to make women 'Dance naked before him'; on one occasion, it emerged, he had 'Kisst . . . and tongu'd' a woman, on another he had 'putt his hands under a Faire Ladye's Coates'. On hearing of James's intention, the fellows petitioned the King (on 9 April) to inform him that Farmer was unqualified, and asked that James either let them make their own choice or recommend a more suitable candidate. Two days later, however, the fellows received a mandate from the King (dated 5 April) requiring them to elect Farmer forthwith and dispensing him from any statutes or customs barring his election. The fellows assumed that the King had been misinformed both about Farmer and of his own rights to dispose of the presidency, and since the College statutes required that a new election be made within fifteen days, in default of an answer to their own petition they proceeded on 15 April to elect Mr John Hough, an existing fellow.[146]

James was furious and instructed the Ecclesiastical Commission to proceed against the fellows. The case was heard in June. In their written plea, the fellows explained that their college statutes and oaths not only obliged them to elect a duly qualified person but also forbade them from consenting to any dispensation. They further pointed out that the King had no right to require them to elect Farmer, since 'the right of Election' was 'in themselves'. Having deferred the election to the last day possible, to give the King a chance to recommend a duly qualified person, they at last elected Hough, in accordance with the procedures outlined in their statues. The commissioners determined that Hough's election was void, though even they had to accept that Farmer was ineligible, especially once their own enquiries revealed him to be 'a very bad man'.[147]

On 14 August James therefore issued another mandate, with the same dispensation as the last, this time requiring the fellows to elect Bishop Parker of Oxford as president, even though Parker had also never held a fellowship at Magdalen or New College. The fellows persisted, however, in maintaining that Hough's election was valid. James visited Oxford on 4 September and ordered the fellows to admit the bishop; the fellows replied that although 'they were as ready to obey his Majesty in all things that lay in their power . . . the Electing of the Bishop of Oxford being directly contrary to their Statutes, and to the positive Oaths they had taken, they could not apprehend it in their power to obey him in this matter'. As the vice-chancellor of the university pointed out to the King the next day, if they did the fellows would be guilty of 'the heinous sin of perjury': 'We must observe our Statutes, being obliged thereunto by Oath', which 'no power under heaven can dispense with'. In mid-October the King appointed a commission, headed by Bishop Cartwright of

Chester, to carry out a visitation of the College; all but three of the fellows persisted in their refusal to recognize Parker as their president, and were deprived of their fellowships. James appointed a number of Catholics as their replacements.[148]

The Magdalen College affair again raised the issue of the scope of the dispensing power. Government propagandists, naturally, insisted that the fellows should have obeyed the King's mandate to elect the Bishop of Oxford, on the reasoning that the dispensation took away the force of the College statutes and freed them from their oath to make an election in accordance with them.[149] Yet the ruling in Godden v. Hales had made it clear that the king's dispensing power applied only to *mala prohibita* (and only then when the dispensation did not intrude on the rights of a third party); perjury was *malum in se*, a crime against God, and therefore no king could dispense his subjects from the obligation to keep their solemnly sworn oaths. Revealingly, even Lord Chief Justice Herbert, the man who had given the ruling in Godden v. Hales, believed that the royal dispensation in the Magdalen College affair was invalid, 'because there was a particular Right and Interest vested in the Members of that Colledge . . . of Choosing their own Head'.[150]

The residents of Oxford were far from pleased with James's efforts to Catholicize the university. When Walker first started holding mass at University College, in the late summer of 1686, a crowd of people assembled outside the College gates making 'cries and shouts' to disrupt the service, until some of the soldiers who were attending mass came out to disperse them. On other occasions Walker (soon nicknamed 'Obadiah Ave-Maria') found his chapel invaded by Protestant scholars, who protested when he threw them out: 'wee do not keep you out of our Chapels and Churches . . . why should you from yours?' In late July 1688 a boy turned up at Walker's chapel with a cat under his coat, which he proceeded to pinch and pull by the tail during the service so the cat produced 'such an untunable noise' that it created 'some disorder', until the celebrants realized what was going on and chased the youth out of the building. When the vice-president of Magdalen, Dr Robert Charnock, announced in January 1688 that mass would now be said in chapel, the local townsfolk began turning up on Sundays in larger numbers than usual to try to prevent it. In this they had the support of the College's president, the Bishop of Oxford. It was not until Parker's death in March and his replacement as president by the popish titular bishop Dr Bonaventure Gifford that Charnock was able to secure Magdalen chapel for Catholic worship. Determined not to let the Catholics have an easy ride, the Protestant men and women of the town would turn up at mass 'to grin and sneare'. The Catholic fellows found that when out in the town the students would pull faces at them and call them 'ill names'; in hall, the students would sit with their hats on as an act of defiance and then drink healths to the confusion of the Pope after the fellows had left high table.[151]

THE CAMPAIGN TO PACK PARLIAMENT

By the summer of 1687 James finally reached the conclusion that it would be impossible to secure the repeal of the penal laws and the Tests from his present parliament. He therefore issued a proclamation dissolving parliament on 2 July[152] and set about trying to secure the return of one that would be favourable to his wishes. To gauge the mood of the country, he made another progress, this time through the West Midlands, leaving Windsor on 16 August, travelling to Portsmouth, Bath, Gloucester, Worcester, Ludlow, Shrewsbury, Whitchurch, and on up to Chester, then returning via Newport, Lichfield, Coventry, Banbury, Oxford and Cirencester before ending back at Bath on 6 September. The London Gazette predictably portrayed the progress as a great success, charting the enthusiastic reception James received wherever he went.[153] Local accounts confirm that the royal visit provided an occasion for festive display and general merriment. At Coventry, for example, the King was treated to a splendid civic reception, the locals were out in force to cheer him as he processed through the city, and the night of his stay saw bonfires 'through the wholl Citie'.[154] Nevertheless, some local observers sensed that all was not as it should have been. At Oxford, both the University and the corporation laid on an elaborate reception, and when the King entered town 'all the streets . . . were most infinitely crowded with all sorts of people, and all windows fild with faces, who made great acclamations and shouts'; Anthony Wood noted ominously, however, that there were no cries of 'Vivat Rex', or long live the king, 'as the antient manner was'. At Banbury James was assailed by a mastiff dog as he progressed through the streets; the King drew a pistol and shot the animal dead, but the noise of the gunshot so startled the Earl of Abingdon's horse that it threw its rider to the ground, leaving the Earl seriously hurt. The episode has an air of farce about it; certainly it must have detracted from the dignity of the occasion.[155]

James used the tour to promote the benefits of his toleration to local leaders and to make the case for a parliamentary repeal of the penal laws and Tests. In this he thought he had been successful: as the Jacobite Life put it, 'the kind and affable reception' the gentry afforded him convinced him that he 'had gain'd in some manner upon their stubborn temper', while 'the awful presence of a Sovereign imposed such veneration upon the generality of the people where he pass'd, that their joyfull acclamations and dutifull acknowlidgments seem'd to be pledg's of their complyance'.[156] The progress did prompt the submission of more addresses of thanks for the Indulgence, some of which combined promises to seek the return of MPs who would support toleration in parliament: of the 33 addresses that came in during the period from 16 August to 17 September, 18 were the result of pressures brought to bear during the King's progress.[157] Some places, however, resisted all pressure to address. Of the 15 major towns and cities James visited, 3 (Chester, Coventry and Gloucester) had presented some form of address prior to the progress; 8 (Bristol, Cirencester, Lichfield, Newport, Oxford, Shrewsbury, Whitchurch and Worcester) were never to present any address; 1 (Portsmouth) did not address until the new year, following further purges of the corporations; leaving only 3 (Banbury, Bath and Ludlow) who presented some form of address that could be said to have been prompted by the royal progress. Halifax thought the progress did not give James 'any great encouragement' with regard to his schemes for toleration, since it had 'grown into a point of honour, universally received by the nation, not to change their opinion'.[158]

To obtain a detailed assessment of the degree of support that existed for a parliamentary toleration, James decided at the end of October 1687 to carry out an extensive poll of all holders of court office, members of the recently dissolved parliament, JPs, deputy Lieutenants, office-holders in the corporations, members of the London livery companies and other minor officials. Three standard questions were to be put to each individual: would they support the repeal of the penal laws and Tests, if elected to parliament; would they help secure the return of MPs who would support a repeal; and would they support the Indulgence by living in peace with those of all religious persuasions? The task of polling the county and urban magistracy fell to the Lord Lieutenants, yet despite a purge of the lieutenancy that summer, many proved far from enthusiastic about carrying out the poll, and either dragged their feet or put their questions in such a way as to discourage positive answers. Further dismissals followed in the autumn and winter: by March 1688, 19 new men had been appointed, 13 of whom were Roman Catholics, and only 14 from the previous summer had managed to retain their posts. When the answers eventually started coming in – and some areas were very late in reporting back – they were far from encouraging. Most of those polled had no trouble promising to live in peace with those of different religious persuasions, but many of the replies to the first two questions were evasive, qualified, or even hostile. All told, just under 27 per cent of the JPs polled answered 'yes' to the repeal of the penal laws and Tests (though this figure includes Catholics), just over 27 per cent 'no', 28 per cent expressed doubts or reservations, while 18 per cent were absent when the poll was being conducted in their area or else had no answer recorded. If we restrict ourselves to the Protestants polled, we find that just over 16 per cent answered 'yes' and nearly 34 per cent 'no'.[159]

Contemporaries recognized that the poll had been a major public relations disaster, so general and so public had the 'non-concurrence' been.[160] 'Before this Inquiry', the Imperial ambassador wrote in April 1688, 'everyone suspected his neighbour of being a partisan of the King and people suppressed their disaffection, which now they express without fear'.[161] Moreover, the results were perhaps predictable, given the fact that most local office-holders were still Tory Anglicans. James now embarked on a wholescale purge of local office-holders. At the end of 1687, a board of regulators set about considering the county commissions of the peace. By late July 1688 all but five counties in England and Wales had received new commissions, with Catholics, dissenters and former Whigs replacing those who had been unwilling to commit themselves to James's scheme for toleration. One third of the deputy Lieutenants and one fifth of the JPs were now Catholics – an extraordinary number, given the small proportion of the population of England and Wales who were of the Catholic faith, and which had been achieved only by including those whose social status would not normally have entitled them to a position on the bench. It was the Anglican squires who lost out: some three-quarters of those who had been JPs in 1685 were no longer on the bench.[162] The Lord Lieutenants, their deputies and the local JPs normally carried considerable electoral influence, especially if they came from the traditional shire elite. Yet James's newly appointed men scarcely possessed the prestige and local standing necessary to carry the shires on behalf of the crown, which were, in any case, notoriously difficult to control, given the size of their electorates.

James realized that his best chance of securing a compliant parliament lay in gaining control over the urban electorate. He began with London. Having intruded a nonconformist Lord Mayor, Sir John Shorter, in August 1687, in September and October he carried out a purge of the London livery companies (who comprised the City's electorate). This resulted in the dismissal of 17 masters, 58 wardens, 79 assistants and 1,795 liverymen, including most of 'the violent tories'; James replaced them with those removed during the remodelling of 1684–5, among them many dissenters, who were given dispensations from the requisite oaths. Even so, the remodelling did not meet expectations, and James needed to undertake a second purge in February 1688, when he dismissed a further 8 masters, 15 wardens, 194 assistants and 656 liverymen, replacing them with 328 named individuals known to be willing to comply with the royal agenda. Still, the campaign was far from an overwhelming success. As noted early, only nineteen City livery companies ended up delivering addresses of thanks for James's first Declaration of Indulgence – out of a total of eighty-four![163]

In November 1687 James established a committee to regulate the corporations, with the aim of removing obstinate local officials and replacing them with his own nominees.[164] Under the terms of the new charters granted under Charles II during the years of the Tory Reaction, the crown did have the right to order removals; it could, however, only suggest replacements and hope that corporations would comply. A body of local 'regulators' was set up under the supervision of the Catholic lawyer Robert Brent to supply the necessary information, carry out the purges, and recruit appropriate replacements.[165] Over the next several months, the crown sent dismissal orders to 103 towns, about half of those incorporated, resulting in the removal of over three-quarters of the members of these corporations. At Bridport, Evesham, Exeter, Nottingham, Saffron Walden and Totnes, the entire corporation was ousted. The crown did not always get it right the first time: 67 of the 103 towns required additional purges, some as many as 5 in total. Indeed, James often found it difficult to obtain the type of corporate membership he desired. Sometimes the removals were never carried out. When they were, those nominated as replacements might choose to decline the offer, or else accept and prove less compliant than anticipated. Some corporations simply failed to install James's nominees. The corporation of York dutifully dismissed its mayor and various other members, but those who remained then protested that they could not elect the King's nominees because these nominees were not freemen and that since York now had no mayor there was no one who could confer the freedom of the city upon them.[166] Hence James found it necessary, like his brother before him, to have recourse to the ultimate threat of *quo warranto* proceedings to bring the more obstreperous corporations into line. *Quo warranto*s were threatened against some seventy English and Welsh corporations: most quickly capitulated, though twenty-five showed themselves prepared to suffer a corporate death at the hands of the law. Between March and September 1688 some thirty-five new charters were granted, containing two new provisions: a royal power not only to remove but also to appoint (rather than just nominate) members; and a *non obstante* clause dispensing all present and future members from taking the oaths of allegiance and supremacy or subscribing the declaration against the covenant. On occasion, James forcibly billeted troops on recalcitrant corporations, in order to force them to comply with his wishes.[167] A few corporations, notably Winchester and Oxford, were dissolved without being reincorporated, their governments being placed under special royal commissions. The main beneficiaries of the attack on the corporations were Catholics, dissenters and occasional conformists. At Chichester, in February 1688, the reconstructed city council unanimously agreed a resolution that 'all the Members' might 'keep on their hats' during meetings, testifying to the fact that many of the new councillors were Quakers.[168] The principal victims were the Church of England men.

Those Protestant nonconformists and erstwhile proponents of Exclusion who now appeared willing to work with James II have usually been styled 'Whig collaborators'. The term, however, needs to be treated with care. After years of political exclusion and religious persecution, many nonconformists and former Whigs were prepared to avail themselves of James's reforms; how far they were prepared to go in backing James's agenda, however, or the extent to which they were fully committed collaborators, varied considerably from individual to individual. Some cooperated with James only because he had some hold over them. The most infamous example is Sir William Williams, the former Whig speaker of the Commons who became James's Solicitor-General in December 1687: Williams had been fined £10,000 in 1686 for having licensed in 1680 (at the bidding of the Commons) the publication of Thomas Dangerfield's narrative of the Popish Plot, and was facing a separate action brought by the Earl of Peterborough for *scandalum magnatum* in respect of the same publication. James ordered Peterborough to drop the suit and also remitted the remaining £2,000 of the fine that Williams had yet to pay. Pardoned Rye House plotters or Monmouth rebels often felt that they had no option but to appear to back James, the best-known individuals in this category being John Hampden and John Trenchard, who cooperated with James as little as they dared and were quick to go over to William of Orange in late 1688. Other Whig collaborators were men who were so committed to the cause of religious freedom that the genuineness of their support for the King's tolerationist stance cannot be doubted. Here we can include William Penn and the Whig propagandist Henry Care. Yet there were many who occupied an uncomfortable and ill-defined middle ground, uneasy about James's ultimate goals but well aware that for the time being they would be foolish to reject what was now on offer. They revealed their hesitancy in various ways. Notable London nonconformist Sir John Shorter accepted James's nomination to be Lord Mayor in 1687, but when he came to assume his office he insisted on taking all the oaths and Tests required by law, even to the point of taking the Anglican sacrament. It was a gesture that gave the government 'some offence', it was reported, 'it being a distrust of the King's favour and encourageing that which his Majesties whole Endeavours' were intended 'to disannull'.[169]

CONCLUSION

In his efforts to help his co-religionists, James asserted his prerogative above the law and acted in ways which his subjects at the time believed to be illegal. Those Whigs who had predicted during the Exclusion Crisis that a Catholic ruler would mean popery and arbitrary government might have had good cause to feel that they had been proven right, after three years of a Catholic king on the throne. James built up a standing army, gave Catholics dispensations from the Test Acts to enable them to hold office, suspended the entire operation of all the penal laws, broke the Anglican monopoly of worship and education as well as of office, and set about trying to put pliant men in place at all levels of the central and local administration and to obtain a packed parliament that would offer no opposition to his will. Moreover, his defenders justified what he was doing on the grounds that he was a sovereign, imperial prince who enjoyed absolute power. This is perhaps not quite the same thing as saying that James had a blueprint for establishing royal absolutism in England. Initially, James had shown that he wanted to work through parliament and the traditional rulers in the localities. It was only as it gradually became apparent that he would not be able to do so that he embarked on a plan to make himself independent of any central and local institutional or informal checks on his power. However, such independence from central or local checks on their power was, of course, precisely what continental absolute monarchs sought to achieve. James's initiatives, therefore, did result in moving the English monarchy in a more absolutist direction. To all intents and purposes, James did try to establish Catholic absolutism in England. And not just in England. The same was true, as we have seen, in Ireland and Scotland, but in an even more transparent way.

Any self-respecting Whig, then, might well have felt entitled to have said, 'I told you so.' But the simple fact of the matter is that – besides the Catholics – it was the Whigs and dissenters who gained most from James's reforms. It was the traditional supporters of the later-Stuart monarchy, in all three of the kingdoms, whom James upset the most, namely the Tory Anglicans in England and the Protestants of the Established Church in both Scotland and Ireland. Many had openly condemned James's initiatives and even done their best to frustrate them through appeal to the law or by various acts of non-compliance. James had not had a smooth ride, by any means; nevertheless, he had managed, just about, to get most of what he wanted. The question was, what would – or could – his Protestant subjects in England, Scotland and Ireland do to try to stop him? It is to a consideration of this question that we now need to turn.

PART TWO

Revolutions in Three Kingdoms, 1688–91

6

Yielding an Active Obedience Only According to Law

You have made a turd pye, Seasoned it with passive obedience,
and now you must eat it your Selves.

Lady Harvey, in conversation with 'several bishops',
November 1686[1]

Though of Passive Obedience we talk like the best,
'Tis prudence, when interest sways, to resist.

'The Clerical Cabal' (1688)[2]

It is a Maxime in our Law, That the King can do no wrong;
and therefore if any wrong be done, the Crime and Guilt is the
Minister's who does it; for the Laws are the King's publick
Will, and therefore he is never supposed to command any
thing contrary to Law.

[William Sherlock], *A Letter from a Clergy-Man in the City,*
To his Friend in the Country, Containing his Reasons For
not Reading the Declaration (1688), p. 2

By the early months of 1688 it seemed to many British Protestants that their worst fears of popery and arbitrary government were becoming a reality. For the time being, they could hold on to the hope that better days would come when James was eventually succeeded by his Protestant daughter, Mary, the wife of William of Orange. This changed, however, when the Queen gave birth to a son in June 1688, giving rise to the prospect of a never-ending succession of Catholic Stuart monarchs. Ultimately the Protestants' deliverance was to be secured by the invasion of England by William of Orange from the Low Countries, who succeeded in ousting James II and thereby precipitating what turned out to be three very different revolutions in each of the three kingdoms.

Part two of this book will examine the causes of the revolutions of 1688–9 and their respective outcomes. The nature of the settlements that were to be worked out in the aftermath of the dynastic coup during the winter of 1688/9 will be the subject of subsequent chapters. In this chapter and the next we shall examine the reasons for James's downfall, focusing on England. Most historians have seen the Glorious Revolution in England as being instigated from above, not from below. Indeed, there has been a trend in recent years to insist that it was essentially the result of a foreign invasion, led by William of Orange; on that reasoning, it was brought about not only from above, but also from outside.[3] Certainly, no one can deny the crucial role played by William of Orange; in order to appreciate why events transpired in the way they did, we need to understand both why he decided to intervene and how it was possible for him to do so, and the answers to these questions need to be sought (in part) in the United Provinces. But to claim that the Revolution came essentially from above and was the result of external factors is seriously misleading. James faced obstruction, opposition and even resistance to his initiatives from broad cross-sections of his people, and by the late summer of 1688 his regime was already in crisis. William was able to conquer England without having to fight a major battle. It was not that he shattered James's power and destroyed his considerable military might; rather, he found James's power already shattered and did not encounter any considerable military might that needed to be destroyed. In the end, James fled without putting up much resistance. Thus to understand why the Revolution happened, we have to explain not just why James deserted England but why his English subjects deserted him, and this puts the focus back on England itself and also takes us beyond the confines of the royal family or the court. In short, developments within England, from below, played a crucial role in James's fall and the eventual success of a revolution that was never simply dynastic or the result of a foreign invasion.

If this is the case, we are left with a number of important questions.

As we have seen, those who were most upset with James's initiatives were Protestants of the Established Church, and yet, as such, they believed in the principles of non-resistance. Did the people of England *actively* resist James II (as opposed merely to engaging in acts of passive resistance), and if so, what forms did this resistance take and how was such resistance justified? How could Tory Anglicans, in particular, loosen their attachment to the traditional teachings of the Church to a sufficient degree to be able to take the type of action they did against James II in all good conscience? Was it only Tory Anglicans who opposed James, or did they manage to persuade Whigs and nonconformists to join with them – and again, if so, how did they achieve this, given that Anglicans and nonconformists had hardly been the best of friends since the Restoration and that Whigs and non-conformists were among the chief beneficiaries of James's reforms? What did those who stood up against James achieve? Did they merely succeed in creating enough instability in England to ensure that William's invasion was likely to succeed, or did they manage largely to defeat James's political and religious agenda prior to William's invasion (helping to bring about a revolution before the actual Revolution, if you like)? And what precisely transpired when William landed: did William merely instigate a peaceful palace coup, or was there a genuinely revolutionary crisis in England in late 1688 that negates any view of the Glorious Revolution as a non-violent and largely non-revolutionary affair?

The present chapter will develop the story up until the birth of the Prince of Wales and the letter sent to William of Orange by the 'Immortal Seven' in the summer of 1688, inviting the Prince to invade England. It will begin by exploring how Anglican apologists justified the types of acts of resistance against James in which they had engaged, before proceeding to analyse how Anglicans sought to appeal to dissenters to stop them supporting James's efforts to undermine the legal security of the Protestant establishment through the use of his royal prerogative. It will then discuss James's fateful decision to reissue his Declaration of Indulgence in April 1688 and the opposition this generated from the Anglican clerical leadership, resulting in the trial – and ultimate acquittal – of seven bishops in June for their stance against the royal suspending power. It will conclude by looking at how the birth of the Prince of Wales fundamentally altered the dynamic of the crisis by putting paid to the strategy of sitting things out until James was eventually succeeded by his Protestant daughter: the presence of a Catholic heir necessitated more drastic measures. Throughout, emphasis will be placed on the crucial role of the Anglican interest, and especially the clerical establishment, in standing up against James's initiatives, although ultimately they were able to carry most of the Protestant dissenters with them. The next chapter will look at the invasion itself and the revolutionary crisis of late 1688 that caused James II to desert his realms.

EATING A TURD PIE — THE CHURCH, THE LAW AND THE DISSENTERS

We have seen that in the face of opposition from the traditional allies of the crown the court began to woo Protestant nonconformists in the hope of forging an alliance between Catholics and dissenters around a shared goal of religious toleration. For Anglican opponents of James, it became essential to break this alliance, and to persuade the dissenters that their interests would be better served by forming a common Protestant front with the Established Church in the face of the Catholic menace. They faced two major intellectual problems: how to justify opposing James's initiatives in a way that could appear consistent with their professed commitment to the principles of non-resistance and passive obedience; and how to convince the dissenters that, despite the Church's track record of religious intolerance, they would ultimately prove better friends to dissent than the Catholics. Court apologists, on the other hand, needed to prevent any wavering of support from the Protestant nonconformists and to discredit those Tory Anglicans who refused to comply with the King, though without alienating any remaining Anglican sympathizers if possible.

James was taken aback by the reaction of Tory Anglicans to his initiatives, since he believed that their views on obedience and the unaccountability of the sovereign would result in their total compliance. Even the most ardent champions of irresistible, divine-right monarchy, however, allowed that there were some limits to obedience.

To appreciate the logic behind Tory-Anglican non-compliance, we have to be clear about two key doctrines: the doctrine of passive obedience, and the maxim that the king could do no wrong. Although one was supposed to 'yield obedience' to the king 'in all Things' that were 'agreeable to God's Commands',[4] the Church had always held that if the king commanded something that was contrary to God's law, one had to obey God rather than man.[5] One should not commit an immoral act even if commanded to do so by the king. Nor should one violate one's oaths – since perjury was a sin as well as a crime – or go against one's conscience. Nevertheless, one could not resist the king, and one had to accept whatever punishment was meted out for non-compliance. Thus the fellows of Magdalen College had no option but to stand up to James II, but they also accepted the consequences, namely ejection from their fellowships. This was a classic example of the application of the principle of passive obedience, although in modern-day parlance it might more accurately be styled passive disobedience.

Yet what if the sovereign asked you to do something that was against the positive law of the land, though not necessarily against God's law? Or if the king himself promoted an illegal act and it was your responsibility, by dint of the office you held, to see that the law was enforced? It was a fundamental maxim of English law that the king could do no wrong. What this meant, however, was that the law knew no means of holding the king accountable for any wrong that he committed: it was impossible to sue or prosecute the king. It did not mean that nothing that the king ever did could be wrong (or that the crown could not commit an illegal act); it meant that if any wrong were done in the name of the king, it was those who had advised him or acted in his name who were accountable. As one contributor to the pamphlet debate over the Indulgence pointed out, rehearsing the arguments of William Sherlock's famous tract on non-resistance of 1684, although the king was 'not bound in his own person to observe the Laws as Subjects are, because no body has any jurisdiction over him but himself', in a limited monarchy such as England's, subjects were 'bound to yield an active obedience only according to Law'. Indeed, it was 'very dangerous', this author contended (quoting Sherlock), 'for any Subject to serve his Prince contrary to Law', for 'though the Prince himself is unaccountable and irresistible, yet his Ministers may be called to an account, and be punisht for it'. Even if these ministers escaped punishment under the present king, they could be held accountable 'under the next Prince', which should make 'all Men wary how they serve their Prince against Law'.[6]

In short, a maxim designed to ensure the legal immunity of the crown at the same time kept the king within the bounds of the law by placing an obligation on the crown's servants not to violate the law in the king's name. If a judge wrongly advised the king that he had the power to dispense with a law, the judge could be held accountable. If Catholics illegally sought to erect chapels for the public celebration of the mass, local magistrates and other law-enforcement agents were obliged to shut them down, regardless of whether or not the king had wanted the Catholic chapels erected in the first place. What should one do, then, if one were a local magistrate, sworn to uphold all the laws currently in force, when faced with a royal declaration suspending all the penal laws against religious nonconformists? Since the penal laws had not been formally repealed by act of parliament, and since Charles II had seemingly acknowledged that the crown did not possess the ability to suspend ecclesiastical laws, then, arguably, one was obliged to continue to enforce those laws until it had been established beyond any legal doubt that their operation had been suspended. Moreover, law enforcement in England was not just the responsibility of magistrates and parish constables. It was the duty of all subjects to assist magistrates and constables in enforcing the law when called upon to do so; if one witnessed a theft or a mugging, one was supposed to come to the victim's aid or help apprehend the criminal. Some laws – such as those against religious conventicles – positively encouraged ordinary subjects to participate in a law-enforcement role by offering rewards for informers. So what was one supposed to do when one saw a group of Catholics illegally assembling for the celebration of the mass? And how was a militia officer or a member of the trained bands supposed to act when ordered by the king to guarantee the ability of Catholics to worship in public even though this was palpably against the law?

The type of opposition to James's initiatives from Tory-Anglican interests that we have encountered so far accorded well with the

Church's stance on non-resistance and passive obedience and conventional constitutional thinking about the king's unaccountability. Whether that remained the case as James's regime veered ever more deeply into crisis – and especially in the wake of William's invasion in the autumn of 1688 – is more questionable. We shall see, as this chapter and the next unfold, that conventional Anglican beliefs about the irresistibility of the sovereign came increasingly under strain. What we need to be alert to, therefore, is where the potential for movement in Anglican views on resistance came from. We find it in the increasing emphasis placed on the obligation to be obedient to the rule of law and even to uphold the rule of law in the face of a sovereign who sought to violate it.

In the face of Anglican non-compliance with James's initiatives, court apologists were quick to accuse members of the Established Church of disloyalty and hypocrisy. As one satire, supposedly written from the perspective of a Church spokesman, put it in 1687: 'whilst the Government takes our Measures, and advances our Interest, we can be very Loyal'; but 'if our Purposes be cross'd', we can 'drop the Doctrine of Passive Obedience, and leave Non Resistance to shift for itself', and act like 'the Tribe of Forty One it self'.[7] *A New Test of the Church of England's Loyalty*, a Catholic piece of the same year, wondered how the Church of England 'dare appropriate to Themselves alone the Principles of true Loyalty'. It was true that Church of England Protestants had been loyal to Charles I during the Civil War, but only out of self interest, whereas the Catholics had been loyal even though they had had nothing to gain whether Charles won or lost. Church of England Protestants, on the other hand, had never been loyal under Catholic rulers: they had set up Lady Jane Grey in opposition to Mary Tudor's succession; 'barbarously murder'd' Mary, Queen of Scots, 'the undoubted Queen of Scotland . . . and the Lawful Heir of the Crown of England'; and were now again 'standing out in opposition to their Sovereign', because he was 'of another Religion'. The author ended by warning that if the Church of England did not 'change her old Principles of Loyalty', she must expect to forfeit 'her Claim to that Royal Protection, which was promis'd upon the account of her constant Fidelity'.[8] Bishop Cartwright of Chester similarly warned that the Church could not expect 'to be back'd or countenanc'd any longer by the king's civil Authority' if it denied James and his co-religionists 'the free Exercise of their own Religion'.[9]

Anglican apologists deeply resented the imputation of disloyalty. Only the Church of England 'did constantly maintain the Doctrine of Non-resistance to the Supream Magistrate and practice according to it', one responded, whereas the Catholics supported the Pope's power to depose heretical kings.[10] Gilbert Burnet, in his answer to the *New Test*, wondered what better testimony to the Church's loyalty there could be than the facts that its members had defended James's 'Right of Succession, with so much Zeal, that she . . . [had] put her self in the power of her Enemies', voted the King a vast revenue at the time of his accession, and supported the Catholic monarch against the threat of the Monmouth rebellion. Burnet scorned the notion that the Catholics were more loyal, pointing to the example of the Irish Rebellion of 1641. But the Church's principles of loyalty, Burnet continued, did not mean that in gratitude for the King's promise of protection Protestants should willingly 'throw up the Chief Security' the Church had 'in her Establishment by Law' and agree to the repeal of the penal laws and Test. 'God and the Laws hath given us a legal Security, and His Majesty has promised to maintain us in it', Burnet clarified, 'and we think it argues no Distrust, either of God, or the Truth of our Religion, to say, that we cannot by any Act of our own, lay our selves open, and throw away that Defence.' In response to the threat that the King would withdraw his protection, Burnet insisted that 'the Laws gave the Church of England a Right to that Protection, whether His Majesty had promised it or not'.[11] The defrocked Anglican clergyman Samuel Johnson, in his answer to the *New Test*, maintained that 'the word Loyal' was 'a term of Law': 'a Loyal Judgment' was 'a Judgment according to Law', and 'a Loyal Man' someone who 'behaves himself according to Law, and observes the Laws of the Land'. Both prince and people were mutually sworn to keep the law, and 'our Allegiance', Johnson claimed, 'binds us to an Obedience according to Law, and no otherwise'. It followed that 'to obey the King himself contrary to Law is Disloyalty, and to disobey the King in Obedience to the Laws is Loyalty', and thus 'the Church of England's carriage and behaviour' was justified, since 'it has been according to the Laws of the Land'. It was therefore wrong to claim that the Church of England could not expect protection until it changed its principles of loyalty, 'for a Legal Establishment has a Right to a Legal Protection, and the King is bound both by his Oath, and by the duty of his Kingly Office, to Protect the Church of England as it is by Law established'.[12] Both Burnet and Johnson, it must be conceded, were that rare breed, namely Whig clergymen; nevertheless, they still had to make their arguments appear consistent with the teachings of the Established Church.

The most challenging dilemma Anglicans faced as a result of James's Declaration of Indulgence was how to deal with the dissenters. Anglicans could scarcely sit back and support the suspension of the penal laws and the Tests which they for so long had been arguing were essential to preserve the Church from the double threat of popery and religious fanaticism. Besides, many had come to feel that the persecutions of the 1680s had been successful in healing the schism, by forcing dissenters to return to the Church; they were unlikely to rejoice now the floodgates were open and dissenters had started rushing to conventicles. Yet at the same time they were aware that if James were successful in forging an alliance between the Catholics and the dissenters around the shared goal of religious toleration, gone would be their privileged position as the Established Church, and their ability to sustain what they took to be the true faith would be seriously undermined. They therefore needed to convince the dissenters that they would be better off rejecting James's toleration and supporting the Established Church in its efforts to resist the Catholic menace. This was no easy task, given the Church's stance on dissent under Charles II, something that supporters of James's plans for toleration were quick to recall. The Quaker William Penn asked 'what security' the Church of England could give Protestant dissenters 'that she will not do what she fears from Popery [i.e. engage in religious persecution], when she has a Prince of her own Religion upon the Throne', given that she 'has made so fair a progress these last six and twenty Years in ruining families, for Non-conformity'? He also ridiculed the Church's claim to be 'afraid of Popery, because of its Violence', since the Church in its turn sought to protect itself by force: was this not 'resisting Popery with Popery'?[13] Others insisted that the Anglican clergy's lukewarm response to the Declaration of

Indulgence showed that they were still in favour of enforcing the penal laws, and that the Church was troubled 'to see all Christians peaceably professing their Religion, without any possibility of Vexation from their Neighbours' because she 'took pleasure in Wracking of Consciences' and 'Persecuting and Imprisoning'.[14]

Anglicans remained deeply ambivalent in their attitudes towards dissent in the aftermath of James's Indulgence. Some were prepared to reach out and make some sort of compromise to keep the dissenters on their side. For example, Bishop Lake of Chichester, upon the issuance of James's Indulgence, decided 'to translate the Sermon into the body of the Church' – a Puritan position, though not strictly speaking 'against the letter of the Rubric' – protesting to his archbishop that the move resulted in 'such an appearance of the most considerable Dissenters in this City' that he hoped his Grace would not be displeased.[15] Shortly after, Lake preached a sermon in which he expressed his concern about 'the danger of Popery', and suggested that the only remedy was to relax and remit 'those points of Conformity and Ceremony' that had caused the breach with the non-conformists, in order to form 'a Coalition with them'.[16] Other Church spokesmen, however, denounced the dissenters for perpetuating the separation and thereby helping to strengthen 'the hands of the Papists', and claimed that the dissenters' support for the Indulgence justified 'the imputations . . . laid upon them as a people that would helpe to bring in Popery'.[17] Some Anglican zealots were determined not to allow the dissenters a peaceful toleration, but thought the law must be enforced despite the King's Indulgence. Thus at York, in February 1688, locals riotously disturbed two nonconformist meetings; in March 1688 an Essex parson preached a series of sermons justifying 'the Lawfulness of prosecuting Dissenters'; at Mildenhall, in neighbouring Suffolk, a nonconformist preacher was threatened with prosecution under the 1670 Conventicle Act; while at Sandwich in Kent, at the end of March and the beginning of April, 'some Malicious Envious Spirits' made a couple of assaults on the local meeting-house, breaking the door off the hinges on one occasion (leaving it in a local stream) and smashing a new glass window on the other.[18]

One of the earliest pamphlets aimed at persuading dissenters not to throw in their lot with the Catholics was Gilbert Burnet's *Ill Effects of Animosities among Protestants in England Detected*. Despite being published with 1688 on its title-page, it was circulating in England by early May 1687[19] and seems to have been written prior to the Declaration of Indulgence, during the period when Catholics enjoyed effective toleration but dissenters were still having to petition the crown for relief from the penal laws. Burnet, by this time, was in self-imposed exile – having chosen to leave England at the beginning of James II's reign, travelling first to France and then through Switzerland and Germany before settling in the Netherlands in May 1686, when the Prince of Orange invited him to live in The Hague. The work was thus an early piece of Orangist propaganda and bears outlining in some detail.

The tract begins by explaining how, ever since the Restoration, both Charles II and his brother had sought to foster divisions among Protestants in order to pursue their design of promoting popery and arbitrary government. The conformists had done terrible things to the dissenters as a result, Burnet admitted, but had now become 'enlightned'. The dissenters should be careful, however, not to do anything to help the papists destroy the Established Church. Protestant nonconformists were a small minority, who would not be able to defend the Protestant religion by themselves if the Church of England were overthrown; it was therefore both their interest and duty 'to help maintain and defend' the Established Church. In particular, Burnet implored the dissenters 'not to be accessory to any thing, through which the legal Establishment of the Church of England may by any Act of pretended Regal Prerogative be weakned and supplanted'. Although he could understand why they might be tempted 'to petition the King to suspend the execution of the Penal Laws' or to give them dispensations for their meetings, they should realize that this was what the court wanted them to do, and they ought not 'betray the Kingdom and sacrifice the legal constitution of the Government to the Lust and Pleasure of a Popish Prince, whom nothing less will serve than being Absolute and Despotical'. Besides, 'the Fanatics' could not be 'so far void of sense' as to believe James bore them any good will; once he had established 'himself into a Supremacy and Absoluteness over the Law' so that he could 'subvert the established Religion, and set up Popery', he would soon resume persecuting the dissenters.[20]

The dissenters could rest assured, Burnet insisted, that the Church of England was committed to upholding the Protestant religion, together with England's laws and liberties. The conformists knew as well as any, he proclaimed, 'that the giving to Cesar the things that are Cesar's' placed them 'under no obligation of surrendering unto him the things that are God's, nor of sacrificing unto the will of the Soveraign the priviledges reserved unto the people by the Fundamental Rules of the Constitution, and by the Statutes of the Realm'. They also understood that 'the Laws of the Land' were 'the only measures of the Prince's Authority, and of the Subjects' Fealty' – 'where they [the laws] give him [the prince] no Right to command, they [his subjects] lay them under no tye to obey' – and observed how it was the 'Theologues and Gentlemen of the Church of England' who had 'generally and with greatest honor appeared for our Laws and Legal Government against the Invasions and Usurpations of the Court'. Although the high-Anglican clergy in recent years had upheld the doctrine of passive obedience, 'as they absurdly put it', and insisted that all that subjects could do in the face of royal tyranny was 'tamely to suffer', there were many clergy and lay Anglicans, Burnet said, who were far from being infected with those 'brutish Sentiments and Opinions', although they had been 'branded with the name of conformable Fanaticks'. Burnet then went on to make the remarkable claim that those of the Church of England knew how far they stood 'bound to a Prince on the Throne' – the allusion to James II was transparent – 'who by transgressing against the Laws of the Constitution, hath abdicated himself from the Government, and stands virtually deposed', since 'by the Fundamental, Common and Statute Laws of the Realm, we know none for Supreme Magistrate and Governor, but a limited Prince, and one who stands circumscribed and bounded in his Power and Prerogative'. (Note the idea that James might have 'abdicated himself from the Government' by dint of the fact that he had violated the constitution: it was to be taken up again over the winter of 1688/9.) Burnet did not at this time make a specific call for resistance. He did, however, recall that the Established Church had always defended the armed resistance of the Dutch against the kings of Spain.[21]

He also offered up the prospect of both comprehension and religious toleration 'were England immediately to be rendered so happy as to have a Protestant Prince ascend the Throne, and to enjoy a Parliament duely chosen, and acting with freedom'. Thus 'should it please Almighty God', he added, 'through denying Male Issue to the King, to bring the Princess of Orange to the Crown', the Church of England could still expect to be 'preserved and upheld as the National Establishment', but 'all other Protestants may very rationally promise themselves an Indulgence'.[22]

In other writings, Burnet warned dissenters not to be taken in by the Indulgence, since Catholicism was a persecuting religion and the Papists would trust the dissenters no longer than they had occasion to use them; he even sought to remove the stigma of persecution from the Established Church by insisting that it was the court that had set the persecution in motion.[23] Another author insisted that the Church of England realized the iniquity of persecuting people simply on account of their religious beliefs, and wanted to secure liberty of conscience by law – though the papists would still be excluded from such a toleration, for popery was not merely a religion but 'a Conspiracy against the Peace of Societies, and the Rights of Mankind', since the pope claimed the right to depose kings and absolve subjects from their due allegiance.[24]

On the nonconformist side, the man who proved most determined to dissuade the nonconformists from throwing in their lot with James II was the fiery Scottish independent divine Robert Ferguson – the erstwhile chaplain to the first Earl of Shaftesbury and both a Rye House plotter and a Monmouth rebel – who, like Burnet, was now in exile in the Low Countries. In a work that appeared in the summer of 1687 (its postscript reveals that it was written before James issued his follow-up Scottish Indulgence of 28 June but published shortly thereafter), Ferguson berated those nonconformists who had welcomed James's toleration: ''Tis matter of a melancholy consideration, and turns little to the credit of Dissenters', he bemoaned, 'that when they of the Church of England . . . are thro being at last enlightned in the designes of the Court' as to 'recover their witts . . . there should be a new Tribe of men muster'd up to stand in their room, and who by their vows and Promises made to the King in their Addresses, have undertaken to perform, what others have the Conscience, and Honesty, as well as the Wisdom, to refuse and decline.' Ferguson was adamant that 'none ought to be persecuted for their Consciences towards God in matters of Faith and Worship', asserting (in a way that echoed the position of the Levellers in the late 1640s) that liberty of conscience was not 'one of those things that lye under the power of the Sovereign and Legislative Authority, to grant or not to grant', but rather that it was 'a Right setled upon Mankind antecedent to all Civil Constitutions and Humane Laws, having its foundation in the Laws of Nature, which no Prince or State can legitimately violate and infringe'. (The Catholics remained an exception, since 'Governors may both deny Liberty to those whose principles oblige them to destroy those that are not of their mind' and regulate the liberty of those whose opinions were 'erroneous and false' and therefore 'dangerous to the Soules of men'.) Nevertheless, the fact 'That Liberty ought to be allowed to men in matters of Religion' was no justification for kings 'giving it in an illegal and Arbitrary manner'. Fortunately, Ferguson pointed out, there were 'many Dissenters' who had preserved themselves 'innocent at this juncture' and not succumbed to temptation, adding that he hoped 'the Nation' would 'be so ingenuous, as not to impute the miscarriages of some of the nonconformists, to the whole party, much less to ascribe them to the principles of Dissenters', as if to try to shame those who had initially welcomed the Indulgence into rethinking whether they really wanted to make themselves complicit in James's attempts to establish arbitrary government.[25]

Not that Ferguson was particularly soft on the Established Church. 'Had it not been for many of the Church of England', he complained, 'who stood up with a zeal and vigour for preserving the succession in the right line, beyond what Religion, conscience, Reason, or Interest could conduct them unto', Charles II could never have 'out-wrestled the endeavours of three Parliaments for excluding [the Duke of York] from the Imperial Crown of England'. Furthermore, 'had it not been for their abetting and standing by him with their swords in their hands upon the Duke of Monmouth's descent into the Kingdom anno 1685, he could not have avoided being driven from the Throne'.[26] Indeed, Ferguson was to go on to offer an explicit justification of resistance. Thanking God that he was 'not tainted with that slavish and adulatory doctrine' of passive obedience, he pronounced that he had 'always thought that the first duty of every member of a Body politick' was 'to the Community, for whose safety, and good, Governors [were] instituted'. It followed that 'the Rules of the Constitution and the Laws of the Republick or Kingdom' were 'to be the measures both of the Soveraign's Commands, and of the Subjects' obedience; and that as we are not to invade what by concessions and stipulations belongs unto the Ruler, so we may not only lawfully, but we ought to defend what is reserved to our selves, if it be invaded and broken in upon'. For 'without such a Right in the Subjects, all legal Governments, and mixt Monarchies, were but empty Names and ridiculous things'.[27] In short, Ferguson couched his appeal to the dissenters with an explicit defence of the right – and even duty – of subjects to resist rulers who acted illegally.

The most famous appeal to the dissenters to appear in print at this time was the Marquis of Halifax's *Letter to a Dissenter*, written in August 1687. It immediately attracted a great deal of attention. 'One of the most admired peces, for stile, close reasoning and Expression that [had] appeared abroad for a long time', according to one contemporary, its price soared from a mere 3d on the first day of publication, to 6d on the second, and subsequently to 5 shillings; by the end of October some 20,000 copies were in print, and the tract had soon gone through six editions.[28] As the government propagandist Henry Care observed, Halifax's *Letter* spread 'industriously' and was soon to be found in every 'Corner of the Land'.[29] Halifax's tone, however, was admonitory rather than conciliatory. He informed the dissenters that it was their 'Duty . . . not to hazard the publick Safety, neither by desire of Ease, nor of Revenge'. They should consider that their 'new Friends', the Catholics, did not make them 'their Choice, but their Refuge'; the Catholics had always 'made their first Courtships to the Church of England' and had turned to the dissenters only 'when they were rejected there'. In fact, the principles of the Church of Rome were fundamentally against liberty of conscience, and the dissenters were 'to be hugged now' so that they might 'be the better squeezed at another time'. Halifax chastised the dissenters for giving thanks for the Indulgence and opening up public conventicles, insisting that because 'the Law is so Sacred . . . no Trespass against it' could 'be Defended':

> To rescue your selves from the Severity of one Law, you give a Blow to all the Laws, by which your Religion and Liberty are to be protected; and instead of silently receiving the benefit of this Indulgence, you set up for Advocates to support it . . . and look like Counsel retained by the Prerogative against your old Friend *Magna Charta*, who hath done nothing to deserve her falling thus under your Displeasure.

The dissenters should therefore think twice before going any further, Halifax warned, since 'the Price . . . for this Liberty' was 'giving up your Right in the Laws'.[30]

Halifax assured the dissenters that the Church of England had realized its 'Mistake' and abandoned 'all the former Haughtiness' towards them, turning 'the Spirit of Persecution, into a Spirit of Peace, Charity, and Condescention'. If the dissenters only waited, they could expect 'ease and satisfaction': parliament, whenever it might meet, was 'sure to be Gentle' to them, while 'the next Heir' had been 'bred in the Country' that the dissenters had 'so often Quoted for a Pattern of Indulgence'. He concluded by insisting that the Church remained committed to the principles of passive obedience and non-resistance. But he expected the present danger would pass away 'by the natural course of things', 'like a shower of Hail', and 'fair weather succeed' – Halifax, after all, was writing before the Queen was to become pregnant with the Prince of Wales. 'Let us be still, quiet, and undivided, firm at the same time to our Religion, our Loyalty, and our Laws', he implored, and the Protestants would eventually triumph, unless 'the Church of Rome, which hath been so long barren of Miracles, should now in her declining Age, be brought to Bed of One that would outdo the best she can brag of'.[31] These last remarks, of course, contained a fateful irony.

The interest that Halifax's *Letter* aroused – as evidenced both by the sales it generated and the fact that it provoked fourteen replies[32] – has often been taken as a measure of its effectiveness.[33] It seems unlikely, however, that either the tone or the types of arguments Halifax advanced would have won over many dissenters. One Baptist respondent said he was unable to resolve whether Halifax's pamphlet 'was designed for a Libel upon the Government, or upon the Dissenters; the Reproach of both being carried on with so even a Thread thro' the whole'.[34] Another reply to Halifax argued that the dissenters would be foolish to reject James's toleration and trust the Church of England to give them relief at some future date, since one only needed to look at the way those of the Established Church had treated dissenters in the past to know that they were the ones who could not be trusted.[35] Penn thought there was not 'any sort of proof' in Halifax's *Letter* 'that Prelacy [had] changed its thoughts' and was any more tender towards Protestant nonconformists than before.[36] Care agreed there was no sign 'that the Sentiments of the Church of England towards Dissenters [had] chang'd, unless it be to a greater degree of Malice', especially when, in some parts of the country, they were continuing to persecute nonconformists.[37]

Yet if James were to succeed in his attempt to get parliament to repeal not just the penal laws but also the Test Acts, what was to stop parliament being packed with Catholics who would then vote to over-turn the Established Church, set up popery, and rescind the toleration of Protestants? To alleviate such concerns, supporters of the court put forward the idea of an equivalent security that could guarantee the protection of the Protestant religion in place of the Tests.[38] For instance, Care suggested a number of alternative safeguards. Why not 'a Civil Test . . . altogether as effectual, and yet not so obnoxious . . . as these Religious ones?' Or what if the same bill that rescinded the penal laws declared liberty of conscience to be 'part of the Constitution of this Kingdom; The natural Birth-Right of every English-Man', which it would be a criminal offence to undermine or subvert? If that seemed too extreme, the penal laws and the Test Act of 1673, which debarred Catholics from office, could be repealed, but the Test Act of 1678 relating to MPs kept in force.[39] In the early months of 1688 both James and Secretary of State Sunderland showed themselves willing to concede the idea that Catholics should continue to be excluded from parliament, although this was an issue over which James himself was to vacillate.[40]

Ultimately, it is impossible to know what impact the pamphlet debate over the repeal of the penal laws and the Tests had on the group whose allegiance was being sought, the dissenters. The furore

over Halifax's *Letter* undoubtedly helped give his arguments a wider
publicity and also to make people aware of the complexities of the
issues involved. It was more complicated, dissenters may well have
been made aware, than simply being thankful for relief after years of
persecution and hoping that parliament would eventually sanction
the toleration afforded them. Yet, at the same time, the debate over
Halifax's *Letter* might have served to harden the antagonism between
the Established Church and dissent, rather than soften it. If Halifax
reproached the dissenters, the dissenters reproached the Church in
return. Care began his reply to Halifax with an attack not just on 'the
high-flown Church-men' who had tried to frighten the gentry by
alleging that the Indulgence would 'blow up the Church of England',
but even on 'the Latitudinarian Divines', those with the 'greatest
Credit and Interest among the Non-Cons', who had sought to 'bug-
bear the Dissenters with a noise of the Snake in the Grass'.[41] In early
1688 Roger Morrice reported how Halifax had 'most highly disobliged the Protestant Dissenters' and was 'distrusted and neglected
by them', and was trying to make his peace with the court. James
and Sunderland started insinuating that the Church had offered to
strike a deal with the court 'to take off the Penall Lawes and the
Test from the Papists if they might be left upon the Protestant
Dissenters', though the King protested he would not 'Comply with
them'. The Church hierarchy vigorously denied this, claiming it was
'an odious Scandall cast upon them to make them odious and increase
Divisions'. For the time being, divisions did indeed appear to be
increasing.[42]

A tract that was probably more effective than Halifax's *Letter* in
persuading dissenters not to accept James's Indulgence was Gaspar
Fagel's *Letter* conveying the thoughts of the Prince and Princess of
Orange on the question of the repeal of the penal laws and the Tests.
James had been trying for some time to get his nephew/son-in-law and
daughter to concur with his plans for repeal; the Princess of Orange
was still next-in-line to the throne and James was well aware that his
efforts to secure toleration for his co-religionists would come to
nought if his successor were immediately to reverse his policy.
William had already told Penn towards the end of 1686 that,
although he disliked religious persecution, he thought the Tests were

an essential legal safeguard. Concerted efforts were made over the course of 1687 to get the Prince to change his mind. James Stewart, a Scottish Presbyterian lawyer and former exile who had returned to England and been reconciled with the court, wrote to Fagel – the Grand Pensionary of Holland and William's trusted political ally – with the aim of trying to show that William had no reason to fear the repeal of the Tests, and holding out the prospect that if William agreed, James would break with France. Fagel's response, dated 4 November 1687, was drafted with the compliance of William; published in Dutch, it was also translated into English by Burnet. The English version enjoyed an initial print-run of some 45,000 copies, and was being distributed in England by William's agents by the beginning of 1688.[43] Fagel's *Letter* made it clear that the Prince and Princess of Orange thought 'no Christian ought to be prosecuted for his Conscience, or be ill used because he differs from the publick established Religion'. The Prince and Princess were even willing to allow Catholics in England, Scotland and Ireland the same liberty they had in the United Provinces, and were therefore ready to give their concurrence to the repeal of the penal laws, provided that the Test Acts excluding them from parliament and public office remained in force, 'as likewise all those other Laws which confirm the Protestant Religion'. It was essential, however, Fagel's *Letter* explained, to exclude Catholics from any share in the government, to ensure they could not do anything 'to the prejudice of the Reformed Religion'. Where they were in power, Catholics had shown that they could never be satisfied just to exclude Protestants from office, but had always sought to 'suppress the whole Exercise of [the Reformed] Religion, and severely persecute all that profess it'.[44] By late January 1688 it was being reported that the numerous copies of Fagel's *Letter* that had been 'industriously spread abroad' had already done the King's affairs 'a great prejudice', it weighing 'much with people'. The Presbyterians immediately held a synod to discuss whether or not the penal laws should be removed, and were said to have had Fagel's *Letter* before them, although for the time being they failed to reach an agreement on the issue.[45]

Such propaganda undoubtedly had some impact. The Spanish ambassador Don Pedro Ronquillo observed in March 1688 that the

King himself was well aware that support for his tolerationist stance was eroding, reporting that some of those who had told James they would back his repeal of the Test had changed their minds and that the Presbyterians appeared now to 'unite with the Anglicans'.[46] Yet what really altered the dynamic was the fact that the Catholic 'miracle', which Halifax thought could never happen, did indeed occur. In the autumn of 1687 the 'long barren' Queen became pregnant, and in June 1688 was 'brought to bed' of a son. Anticipating before the birth that the Queen would provide him with a male heir, James became even less conciliatory, and even more determined to take on the Church of England by reissuing his Indulgence and proceeding full pace with his plans to pack parliament. Anglicans now had to decide how to act; the wait-and-see strategy was no longer a viable option. Likewise, dissenters could no longer hedge their bets; they had to come down on one side or the other. And William of Orange had to make up his mind whether he could afford to allow England, Scotland and Ireland, which had hitherto been his wife's inheritance, to become subject to a potentially never-ending line of Catholic monarchs and perhaps, thereby, drawn into a firm alliance with the United Provinces' main enemy, France.

JAMES'S SECOND DECLARATION OF INDULGENCE AND THE TRIAL OF THE SEVEN BISHOPS

On 23 December 1687 James issued a proclamation announcing the Queen was 'with issue' and appointing 15 January (in London) and 29 January (elsewhere) as days of thanksgiving.[47] Local records confirm the days were appropriately commemorated with church services and peals of bells, but with how much enthusiasm remains open to question.[48] The Earl of Clarendon attended the service at St James's, Westminster, on the 15th, noting that 'there were not above two or three in the church who brought the form of prayer with them' and noting that 'the Queen's belly' was 'every where ridiculed, as if scarce any body believed it to be true'.[49] Danby recalled with suspicion in March how 'many of our ladies, say, that the Queen's great belly

seems to grow faster than they have observed their own to do'.[50] In
Oxford, a libel was soon circulating 'containing an account of 3
women to be brought to bed' and if any of them were to have a son
'he must be nursed up and be king'; come the 29th, only Christ
Church and Magdalen rang their bells during the day, although the
University church did ring at night and a few colleges staged bonfires.[51] Likewise a 'notorious Libell . . . on her Majestie's being with
child' (possibly the same one) rapidly began to spread through the
capital; the King himself found one copy behind the mirror in his bedchamber, at which he was said to be 'Extreamely displeased'.[52] There
was the odd bonfire in the provinces on the 29th, and also on
6 February, for the anniversary of James's accession.[53] However, in
the capital Clarendon noted that the church he attended on
6 February was 'extremely empty: no more than ordinarily at prayers
upon a week day'.[54]

On 27 April James decided to reissue his Declaration of Indulgence, and backed it up with an order, on 4 May, requiring the
bishops to instruct their clergy to read it in their churches on two suc-
cessive Sundays (20 and 27 May for the London area, 3 and 10 June
elsewhere).[55] His strategy was transparent. He had been disappointed
with the Church's response to his Declaration of Indulgence of the
previous year, and hoped that by now forcing the clergy to read the
Indulgence, they could be made to seem to approve of the suspension
of the penal laws and Tests. He expected the Church's teachings on
non-resistance would mean that most would comply; if a few did
refuse, they could be removed from office and their opposition
thereby neutralized.

It proved a serious miscalculation. The clergy of London – among
them Sherlock, Patrick, Stillingfleet, Fowler and Tillotson – held a
series of meetings to discuss how they would respond and, after consulting with leading Anglican politicians (such as Danby, Halifax and
Nottingham) and a number of bishops (including Sancroft of
Canterbury), overwhelmingly decided not to read the Indulgence. As
one of these clerics pointed out, if they did they would 'be in the Scorn
of the Papists, and Fanaticks'. 'The designe' was 'too obvious to all',
namely 'to ridicule us as unstable complying men . . . when our places
are in danger'. Reading the Indulgence would imply an acceptance of

its legality, or at least 'an owning of a power to Command the publishing of things that are against Law'; it would make it hard for the clergy to defend their refusal to vote for MPs who would 'pass this Declaration into a Law'; and the clergy might in future be asked to approve other things, which they would not be able to object to because they had supported this. Besides, most of the clergy thought that the Indulgence was illegal: 'such a Declaration' had 'been solemnly declared in Parliament to be illegal', and the clergy's compliance would in itself be 'unlawful', since they were 'abundantly satisfied that an unlimited Tolleration' was 'pernicious to Religion and the Soules of men'.[56]

As a result of these discussions, Archbishop Sancroft and six of his bishops – Francis Turner of Ely, Thomas Ken of Bath and Wells, John Lake of Chichester, Thomas White of Peterborough, Jonathan Trelawney of Bristol and William Lloyd of St Asaph – decided to petition the crown to ask not to be forced to require their clergy to read the Indulgence (it was said that the bishops of Gloucester, Norwich and Winchester were also privy to and agreed with the petition). The six bishops presented the petition to the King at Whitehall on Friday 18 May; ill-health prevented Sancroft himself from attending, although the petition was in his handwriting. The bishops insisted that their opposition proceeded neither from 'any want to duty and obedience' to the King, nor from 'any want of due tendernesse to dissenters, in relation to whom' they were 'willing to come to such a temper as shall be thought fit, when that matter shall be considered in parliament and convocation'. However, given that the Declaration was 'founded upon such a power as hath been often declared illegal in Parliament', their petition maintained, they felt they could not 'in prudence, honour, or conscience . . . make themselves parties to it'. (A similarly worded document circulated among the London clergy as a justification of why they themselves would refuse to read the Declaration.)[57] James was outraged that the bishops should dare petition against 'his Dispensing power, which Almighty God had placed in him', and it was said 'that his countenance sunke and he looked pale'. He certainly began to lose his cool, blurting out that 'this was a Step towards a Rebellion' and insisting that 'he would be obeyed'. As the bishops moved out of earshot he apparently added that 'they [the Bishops] neither loved him nor his father, but he [Charles I] dyed for them but they fought for themselves, and not for him' – a highly revealing remark which shows how the memory of the Civil War and the regicide still haunted James and coloured his attitude towards politics.[58] The Jesuit Father Petre was said to be delighted that James now seemed set to break with the Church of England, predicting they 'should be made to eat their own dung'.[59]

Very few of the clergy did obey the King. The Declaration was read in just seven churches in the whole of the metropolitan area, and in at least three of these (Westminster Abbey, St Gregory's by St Paul's, and St Matthew's, Friday Street) the congregation walked out in protest. Most of these churches subsequently declined to read it on the following Sunday. Across the country as a whole, no more than 200 churches (out of over 9,000) saw the Declaration read.[60] At Chislehurst in Kent, one of the ejected fellows of Magdalen College, instead of reading the Declaration, preached a sermon praying for deliverance 'From the fury of the Papists, and the dread of the Fanaticks'.[61] In the diocese of Oxford, without a bishop since the death of the ultra-loyal Samuel Parker in March, only six read it; in Oxford itself, not one did so.[62] Only six of the bishops instructed their clergy to read the Declaration – Durham, Lincoln, Hereford, Rochester, Chester and St Davids – yet even then their diocesan clergy, for the most part, refused to comply.[63] The Bishop of Durham had to suspend thirty ministers for non-compliance, including his archdeacon. The diocese of Chester provides a rare example where 'a great part of the Clergie' complied with their bishop's order, but even they later addressed the King to explain that they had acted out of duty, not because they approved of 'the Matter of the Declaration'.[64] Similarly, Bishop Croft of Hereford wrote a tract arguing that the reading of the Declaration did not imply consent to it, and that people had to 'submit unto his Majesties Will and have patience', even though if the King had asked for his opinion on this matter he would have beseeched him 'not to use his Dispensing Power in that high manner'.[65]

The loyalist press was quick to pour scorn on the bishops and clergy who refused to read the Indulgence. One author condemned the refusal as 'an unquestionable Act of Disobedience to the command of the Soveraign Authority, than which there cannot be a greater mark of that Disloyalty which the Clergy of the Establish'd Religion so much disown'.[66] Another adduced various legal arguments for why the clergy had to obey the King, assuring them that if they obeyed unjust commands they were not at fault.[67] One poet asked, 'if conscience be thought a sufficient pretense, / Why should it not salve the Dissenters' offense?', and suggested that, despite the Anglican clergy's talk 'of Passive Obedience', they clearly thought it prudent, 'when interest sways, to resist'.[68]

Anglican apologists were quick to defend the non-compliance. One author stated that he was prepared to leave consideration of the dispensing power to others more expert, and also claimed that he did not begrudge the King the right to make use of his Catholic subjects. But he did wonder why, given that there were 'no Penal Laws to which our Congregations are obnoxious', the reading of the Indulgence should be imposed upon the Anglican clergy, since that could only be construed as 'solliciting and tempting our own people to forsake our Communion'. However the clergy could not in conscience, he continued, read a declaration which stated that the King wished all his subjects 'were Members of the Catholick Church' and which suspended 'all manner of Penal Laws, in matters Ecclesiastical', including, by implication, those against fornication, adultery, incest, blasphemy, prophaneness and 'open derision of Christian religion'; this was 'not out of any unreasonable opinion of our selves, nor disaffection to Protestant Dissenters', but stemmed from 'a tender care of the Souls committed to us, especially those of the weaker sort, to whom we dare not propose an Invitation to Popery, and much less any thing that may give countenance or encouragement to Irreligion'.[69]

The strongest statement against reading the Indulgence came from William Sherlock, a prominent participant in the meetings the clergy held in London in May, in a pamphlet dated 22 May. 'By our Law', Sherlock wrote, 'all Ministerial Officers are accountable for their Actions: The Authority of Superiors, though of the King himself, cannot justifie inferiour Officers, much less the Ministers of State, if they should execute any illegal Commands.' It was a maxim of our law, he explained, that 'the King can do no wrong; and therefore if any wrong be done, the Crime and Guilt is the Minister's who does it'. The laws were 'the King's publick Will' and the king could never be 'supposed to command any thing contrary to law'; if any minister commits an illegal action, he is not 'allowed to pretend the King's Command and Authority for it'. Ministers of religion had 'a greater tye and Obligation than this', Sherlock continued, being responsible for 'the care and conduct of men's Souls', and thus were obliged to ensure 'what they publish in their Churches be neither contrary to the Laws of the Land, nor to the good of the Church'. Moreover, their reading the Declaration would undoubtedly imply their consent to it; the clergy were not 'common Cryers', but what they read they might be 'supposed to recommend too'. The Indulgence, Sherlock further claimed, was 'against the Constitution of the Church of England', which was 'established by Law' and to which the clergy had subscribed, so they were 'bound in Conscience to teach nothing contrary to it'. Yet to read the Indulgence was 'to teach an unlimited and universal Toleration, which the Parliament in 72 [i.e., February 1672/3] declared illegal, and which has been condemned by the Christian Church in all Ages'. It was 'to teach my People, that they need never come to Church more'; it was 'to teach the dispensing Power, which alters, what has been formerly thought, the whole Constitution of this Church and Kingdom: which we dare not do, till we have the Authority of Parliament for it'; it was 'to recommend to our People, the choice of such persons to sit in Parliament, as shall take away the Test and Penal Laws, which most of the Nobility and Gentry of the Nation have declared their judgment against'; and it was to condemn those patriots who had forfeited their favour with their prince because they would not consent to taking away the Tests and the penal laws.[70]

The moderate dissenters (especially the Presbyterians), after a series of meetings with some of the Church's representatives, decided to support the stance taken by the seven bishops, preferring to 'remain under the persecution of the penal Laws, in the hopes and expectation of receiving at the proper period some alleviation, than by separating from the English church, to go surely the one after the other to the ground'.[71] The King and his advisers thought of ordering dissenting ministers to read the Indulgence in their meetings, but backed down when informed there would be considerable opposition. Instead, working through Penn and Stephen Lobb, they tried to bring pressure on the nonconformist leaders to present an address, but found no dissenters 'of Condition or quality' would support it, since they wanted 'Liberty by a Law' and were 'utterly against letting Papists into the Government'.[72] A mere twenty-one addresses of thanks came in for the Indulgence of 1688, mostly from purged corporations and magisterial benches – although most corporations and benches that had been purged declined to address. Even the members of the recently purged Chichester town assembly, who had voted unanimously the previous February to allow themselves to hold meetings with their hats on (a concession to Quaker scruples), voted down a proposal to address the King 'for this declaration for toleration'. (A further purge of the corporation predictably followed a couple of weeks later.)[73] The Quakers, at their yearly meeting in London, were the only group of dissenters to draw up an address.[74]

James summoned the seven bishops to Whitehall on 8 June to explain their actions, but they refused to answer the King's questions, protesting that by the laws of the land 'no Subject was bound to accuse himselfe', as the Bishop of St Asaph put it. Furious, James demanded they give bail to appear at King's Bench; they again refused, claiming that as peers of the realm they could not be required to post bail, but offered to give their personal promise, as clergymen, to appear. James, his patience exhausted, ordered them to the Tower. Crowds of people gathered to pay their respects as the seven were escorted out of Whitehall and taken by river to their imprisonment, falling to their knees and shouting 'God bless the Bishops'; even the soldiers at the Tower did the same.[75] The bishops appeared at Westminster Hall on 15 June, accompanied by twenty-one noblemen who came to put up bail, if needed (among them Halifax, Danby and Clarendon). The bishops were charged with publishing a seditious libel against the King and government. They pleaded not guilty and were released on their own recognizance (£200 for the archbishop, £100 each for the others) to await trial on the 29th; the reason why they were now prepared to give bail when they had not before, they said, was that having tried to assert the privilege of peerage but having been overruled by a court of justice, they deemed it appropriate to submit. A rich Quaker from Wells also appeared, offering to be bail for the Bishop of Bath and Wells, and stating that 'tho he could not Swear, he was worth 10,000 li. [and] he would substantially prove it'.[76] Again, crowds of people cheered the bishops as they left Westminster Hall, falling to their knees to beg their blessing, while that evening there were numerous bonfires throughout the capital to celebrate the bishops' release.[77] Indeed, 'the generality of people' were in such 'a humour . . . about the Bishops' that the bishops dared not even 'stir abroad' during the two weeks leading up to the trial, for wherever they went 'crowds of people flocke[d] about them to aske them blessing'.[78]

On the day of the trial, throngs of people gathered in Westminster Hall and in the streets outside the courtroom, providing an intimidating environment for those who came to make the case for the prosecution. The Solicitor-General, Sir William Williams (a Whig turncoat) and others associated with the government were treated with 'the utmost disrespect'. Sunderland, who had announced his conversion to Catholicism only the day before, was kicked 'on the breach so severely' as he came through the hall to give his evidence 'that he cryed out "Oh"'; someone even held 'his fist up' to the Secretary of State as if 'to strike him over the face'. When Sunderland left the courtroom he was greeted with cries of 'Kill the new Popish Dog'. The Bishop of Chester, who turned up at the trial 'to satisfy his curiosity', was not only saluted with chants of 'Grasping Woulf in sheep's attire', but – being 'a tall and Corpulent Gentleman' – was also jeered from all directions with shouts of 'make room', since 'he had the Pope in his belly'.[79]

The indictment accused the bishops of conspiring 'to diminish the regal authority, and royal prerogative, power and government' by framing and writing a 'pernicious and seditious Libel' concerning the King's Declaration of Indulgence 'under pretence of a Petition', which they 'published' in the presence of the King. Although the bishops had not printed their petition, the presiding judge, Lord Chief Justice Wright, ruled that merely bringing the petition to the King constituted publication. The main thrust of the defence's case was that the bishops' petition could not have been an affront to the royal prerogative because the King did not possess the suspending power: parliament had in the past condemned the suspending power, and Charles II, on withdrawing his Indulgences of 1662 and 1672 had acknowledged that he possessed no such power. Sir Robert Sawyer insisted that the bishops had simply told the King what parliament had declared (they did not offer this as their own judgment), so how could this be construed as an attempt 'to diminish the king's prerogative and regal power'? Sawyer further maintained that the bishops had 'done their duty' in this matter, since the Elizabethan Act of Uniformity had made bishops 'special guardians of the law of uniformity', so that they were 'obliged to see it executed'. Heneage Finch argued that only the legislature – the king, Lords and Commons – had the 'power to abrogate the laws' and that Charles II had accepted, when he withdrew his Indulgences, parliament's reasoning that he could not suspend the penal laws in matters ecclesiastic without an act of parliament. When the king is 'misinformed, or under a misapprehension of the law', Finch went on, the bishops, as peers of the realm, had the right 'humbly to advise the king' and a 'duty . . . to make known their reason why they could not obey that command'. Sir Henry Pollexfen insisted that the royal dispensing power, as vindicated by Godden v. Hales, could not sanction the suspending power, but proved 'quite the contrary'. 'For why should any man go about to argue, that the king may dispense with this or that particular law', Pollexfen asked, 'if at once he can dispense with all the law, by an undoubted prerogative?' Sir John Somers concluded that the bishops, in petitioning against the suspending power, thus had 'no design to diminish the prerogative, because the king hath no such prerogative'.[80]

The prosecution refuted such claims, arguing that in withdrawing his Indulgences Charles had never made a formal disclaimer of his right, and pointing out that what the defence alleged had been declarations in parliament (concerning the suspending power) had, in fact, been no more than the declarations of one part of parliament (either the Commons or the Lords), which had never received the concurrence of the principal part, the king. Furthermore, it was irrelevant whether what the bishops had said in their petition was true or not; the only thing to consider, they maintained, was whether the petition was 'reflecting and scandalous'.[81] In his summing up, Wright insisted that the suspending power was irrelevant to the case, and refused to give his opinion as to whether it was legal or not. For Wright, the key issues were whether a publication had taken place and, if so, whether there had been a libel. Since 'any thing that shall disturb the government, or make mischief and a stir among the people' could be construed as libellous, then the bishops' petition did, in his determination, constitute a libel. Because this involved a question of law, however, the other three judges of King's Bench were allowed their say. Justice Holloway concluded that he did not think the bishops' petition was a libel, Justice Allibone that it was; both remained silent on the issue of the suspending power. Justice Powell, however, argued that 'if there be no such dispensing power in the king', then the petition was 'no libel', and invited the jury to base their decision on whether they thought the power the King claimed in his Declaration of Indulgence was legal. At ten o'clock the next morning – 30 June – the jury returned a verdict of 'not guilty'. They would have brought in their verdict the previous day, within half an hour of the trial concluding, were it not for the obstructionist tactics of one Mr Arnold, the King's brewer, and a Mr Done, a macebearer, who refused to concur with the majority.[82]

Large cheers resounded both inside the courtroom and on the streets outside as soon as the verdict was announced. As the nobility who had attended the trial made their way home, they threw money out of their coaches, urging 'the poor people . . . to drink the Health of the King, the Prelates, and the Jury'. That night there were bonfire and firework celebrations throughout the metropolitan area, and even a number of pope-burnings. Crowds stopped passers-by to demand contributions towards their festivities; those who refused stood the risk of being robbed or beaten up. 'Almost all the Papists in London', one correspondent reported, 'had bonfires made at their doors', and were made to pay for them; there was at least one fatality, when Lord Salisbury's servants fired at the crowd that constructed a bonfire outside his residence.[83] Contemporaries reported similar displays throughout the country as news of the bishops' acquittal spread: in Bedford, Bristol, Cambridge, Gloucester, Lichfield, Norwich, Oxford, Tamworth, and in many towns and villages in Buckinghamshire and Leicestershire.[84] When news reached the army camp at Hounslow Heath, there were loud huzzas, and the soldiers rejoiced by drinking the health of the bishops. It was an ominous portent.[85]

The dissenters also, by and large, rallied behind the bishops. Ten nonconformist ministers visited the bishops during their initial detention in the Tower, proclaiming that 'they could not but adhear to them as men constant to the Protestant faith'.[86] Halifax told William of Orange that the business of the bishops had 'brought all the Protestants together, and bound them up into a knot, that cannot easily be untied'.[87] When the bishops were acquitted, the dissenters were observed to be not 'backward in showing themselves well pleased with the verdict'.[88] The bishops even received letters from the Presbyterians in Scotland, for so long bitterly hostile to prelacy, assuring them of their sympathy.[89] Indeed, the seven bishops became the iconic figures of successful resistance to James's innovations. A medal was coined with the seven bishops on one side, and a Jesuit and a monk on the other, digging away at the foundations of the Church of England, with the words 'The gates of Hell shall not prevail against her'.[90]

The trial of the seven bishops had been a disaster from the crown's point of view. James had not only failed to bring the bishops into line, but, by forcing the issue, he had made it apparent that public opinion was overwhelmingly against his attempts to establish a general toleration through the use of the suspending power. Moreover, the verdict itself seemed to affirm that the suspending power was indeed illegal. As a result, judges at the assizes resumed prosecutions against Catholics for being in violation of the penal laws.[91] James made desperate efforts to salvage some credibility, but to little avail. Some of those arrested for making disturbances on the night of the bishops' release were convicted at the City of London's sessions, being either fined or sent to the house of correction. Those brought before the Middlesex sessions at Hickes Hall, however, had their bills of indictment thrown out by the grand jury (in a way reminiscent of the infamous Whig '*ignoramus*' juries of the Exclusion Crisis). Moreover, the Hickes Hall grand jury comprised precisely those types whom James had brought into positions of authority in order to win support for his policy of religious toleration: the foreman was a Baptist and the rest said to be 'of the same stamp'.[92] The King tried to encourage addresses in abhorrence of the bishops' petition, but these had difficulty getting off the ground, despite the purges of recent months.

Although eight members of the Middlesex grand jury subscribed an abhorrence in July, for example, the other thirteen refused.[93] James sacked the two judges (Holloway and Powell) who had argued that the bishops' petition did not constitute a libel and toyed with the idea of bringing the seven bishops before the Ecclesiastical Commission for refusing to read his Declaration, although no such proceedings were ever instituted. The commissioners did instruct chancellors, archdeacons and commissaries to launch inquiries into which clergy had read the Indulgence and to report those who had refused, but on the whole they refused to cooperate.[94] Bishop Sprat of Rochester resigned from the Ecclesiastical Commission in mid-August, because he thought it was wrong to proceed against those clergy who, out of conscience, had refused to read the Indulgence, even though Sprat himself had backed the King's order to that effect.[95]

THE BIRTH OF THE PRINCE OF WALES AND THE INVITATION TO WILLIAM OF ORANGE

The drama of the trial of the seven bishops upstaged what for James was the most momentous event of that summer, the birth of the Prince of Wales on 10 June. The King immediately issued a proclamation announcing the news, ordering the Lord Mayor of London to promote bonfires and setting aside two days of public thanksgiving (17 June in London, 1 July elsewhere).[96] The court and its agents in the localities did their best to encourage suitable public displays, while the *London Gazette* published accounts of celebrations brought to its attention in an effort to convey the impression that the nation was rejoicing with the King.[97] The evidence in fact suggests that the nation at large hardly found this a time for rejoicing, and those celebrations that did take place looked to all the world to be staged events. One loyalist newswriter wrote of the inexpressible 'joy for this happinesse' shown in London on 10 June, and reported how people feared they 'should have been burnt . . . with bonfires and drowned with wine' – his account making it clear not only that there was an abundance of alcohol to encourage the crowds to come out but also that he was one of the participants and scarcely an unbiased observer of the events he was purporting to describe.[98] At Oxford that same day there was one bonfire at Carfax, while the officers of the regiment stationed in town made another at the Cross Inn and provided a barrel or two of beer for the locals to try to put them in a celebratory mood. Magdalen College and Christ Church also lit bonfires, but no other colleges commemorated the event, 'knowing full well', the Oxford antiquary Anthony Wood tells us, that if the Prince lived 'the crowne of England and popish religion' would 'never part'. The initiation of *quo warranto* proceedings against the city of Oxford a few days later enabled the government to bring pressure to bear to ensure that the official day of thanksgiving on 1 July was better observed: the commissioners responsible for regulating the corporation ordered all the church-wardens to ring their bells, and the commissioners themselves and every army officer in town sponsored their own bonfires, as did many of the troopers. The colleges also seemed to join in the general celebrations, with all except Merton staging bonfires. But, according to Wood, it was a subterfuge: the joy that 'many protestants thus shew'd . . . under pretence of thanksgiving for the prince his birth' was really for 'the deliverance and quitting' of the seven bishops.[99] Indeed, a number of contemporaries, including those sympathetic to the court, observed that there were more bonfires in support of the bishops than for the birth of the male heir. Some communities were prepared to draw up congratulatory addresses, out of a sense of duty and good manners, but invariably in the face of considerable local opposition.[100] James staged an elaborate firework display on the River Thames on the night of 17 July to celebrate the birth and the Queen's safe delivery and return to health, which attracted some 100,000 spectators from the London area and surrounding countryside, but this also appears to have backfired. There were three mechanical figures in the display – two females representing fecundity and loyalty, and Bacchus – but according to the government newspaper, the *Publick Occurrences*, some local wits remodelled the effigies in advance to make them look like Queen Elizabeth, Anne Boleyn and Henry VIII, and then started spreading the rumour that these were 'to be publickly blown up, as an Emblem that all that they did, shall now be Revers'd'.[101]

The birth of the Prince of Wales put an end to the 'wait-for-better-times' strategy advocated by the likes of Halifax, since there was now little likelihood that James's policies would be reversed by his successor. As we have seen, doubts had been raised from almost as soon as the pregnancy had been announced as to whether the Queen were genuinely pregnant; now rumours began to spread that the Queen had not in truth been brought to bed of a son but that the infant had been smuggled into the delivery room in a warming pan. Shortly after the Prince's birth, James's own daughter, Anne, wrote to her sister Mary stating that she did not believe the Queen had been with child and 'where one believes it, a thousand do not'.[102] According to one anti-Catholic satire, soon 'the whole Kingdom' was laughing 'at the Sham', and 'the People' were saying that 'the Queen lay under such Circumstances at the time of the report of her Conception, that not all the Stallions in Europe could have got her with Child'.[103] If the warming-pan story were true – there is no way to know for sure, but the balance of evidence suggests that it almost certainly was not – then James was not only seeking to foist a Catholic successor on the nation by underhand means, but he was also defrauding his Protestant daughter, Mary, and her husband, William of Orange, of their rightful inheritance.[104]

On the day that the seven bishops were acquitted the earls of Devonshire and of Danby, Bishop Compton, the Earl of Shrewsbury, Lord Lumley, Edward Russell and Henry Sidney sent a letter to William of Orange inviting him to intervene in English affairs. The seven represented specific constituencies that William would need to be convinced would be on his side before he could engage in such a risky venture: Devonshire and Danby both were landed magnates who might expect to command substantial followings in their respective territorial spheres of influence, one a Whig, the other a Tory; Compton, the suspended Bishop of London, represented the Church; Shrewsbury and Lumley (both of whom, like Danby, had stood bail for the seven bishops) had been removed from the army for their opposition to James's intrusion of Catholic officers, and might be expected to represent disaffected opinion within the armed forces; Russell and Sidney represented the navy. Their letter assured William that 'the people' were 'so generally dissatisfied with the present conduct of the government' that 'nineteen parts of twenty . . . throughout the kingdom' desired a change, and 'would willingly contribute to it, if they had such a protection to countenance their rising, as would secure them from being destroyed'. It was 'no less certain', the letter continued, 'that much the greatest part of the nobility and gentry' were 'as much dissatisfied', and 'that some of the most considerable of them' would join William at his landing and use their interest 'to draw great numbers to them'. If William landed with a force sufficient 'to defend itself and them, till they could be got together into some order', they would soon have double the number of James's army, which they predicted would not remain loyal to the King in any case, since the officers and the common soldiers were 'so discontented'. It was important, however, for William to act now, before the court changed the officers and soldiers of the army, procured the meeting of a packed parliament, or began to proceed by more violent means.[105]

William was indeed to act quickly. The question was, would 'the people' prove to be 'so generally dissatisfied' as the Immortal Seven predicted?

7

The Desertion

In case Popery should intirely obtain here both in Church and State it would be so fatall to the Dutch Interest that is founded upon Protestancy, that some conceive they would be aggressors upon us not only by Sea but by Land, knowing that they cannot subsist if we entertaine Popery, and if they should, the Kingdome generally would stand well affected to them.

Roger Morrice, 26 November 1687[1]

The Acclamations of the People in England, the Desertion of the Army, and the general adherence of the Nobility and Gentry to the Prince of Orange at His Landing, prevented a Civil War, and the Effusion of Blood, and the present King became quietly vested in the Throne, and Government.

G[eorge] P[hilips], *The Second Apology for the Protestants of Ireland* (1689), p. 8

About the end of this year [1688] happen'd here in England the greatest revolution that was ever known. I mean by that most bold and heroick adventure of the most illustrious and famous . . . Prince of Orange, who soon turned the scale of affairs, and delivered us out of all our fears of tyranny and popery, which, as farr as I can possibly see, would have faln upon us.

Diary of Adam de la Pryme, p. 14

William had his invasion force ready to depart by mid-October. Bad weather frustrated his first attempt to depart, and the continuation of

adverse winds meant that his armada did not finally set sail until
1 November. His fleet was to drop anchor in Tor Bay, off the south
Devon coast, on 5 November. By any reckoning, William's decision to
invade England was a huge gamble – he was playing a high-stakes
game that could very easily have ended in disaster both for him and
for the Protestant interest in north-west Europe. It was indeed a
heroic adventure; and it was to trigger a remarkable transformation
(a great revolution, as contemporaries would have styled it) in the
political and religious affairs of England.

To understand why William chose to accept the invitation from
Devonshire, Danby et al. and how he was able to put together and
fund an invasion force we need to look both to the United Provinces
and also at developments on the Continent. Those who have criticized
conventional accounts of the Glorious Revolution as being too
focused on England and stressed the need to explore the European
dimension unquestionably have an important point. William was
concerned about the balance of power in Europe, and the threat that
the French posed to his own homeland. He had been planning the
invasion since April, and the so-called invitation of July was merely
the assurance of English support that he had long been seeking. Both
the context and the stakes were international; it was not only the
English, nor even just the inhabitants of the three Britannic kingdoms,
who were concerned.[2]

It would be wrong, however, to go too far and suggest that the
European dimension alone explains why the Glorious Revolution
happened, or that James was toppled purely as a result of a successful foreign invasion, the logic for which was dictated by the preoccupations of policy makers in the United Provinces. William, it is true,
invaded England with a large, professional army: some 10,692 regular infantry and 3,060 regular cavalry, plus various English, Scottish,
Huguenot and Dutch volunteers (many of whom were professional
soldiers). One scholar has claimed that William's total army may have
been as large as 21,000 men, although this is now largely agreed to be
an overestimate; somewhere in the region of 15,000 is closer to the
mark. What is clear is that William's army was numerically vastly
inferior to James's, which on the eve of the invasion numbered some
40,000 (including Scottish and Irish troops). James was able to send

24,000 English soldiers, plus 2,964 Scottish and 2,820 Irish troops (nearly 30,000 in total) to rendezvous at Salisbury Plain to meet the invasion force, while he had another 4,000 to 5,000 troops stationed in garrisons and a further 4,400 newly raised men who could be brought into action once they had completed their training. Moreover, William's troops had faced not just one but two sea voyages (having lost vital supplies – and especially horses – in the first abortive attempt) and were thus tired and seasick and in need of rest to regain full fighting fitness. By comparison, James's men were well-rested, well-fed and well-accommodated.[3] With nearly twice the forces at his disposal and the advantage of fighting on home soil, James should have had the upper hand, even granted that William's troops were more experienced and better trained.

Yet the simple fact is that William succeeded without having to engage James's troops in battle, although there were some skirmishes (notably at Wincanton and Reading) that resulted in fatalities, which belies the notion that the Revolution, even in England, was bloodless. It was not that William's invasion force proved superior to James's in battle, or even that William's army posed such an intimidating threat that English people realized they were fighting a lost cause and threw in the towel. Rather, James threw in the towel – in the face of desertions among the nobility and gentry, the mass of the civilian population, and even within his own military. This chapter will therefore examine why James's regime collapsed so easily and so quickly in the face of the foreign invasion. It will start by looking at how James responded to the threat of William's invasion and show how the crisis enabled the Tory-Anglican interest to force James to undo most of his controversial policies even before William had set foot on English soil. There was an Anglican revolution in the autumn of 1688, in other words, which preceded the ultimate Williamite revolution – though in this respect it was a revolution closer to the astronomical meaning of revolving back to the position where things had started from. The chapter will then proceed to look at how the people of England responded to William's invasion, looking at the various resistance movements to James that developed, particularly in the north of England; the increasing desertions to William as the Prince made his way from the West Country towards London; and the crowd unrest that erupted in opposition to the pro-Catholic policies pursued by the King and his advisers. We shall see that the overthrow of James II was no mere palace coup, peacefully engineered from above as a result of a dispute within the royal family. Instead it involved the active, and at times quite violent, resistance of broad cross-sections of the English population, and it was this which caused James to panic and to flee the realm without putting up a fight. In that sense it was not so much William's invading army that brought James down – although the importance of the Williamite invasion in shaping the way events were to unfold should not be downplayed – but rather the people of England.

WILLIAM'S INVASION AND THE COLLAPSE OF JAMES'S REGIME

James was not oblivious to the military build-up in the United Provinces, but seems to have thought it inconceivable that William would contemplate an offensive campaign so late in the season or over the winter, or indeed that his own nephew and son-in-law would act against him. As late as 8 September, Sunderland could report that despite 'the noise of the preparations made by our neighbours' the King remained 'very well assured' that there was no design against him.[4] James therefore continued with his plans to secure a parliamentary repeal of the penal laws and Tests. On 24 August he had announced that parliament would meet on 27 November, and government agents busied themselves trying to drum up support for religious toleration.[5] It was not until after the electoral writs had been issued on 18 September that James began to sense the degree of danger he was in. From the 21st he started sending out instructions to increase the size of existing regiments in his army and issuing commissions for the raising of new regiments. He also began making concessions on the domestic front. On the 21st he issued a proclamation designed to assuage Anglican doubts about his plans for toleration, promising he would 'inviolably . . . preserve the Church of England' and confirming that Catholics would remain barred from sitting in the Commons. The following day he wrote to the Lord Lieutenants inviting them to restore those deputy Lieutenants and JPs who had recently been removed from office, though the fact that the King spoke in terms of hoping to secure their support in the forthcoming parliament reveals that, even at this late stage, James was not anticipating a Dutch invasion that might cause him to put his domestic programme on hold. It was only from the 24th that James began to speak of the invasion being imminent. On the 27th he sent for military reinforcements from Ireland (some 2,800), ordered the standing army in Scotland (another 3,700) to march south into England, and the next day issued a proclamation recalling the parliamentary writs and inviting his English subjects to assist him in opposing the Dutch.[6]

In a desperate attempt to build up more support at home, James now made a complete U-turn. In a meeting at Whitehall on 28 September, he informed the bishops that he was willing that 'things past should be buryed in perpetuall oblivion', and pledged to restore the Bishop of London, readmit the dismissed fellows of Magdalen College, terminate the Ecclesiastical Commission, restore the corporations and allow the dispensing power to be determined by (a regularly elected) parliament, which he would call immediately.[7] His first gesture came on 2 October, when he restored London's charter (which had been taken away in 1683 during the height of the Tory Reaction).[8] On the 3rd the Archbishop of Canterbury and the bishops of Bath and Wells, Chichester, Ely, London, Peterborough, Rochester, St Asaph and Winchester presented the King with an address in which they outlined their demands for reform. Picking up on James's promises of 28 September and adding their own refinements, they asked that James place the government of the counties in the hands of those qualified by law, annul the Ecclesiastical Commission and promise never to set one up again in the future, stop all dispensations and cancel those granted since he came to the throne, restore the president and fellows of Magdalen College, suppress the Jesuit schools, 'desist from the Exercise of such a Dispensing power, as hath of late been used, and to permitt that point to be freely, and calmly debated, and argued, and finally settled in parliament', stop the *quo warranto* proceedings against the corporations and restore the old charters, and issue writs for a free and regular parliament, 'in which the Church of England' might 'be secur'd according to the Acts of Uniformity' and provision be made 'for a due Liberty of Conscience, and for securing the Liberties, and properties of all your Subjects'. In short, the bishops asked James 'to restore all things to the State in which he found them when he cam to the Crowne'.[9] Morrice observed how the government seemed 'now to be like a Vessell tossed up and down at sea, and ready to sinke'; the bishops had 'given the Vessell a Twigg to take hold on whereby it may draw it selfe to Land', but they seemed 'yet to keepe the Hatchet in their own hand, by which they can cut off that Twigg at their pleasure'.[10]

James immediately began to comply. He abolished his Ecclesiastical Commission on 5 October; on the 11th he instructed the Bishop of Winchester, the visitor of Magdalen College, to settle the College 'regularly and statutably', and on the 17th he issued a proclamation restoring the corporations (with certain exceptions). He also began restoring JPs who had been on the bench in 1687 and even (in a few counties) removing some of the recently appointed Catholic and nonconformist magistrates.[11] It appeared that the bishops had brought James to heel. If their programme had been carried out in full, there would have been an Anglican revolution that would have effectively resulted in a return to the *status quo ante* (though with some degree of religious toleration established by parliament) and which would have left James on the throne. This attempted Anglican revolution was scuppered, however, by William of Orange's invasion and the consequent collapse of James's government.

There has been endless debate over whether or not the Prince of Orange had always intended to seize the English throne (and thus also the Irish and Scottish thrones) for himself. In fact, William's number one priority was to make sure that England was not only detached from France's orbit but also brought into his continental alliance (the League of Augsburg) against Louis XIV. He may, for a while, have thought that he could achieve this without necessarily having to set himself up as king of England, Scotland and Ireland in James's stead, though it seems unlikely that he still believed this by the autumn of 1688. He needed to be careful, however, about how he justified his invasion to British Protestants, so that he could sustain their support and not frighten them into rallying behind James II in the face of a foreign threat. He would need a very carefully worded invasion manifesto.

William's English friends sent him such a draft manifesto in late August, which was primarily the work of Danby and which laid out the grounds for the invasion in a way designed to appeal to the broadest possible cross-section of the population. The manifesto concentrated on developments that had happened since the accession of James II in 1685, turning a blind eye to any alleged abuses of royal power under Charles II. The draft provoked considerable debate when it reached William in The Hague. Danby was, of course, a Tory Anglican, and it was the Tory Anglicans whose loyalty to the crown had been dislodged as a result of James II's political and religious initiatives. Many of those with William in the Low Countries, however, were Whigs who had been forced into exile during the years of the Tory Reaction or in the aftermath of the Argyll and Monmouth rebellions. They included English radicals, such as John Wildman, as well as more extreme Whig peers, such as the Earl of Macclesfield and Lord Mordaunt. There were also more moderate influences, such as Gilbert Burnet, a Scots-born clerical Whig who put the interests of the Anglican Church first. Then there was a group of dissident Scots, including Sir James Dalrymple of Stair and William Carstares. Wildman objected to Danby's draft, and urged that William's manifesto should rehearse grievances not just against James but also against Charles, implicating Tory Anglicans in the process and thereby limiting the appeal specifically to Whigs and dissenters; he believed that 'as the Declaration was [currently] penn'd, all the Tory party would probably come in and be receiv'd by the Prince', and the chance of more far-reaching reform would be lost. Burnet, among others, argued that Wildman's proposal would be a tactical mistake, since it would undoubtedly alienate those who had sacrificed so much in standing up against James's innovations and thereby seriously jeopardize the success of the expedition. In the end William and his advisers decided to accept Danby's draft, with slight modifications.[12]

William's *Declaration . . . Of the Reasons Inducing him to Appear in Armes in . . . England* was published in The Hague on 30 September. It was, in essence, a catalogue of all the allegedly illegal acts committed by the crown during James II's reign, though instead of attacking James himself it blamed the King's counsellors, accusing them of overturning 'the Religion, Laws, and Liberties' of England, Scotland and

Ireland, promoting 'Arbitrary Government', and endeavouring to introduce 'a Religion which is contrary to Law'. To advance this design, these evil counsellors had, it was claimed, invented the king's suspending power; purged the judicial bench to get a ruling in favour of the dispensing power; procured the appointment to public office of Catholics, who were rendered by law 'Incapable of all such Employments'; set up an Ecclesiastical Commission against law; turned out the President and fellows of Magdalen College 'contrary to Law'; promoted Catholic worship against 'many expresse Lawes'; set up several Jesuit schools; purged the lieutenancy, magisterial bench and town corporations of those who refused to agree to a repeal of the Tests and penal laws; and attempted to interfere with the freedom of parliamentary elections. 'The dismall effects of this subversion of the established Religion, Lawes and Liberties in England', the *Declaration* continued, were even more apparent when one looked at Ireland, where 'the whole Government' was currently in 'the hands of Papists', and where the Protestant inhabitants lived in daily fear 'of what may be justly apprehended from the Arbitrary Power which is set up there'. These evil counsellors had also supposedly 'prevailed with the King to declare in Scotland' that he was 'clothed with an Absolute power' and that all his subjects were obliged 'to obey him without Reserve', thus enabling James to assume 'an Arbitrary power' over both 'the Religion and Lawes of that Kingdome'. From all this it was apparent what was 'to be looked for in England'. The *Declaration* predictably condemned the supposititious Prince of Wales, who it claimed 'was not born by the Queen'. It insisted, however, that William's design was 'no other' than 'to have a free and lawfull Parliament assembled as soon as possible', so as to address the grievances identified. William would also secure the calling of a parliament in Scotland, 'for the restoring the Ancient Constitution of that Kingdom, and for bringing the Matter of Religion to such a Settlement, that the people may live easy and happy', and 'study to bring the Kingdome of Ireland to such a state, that the Setlement there may be religiously observed' and 'the Protestant and British Interest there . . . Secured'.[13] Following his invasion, upon establishing a power base in the West Country, William issued a second declaration, adding the charge that James had formed a private league with France, which William claimed he had not mentioned earlier merely out of deference to James, who had publicly avowed that he had done no such thing.[14]

In the face of the Dutch invasion, some people rallied behind their beleaguered king. In early October, the grand jury for the county of Cumberland drew up an address against the Dutch, and similar addresses followed from the city of Carlisle and the common council of Exeter. Several members of the nobility and gentry pledged their support for James, offering to raise men on his behalf, though for some this was merely a subterfuge: the *London Gazette* announced that one of those who had pledged was Danby.[15] One manuscript poem, which circulated in the West Country and seems to have been designed to appeal to dissenters, urged 'Good people' to 'Throw the Orange away', since it was 'a very sowr fruit': 'Lob, Pen and a Score / Of those honest men and more', the rhymester predicted, 'Will find this same Orange exceedingly sowr'.[16] What impresses, however, is the speed and ease with which William gained control over England following his landing. It would certainly be wrong to imply that the English immediately, and en masse, went over to William. There were many whose instincts were to be loyal to their king and who tried to do what they could to resist the Dutch invader; there were even more who initially were unsure how to act and were reluctant to engage in an act of treason by declaring themselves for William until they could see which way the tide was turning. Rather, we should think in terms of an expedition that quickly developed a momentum of its own: William's initial successes, together with early manifestations of support for him, soon induced more and more people to declare their sympathy or go over to his cause, until in the end James himself came to realize that there was no way he could halt the Dutch advance.

William did not, of course, just invade and hope for the best. He and his agents had been conspiring for some time with leading dissidents in England to ensure that he would meet with limited resistance from James's armed forces and that leading members of England's politically and economically important classes would rally to his cause. Such was the disillusionment with James among the English merchant community that many helped provide funds to finance William's invasion, pouring some £200,000 into William's coffers in just six weeks in July and August 1688.[17] A Williamite conspiracy within the navy was designed to ensure that William met with limited resistance as he attempted to cross the Channel. Arthur Herbert, the former admiral whom James had replaced with the Catholic Roger Strickland, had gone over to William in the summer and was to lead the Dutch invasion force; he was also able to ensure that many of the sea captains who had previously enjoyed his patronage pledged not to fight William. In the end, the fruits of the conspiracy were never put to the test, since unfavourable winds meant the English fleet was unable to get out of the Thames estuary and engage the Dutch.[18] Disaffected nobility in the north of England were also conspiring to secure the north of the kingdom for William.[19] However, again, the wind dictated that William's armada did not head up the east coast to link up with these dissidents, but instead sailed down the English Channel. William also came over with a sizeable contingent of discontented English and Scottish exiles – 'disgruntled peers, redundant MPs, proclaimed traitors, escaped spies, fugitive rebels, suspected republicans, renegade officers, and mischievous divines' – among them lords Cardross, Leven, Macclesfield, Mordaunt, Shrewsbury and Wiltshire, Sir Rowland Gwynne, Sir John Hotham, Sir Robert Peyton, Sir William Waller, Sir James Dalrymple of Stair, Gilbert Burnet, Robert Ferguson, Andrew Fletcher of Saltoun, John Locke, Edward Russell, Henry Sidney and John Wildman, to name but a few.[20] This was not merely a foreign invasion force, akin to the Spanish Armada of 1588. Rather, this was a British conspiracy in which discontented English and Scots utilized the resources available to a man who, although head of a foreign state, was nevertheless married to the next-in-line to the English, Scottish and Irish thrones (barring the supposedly supposititious Prince of Wales) and who was third-in-line himself, in order not to subject the three kingdoms to foreign rule but rather to free them from perceived tyranny, in accordance with the desires of the vast majority of British Protestants. To claim that 1688 should be seen 'as an instance of what had last been seriously attempted a century earlier' is to get it seriously wrong.[21]

Upon landing, William managed to secure control over the West Country fairly easily. He gained Exeter on 9 November, and although the magistrates of the recently restored corporation tried to stop him from entering and the clergy subsequently refused to read his *Declaration* in their churches, the ordinary citizens gave him a tumultuous reception.[22] William was to stay at Exeter until the 21st, 'to refresh the Army after it had been so long on Shipboard, and to recover the Horses to their former Strength, as also for the Gentlemen of the Country thereabout to come and join his Highness there', as one of the chaplains of his expeditionary force put it.[23] He was soon joined by the Whigs Lord Colchester, Lord Edward Russell and Thomas Wharton (the sons and heirs of the Whig peers Earl Rivers, the Earl of Bedford and Lord Wharton), and the Tories Sir Edward Seymour and William Portman. To cement support for William across the nation, Burnet, at the instigation of the Tory MP Sir Edward Seymour, penned an Association for 'pursuing the ends of the prince's declaration', which was then printed and circulated for general subscription. Edward Russell and Lord Leven negotiated the surrender of the garrison at Plymouth from the Earl of Bath on 18 November, Bath himself going over to the Prince, while Shrewsbury was sent to secure Bristol. With William's rear now safeguarded, the way was clear for a march on London.[24] Lord Lovelace was foiled in his attempt to bring some seventy 'well appointed men' to link up with William by the Gloucestershire militia under the command of the Duke of Beaufort, the only Lord Lieutenant to make any concerted effort to stop supporters from joining the Prince; they came to blows, and a couple of the militia men were killed and half a dozen more were injured, but Lovelace and thirteen of his followers were taken and sent to Cirencester jail and, subsequently, Gloucester castle.[25] However, in Dorset, the local nobility and gentry began to organize the militia and the collection of taxation for the benefit of the Prince, while 'many of the greatest quality and estates' in Somerset and Devon also joined with William, as did the local populace.[26]

By the end of the third week in November it was said that William had enlisted some 12,000 recruits, so great an army that he wished many would offer 'to repair home' until he told them they were needed.[27] What he wanted was not civilians but deserters from James's army, as promised in the letter inviting him to invade, and he expected much from a Williamite conspiracy brewing amongst certain army officers. The first of the major desertions occurred on

12 November, when Viscount Cornbury, Clarendon's eldest son and commander of the royal dragoons, and Thomas Langston, with the Duke of St Alban's regiment of horse, deserted the royal army at Salisbury Plain and crossed into enemy lines, although in fact they carried few of their troops with them. Others began to run from their colours over the next few days. The most significant blow came in the third week of November: in the early hours of Saturday the 24th, Lord Churchill, the Duke of Grafton and Colonel Berkeley crossed into enemy lines, and they were rapidly followed by the young Duke of Ormonde (the grandson of the former Lord Lieutenant of Ireland who had died in July 1688), the Duke of Northumberland, Prince George of Denmark (the husband of James's daughter, Anne) and Lord Drumlanrig. The total number of desertions was not particularly large. The effect on morale within the army camp, however, was devastating, as no man could be sure of the loyalty of his neighbour or of his commanding officer.[28] The mood of the army was further swayed by the publication, in October 1688, of Thomas Wharton's anti-Irish song 'Lilliburlero'. Although originally written in early 1687 in condemnation of Tyrconnell's appointment as Lord Deputy of Ireland, it was now printed for the first time and enjoyed enormous popularity. A sequel was immediately published, making direct references to the events of the autumn of 1688, while supporters of James II even wrote some anti-Dutch words to the tune, although the attempt to appropriate the song for the government seriously backfired since it only served to remind the public of the original. Burnet, despite thinking 'Lilliburlero' 'a foolish ballad', nevertheless admitted that it 'made an impression on the [King's] army that cannot be well imagined by those who saw it not', and observed that 'the whole army, and at last all people both in city and country, were singing it perpetually'. Wharton himself boasted that the tune 'sung a deluded Prince out of three kingdoms'.[29]

There was a series of risings in support of William in the north of England, where William had initially been expected to land. Lord Delamere raised a regiment of some 300 'Noblemen and divers Gentlemen of great Quality' in Cheshire and declared for the Prince on 15 November; 'great numbers' of countrymen and freeholders apparently volunteered to join with him, but Delamere sent them home, 'promising to give them notice' if he had 'any further occasion of their service'. Not that the upper-class nature of his regiment meant that it acted in a particularly respectable way; according to one report, Delamere took to riding about the country 'like a mad man', seizing horses belonging to Catholics and despoiling their chapels. The Earl of Devonshire raised his tenants and marched into Derby on 17 November, where he declared for a free parliament, before proceeding to Nottingham, which he entered on the 20th and where he was joined by Delamere the following day. On the 24th Delamere and his supporters headed south to join up with the Prince, passing through Lichfield, Birmingham and Worcester, before arriving at Bristol (which was by now under Williamite control) on 2 December. Devonshire remained in Nottingham, where he was joined by reinforcements from the south Midlands (particularly Northamptonshire and Buckinghamshire) on 29 November and then, on 2 December, by James's own daughter, Princess Anne, and Bishop Compton of London (who had fled the capital a few days earlier). On 22 November, Danby seized York and declared for 'a free parliament and the Protestant religion and no Popery', and by the beginning of December he had also secured the capitulation of the important garrison at Hull. Other areas followed suit. On learning the news of William's landing, William Rowland of Hexham in Northumberland gathered together a band of Protestants and proceeded to disarm all the papists' houses in the vicinity. Rowland then went off to London, presumably to assist in the campaign against popery in the south. In East Anglia, the Duke of Norfolk raised the militia for William and took Norwich and King's Lynn, 'whereupon the Tradesmen, Seamen and inferior sort, put Orange Ribbons in their Hates, shouting and echoing Huzzas for the Prince of Orange and the Duke of Norfolk'. On the Welsh borders, Lord Herbert of Cherbery and Sir Edward Harley, together with 'most of the gentry of Worcestershire and Herefordshire' entered Worcester and seized Ludlow castle. Everywhere the insurgents took measures to disarm the local Catholics.[30]

Others joined in the demand for a free parliament. Those close to the King saw it as the only hope for a peaceful solution to the crisis. Thus on 17 November, seven bishops (including the Archbishop of Canterbury) and twelve temporal peers (among them Clarendon and

Rochester) petitioned the King for a free parliament as 'the only Visible way to preserve your Majesty and this your Kingdom' and avoid 'the Effusion of Christian Blood'; the King replied that he could not call a parliament while there was an invading army in the West, but he would do so 'as soon as the present troubles were appeas'd'.[31] Similar addresses came in from across the country: from Westmorland and Cumberland and Lancashire in the north, to Norwich in the east, and Gloucestershire and Devon in the west.[32] By early December, as the Countess of Huntingdon put it, the nobility and gentry were up 'in all Counties', having all declared 'for a free parliament and the protestant religion and many for the Prince of Oreng'.[33]

How did those who had orchestrated the uprisings on William's behalf justify engaging in active resistance against their king? For Whigs this was fairly straightforward, since they had always held that tyrants who broke the law could be resisted. Justifying his active resistance in a speech to his tenants in Cheshire in November 1688, Delamere proclaimed that he had to choose whether he would be 'a Slave and a Papist, or a Protestant and a Freeman'; if the nation were to be delivered, 'it must be by force or by miracle', he said, but 'it would be too great a presumption to expect the latter, and therefore our Deliverance must be by force'.[34] In their declaration, the nobility, gentry and commons assembled at Nottingham claimed that although it was rebellion 'to resist a King that governs by Law . . . he was always accounted a Tyrant that made his Will the Law; and to resist such an one' was 'no Rebellion but a necessary Defence'.[35]

For others who joined with the Williamite resistance movement, however, the situation was a little more complicated. Let us take Gilbert Burnet, for example. He was one of William's chief propagandists and thus clearly a Whig in his politics. Yet he was also a churchman who, after earning his MA in his native Scotland, had served as a licensed preacher in the Scottish Episcopalian Church and then as Professor of Divinity at the University of Glasgow before moving to England, where he had been a royal chaplain and then chaplain to the Rolls Chapel and a lecturer at St Clement Danes, London, before falling out of royal favour and opting to withdraw to the Continent upon the accession of James II. Under William he was to become Bishop of Salisbury. A self-appointed apologist for the

Church of England against the errors of Rome, back in December 1674 he had even preached a sermon entitled *Subjection for Conscience Sake Asserted*.[36] One of the first to hint at the necessity of resistance to James II in print, in the autumn of 1688 he produced his *Enquiry into the Measures of Submission* to complement William's invasion manifesto of 30 September. It was quite overtly an Anglican resistance tract.

Burnet began by asserting that all men were 'born free' and had a 'duty of Self-preservation'. Although 'Considerations of Religion' did indeed 'bring Subjects under stricter Obligations, to pay all due Allegiance and Submission to their Princes', they did 'not at all extend Allegiance further than the Law carries it'. Under the English system of government, the king's authority was limited: if he acted 'beyond the limits of his Power', subjects lay under no obligation to obey; and if any, acting illegally in the king's name, sought to 'Invade our Property' they were 'violent Aggressours' and the principle of self-preservation allowed for 'as Violent a resistance'. Burnet was also adamant that England was 'a free Nation' with 'its Liberties and Properties reserved to it by many positive and express Laws'; if 'we have a right to our Property, we must likewise be supposed to have a right to preserve it . . . against the Invasions of the Prerogative'.[37]

The difficulty was that there were 'many express Laws' that made it 'unlawfull upon any pretence whatsoever to take Arms against the King, or any Commissioned by him', and that all office-holders in Church and state had sworn an oath to this effect. 'And since this had been the constant Doctrine of the Church of England', Burnet continued, in a vein designed to reveal his own sincere commitment to the teachings of the Anglican Church as well as his intent to reach out to those with Anglican convictions, 'it will be a very heavy Imputation on us, if it appears, that tho we held those Opinions, as long as the Court and the Crown have favoured us, yet as soon as the Court turns against us, we change our principles'. There was a tacit exception, however, Burnet insisted: whenever liberty and resistance came into conflict, liberty took priority. 'The not resisting the King' applied only 'to the Executive Power', that is, we could not resist upon 'pretence of ill Administrations in the Execution of the Law'. But this did not extend 'to an Invasion of the Legislative Power, or to a total

Subversion of the Government', for the law 'did not design to lodge that Power in the King'. It followed that if the king tried 'to Subvert the whole Foundation of the Government . . . he annuls his own Power; and then ceases to be King, having endeavoured to destroy that, upon which his Authority is founded'. Burnet then went on to consider whether the foundations of the government had been struck at under James, and concluded that they had, rehearsing in full the case made against James by William's invasion manifesto.[38]

For Danby, who led the resistance movement at York, the problem was especially intellectually taxing. In effect, Danby had been the original Tory: the founder of the Church and King party under Charles II in the mid-1670s and, as the leading minister at the time of the Popish Plot, he was the focus of the Whigs' wrath during the earliest phase of the Exclusion Crisis. His motives are easy to understand. In the mid-1670s, he had sought to tie the crown to a pro-Anglican and anti-French policy; he had arranged the marriage between William of Orange and James's daughter, Mary, to whom he expected the succession would pass after James's eventual demise; and he had even proposed limitations on a popish successor to guarantee the Church would be safe should James inherit the throne. James's policies as king had undermined his entire political agenda. He had also been made a sacrificial lamb in the wake of the Popish Plot, when the Commons had tried to impeach him for allegedly trying to introduce an arbitrary and tyrannical form of government, and although he had escaped impeachment, he had spent five years in the Tower and was not to regain royal favour after his release. Yet back in 1675, Danby had sought to impose a non-resistance oath on those who sat in the Lords and had launched a propaganda offensive designed to promote the English sovereign as a divine-right, absolute monarch. One might think this should have made it impossible for him later to contemplate active resistance to James.[39]

A justification of Danby's northern resistance movement appeared in print in 1689. Published anonymously, it has been attributed to Danby himself, and it was certainly intended to offer a vindication of the justice of the undertaking that could appeal to Tory-Anglican consciences. Laws, the author states, were supposed to be supportive, not destructive, of man. When a man cannot defend himself by law, 'he may by the Law of Nature . . . smite his Adversary to save his own life'. If some set about trying 'to destroy the Rest' it was 'lawful by the Laws of God and Man, for the injured to defend themselves'. 'Arbitrary Princes' might have 'a Political power to treat a Subject cruelly and inhumanely', but this was not true of those supposed 'to rule by Laws made for the Publick Good, and such as render the Subjects Freemen, not Slaves; such as secures their Religion, Liberty and Property'. If such princes, 'contrary to Law', imprison their subjects or seize their estates, 'they do it unjustly, without God's Warrant, or any Political Authority, and may be resisted'. The author accepted that government was ordained by God; but God had left it to the people to decide which type of government to erect. If the governor tried to assume more power than his people had given him, then 'Subjects may by the Laws of God and Man deny to yield to it'. In answer to the Pauline injunction that 'the powers that be' were ordained of God and thus could not be resisted, the author maintained that governments had 'God's warrant to proceed according to the Frame of the Government, to the End of the Government, which is the publick Good', but 'if the Governor proceed neither according to the frame of the Government, nor to the End, but against it, such Process cannot be the Ordinance of God'. It did not follow that 'because I may not resist the Ordinance of God, that I may not resist the powerless and inauthoritative, unjust, Attempts of Superiors upon me'. Thus 'resistance (for the Publick Good) of Illegal Commission'd Forces, is not resisting the King's Person, but his Forces; not his Power, but his Force without power'. One certainly should not wittingly or wilfully kill the king, however, even if he joins with wicked men. Regicide was not an option.[40]

The author then proceeded to direct his argument more specifically to the English context. England had a limited monarchy, where the king was bound, by his coronation oath, 'to Govern by the Laws'. If a king acted against law, and not for the public good, then he was guilty of injustice. 'Illegal force . . . must be resisted', though resistance must be a last resort, and only engaged in if the cause is good and can achieve the desired end. It is not rebellion, however, because 'Rebellion is resisting the just Power of the Government'. To the objection that only the king possessed the power of the sword, the author insisted that 'If force be offered that wants Political Power, who ever does it, does it but in the Nature of a Private person, and Private persons may resist such.' As for our oaths of allegiance, the author maintained that we swore to give allegiance to the frame of the government and that our allegiance was therefore 'bounded by our Laws', to which the king also owed allegiance, having sworn to observe them in his coronation oath. Although the king undoubtedly possessed prerogative powers, the royal prerogative could not be used against the frame of the government or the public good. 'A Prerogative therefore cannot destroy a Law, but it may supply its defects, pardoning a Condemned innocent, or a hopeful penitent, or dispensing with a Law, to one, that by particular Accident, the Law in its rigour would undo.' (Danby himself, of course, had received such a royal pardon back in 1679.) 'But no Prerogative', he continued, 'can Impower the King to destroy the people's Liberty or Property. That dispensing Power, that . . . casts all the Laws asleep', he was adamant, in allusion to James's Declarations of Indulgence, 'is no Prerogative belonging to the Crown of England'. 'Resisting Illegalities, and Misgovernment', he concluded, was therefore 'the way to preserve Government', as long as the king remained safe.[41]

THE CROWD AND THE REVOLUTION OF 1688

Along with the uprisings in the north and Midlands, and the desertions to William amongst the nobility, gentry, merchants and armed forces, there was also an outbreak of anti-Catholic rioting in the autumn. There had been periodic unrest earlier in the reign, revealing that in many communities tensions between Protestants and Catholics lay not far beneath the surface. Thus, as we saw in Chapter 5, there were riots in London and a number of provincial towns in the spring of 1686 upon the first opening of public Catholic chapels (see p. 200). A serious incident happened at York on Shrove Tuesday 1688. It started innocently enough, when some youths gathered in the Minster Yard to indulge in the traditional holiday pastime of throwing at cocks – a rather barbaric pastime whereby participants took turns at throwing a club at a cock that was tied by one leg to a stake in the ground (the winner, i.e., the one who killed the cock, got to take it home for dinner). A local Catholic homeowner came out to complain about the noise and the dispute escalated when the man assaulted a couple of the youths and they replied by throwing stones, breaking the window of a Catholic chapel which happened to be inside the man's house. Whether this was a premeditated attack on a Catholic mass or holiday high spirits that got out of hand depends on which account one reads. The homeowner, however, believed that he was being victimized because of his religion and sent for the Catholic troops that were stationed in the city: these not only proceeded to arrest some of the youths and a number of citizens who were innocent bystanders, but made their detainees ride the wooden horse – a military punishment that should not have been inflicted on civilians.[42]

Anti-Catholic agitation escalated dramatically as James's regime plunged deeply into crisis in the final months of 1688. Trouble erupted in London on 30 September at the chapel in Lime Street, when the Jesuit priest Charles Petre (the brother of James's Jesuit privy counsellor) spoke disparagingly of the King James Bible in his sermon. A large crowd quickly assembled. They pulled Petre from the pulpit, smashed the altar, and would have gone on to demolish the chapel completely had not the Lord Mayor taken swift action to restore the peace.[43] The respite was only temporary. The following week an angry crowd once more forced its way into the chapel, causing considerable damage before the Lord Mayor and local constables managed to restore order; in addition there was a violent assault on the Catholic chapel in Bucklersbury and on the friary in Lincoln's Inn Fields.[44] The Lime Street chapel was the scene of further trouble two weeks later, when a group of youths began to torment a couple of Irish soldiers who happened to come by even though the chapel was shut. The soldiers charged at the youths with their swords, whereupon a large crowd assembled and chased the soldiers off. The Irishmen then ran into a nearby church, causing mayhem: the congregation shouted 'massacre' and immediately fled the church in panic, some of them leaping out of windows; one individual broke his leg in the fall.[45] On Lord Mayor's day (Monday 29 October), traditionally a public holiday in London, 'the Mobilee went from their Bonefires to the

Masshouse in Bucklersbury', broke in and proceeded to deface it, removing vestments, copes, ornaments and trinkets, which they burned in the street.[46] The King ordered the Lord Mayor and sheriffs to make sure nothing like this happened again, and the following Sunday the trained bands were out in force to stop the youths from assaulting the Catholic chapels in Lincoln's Inn Fields and Lime Street.[47] However, there was further violence on Sunday 11 November, occasioned by the spread of a rumour that 'gridirons, spits, great cauldrons' and other 'very strange and unusual instruments of cruelty' intended for use on Protestants were being stored in the recently opened Benedictine priory in Clerkenwell. A crowd of youths stormed the building and tried to pull it down, and with the city authorities finding it impossible to hold the crowd at bay, the horse guards were sent for, who fired into the crowd, killing about four of the rioters and injuring many more.

James at last realized he would have to back down. Following the trouble on the 11th, he immediately ordered the closure of all Catholic chapels in London, except those belonging to the royal family and foreign ambassadors. Even this gesture was not enough to bring quiet to the streets. When the monks of Clerkenwell began to remove their effects for safe-keeping on the 12th, a crowd of youths seized three cartloads of their goods in Holborn and burned them publicly in the streets, and it took extensive policing of the establishments that remained open to ensure that no further attacks happened over the next couple of weeks.[48] A heavy armed presence did at least prevent a planned pope-burning on 17 November (the anniversary of Queen Elizabeth's accession): the apprentices, it was reported, had divided themselves into three regiments with banners bearing the inscription 'No Pope, No Popists', and had even planned to attack the houses of Lord Salisbury and other Catholic converts around London, but the trained bands and king's guards were out in force that day and managed to prevent any disturbances.[49]

There were also attacks on those associated with James's policies. In early October, Solicitor-General Sir William Williams, one of the prosecutors in the trial of the seven bishops, had the windows of his chambers in Gray's Inn smashed and 'reflecting inscriptions' fixed over his door.[50] The house of the King's printer, Henry Hills, was attacked on three different occasions in the first two weeks of November, on the last by a crowd of over a thousand, who broke his windows and threatened 'to do him more mischief', before the King finally ordered the Lord Mayor to station a strong guard outside Hill's establishment to prevent any further trouble.[51]

Similar unrest broke out in the provinces. In Norwich on 14 October (James's birthday), a crowd of about a thousand people, mainly adolescent males, attacked a Catholic chapel and used the priest 'very ill' before being dispersed by the mayor and sheriffs.[52] At the end of the month a group burned the Catholic chapel in Birmingham and proceeded, we are told, to 'secure the Papists', making sure they could not be a threat, while in Oxford on 5 November (Gunpowder Treason Day), although there were no riots, there were 'more bonefiers at Colleges and in the streets' than ever before 'in spite to the papists'.[53] The risings of the Williamite peers in the north and Midlands also brought in their wake anti-Catholic violence, as the insurgents ransacked the houses of local Catholics in the search for priests, arms and horses, and destroyed places of Catholic worship. News reached Oxford on 26 November that Delamere 'was about Northampton burning all popish chapel stuffs and defacing popish chappells' and would soon be in Oxford, which caused several of the University's Catholics to decide that the time had come to get out of town as quickly as possible.[54] On Friday 30 November, a crowd in Cambridge broke into Father Francis's chapel in Sidney Sussex College and carried away vestments and all the ornaments for saying mass, which they then publicly destroyed in a bonfire in the street. They also went after a priest in Bennett's College, who had to hide 'in a bogg house' to 'escape their fury', made a Catholic 'dance naked in a ditch till he promised to change his religion', pulled 'divers new Converts . . . through the dirt', and smashed all the windows of the house of the Catholic former mayor, whom they dragged out of bed and whose scarlet gown they 'burnt . . . upon a Pole'.[55] At Oxford on the afternoon of 4 December a crowd of 200 people, mainly boys, went to every popish house in town and smashed the windows, starting first with the Mitre Inn, whose owner had openly condemned those who had gone over to William and stated that 'he hoped to see Oxford in ashes before Christmas'.[56] By the beginning of the second week of December many urban centres had witnessed attacks on Catholic chapels and the residences of Catholics: in addition to London, Northampton, Norwich, York, Oxford and Cambridge, we could add Bristol, Bury St Edmunds, Gloucester, Hereford, Ipswich, Newcastle upon Tyne, Shrewsbury, Stafford, Sudbury, Wolverhampton and Worcester.[57]

The general anti-Catholic fever was further fuelled by the publication of a spurious third Declaration issued in William's name – dated 28 November but published in London on 4 December and dispersed 'over most Parts of the Kingdom' – alleging that 'great Numbers of Armed Papists' had lately made their way towards London either to fire the city or massacre the inhabitants, calling upon all magistrates to take speedy action to disarm Catholics, and warning that any Catholics found in possession of arms or in any military or civil office would be treated by the Williamite forces as 'Robbers, Free-booters and Banditi'. The Whig Hugh Speke later claimed to have written the Declaration, together with 'another Gentleman', though other contemporaries believed this a vain pretence; John Oldmixon thought it had probably been penned by Samuel Johnson. William, although disowning it, nevertheless 'seem'd not at all displeas'd with the Thing', while most soon realized 'it did his Highness's Interest a great deal of Service'.[58] In London, the phoney Declaration was brought to the Lord Mayor, who was asked to execute it, while at the Middlesex sessions at Hickes Hall a grand jury drew up a presentment against the earls of Sunderland, Salisbury and Peterborough 'and all other English Papists that were reconciled to the Church of Rome as Guilty of High Treason' (though they were subsequently persuaded to let it drop).[59] The Declaration had the effect of terrifying Catholics, and many Catholic office-holders immediately laid down their commissions and fled, prompting the diarist John Evelyn to remark 'it lookes like a Revolution'.[60] It also prompted 'Protestants everywhere' to stand 'on their Guard' and to proceed 'in most Places' to disarm 'the Papists' so that 'ever after that', Speke boasted, the Catholics did not 'make any shew of Resistance in any Part of England'.[61]

James was clearly unnerved. Initially hoping to contain William in the West, he dispatched troops to establish a forward position at Salisbury Plain, which he appointed as the general rendezvous of all his forces, and set off from London on 17 November to join them, arriving two days later. Yet faced with open revolt in the west and in the north, anti-Catholic rioting in London and some provincial towns, and desertions within the army, he panicked. By now suffering from frequent nosebleeds and clearly on the verge of a nervous breakdown, he accepted the advice of a council of war held on 23 November that he should order his army to withdraw and retire behind the Thames to Reading. Churchill was still in favour of advancing, but Churchill, as we have seen, had other motives; it was on that night that he and some other army leaders were to go over to the enemy. James's nosebleeds might possibly have saved him from what would have been an audacious attempt to deliver him into the hands of the Dutch invaders: one London newswriter reported that Churchill had been planning to seize the King and carry him off to the Prince of Orange when James reviewed his troops on the 22nd, 'but was disappointed by his Majesties Bleeding at nose that night', so that the review was undertaken by Lord Feversham instead. James ordered the retreat to begin on the 23rd and himself arrived back in London on the 26th. The following evening he summoned the bishops and nobles about town to Whitehall to ask them what he should do. Halifax advised calling a parliament immediately, and James issued a proclamation to this effect on 30 November.[62]

Desertions within the army continued, and William and his troops were able to continue their slow march to London largely unimpeded. The campaign saw a few minor armed skirmishes. The first was at Wincanton, on 21 November, when an advance guard of William's army, foraging for transport, had been confronted by 120 Irish soldiers under the command of Colonel Sarsfield, leaving perhaps 30 dead. In revenge, the Duke of Schomberg in William's army refused to offer quarter to a party of King's Horse it stumbled on outside Dorchester, killing fifty-three. The last incident was when Dutch troops took Reading early on Sunday 9 December, killing some thirty to fifty Irish troopers.[63] With an attempt to reach an accommodation with William on 8–9 December having failed – James had offered to do anything William desired to secure the meeting of a freely elected parliament if William and his men stayed out of London – effectively the game was now up.[64] In the early hours of Monday 10 December the Queen made her escape to France disguised as a laundry woman, taking her infant son with her.[65] At three o'clock on the morning of the 11th, after further unrest the night before, which had seen the destruction of the Catholic chapel in the Tower, James fled the capital himself, accompanied by Sir Edward Hales and another Catholic, Ralph Sheldon. He had seemingly contemplated heading north and throwing himself on the mercy of the rebellious lords and gentlemen up there, who, he was assured, would never harm his person; instead, 'the Papists and priests prevailed with him to quit his kingdoms to make their fall appear more glorious'. He therefore made for the Kent coast where he intended to take a boat to France. James explained to Lord Dartmouth that he was 'resolved to venture all rather than consent to anything in the least prejudicial to the crowne', but 'having been basely deserted by many officers and soldiers' in the army and finding 'the same poysone is gott amongst the fleet' he felt he could no longer expose himself to what he 'might expect from the ambitious Prince of Orange and the association of rebellious Lords'; he had therefore 'resolved to withdraw' until this 'violent storme' was over, which he predicted would be 'in God's good time'. At his departure, he deliberately tried to create a government vacuum, dropping the Great Seal into the Thames and giving orders for the disbanding of the army.[66] Following James's flight, the lords spiritual and temporal who were in London at the time immediately established themselves as a provisional government, and resolved to assist the Prince of Orange in obtaining a free parliament to secure 'Our Laws, Our Liberties and Properties' and 'the Church of England in particular, with a due Liberty to Protestant Dissenters', as well as 'the Protestant Religion and Interest' more generally 'over the whole World'.[67]

The King's departure became the cue for further rioting. On the night of the 11th huge crowds, numbering several thousand, attacked all houses in London where they suspected mass was said or priests were lodged, including not only those that had recently been closed but also the residences of foreign ambassadors. They levelled the Catholic chapels in Lincoln's Inn Fields, Clerkenwell, Bucklersbury and Lime Street, ripping out the wainscotting and seats, and carrying out all the furnishings and paraphernalia for saying mass 'in mock procession and triumph, with oranges on the tops of swords and staves' and 'great lighted candles in gilt candlesticks' to be committed to a huge bonfire outside. They demolished the Spanish ambassador's residence at Wild House, destroying furniture, pictures, books, plate, three coaches and other valuables in the bargain, and afterwards 'marched down the Strand with Oranges upon their Sticks, crying for the Prince of Orange'. What could not be accomplished that night was reserved for the next. On the evening of the 12th they attacked the Florentine ambassador's residence in the Haymarket, burning 'every thing but the walls', saying it was 'a Mass House, where many Catholics daily performed their Devotion, and that they would now eradicate the Tree and Roots of Popery'. They also entered the French ambassador's residence, though a combination of the presence of the trained bands and monetary gifts from the ambassador's landlord succeeded in inducing the crowd to desist. The houses of those who served the crown were also attacked. Crowds did considerable damage to Henry Hills's printing house in Blackfriars and the residence of James's electoral agent, Robert Brent; they threatened the Earl of Huntingdon's town house and pulled down some private houses in and about the capital, including two large country houses just outside Southwark that belonged to Catholics. Some 5,000 people gathered outside the London residence of the Catholic convert Lord Salisbury as it was searched for arms, and another group went to attack the home of the Catholic privy counsellor Lord Powis, although ultimately they decided to leave it alone because he had been against sending the bishops to the Tower. In the early hours of the 12th Lord Chancellor Jeffreys was seized by a crowd in Wapping, disguised as a seaman and trying to make his escape to France, and handed over to the Lord Mayor. Jeffreys was sent to the Tower and placed under a heavy guard to protect him from the mob, who threatened 'to pull him to peces before he be brought to public justice'. At Canterbury a crowd besieged Sir Edward Hales's house as soon as they learned he had fled with the King, entirely destroying his great library and everything else that was valuable, and also seizing several Jesuits and priests who were making their escape.[68]

Catholic peers had their country homes raided by mobs searching for secret stores of weapons. In Hertfordshire, the 'country Mobile' rose and demolished the house of the Catholic Lord Aston, where they had heard he had 'stor'd up great quantities of Provisions', and set fire to all the furniture. The Cambridge 'Mobile' joined up with 'their Brethren' of Bury St Edmunds to attack Lord Dover's house at Cheveley, and after having demolished the chapel and inflicted considerable damage on the house, furniture and deer park, they went to Balsham in search of the Bishop of St Davids, Thomas Watson – who was also still rector of Burrough Green, Cambridgeshire, and who had shown himself to be a committed supporter of James II – whom they seized and led back to Cambridge 'in a triumphant Manner' on 'a paultry Hourse, without Saddle or Bridle', to be secured in the castle. In Bury it was said that 'the poor Mobile that had nothing to hazard or loose' styled themselves 'the Protestant Reformers' and went 'rambling about Town and Country, sometimes in a formidable Body, and sometimes in Parties, imposing on some Taxes, Rifling both Papists and Protestants, Test-men and Anti Test-men, without any Distinction', and plundered the houses of several eminent Catholics. In Northamptonshire 'the Rabble . . . demolished all the Papist Chappels, and most of the remarkable Papist Houses', before finally setting upon the Earl of Peterborough's house at Drayton. Here they seized the Earl's steward, tying him to a stake, 'piling Faggots and other combustible matter about', and threatened to burn him if he did not reveal where his lordship had hidden his sizeable cache of arms. The crowd actually set fire to some of the loose fuel before the steward finally revealed he had thrown them in the estate's fishponds. In Caernarvonshire, local constables defaced the private Catholic chapel of Robert Pugh of Penrhyn Creuddyn.[69]

The way in which James had disbanded his troops merely served to contribute further to the general mayhem. Those Irish soldiers who had been brought over as reinforcements had no option but to try to make their way back to their homeland as best they could. As they journeyed from where they had been stationed in the south and east (mainly Portsmouth and Tilbury) towards the seaports on the Irish Sea, still in possession of the weapons with which they had been issued, rumours began to fly that the Irish had risen and were committing all manner of outrages. The alarm reached the metropolis late on the night of 12 December and in the early hours of the 13th, with reports coming in from the countryside of 'the Irish being up in a great body, burning and killing all as they came along', prompting Londoners to leave their beds, illuminate their windows, and take to the streets with whatever weapons they could lay their hands on. Soon much of the kingdom was in a state of panic. By midnight on the 12th, the inhabitants of Ampthill in Bedfordshire, having been informed by messengers on horseback that Irish papists had fired the nearby towns of Bedford, Luton, Dunstable and Woburn, barricaded the five entrances into town with overturned carts, so 'senseless and affrighted' were they that they did not stop to wonder why they could not see any smoke in the air. At Wendover in Buckinghamshire the locals were alarmed with reports of 'some thousands of Irish Soldiers being . . . within a few miles of the place, Robbing, Burning, and Murdering Man, Woman, and Child', which caused panic for several hours until they were eventually informed it was a false alarm. On the 13th, the Earl of Ailesbury encountered workmen at Rochester cutting down the wooden bridge, 'to hinder the Irish Papists from cutting their throats', they having heard that nearby Dartford 'was on fire, and the streets ran with blood'. As he passed through Chatham and Sittingborne, Ailesbury saw women 'crying at their doors . . . with their children by them', preferring, so they said, 'rather to be murdered there then in their beds'.[70]

One correspondent reported how once 'the Irish part of the King's army' that had been at Reading had 'got some considerable distance from the Prince's [army]' they began 'to plunder, kill and destroy'. The city of Oxford received a similar report that 'a great Body of Irish were coming . . . to Plunder' the place, upon which the locals immediately took to arms, closed the drawbridge, and secured the avenues leading into the city. Soon a rumour was flying that Birmingham had been burned and that the Irish were heading off to Wolverhampton to continue their acts of terror, and before long news had spread from town to town across the Midlands 'that the Irish were Cutting of Throats', with Lichfield in Staffordshire on fire and nearby Burton 'attempted upon'. The reports were false, but an enraged rabble seized a local Catholic gentleman, together with his priest (both of whom were lucky to escape with their lives) and proceeded to burn his new chapel to the ground and turn out all his deer. 'A great concourse of Country People' who lived along the Lincolnshire sea coast flocked into Lincoln on the 14th, 'upon an Alarm, That a great Number of Irish were landing upon them'. By the 15th the northern counties were 'universally alarmed' by reports that 'the disbanded Irish Papists would cut all their throats': someone brought the news to Wakefield that they had fired Birmingham and slain men, women and children; another that Nottingham had been fired. In the early hours of the 19th, the residents of Yeovil in Somerset heard 'that some thousands of the Irish were coming Westward' and 'had burn'd Portsmouth, Lymington, and Basingstoke'; the whole county, as far as Taunton, was up in arms, before it was finally revealed to be a false alarm. The fright hit East Anglia. At Bury St Edmunds, a rumour that some Irish were 'approaching with Fire and Sword' resulted in more than 500 local inhabitants appearing in arms 'in an instant', 'Fortifying and Barricading the Town Gates and Avenues leading thereto'. There was also trouble in Wales. In Pembrokeshire, angry crowds thwarted the efforts of disbanded Irish troops to cross the Irish Sea, while at Dolgellau in Merionethshire local inhabitants mistakenly fired on some excise commissioners believing them to be Irish soldiers. Not that the Irish soldiers were always totally blameless. They committed 'some small Rudeness and Outrages . . . in some places', one correspondent wrote, in attempts to get food. Yet imaginations clearly ran riot as to what the demobbed Irish might be up to, especially when they were known to be nearby but not quite within immediate view.[71]

Many observers were shocked by the unruliness and violence of the anti-Catholic crowds. The Essex JP Sir John Bramston thought some of the participants in the London disturbances of 11 December were 'common theeves', and it was they who 'set the boys to work', while one pamphleteer insisted that anyone who tried to justify the 'base and villainous Actions' of that night 'must be degenerated from common Humanity'.[72] Historians have also condemned 'the indiscriminate orgy of looting and destruction' unleashed by James's flight, and have tended to convey a picture of an anarchic mob, fuelled by anti-Catholic bigotry and reinforced by members of the criminal underworld, bent on pillage and destruction.[73] In fact, a closer examination shows that there was a considerable degree of structure and discipline behind much of the rioting and that the crowds were clearly seeking to make specific political points. This is not to sanitize the crowd. The spectacle of large numbers of people roaming the streets of densely populated urban centres, pulling down timber-framed houses and burning everything they found within, was undoubtedly terrifying. The scale of the destruction was extensive: some £400 worth of damage was done to the altar furnishings of the chapel in Bucklersbury on 29 October, while the Spanish ambassador is reported to have suffered losses amounting to between £15,000 and £20,000.[74] Yet the crowds acted in ritualized ways, removing the furnishings from the buildings and burning them in the open street. They were making a public statement. It would be naïve to assume that there was no indiscriminate plunder, although according to some contemporaries, at least, there was remarkably little. Thus the contemporary Whig historian John Oldmixon (who was fifteen in late 1688 and living in London, and may well have been a participant in the riots) tells us that such was the 'justice' shown by the crowds that if anyone did try to purloin something, 'they were immediately taken hold of, and us'd in a worse manner than the Law uses Pilferers'. Burnet also commented on the discipline of the crowds, even those in London on the night of 11 December, writing that 'Never was so much fury seen under so much management', since 'none were killed, no houses burnt, nor were any robberies committed'.[75]

In fact, rather than seeing the crowds as seeking to take advantage of the collapse in royal government to loot and pillage, we can almost view the attacks on Catholic chapels as law-enforcement riots. The verdict in the trial of the seven bishops had seemed to confirm that the King did not possess the suspending power. If so, then the Indulgence that was based on this supposed prerogative was nullified, and the laws against Catholic worship remained in force. Furthermore, the Restoration government had on occasion ordered the destruction of houses that were known to host religious conventicles outlawed by law. What we see happening in England in the autumn of 1688, then, is crowds appropriating a government sanction against religious assemblies that, following the trial of the bishops, were widely believed to be in violation of the law. William's invasion manifesto of 30 September, as we have already seen, had specifically alleged that the attempts to set up churches and chapels for the exercise of the

Catholic religion had been against the law. Significantly, two juries, which sat to consider the shooting of some of those who attacked Catholic chapels in London on 11 November by the King's soldiers, concluded that the rioters were 'loyal persons' and the Catholics 'traytors and enemies to the nation' who met 'contrary to the Lawes of this Land'.[76] Indeed, the fact that James himself ordered all Catholic chapels (except those belonging to the royal family and foreign ambassadors) to be closed down following the disturbances on 11 November, appeared almost tantamount to an admission by the King that his promotion of Catholic worship had been illegal. Subsequently, an indictment was brought against the Earl of Craven, the Lord Lieutenant of Middlesex, for protecting popish priests and 'suppressing the well meaning Mobile and murdering 2 or 3 of them'.[77]

If such an interpretation is valid, how then do we account for the attacks on the foreign ambassadors' chapels following the King's flight on 11 December? Foreign ambassadors undoubtedly were allowed to keep chapels for their own private worship, and many contemporaries saw the crowd attacks as a violation of the law of nations. However, it was widely known that the ambassadors' chapels were being employed not just for private use but for public worship, and this was illegal. In addition, a number of court Catholics had chosen to store their valuables in the residences of the foreign ambassadors, hoping that they would be safe from the fury of the mob. In a sense, the attacks on the ambassadors' chapels were really attacks on the King's evil counsellors, who had been responsible for various illegal acts committed by the government under James II, and might be seen on a par with the attacks on other servants of the crown committed at this time. Finally, William's third Declaration – the authenticity of which no one at the time had cause to doubt – further seemed to sanction the crowds' actions in disarming Catholics: the crowds were, in effect, acting upon what they believed were William's instructions following the flight of their own king.

What we see in the crowd unrest of the autumn of 1688, in other words, is a rejection of the men and measures of James II. However, this was not necessarily tantamount to a rejection of James himself. Support for William of Orange was unquestionably widespread,

1. English Protestant identity in the seventeenth century was powerfully shaped by a fear of Catholic conspiracy that was in part rooted in history. This print dates from 1621 and depicts England's double providential deliverance from the Spanish armada of 1588 and the Gunpowder Plot of 1605. An embellished version of this print was published in 1689 to celebrate England's most recent 'deliverance'.

2. A woodcut from 1685 depicting royalist victory over the Monmouth rebels at Sedgemoor.

Titus Oates, *Anag.* Testis Ovat.

Testis ovat fallor fractus dum Crimine lingua,
Et reforma Satira premia Testa ovat.
Testa ovat, plures laceat tria Regna, deliro
Author quam Sinco lumine Testa ovat.
Testa ovat, quid-Urea perit, ruit Anglia, viret
Quid nimit proprius Scotia, Testa ovat:
Testa ovat latua magnos disjungere Fratres,
Et paste e Patria Caslum Testa ovat.
Testa ovat necat dum pena pilstior infans;
Ebrius innocua Sanguine Testa ovat.
Testa ovat; falsa sed quale ruatio lingua;
Qui quod iniquus, ovat, quam male Testa ovat.

Thus rendred.

PAid for his Crimes the Perjur'd Witness swears,
And shews what for rewards his false Tongue dare
Swears till three Kingdoms mourn; whilst o'er the prin
Our Witness triumphs with relentless Eyes.
Swears on till *Ireland* perish, *England* fall,
And *Scotland* in one common Funeral.
Swears still, dreadless of Hell, nor fearing Heaven,
Till the great *TOR R* be from his Countrey driven.
Wrong'd Innocence by Perjur'd Witness dies,
Who drunk with guiltless Blood still Swears and lies:
Then since our Witness has this hardned face,
Let the false Wretch the Pillory disgrace.

London, Printed for *J. Hindmarsh,* at the *Golden-Ball* over against the *Royal-Exchange.* 1685.

3. The infamous Popish Plot informer Titus Oates, convicted on two counts of perjury at the beginning of James II's reign, was sentenced to two public whippings, perpetual imprisonment, and annual stints in the pillory. The Revolution brought him a pardon and a pension. The clause in the Declaration of Rights condemning excessive and unusual punishments alluded to the treatment meted out to Oates.

4. James's right-hand man in Ireland, Richard Talbot, Earl of Tyrconnell. A long-standing friend of the king, he was an embittered enemy of the Restoration land settlement and the champion of the Catholic interest in Ireland.

5. The seven bishops who petitioned against James's second Declaration of Indulgence of 1688. Tried for publishing seditious libel and found not guilty by a London jury, their opposition marked the beginning of the end for James II's regime.

6. A Dutch painting depicting the embarkation of the Dutch fleet in the autumn of 1688. A 'Protestant wind' was to blow the fleet down the Channel towards Torbay.

The Mass house at S.t Ioness pulling it down &.ct

Burning y.e Popish Chaple in Lincolns Inn Fields.

7. Illustrated playing cards from a pack produced to commemorate the Revolution of 1688–9. The II, III and X of diamonds depict the attacks on Catholic chapels in London in late 1688. The knave of diamonds shows an entirely fictional scene of Catholic clergy singing the mass in the mistaken belief that the French had landed to support James's tottering regime.

Singing of Mass thinking that the French had landed.

Lime Street Chaple pulling down and burnt

8. A contemporary engraving depicting the arrest of George Jeffreys, James's Lord Chancellor and the judge who had presided over the 'Bloody Assizes', at Wapping on 12 December 1688.

9. An illustrated ballad celebrating the return of James II to the capital on 16 December 1688, following his first abortive flight. Even at this late stage, some Protestants hoped that redressing their grievances might not necessitate the overthrow of their king.

10. William of Orange was to make his own triumphal entry into London two days later, on 18 December. By this time James had once again been forced to leave the capital.

11. An illustrated broadside of 1689 rejoicing at the downfall of the Jesuit priest and privy counsellor Father Edward Petre. Such was Petre's influence with the King that he was considered by many to be 'the first minister of state' in 1687–8.

12. An allegorical design depicting England's deliverance from 'French tirany and Popish oppression' by William of Orange. Oranges falling from the tree in the centre knock down Jeffreys (to the right) and topple the crown from James II's head (to the left). The Queen flees with her infant son, while Louis XIV of France is shown murdering his own (Protestant) subjects. Note the watching eye of Providence, reminiscent of the print in Plate 1.

13. The front page of a pamphlet of 1689 celebrating the coronation of William and Mary on 11 April 1689.

14. Illustrations from a Protestant propaganda tract of 1689 recalling alleged brutalities committed by Irish Catholics against Protestants during the Irish Rebellion of 1641.

15. Dutch painting depicting William of Orange at the Battle of the Boyne on 1 July 1690. The image of William on a white horse has, of course, become iconic in Northern Ireland, but in all likelihood William rode a brown horse: a white one would have made him too visible a target for the enemy.

but William had come to rescue English liberties and the Protestant religion; he had given no public intimation that his ultimate goal was to seize the crown for himself. To be sure, there were some committed Orangists who wanted James off the throne. Thus when Lord Lumley took Newcastle in early December, for example, the statue of James that stood on a lofty marble pedestal was pulled down and thrown into the Tyne.[78] However, not everyone anticipated the fall of the King. Indeed, there was to be one last show of support for James before he finally escaped to France.

James, who had failed in most of what he had set out to accomplish during his reign, was even unsuccessful in his last act of desperation. His party was stopped by seamen at Faversham in Kent at about eleven o'clock on the night of the 11th as they waited onboard their vessel while it took on ballast. The seamen were on the lookout for escaping Catholics and thought they had found some likely suspects. Indeed, they recognized one of the men in the party – Sir Edward Hales, who was a local man – but they failed to recognize the King himself, who was wearing a minimal disguise. Taking James to be Hales's Jesuit confessor, they called him an 'old Rogue', an 'ugly, lean-jawed hatchet-faced Jesuite', and a 'popish dog', and even pulled down his breeches to see if he had any treasure concealed about his person. It was only when the would-be escapees were taken back to a local inn that the King's true identity was revealed. Realizing their mistake, the crowd gave the King back what they had taken, though in a final act of generosity James distributed all his gold amongst the local inhabitants.[79] At the behest of the provisional government that had set itself up in London following James's flight, the Earl of Winchelsea and various other leading gentry went to Kent to provide a military escort to bring the King back to the capital. James entered the City to a rapturous reception on 16 December. 'Multitudes of people', most accounts agree, lined the streets, cheering at their King's return. Ailesbury recalled how the streets from Southwark to Whitehall were so crowded, 'there was scarce room for coaches to pass through, and the balconies and windows besides were thronged'. The day concluded with ringing of bells and bonfires. James was later to write that it was 'liker a day of triumph'; even Burnet was taken aback by the 'expressions of joy' from such 'great numbers', and could only conclude that 'the multitude' was a 'slight and unstable thing . . . and so soon altered'.[80]

Some contemporaries tried to downplay the show of support for James. Oldmixon recalled that he remembered it well, but was rather dismissive, stating 'that there was some shouting, by Boys, and that some of the Guards bid them hollow'. Edmund Bohun, in a work written in defence of the Revolution, claimed that 'a Set of Boys' followed James through the City, 'making some Huzzas, whilst the rest of the People silently looked on'; in his autobiography he wrote that 'there was much gaping but no rejoicing'. One London-based newsletter writer claimed that it was 'the Papists' who made the bonfires that night. Yet we do not necessarily have to conclude either that the crowd was fickle or that contemporaries misrepresented the enthusiasm with which James was welcomed back to his capital. The riots and demonstrations of late 1688, indeed the whole of the resistance movement to James, including (ostensibly) the Williamite invasion itself, had been directed against the illegal acts committed in the name of the crown and promoted by the King's evil ministers. The struggle had not necessarily been to overthrow James himself, but to bring him to terms, and make him rule in a way that would guarantee the security of the Protestant religion and protect the liberties and rights of the people. As the Essex JP Sir John Bramston wrote in his *Autobiography*, 'the people huzzainge as he came, put hopes into his Majestie that the anger was not at his person, but at his religion'. For the author of a congratulatory poem written to commemorate the King's return to Whitehall, evil ministers were to blame: 'Let Achan fall, the Troubler of the Land' and 'Dagon tumble', he implored, 'but let Cesar stand'. The poet also hinted that the King was given such an enthusiastic reception because it was anticipated that his return would lead to a restoration of law and order after days of rioting. Indeed, as soon as he got back to Whitehall, James issued a proclamation against riots.[81]

James's return had been an embarrassment for William, however. Indeed, the retrospective Jacobite *Life of James II* alleged that William 'was in such a surprise . . . at the joyfull reception [James] met with at his arrival, as made him stand at a gaze in some doubt with himself what was next to be done', apprehending 'extreamly this sudden change and the unsettled genius of the people'. William refused James's request for an interview, but instead, on the evening of the 17th, sent some of his own Dutch troops to 'take the posts' at the royal palace at Whitehall, where the King was now staying. Again according to the *Life*, James 'now perceivd he was absolutely the Prince of Orange's prisoner'. Shortly after midnight James was awoken by the Earl of Middleton with a message from the Prince, the substance of which was 'That to avoid the disorder which his Majesty's presence might cause in London', he should leave the capital that very morning. William's suggestion was that James should retire to Ham House. James objected on the grounds that the place was cold in winter and unfurnished, but he offered to go to Rochester instead. William agreed, but sent some of his own troops to make sure that James reached his destination. James's party left London by barge, but, delayed by the tide, had made it only as far as Gravesend by the evening. Forced to stop for the night, the King found that William's troops 'kept very strict watch about the house' where he stayed. When he reached Rochester on the 19th, however, James found his guards 'were not So exact', which led him to conclude 'that the Prince of Orange would be well enough contented he should get away'. In the early hours of 23 December, James managed to slip away quietly to France, where he arrived on Christmas morning. He recognized that if he had chosen to remain it would have made things more awkward for the Williamites, who might have found it more difficult to dethrone him, but by now he clearly did not trust the Prince and feared for his own life: he did, after all, have the precedent of what had happened to his own father in 1649 to think about. As James explained in a paper he left behind: 'How could I hope to be safe, so long as I was in the Power of one, who had not only done this to me [i.e. sent his guards to take the posts at Whitehall], and Invaded my Kingdoms without any just occasion given him for it, but that did by his first Declaration lay the greatest Aspersion upon me that Malice could Invent, in that Clause of it which concerns my Son'.[82] The desertion was at last a reality; England was without a king.

James's departure from London had enabled William to enter the capital on the 18th. He too received a rapturous reception from 'vast crouds of people' who had gathered in the streets, and this despite the appalling weather on that day. Bishop Compton of London rode at the head of a troop carrying the motto '*Nolumus leges Angliae mutari*' ('We are unwilling to change the laws of England') on its banner. In Ludgate, just outside the city walls, an orange woman 'gave baskets full of Oranges to the Prince's Officers and soldiers as they marched by to testifie her affection towards them', and various other 'ordinary women . . . shooke his soldiers by the hand as they came by and cryed, "Welcome, welcome, God blesse you, you come to redeeme our Religion, Lawes, Liberties and Lives, God reward you."' Again, the day concluded with bells, bonfires, and even the burning of popes, with 'such shouts and Huzzas as are not to be Expresst'. Evelyn concluded that 'all have now it seems submitted', and thought the bells and bonfires proclaimed 'as much Joy and Satisfaction, as those are capable of, who have beheld so many changes and Revolutions, without being able to divine how all this will conclude at last'.[83] On 21 December a contingent of Anglican clergy, led by the Bishop of London, together with four nonconformist divines, presented an address to William thanking him 'for his great and noble Attempt to deliver them from Popery and Slavery' and promising him 'their utmost assistance' to help him achieve that end. Although some of the clergy had wanted the address to include a clause imploring the Prince 'to have speciall respect to the King And to preserve the Church of England Established by Law', ominously the bishop chose to omit the words 'Respect to the King' and 'Established by Law'.[84]

The question was, what would happen next? Even a diehard Anglican such as John Evelyn could look forward with some optimism to what the 'approaching Revolution' might bring; yet he also remained sceptical as to whether there would be any 'Improvement of mankind in this declining Age'. 'A Parliament (Legaly Cal'd) of brave, and worthy Patriots, not Influenced by Faction, nor terrified by Power, or Corrupted by selfe Interest', he had no doubt, 'would produce a kind of New-Creation amongst us.' But he feared things might 'dissolve to Chaos againe, unless the same stupendious Providence (which has put Opportunitie into men's-heads, to make us happy) dispose them to do Just and righteous things, and to use their Empire with Moderation, Justice, Piety, and for the publiq good.'[85] It is to a consideration of exactly what sort of 'New-Creation' the anticipated 'Revolution' brought about in England, Scotland and Ireland that we must now turn.

8

'The Greatest Revolution that was Ever Known': The Revolution Settlement in England

Concerning the Violations and Outrages committed on the English Government, all of which . . . have had according to their respective proportions a considerable influence towards the present Revolution: I have seriously reflected on these last three years, but to derive them to the original source, I find it of absolute necessity to resort further back, though in common opinion the remoter a cause is the less is its influence, and unthinking men generally imagine the last and next immediate causes of things to be the onely engines and movements deserving of enquiry, but wiser men look further, and can see causes and consequences at a greater distance.

A Letter to a Gentleman at Brussels (1689), p. 3

We have seen that it is misleading to characterize the Revolution in England as coming solely from above, or to suggest that by 1688 James II's position was so strong that he could only have been brought down as a result of a foreign invasion. James's regime collapsed from within; indeed, there was such widespread opposition to James's ambitious measures to help his co-religionists prior to William's invasion that there would have been some sort of revolution in the autumn of 1688 even if William had never set foot on English soil. Even William's 'conquest' of England can, in many respects, be regarded as being effected from below, since James was not overcome in battle by a foreign army but, rather, he fled in the face of widespread disaffection amongst his subjects.

Yet what of the settlement that followed in the wake of the

Williamite conquest and James's desertion? There has been considerable debate amongst historians as to how to see the Revolution settlement of 1689. Was it a Whig victory, which fundamentally changed the nature of the monarchy in England, or no more than a palace coup, which changed very little? Since the 1950s, conservative views of the Revolution settlement have tended to predominate. Such accounts have stressed the important role of the Tories in helping to bring about the Revolution and argued that a combination of conservative forces within parliament and opposition from the Prince of Orange himself served to frustrate any initiatives for radical reform. In this view, the most radical act of 1689 was the transfer of the crown, though the significance of this should not be underestimated. The Declaration of Rights, which accompanied the offer of the crown to William and Mary, by contrast, did little more than assert ancient rights and liberties, and besides, the offer of the crown was not even conditional upon William and Mary's acceptance of the Declaration.[1] Such a view still retains considerable currency; as one leading historian has written, 'The Sensible Revolution of 1688–9 was a conservative Revolution'.[2]

The last couple of decades, however, have seen renewed attempts to invest the Glorious Revolution in England with more Whiggish – and more revolutionary – credentials. For one leading modern authority, it was an 'Unexpected Whig Revolution' – Whig, that is, not so much because it redefined the powers of the monarchy, but because it marked a break in the succession, and therefore a belated victory for Exclusion, and because the dynastic coup revolutionized England's domestic politics and foreign policy.[3] The author of our most detailed study of the Declaration of Rights has concluded that the Revolution was a victory for Whig principles and changed 'not only the English king, but also the kingship': Whigs dominated the committees that were responsible for drawing up the terms upon which the crown was to be offered to William and Mary, and although some compromises had to be worked out along the way, the Declaration of Rights nevertheless significantly altered the existing powers of the crown and helped establish limited monarchy in England.[4] Likewise, an important study that appeared on the occasion of the tercentenary in 1988 argued that significant inroads were made on the prerogative by the Revolution settlement, and that 'the debate on the nature of the monarchy' ended 'decisively in 1689 with the victory of those who argued it was limited and mixed'; the Declaration of Rights, rather than asserting ancient rights and privileges, 'made new law under the guise of declaring the old'.[5] Most recently, one historian has argued that England's revolution of 1688–9 was 'quite revolutionary', and 'fundamentally transformed the policies and ideology of the English state'.[6]

The extensive disagreement amongst scholars stems partly from the ambiguities inherent in the Revolution settlement itself. The settlement of 1689 involved not only some degree of compromise but also a certain amount of fudging, lending itself to a plurality of readings as a result. Contemporaries could interpret what had transpired within a Whiggish framework or subscribe to a more Tory reading of events, depending upon their personal political agendas and how they felt they needed to salve their own consciences: 1689 could both be seen as having changed quite a lot and as having altered very little – as a victory for popular sovereignty or as a miraculous deliverance wrought by God. The ability of the Glorious Revolution in England to appear all things to so many different types of people, of course, goes a considerable way towards explaining its success. Acknowledging this should not obscure the fact, however, that there remain certain key interpretative issues that need to be resolved.

In order to understand the nature of the Revolution settlement and evaluate how radical it was and whether or not it marked a victory for Whig principles, a number of issues need to be addressed. The first is: how do we get from 1688 to 1689? A desire to defeat the trend towards popery and arbitrary government under James did not necessarily amount to wanting to dethrone the reigning monarch and replace him by his daughter and son-in-law; it is thus necessary to investigate the extent to which the virtually united front in support of William's endeavours to rescue English liberties of late 1688 translated into positive support for the transference of sovereignty from James to William and Mary. Do we see the bi-partisan front sustained throughout or did the Revolution become more of a partisan affair as it progressed? We also need to re-examine the constitutional significance of the Declaration of Rights in the light of what we now know about politico-constitutional developments under the Restoration monarchy in general, and during the reign of James II in particular. At the same time, it is essential to acknowledge that the Declaration of Rights was not the entirety of the Revolution settlement, and nor was it intended to be, since the makers of that settlement always recognized that further reforms were desirable, which would require fresh legislation and which therefore could not be achieved via the means of such a Declaration. Moreover, we need to think about the implications of the dynastic shift that occurred in 1688–9 and the extent to which these might have been revolutionary. The mere change of the monarch had dramatic consequences in and of itself, for both England's domestic and foreign policy, and also for the two other kingdoms that were part of the Stuart multiple-kingdom inheritance. Some of these consequences might have been unforeseen; others, however, were not, but were, rather, precisely what those who supported the dynastic change were hoping to achieve (notably the revolutionary shift in England's foreign policy). This chapter will restrict itself to looking at the settlement in England over the course of 1689–90. Subsequent chapters will deal with Scotland and Ireland. A final chapter will take a longer perspective, taking the story for the three kingdoms into the eighteenth century in order to consider how the changes wrought by the upheavals of 1688–9 helped revolutionize the British state.

THE CHALLENGE OF THE COMMONWEALTHMEN

The events of December 1688, and James's flight on the 11th, created a power vacuum at the very heart of the government. On learning of the King's withdrawal, the Earl of Rochester (James's brother-in-law by his first marriage) immediately summoned the spiritual and temporal peers to meet at the London Guildhall to form a provisional government; on the 12th, James's privy counsellors were invited to join them. Attendance fluctuated between twenty-two and thirty-eight, depending on the day and hour. The King's old friends, led by Rochester and the bishops, found they could count on the support of the majority, although there was a strong minority of 'violent' Whigs and 'angry' displaced courtiers whose sympathies lay with William. It was this body which, indirectly at least, was responsible for bringing James back to London on the 16th.[7]

When William himself arrived in the English capital on the 18th, 'the greatest Lawyers, and those that came in with the Prince' advised that William and his wife Mary should simply assume the title of king and queen, following the example of Henry VII after the battle of Bosworth Field (1485). Legally this had a number of advantages. It would legitimize all acts of resistance, since legislation from Henry VII's reign – the so-called *De Facto* Act of 1495 – granted indemnity to all persons who obeyed a *de facto* king or who fought for one against a *de iure* king. It would also enable William to call a parliament, which could be summoned only by a king. William refused to assume the crown, however, since he had promised in his invasion manifesto to refer the settlement of the nation to parliament. Instead, he called another assembly of peers, to meet on 21 December at the Queen's Presence Chamber in St James's, to give their advice on the best manner of pursuing his declared objectives. This proved to be a divided body and, with the *de iure* king as yet still in the country, did nothing to address the question of how to obtain a parliament. The Earl of Nottingham insisted that only James could issue writs for a parliament and suggested that he should be brought back with his authority specifically limited. In order to hear the voice of the commons, William decided to call a meeting for the 26th of the surviving MPs from Charles II's reign, together with the Lord Mayor, aldermen, and fifty representatives of the common council of London. Significantly, the members of James's 1685 parliament, an overwhelmingly Tory body, were ignored – presumably because, following the purges of Charles II's final years, this was not deemed a freely elected body. James's second flight on 23 December, however, changed the dynamic amongst the peers. Nottingham made a last-minute attempt to secure a conditional restoration of King James, proposing that there should be annual parliaments, to sit for a minimum of thirty days; that James should be required to take parliament's advice on religious and constitutional issues; and that William should serve as guarantor for what parliament demanded (in effect, in the capacity of a regent). Nottingham's motion was not carried. Instead, on Christmas Day the peers agreed to two addresses: one inviting William to issue writs for electing a convention to meet on 22 January; the other asking him to assume the direction of the government in the meantime. The following day the assembly of commoners followed suit with similar addresses, and William assumed the responsibilities of government on the 28th.[8]

The elections to the Convention were relatively tranquil, at least compared to the turbulent general elections of the Exclusion era or the fierce partisan disputes that were to characterize the reigns of William and Anne. It is true that there were a few fervent contests, fuelled by partisan campaigning and divisions amongst the electorate over the dynastic issue. All told, however, there were just 50 contests, compared to 101 in March 1679, 77 in October 1679, 54 in 1681 (when many Tories had decided not to compete rather than face inevitable defeat at the polls), and 79 in 1685. Some constituencies managed to avoid contests in 1689 by agreeing in advance to return one Whig and one Tory unopposed. The result was a House of Commons in which the two parties were fairly evenly matched: out of a total of 513, there were 174 known Whigs to 156 known Tories, along with 183 new members.[9] It is usually assumed that the Whigs had an overall majority, since the House chose the Whig Henry Powle as speaker in preference to the Tory candidate, Sir Edward Seymour. Yet Powle was a moderate Whig, who had voted against Exclusion in 1679 and who had consistently favoured a policy of limitations on a popish successor. He was chosen less for his partisanship than because he was the one candidate likely to be acceptable to all. The Tories held the ascendancy in the Lords. Significantly, however, the upper House chose the Marquis of Halifax, the self-styled 'Trimmer' (i.e., one who trimmed between the two extremes), as their speaker.[10]

The build-up to the meeting of the Convention saw a heightened public debate about how to settle the government. Contemporaries noted how 'people began to divide into different factions' as pamphlets flowed from the presses in an attempt to influence opinion both within the Convention and outside it.[11] Although the Licensing Act, which had been renewed in 1685, technically remained in force, there was no way of effectively enforcing its provisions at this juncture. According to one estimate there were at least 300 pamphlets and other printed works in circulation between the autumn of 1688 and the end of February 1689, though this is probably on the conservative side; according to another estimate, some 2,000 titles appeared over the course of the year 1689.[12] Some of the works were for settling the throne on William and Mary jointly, or even on William alone; others 'for declareing the government dissolved and beginning all de Novo'; still others for some sort of solution that would have preserved James as king, at least in title, either by recalling him on terms, or else by making the Prince and Princess of Orange regents during the remainder of his life; and some maintained that if there had to be a breach in the succession, then Mary, as James's immediate heir (assuming one believed in the 'warming pan' myth) should reign alone.[13]

Most Whig writers appealed to contract theory in order to justify the overthrow of James II. A number of pamphlets merely echoed the case against James made by William's invasion manifesto of October 1688 and reiterated by Burnet in his *Enquiry into the Measures of Submission*, though in the process often highlighted the three-kingdoms dimension to the crisis. *The Anatomy of an Arbitrary Prince*, for example, complained how James had 'broken his Oath before God and Man, and the Laws of the Land, and his repeated Promises of Keeping them inviolable' by erecting Catholic chapels and schools, appointing Catholic judges and magistrates, setting up the Ecclesiastical Commission, suspending the Bishop of London, attacking Magdalen College, seizing town charters, keeping a standing army, and also 'By Invading the Fundamental Constitution of Scotland . . . altering it from a legal limited Monarchy, to an Arbitrary Despotick Power' and by removing Protestant officers in Ireland and putting in Catholics.[14] A belief that James had broken his contract could lead to one of two possible conclusions: either that the king had deposed himself, or that his subjects had the right to depose him. The first was more commonly reached; the second was intrinsically more radical. Thus Burnet, as we have seen, had insisted in the autumn of 1688 that a king who subverted 'the whole Foundation of the Government' annulled his own power and ceased to be king.[15] Robert Ferguson, in defence of William's invasion, similarly argued that if the sovereign subverted 'the Fundamental Laws of the Society' he thereby annulled 'all the Legal Right he had to Govern, and Absolve[d] all who were before his Subjects, from the Legal Engagements they were under of yielding him Obedience'. Yet Ferguson went on to argue that 'our Predecessors and Ancestors' had always reserved to themselves a right 'of inspecting his Administration . . . and of abdicating him from the Soveraignty, Upon universal and egregious faileurs [sic] in the Trust that had been credited and consigned unto him', citing parliament's deposition of Richard II as an example. Asking whether a king of England could 'so misbehave himself in Office' that he could be 'Degraded and Deposed from his Regal Dignity', Ferguson pointed out that even 'the highest Assertors of Monarchy and Regal Prerogative' allowed that there were various cases in which kings might 'both abdicate themselves from their Power and Authority, and be renounced and degraded by others', and insisted that James's misbehaviour had been such as not only to justify resistance but also to 'render it now Just and Expedient to Abdicate him'.[16]

Most who embraced contract theory argued that William alone should be made king. Thus one author claimed that since James had subverted the government, the people were free to settle the exercise of government themselves, and that they should make the Prince of Orange king: William deserved the crown, for all he had done, and England needed a strong king to fight the war against France, whereas to offer the crown to both William and Mary would be to engage in a risky experiment of 'joint-power in governing', of which England had no experience.[17] Similarly Ferguson, despite taking the more radical line that subjects could depose their king, nevertheless opted for the constitutionally conservative solution that the deposed king should be replaced by another member of the royal family who agreed to uphold the existing constitution, and that 'a Democratical Republick' was an 'impracticable' solution which would not suit the temper of the English people. Parliament should settle the crown as expeditiously as possible and keep it within the royal line and family, Ferguson thought, although parliament did not have to give it to the next heir. He was also adamant that although the Princess of Orange deserved to have the royal title, sovereignty could be vested in only one person, and that 'Reason of State' dictated that it should be lodged 'where it may be most for the publick good', namely in the Prince of Orange.[18]

There was a group of radical or 'true' Whigs – or commonwealth-men, as they were sometimes called – who believed that it was not enough simply to replace one king by another but instead saw the need for fundamental constitutional reform. The three central figures in this group were John Wildman, the one-time Leveller agitator turned Whig plotter, who sat in the Convention for Great Bedwyn, Wiltshire; John Hampden, an Exclusionist MP and Rye House plotter, who was MP for Wendover, Buckinghamshire; and Samuel Johnson, the defrocked former chaplain to the late Lord Russell (the Earl of Shaftesbury's right-hand man in the Commons during the Exclusion Crisis) and author of the influential *Julian the Apostate* (1682) and *A Humble and Hearty Address to all English Protestants in this Present Army* (1686). They had important friends in the upper House (among them lords Bolton, Delamere, Lovelace, Macclesfield, Mordaunt and Wharton), as well as in the City of London (especially among the dissenters), while they also cultivated the support of a number of dissident clergymen (including the Presbyterian minister John Humfrey, the eccentric Anglican clergyman Edmund Hickeringill, and the lawyer-turned-cleric Edward Stephens). They took advantage of the breakdown in licensing controls to argue their case in the press: at least fifty-one 'rights and reform' pamphlets (including new works and reprints of earlier tracts) appeared in late 1688 and early 1689, although most of these were published anonymously and it is not always easy to ascribe authorship.[19]

The commonwealthmen argued that the events of 1688 had resulted in a dissolution of the government and that the people were therefore free to erect a new system of government if they desired. As Humfrey explained, since England's government was mixed, with power vested in king, Lords and Commons, the fact that the King was 'now gone' meant that this 'one Corporation' was 'now broke'. The same was true regardless of whether one thought that James had forfeited his crown by attempting to introduce popery and arbitrary government, or had simply departed from his government by going from his people. 'Supreme Power', Humfrey argued, therefore reverted into 'the hands of the People', who could 'place it as they will', and 'bound and limit it as they see fit, for the publick Utility'. If they did not take this opportunity to deliver the people from slavery, Humfrey warned, 'the Ages to come' would 'have occasion to blame them for ever'.[20] Wildman argued that if James's 'Desertion of the Government' amounted 'to a Demise, or Civil Death', then 'the next Heir ought immediately to be Proclaim'd, and must Inherit the Crown with the same inseperable Prerogatives that heretofore belong'd to it, and all Laws or Acts of Parliament made to limit and abridge them' would be 'null and void'. But if, as Wildman himself maintained, 'the Departure of the King' amounted to a dissolution of the government, then power reverted to 'the People', who might erect a new system of government, 'either according to the old Modell, if they like it so well, or any other that they like and approve of better'.[21]

A few commonwealthmen favoured the abolition of the monarchy. One author, debating 'Whether Monarchy or a Common-wealth be best for the People', argued that although 'a good King' might be 'better', good kings were 'so rarely to be found', and bad ones 'so pernicious and destructive', that 'Wise men' thought it best 'to take up with the mediocrity of a Common-wealth'. This particular author seems to have had in mind the idea of restructuring the English state along the lines of the governments of cities and corporate towns (such as London, with its Lord Mayor, court of aldermen and common council), which he described as being really commonwealths, with sovereignty vested in a representative body.[22] The author of *Now Is the Time* proposed a republican regency for the remainder of James's reign. During this time, he suggested, a grand committee of the Lords and Commons (forty from each, half of them serving for life, half by a system of biennial rotation), presided over by the Prince of Orange (or whomever he appointed as his deputy), should form a council of state or governing senate, while parliaments should 'be Chosen Triennially' and 'meet Annually'. 'Such a Constitution', this author believed, 'would effectually Secure us . . . from Popery and Tyranny', though these arrangements need continue only 'during the Life of the King', and not under 'a Protestant Successor'.[23]

Typically, however, the 'true' Whigs argued for a limited monarchy. The English constitution was 'defective', Wildman maintained, and in need of 'some touches of . . . Legislative Skill to help it out'. For example, 'every Well-Constituted Government' ensured that the legislative power should meet frequently; yet in England the king, through his prerogative, had the power 'to keep off Parliaments' as long as he pleased. Wildman also thought it wrong that the king should have the right to appoint and dismiss judges at his pleasure, but he also insisted that changing judges' commissions to good behaviour would not improve things, since this would only make the king more careful to appoint men who would always 'stand firm to the King's Interest' in the first place. Instead, Wildman proposed, judges 'should be chosen by Them who are chiefly concern'd, and for whose benefit and protection both the King and Laws were first made and intended' – by which he clearly meant the people, with presumably their choice vested in their representatives in parliament. Indeed, Wildman insisted that those who censured James II for breaking his promise to govern according to law were wrong to do so, since 'the present Laws and Constitutions of England' did 'undoubtedly give the King a Power to make the Judge, and to the Judge a power to pronounce the Law', and James II had never done anything without 'the Opinion and Concurrence of his Judges'. Wildman further thought it 'very incongruous' that the king should have 'the absolute power of Peace and War . . . whilst the power of maintaining it', through voting taxation, was 'in the People'. He also argued the need for electoral reform: the property qualification for voters should be raised from the 40 shillings mark to a £40 freehold to ensure that electors were less open to bribery; there should be a redistribution of parliamentary seats, to do away with rotten boroughs and the over-representation of relatively underpopulated areas (like Cornwall, with its numerous corporations); and a secret ballot should be introduced. As a sop to Williamite sentiment, Wildman finished by saying that if the matter were left to him alone, 'the Government should be Monarchy, and this Monarchy should be Absolute and Arbitrary, and the Prince should be my King'. 'But the Honour I have for Him', Wildman concluded, did not extend 'to His Posterity'; just as 'a good Man' might have 'a Profligate Son', so Wildman himself would 'be loath to Repose such a Trust . . . in the hands of any one' he did not know.[24]

Similar reforms were suggested in other commonwealthmen tracts. Humfrey thought the control of the militia and the power of appointing judges should be given to parliament, and also that the questions of the royal veto and the king's prerogative to call and dissolve parliament should be addressed.[25] *A Letter to a Friend* (possibly also by Wildman) argued that the people should set up a limited monarchy wherein control of the militia, the right to declare war and peace, and the appointment of judges, sheriffs and other officers were lodged in the legislature, namely king, Lords and Commons, since this would 'necessitate frequent Parliaments, and make it impossible for the Monarch to enslave us'.[26]

Most Tories, and the majority of the bishops, found it difficult to countenance any idea of a breach in the succession. They favoured either restoring James upon terms, or a regency (with James keeping the title of king); failing either of these, they would have preferred settling the throne on Princess Mary alone. Archbishop Sancroft took the lead, summoning a meeting of all the bishops who were in the London area at Lambeth Palace on 26 December, where they discussed plans 'to call back the King', whom they proposed to 'bind hand and foot' so that he would 'never be able again to break in upon them, or put the Papists into their preferments'. Early in the new year this group, following consultations with certain London divines (amongst them William Sherlock), decided to draw up an address to William to ask either that he send 'Propositions' to the King or that William allow them to do so. Some eighteen bishops were involved in this 'conspiracy' to seek a conditional restoration of James, though Bishop Compton of London himself would have nothing to do with it; they were joined by some thirty temporal lords (amongst them Nottingham, Clarendon and Rochester) and fifty commoners.[27]

In the end, 'this Hierarchicall party' backed down from either addressing James or seeking William's permission to do so. They did, however, make their case in print. One broadsheet, purporting to be a speech to the Prince of Orange by 'a True Protestant' of the Established Church, thanked William for his undertaking to restore English liberties and secure the Protestant religion, but advised that his 'honour' lay in keeping close to the sense of his first Declaration, which obliged him to 'refuse the false glitterings of a Crown'. If he let himself or his wife be crowned, he would blemish the Protestant religion with the deposing doctrine, unite the forces of international popery, strengthen the French king, and create strong factions against him. It was in William's power, the author continued, 'to prevail with the King to give so much into the People's hands, as will make them safe'; if James, however, were to return 'by a high hand' (presumably with foreign backing), he would then be able to 'act without controul'.[28] Sherlock, in a pamphlet purporting to be a letter to a newly elected member of the Convention, insisted that it was essential to stick to the old establishment as near as possible, and favoured inviting James back 'under such legal restraints' as to 'put it utterly out of the king's power to invade our Liberties or Religion'. It would be wrong to judge how many were for James by the late defection, Sherlock asserted; the reason why 'the whole Nation . . . was very unanimous for the Prince' was 'not that they were willing to part with the King, and set up another in his room, but because they were horribly afraid of popery, and very desirous to see the Laws and Religion of the Nation settled upon the old Foundations by a Free Parliament, which was all the Prince declared for'. Yet 'many who were well-wishers to this Design', Sherlock contended, 'will not renounce their Allegiance to their King; and now they see what is like to come of it, are ashamed of what they have done . . . and are ready to undo it as far as they can'. Sherlock was most worried about what would happen on the religious front. Anglicans were glad to be rid of popery, but they would 'not be contented to Part with their Church into the bargain'; the dissenters were likewise glad to be rid of popery, but now they expected 'glorious days for themselves'. 'Consider how difficult it will be,' Sherlock implored, 'for any Prince who has but a crazy Title to the immediate possession of the Crown, to adjust this matter so, as neither to disgust the Church of England, nor the Dissenters.' If either of them should be disobliged, there would be 'a formidable party' against such a prince. 'Should any King be deposed, and any other ascend the Throne,' Sherlock predicted, it would 'be necessary for them to keep up a standing Army to quell the Discontents.'[29]

ABDICATION OR DESERTION? THE DEPOSING OF KING JAMES

In his letter to the Convention, read on 22 January, the opening day of the session, William told those assembled that he had 'endeavoured to the utmost of [his] Power to perform what was desired' of him and that it was now up to them 'to lay the Foundations of a firm Security' for their religion, laws and liberties, claiming that all he wanted was to see 'the Ends of [his] Declaration . . . attained'. William did, however, urge the need for unity and speed, since 'the dangerous Condition of the Protestant Interest in Ireland' and 'the present State of Things Abroad' meant that delay could be fatal. Despite this, the Commons decided, on the intervention of Tory member Sir Thomas Clarges, to defer beginning the debate on the state of the nation until 28 January, to give members more time to assemble. In the meantime, the Convention set aside 31 January (in London and Westminster) and 14 February (elsewhere) as days of thanksgiving for God's making the Prince of Orange 'the glorious Instrument of the great Deliverance of this Kingdom from Popery and Arbitrary Power', thereby explicitly casting what had happened so far in a providential light.[30]

In reaching its resolutions concerning the settlement of the crown, the Convention managed to sustain at least the appearance of a broad degree of consensus. However, the debates reveal significant divisions not only between Whigs and Tories but also within the parties, as well as disagreements between the Commons and the Lords. This ability to maintain consensus in the face of severe political disagreement was something that eluded the Scots, and goes a long way towards explaining why the constitutional settlement in England was very different from that which was to be worked out north of the border.

In discussing how revolutionary the Glorious Revolution was, and whether or not it was a victory for Whig principles, historians have typically focused on the significance of the legal restraints placed on the crown by the Declaration of Rights. However, arguably the most radical act of 1689 – and certainly the most unequivocally Whiggish – was the transfer of the crown itself from James to William and Mary. Tories had always held, as Secretary of State Sir Leoline Jenkins had put it during the Exclusion Crisis, that it was 'impossible for subjects to renounce or divest themselves of the allegiance they were borne under';[31] but that, of course, was exactly what the English did in 1689. However, it is usually argued that they did so in the most conservative way conceivable. Thus the Convention did not depose

James, but determined that he had abdicated, thereby leaving the throne vacant and in need of being filled. A look at the debates on the vacancy, and an examination of the various options that were considered but rejected, forces us to question whether a conservative reading is appropriate.

The debate in the Commons on 28 January was opened by Gilbert Dolben, a Tory, who argued that 'the king is demised' and James II no longer 'King of England' as a result of his having withdrawn himself 'from the administration of the government, without any provision to support the commonwealth'.[32] By 'demised', Dolben insisted, the law meant 'deserted the Government', the Latin *demisio* meaning 'laying down'; he also used as synonyms 'abandoned' and 'forsaken', and was adamant that James's forsaking the government had been voluntary. Dolben did not mention any maladministration on James's part, but seemed to think that the King's fleeing the realm and consequent absence from the kingdom constituted the demise, although in a later speech he qualified himself by saying that 'if the King would not stick to his Laws, nor redress the grievances of his people', he would call that 'a voluntary Demise'.[33] Since a demise was equivalent to the death of the king, there was no reason that this should affect the succession, and thus presumably the crown passed to the next heir.

The first to make the case for abdication was the radical Whig Sir Robert Howard. He began by outlining James's misdeeds, comparing him to Richard II (who had, of course, been deposed), and claiming that although there was 'a Maxim in the Law that the King can do no Wrong', many able lawyers of old took this to mean that if a king did wrong of his own volition 'he thereby ceases to be King'. 'The Originall of Power', Howard continued, was 'by Pact and Agreement from the People', but there had been 'such Violences offered to our very Constitution' that it was clear the pact had been broken. He therefore thought it 'to be above a Demise, A very Abdication of the King', and insisted that the people now had the right 'to new form themselves, under a Governor Yet to be Chosen'. Moreover, Howard added, James had not just broken the original contract with his people, he had also refused to govern them 'by withdrawing the Seals and making no Provision for the Government in his Absence'. Was not this 'an Abdication of it'? The Whig Henry Pollexfen spoke next, saying that in his opinion the King had 'forfeited his Right to the Crown of England before he went away'.[34] Other Whigs linked contract theory with abdication. For example, Sir William Pulteney maintained that 'there is an Abdication and . . . the Crown is void'; 'the Office of the King', he went on, was 'originally from the People' and if the king endeavoured to destroy those he was entrusted to preserve it was a breach of trust. 'I know there is a Maxim That the King can do no Wrong,' Pulteney added, 'but I would fain know Whom to blame else for the Wrong that has been Done us: it has been originally and primarily by no other but the King.'[35] Moreover, it was not just the wrongs that James II had committed in England that were causes of concern; some MPs also complained how James had given Ireland away to 'the Irish papists' after it had only recently been recovered following the 'bloudy Massacre' of 1641.[36]

The Tories were unhappy with where the Whigs were taking the debate. Sir Robert Sawyer tried to blur the issue of terminology, arguing that demise and abdication meant the same thing. In his opinion the King's departure was an abdication, as was James's refusal to govern according to law; what he was against was the inference that an abdication constituted a 'Dissolution of the Government'. The disposal of the crown was not in the people, he insisted; besides, the Convention did not represent a quarter of the people of England, while members should also consider 'the Relation which wee have to Scotland and to Ireland', which the Convention did not represent at all. 'If the Crown be faln', Sawyer said, it was 'just as if the King were dead', and so the privy council should simply proceed to proclaim the next heir, according to standard practice whenever a king died. The people could not choose whomsoever they wished to be their king, though if there was a dispute over who was the next heir, they might choose from among the several competitors – which was presumably Sawyer's way of getting around the problem of the Prince of Wales.[37] Heneage Finch wanted to know whether it was 'the maleadministration or the going away of the King' that amounted to an abdication. Finch was adamant that there had been no dissolution and insisted that the English monarchy was not elective but hereditary. 'By neglect, or male-administration', a king could 'forfeit no more than is in him'; the consequence was therefore 'no more, than that his personal exercise of the Crown is gone; but still it must subsist somewhere'. Finch suggested establishing a regency during James's life, as if the King were a lunatic.[38] Sir Christopher Musgrave wanted to know whether the intention was 'to depose the king'. He denied that James had subverted the government, but questioned whether, even if James had 'forfeited his Inheritance to the Crown', the Convention had the power to depose him. Musgrave also said that he was concerned about the trouble the Scots might cause, if they did not concur with the English Convention.[39] The Whigs tried to sidestep this issue by insisting that it was not a question of 'whether we can depose the King; but, whether the King has not deposed himself', as Sir John Maynard put it. Besides, as Sir William Williams pointed out, the plain fact was that James was gone and had 'deprived this Nation of the Exercise of Kingly Government'. It was essential to declare the throne void, Hugh Boscawen maintained, because there was now a 'little one beyond sea too' (namely the Prince of Wales).[40]

In the end, the House agreed to the following resolution:

That King James the Second, having endeavoured to subvert the Constitution of the Kingdom, by breaking the Original Contract between King and People; and, by the advice of Jesuits, and other wicked Persons, having violated the fundamental Laws; and having withdrawn himself out of this Kingdom; has abdicated the Government; and that the Throne is thereby vacant.

The syntax is awkward and may have been designed to cloud some of the deep disagreements that existed among members. It is notable, however, that neither the word demise nor desertion appear in the resolution. Although many members were reported as being unhappy with the resolution, only three voted against it – though one did walk out before the vote was put. On the following morning, the 29th, the Commons passed a further resolution, 'That it hath been found, by Experience, to be inconsistent with the Safety and Welfare of this Protestant Kingdom, to be governed by a Popish Prince'.[41]

When the Lords convened to discuss the state of the nation on the 29th, it unanimously concurred with the Commons' vote against a Popish prince. Bishop Turner of Ely, however, then introduced a motion for a regency, arguing 'that the King was in being and so was his Authority', but by reason of being a Catholic 'was uncapable of Administring the Government'. It received powerful support from the likes of Clarendon, Rochester, Ormonde, Nottingham and all the bishops in the House except Compton, and was only narrowly defeated by a vote of 51 to 48.[42] The Lords turned to the resolution on the vacancy on the 30th, and after a long and heated debate, lasting until 10 o'clock at night, eventually agreed to the clauses about the original contract (by a vote of 56 to 48), James's violation of the fundamental laws (by a majority this time of 11), and James's having withdrawn himself out of the kingdom, but objected to the word 'abdicated' in the penultimate clause, which they changed to deserted. On the following day they voted down the final clause, concerning the vacancy of the throne.[43]

This was now a critical moment for the Revolution. It was more than seven weeks since James's initial flight and the nation was no nearer to settling the throne. The situation in Ireland was rapidly deteriorating, while the European situation – with Louis XIV of France, having just invaded the Rhineland Palatinate, threatening to dominate Germany and overrun the Dutch – demanded speedy action. Delay could only play into James's hands, giving him the time he needed to launch an attempt to regain his three kingdoms with a French-backed invasion of Ireland. To many in England, until the Convention ruled on the succession, James remained technically their king. When Dr Sharp, the man whose anti-Catholic sermonizing under James II had been the catalyst for the establishment of the Ecclesiastical Commission, preached before the Commons on 30 January to mark the anniversary of Charles I's execution, he formally prayed for James II as 'King and Supream Governour in all Causes and over all persons', and maintained 'that deposing Kings was popish doctrine'.[44] There were sermons, bells and bonfires in London on the 31st to mark the day of thanksgiving, though Reresby remarked that 'the rejoiceing was not soe great . . . as was expected'. Indeed, Morrice noted that there were 'severall Sermons' in favour of restoring James II, the most 'conspicuous' being that by Bishop Lake of Chichester before the Lord Mayor at Bow Church, who reminded his listeners that 'The Church of England teacheth us to be obedient in all things to Kings', 'that Kings can no way be set aside, no way limited, no way restrained', and that therefore 'We must return to our duty and invite him in againe'. Morrice heard that the sermon 'had given universall offence to the very body of the City of all persuasions' and ruined the bishops' 'interest throughout the City and Kingdome'. Nevertheless, Sherlock and a dozen or so other divines were said to have preached similar sermons on that day.[45]

Concern about the failure of the Lords and the Commons to agree over the issue of the vacancy, and fear that the violence of the debates might drag England into civil war, prompted William's supporters in London to petition both Houses on Saturday 2 February, urging that the Prince and Princess of Orange 'be speedily settled in the throne'. Two groups of about twenty citizens presented separate petitions to the two Houses, with Lord Lovelace heading the contingent to the Lords and Anthony Rowe, member for Penryn, that to the Commons; they were accompanied by crowds of people who assembled outside the Convention and jeered those members believed hostile to a Williamite settlement. To avoid stirring up too much commotion, the petitioners had decided not to collect signatures, but this merely gave the Lords and the Commons the excuse to reject the petitions on the grounds that they were not signed. Thus Serjeant Maynard (a Whig) protested in the Commons: 'Here's a Petition proferred you from you know not whom . . . if you read it, the Parliament is without doors and not here.' Sir Edward Seymour (a Tory) articulated his concern that the petitioners made use of 'miserable people' and his worry that pressure out-of-doors might interfere with the freedom of parliamentary debate: 'If your Debates are not free, there is an end of all your proceedings . . . What comes from you is the result of reason, and no other cause. As your Debates must be free, so must your Resolution upon them; which cannot be unless some care be taken to preserve you from the Mob.' Lovelace and his allies therefore immediately set about obtaining signatures, an action hardly likely to assuage the fears of the likes of Maynard and Seymour; they allegedly collected some 15,000 and it was reported that a crowd of 10,000 was intending to descend on Westminster with the petitions on Monday the 4th. Conservative peers, fearing that the opposition to the Commons' resolution might collapse in the face of such pressure from out-of-doors, urged William to have the petitions suppressed. William agreed, partly to forestall any possibility of riotous unrest, but also because he wanted to ensure there could be no grounds for thinking that the Convention had been coerced into offering him the crown by an unruly rabble.[46]

This pressure from out-of-doors appears not to have had any immediate impact on opinion in the Convention. The Commons unanimously decided, on 2 February, to reject the Lords' amendments to the resolution about the vacancy and called for a conference with the Lords on the 4th. Here, John Hampden explained that the word 'deserted' did 'not fully express the Conclusion necessarily inferred from the Premises': 'deserted' respected 'only the Withdrawing', but 'abdicated' applied to 'the Whole' (namely James II's endeavouring to subvert the constitution by breaking the original contract and his violation of the fundamental laws, as well as his withdrawing himself). Hampden also insisted that the throne was vacant, since there was no person on the throne 'from whom the People of England' could 'expect regal Protection' and to whom, therefore, they owed 'the Allegiance of Subjects'. The Lords decided, by a vote of 54 to 49, to adhere to their choice of 'deserted', although the question of whether to agree with the Commons that the throne was vacant was defeated by a vote of just 55 to 54. The next day, the Lords explained that they objected to 'abdicate' partly because it was not a term known to common law and partly because it implied 'a voluntary express Act of Renunciation', which there had not been in this case and which did not follow from the premises. With regard to the vacancy, the Lords insisted that the English monarchy was not elective but hereditary, and although government by King James had ceased (by dint of his desertion), no act of the king alone could bar or destroy the right of the heirs to the crown. If the throne was therefore vacant of James II, allegiance was due 'to such Person as the Right of Succession does belong to', implying, in their mind, the Princess of Orange.[47]

Inspired by the Lords' resolution, Mary's supporters in the Commons seized the opportunity to challenge the notion that the throne was vacant, often invoking the British dimension to show why the Convention could not simply declare in favour of William. 'We are not debating for ourselves', Clarges protested, 'but for all the

King's dominions'; the crown was hereditary, not elective, and should go 'to the next Protestant Heir'. Likewise, Sir Joseph Tredenham, another self-professed Maryite, pointed out that 'Scotland must have a Share in this Election', adding that 'as long as we stand firm to the Succession', Scotland would surely concur with what England did. In the end, the Commons rejected the Lords' amendments, though this time by a vote of 282 to 151, and called for an open conference with the Lords on the following day to explain their reasoning.[48] The Whig lawyer John Somers argued that although abdication was not a word known to common law, neither was desertion. Both were Latin words, though with distinct meanings. Abdication signified 'entirely to renounce, throw off, disown, relinquish any thing or person, so as to have no further to do with it', either 'by express words or in writing' or 'by doing such acts as are inconsistent with the holding or retaining the thing'. A desertion, by contrast, 'was temporary and relievable'. The Commons had insisted that James had abdicated the government, therefore, to make it clear that he had 'no right of return to it'. The Commons' spokesmen also insisted that this would not make the crown of England 'always and perpetually elective', since the constitution, notwithstanding the vacancy, remained the same; as a result of the abdication, the Convention had to supply a defect, but 'only for this Tyme'. Despite spirited speeches by Nottingham, Clarendon, Rochester, the Earl of Pembroke and the Bishop of Ely in defence of the amendments, the Lords capitulated. Opinion in the upper House was further swayed by the fact that William, in a meeting with Halifax, Danby and other peers on 3 February, had made it clear that he would return to Holland if the Convention decided on a regency or to make his wife queen alone, while Mary herself had let it be known that she did not want the crown for herself, but would only rule jointly with her husband. On the morning of the 6th, after a brief debate lasting half an hour, the Lords decided by a vote of 65 to 45 to agree to the Commons' resolution. News that the two Houses had finally reached agreement over the vacancy was celebrated with 'bonefires at many noblemen's doores, and in many places all over the town', and with the ringing of church bells.[49]

THE DECLARATION OF RIGHTS

The Convention had determined, then, that James's abdication followed from his having broken the original contract, endeavoured to subvert the constitution, and violated the fundamental laws of the kingdom, as well as from his having withdrawn himself without providing for any government in his absence. He was taken to have abdicated, in other words, because he had shown that he was no longer willing to rule his kingdom of England in accordance with its constitution – a Whig interpretation of events. This amounted to a self-deposition; James had un-kinged himself. The Convention did not claim to have deposed James, although one might argue that the mere fact that the Convention imposed this particular interpretation on events meant that, in effect, they had.

Yet if the resolution concerning the abdication and vacancy was a clear-cut victory for the Whigs, the same cannot be said of the decision to accompany the settlement of the crown with a Declaration of Rights. On 29 January, the day after the Commons had determined that the throne was vacant, Lord Wharton, a Whig, urged the lower House to offer the crown to the Prince and Princess of Orange and resettle the government 'as near the ancient Government as can be'. He was challenged by Lord Falkland, a Tory, who said that before members decided whom to put on the throne, they should take care to secure themselves 'from Arbitrary Government' and consider 'what powers we ought to give the Crown'.[50] It has been suggested that Falkland's interjection was a delaying tactic, designed to divide the House and give conservative forces within the Convention time to manoeuvre on the question of who should head the government.[51] It certainly caused a delay. A number of Whigs rushed to support Falkland's proposal, arguing in the process the need to address problems dating back to Charles II's reign as well as those that had occurred under James II. William Garroway said 'we have had such Violation of our Liberties in the last reigns' that the Prince of Orange could not 'take it ill, if we make conditions, to secure ourselves for the future'. Hugh Boscawen agreed that 'Arbitrary Government was not only by the late King that is gone' but had been 'farthered by the extravagant Acts' of Charles II's Cavalier Parliament. William Sacheverell insisted that, God having 'put this opportunity into our hands', the whole world would 'laugh at us' if we made 'a half settlement', and saw the need to 'look a great way backward': indeed, he thought there were not three laws from the last twenty years or more that deserved to be continued. Whig lawyers, such as Somers, Treby, Pollexfen and Maynard, however, were concerned that discussing conditions would take up too much time, 'whereby Ireland might be destroyed and Holland hazarded'. Pollexfen suggested that Falkland's proposition was made 'to confound' the House. Claiming to be 'as much for Amendment of the Government as any man', he protested that going about it in this way would 'not settle the Government, but restore King James': one kingdom (i.e. Ireland) was 'gone already'; the clergy were divided; and the more the English divided amongst themselves, the more they would make way for the popish interest. Besides, Pollexfen continued, it was impossible to make new laws until there was a king: 'A Law you cannot make till you have a King', he proclaimed. The whole idea was 'not practicable'.[52]

Nevertheless, it would be wrong to dismiss Falkland's proposal as insincere. As we have seen, Tories had been concerned about abuses of royal power under James II; they also saw the need to establish further guarantees for the Anglican establishment to ensure that it could not be undermined by a future monarch, especially if that future monarch was to be another non-Anglican – the Calvinist William of Orange. Hence Falkland was joined by another Tory, Sir Edward Seymour, a fierce critic of James II in the 1685 parliament, who asked his fellow members whether they would 'let men go on in the same practices they have formerly' and 'establish the Crown', but not secure themselves, adding that 'theire business there was to secure themselves from Tyranny'. Falkland himself reiterated the point later in the debate, saying 'we must not only change hands, but things; not only take care that we have a King and Prince over us, but for the future, that he may not govern ill'. The idea that he was merely trying to delay matters to allow conservative forces in the upper House to frustrate the Whig initiative in the Commons on the vacancy, is belied by the fact that Falkland objected to the Lords' amendments to the Commons' resolution on the vacancy in the debate in the House on 2 February, insisting on the word abdicate because it 'relates to breaking your Laws', whereas desertion left open the possibility that James might 'come again, and resume the Government'. After a lengthy debate, the Commons agreed that before they filled the throne, they should appoint a committee 'to bring in general Heads of such things' as were 'absolutely necessary . . . for the better securing our Religion, Laws, and Liberties'.[53]

The committee, which comprised twenty-eight Whigs and twelve Tories and was chaired by the Whig lawyer Sir George Treby, identified some twenty-three 'Publick Grievances of the Nation' that needed redressing, which they brought to the House on 2 February. Five more grievances were added to the list during the debate that day. These twenty-eight 'Heads of Grievances', as they are normally known, identified a number of concerns that would have been shared by Whigs and Tories alike. Thus they declared the royal suspending power, the dispensing power, the Ecclesiastical Commission, extra-parliamentary taxation and the keeping of a standing army in peacetime without parliamentary consent to be illegal. They also proclaimed against the *quo warranto* proceedings and interference in the freedom of parliamentary elections; called for frequent parliaments; demanded a number of legal reforms (concerning the appointment of sheriffs, impanelling of juries, levying of bail, regulation of treason trials, and the tenure of judges); complained about oppressions and abuses in the collection of the hearth tax and the excise; defended the right of subjects to petition the crown; insisted that no member of the royal family should be allowed to marry a papist; suggested that future monarchs be required 'to take an oath for maintaining the Protestant religion, and the laws and liberties of the nation'; and that 'effectual provision . . . be made for the liberty of Protestants in the exercise of their religion and for uniting all Protestants in the matter of public worship as far as may be possible' (something which most Anglican spokesmen had come to deem necessary in the wake of James's attempt to appeal to the dissenters). Some of the items on the list were thought of as being merely declarations against the alleged illegal activities of James II. Others were demands for reform that would have required fresh legislation. Several of the grievances had a distinctively Whiggish appeal. Thus the Heads of Grievances asserted not only 'that Parliament ought to sit frequently' but suggested 'that their frequent sitting be preserved'; that there should be 'no interrupting of any session of Parliament, till the affairs that are necessary to be dispatched at that time are determined' (an allusion to how Charles II had managed to frustrate the demands of the Whigs during the Exclusion Crisis); 'that the too long continuance of the same Parliament be prevented' (to avoid a repeat of Charles II's Cavalier Parliament of 1661–79); that 'no pardon . . . be pleadable to an impeachment in Parliament' (an allusion to Danby's pardon in 1679); that 'the acts concerning the militia' were 'grievous to the subject'; that judges should hold their commissions *quam diu se bene gesserint* (on good behaviour, rather than at royal pleasure); and even that judges be paid salaries out of the public revenue (so as to ensure the independence of the judiciary from the crown).[54] Such concerns had been raised by the country opposition to Charles II in the mid-1670s, by the Whigs of the Exclusion Crisis, and by the Rye House plotters of 1683 and the Monmouth rebels of 1685.

When the Commons came to debate the Heads of Grievances on 4 February, the Whigs were divided as to how to proceed. Colonel Birch was for sending the Grievances to the Lords immediately. Wildman, however, suggested that they should split them into two, separating out those clauses that were declarative of old law and those that would require fresh legislation, arguing that when the Commons had framed the Petition of Right (1628), they had 'refused to have new Laws, but claimed what they demanded *ab origine*'. Sir Thomas Lee agreed that some of the heads could only be remedied by new laws and that the House would need to reframe the document they sent to the Lords. The Commons therefore decided that the same committee that had drawn up the Heads of Grievances should re-draft the document, distinguishing such as were 'introductory of new Laws' from those that were 'declaratory of ancient Rights'. They seem to have been influenced in part by the realization that pressing for further radical reform, at a time when the Lords would not even agree that the throne was vacant, would create further division between the two Houses, as well as by an appreciation that William himself was opposed to limitations. Yet members also appear to have accepted Pollexfen's point – made in opposition to Falkland's original motion

– that the Convention did not have the power to make new law, which would require the royal assent.[55]

Late on the afternoon of the 6th, having finally accepted the Commons' resolution concerning the abdication and vacancy, the Lords proceeded to discuss who should fill the vacant throne. The Marquis of Winchester proposed declaring William and Mary king and queen of England, and was supported 'with great Vigour' by fellow Whig peers Devonshire and Delamere. Nottingham made a last-ditch attempt to sabotage the settlement, saying that this 'could never be justified by reason or Law, but only by the Sword', that it would lead to a lengthy war, was contrary to all oaths, and would make the monarchy elective. Clarendon, Rochester and many of the bishops concurred. The Williamite peers replied that declaring William and Mary king and queen was the only way to prevent the mischiefs Nottingham had enumerated, because it would make England so strong by a union at home and with 'the Reformed interest' abroad that England's enemies would be 'unlikely to make a War upon' her; that it was 'most highly reasonable' to 'set him upon the Throne that had delivered us'; and that there were many precedents for the two estates departing from the strict line of succession but this had never made the crown elective. Nottingham then raised the issue of Scotland, reminding peers that this 'was a free Kingdome and might as well constitute a King to Reigne over England, as England might constitute one to Reigne over Scotland'. Halifax tried to calm concerns on this point by proposing that they should crown the prince and princess 'King and Queen of England with all the appurtenances thereunto belonging' and 'afterwards Consult with Scotland'. The House accepted without a division the resolution that William and Mary should be crowned jointly, and Nottingham was even induced to chair a committee to redevise the oaths of allegiance and supremacy, which would allow for the acceptance of William and Mary as monarchs *de facto* rather than *de iure*.[56]

On the afternoon of 7 February, the Commons' committee that had been assigned to separate the Heads of Grievances into two reported back with a declaration of ancient rights, together with a demand for new legislation by a future parliament to remedy the other 'Defects and Inconveniences'. The following day, the Commons voted to amend the resolution in favour of crowning William and Mary jointly with a proviso placing executive power in William alone, and appointed a new committee – this one chaired by the Whig lawyer John Somers and comprising sixteen Whigs and five Tories – to consider what amendments to make to the Lords' vote of the 6th, and to connect that to the declaration of ancient rights. Before the end of the day this committee had produced the draft of what was to become the Declaration of Rights; gone was the demand for future legislation to remedy those grievances which were not declarative of ancient rights. The Lords then reviewed the draft, suggesting various amendments, some of which the Commons accepted, and the final text of the Declaration of Rights was approved by the Convention on the 12th.[57] William and Mary were then proclaimed king and queen of England in London and Westminster on the 13th, and shortly thereafter in the rest of the kingdom.[58]

It has been suggested that because the committees that were responsible for framing the Declaration of Rights were dominated by Whigs, and the offer of the crown to William and Mary was accompanied by a statement of rights, the constitutional settlement of 1689 should be seen as a Whig victory (albeit a qualified one, since some of the more radical demands for reform were omitted in the face of opposition from William and conservative opinion in the Convention). Such a view seems questionable. As we have seen, as the crisis of 1688–9 unfolded, Tory Anglicans had not shown themselves shy of seeking additional legal safeguards from the crown, whether as the price of James keeping his throne or of William getting it. At the same time, many Williamite Whigs had seen no need for limitations on the new monarch, since in William they had a king of their own liking. Furthermore, a close examination of the Declaration of Rights suggests that there was little that was distinctively Whiggish about it – the wording it adopted, and rights it proclaimed, would in the main also have been agreeable to Tory-Anglican opinion.

The Declaration began by asserting that James II, 'by the Assistance of divers Evil Counsellors, Judges, and Ministers . . . did endeavour to Subvert and extirpate the Protestant Religion, and the Lawes and Liberties of this Kingdome'. It then listed eight means whereby he had sought to do this, followed by a further five abuses deemed to have been committed 'of late Years' (that is, under Charles II as well), all of which were determined to have been 'utterly and directly contrary to the knowne Lawes and Statutes and freedome of this Realme'. The Declaration did not however claim, as the Commons had initially resolved on 28 January, that James had broken his original contract with the people. Instead, it stated that James had 'abdicated the Government' and left the throne 'vacant', and that the Prince of Orange, who had been raised by God to be 'the glorious Instrument of delivering this Kingdom from Popery and Arbitrary Power', had, on the advice of the Lords and principal members of the Commons, called a parliament to effect 'such an establishment as that their Religion Lawes and Libertyes might not againe be in danger of being subverted'. This body, the Declaration continued, seeking the best way of 'vindicating and asserting their antient rights and Liberties', decided to declare a series of 'premises' that they insisted were 'their undoubted Rights and Liberties'. They listed thirteen in total, which were intended to address the abuses of power identified in the first half of the Declaration, though there is an asymmetry, since, clause by clause, the second half of the document does not exactly correspond to the first.[59]

Did the Declaration of Rights merely vindicate and assert ancient rights and liberties, or did those who framed it deliberately set out, as some historians have claimed, to make new law under the guise of proclaiming the old? Despite being drawn up in committees dominated by Whigs, the Declaration of Rights had to be approved by the Convention as a whole, which was more evenly balanced between the two parties. The Lords, which had shown such legal tetchiness over the Commons' use of the word 'abdication', had the judges review the Declaration carefully, to ensure that nothing was declared illegal that patently was not so, and insisted on a number of modifications to the wording of the Commons' draft as a result.[60] Moreover, there was also the concern that any new limitations imposed by the Convention before William and Mary were proclaimed king and queen could subsequently be deemed null and void. Indeed, in 1660 the Convention Parliament that had recalled Charles II had determined that all legislation enacted over the preceding two decades that had not received the royal assent, freely given, was null and void, while one of the main arguments used by Whigs against the court's offer of limitations during the Exclusion Crisis had been that such limitations imposed on the Catholic heir before he became king would be rescinded immediately upon his accession, since a king could not have his prerogative given away before he came to the throne.[61] Furthermore, since the Convention of 1689 was not a true parliament, if it had tried to proclaim new laws under the guise of asserting ancient rights and liberties, its innovations would never have stood up in a court of law if subsequently challenged. There are good grounds for thinking that what the Declaration of Rights proclaimed to be existing law was genuinely believed, by those who helped frame the document or else gave their consent to it in the Convention, actually to be existing law. It is conceivable that they were wrong, or deceiving themselves in order to vindicate the overthrow of a king they disliked (James II, as we have seen, had always claimed that he was acting within his legal rights), though the fact that the Declaration passed a bi-partisan and bi-cameral Convention shows that, if this was the case, there must have been a wide degree of consensus underpinning this self-deluding desire to believe in a particular (though erroneous) interpretation of the constitution – something which further undermines the argument that the Declaration of Rights marked a victory for one particular party.

What particular ancient rights and liberties, then, did the Declaration of Rights vindicate and assert, and which, if any, broke new constitutional ground? Controversy has hinged in particular on the first three resolutions in the second half of the document, namely those against the suspending power, the dispensing power and the Ecclesiastical Commission, and the sixth resolution, that against keeping a standing army in peacetime without parliamentary consent. Before examining them more closely, two things need to be emphasized. The first is that these were as much Tory grievances as they were Whig ones. The bishops had led the attack on Charles II's attempt to use the suspending power to establish some degree of liberty of conscience in 1662 and 1672 (whereas, in fact, the future Whig leader, the Earl of Shaftesbury, had supported Charles's use of the suspending power in this context),[62] and it was the bishops, again, who had led the opposition to James's II's subsequent attempts in 1687 and 1688. The dispensing power had been challenged by the Tory-dominated parliament of 1685 and by the fellows of Magdalen College, Oxford, and James's Ecclesiastical Commission had been set up to discipline recalcitrant Anglican clergymen. The Tories had also challenged James's build-up of a standing army in the parliament of 1685; indeed, Cavalier-Anglican opposition to standing armies stemmed from their hatred of the Long Parliament's New Model Army of the 1640s and military rule under Cromwell, and those who were later to emerge as Tories had criticized Charles II's attempts to establish a peacetime standing army in the late 1660s and 1670s. The second point to emphasize is that contemporaries genuinely appear to have believed that all of these were illegal; indeed they had already challenged their legality long before the framing of the Declaration of Rights. In believing this, they were arguably correct. It would certainly be wrong to imply that those who sat in the Convention seized the opportunity provided by the breakdown in royal authority to declare illegal powers which they believed the crown legally possessed.

The first resolution forthrightly declared that 'the pretended power of suspending of Lawes or the execution of Lawes by Regall Authority without Consent of Parliament is illegal'. This was an implied condemnation of James's Declarations of Indulgence, and seems relatively uncontroversial. Contemporaries had long thought that the only body capable of suspending laws was the same body that had enacted them – namely parliament: king, Lords and Commons acting together. Charles II had tried to claim that, as head of the Church, he had the right to suspend ecclesiastical laws, and this was the rationale behind his Declaration of Indulgence of 1672. Parliament had told him that he was misinformed and made him withdraw the Indulgence in 1673. Charles's action in 1673 was interpreted as an explicit acknowledgement by the crown that it did not possess any such power, and was repeatedly cited by those who condemned James's attempts to establish a suspending power.[63]

The second resolution – that against the dispensing power – is somewhat more complicated. The original draft of the Declaration of Rights had condemned it outright. The Lords took exception, however, arguing that the king did possess such a power and that the granting of *non obstantes* (dispensations) could, in fact, be beneficial to the subject. It was the way that the dispensing power had been extended under James II that was the problem. The Commons therefore changed the wording, so that the final text of the Declaration of Rights read 'that the pretended Power of dispensing with Laws, or the Execution of Laws, by Regal Authority, as it has been assumed and exercised of late, is illegal'.[64]

Yet had the way the dispensing power been exercised 'of late' been illegal? James, after all, had obtained a judicial ruling in favour of his right to give dispensations from the Test Act in the case of Godden v. Hales of 1686. In 1688 Lord Chief Justice Herbert, the judge who presided over Godden v. Hales, published a detailed justification of his ruling. Here he repeated the distinction between things that were *mala in se* (evil in themselves, which the king could not dispense with) and those which were *mala prohibita* (that is, which had been legal until prohibited by parliament, which the king could dispense with). Herbert also insisted (citing Coke) that nothing could 'bind the King from any Prerogative' which was 'sole and inseparable to his person', such as his 'Sovereign Power to command any of his Subjects to serve him for the publick weal', and further claimed that the king could even dispense with statutes made *pro bono publico* ('for the public good', as some had argued the Test Act was), if no particular damage arose to a particular person as a result. Addressing the issue that Godden v. Hales had been a feigned action (which he claimed he had been unaware of at the time), Herbert said this did not invalidate the ruling: feigned actions were often directed out of Chancery to settle 'great and difficult Points of Law', so why might not the king 'direct such an Action to be brought, to satisfie himself whether he had such a Power'? Yet the ruling had not 'given up our Lives, Liberties, and Estates, to be disposed of at the King's pleasure', Herbert insisted, since the king could not 'dispense one tittle with Magna Carta or any of the other laws whereby the lives, liberties or interests of any subjects are confirmed'.[65]

However, several observations need to be made before we conclude that the declaration against the dispensing power broke new legal ground. The first is that 'the pretended power of dispensing with laws . . . as . . . exercised of late' was not solely an allusion to James's dispensations from the Test. James had used his dispensing power in other ways during his reign – for example, to dispense the fellows of Magdalen College from their college statutes laying down the procedure for the election of a new president; even Herbert thought that James's attempt to use the dispensing power in this case was illegal.[66] Secondly, as we saw in Chapter 5, many contemporaries thought the decision in Godden v. Hales was wrong. Not only was it a feigned action, set up to achieve a judicial ruling in favour of the dispensing power, but the judicial bench had been purged in advance to ensure the right result. As one pamphlet, dated 22 December 1688, somewhat colourfully put it, the judgment had been procured 'by packing a dozen Judges, and knowing their opinions beforehand, and turning out those who dissented, and putting in a parcel of Blockheads who should agree'.[67] It was also arguable that Herbert had misinterpreted his case law. In 1689 the Whig lawyer, historian and polemicist William Atwood produced a lengthy tract responding to Herbert's self-vindication, claiming that Herbert had misinterpreted both the precedents and the authorities he had cited. With regard to statutes *pro bono publico*, Sir Edward Coke had said that the king could dispense with the penalty granted to himself, not with the statute itself. Nor was it the case that the king could dispense with all things that were *mala prohibita*. There were 'many things in Magna Charta', Atwood stated, that were 'but *mala prohibita*', but even Herbert conceded that the king could not dispense with one tittle of that. The reasoning upon which Herbert had based his initial judgment, namely that Henry VII had nevertheless dispensed with an act of Henry VI's reign against the appointment of sheriffs for more than one year, even though the act had included a provision against *non obstantes* with regard to the sheriffs, was faulty, Atwood claimed, since the particular case in question related to the county of Northumberland, an ancient liberty, where the shrievalty was inheritable for life with a fee to the crown. Moreover, it could not be shown that any sheriff had held office for more than one year by the same patent (and even if it could be, this would not create a right). The Test Act could not be dispensed with, Atwood insisted, because doing so would violate the interests of private persons, since the Test Act declared and confirmed 'an Inherent Right, and Interest of Liberty, and Freedom in the Subjects of the Realm', namely a freedom 'from Popish Slavery and

Tyranny'. Indeed, Calvin's case of 1608 had established that the king could not dispense with an act of parliament which 'disableth any Person, or maketh any thing void, or tortious, for the good of the Church or Commonwealth', because 'in that Law all the King's Subjects have an Interest.' In Atwood's view, the resolution in Godden v. Hales was worse than the infamous ship-money verdict of 1637, which had sanctioned Charles I's imposition of an extra-parliamentary levy on the grounds of emergency: for though on this occasion the judges 'made the King the sole Judge of the Kingdom's Necessity, yet they suppos'd it to be at a time when there was a real Danger', while with James the dispensing power was 'abus'd to the bringing in what the Parliament labour'd to prevent'. If Herbert had done his research, he would have found that it was 'far from being a setled Point, That the King might dispense with particular Persons as to whatever is not prohibited by the Law of God'. *Non obstantes* had long been in dispute, and several parliaments had been against them. Atwood concluded by demanding that Herbert should be prosecuted for treason for deliberately subverting the law.[68]

A final observation follows from this last point. If a judge made a bad ruling or misinterpreted the law, the appropriate body to correct such an error was parliament. Herbert, in his self-vindication, had protested that if he had been wrong he had nevertheless made the best judgment he could in light of how he understood the law, and would cheerfully submit to parliament's determination 'whether the ruling he had given was consonant to Law'; indeed, he thought it 'very fit that this dark Learning . . . of Dispensations, should receive some Light from a determination in Parliament'.[69] Similarly, James II himself, when he started to backtrack in the autumn of 1688, had promised he would 'lay his dispensing power to be determined by the arbitrement of Parliament'.[70] In 1689, the Lords and Commons did arbitrate on the dispensing power and declared that, as it had been exercised of late, it was illegal. This, in itself, was not constitutionally innovative, although it was done, one must concede, by an assembly of Lords and Commons that had not been summoned by the king and was therefore not technically a legal parliament.

The third resolution of the second half of the Declaration of Rights declared that 'the Commission for erecting the late Courte of

Commissioners for Ecclesiastical Causes and all other Commissions and Courts of like nature' were 'illegal and pernicious'. As we saw in Chapter 5, there are good grounds for believing that James's Ecclesiastical Commission was an illegal court, since it was set up in violation of an Act of 1641, confirmed at the Restoration, which had abolished Charles I's High Commission and voided in perpetuity the crown's right to appoint commissioners under the great seal to exercise any manner of spiritual or ecclesiastical jurisdiction. Many contemporaries, as we have seen, firmly believed James's Ecclesiastical Commission to be illegal; indeed, its first victim, Bishop Compton, refused to acknowledge the authority of the court, having been informed it was 'directly Contrary to Statute Law'.[71]

Where the Declaration of Rights perhaps did break new constitutional ground was in declaring that 'the raiseing or keeping a Standing Army within the Kingdom in time of Peace unlesse it be with consent of Parliament' was 'against Law'. There was no law, as such, that explicitly forbade the keeping of a standing army in times of peace without parliamentary consent. Moreover, the Militia Acts of 1661 and 1662 had confirmed the right of the crown to control all armed forces within the country. It should be said, however, that these acts were primarily concerned with the militia (the part-time and unpaid county trained bands mustered by the Lord Lieutenants and their deputies); the framers of the legislation of 1661 and 1662 were not envisioning a large, professional standing army such as James assembled. Contemporaries clearly saw the militia and the standing army as separate issues; in the original Heads of Grievances complaints about the two were listed in separate clauses. However, the legislation enacted in 1660 to disband the republican army provided that all officers were to be cashiered 'except such . . . as his Majesty shall thinke fit otherwise to dispose and provide for, at his own Charge'.[72] This seemed to imply that the king was free to keep as large an army as he could afford. In fact, the framers of the act were probably thinking of a small coterie of personal guards. It was clearly expected at the time of the Restoration that the crown, by itself, would not have the means to finance a large standing army, and that it would need to come to parliament to seek funding for any expenditures on the military. Still, this was only an informal check on the king's power, not a legal restraint; James II showed that the crown could, by itself, finance a large military establishment.

Nevertheless, there were other legal restrictions on maintaining a standing army in peacetime, namely those stipulated by the Petition of Right of 1628, which had provided against the billeting of troops on private householders and the imposition of martial law. Charles II, when he tried to build up his standing forces, found that he had no option but to violate the provisions of the Petition of Right. Parliament took a number of stands against standing armies in the late 1660s and 1670s, and on 1 April 1679 finally resolved 'that the continuing of any standing forces in this Nation, other than the Militia' was 'illegal', complaining in particular of the fact that Charles's army had been billeted in private houses. This resolution was followed in May by an act disbanding Charles's forces and confirming that it was illegal to force private householders to receive soldiers into their homes without their consent (see p. 188). James nevertheless went on to build up a sizeable peacetime standing army, in spite of the Disbanding Act, and proceeded to billet troops in private houses and impose martial law. There had, then, clearly been legal violations here. The problem was, what was the best way of redressing them?

Here it is important to notice a slight difference in wording between the first and the second halves of the Declaration of Rights. In the draft originally sent to the Lords, the first half of the Declaration identified that one of the means whereby James had endeavoured to subvert the laws and liberties of the kingdom was 'by raiseing and keeping a standing army in time of Peace without Consent of Parliament'. The Lords insisted that the words 'and quartering Soldiers, contrary to Law' be added, as 'an Aggravation of the Grievance'.[73] There is no doubt that, thus worded, the Declaration of Rights was correct in alleging that James had acted illegally. It was clear, in other words, that attempts by both Charles II and James II (particularly the latter) to establish a standing army in peacetime without parliamentary consent had led to violations of the law and of the people's ancient rights and liberties. How was the Convention going to attain the desired ends of vindicating and asserting these ancient rights and liberties in this regard? The solution it came up

with was simply to declare that raising or keeping a peacetime standing army without parliamentary consent was illegal. Here one might
suggest that the emphasis should be placed more on the verb 'to vindicate' than 'to assert': such a declaration was indeed the only way to
guarantee that the people's rights and liberties would not be violated
in future. Although technically the resolution might have enunciated
a new position at law, it was done with the intent of vindicating the
legal rights that the English people were already believed to possess.

The remaining provisions of the Declaration of Rights are less controversial.[74] Clause four, which condemned as illegal the 'levying of
money . . . by the pretence of Prerogative without Grant of Parliament
for longer time or in other manner, than the same is or shall be
granted', referred to James's levying of the excise in the first few weeks
of his reign, prior to the meeting of the 1685 parliament, which had
technically been illegal even though many had accepted it as necessary
at the time. Clause five affirmed 'the right of the Subjects to petition
the King' and that 'all Commitments and prosecutions for such petitioning' were illegal – a reference to the seven bishops' case of 1688.
(The first half of the Declaration of Rights also listed as one of James's
illegal acts prosecuting in the court of King's Bench causes which were
'Cognizable only in Parliament', another allusion to the proceedings
against the seven bishops.) Clause seven affirmed that 'Subjects which
are Protestants may have Armes for their defence Suitable to their
Condition and as allowed by Law'. This was in response to a charge
made against James II in the first half of the Declaration of Rights that
he had disarmed Protestants at a time when Catholics 'were both
armed and Employed contrary to Law'. (This was probably in particular an allusion to what had gone on in Ireland.) It has been claimed
that the Declaration of Rights established a new right to bear arms.[75]
In fact, clause seven does not use the term 'right' and seems clearly to
state that no new legal privilege is being granted here. It explicitly
confirms existing limitations on who was allowed to possess arms
and, if anything, should more accurately be seen as a gun-control
measure.[76] Clauses eight and nine state 'that Elections of Members of
Parliament ought to be free' and 'that the freedome of Speech and
debates or proceedings ought not be impeached or questioned in
any Courte or place out of Parliament'. Both were time-honoured

principles. The first was a reference to James's attempt to pack parliament in 1688 – the first half of the Declaration of Rights explicitly listed this as a grievance against James II – though some Whigs might have read it as also applying to Charles II's interference in borough franchises in the years of the Tory Reaction. The second referred to the prosecution of Sir William Williams in 1686 for licensing a pamphlet when Speaker in 1680, which King's Bench judged to be a seditious libel.

Only clauses ten to twelve – insisting that excessive bail, and excessive and unusual punishments, ought not to be imposed; demanding that jurors be duly impanelled and that jurors in trials for high treason must be freeholders; and outlawing 'all grants and promises of fynes and forfeitures of particular persons before conviction' – alluded to grievances that pre-dated the accession of James II. (In the first half of the Declaration the corresponding clauses are nine to thirteen and are introduced by the phrase 'And whereas of late years', to distinguish them from the earlier clauses, which had been introduced as charges specifically against James II.) Clause ten condemned a trilogy of wrongdoings, which had been listed as separate clauses in the first half of the Declaration. The first was the imposition of excessive bail, a reference to the huge sums (anywhere between £10,000 and £60,000) that had been set in the final years of the Tory Reaction and at the time of the Monmouth rebellion as a way of keeping those suspected of disaffection (but whose offences were bailable) in prison – though one must also not forget the £30,000 bail set for Danby's release from prison in February 1684, reminding us that this clause addressed Tory as well as Whig grievances.[77] The second was excessive fines. Here the framers presumably had in mind the £10,000 fine imposed on Sir Samuel Barnardiston in 1684 for writing seditious letters, the £40,000 meted out to John Hampden in 1684 for his alleged involvement in the Rye House Plot, and the £100,000 imposed on both Thomas Pilkington and Titus Oates in 1682 and 1684 for *scandalum magnatum* upon the Duke of York, though it should be remembered that even the fines of £500 each imposed on the Whigs Benjamin Harris in 1679 (for seditious libel) and Thomas Dare in 1680 (for sedition) had been regarded as excessive at the time.[78] The third was unusual punishments, and referred to Oates's being sentenced to two whippings and two stints in the pillory and then to stand in the pillory four times a year for the rest of his life, following his condemnation on two counts of perjury in 1685, and the flogging and pillorying of Samuel Johnson in 1686 for publishing seditious libel – punishments that might well have proved fatal when the crime did not carry the death penalty. Clause eleven, concerning the proper impanelling of jurors (more precisely explained as the returning of 'partial corrupt and unqualified persons' in the first half of the Declaration), was aimed at abuses during the years of the Tory Reaction, while the specific stipulation that jurors in trials for high treason be freeholders alluded to the use of non-freeholders in the trials of the Rye House plotters in 1683, notably that of Lord Russell. Existing law was not clear on this last point, though the clause was certainly in the spirit of existing law; Russell's counsel in 1683 had cited an act from Henry V's reign stipulating that jurors in capital offences be forty shilling freeholders (and it was recognized at law that trial jurors at assizes had to be freeholders, with an act of 1665 raising the qualification to the possession of a freehold worth £20 per year), but the prosecution had insisted that Henry V's act did not specifically mention cases of high treason and also did not apply to jury panels in corporations.[79] Clause twelve, outlawing grants of fines and forfeitures prior to conviction, alluded in particular to the way the estates of some of those Monmouth rebels sentenced to transportation had been promised to bidders before formal conviction. James II had not invented the practice, and the framers were probably also thinking of similar incidents under Charles II (though it should be pointed out that the practice had a long history, and had even been followed by rulers whom the Whigs and commonwealthmen regarded more favourably, such as Queen Elizabeth and Oliver Cromwell). However, it had been denounced by medieval statutes, while the great early seventeenth-century jurist Sir Edward Coke was quite clear that the king had no right to do this.[80]

Clause thirteen of the Declaration of Rights asserted 'that for redress of all grievances and for the amending, strengthening and preserving of the Lawes, Parliaments ought to be held frequently'. The infrequent meeting of parliament had not been identified as one of the abuses in the first half of the Declaration, and this clause was clearly inserted at the end in the hope of ensuring that no such abuses of executive power, such as had occurred in the 1680s, could be repeated and that the ancient rights and liberties claimed by the Declaration could be guaranteed. It might have been an allusion both to Charles's failure to call parliament during the last four years of his reign (which was technically in violation of the Triennial Act of 1664) and also James's failure to meet with parliament again after November 1685. Yet revealingly there was no attempt to secure the frequent meetings of parliament, even though the country opposition of the 1670s, the Whigs of the Exclusion Crisis and the Rye House and Monmouth rebels had claimed that medieval statutes provided for the annual meeting of parliament; nor was there even a statement that parliaments should meet every three years, as spelled out by the Triennial Act.

The final section of the Declaration of Rights resolved that William and Mary should be declared king and queen of England, France and Ireland 'and the Dominions thereunto belonging . . . during their lives and the life of the Survivor of them', with the exercise of regal power vested in William alone, and that after their deaths the crown should pass to the heirs of the Princess of Orange or, if she remained childless, to James II's second daughter, Princess Anne of Denmark and her heirs. The Declaration then stipulated two new oaths to be taken by all people previously required to take the oaths of allegiance and supremacy: one to 'bee faithfull and bear true Allegiance to their Majesties King William and Queen Mary'; the other abjuring the doctrine 'That Princes Excommunicated or Deprived by the Pope or any Authority of the see of Rome may be deposed or Murdered by their Subjects' and declaring 'that noe foreign Prince, Person, Prelate, State or Potentate hath or ought to have any Jurisdiction, Power, Superiority, Preeminence or Authority Ecclesiastical or Spiritual within this Realme'.

Scholars have disagreed over whether the offer of the crown to William and Mary was conditional upon their acceptance of the Declaration of Rights.[81] Strictly speaking, it was not. The crown was offered at a special ceremony involving the new monarchs and the members of the Convention, which took place at the Banqueting House on 13 February. Halifax, as speaker of the Lords, asked William and Mary for permission to read the Declaration; they agreed, the clerk of the Lords then read it, and after that the crown was offered. However, William replied with a short speech in which he first accepted the crown, and then told the members of the Convention that as he 'had no other Intention in coming hither, than to preserve your Religion, Laws, and Liberties', so they could rest assured that he would 'endeavour to support them', adding that he would 'concur in anything that shall be for the Good of the Kingdom' and do everything in his power 'to advance the Welfare and Glory of the Nation'.[82] William did not take a formal oath promising to uphold the provisions of the Declaration. Nor was the reading of the Declaration and the offer of the crown linked to the taking of the coronation oath, as it was to be in Scotland; William took the English oath at his coronation on 11 April. There was certainly no attempt to link the offer of the crown with a request that those grievances which did not find their way into the Declaration of Rights be remedied – again, in contrast to what was to happen in Scotland. Furthermore, we might wonder in what sense the offer of the crown could have been made conditional upon the acceptance of the Declaration if, as has been argued here, the framers of the Declaration did not think they were imposing any new conditions on the crown.

Yet framing the issue like this puts a whole new light on the question. It was not that the members of the Convention were offering the crown to William and Mary on the condition that they relinquish certain royal prerogatives that all previous monarchs had enjoyed. Rather, they were spelling out to William and Mary that the people of England possessed certain rights and liberties that James II had violated, and that there were certain things that English monarchs could not legally do, notwithstanding anything James II had done to the contrary. William and Mary took the crown on the same terms that James II and all previous monarchs were presumed to have taken it – they were supposed to rule according to law. We have to remember, however, that not ruling according to law had cost James his throne. He was taken by the Convention as having abdicated the government, not just by his withdrawing himself, but by his refusal to respect the constitution. The Declaration of Rights did not link James's abdicating the government so explicitly with his subverting the fundamental laws as had the Convention's original resolution on the vacancy, so it was possible to read the Declaration of Rights as meaning either that James had ruled illegally and (coincidentally) also abdicated the government, or that he had abdicated the government by dint of the fact that he had ruled illegally. Yet it was certainly possible to interpret the reading of the Declaration to William and Mary prior to the offer of the crown as a warning that, if they did not rule according to law, they too would un-king themselves.

THE POST-DECLARATION OF RIGHTS SETTLEMENT

The fact that in framing the Declaration of Rights the members of the Convention chose to defer addressing those grievances which would require fresh legislation until after the crown had been settled means that we cannot see the Declaration by itself as the entirety of the Revolution settlement. It was always expected that further reforming legislation would follow once a legal parliament had been called into existence. This was achieved on 23 February when the Convention passed a bill, which received the royal assent, turning itself into a parliament. Although the Tories would have liked fresh elections, William and his Whig allies thought that calling a new parliament would cause a dangerous delay, given the international situation and the necessity of raising money speedily for the impending wars in Ireland and on the Continent.[83]

The first grievance to be addressed that did not find its way into the Declaration of Rights was the hearth tax – a levy imposed on fireplaces at the Restoration, on the assumption (not always correct) that the more hearths one had the more wealth one possessed, which had been very unpopular. On 1 March, in an attempt to persuade parliament to be more generous when voting supplies, William informed the Commons that he understood 'the Chimny mony was very grievous and burdensome to his good Subjects' and that he was content it should be removed. The announcement was well-received in both the House and the nation at large, and the Commons immediately appointed a committee to bring in a bill for the abolition of the tax.[84]

In March Parliament turned its attention to devising a new

coronation oath – again, something that had been deemed necessary by the Heads of Grievances – to oblige the new sovereign to rule according to law. In the traditional oath, which James II had taken in 1685, the monarch promised to 'grant and keep and . . . confirm to the people of England the Laws and Customs to them granted by the Kings of England'. The 1689 oath removed the notion that the people enjoyed their laws and customs as a grant from the king. Thus at their coronation William and Mary solemnly swore and promised 'to Governe the People of this Kingdome of England and the Dominions thereto belonging according to the Statutes in Parlyament agreed on and the Laws and Customs of the same'. That part of the traditional oath asking the monarch to 'keep peace, and godly Agreement . . . to the holy Church, the Clergy, and the people' (which was vague and potentially carried Catholic overtones) was also dropped and replaced by an explicit promise 'to Maintaine the Laws of God, the true Profession of the Gospell, and the Protestant Reformed Religion Established by Law'. The Whigs had wanted to use the words 'as shall be established', to allow for the possibility of further reform in the Church, though Tories insisted on their preferred formula and carried the vote by 188 to 149.[85] On 24 April the Convention passed legislation abolishing the old oaths of allegiance and requiring all civil and ecclesiastical office-holders to take the new oaths prescribed by the Declaration of Rights by 1 August or, after a six-month grace period, face deprivation of office.[86]

On 5 March it was proposed in the Commons that a bill should be prepared for enacting the Declaration of Rights into law and to prevent a papist from coming to the throne.[87] Partisan disputes, and a preoccupation with other issues (such as funding the war), meant that no agreement had been reached before parliament adjourned for the summer on 20 August. The bill was revived in the autumn, however, and eventually enacted on 16 December. The Bill of Rights, as it is normally known, gave statutory force to the Declaration of Rights, and further asserted that William and Mary 'did accept the Crowne . . . according to the Resolution and Desire of the . . . Lords and Commons contained in the said Declaration'. The wording is again ambiguous: was the 'Resolution and Desire' alluded to simply that William and Mary accept the throne, or was it the entire list of premises spelled out at the beginning of the Declaration intended to vindicate ancient rights and liberties? The Bill of Rights nevertheless continued, in this respect, to insist that all the 'Rights and Liberties asserted and claimed' in the Declaration of Rights 'were the true auntient and indubitable Rights and Liberties of the People of this Kingdome'. The Bill of Rights, however, did go beyond the Declaration of Rights by further stipulating that no one could come to the throne who was, or ever had been, a Catholic; that a king or queen might not marry a Catholic; and that any future monarch who came to the throne must take the Test Act oath of 1678. This was because, the Bill states (reiterating the wording of the Commons' resolution of 29 January), 'it hath been found by Experience that it is inconvenient with the Safety and Welfare of this Protestant Kingdome to be governed by a Popish Prince or by any King or Queene marrying a Papist'. The Bill of Rights also placed further limitations on the dispensing power, stipulating that in future no royal dispensation could be used against any act of parliament that had not specifically included a provision allowing for such.[88]

Some progress was also made towards addressing clause sixteen of the Heads of Grievances – that effectual provision be made for Protestants to have freedom of worship and that Protestants be united in matters of public worship as much as possible. It was widely recognized that something would have to be done to help the Protestant dissenters;[89] after all, Anglican leaders had already promised the dissenters some form of relief from a future parliament in return for their agreeing not to back James's Declarations of Indulgence. Nottingham proposed a scheme to broaden the basis of the national Church by comprehending the more moderate dissenters, while conceding a very limited toleration to those who remained outside. In the end, however, the plans for comprehension got separated from the provision for freedom of worship. At William's insistence, a Toleration Bill went through parliament fairly quickly in the spring. This did not repeal the penal laws, but gave Protestant dissenters immunity from prosecution for holding their own religious services if they licensed their meeting-houses and kept their doors open when they met (the latter to meet the charge, frequently made during Charles II's reign, that dissenters met in private to plot sedition against the state), subscribed the declaration against transubstantiation (contained in the Test Acts of 1673 and 1678), and took the oath of fidelity and allegiance and that against the pope's deposing power (prescribed in the Declaration of Rights).[90] It was decided, however, that comprehension was a matter more appropriately taken up by Convocation. The latitudinarian divine John Tillotson proposed a certain degree of liturgical reform and a relaxation of the demand for ceremonial conformity as a way of enticing dissenters back into the fold.[91] Yet the High Anglican clergy proved reluctant to make any concessions, their fears for the security of their Church having been heightened by the abolition of episcopacy north of the border as part of the Revolution settlement in Scotland. One Jacobite pamphleteer itemized among 'the Train of Mischiefs' that would 'follow this Revolution' the 'Scandal and Change it brings to our Church'. Comprehension and changes in the liturgy seemed likely to follow, something to be particularly concerned about 'because of what has happened to the Church of Scotland'. The author's dire prediction? 'We must be more Presbyterian, and our Sacramental Test must be abrogated.'[92] One correspondent, commenting in a letter to the Tory-Anglican Edmund Bohun on the 'good newes' of the Scottish government's success in putting down the Jacobite rebellion north of the border in early May 1690, nevertheless expressed his concern that the Scots were 'of such a restless temper' that if they were short of things to do at home they would 'com and help their dear brethren in England (as they once before did) to pull down our popish establishment, and erect their super-fine protestant discipline in the room of it'.[93]

The toleration established was thus quite limited. Papists and anti-Trinitarians were explicitly excluded from the Act's provisions. Nor was one free to opt out of religious observance altogether: one was allowed not to go to Church on Sunday only if one chose to go to a dissenting meeting instead. This was not religious toleration in our modern understanding of the term. The Test Acts remained on the books (there was an abortive attempt at repeal in March 1689),[94] which meant that not only Catholics but also nonconformists, including those more moderate types who might have hoped to benefit from comprehension, remained excluded from office. In theory, the state remained as narrowly confessional as ever, although some dissenters were able to gain access to office through the practice of occasional conformity. Quakers continued to be the most vulnerable group, not least because of their refusal to swear oaths; although the Toleration Act allowed Quakers to subscribe the declaration against transubstantiation and the declaration of fidelity to William and Mary and against the pope's deposing power, there remained the problem of oaths that were required to engage in a wide variety of legal and commercial transactions.[95]

Other attempts to secure legal redress for those grievances not covered by the Declaration of Rights, however, came to nought, at least in the short term. The Lords did introduce a bill to regulate the trials of peers, including treason trials, in late February 1689, to address concerns raised by article seventeen of the Heads of Grievances, but it was lost due to disagreement between the two Houses; it was not until 1696 that any reforming legislation was successfully enacted. William personally chose to comply with the request in article eighteen of the Heads of Grievances that judges' commissions be held on good behaviour, not at royal pleasure, yet so too had Charles II at first; there was nothing at law requiring the monarch to appoint judges on these terms until the passage of the Act of Settlement in 1701, which did not come into effect until the Hanoverian Succession of 1714. In June 1689 the Commons introduced a bill to reform the militia (in accordance with article five of the Heads of Grievances), but this got held up in the Lords and was lost when the parliament was dissolved early in the new year. Parliament also considered various versions of a bill to restore corporations as they had existed in 1675, to meet the demand in article thirteen of the Heads of Grievances that the corporations be restored to their ancient rights, but with the Whigs pressing for the inclusion of a clause that would have barred from office all those who had supported the *quo warranto* proceedings of the 1680s in the face of opposition from the Tories and also the King, the bill finally was lost when William prorogued and then later dissolved parliament in late January, early February 1690. When discussing the Bill of Rights in November 1689 the Lords, in order to meet the request in the Heads of Grievances that the frequent meeting of parliament be secured (article nine), did consider reviving the Triennial Act of 1641, but again this measure was lost with the dissolution. A Triennial Act was not to be passed until 1694, but even then it did not include the provisions in the 1641 act that guaranteed the meeting of parliament even if the king failed to call one.[96]

The preferred means of keeping the crown dependent upon parliament seems to have been through the power of the purse. Thus Whigs and Tories combined to ensure that the revenue eventually settled on the crown in 1690 was temporary (parliament granted customs for a term of four years) and inadequate (William and Mary received for the term of their lives half the excise given to Charles II and James II), in order to put the people 'out of fear', as Sir Joseph Williamson put it, 'of not meeting the king frequently in parliament'. William had further lost out, of course, by having already relinquished the hearth tax. The end result was that whereas the crown's revenue had been about £2 million per annum during the reign of James II, by 1692–4 it was only £942,179.[97] Ultimately, however, it was the financial revolution that came in the wake of William's wars, and the resultant national debt which had to be serviced by regular grants of parliamentary taxation, that guaranteed regular meetings of parliament after the Glorious Revolution (see pp. 491–2).

It is hard to agree that the Revolution settlement created a new type of monarchy. Most of the powers of the crown were left intact. Thus, as had been the case before 1689, the monarch had the right to determine all questions of policy (both foreign and domestic), choose his own ministers, veto parliamentary legislation, and determine when and for how long parliament should sit. The Declaration of Rights, in essence, did little more than vindicate and assert what the framers undertook to be ancient rights and privileges. In the short term, only a limited number of those Grievances omitted from the Declaration of Rights because they required reforming legislation were addressed.

It would be wrong, however, to see the Revolution settlement as of limited constitutional significance. The Declaration of Rights, given statutory force with the passage of the Bill of Rights, settled a number of issues that had been matters of dispute between the crown and parliament over the course of the seventeenth century, and settled them decisively in parliament's favour. No longer could the crown claim to be above the law or exploit areas of legal ambiguity in order to exalt its own authority. The Declaration thus provided the sort of legal clarity on a number of points of controversy that would make the types of experiments in royal absolutism that the Stuarts had engaged in impossible in the future. The Bill of Rights, moreover, included the additional provision debarring Catholics from coming to the throne as well as a further limitation on the dispensing power. Nor should we minimize the significance of the Toleration Act. Limited though it might have been, it nevertheless did establish a legal liberty of conscience for those Protestant groups that had suffered persecution during the reign of Charles II and at the beginning of James II's reign, and helped ease many of those religious tensions that had been one of the major sources of political instability during the seventeenth century. When John Somers boasted in 1690 that 'Our happiness' stemmed from the fact that 'our Princes' were 'tied up to the law as well as we', adding that 'our Government not being Arbitrary, but Legal, not Absolute, but Political, our princes can never become Arbitrary, Absolute or Tyrants', he was making points which many constitutionalists might have thought were true in theory prior to the reign of James II. The achievement of 1688–9 was to ensure that they would also henceforth be true in practice.[98]

REACTIONS TO THE REVOLUTION

The Revolution settlement in England, then, was a compromise. It was not a victory for one particular party; indeed, Whigs, Tories, high Anglicans, Latitudinarians and dissenters alike would have had reason to feel disappointed in not getting the settlement they desired. Yet at the same time the settlement reached was the product of bi-partisan negotiation. The political elite held together in the face of severe partisan disagreement. No one party decided to walk out of the proceedings of the Convention (as was to be the case in Scotland), and although no one party got everything its own way, no party could feel that they had lost out entirely. So how was the Revolution settlement received? Was it generally welcome to the nation at large? Or was there a significant undercurrent of disaffection, amongst either the political elite, or the mass of the population?

We can get a sense of the mood of the population as a whole by looking at public celebrations and demonstrations. Many contemporaries commented on the widespread enthusiasm for the settlement of the crown on William and Mary in February. The Princess of Orange appears to have been a popular figure. When she arrived in London on 12 February – she had remained in the Netherlands so long not, as some contemporaries insinuated, because William wanted to keep her out of the way until he had achieved both the crown and sole regal authority for himself, but because the bad winter had kept the ports frozen – she was greeted with bells, bonfires and 'the lofty Shouts and Acclamations of huzzaing Throngs and Multitudes, who doubly rejoiced', we are told, 'for her safe Arrival, and for her being declar'd Queen'. There were similar celebrations in London the next day when William and Mary were proclaimed King and Queen, first at Whitehall, then at Temple Bar, Cheapside, and finally at the Royal Exchange. 'Each Proclamation', the *London Gazette* tells us, was 'Ecchoede with Universal Acclamations of Joy by the Multitudes of People which crowded the Streets, Windows and Balconies.' Again, the evening concluded with bonfires and bells; Roger Morrice noted there 'were very great and Universall Bonefires in every streete, and very many in severall, and at many particular persons doors'.[99] There were bonfires in some provincial towns on the 14th, to celebrate the day of thanksgiving for deliverance from popery and arbitrary government, while there are numerous accounts of joyous celebration throughout the county and market towns of England as the new monarchs came to be proclaimed in the provinces over the course of the next couple of weeks. At Whitehaven in Cumberland, William and Mary were proclaimed, it was said, 'in the presence and auditory of twenty times as many more people at the least than were present for the proclamation of King James the Second'.[100] The royal coronation on 11 April provided another occasion for London and the provinces to celebrate the accession of the new monarchs to the throne. Luttrell noted the 'great splendour and joy' at places such as Oxford, Worcester, Rye, Brecknock, Exeter, Lyme and Coventry.[101] A rather elaborate ritual took place at Bath, as young men and women processed through the town to commemorate England's 'happy deliverance from Popery and Slavery' to the 'acclamations of unforced Joy, exceeding what was ever seen in that City'.[102]

A certain degree of scepticism is needed in dealing with such accounts. The *London Gazette*, as much the official organ of the new government as it had been of the old, was bound to put the most positive gloss it could on reactions to the proclamations and the coronation, since it wanted to create the impression that the new regime was universally popular. Moreover, these demonstrations were clearly sponsored from above – starting, as they normally did, with a formal solemnity involving local dignatories and civic authorities, who in turn provided money for bonfires and alcohol. To give a typical example, when William and Mary were proclaimed at Hereford, there was a civic display, accompanied by the firing of cannon and the beating of drums by the local militia, and one of the members of the area's leading gentry family, Robert Harley, provided 'a bonfire . . . and a hogshead of cyder'.[103] Often it was the local town authorities who gave money for beer, wine and even tobacco to make sure that the proclamation and coronation were celebrated in the right spirit.[104] This does not mean we should doubt whether such public professions of support for the new monarchs were sincere. In fact, there are plenty of independent, local accounts to suggest that there was a considerable degree of genuine enthusiasm, throughout much of England, for the proclaiming and crowning of William and Mary.

Nevertheless, we also have isolated reports of disaffection. Much of the alleged disaffection came from predictable sources: soldiers in the army who had served under James II, and the high-Anglican clergy. The Whig MP for Cirencester, John Howe, complained in the Commons on 25 and 26 February that he had received letters from his corporation stating that the soldiers quartered there would 'not let the People make Bonfires at proclaiming the King' and had themselves proclaimed King James and drunk 'King William's and Queen Mary's Damnation'. The town clergy had also refused to appear at the proclamation.[105] The Whig MP for Cornwall, Hugh Boscawen, complained in the House on 1 March that he had learned 'that the Soldiers in Cornwall' were 'as bad as the rest; and when the Magistrates rejoiced at the happy change', they 'killed a man'.[106] At Oxford, Morrice heard, the University vice-chancellor 'was very backward and unwilling to proclaime the King and Queene', though the mayor did so 'with all readynesse and great solemnity'. Morrice also learned that the clergy in many dioceses refused to keep the public day of thanksgiving for William and Mary's accession to the crown.[107] In Stamford, the mayor sought to frustrate celebrations for the royal coronation on 11 April by cutting the bell ropes of the church and issuing an order to prevent bonfires.[108]

Even in London there are hints of disaffection. Laurence Echard, in his early eighteenth-century history, tells us that the 'Torrents of Joy' that filled 'the whole City and Suburbs' when William and Mary were proclaimed on 13 February 'totally drown'd all the little Discontents and Murmurings that began to appear upon this Mighty Change'.[109] Not quite totally, it seems. Morrice heard how, in late Feburary, a London divine counselled his auditors 'to keepe their loyalty untainted . . . against Dutch against Devill'.[110] The London court records provide a number of cases of seditious words in the early months of the new regime. George Smith, who had formerly held a commission under James II, although now he held one from William III, was fined 3s 4d and sentenced to stand in the pillory for saying in Coleman Street in the heart of London on 22 June: 'God Damn all the Dutch Men, they were but a Handfull, Bake them in An Oven and Broile them on A Gridiron.' Joseph Sheere was fined £6 8s 4d and sentenced to stand in the pillory for saying, on 19 May, 'that King James was now in Scotland and had almost conquered it' and that 'He hoped to see the same in England'.[111] In November someone defaced William III's portrait in the London Guildhall 'by cutting out the crown and scepter'.[112] A man called Michael Ferrer allegedly told an acquaintance at the Royal Exchange on 21 November that he was upset 'King James was turned out', and felt 'that he [King James] had not Right done him'. 'King William set forth in his Declaration, that he came to preserve the Laws', Ferrer grumbled, 'but instead of that he had altered them'; he said 'he came to maintain our Rights, but instead of that he came for the Crown'. In this particular case, there might have been an element of malicious prosecution; Ferrer was at least able to call credible witnesses at his trial the following January to testify to his reputation, and he secured himself an acquittal.[113]

To what extent, then, were people able to make their peace with the new regime, and how did they do so? How easy it would prove to embrace the Revolution depended not only upon an individual's political or religious opinions, but also on the meaning one chose to ascribe to the events of 1688–9 and whether one was happy with what one understood to be the outcome.

A major pamphlet controversy arose, designed to influence public opinion over whether or not to give allegiance to the new regime. Some 192 pamphlets relating to the allegiance controversy appeared between 6 February 1689 and the end of 1694. Of these, 89 were Whig, 50 Tory and 53 Jacobite; some 80 appeared in 1689 alone. The 139 loyalist pamphlets embraced a range of different reasons for adhering to the Revolution settlement, which can be split into six broad categories: contractual resistance; possession; abdication/ desertion; conquest; providence; and resistance *in extremis*. Many pamphleteers used more than one type of argument to try to sell the Revolution to the public.[114]

As one might expect, it was the Whigs who had least difficulty in accepting the legitimacy of the Revolution. Most willingly embraced contract theory: of the 89 Whig pamphlets, 68 appealed to some form of contractual resistance; naturally no Tory pamphlets did. There were moderate and more radical strands to the way contract theory was used, however. Twenty-three pamphlets took the line that English history showed the contractual roots of the polity and that James had violated his contract by failing to rule according to the constitution; fourteen took the more radical approach of basing the original contract in natural law and arguing that resistance was legitimate because James had violated his subjects' natural rights. This was the line argued by John Locke in his *Two Treatises of Government*, a tract which had been drafted in the early 1680s to legitimize the conspiracies of the radical Whigs against the government of Charles II, but which was revised and published (for the first time) in the autumn of 1689 to offer a defence of William and Mary's title to the crown. Regardless of whether one took a historical or natural law approach, Whig contract theorists tended to the view that James had un-kinged himself as a result of violating his contract. Of the 68 pamphlets embracing contract theory, only 22 maintained that James had been deposed. Furthermore, of those 68 tracts, only 34 used contractual arguments alone; the others also embraced other theories to legitimize the Revolution settlement. Among defences of the Revolution as a whole, by contrast, contract theory was less significant. Thus, only 49 per cent of the loyalist tracts (68 out of 139) embraced contract theory, and only 16 per cent (22) argued that James had been deposed. Some 76 per cent (105) appealed to arguments other than contract theory to justify what had transpired.[115]

Accepting the legitimacy of what had taken place in 1688–9 posed a much greater moral and intellectual problem for Tory Anglicans, since they had for so long upheld the principles of indefeasible hereditary succession, non-resistance and the inviolability of oaths. One Worcestershire cleric wrote that 'he was amazed at the proceedings of the Convention, that they should depose the King', since 'Deposing Kings and absolving subjects from theyr allegiance' were 'some of the grand doctrines for which we quarrel with the Papists'.[116] In the end, however, very few Tory Anglicans refused to swear allegiance to the new monarchs. Some, it should be said, procrastinated for an awfully long time: William Sherlock did not capitulate until August 1690, though prior to then he continued to lecture in St Dunstan's in the West in London and to offer prayers for William and Mary as *de facto* monarchs.[117] Jacobites were fiercely critical of the apparent hypocrisy of those clergy who took the new oaths: 'there never was so sudden and so shameful a Turn of Men professing Religion', bemoaned the Protestant Irish Jacobite Charles Leslie. Indeed, Leslie reported that 'the Common People' joked 'that there was but one thing formerly which the Parliament could not do, that is, to make a Man a Woman: But now there is another, that is, to make an Oath which the Clergy will not take'.[118]

Tories who threw in their lot with the Revolution inevitably insisted that the Convention had not deposed James II and distanced themselves from resistance theory. They did not eschew resistance theory altogether. As we saw in the previous chapter (and as we shall see again when we look at Scotland and Ireland), some Tory Anglicans were willing to embrace a theory of limited resistance, in exceptional circumstances. Of the thirteen allegiance controversy pamphlets that appeared between 6 February 1689 and the end of 1694 that allowed for resistance in extreme cases, nine were Tory (or

18 per cent of the total number of Tory pamphlets that appeared at this time).[119]

The majority of Tory Anglicans, however, denied that the people had engaged in any acts of resistance in 1688–9. One solution was to maintain that the Revolution had come about as a result of God's Providence. Care is needed, however, when discussing the use of providentialist justifications. It was quite common for people across the political spectrum to employ some form of providentialist rhetoric when justifying the Revolution. When the Convention proclaimed William and Mary King and Queen on 13 February, the nonconformist Sussex merchant Samuel Jeake wrote in his diary that 'now, through the mercifull Providence of God, we were freed from the fears of Popery and Persecution'.[120] The trimmer Sir Richard Temple, in a manuscript tract written in c. 1690 condemning the Whigs for allegedly supporting James II's efforts to overthrow the penal laws and the Test Act, recalled that we were 'Saved by God's Providence'.[121] The author of the very Whiggish *Four Questions Debated*, having first maintained that James had 'totally Subverted' the government of England by his misrule, that the exercise of the government was therefore dissolved and the people had the right to choose the successor, and that they should not follow the lineal descent but settle the throne on William alone, nevertheless sought to bolster the case for William by appealing to 'the extraordinary Providence of God': God's wonders could be seen in how He preserved William and the fleet 'in the Deeps' and by 'what we have heard and seen since he came ashore', and so it was 'apparent that the Lord hath sent him'.[122] Yet a thoroughgoing theory of a divine right of Providence, holding that subjects must acquiesce in the divine interventions of God and that a monarch thus installed was ruler *de iure* and not just *de facto*, was regarded as too 'enthusiastic', and only 14 pamphlets in the allegiance controversy took such a line – and even then, only 6 were Tory and 8 were Whig.[123]

Tories tended to salve their consciences by arguing that James had abdicated or deserted and that they owed *de facto* allegiance to the new monarchs who were in possession of the throne. Sixty-five out of the 139 loyalist pamphlets in the allegiance controversy (47 per cent of the total) sought to justify allegiance by appeal to possession; 38 of these were Tory tracts (76 per cent of the total number of Tory loyalist tracts). Forty-five pamphlets appealed to abdication: 17 were Whig tracts, 28 Tory (with the Tory tracts tending to see abdication as equivalent to desertion). The trouble with the above arguments, however, is that they did not recognize William and Mary as *de iure* monarchs, simply as monarchs *de facto*. The way this was resolved was by an appeal to conquest theory, as based on the international law arguments of the Dutch humanist Hugh Grotius. Thus it was argued that William had a legitimate title to the throne because he had won it through conquest in a just war – the reason why the war was just being that James had attempted to defraud William of his hereditary property rights by endeavouring to change the English government and by presenting the supposititious heir to the throne. Since William was an independent prince and head of a sovereign state, international law regulated the relationship between himself and James II; he could therefore use arms to defend his rights and victory conferred a *de iure* title to the throne. The beauty of this was that the theory was compatible with the view that James II's English subjects themselves had never engaged in any acts of armed resistance.[124]

The theory clearly appealed to the new Williamite regime. The government hack, James Welwood, took this line in his Williamite periodical *Mercurius Reformatus*. Thus, on 17 July 1689, he insisted that the Prince of Orange 'had the justest ground imaginable to make War upon a Prince that had so abused his Power, and endeavoured to defraud him and his Princess of their just Right of Reversion to the Crown; and this he might do . . . since King James and he were upon equal ground, as to a Right of making War one upon another, being both Sovereign Princes, and independent of one another'.[125] Similarly, the government's chief propagandist Gilbert Burnet published a *Pastoral Letter* in 1689, in which he argued that 'it was a just war the Prince of Orange had made against the King, who by going about to change the government of the Kingdom wherein the Prince had an expectancy, and by putting a supposititious heire upon him, had endeavour'd to disapoint his succession'.[126] It was an argument that was also used by Edmund Bohun (who combined it with a view that James had deserted), and by William Sherlock (who combined it with providential theory) when he eventually decided to take the oaths. A total of thirty-two of the allegiance controversy tracts embraced conquest theory (fifteen were Whig, seventeen Tory), but it has been suggested that it was perhaps this argument, rather than any of the others, that had the greatest effect in bringing people over to the new government.[127]

In fact, the vast majority of English people accepted the validity of the dynastic shift that had occurred in 1688–9. By the end of 1690, most prominent laymen and clergy had sworn allegiance to the new regime. Those who felt a particular bond of loyalty to James – his close political advisers, personal servants, co-religionists and some (at least) who had served him in the armed forces – as well as devout Anglicans who believed in the absolute inviolability of oaths, could not accept the legitimacy of the new regime and persisted as Jacobites or Nonjurors. Some followed James into exile at St Germain-en-Laye near Paris, where they conspired to bring about a Stuart Restoration, the leading figure here being James's erstwhile Secretary of State, the Earl of Middleton. A minority of lay office-holders and about 400 clergymen (about 3.5 per cent of a total clerical estate of about 12,000) refused the oaths and became Nonjurors. This group included ten peers (among them the Earl of Clarendon), sixty-one former or present MPs, and nearly half the episcopal hierarchy (including Archbishop Sancroft of Canterbury and Bishop Turner of Ely). Many English Catholics also remained deeply committed to a Stuart Restoration. Nevertheless, despite the existence of some high-profile Jacobites, Jacobitism was not a significant force in England in the immediate aftermath of the Glorious Revolution. It was to become more significant over time, as people grew disillusioned with developments under the post-Revolution regimes, with even some radical Whigs, disappointed by the conservatism of the Revolution settlement, looking to a conditional restoration of James II as a way of implementing some of their much-desired constitutional reforms. However, in 1689–90 the Jacobites did not enjoy anywhere near the level of support necessary to enable them to mount a successful challenge to the post-Revolution regime. Even the majority of Nonjurors were scarcely Jacobites in any meaningful sense – many had opposed James when king and would scarcely have relished his return, and few were willing actively to seek his restoration; they merely believed that their oaths prevented them from renouncing their allegiance.[128]

Thus in England consensus was sustained. Most Tories and Whigs, conformists and nonconformists, made their peace with the Revolution, even if they were able to do so only because the very ambiguity of the Revolution settlement enabled it to be different things to different people. The situation was to be very different in Scotland and Ireland, and the revolutions in both were to take on very different hues as a result.

9

The Glorious Revolution in Scotland

In Scotland the Revolutions and changes were neither small nor few . . . The Stroak which was given to papists and their Idolatry was not the Result of long contrived Counsells, nor begun nor effectual by great and wise men, but done in a sudden, by Children and others not much esteemed.

Alexander Shields, contemporary historian
of the Society People[1]

The Prelate being, 1. A Monster in the State; 2. A Mischief in the Church; and 3. The great Obstruction of the Happiness of both . . . were it, not then, 1. for the King's Honour and Emolument, 2. for the Kingdoms Welfare and Tranquility, and 3. for the Churches Happiness and Unity, to have this burthen removed, this Idol of Jealousie cast down, and this Stumbling-block taken out of the way?

The Great Grievance of Scotland
(Edinburgh, 1689), pp. 1, 4

The Revolution in Scotland has traditionally been seen as more radical than that in England. The Scottish Convention of Estates, which met on 14 March 1689 to determine the settlement of the throne following James's 'abdication' in England, came to be dominated by Whigs and Presbyterians, who forged a radical settlement resulting in the restructuring of the powers of the Scottish monarchy and the replacement of Episcopalianism with Presbyterianism. Yet if there was a revolution in Scotland, it has been widely accepted that the

Scots were 'reluctant revolutionaries'.[2] As one influential survey puts it, 'there were no indications of any readiness on the part of the Scots by themselves to initiate a revolution, even when the permanence of the regime seemed to be assured by the birth of a son to James's queen' in June 1688; 'the Revolution was made in England and imported into Scotland'.[3] Similarly, another scholar, summarizing conventional wisdom, has maintained that 'discontent in Scotland remained passive'; 'in striking contrast to the events precipitating the Great Rebellion, the Revolution of 1688–9 was solely made in England'.[4] In recent years, historians have even begun to question the revolutionary credentials of what transpired in Scotland, urging that the Revolution should be seen in a more conservative light – backward-looking and limited in scope. According to this view, the 'participants in the Scottish Revolution of 1688' had no gripes with the traditional monarchy in Scotland – it was the King who was the radical – and they therefore deliberately shunned 'the formulation of new paradigms', choosing instead to reach back 'towards old, indeed almost antiquarian, and always conservative formulations to articulate their position'. Some would now hold that the Scots were not just reluctant revolutionaries, they were not revolutionaries at all.[5]

The Glorious Revolution in Scotland has been poorly understood because it has been so little studied. No full-scale treatment of the events of the winter and spring of 1688–9 exists that is comparable to those we possess for England, and we have no scholarly analysis of the Scottish constitutional settlement of 1689 (as encapsulated in the Claim of Right and Articles of Grievances) on a par with what we have for the English Declaration of Rights. This chapter aims to address these deficiencies. In doing so, it will offer a reading of the Revolution in Scotland that is significantly different from what we have been taught in textbooks. One certainly cannot deny that the triggers for the Revolution in Scotland came from initiatives taken in England. In this respect, 1688–9 provides a striking contrast with the mid-century revolution, which was precipitated by a rebellion that happened first in Scotland. Moreover, when we recall that the Scots had three times risen in rebellion since the Restoration – in 1666, 1679 and 1685 – their relative passivity at a time when the English were conspiring with William of Orange against James II might seem all the more remarkable. Yet to describe the Scots as reluctant revolutionaries, as if this applied to all Scots, is unhelpful. Against those who were reluctant there were many Scots who were keen to see the downfall of James VII and who took an active part in trying to restructure the political and religious system north of the border. Such activism can be detected both at the level of the political elite and also out-of-doors – indeed, the crowd unrest in Scotland was more extensive and considerably more violent than that in England – and it led to a settlement in Church and state that was, in a genuine sense, revolutionary. Nor should we conclude that the Revolution was essentially imported into Scotland from England. In essence, the English had reacted against what they saw to be the violations of the law by the crown in the 1680s, and by James II in particular, and in the process they had sought to provide additional safeguards for the rule of law and the security of the Protestant religion; they did not undertake a fundamental restructuring of the existing political system. The Revolution in Scotland, by contrast, was a self-conscious indictment of the Stuart polity in Church and state as legally constructed since the Restoration. Why the Scottish Revolution took the course it did, even though there were some Scots who would have welcomed an English-style revolution settlement, was related to particular historical developments north of the border, particularly the bitter legacy of political and religious tensions generated as a result of the various policies pursued by the government in Scotland since the Restoration. In this sense the Scottish Revolution was very much one made in Scotland: not only did it end up being quite different from the English one, but it was shaped by issues deeply rooted in the Scottish past and which were of a distinctively Scottish nature.

RELUCTANT REVOLUTIONARIES?

Were the Scots reluctant revolutionaries? It seems questionable whether they were any more reluctant than their English counterparts. Let us remind ourselves what the English did. Although there had been a marked loyalist reaction in the final years of Charles II's reign, and considerable support for the Catholic James when he came to the throne in 1685, this support quickly evaporated as soon as James began to use his prerogative to promote the interests of his co-religionists. There was opposition to James's initiatives at all levels of English society, and when the birth of the Prince of Wales held out the prospect of a never-ending succession of Catholic Stuart rulers, the English conspired to bring over William of Orange to help rescue their political and religious liberties. Many people deserted to William after he had landed at Torbay in November 1688, and as James's regime began to collapse there was considerable anti-Catholic agitation and rioting, as people made clear their rejection of men and policies under James II. It is unclear how the Scots acted any differently. As we saw in Chapter 4, James VII had managed to alienate a significant proportion of his Scottish subjects, both Episcopalians and Presbyterians, by the middle of 1688. We shall see here that many Scots actively conspired with William of Orange to overthrow James's regime and that in Scotland there was also considerable anti-Catholic rioting from crowds protesting against men and measures under James VII. If anything, the Scots were more engaged revolutionaries than their English counterparts – or rather, there was a more active commitment to a higher degree of revolutionary change among certain sections of the Scottish population than can be discerned among the English.

The low level to which support for the crown in Scotland had sunk by June 1688 is indicated by the trouble the Scottish council had in encouraging public celebrations for the birth of the Prince of Wales. There were staged demonstrations in Edinburgh and Glasgow on 13 and 14 June, though troops had to be out in force to prevent possible disorder and to ensure that bonfires were actually lit.[6] Very few of the nobility attended the official day of thanksgiving at Edinburgh on 21 June, and when Lord Chancellor Perth acclaimed the new prince, scarcely any of the spectators seconded him 'in his acclamations of joy'. Although many householders did light bonfires, under threat of being fined, it was said that the maidservants often refused to bring materials for the fires, protesting that 'there was no reason for such joy'.[7] Within a few weeks of the birth, many of the Episcopal clergy, doubting the legitimacy of the new prince, stopped praying for him in their services, and instead began 'to insinuate in their People fears of Popery and Arbitrary Government'.[8]

Although the invitation to William of Orange came from England, a number of Scots played an active part in the Williamite conspiracy that developed in the summer and autumn of 1688. Several exiled Scots were influential in William's entourage at The Hague, and joined with William's invasion force in November. The most well-known examples are Gilbert Burnet and Robert Ferguson, though one could argue that their political preoccupations at this time centred on England rather than on their native land. Yet in addition to these there were men like Sir James Dalrymple of Stair, who had fled to Holland following his stance against the Scottish Test Act of 1681, and William Carstares, the tortured Rye House plotter and now William's chaplain. Stair and Carstares were responsible for Scottish intelligence, and sent over a number of agents both to gather news and distribute propaganda, among them William Cleland and Dr William Blackadder, veterans of both Bothwell Bridge and the Argyll rebellion. The tenth Earl of Argyll was also in Holland, and pledged William the support of his clan to fight against the family that had put both his father and grandfather to death, as were veterans of the 1685 rebellions, such as Andrew Fletcher of Saltoun and Lord Pollard, and those who had been mixed up in the Rye House intrigues, such as Sir Patrick Hume, Lord Cardross and the Earl of Melville. Due to ill health, Melville himself was unable to join William's expeditionary force; he was not fit enough to travel to England until late February 1689. Melville's son, the Earl of Leven, however, did come over with William and raised a regiment for Orange at his own expense. Indeed, the English and Scottish squadron that comprised part of William's invasion force was commanded by a Scotsman, Major-General Hugh Mackay. Nor is this list exhaustive. Within Britain, the Scottish dimension to William's campaign was managed by two men – Stair's son, Sir John Dalrymple, who sat on the Scottish council in Edinburgh, and the Earl of Drumlanrig, son of the Duke of Queensberry and son-in-law of the Earl of Rochester, in London.[9]

William was well aware from the beginning that any actions taken against James would have ramifications for all three Stuart kingdoms.

His *Declaration of Reasons* of 30 September 1688, justifying his reasons for invading England, also blamed 'Evill Councellours' for prevailing with the King to declare in Scotland that he was 'clothed with an Absolute Power' and promised to call a parliament in Scotland to restore that kingdom's 'Ancient Constitution' and settle 'Matters of Religion' so that the people might 'live easy and happy'.[10] In addition, William issued a separate *Declaration . . . for . . . Scotland*, penned by Ferguson and other Scottish advisers at The Hague. A hostile author, writing in 1690 after the implications of the Williamite revolution had become apparent in Scotland, maintained that the Scottish declaration was 'purely Presbyterian'.[11] In fact, the authors strove to avoid blatant partisanship, and William certainly did not stand on a radical covenanting platform as Argyll had done in 1685. Thus the Scottish Declaration did not directly attack James; instead, like its English counterpart, it blamed 'Evil Councellors' for overturning 'the Religion, Lawes and Liberties' of the kingdom and setting up 'Arbitrary Government'. It then rehearsed the 'lamentable Effects' of their misgovernment in Scotland in detail: the king had been declared absolute; the 'Laws, Priviledges and Rights of the Kingdom . . . overturned'; popery openly encouraged and papists promoted to positions of authority; burgh elections hindered; and a declaration (namely the Indulgence of 1687) issued making 'all Parliaments unnecessary, and taking away all defences of Religion, Liberty and Property, by an assumed and asserted Absolute Power', to which obedience was required 'without Reserve'. William's *Declaration . . . for . . . Scotland* did allude to the religious persecution of Charles II's reign, when it complained about the imposition of bonds, exactions of oaths, free-quartering of troops, and the killing times of 1684–5. Yet it did not limit its appeal to those Protestants outside the Established Church; indeed, it also recalled how Protestants who were hostile to the attempts to abolish the penal laws (that is, Episcopalians) had been removed from places of public trust under James VII. The *Declaration . . . for . . . Scotland* insisted that all William wanted to do was to free 'that Kingdom from all hazard of Popery and Arbitrary Power' and settle a parliament to redress the above-mentioned grievances, and it concluded with an appeal for consensus, expressing the hope that William's actions would be 'accompanied with a chearfull and universall concurrence of the whole Nation'.[12]

When news of William's invasion plans became known, some groups in Scotland rallied behind the crown. On 3 October the privy council wrote to James pledging 'their lives and fortunes' in defence of the King, the Queen, and their new-born son, while on 3 November the archbishops and bishops sent the King a fawning letter, congratulating him on the birth of the Prince of Wales and expressing their abhorrence of the Dutch invasion, signed by all but the bishops of Argyll and Caithness.[13] James certainly believed his northern kingdom was secure, and on 27 September he ordered the standing forces in Scotland, with the exception of the chief garrisons, to march south to Carlisle to assist in the defence of England. To compensate, the shire militias were raised and placed in a posture of defence. Some Scots enthusiastically embraced the call to come to the defence of their king and country. At a meeting on 11 October, the merchants of Glasgow unanimously agreed to a government recommendation to raise ten militia companies, while the noblemen and gentlemen of Fife offered to raise 400 foot soldiers and a troop of horse at their own expense.[14] In mid-November, in response to the news of William's landing at Torbay, loyal addresses came in from the Argyllshire militia and the convention of Scottish burghs.[15]

In some areas, however, the loyalty of the local population was clearly in doubt. In Dumfriesshire, for example, many local landowners absented themselves from serving in the militia.[16] Indeed, James's decision to move the army to England proved a grave error. There was much more support for William in Scotland than James had suspected, and leaving the kingdom's defences seriously weakened at this crucial time allowed William's supporters to mobilize on his behalf. Initially, the greatest support for William appears to have been in the Presbyterian heartland of the south-west. One Williamite agent reported back to Holland in the late summer that 'the body of the Nobility, Gentry and Commons of the South and West parts' were 'zealous for the interest of the Protestant successors', and that the nonconformist ministers were 'much devoted' to the Prince and Princess of Orange.[17] The contemporary historian of the Society People (or Cameronians), Alexander Shields, later wrote that 'the Generality of people' longed 'for the landing of the Dutch', though he admitted that 'many knew not wherefor they desired them'. The

Society People themselves determined at a General Meeting held on 24 October that in the event of a Dutch landing in Scotland they too would rise, although they would not place themselves under the leadership of the Dutch, whom they regarded as 'a Promiscuous Conjunction of Reformed and Lutheran malignants and sectaries', which it was 'against the Testimony of the Church of Scotland to joine'.[18] The withdrawal of the Scottish army, however, allowed the disaffected to move to Edinburgh and make the Scottish capital the base for their activities. Here 'the Presbyterians and discontented Party' from all over the kingdom started meeting publicly to discuss what to do. Among them were the Earl of Glencairn and Lord Ross, former privy counsellors who had been removed by James for their opposition in the parliament of 1686; the Earl of Crawford (the son of the ex-Covenanter who had served briefly as Treasurer in the early years of the Restoration); the Earl of Dundonald, the Duke of Hamilton's son-in-law, who had been brought on to the council and subsequently ejected by James; Sir James Montgomery of Skelmorlie, a Presbyterian and radical who was to play a crucial part in the events of 1689; Lord Shaw of Greenock, whose people had been responsible for the capture of Argyll in 1685; and Sir James Murray of Philiphaugh, the alleged Rye House plotter, who undertook to intercept correspondence between the King and his Scottish council.[19]

In Scotland, as in England, people began deserting James as the crisis unfolded to join with William in his endeavour to rid their country of popery and arbitrary government. By early December, an anti-Perth faction had emerged within the council, centred around Atholl, Tarbat and Sir John Dalrymple. After first forcing Perth to disband the militia, on the grounds that William had declared the keeping of armed forces in times of peace to be illegal, they eventually secured Perth's resignation in the second week of December following the outbreak of violent anti-Catholic rioting in the Scottish capital (discussed below).[20] On 13 December, with Atholl now in effect head of the Scottish government, the council voted in favour of a free parliament, in accordance with William's Scottish declaration.[21] They followed this on 24 December with a letter to William thanking him for his efforts on behalf of the Protestant religion and the 'good intentiones' he had expressed for Scotland, and asking for his assistance 'in procureing a free parliament . . . in which our religion may be secured in the most comprehensive terms for including and uniteing all Protestants' and 'the just rights of the crown, the property and liberty of the people . . . established upon such solid foundations as may prevent all fears of future attempts upon our religione'.[22]

Scots in England were quick to join with William as he marched from the West Country to London. In early December, a Scottish battalion under the command of General Douglas deserted to William as the Prince reached the outskirts of Maidenhead. The Earl of Drumlanrig, who was already in London, likewise joined with the Prince. By Christmas there was a large number of Scots in London waiting on the Prince, over and above those who had been part of the invasion force. Among them were Hamilton, his sons-in-law Dundonald and Lord Murray (the latter also being Atholl's son), Crawford, Drumlanrig, Ross, and Lord Yester. On 25 December Hamilton and rest of the Scots in London had a meeting with William at which they thanked him 'for his glorious Enterprize', offered him their service, and requested he take over the civil and military administration of Scotland.[23]

The removal of the army from Scotland in late September made it increasingly difficult to police the mass of the population north of the border. As with England, there was an outbreak of anti-Catholic demonstrations in the autumn of 1688. In mid-October Luttrell heard reports of 'some disturbance in Scotland, occasioned by the masse houses there', and of 'some violence' offered to Chancellor Perth.[24] At Glasgow on 30 November, St Andrew's Day, the Earl of Loudoun and several university students burned effigies of the pope and the archbishops of St Andrews and Glasgow, apparently 'without any Opposition'.[25] In early December, the students of Edinburgh University conducted their own pope-burning at the Edinburgh town cross, despite attempts by those in authority to prevent it. Two days later they marched on the parliament house, in the middle of the day, shouting 'No Pope, No Papist'. They forced their way in and proceeded to conduct a mock trial of 'his Holiness', condemning the pope 'to be burnt publickly at the Cross' on 25 December next.[26]

Serious unrest broke out in the Scottish capital in the second week of December. On Sunday the 9th rumours spread through Edinburgh that large numbers of Catholics had come to town with the design 'to burn it that Night'. The university students and the local apprentices sounded the alarm by beating drums and running through the streets crying 'No Pope, No Papist, No Popish Chancellor, No Melfort, No Father Petres'. On this occasion the magistrates prevented an anticipated attack on the Catholic chapel at Holyroodhouse by shutting the gates of the city and confining the crowds within the city walls; the youths had to content themselves with going to the town cross and proclaiming the offer of a £400 sterling reward to any who should bring in Perth or Melfort 'dead or alive'.[27] Fearing for his life, Perth fled the capital the next day and headed towards the Highlands; he was seized on board a boat disguised in women's clothing as he tried to make his escape to the Continent on 20 December and, after a brief spell in the Edinburgh tollbooth, he was dispatched to Stirling Castle.[28] On the evening of the 10th, following the Chancellor's flight, crowds gathered again in Edinburgh – not just 'boys', as before, but 'all sort of men' armed with staves, swords and firearms – and marched straight through the gates of the city to Holyroodhouse. A Captain Wallace, who kept guard at the palace, ordered his troops to open fire, killing a dozen rioters and wounding many more; the council responded by sending the trained bands to secure Holyroodhouse from Wallace, at the cost of further bloodshed. The crowd, now allegedly some 2,000–3,000 strong, then stormed the palace, killing several soldiers in revenge. They proceeded to deface the Catholic chapel and the Abbey church, tearing down any 'monuments to idolatry', breaking the organ to pieces, and carrying their prizes 'up to the Town in Processions through the Streets', before burning everything combustible in a huge bonfire in the Abbey close. They also fell upon the house where the Jesuits lived, ransacked the lodgings of the Earl of Perth and the residences of a number of other leading Catholics, and destroyed the Catholic printing office run by Peter Bruce. The next day the youths went to the houses of all known Catholics in the city, seized their books, beads, crosses and images, and solemnly burnt them in the street.[29]

There were similar attacks on the residences of Catholics elsewhere in Scotland. Crowds besieged the Earl of Traquair's house in Peebles and the Laird Maxwell's in Dumfriesshire, seizing a variety of

'Romish wares' (an altar, crucifixes, eucharist cup, wafers, a box of relics, images, candles and a large number of popish books), which they then proceeded to carry several miles to the towns of Peebles and Dumfries respectively so as to burn them at the market cross.[30] According to Shields, the crowds restricted themselves to 'searching for Idolatrous things' and did not pilfer any of the other possessions of the Catholic lords or take any of the more valuable Catholic paraphernalia for themselves; their intent was solely to bring them to the public market crosses in order to destroy them 'before many witnesses'.[31]

The anti-Catholic agitation continued through December and into the new year. On Christmas Day the students of Edinburgh University held their planned pope-burning at the town cross before thousands of spectators, among whom were a number of privy counsellors and local magistrates.[32] Scotland also suffered its equivalent of the Irish scare. Shortly before Christmas, rumours spread that Irish Catholics had landed in Galloway and were 'Putting all to Fire and Sword'. The local inhabitants began to arm themselves in self-defence and set about apprehending local Catholics. At Dumfries, for example, they seized the provost and several other papists and priests, and threw them into prison.[33] There was a particularly elaborate pope-burning procession at Aberdeen on 11 January 1689, intended to commemorate the restoration of local elections in the burgh and the return of committed Protestants to serve as magistrates and town councillors in place of those who had been imposed on the town by James VII, which was organized by the students of the university. The students had even taken the precaution of writing to the town authorities in advance about their plans, inviting them to attend and giving assurances that the demonstration would be peaceful. After a long procession through the town centre of people dressed up as Catholic clergymen, and a short play depicting the downfall of the 'Scarlet Whore' and the kingdom of Babylon, the students held a mock trial of the pope for his 'High Treason against . . . God' and being 'an enemy to Religion, Monarchy and Government, and an open and avowed Murderer of Mankind', before sentencing him to be burnt to ashes at the market cross. The evening ended with fireworks and the ringing of the bells of Trinity Church, now restored to Protestant worship after it had been given over to the Catholics in James VII's reign.[34] There were further attacks on mass-houses north of the border in mid-January.[35]

The pattern of anti-Catholic unrest described here is very similar to that which took place in England in late 1688. In both countries we see people celebrating the demise of James's pro-Catholic policies and attempting to take advantage of the collapse of royal authority to suppress what they still regarded as illegal forms of religious practice. Moreover, as with England, this crowd activity reveals a shared desire among all Protestants in Scotland to be rid of popery. Presbyterians, and especially the Society People, were certainly active in these outbreaks, as they later acknowledged.[36] On the other hand, the prominent role played by students from the universities of Glasgow, Edinburgh and Aberdeen suggests a significant Episcopalian presence. And although some of those who participated in the anti-Catholic agitation might have been looking forward to the eventual dethroning of James VII and a subsequent reconstruction of the ecclesiastical settlement, others saw themselves as rejecting no more than the illegal measures pursued by their Catholic king. The rioters at Edinburgh in early December, for example, condemned popery and James's popish ministers, but they did not mention the King himself; instead, in accordance with William's *Declaration . . . for . . . Scotland*, they asked merely for 'A Free Parliament'.[37] Some groups, to be sure, firmly identified themselves with William's position. One report from Edinburgh on 15 December claimed that Protestants were 'up in Arms in several parts of this Kingdom, Declaring for the Prince of Orange, for the Protestant Religion and a Free Parliament'.[38] In Glasgow, at the very end of December, the radical covenanting minister Mr Boyd, together with others of the Society People, read William's declaration and publicly proclaimed him 'the Protestant Protector', and 'the whole Country' was said to be 'up for the Prince'. William was similarly proclaimed at Irvine and at Ayr, while on 1 January the Edinburgh magistrates had William's Declaration read and started 'putting on bonfyrs'.[39] The students of Aberdeen University, by contrast, couched their ritual of 11 January in explicitly loyalist language. In their letter to the town magistrates, they stated that they wished 'Prosperity and Safety to all the Maintainers of the True Protestant Religion' and 'the Preservation of His Sacred Majesty', while in their play those who witnessed the downfall of the pope not only promised to countermine all of Rome's plots, but also shouted that they would 'ever pray for Religion and our King'.[40]

However, starting on Christmas Day 1688, and continuing through the first half of 1689, there were also a series of attacks throughout the south-western shires on conformist, Protestant clergy, as local Presbyterians sought to drive Episcopalian ministers out of their livings. These 'rabblings', as they have come to be known, followed a common, ritualized pattern. Typically, the crowd would carry the minister out of his house into the churchyard (or some other public place) where they would 'expose him to the People as a Condemned Malefactor'. They would then forbid him to preach 'any more in that place', tear up his gown and throw the pieces over his head, burn his Common Prayer Book (which they styled 'the Mass in English'), seize the keys to the church, lock the doors, and eject him and his family from the manse.[41] At Badernock (now Baldernock) in Dunbartonshire, on Christmas Day 1688, a crowd of Presbyterians, finding that the minister had already made his escape, picked on the minister's wife and told her that 'they would cut off her Papish nose and rip up her Prelaticall belly'. At Cathcart, in the presbytery of Glasgow, they turned the minister's wife and her small children out of the manse and kept them in a stable all night, where three of the children nearly died 'through the Fear and Cold'. Episcopalians complained that the crowds were often quite violent. At Ballantrae, in Ayrshire, according to one account, the minister's wife, who was 'big with Child', was beaten to the ground and the minister himself 'wounded . . . with a small Sword' and beaten 'severely with Cudgels'. Sometimes, however, it was crowds of Presbyterian women who attacked Episcopalian men. At Glasgow on 17 January, for example, 'a great Multitude of People, for the most part Women, came to Church, with a design to have drag'd the Minister out of the Pulpit'. The minister, having been tipped off in advance, chose not to enter the church and tried to slip away quietly, but he was 'fallen upon most barbarously, beaten, and had his Gown and other Cloaths torn in many pieces' – though whether by the women who had intended to ambush him inside the church or by the menfolk of the parish lying in wait outside our account does not make clear.[42] One of the ministers 'rabbled' was John Birnie of Broomhill, who in the summer of 1686 had turned down the offer of a bishopric as an inducement to support the repeal of the penal laws, and who was under such suspicion from James VII's government by the autumn of 1688 that his manse was 'twice severely searched' for concealed arms by government troops under the command of a Catholic officer. When a crowd of about forty well-armed Presbyterians came to eject Birnie from his manse at Christmas, his wife told them they should be ashamed 'to come with a design to spoil and search their house as papists had done' out of some pretended zeal for the Protestant religion. Birnie kept his cool and welcomed the armed men in, giving them food and drink; they left peaceably, after having made Birnie promise that 'with due convenience' he should quit his manse and move into a gentleman's house in the parish which was then empty, which Birnie did.[43]

Although Presbyterians of all types appear to have been involved in the rabblings, the Society People were the 'most active'. Indeed, the Society People subsequently issued guidelines instructing their members how to proceed. At their meeting of 3 January, responding to reports that 'Episcopall Curats' had been robbed of their horses, arms, money and other household possessions, they framed an 'Apology', to be published at market crosses throughout the countryside, asserting that although they felt themselves duty bound 'to endeavour by all approven means the extirpation of Prelacy as weell as Popery' and that they would therefore do all they could to dispossess 'the Prelatick Curats from the Churches upon which they are intruded', they did not approve of taking any of the curates' possessions. At their next meeting, held on 23 January, they drew up a paper for parishioners to present in advance to their curate, which warned the curate to cease his ministry and vacate the church, and threatened force if he refused.[44] These guidelines appear to have been followed exactly. On 1 February 1689, for example, the Presbyterians of Livingston, in Linlithgowshire, delivered precisely such a paper to the minister's wife (again the minister was away from home) before they seized control of the church.[45]

These rabblings signified a rejection of the Restoration settlement of the Church – an attack on a particular type of Protestant settlement – and not just a rejection of Catholicism. Moreover, unlike the anti-Catholic rioting, which was directed at illegal activity, the Presbyterian crowds sought to overturn a legal Church establishment and restore the one that had been disestablished at the Restoration. They were also acting in direct contravention of an act of 1685, which had made invading the houses of ministers of the Established Church a capital offence.[46] These were self-consciously revolutionary crowds, unlike anything seen in England. As the group that deprived the minister of Cumnock, Ayrshire, on Christmas Day 1688 stated: 'this they did not as States-Men, nor as Church-Men, but by violence and in a Military way of Reformation'.[47] They were free to act, they felt, because the government had been dissolved as a result of James's flight.[48] 'These things were acted in an Interregnum', one Presbyterian apologist claimed, 'When we had no Civil, nor Church-Government. When one King was removed, and another not yet set up.'[49] In short, the Presbyterian crowds seized the opportunity provided by the collapse of the government to promote their own agenda for reform. When the Laird of Bridgehouse tried to warn one group of Presbyterians 'that their appearing in Arms and abusing the Clergy in this Hostile manner, were but insolent outrages against all the Law of the Nation' and that they would 'do well to remit their Illegal forwardness', they told him 'to stand off and forbear giving Rules to them', adding that 'they would not adhere to the Prince of Orange, nor the Law of the Kingdom, any further than the Solemn League and Covenant was fulfilled and prosecuted by both'.[50] The Presbyterian radical Sir James Montgomery of Skelmorlie thought it was hardly surprising that such rabblings took place, when one reflected upon the terrible persecutions these people had suffered and the fact that many of the clergy thrust out had acted the part of informers.[51] In the absence of reliable evidence, the precise number of those driven out will remain unknown; contemporaries thought the figure was in the region of two or three hundred.[52]

THE BALANCE OF FORCES IN THE
WINTER OF 1688/9

It is difficult to sustain the argument, then, that the Scots remained passive in the autumn and winter of 1688/9, or that they were reluctant participants in the movement to rid the British realms of popery and arbitrary government. Some actively intrigued with William, many more declared for him after he landed in England, while others took to the streets to demonstrate their hostility to Catholicism and even to the existing Church establishment. James had alienated considerable sections of the Scottish population by late 1688, and there was widespread support among people of all classes and political and religious persuasions for William's expressed goal of securing Scotland's religion, laws and liberties. The trouble was that in Scotland there existed no consensus as to how these should be secured. Unlike England, therefore, it proved impossible to achieve a compromise settlement round which the majority of the nation could unite.

By the beginning of the new year many leading Scots had come south to England to treat with William concerning the future of their country. William assembled all the Scottish peers and gentry then in London at St James's on 7 January and asked their advice concerning what should be done 'for securing the Protestant Religion, and Restoring [their] Laws and Liberties'. A group of thirty peers and eighty gentlemen withdrew to Whitehall and, having elected Hamilton as their president, proceeded to discuss over the next few days what direction they should take. Hamilton's son, the Earl of Arran, while acknowledging the debt the Scots owed William for their 'Delivery from Popery', nevertheless insisted on the need to distinguish between James's 'Popery and his Person'. 'I dislike the one', he maintained, 'but have sworn and do owe Allegeance to the other'; he therefore suggested the Scots ask William to invite James to return and call a free parliament 'for the Securing [their] Religion and Property, according to the known laws of that Kingdom'. His motion met with no support. Instead, on 10 January, the assembly unanimously agreed to invite William to assume the running of all civil and military affairs for the time being and to call a Convention of Estates to meet at Edinburgh on 14 March to settle the government.[53]

Trying to make sense of the pattern of political allegiances in Scotland during the period of the Revolution is no simple task. Not only can we detect a variety of contending political and religious positions, but we also see apparent shifts in political allegiance over short periods of time. Considerations of self-interest certainly played their part in shaping the reaction of the Scottish elite, as leading magnates jockeyed for position and sought to promote their personal ambitions.[54] Yet it would be wrong to take too cynical a view; conviction did play a part. Some put loyalty to an individual first, whether that individual be James, William or themselves, while others were motivated more by a desire to achieve particular religious or constitutional objectives.

At one extreme were the inevitable Jacobites, people who for reasons of personal loyalty or political commitment were always going to remain true to James VII: men like the Catholic Duke of Gordon, Governor of Edinburgh Castle, and the Protestant earls of Balcarres and Claverhouse (the latter recently created Viscount Dundee). When ordered by the council on 22 December to surrender Edinburgh Castle, Gordon refused, saying that as his commission came directly from the King, he could not lay it down until the King instructed him.[55] Gordon was to hold on to the Castle in the name of King James until mid-June 1689. In February 1689, after the English had settled the throne on William and Mary, Balcarres and Dundee were reported to be openly drinking to 'King William's confusion and King James's restauration';[56] indeed, Dundee was soon to launch a rebellion to restore James. There were also those, such as Arran, who disliked the measures pursued by James as king and welcomed the fact that William had come to deliver Scotland from popery and arbitrary government, but who hoped that a settlement might be achieved that could preserve James's Scottish crown.

Those who remained unswerving in their loyalty to James right from the start, however, were in the minority. There was a significant group of waverers, from the politically unscrupulous through to the politically flexible and politically timid. There were certainly those who were prepared to pursue the course of action that seemed most likely to promote their own political ambitions – men like Atholl and Tarbat, who had held high office under both Charles II and James VII, who deserted to William when the chance came to strike at Perth towards the end of 1688, and who flirted with Jacobitism when they did not achieve the recognition they expected under the new regime. We also have a number of less spectacular figures, political realists who could bend with the times to support the most pragmatic and therefore most workable solution.[57] Some might have started off preferring a solution that would have kept James on the throne but moved firmly into William's camp once it became obvious which way the tide was flowing. If we take the Episcopalians as a group, although some were committed Jacobites (such as Balcarres, Dundee and the bishops themselves), others were more flexible and showed themselves for a time willing to try to work with William to try to achieve a settlement that would have preserved episcopacy and left the powers of the monarch undiminished: men like the Duke of Queensberry, Sir George Mackenzie of Rosehaugh and, on a less cynical reading of their motives, Atholl and Tarbat.

Among the Williamites we can identify a variety of positions. There were the Presbyterians – men such as the earls of Crawford, Argyll and Sutherland, and Sir Patrick Hume – who sought fundamental reforms in both Church and state. There were also various types of trimmers, people who were committed to William and would remain loyal to the new regime whatever settlement was achieved, but who tried to bring about a more moderate settlement than that desired by the Presbyterians in order to make the Revolution less partisan and to win the support of the broadest possible cross-section of the population. These included men like Tweeddale, Sir James Dalrymple of Stair and his son Sir John, but also Hamilton (whose service to William and to himself came before any particular partisan agenda), and even perhaps the Earl of Melville, William's first Scottish Secretary of State (though Melville was more recognizably in the Presbyterian camp). Finally we have the radical extreme, those people who sought a revolutionary settlement in either Church and state (or both), and who began to distance themselves from the new regime when the sort of reforms they desired were not instituted. Here we would include the Cameronian Society People, and also the radical

Presbyterian politicians, such as Sir James Montgomery of Skelmorlie, who out of frustration with the working out of the Revolution settlement himself turned to Jacobitism.

In between James's flight in December and the eventual meeting of the Scottish Convention in March, various interests sought to lobby William concerning their preferred settlement. The most organized group were the Presbyterians. By late December 1688, they were busy promoting an address to William, in which they rehearsed their sufferings under episcopacy during the last two reigns – the Highland Host, exorbitant fines, torture, and the summary execution of field conventiclers – and asked him to call a free parliament, procure 'the Extirpation of Prelacie' and the 'Reestablishment of the Presbyterian Government of the Kirk', and to restore those ministers evicted at the Restoration. The address appears to have been a first draft and was thus never presented in quite this form. However, it was superseded by another to much the same effect, drawn up in January at a general meeting of the Presbyterian ministers convened at Edinburgh and subsequently signed by various nobles, knights and gentlemen (including the earls of Crawford, Argyll, Sutherland and Cardross, and by Stair and Hume), and which was eventually presented to William in London on 27 February.[58] Another address calling for the abolition of episcopacy, purportedly signed by 40,000 people ('Nobility, Gentry and Commons'), was being readied for presentation to the Scottish Convention in mid-March; this also asked that the government be settled on William of Orange and that 'the Executive Power of the Laws' be put in the hands of God-fearing men, although there is no record of it having been presented.[59] The Society People likewise drew up a petition to the Convention, asking it to free the Church from the 'yoak of prelacie, popery and erastianisme by annulling the lawes that have rescinded the most just and laudable establishment of presbyterian government'. This too was never actually delivered.[60]

At the other end of the spectrum were those who wanted to preserve diocesan prelacy. Many of the Scottish nobility and gentry, and the vast majority of the population north of the Tay, favoured episcopacy. The bishops themselves frantically began lobbying the English bishops in a desperate attempt to preserve their order. On

20 December, Archbishop Paterson of Glasgow wrote to the Archbishop of Canterbury asking him to forgive 'anie yeeldings or condescensions latelie made by anie of our order to the King's most importunat desires' – which he blamed on the fact that the Scottish bishops did not enjoy the same security of tenure as their English counterparts, but could be dismissed at will by the king by virtue of the Act of Supremacy of 1669 – and insisting that William would not be able to secure the monarchy in Scotland 'without a setled Episcopacie in it'. The Archbishop of St Andrews made similar points in a letter to Archbishop Sancroft four days later, in which he further warned that the peace of the Anglican Church depended upon the preservation of the Church in Scotland. Paterson also petitioned William to protect the Episcopalian clergy in the western division of his diocese from the forcible ejections by the rabble.[61] Yet, even if the Scottish bishops were prepared to appeal to William for protection, they would not commit to a solution that would place him on the Scottish throne. Instead, they insisted that they would serve him only 'so far as law, reason, or conscience would allow', as the Bishop of Edinburgh, William Rose, bluntly told the Prince.[62]

The leaders of the lay Episcopalian interest, however, were willing to be more accommodating. The key activists here were the Duke of Queensberry, Charles II's Treasurer in the 1680s who had been brought down by the Perth faction shortly after James's accession, Sir George Mackenzie of Rosehaugh, the former Lord Advocate who had been removed in 1686 for his opposition to James's attempts to repeal the penal laws, and Viscount Tarbat (also a George Mackenzie). All three were in London in the early months of 1689 lobbying in defence of the bishops.[63] In January, the two George Mackenzies produced a *Memorial* for the Prince of Orange, advising William that since he had 'come to support our Laws', he was 'in honour bound to support Episcopacy', which was 'confirmed by twenty seven Parliaments'. They also warned that 'Episcopacy' in Scotland was 'necessary for support of the Monarchy', since the Scottish Presbyterians harboured anti-monarchical principles.[64] Queensberry's protégé, Alexander Cairncross, the deprived Archbishop of Glasgow, was also in London in the early months of 1689 representing the cause of his order at William's court.[65] In the Convention, Atholl and Tarbat said they were willing to support William as king, but at the same time continued to lobby William to try to persuade him to preserve episcopacy.[66]

Modern historians have emphasized that an ideological commitment to the theories of indefeasible hereditary succession, divine right and passive obedience made it extremely difficult for Scottish Episcopalians to jettison their support for James.[67] For the Episcopalian interest to be won over to William, means had to be found of justifying the overthrow of James VII which could be made to appear compatible with their professed beliefs in non-resistance, and which maintained a healthy distance from Presbyterian theories of resistance. The way forward was shown by James Canaries, the Episcopalian minister of Selkirk. Canaries had championed James's accession in 1685, but, by February 1686, had turned against the new regime and had preached a violent sermon attacking both Catholics and Protestant fanatics for their 'disloyal Principles', for which he was suspended from his living (see pp. 58–9, 150–51) Now, in a sermon preached in Edinburgh on 30 January 1689 (the 40th anniversary of the regicide), which was later published in an extended form, Canaries articulated a theory of limited resistance – one that condemned both popish and Presbyterian principles and sought to make the religious duty of subjection compatible with the secular right of people to hold their sovereign accountable if he violated the law. His ingenious argument certainly involved the formulation of what were, for Scottish Episcopalians, new paradigms, and belies the view that the Scottish Revolution was ideologically sterile.

Canaries began by affirming the Pauline doctrine of non-resistance and that people had to be subject to the supreme authority for conscience sake.[68] Yet subjects, he claimed, were 'upon their Conscience to yield their Soveraign all those Rights and Dues which by the peculiar Constitution in which they live, He can Legally exact of them', but no more 'than what by the established Form of the Government he has a just Title to'. Although 'the King be Superiour to the whole Body of the Subjects, when he Rules according to Law', Canaries asserted, 'when he deserts the Laws, and takes up his own Arbitrary Will in lieu of them; then the Subjects may look to themselves'. No 'private Subject' was allowed 'to resist' the government he lived under for any private act of injustice he suffered. But 'when the Subjects

Right in general is Invaded, and the Injustice reaches the Publick Interest of them all', then 'every particular Subject not only may', Canaries said, but 'ought to do whatever he can to contribute the relieving the whole Subjects Right in the Laws, from that Tyranny and Oppression it is falling, or fallen under'.[69]

Canaries, nevertheless, distanced himself from the Presbyterian theory of resistance. He condemned those who used pretended zeal for God or religion to justify overthrowing princes who did not share their religious outlook: Christ did not allow such a thing, and 'Subjects must cease to be Christians' if they sought 'to dethrone Princes meerly for the sake of their Religion'.[70] The Church of Rome had been responsible for propagating this rebellious doctrine, although many who called themselves Protestants had also followed this popish principle – such as those who were responsible for the regicide.[71] Nevertheless, it was 'quite another thing for Subjects to vindicate the Legal Right they have to profess their Religion', since 'the Religion of no Subjects that is established in this manner, can ever be invaded, without the Constitution of their Government' being so too. It was an ingenious argument, which allowed Episcopalians the right to resist but denied it to Presbyterians.[72]

Given the balance of forces between Presbyterians and Episcopalians in Scotland, and the apparent willingness of some Episcopalians to work with William, some came to feel it best to seek a compromise settlement in the Church. In their letter to William of 24 December, the Scottish council had expressed their hope for a comprehensive Church settlement.[73] William himself was not averse to maintaining episcopacy and desired a solution that would offend as few people as possible.[74] Some thought the priority should be to achieve a suitable political settlement, putting the more contentious religious issues on the back burner until a later date. It was in this context that the idea of a political union between England and Scotland, uniting the two crowns and the two parliaments in one, came to be revived. Its main advocate was Tweeddale, who had been in self-imposed semi-retirement since February 1687 rather than be associated with James's pro-Catholic policies. Tweeddale was a trimmer who hoped to establish an alliance of the centre as a way of preventing the seizure of power by either extreme, and who saw a union as the best way to guarantee military and political security and a moderate settlement in the Church.[75] Political union would also prevent the possibility of the Scots going their own way in 1689 and breaking up the union of the crowns that had existed since 1603. On 29 December, the noblemen, gentlemen and royal burghs of Haddingtonshire, at Tweeddale's instigation, drew up an address to William inviting him to consider how the kingdoms of Scotland and England might be united 'in a more strict and inseparable union', which would, in their opinion, prevent Scotland's enemies in the future from taking advantage of 'our distinct and different Laws and Customs and exercise of Government . . . to raise Standing Armys in either Kingdome by which the other may be thretned or enforc'd to submit to Alterations in their Religion or diminution of there [sic] Liberty' or from bringing in foreign forces 'for the subversion of the Religion and Liberty of both'.[76]

The Presbyterians, however, suspected that the proposal of uniting with a country where the episcopalian interest was dominant, before the Scots had achieved a settlement in their own Church, was an underhand way of seeking to preserve episcopacy in Scotland.[77] Although the Haddingtonshire address did not express a preference with regard to the settlement in the Church, it was certainly the case that Episcopalians, such as Queensberry and Tarbat, found the idea of a union attractive.[78] Tarbat and Mackenzie warned William in their *Memorial* that if Scotland were subjected to Presbytery, it would destroy any chance of union with England, since the English were for episcopacy.[79] William himself favoured a union and claimed that many of the Scottish nobility and gentry he had met with in London looked upon 'an Union of both Kingdoms . . . as one of the best Means for procuring the Happiness of these Nations, and settling a lasting Peace amongst them.'[80]

THE MEETING OF THE SCOTTISH CONVENTION

Most Scots, then, by the winter of 1688/9, were looking to William of Orange in the hope that he, by calling a free parliament, might help deliver their kingdom from popery and arbitrary government. There were some, undoubtedly (as there were in England) who hoped that this could be achieved while still preserving James VII on the throne. Yet at this stage it appears that many Episcopalians could have been brought to agree to a settlement in favour of William if suitable measures were taken to address their religious concerns. There were others who saw the value of compromise, and who wanted, in particular, a moderate settlement in the Church. Some believed that the best way forward was for a political union with England. There were significant numbers in Scotland, in other words, who might have welcomed an English-style settlement, and even those who wanted simply to import the Revolution settlement made in England. In the end, however, compromise was eschewed. The balance of power within the Convention, which assembled in Edinburgh on 14 March, was to tip decidedly in favour of the Whigs and Presbyterians, who sought fundamental reforms in both Church and state. Why then, given the balance of forces that we have identified in the winter of 1688/9, did the Convention end up being such a partisan body?

In large measure it was due to the fact that committed Whigs and Presbyterians were more successful in getting returned to the Convention than Jacobites or Williamite Episcopalians. Given that James's remodelling of the royal burghs had enabled him to place his own men in control of the process for returning burgh representatives, it was clear that to meet the desire for a free parliament the members of the Convention would have to be elected on some kind of restructured franchise. At their meeting in London in January, the Scots agreed that although the shire franchise could remain the same, burgh elections should be made by a general poll of all burgesses. They also decided that only Protestants would be allowed either to vote or to stand for election, although the operation of the Test Act was to be suspended – a move that opened up the poll to the Presbyterians.[81] The Presbyterians appear to have been very active at the polls, particularly the Society People, who canvassed on behalf of their favoured candidates and circulated papers urging people to choose those who would vote for the repeal of the Scottish Supremacy Act of 1669 (which had made the king the head of the Church in Scotland) and for the overthrow of episcopacy.[82] According to

Episcopalian apologists, many Episcopalians decided to boycott the elections, refusing to put themselves forward as candidates for those constituencies they had always represented, or even to participate in the poll, believing it would be a violation of the Test oath to meet to consult about the affairs of the nation without the consent of the king.[83] Such claims might have been disingenuous, an *ex post facto* rationalization of defeat. The Presbyterian political radical Montgomery of Skelmorlie, for example, claimed that Episcopalians 'bestirr[ed] themselves more vigorously about Elections' than anyone, riding 'Night and Day begging Votes' in counties and burghs, and using 'all the indirect wayes imaginable', including physical intimidation, to get their own men elected.[84] What is clear, however, is that the Episcopalians did not do well in the elections.

Moreover, of those Jacobites and Episcopalians who were returned to the Convention, several were either to withdraw or were driven out. Some left right at the beginning, seeing the way the tide was turning when Hamilton won the election for President of the Convention, defeating Atholl (who was the bishops' candidate) by fifteen votes. Others were displaced by the committee of elections, set up under the chairmanship of Sir John Dalrymple and dominated by Presbyterians and committed Williamites, which was blatantly partisan in determining disputed elections. By contrast, at least two peers (Argyll and Melville) and two shire representatives were allowed to take their seats even though they were under the sentence of forfaulture and therefore legally debarred.[85]

James himself must also take some responsibility for undermining his own cause within the Convention. On 16 March, two days after its assembly, the Scottish Convention heard two letters, one from William, now king of England, the other from James. The Convention decided William's should be read first, since 'it could not Dissolve the meeting, as the King's letter might doe'. It proved moderate in tone, and simply invited those assembled 'to enter upon such Consultations as are most probable to setle you on sure and Lasting foundations' and to act 'with regaird to the Publick good, and to the generall Interest and Inclinations of the People'. It did not make any positive demands, beyond expressing William's belief in the usefulness of a union. The Convention agreed to allow James's letter to be read only after passing an act asserting that they were 'a frie and lawful meeting of the Estates', and would 'continue undissolved' until they had settled and secured 'the Protestant Religione, the Government, lawes and liberties of the Kingdome'. James's letter was most uncompromising. It charged that the Convention had been summoned 'By the Usurped Authority of the Prince of Orange' and demanded that those assembled support his 'Royall interest', as loyal subjects should, threatening to 'punish with the rigor of Our Law' all who remained in rebellion; the Scots, the letter stated, would have to wait for the opportunity to secure their 'Religion, laws, Propertys, libertys and rights' until it became possible for James to summon a parliament. According to the *London Gazette*, James's letter 'rather served to make the Convention more unanimous for the setling the Government' on William.[86]

Pressure out-of-doors also had an impact in determining the eventual political complexion of the Convention. The population of the capital had been swelled by the arrival of a volunteer force of some 2,000 men from the south-western shires, many of them Society People, who had come to provide a guard for the Convention at a time when Edinburgh Castle was still in the hands of the Catholic Duke of Gordon. The Convention decided to accept their services temporarily, placing them under the command of the Earl of Leven; they were eventually disbanded at the end of March following the return from England of some Scottish regiments under the command of Major-General Mackay. Their presence helped make the Scottish capital a decidely hostile environment for open Jacobites. The bishops, who had insisted on praying for King James when the Convention opened, found themselves 'rail'd at, threatned, baffled and affronted' by angry crowds whenever they made their way through the streets of Edinburgh, as did many of their lay supporters. A report on 18 March that Dundee was conspiring with Gordon to launch an attack on the Convention led Hamilton to order the doors of the house to be shut, warning that 'there was danger within as well as without doors', and to call on Leven to raise his volunteers to protect the city. Large numbers gathered with arms in the square adjoining the parliament house, and when the immediate threat from the Castle appeared to have passed and the doors of the house were finally opened, the Jacobites and Episocopalians had to face the terrifying prospect of walking out through a hostile crowd who greeted them with threats and curses, while the known Williamites and Presbyterians found they were received with cheers and acclamations. In the face of such intimidation, several Jacobites and Episcopalians decided to quit the Convention. Furthermore, many of those who had been sitting on the fence felt that the time had now come to identify themselves firmly with the Williamite camp.[87]

The roll of the Convention lists 188 who were called to sit in the assembly: 9 clergy (including the 2 archbishops), 58 nobles and 121 commissioners for the shires and burghs.[88] The elections themselves had the biggest impact on the composition of the assembly, the result of a combination of the restructured franchise and the altered political mood of the country. Of the 56 shire commissioners, only 12 had sat in the parliament of 1686, and only 13 of the 65 burgh commissioners. According to Tarbat, it was the burghs, under the new method of election, that held the key to Presbyterian success; the majority of the nobles and barons, he claimed, were 'not for Presbitery'.[89] Displacements or withdrawals were only minor factors in determining the political complexion of the Convention. The committee of elections, in fact, heard a total of only ten cases of disputed or double returns.[90] At the end of March, the official English account of the Convention's proceedings reported that 6 bishops, 9 earls, 3 viscounts, 7 lords and 10 gentlemen had chosen to absent themselves from the Convention, making a total of 35. The withdrawals were not necessarily permanent; some of those who left were later to return, including a few of the bishops. There were others, however, who were to absent themselves on crucial days, feigning indisposition or illness.[91]

For these various reasons, therefore, the Convention came to be dominated by those who wanted to free 'ther Church from Prelacie' and 'ther State from arbitrarie Government'. Of those who remained to work out the Revolution settlement, a minority were for offering the throne to William and Mary without any conditions attached, though they were easily voted down. Others were for following up on William's suggestion of a union with England. The two Dalrymples (Stair and his son Sir John) and Tarbat proposed the two countries should be represented by one parliament, though Scotland should retain its own municipal laws and keep the existing Church polity, which could then be modified by the present Convention or an ensuing parliament. The scheme appealed to those 'that had a Mind to trim', seeing the advantage of delaying the contentious issue of the Church settlement until after the crown had been settled. Darlymple and Tarbat also tried to appeal to the remaining Jacobites in the Convention, alleging that it would take months before any treaty could be concluded and that the buying of such time could only serve James VII's interests. Yet the Convention voted the proposal down. King James's friends would have nothing to do with it, realizing that a union could only work for the Prince of Orange's interests, who was already king in England. Hamilton and his supporters also opposed the idea, believing it would threaten their own ambitions for political dominance within Scotland. The Presbyterians feared that a union with a country 'where the Church of England was the strongest party' would be 'of ill consequence to their Kirk', and demanded that episcopacy be abolished first. The political reformers worried that a union would deny them the opportunity 'of distinguishing any rights or priviledges that belonged' to the Scots 'as a people'. The idea of a union was not totally abandoned. Some Presbyterians were prepared to consider it later in the session, once their political and religious agenda had been achieved, and on 23 April the Convention did nominate commissioners to negotiate with the English concerning a union of the two kingdoms. By then it was too late, however, since the Revolutions in the two countries had taken significantly different paths, and the English parliament was no longer interested in pursuing the idea.[92]

THE MAKING OF A REVOLUTIONARY SETTLEMENT

During the first two weeks of April the Scottish Convention forged a Revolution settlement that was much more radical than that adopted by the English. The first significant step was taken on 4 April, when the Convention declared the throne vacant. It was impossible to follow the English example and maintain that James, by fleeing the realm, had abdicated, since Scottish kings had not resided in their native land since James VI had inherited the English crown in 1603. As Arran had pointed out to the Scottish assembly in London on 8 January, the King's 'present absence from us, by being in France, can no more affect our Duty, than his longer absence from us in Scotland has done all this while'.[93] One way forward would have been to follow the path advocated by the Whigs in England and maintain that the throne had become vacant as a result of James having broken the original contract between the king and his people. One pamphleteer argued that 'by the Constitution of the Government' of Scotland, 'there was an Original Contract betwixt the King and the People, by which their Kings were obliged to Rule by Law', and that history showed that 'when the Kings made Invasion upon Religion, and the Law and Liberties of the Subject', the Estates had convened 'by their own Authority, and called their Kings in question for it'.[94]

The declaration of the vacancy agreed to by the Convention did not, however, use the language of the original contract. Instead, it concluded that James, by 'Inverting all the ends of Government', had 'Forefaulted the right to the Croune'. This was because James, 'being a professt Papist', had assumed 'the Regall power and acted as King' without ever taking the coronation oath as required by law, and 'by the advyce of evill and wicked Councillors' had 'Invaded the fundamentall constitution of this Kingdome', altering it from 'a legall limited Monarchy, to ane Arbitrary despotick power', using his power to subvert the Protestant religion and violate 'the lawes and liberties of the Natione'. The declaration also charged James with having committed a series of acts the Convention deemed were contrary to law: he had 'asserted ane absolute power to Cass, annul and Disable all the lawes, and particularly arraigneing the lawes establishing the Protestant Religion'; set up Jesuit schools; allowed the public celebration of the mass; converted Protestant chapels and churches into public mass-houses; disarmed Protestants and appointed Catholics to civil and military office; established a popish printing press; sent the children of Protestant nobles and gentry abroad to be brought up Catholics; bestowed pensions upon priests; bribed Protestants to change their religion by granting them offices and pensions; imposed oaths contrary to law; given gifts and grants for exacting money without the consent of parliament or the Convention of Estates; raised a standing army in time of peace, without the consent of parliament; employed officers in the army as judges, whereby many people were put to death summarily, without legal trial, jury or record; used inhuman torture without evidence and in non-capital offences; imposed exorbitant fines; imprisoned people without cause; forfaulted several persons upon stretches of old and obsolete laws, notably the Earl of Argyll; subverted the rights of the royal burghs to choose their own magistrates, so that he could control whom they returned to parliament; changed judges' commissions from life to royal pleasure, so that he could turn them out of office when they did not comply with his wishes; and granted individuals personal protection from civil debts.[95] Some of the crimes alleged, in fact, had been committed by Charles II rather than by James VII as king.

We should not confuse the word 'forfault' with our modern word 'forfeit': the former was a technical legal term, normally applied to fiefs, and its use in the declaration of the vacancy suggests that the Scots were embracing a feudal conception of their monarchy rather than a more modern contractarian one. It does not follow, however, that the Scots were therefore adopting a conservative rather than a radical position, as one scholar has maintained.[96] There appear to have been specific reasons why the Convention opted for a forfaulture. According to Balcarres, the Convention insisted 'that they intended not to forfeit [James] as a Traitor', but only to declare him 'forefeited', since this was a sentence that would reach to James's family 'and take off any pretensions the Prince of Wales might afterwards have'. It is revealing to note, however, that Balcarres thought this a 'Childish distinction'.[97] Moreover, it was one that created further problems, since it would have involved the exclusion from the succession not just of the infant Prince of Wales but also of James's other children, including William's wife, Mary. The Convention therefore decided that the word 'forfault' in their resolution 'should imply no other alteration in the succession to the crown, than the seclusion of King James, the pretended Prince of Wales, and the children that shall be procreated of either of their bodies'.[98]

In fact, in opting for a forfaulture the Convention might have deliberately been seeking the more radical solution. Stair thought 'the terme of forfating the King's right' was too 'harsh', because it implied that 'the Conventione had a superiority of jurisdictione'. He would have preferred the Convention to have opted for a straightforward breach of contract, declaring that since James 'had violat his pairt of the mutuall engagements, they [the Scottish people] wer frie of ther pairt'.[99] There was a conservative construction of the term forfault that would have avoided these radical implications, but significantly this was not adopted. Thus some in the Convention, Balcarres informs us, 'were for making use of an old obsolete Word, Forfeiting, used for a Bird's forsaking her Nest'; it was rejected, however, in favour of the proposal that the king, by committing certain acts, had 'forfeited' his right to the throne.[100] Ferguson concluded that parliament had deposed James VII 'for his violating the original Contract'.[101] Other contemporaries did not see the forfaulture of James VII as a conservative act, but as more in accordance with the principles of radical Presbyterians. Montgomery of Skelmorlie, for example, concluded that 'King James was . . . forfaulted by our States', where the Presbyterians were in the ascendancy, 'upon the same grounds' as Mary Queen of Scots in 1567 'was forfaulted by the Protestant States of this Kingdom (who were generally Presbyterians) for her practises and Designes against Religion and Liberty'.[102] The Society People believed that the Convention, in proclaiming King James 'to have forfait his right to the Crowne', gave the same reasons for doing so as the United Societies had against the proclaiming of him king in the first place.[103]

The declaration of the vacancy was passed by a large majority, with only twelve dissenting voices, among them Mackenzie of Rosehaugh and the seven bishops who were present for the vote.[104] The Convention then decided to offer the Scottish crown jointly to William and Mary, with sole regal power – as in England – vested in the king alone. Queensberry and Atholl, who had absented themselves for the vote on the vacancy, found they could support this, telling the Convention that though 'not fully convinced of their Right in declaring the Crown vacant', since they had done it, they were prepared to acquiesce, and thought that 'none deserved so well to fill it as the Prince of Orange'.[105]

The terms on which the Scottish crown was offered to William and Mary were laid out in the Claim of Right on 11 April, which the Scots regarded as their 'Instrument of Government'.[106] In structure, it was similar to the English Declaration of Rights. The first half outlined the various alleged illegal acts committed by James VII, and simply reproduced the reasons offered on 4 April for why he had forfaulted his right to the throne. The second half established guidelines for future royal behaviour by declaring certain things illegal or laying down prescriptions for what ought to be done, and was, in essence, a restatement of the first half in positive terms, with a few additional rights and prescriptions added. Like the English Declaration of Rights, the Scottish Claim of Right purported to be doing no more than 'vindicating and asserting . . . antient rights and liberties'.[107] In its condemnation of popery and arbitrary government, however, the Claim of Right also condemned policies pursued by Charles II (to a much greater extent than its English counterpart, and this despite the fact that the document laid the blame solely on James VII) and found it necessary to declare certain things illegal which the kings in Scotland unquestionably had a legal right to do. This is not to say that the pretence to be vindicating and asserting ancient rights and liberties was disingenuous. The framers of the Claim of Right appear to have been invoking an earlier constitutional framework – the reform programme of 1640–41 carried out during the Covenanting Revolution – that had been superseded by legislation enacted since the Restoration.[108] But the Claim of Right was not just a rejection of the illegal measures pursued by Restoration monarchs (as was the English Declaration of Rights); it also sought, in crucial respects, to redefine the powers of the Scottish monarchy as it had been legally reconstituted after 1660.

The second half of the Claim of Right began by dealing with the problems of a Catholic king and the promotion of popery under James VII. Thus, it asserted that, 'By the law of this Kingdome no Papist can be King or Queen of this realme, nor bear any Office whatsomever therin; nor can any protestant successor exercise the regall power, until he or she swear the Coronation Oath.' This was a dubious claim at best. It is true that an act of 1567 required all monarchs to take an oath promising to protect the true religion 'at the tyme of their coronatioun, and ressait [receipt] of thair princely authoritie', and this had seemingly been confirmed by an act of 1681 ratifying all laws passed since 1567 for the security of the Protestant religion. Yet the Succession Act of 1681 had explicitly stated that the heir to the throne could not be debarred from the succession on the grounds of his religion and that upon the death of the king the administration of the government immediately devolved upon the heir, thus in effect rescinding the requirement to take the coronation oath.[109] In a tract published in 1684, the then Lord Advocate, Mackenzie of Rose-haugh, had insisted that the Coronation Act related only to the crowning of the king, not to the succession; that a coronation was not absolutely necessary, since a king was still a king without being crowned, and there was no clause in the Coronation Act 'debarring the Successor, or declaring the Succession Null, in case his Successor gave not this Oath', and that the Succession Act of 1681 had, in any case, abrogated the Coronation Act.[110] Even the Whiggish lawyer Sir John Lauder of Fountainhall had acknowledged in 1685 that under Scottish law the coronation of the king was not legally required.[111]

The Claim of Right then declared that 'all Proclamationes assert-ing an absolute power to Cass, annull and Disable lawes', the erect-ing of Jesuit colleges, converting Protestant churches into mass-houses, and allowing mass to be said, were contrary to law. Whether they were, however, is again questionable. It is true that the mass had been declared idolatrous by two acts of 1560 and 1567, attendance at which was punishable by death at the third offence, and an act of 1592 against Jesuits, seminary priests and trafficking papists – the essence of which had been confirmed by a similar act passed in 1661 – had made the saying of mass treason.[112] Yet the Scottish Act of Supremacy of 1669 had established that it was an inherent right in the Scottish Crown to order 'the Externall Government and policie of the Church' and that Charles II and his successors could 'setle, enact, and emit such constitutions, acts and orders, concerning the administra-tion of the externall Government of the Church, and the persons imployed in the same, and concerning all ecclesiasticall meitings and maters' as they thought fit. It had also rescinded and annulled all pre-vious laws that were inconsistent with this royal supremacy.[113] Under the terms of the Supremacy, as royal apologists had argued back in

1686, the Scottish king did possess the right, through his prerogative, to redefine Scotland's ecclesiastical establishment, including dispensing with or suspending penal statutes against Catholic or Protestant nonconformists and turning over Protestant churches to Catholic worship (see p. 155). Those critical of the plans for Catholic toleration in 1686 had been chary of discussing the royal prerogative, and had even been prepared to admit that the king of Scotland could not be tied to the laws (see p. 157). Furthermore, the Excise Act of 1685 had explicitly recognized the Scottish monarchy as 'absolute'. Admittedly, this had been passed at the time of Argyll's rebellion, and was intended to affirm that the Scottish king could not legitimately be resisted by his subjects, not to establish the principle that he possessed 'an arbitrary despotick power' to act 'in violation of the laws', which is what the Claim of Right criticized James for doing. Nevertheless, the charge made in the declaration of the vacancy and repeated in the Claim of Right that James had invaded 'the fundamental constitution of this Kingdom', which was of 'a legal limited monarchy', ran contrary to the fact that an act of parliament had established that the monarchy in Scotland was not a 'legal limited' one.

The next three clauses proceeded to condemn as contrary to law the means whereby James VII had sought to promote popery in Scotland: by 'allowing Popish bookes to be printed and Dispersed'; sending the children of noblemen, gentry and others abroad 'to be bred Papists', making donations to popish schools and colleges, bestowing pensions on Catholic priests, and persuading Protestants to convert by offering them 'places, preferments, and pensiones'; and 'the Disarming of protestants and Imploying papists' in both civil and military office. All three clauses were clearly in accordance with the spirit of existing laws designed to protect and uphold the Protestant religion. Although Scotland did not have the same sort of centralized system of press regulation as did England, in November 1661 the Scottish council, in accordance with long-established Scottish laws against treason and heresy, had prohibited the printing of political and religious material without license, while in 1671 Charles II's government had granted a monopoly of Scottish printing to Andrew Anderson; the Catholic printing press established at Holyroodhouse under James VII had thus required a special dispensation from the

King. And certainly, in giving offices to Catholics, James had acted in violation of the Test Act of 1681, which required all office-holders to swear an oath pledging their commitment to the Protestant religion. It was arguable, however, that as an absolute monarch in Scotland, James was 'so far above' the laws that he did have the power to 'dispence with them', as Lord Chancellor Perth had advised the King at the time.[114]

The remainder of the Claim of Right condemned various executive actions under both Charles and James that seemed to undermine the authority of parliament or pervert the course of justice, thereby seeking to make the royal government of Scotland more accountable to parliamentary control. Some of its provisions were less controversial than others. Most exposed what were clearly ambiguities in Scottish law. A few, however, declared illegal practices which had hitherto been perfectly legal. Several clauses condemned those initiatives taken to deal with the problem of political and religious dissent during the 1680s.

The clause stating that James had acted illegally by imposing oaths without the authority of parliament was most obviously an allusion to the oath in James's Scottish Indulgence of 1687, which bound subjects to maintain the king and his heirs in the exercise of their absolute power and authority; the framers might also have had in mind the Abjuration Oath of 1684, however, which the Scottish council had ordered to be tendered to anyone suspected of supporting the Cameronian *Apologetick Declaration* of that year calling for the overthrow of Charles II (the penalty for refusing which was death). Ferguson, in a tract published first in 1687, when condemning the Indulgence oath, had asserted that 'the imposing an Oath upon subjects' had always been 'look't upon as the highest Act of legislative Authority' and that no Scottish king had ever 'pretended to a Right of enjoining and requiring an Oath that was not first Enacted and specified in some Law'.[115] The Claim of Right also asserted that charging lawburrows 'at the King's instance' and imposing bonds 'without the authority of Parliament' were contrary to law – an allusion to Charles II's bond of 1674 and 1677 (which required landlords to get their tenants to take out a bond promising not to violate the laws against conventicles or face punishment for the offence themselves) and his use of lawburrows in 1678 (which were essentially sureties to keep the peace imposed upon those who refused to subscribe the bond, under penalty of a fine valued at the equivalent of two years' rent). The legality of Charles II's bond and his particular use of law-burrows had certainly been contested in 1678, though the government itself had felt it was on firm legal ground and could cite appropriate parliamentary legislation to justify its actions.[116]

Other clauses declared 'the putting of Garrisones in privat men's houses in tyme of peace without their Consent, or the authority of Parliament' (a policy pursued by the Scottish council in 1675 to meet the Presbyterian challenge in the south-west) and 'the Sending of ane army in ane hostile manner upon any pairt of the Kingdome, in a peaceable tyme' and exacting 'any manner of free quarters' (an allusion to the way the Highland Host had been sent to police the Presbyterian heartlands in early 1678) to be illegal. The Scottish Militia Act of 1661 had asserted that the power to raise and command the people of Scotland in arms and to command all forts and garrisons resided in the king alone, and this was confirmed by another act of 1663; on the other hand, the 1661 Act had stated that the king's subjects should always be 'free of the provisions and mantenance of these forts and armies', unless approved by parliament or a Convention of Estates. And although the 1663 Act had allowed the king to send his army 'to any parte of his dominions of Scotland, England or Ireland', this was 'for suppressing of any foraigne invasion, intestine trouble or insurrection or for any other service whairin his Maiesties honour Authority or greatness may be concerned'; sending in the army 'in ane hostile manner . . . in a peaceable tyme' arguably did not fit these criteria. Whether Charles II's policy of quartering troops in the Presbyterian strongholds of the south-west had been illegal, however, is another matter, since the government here was dealing with 'intestine trouble or insurrection'.[117]

The clauses condemning 'useing torture without evidence, or in ordinary Crymes' and forcing subjects 'to Depone against themselves in capitall Crymes, however the punishment be restricted', highlighted the abuses in the dealings with the Scottish Rye House plotters William Spence and William Carstares in 1684. The rules governing the use of torture were, in fact, unclear, although with regard to both

Spence and Carstares the government had ignored convention when torturing the same individual more than once and where there existed no solid presumption of guilt for a capital crime. Furthermore, both Carstares and Spence had refused to swear an oath to answer all charges against them, on the grounds that it was illegal to force them to incriminate themselves (which it certainly was in capital offences), but the Scottish authorities took this to be equivalent to their implicating themselves, thus providing a sufficient presumption of guilt to justify the use of torture. The government's rationale for tendering the oath had been that they were not intending to charge Carstares and Spence with a capital crime; yet either this meant that Carstares and Spence were subsequently tortured for a non-capital crime or that they had been asked to incriminate themselves in a capital offence. The Claim of Right also declared that changing judges' commissions from *ad vitam aut culpam* (for life) to *durante bene placito* (at royal pleasure) was contrary to law, and re-established the principle laid down by an act of James VI's reign that had been violated when Charles issued a new commission for the Lords of Session in 1681.[118]

If the above clauses addressed what were ambiguities in Scottish law and condemned practices which, if not technically illegal, were at least against the spirit of the law, others condemned actions that had been sanctioned by parliamentary statute or were otherwise quite clearly legal. The clause stating that employing officers of the army as judges or putting subjects to death summarily without legal trial were contrary to law sought to confirm basic legal rights and the principle of due process, which had been violated during 'the killing times' of the 1680s. Yet in fact the Scottish king's right to allow any commissioned by him (including army officers) to 'take cognizance and decision of any Cases or causes he pleases' had been acknowledged by an act of 1681.[119] The declaration against 'fyneing husbands for ther wives withdrawing from the church' flew in the face of an act of 1685 which had confirmed that it was legal to fine husbands for their wives' withdrawing from church and ordained that this practice should be observed in all time coming.[120] The clause condemning arbitrary imprisonment (without express cause shown) and delaying putting prisoners to trial again sought to address abuses committed by the government in the 1680s in its dealings with political and religious dissidents. However, there was no habeas corpus act in Scotland, so the government had not acted contrary to law in this respect. Similarly, the Claim of Right broke new ground when it proclaimed the illegality of imposing 'extraordinary fynes' and exacting 'exorbitant Baile', because Scottish law had allowed for the imposition of heavy fines.[121]

The framers of the Claim of Right also had no compunction about overturning legal precedents set by the courts. The clause proclaiming the illegality of forfaultures 'upon stretches of old and obsolete lawes' and 'frivolous and weak pretences', as in the case of 'the late Earl of Argylle', reversed a previous legal judgment by the highest criminal court in the land. The Claim of Right further declared that the opinion of the Lords of Session in two specific cases (concerning more obscure aspects of the Scottish law of treason) were wrong, and asserted that subjects had the right to appeal to king and parliament against sentences pronounced by the Lords of Session. From here it went on to make the more general claim that it was 'the right of the subjects to petition the King' and to declare that 'all Imprisonments and prosecutiones for such petitioning' were contrary to law. This, of course, paralleled the clause in the English Declaration of Rights which referred to the arrest of the seven bishops in England for refusing to instruct their clergy to read James's second (English) Declaration of Indulgence in 1688. It is, however, inconceivable that the framers of the Claim of Right could have had this case in mind, not only because it had nothing to do with Scotland but also because the framers themselves (as we shall soon see) were no friends to episcopacy. Instead the clause seems to have alluded to an incident that happened back in 1660, when a group of Presbyterian ministers had been 'cruelly incarcerate[d]', as one Presbyterian apologist writing before the Revolution had put it, for daring to remind Charles II that he had previously taken the Covenant and lay under certain obligations as a result. Likewise the Scottish Presbyterians, in the immediate aftermath of the Revolution, complained how they had not even been allowed to petition for relief from the harsh persecutions under which they had suffered at the hands of the Restoration regime.[122]

The cumulative effect of the provisions of the Claim of Right was to bolster the position of parliament within the Scottish constitution at the expense of the royal prerogative. Two further clauses aimed to ensure the independence of parliament. One determined that parliamentary elections should be free, and declared illegal James's attempts to nominate town magistrates or councillors in order to ensure that the burghs returned members to parliament who were to his liking. In fact here James could claim to have been following the precedent of his grandfather, James VI; there had, however, been no *quo warranto* proceedings in Scotland, as there had in England, to lend the colour of law to the crown's actions.[123] The other clause condemned 'the giveing gifts or grants for raiseing of money without the Consent of Parliament or Convention of Estates'. This was probably less a complaint against extra-parliamentary forms of taxation – although in England James had illegally collected customs and excise in the opening months of his reign without parliamentary sanction, in Scotland an act of 1681 had allowed for the continued collection of the excise for five years after Charles II's death[124] – but more a criticism of the Scottish system of tax farming, especially as practised under Charles II by Lauderdale, who had been notoriously partial in granting tax farms and monopolies to his friends and clients.[125]

The Claim of Right also made two recommendations. One was that 'for redress of all greivances, and for the amending, strenthneing [sic] and preserving of the lawes, Parliaments ought to be frequently called, and allowed to sit, and the freedom of speech and debate secured to the members'. There is an obvious parallel here with the English Declaration of Rights, and the demand for frequent parliaments that might be allowed to sit is one that we more readily associate with the Whig opposition to Charles II in England during the Exclusion Crisis than with anything heard in Scotland under either of the two post-Restoration monarchs. This clause was no English import, however. Instead, it harked back to the reforming legislation of the Covenanting Revolution of the mid-century, particularly the Scottish Triennial Act of June 1640 (guaranteeing that parliaments meet every three years), which had claimed that frequent parliaments had been the norm in Scotland prior to James VI's departure for England in 1603.[126] The other recommendation was that prelacy ought to be abolished, since it was 'a great and insupportable greivance and trouble to this Nation, and contrary to the

Inclinationes of the generality of the people'. Again, this looked back to the reforming legislation of 1640, which had abolished episcopacy and revived an act of 1592 in favour of Presbyterian Church government.[127] Burnet thought it 'an absurd thing to put this in a claim of rights; for which not only they had no law, but which was contrary to many laws then in being'. The demand was included here, however, and not in a statement of grievances, where it more properly belonged, as a deliberate strategy to ensure that the new monarchs would be required to abolish the institution of episcopacy. Those who drew up the Claim of Right had concluded that prelacy was 'the occasione of most of ther trouble and disqwiet' and wanted to make 'presbytery a foundation ston of the government'.[128] The Claim of Right concluded by abrogating the existing oath of allegiance and all other oaths and replacing them with an oath to 'be faithfull and bear true allegiance to their Majesties King William and Queen Mary'.

The Convention followed the Claim of Right by agreeing on 13 April to thirteen Articles of Grievances, requesting specific reforms designed to strip the Scottish monarchy of certain legally acknowledged powers that had led to perceived abuses under the Restoration monarchs. The document opened by condemning the Lords of the Articles (the steering committees that had enabled the crown to control legislative initiatives in parliament and which had been reconstituted by an act of 1663), asserting that 'there ought to be no Committees of Parliament but such as are freely chosen by the Estates to prepare motions and overtures that are first made in the house'. The second article stated that the Supremacy Act of 1669 'ought to be abrogated', because it was 'Inconsistent with the Establishment of the Church Government now desyred'. Subsequent articles declared various other laws enacted since the Restoration to be grievances: the act of 1681 'Declareing a Cumulative Jurisdiction' in the crown (which, according to one pamphleteer, had given 'the King the greatest latitude of Arbitrary Power imaginable, and more than is practised in any place of Europe'); the act of 1663 giving the king power to impose customs on foreign trade, which was 'prejudiciall to the trade of the Nation' (and which, as the same pamphleteer pointed out, had enabled the kings of Scotland to 'Supply themselves without being beholden to Their Parliaments'); and 'most of the lawes' enacted by the parliament of 1685, a body which had passed a series of brutal measures against Presbyterians, including the imposition of the death penalty on those who preached at house conventicles or who were merely present at field conventicles, and an Excise Bill, containing a preamble declaring the Scottish monarchy to be absolute. The Grievances further declared that 'the levieing or keeping on foot a standing army in tyme of peace without consent of Parliament' was a grievance – in effect a request for the repeal of the 1661 Militia Act. Various other legally accepted practices came under attack because they had been abused by the crown in the Restoration period. For example, the fifth article stated 'that Assyses of Error' were a grievance, a reference to the fact that under Scottish law jurors could be prosecuted for wrongly acquitting a criminal. The third article reported that 'forefaultors in prejudice of vassalls, Creditors and aires of entaile' were 'a great greivance'. Forfaultures had been resorted to quite frequently by the Crown in the 1680s to deal with those accused of treason, and required the forfeiture of the rebel's estate to the king 'in the same condition that it was Originally given out, without the burden of . . . Debt, or Regard to . . . any Deeds or Alienation made before the Crime'. In the process, a forfaulture hit not only the accused but also many others who had no share in his guilt, such as the traitor's lawful creditors and his innocent vassals. The Grievances also called for further legislation to protect the Protestant succession by asserting that 'the marriage of a King or Queen of this Realme to a Papist' was 'dangerous to the protestant religion and ought to be provyded against'.[129]

Finally, on 18 April the Convention devised a new coronation oath. This required William and Mary to swear to 'maintain the true Religion of Christ Jesus, the preaching of his holy word and the due and right ministratione of the sacraments now receaved and preached within the Realme of Scotland'; abolish 'all false religion, contrary to the same'; rule 'according to the loveable lawes and constitutiones receaved in this realme'; and 'roote out all hereticks and Enemies to the true worship of God that shall be convicted by the true Kirk of God' from Scotland.[130]

Scholars disagree over whether the offer of the crown to William and Mary was made conditional upon their acceptance of the Claim of Right and the Articles of Grievances. After agreeing to the Claim of Right on 11 April, the Convention decided that William and Mary should immediately be proclaimed king and queen of Scotland from the market cross in Edinburgh. The ceremony was performed with due solemnity that afternoon, and that evening there were bells, bonfires and other celebrations in the Scottish capital. Two days later the Convention ordered that William and Mary be proclaimed in all the royal burghs. Nevertheless, the Convention made it explicit, in a separate act declaring that 'the Estates [were] to continue in the Government untill the King and Queen of England accept the throne', that William and Mary were not to be admitted to the full exercise of the regal power until they had accepted the crown 'according to the Instrument of Government' and had taken the coronation oath.[131] It seems clear, then, that the Convention viewed the offer of the crown as conditional at least upon the acceptance of the Claim of Right.

The Grievances were another matter. As one Williamite tract pointed out, since 'their Majesties were . . . proclaimed King and Queen of Scotland before the Grievances were framed . . . they could be no Condition . . . of their Right'; they were merely humbly 'represented to the King . . . to be redressed by him in Parliament'.[132] Yet since William and Mary could not exercise the full regal power until they had taken the coronation oath, we need to look more closely at the circumstances under which they took that oath to see under what conditions they finally accepted the crown. The Scottish Estates sent three commissioners – Argyll (representing the nobility), Montgomery of Skelmorlie (for the knights) and Sir John Dalrymple (for the burghs) – to London to make the offer of the crown to William and Mary and to present William with the Claim of Right, the Articles of Grievances and a request that the Convention be turned into a parliament (so that it could enact the necessary legislation to redress the Grievances). William was formally admitted to the government of Scotland in a ceremony that took place at the Banqueting House on 11 May 1689. His chief Scottish adviser at court, the Earl of Melville, we are told, 'strugled hard to defeat the grivances', proposing that they should not be read until after the King had taken the coronation oath. The commissioners, however, had explicit instructions about the order to be followed. In the end, the Claim of Right, the

Grievances and the request for a parliament were read before the tendering of the coronation oath. William even gave a commitment that he would 'redress all Grievances, and prevent the like for the future by good and wholesome Laws' before he took the oath. The only element of the proceedings to which William took exception was the clause in the coronation oath concerning rooting out heretics, saying that he did not understand himself obliged 'to become a Persecutor'. The commissioners reassured him that the phrase was merely form, and that 'by the Law of Scotland no man was to be persecuted for his private Opinion'.[133]

Following his acceptance of the crown, William established his new Scottish administration. His choice of men reveals his continued desire to pursue a policy of accommodation. He made Melville, a moderate Presbyterian, his Secretary of State for Scotland, and appointed Hamilton, a man who had often emerged as the champion of political and religious freedoms under Charles and James but who had never committed himself to the Presbyterian platform, commissioner to the Scottish parliament. Hamilton's appointment was balanced, to some extent, by that of the Presbyterian Earl of Crawford as president of the parliament, and subsequently also as president of the council. But William's council also included four men – Atholl, the Earl Marischal, and the earls of Erroll and Kintore – who, according to their Presbyterian critics, had not only been 'greivous in the late state' but had also opposed William's interest in the Convention. The key places in the judiciary went to the Dalrymples: Stair was reinstalled as president of the Court of Session, and Sir John became Lord Advocate.[134]

William promised members of the Convention that he would assist them in making laws to secure their 'Religion, Liberties, and Properties' and gave his commissioner detailed instructions concerning what legislation he should agree to in order to redress the Grievances.[135] The Convention was formally turned into a parliament on 5 June, through an act which established that the three estates were to consist of the noblemen, barons and burgesses, thus excluding the bishops.[136] To fulfil the demand laid down in the Claim of Right, parliament abolished prelacy on 22 July 1689.[137] However, William and his Scottish advisers did not feel themselves obliged to meet every demand of the Grievances, insisting that the King had made only a general engagement to redress things that were 'truly grievous to the Nation'. In particular, they did not want the total abolition of the Lords of the Articles, since there was a value to the court in keeping some form of steering committee; they would have preferred to have kept a modified version, making it an elected body rather than a nominated one.[138] With regard to the Church, although William and his advisers accepted that episcopacy would have to be abolished in accordance with the Claim of Right, they hoped to avoid a rigid Presbyterian system and to accommodate as many Episcopalian clergy within the new settlement as were prepared to conform.[139] Parliament, however, remained committed to its agenda, and approved legislation abolishing the Articles and the royal supremacy and restoring those ministers turned out for not complying with prelacy or for taking the Test in 1681. It also voted in favour of an act incapacitating those who had employments under the late government. Hamilton withheld the royal assent and the session was adjourned on 2 August with none of these measures having passed into law.[140]

In order to win parliamentary support for much-needed taxation, William found it necessary to give ground on the Grievances when the Scottish parliament reassembled in the spring of 1690. He appointed Melville as commissioner, giving him specific instructions to agree to the abolition of the Articles and the royal supremacy and the restoring of Presbyterian ministers, and to pass the legislation parliament proposed for settling the government of the Church.[141] On 25 April 1690 parliament abolished the royal supremacy and restored Presbyterian ministers who had been deprived of their livings since 1661, and on 8 May it abolished the Lords of the Articles. On 7 June it established the Confession of Faith of 1643 as 'the summe and substance of the doctrine of the reformed Churches', and restored the Presbyterian system of Church government in accordance with the provisions of an act of 1592, giving the General Assembly of the Church the power to purge ministers who were 'insufficient, negligent, scandalous and erroneous'. On 19 July parliament abolished lay patronages and replaced them with a system of election by heritors and parish elders.[142]

There were certainly limitations to what the Revolution achieved in Scotland. The changes introduced were not as far-reaching as those instituted by the Covenanter revolution of the late 1630s and early 1640s, which had seen not only the overturning of episcopacy but also a radical restructuring of the powers of the monarchy in Scotland (depriving the King of the right to choose his own ministers, to call parliament, or to control the armed forces). The act re-establishing Presbyterianism was silent on the issue of the National Covenant of 1638 and the Solemn League and Covenant of 1643, and parliament made no attempt to undo the Rescissory Act of 1661 (which in turn had undone the reforming legislation in Scotland passed during the mid-century revolution) or the act against the Covenants of 1662. A grand committee of the Convention had tried to insert a proviso in the Claim of Right that the king should not be able to name judges, privy counsellors, or other officers of state without the consent of parliament, but this motion had been rejected 'as an unreasonable Incroachment upon the Monarchy'; only three favoured the proposal, and in the end even they backed down. An attempt to revive legislation of 1641 stating that the king could only appoint officers of state with parliamentary consent also failed, as did efforts to secure freedom of speech and regular meetings of parliament.[143] Nevertheless, it is hard to agree with those who claim that the Revolution was a conservative affair and that the makers of the Revolution settlement had no gripes with the traditional monarchy in Scotland. Mackenzie of Rosehaugh, who had served as Lord Advocate under both Charles II and James VII, bemoaned in May 1689 how 'our just, noble, and antient government' had been 'pull'd to peeces'.[144]

Although the Revolution in Scotland was undoubtedly more Whiggish than its English counterpart, it was possible to interpret what had happened north of the border in various ways. As in England, there was a lively pamphlet debate over how to justify transferring allegiance to William and Mary. Most Scots who supported the Revolution held that James had un-kinged himself, because he had invaded the constitution and violated the laws and liberties of the nation. Some, as we have seen, interpreted the Convention's forfaulture of James as an act of deposition. Yet there was a general reluctance in print to embrace radical contract theory – the view that it was the Scots who had un-kinged James – or to endorse individual rights of resistance; most instead held that resistance was allowable only in cases of extreme necessity. Indeed, some writers even sought to make the Scottish Revolution compatible with the principles of passive obedience and non-resistance, either by insisting that it had been brought about by God's Providence or, more powerfully, by claiming that William had conquered Scotland in a just war and that allegiance was now due to him as *de facto* monarch.[145] The types of argument, in other words, that allowed Tory Anglicans in England to make their peace with the dynastic shift were articulated north of the border. The trouble is, they failed to have the same effect in Scotland, because Episcopalian royalists found it very difficult in practice to accept what was indeed a much more partisan settlement north of the border.

THE BATTLE OVER THE REVOLUTION: JACOBITES, PRESBYTERIANS AND EPISCOPALIANS

The Scottish Revolution settlement, then, introduced sweeping changes in Church and state. Inevitably, it did not go uncontested. The new regime faced a significant Jacobite challenge, which was not to be successfully contained until the spring of 1690. The Duke of Gordon, holed up in Edinburgh Castle and isolated from potential supporters, never posed any real threat and finally surrendered on 13 June 1689.[146] A more serious challenge came from a rebellion launched by Viscount Dundee, who withdrew to the Highlands and declared for King James.[147] In June, James VII issued a proclamation declaring all those assembled in the Scottish parliament rebels and commanding his subjects to join with Dundee, granting warrants to seize the estates, goods and persons of those who resisted and to secure the revenues and excise for their subsistence.[148] James was initially hoping to join with the Jacobite forces in Scotland himself with an army from Ireland, although developments in Ireland were to prevent him from doing this.

The Jacobites believed that 'three partes of four' in Scotland wished for the restoration of their King 'and would heartily concur in it if there were a body of men to cover their riseing', and that the

'King's friends' in Lancashire, Yorkshire and the northern parts of England would join with them.[149] Yet Dundee came nowhere near obtaining the level of support necessary for success. Indeed, it is noticeable that very few of the leaders of the Episcopalian interest in Scotland were prepared to join his enterprise. Powerful magnates in the north, such as Atholl and Tarbat (who were upset because they had failed to receive the recognition they expected under the new regime), were prevailed upon to give Dundee no resistance as he tried to enlist recruits, though their own commitment to his cause is questionable. Tarbat, in fact, managed to obtain an exoneration for the part he had played in the previous administration, and although for a brief period he maintained links with the Jacobites, he quickly and successfully transformed himself into a Revolution Tory. Atholl retired to Bath, allegedly for his health. Mackenzie of Rosehaugh fled to York, fearing that his known 'bigotrie for the royall familie and monarchie' would prompt the new regime to seek retribution against him. Balcarres was kept under close imprisonment in his house, though he swore he had never had anything to do with Dundee since leaving Edinburgh, and he likewise pleaded to be allowed to go to England for his health. Mar died suddenly at his home in Alloa in May.[150] Although several clans from the Highlands joined with Dundee, he managed to gather an army only about 2,000 strong.[151] Meanwhile, loyalists began to mobilize in defence of the Revolution. In the south the Society People raised a volunteer regiment and declared themselves ready to act for the preservation of the Protestant religion and 'the work of reformation in Scotland, in opposition to popery, prelacy, and arbitrary power'.[152] Various nobles and landowners from the Selkirk area, near the English border, petitioned to be allowed 'to put themselves in a postur of defence' so that they could suppress any insurrections at home and oppose any invasion by Catholics from the north of England; the council authorized them to put together a regiment of horse and foot of such men who were willing to enlist themselves. Likewise, the Earl of Monteith received permission to keep his vassals and tenants in arms to protect against the threat posed by persons disaffected to the present government.[153]

The government sent an army under Major-General Mackay to put down the rebellion. Dundee, an experienced military commander of some skill, did win a notable victory over Mackay's forces at Killiecrankie on 27 July 1689; however, Dundee himself fell at the battle, and without his leadership there was never any hope that the small, ill-trained and ill-equipped Jacobite army he had raised could prevail in the long run against Mackay's superior forces. On 21 August the Society People regiment inflicted a telling defeat on the rebel forces at Dunkeld, and although the rebellion dragged on, it was finally put down at Cromdale on 1 May 1690.[154]

It was not just the hard-line Episcopalians and the Highland clans who looked for a Jacobite restoration in 1689–90. A group of radical Presbyterians, known as 'the Club', disappointed at the slow pace of reform and at the frustration of their own political ambitions, began to engage in Jacobite intrigue. They were led by Montgomery of Skelmorlie, one of the commissioners who had been sent to London with the offer of the crown to William and Mary. Described by Burnet as 'a gentleman of good parts, but of a most unbridled heat and a restless ambition',[155] he was undoubtedly a man of genuine political convictions, but he was angry at having been passed over for the job of Secretary of State for Scotland in favour of Melville. He was joined by the Earl of Annandale and Lord Ross, who were likewise resentful for not being given employments under the new regime, the Episcopalian leaders Atholl and Queensberry, and the radical Whig plotter Robert Ferguson.[156] In October 1689 they addressed William, complaining that 'in this Revolution . . . the People did only observe a change of Masters, but no ease of Burden, or redress of Laws'.[157] They conspired with known Jacobites, trying to persuade them to take the oath of allegiance and assume their seats in parliament, so that between them they could put pressure on the new regime. Their tactic was to frustrate the voting of supply and thereby cripple the government financially. A trade depression brought about by the political upheavals had meant that customs and excise had fallen to almost nothing, and Mackay's army was already being forced to live upon free quarter because the administration could not afford to pay it, producing complaints 'from evrie corner' of the country. Denied adequate funds, the Club predicted, the government's unpopularity would increase to the point where the kingdom would declare against it, and then they would be able to 'bring home King James in a

Parliamentary way'. The conspiracy failed, partly because the Club could not persuade enough of the 'King's friends' to re-enter parliament and partly because the need for funds compelled the government to concede to all the demands set forth in the Grievances in the spring and summer of 1690. Most of the radicals deserted Montgomery once the government had agreed to their political agenda.[158] Montgomery fled to London, but continued to engage in Jacobite intrigue, and in late 1691 tried to encourage a rising of Presbyterian extremists in the Scottish south-west. In 1692 he published a pamphlet accusing William of committing all the crimes that James had been accused of and worse, and arguing that if 'we placed the Prince upon the throne' in order 'to preserve our Liberties from the insults of King James', we had 'either mistaken the Disease or the Cure'. Montgomery was to end his days at the exiled Jacobite court at St Germain in 1694.[159]

If the political and military challenge of Jacobitism was successfully suppressed, the battle for the hearts and minds of the Scottish people proved much more difficult to win. Latent disaffection to the new regime was always going to be much greater in Scotland than in England because of the partisan nature of the Scottish Revolution. There were simply too many who had lost out and who could only regret the changes wrought in 1689–90. The greatest problem was with the way the religious settlement came to be worked out in Scotland. Both toleration and comprehension were rejected, and most of the Episcopalian clergy ended up being driven out of their parishes. The result was that there was no easing of tensions between Presbyterians and Episcopalians, but instead an intensification of the religious divide.

The campaign against the Episcopalian clergy was conducted in a series of stages. The first ejections, as we have seen, had been brought about as a result of the 'rabblings' that had started on Christmas Day 1688. On 13 April 1689 the Convention determined that those who were at that time 'in possessione and exercise of their ministrie' and 'behaveing themselves . . . under the present government' should be immune from 'any injury', thus in effect sanctioning the 200–300 deprivations carried out by the rabble. Final confirmation was provided by an act of 7 June 1690, declaring that the rabbled ministers had deserted their livings which had thereby become vacant. Also on

13 April 1689 the Convention decreed that those clergy who were in place should, under pain of deprivation, stop praying for King James and instead offer their prayers for William and Mary and read a proclamation from their pulpit declaring William and Mary king and queen.[160] This was backed up by a council order of 6 August inviting members of congregations to denounce those ministers who did not pray for their new sovereigns. By November 1689 the number of Episcopalian clergy who had been deprived for noncompliance had reached 182.[161]

Some of the deprived Episcopalian ministers undoubtedly harboured Jacobite sympathies. William McKechnie, minister at Bonhill, near Dumbarton, affirmed that 'seing he hade sworne alledgance to King James' he could not 'give obedience to King William's authoritie'. John Lumsdean, minister at Lauder in Berwickshire, not only declined to pray for William and Mary but instead prayed every day that God would give King James 'the necks of his enemies and the hearts of his subjects'. Similarly, James Aird, minister of Torryburn near Dunfermline, refused to read the declaration proclaiming William and Mary king and queen and expressly prayed for King James, saying that he hoped 'the Lord would put a hooke in the nose of that usurper [William], and send him back the way he came, and restore the other to his right'.[162] Some clergy were reported as rejoicing at the Jacobite victory at Killiecrankie: William Murray, minister at Crieff in Perthshire, for example, had his congregation sing the words for Psalm 118, v. 24, 'This is the day God made, in it we'll joy triumphantly'.[163] Alexander Lindsay, minister at Cortachy in Angus, was accused of preaching treasonable and seditious doctrines in his sermons. On one occasion he allegedly said that 'he would never forgive nor forgett' what 'evill the Presbyterian partie hade done in killing their king [i.e., Charles I] and murdering their high preists, and that they could never be the builders of the church that ware the distroyers of it and layers of it wast'. On another he taught that 'the government hade made great wastes and great devastationes in the kingdome makeing new lawes and repelling just ones formerly made', bemoaning the fact that whereas it was once 'accompted religione . . . to preach up obedience to the supreme magistrat', now 'on the contirar actually rebellione was accompted religione and to depose and dethron kings is accompted a dutie'. Lindsay was also accused, it should be said, of being an habitual drunkard, who used to 'sitt up on Saturday nights with baggpypes, drinking and playing till day light'.[164] He was not alone among accused Jacobites of being suspected of moral depravity. Robert Young, minister at Kippen in Stirlingshire, along with not praying for William and Mary was accused of drunkeness, profaning the sabbath, 'useing the airt of magick with his Bible and a key', appropriating the money in the parish poor box for his own use, and threatening violence against anyone who stinted him over the payment of tithes. John Edmonstone, minister at nearby Gargunnock, was cited by his parishioners for praying that God would restore King James, and also for 'being a persone most insufficient for the ministrie', imposed upon them without the consent of anyone in the parish. By all accounts Edmonstone was a most unsavoury individual, another habitual drunkard who was known to urinate and excrete in his breeches; no wonder only a tiny handful of people would bother to go to hear him in church.[165]

A significant number of those Episcopalian clergy who found themselves under attack, however, were Williamites, who would have been happy to acknowledge the legitimacy of the new regime.[166] Some protested that the only reason why they had failed to read the Convention's proclamation requiring them to pray for William and Mary on the day appointed was because they did not receive it in time; others claimed that they did not receive it at all or else that they were forcibly prevented from reading the proclamation, even though they expressed their willingness to pray for William and Mary and submit to the government. Several were able to prove that they had indeed read the proclamation, and as a result were reprieved by the council, suggesting a certain amount of malicious prosecution.[167] James Canaries at Selkirk was accused by some of his parishioners of having prayed for William and Mary but without calling them king and queen, and for continuing to pray for the late King James. The council found the charges against Canaries not proven, and allowed him to continue his ministry. However, it appears that a Presbyterian faction at Selkirk wanted to remove Canaries and install their own man. They thus tried to prevent Canaries taking possession of the manse the parish was building for the resident incumbent, by seizing the keys to deny him access and breaking the windows and doing other damage to the property to ensure that it was uninhabitable.[168]

Further deprivations followed the meeting of the General Assembly of the Church in October 1690. William hoped that Episcopalian ministers who took the oath of allegiance and read the proclamation of William and Mary as king and queen would be allowed to continue in post.[169] The core of the Assembly, however, was made up of some sixty so-called antediluvian ministers who had been deprived since 1661, together with fifty-six ministers they had ordained (there were an additional forty-seven elders), and they proved intransigent. Not only the Church but also the universities were purged of all those who would not take the oath of allegiance, subscribe to the Westminster Confession, accept the new Church government, or who were otherwise thought unfit to exercise the ministry. Although the crown made various efforts between 1692 and 1695 to achieve a more comprehensive settlement, these largely came to nothing. A mere 116 former Episcopalian ministers conformed to the new Church. In the period from 1688 to 1716, a total of 664 ministers out of 926 parishes were ejected, the majority of those ejections occurring in the first couple of years following James's flight in December 1688.[170]

Some deprived clergymen managed to hold on to their livings with the support of their parishioners or local landlords, particularly in the north-east. When the newly appointed Presbyterian minister of Glenorchy in Argyllshire arrived to take over from the ousted Episcopalian David Lindsay, none of his parishioners would talk to him. When the new man tried to give his first service, he found his entry to the church blocked, and twelve armed men escorted him back out of the parish and made him swear on the Bible that he would never return. He kept his oath, and Lindsay survived as minister for Glenorchy until his death thirty years later.[171] William Smyth, Episcopalian minister of Moneydie in Perthshire, despite being deprived in 1693, continued to hold services in his parish or nearby until 1709.[172] Some 113 former Episcopalians were still in the parishes as late as 1710. It was not until 1720 that the Presbyterian Church finally gained possession of all the churches.[173]

The deep tensions that existed between Presbyterians and Episcopalians were reflected in a bitter press campaign of mutual recrimination fought out in the aftermath of the Revolution. Episcopalians protested that they were suffering persecution on a scale similar to that being experienced by the Huguenots in France.[174] One author complained how those very persons who, in the previous reign, had 'Addressed for Liberty of Conscience . . . do now Usurp, Tyrannize over others, and deprive them not only of their freedom in Religious concernments, but of their Possessions', merely for adhering to that holy doctrine that had been established by the laws of the kingdom; in all this, they had 'come near to, if not outdone the merciless fury of French Dragooning'.[175] The Anglo-Irish Protestant Nonjuror Charles Leslie alleged that 'these new modell'd Presbyters, invested with Episcopal Power, in Opposition to Episcopacy, did exercise it with a Tyranny and Lordliness the Bishops had never shewn'.[176] Long accounts were produced detailing the sufferings of the Episcopalian clergy and the alleged atrocities committed against them and their supporters by the Presbyterian rabble.[177] One man, whose only sin was to have married a relation of a bishop, was allegedly 'set upon in his House' and 'dragg'd out into the Ditches, his Books burnt or spoiled, and his poor Wife (at that time in Child-bed) miserably abused'. One Episcopalian minister allegedly had his face daubed with excrement, another even lost his life to an angry crowd. Presbyterian apologists, of course, were quick to deny such reports, alleging that these 'hear-say Violences used to their Clergy' were nothing but 'Hellish Prelatical Lyes'.[178]

Episcopalian apologists challenged the assertion made in the Claim of Right that prelacy had been 'a great and insupportable greivance' and 'contrary to the Inclinations of the generality of the people'. In the first place, they maintained, it was clear that 'the Church Party, both for number and quality was predominant in the Nation'. The greatest part of the nobility and gentry favoured episcopacy, as did most of the people, especially towards the north, while the Presbyterians drew their support mainly from 'the meaner and vulgar sort, and those only in the Western parts of the Kingdom'. As another writer put it, if by 'people' the authors of the Claim of Right meant 'the Commonalty, the rude, illiterate Vulgus, the third Man through the whole Kingdom is not Presbyterian'; if they meant 'Persons of better Quality and Education', whose sense, this author thought,

'ought in all reason, to go for the sense of the Nation', then not one-thirteenth were Presbyterian.[179] They denied that the Episcopalians had been persecutors under Charles II. The penal laws enacted against dissenters after the restitution of episcopacy had been necessary because the Presbyterians advocated resistance and engaged in rebellion against the state. As Tarbat and Mackenzie put it, 'The Severity of our Laws never appeared against Dissenters for having different Opinions from the established Church'; nor was it possible to 'instance any one that suffered either Ecclesiastick or Civil Censure, only upon that account, but for High Treason against the State'.[180] It was not true, another pamphleteer proclaimed, 'that the Presbyterians have suffered any thing for Conscience sake, these twenty seven years by-past': the state had simply made laws for curbing people of 'seditious and ungovernable tempers' and to prevent them 'from breaking out daily into open Rebellion'.[181] In order to substantiate such allegations, in 1692 Alexander Monro produced an abridgement of Alexander Shields' *The Hind Let Loose*, a tract of 1687 detailing both the sufferings and the activities of the radical Presbyterians, and invited his readers to judge for themselves 'whether the Severity of Laws against such Enthusiasts, be not the most Christian compassion towards the State, rather than Cruelty, Tyranny, or Oppression'.[182]

The Episcopalians also denied that they had played any role in the promotion of popery in Scotland. Indeed, they reminded people how they had resisted court designs to establish toleration for Roman Catholics under James VII: 'the Penal Statutes were still kept on foot by that Episcopal Parliament . . . and some of the Bishops too were active in the matter'.[183] Instead, it was the Presbyterians, they claimed, who were guilty of promoting popish principles. Tarbat and Mackenzie wished the Presbyterians would 'renounce that absolute Supremacy or Papacy which the Kirk hath always claimed over Kings, and Civil Powers', and suggested that 'the Papacy of the Scots Presbytery' was inconsistent 'with any Form of Government, except that of Popery, which arrogantly presumes (as they also do) to punish and persecute all Governors in the State at their pleasure, and manage all secular Interests'.[184] William Strachan thought that the Presbyterians were like the Papists in carrying the jurisdiction of the

Church to such a height 'as to encroach upon the Rights of the secular Magistrates, and to subject the State to the Church, not only in Spirituals, but likewise in Temporals'.[185]

Episcopalian apologists also sought to refute allegations that their clergy had ever been negligent or lived an immoral lifestyle. In answer to one Presbyterian pamphleteer, who had alleged that under James VII the Dean of Hamilton had been accused not only of sodomy, but also 'of buggering a Mare' and 'lying with several men's Wives', Strachan pointed out that the dean was never accused of buggery or adultery at all; the charge was of sodomy alone and even that was never proven.[186] Instead, charges of immorality were turned back against their opponents. Gilbert Crockatt and John Munro compiled numerous stories of alleged scandalous behaviour by Presbyterians – most of them, no doubt, no more true than similar accusations levelled against the Episcopalians – in a tract first published in 1692, and which was popular enough to be published in a new edition, with additions, the following year. To prove that Presbyterian ministers promoted impiety, Crockatt and Munro cited the example of one Mr Selkirk who, when preaching at Musselburgh, near Edinburgh, assured his congregation that God saw no sin in his chosen ones: 'be you guilty of Murder, Adultery, Bestiality, or any other gross sin, if you be of the Election of Grace, there is no fear of you, for God sees no sin in his Chosen Covenanted People'. Crockatt and Munro also asserted that the Presbyterians' conventicles 'produced very many Bastards', because they believed that 'Where Sin abounds, the Grace of God superabounds' and that 'To the Pure all things are pure'. To illustrate Presbyterian hypocrisy, he recounted the alleged story of a married Presbyterian woman from near Edinburgh, who although having suffered several fines for not going to church, 'scrupl'd not to commit Adultery with one of the Earl of Marr's Regiment', and then proceeded to bemoan the fact that none of the soldiers was 'Godly', being that they were 'great Covenant-breakers'.[187] These were matters in which Crockatt had a certain amount of expertise; according to the Earl of Crawford, Crockatt had some years previously been forced to give up his position as a regent of St Andrews 'upon misfortun of one or more fornications'.[188]

What, then, was the significance of these anti-Presbyterian diatribes, beyond letting off steam and heaping vitriol upon those who had now taken over the Church establishment and were thus in a position to seek revenge against their former Episcopalian persecutors? The earlier Episcopalian apologias, certainly, were produced with the intent of trying to influence the outcome of the eventual settlement in the Church in Scotland. Tarbat and Mackenzie's *Memorial*, as we have seen, was written before William of Orange was offered even the English crown, and was designed to convince the Prince not to sacrifice the bishops. Those tracts that appeared immediately following the abolition of prelacy might have been intended to try to forestall the establishment of a fully fledged Presbyterian system or to persuade those in power to lend more protection to the suffering Episcopalian clergy. However, it seems that much of this literature was aimed primarily at an English, not a Scottish audience.[189] Within Scotland itself, such propaganda merely served to harden the lines of division, not to mitigate a religiously polarized situation, and might therefore be deemed counterproductive. The main goal, however, was to discredit the Scottish Presbyterians and the Scottish Revolution settlement in the eyes of William and the key policy makers in England. Such propaganda also served to warn the English of a similar threat to their establishment south of the border and that they would be well-advised to try to prevent the official establishment of Presbyterianism in Scotland. Writing in 1690, Thomas Morer observed 'what bitter Reflections' the Scottish Presbyterians were 'daily casting upon [the] Church of England', condemning her clergy 'for deserting the Principles of Passive Obedience and Non-resistance' they used 'to glory so much in', and boasting 'that King William loves Episcopacy as ill in England, as in Scotland, and would be content to have it away . . . if he could get it done'.[190] In a tract published that same year, before the final establishment of Presbyterianism in Scotland, John Sage adopted a three-kingdoms perspective, and pondered whether 'considering that their Solemn League and Covenant obliges them to root out Episcopacy in England and Ireland . . . the Settling Presbytery in Scotland be reconcilable to the Securing Episcopacy in England?'[191] Montgomery of Skelmorlie suggested that the bishops and their clergy were well aware that their credit had sunk so low in Scotland 'by their monstrous unheard of Cruelties and persecutions that it was not possible to prevent their being rooted out by a justly incensed people . . . unless they were able to form a support to themselves in England'. They thus began 'to vilify the Presbyterians', in the hope of making William and the people of England the Presbyterians' enemies.[192] Indeed, the wranglings that occurred in Scotland partly explain why plans for religious comprehension failed in England, 'the rigour' used against the Episcopalians north of the border being a major reason why the English Convocation proved unwilling to compromise with their own nonconformists.[193] As Strachan pointed out in 1694, the 'cruel Treatment which their Brethren in Scotland received from that Dissentient Party' justly alarmed 'the English Clergy to expect the same usage from the Presbyterians' in their own country, and given how much influence the Presbyterians had in the English parliament of 1689, 'it was no ways safe' for the Convocation to 'consent to the Dissolving of the present Act of Uniformity'.[194]

The Presbyterians were quick to respond to this Episcopalian attack, the way being led by the Presbyterian divine Gilbert Rule, himself a sufferer under Restoration episcopacy, who produced two lengthy tracts in vindication of the new Scottish Church establishment. On the numbers issue, Rule simply asserted that Scottish Presbytery was agreeable to the general inclinations of the people, and that he wished the matter could be put to a poll amongst the more sober and religious sort in order to prove it. His qualifications were such, however, as to make it apparent that the Presbyterians themselves were aware that there were large sections of the Scottish population they did not carry with them. 'We do not grudge them [the Episcopalians]', Rule continued, 'a multitude of debauched Persons, who hate Presbytery, as the Curb of their Lusts', and also 'a sort of Men, who had their dependence on the Court, or on the Prelates', as well as 'the Popishly affected, who were but Protestants in Masquerade'. Rule was even prepared to concede that 'there may be found both among the Ministers and People some sober and religious Persons, who are consciously for Prelacy', and that the numbers of these had greatly increased since 1662 because of people having been brought up under episcopacy. Nevertheless, he believed this last group was still a small minority when compared to those who supported Presbyterianism.[195] Rule also refuted the charge that the

Presbyterians were guilty of persecution. The Episcopalians were not 'Persecuted for Worshipping God, as we were by them', he insisted; 'What Possessions have any been deprived of, unless for Crimes against the State?'[196] Indeed, this was the official line. As Crawford, the president of the council, put it in January 1690, 'no Episcopal man, since the late happie revolution' had suffered 'upon the account of his opinion in Church matters' but only 'for their disowning the civil authority, and setting up for a cross interest'.[197] The Presbyterians had suffered much more in the past than the Episcopalians alleged they were suffering now, one pamphleteer protested, for among other things the Presbyterians were subjected to 'Rapes, Rapine, Murder, Hanging, Drowning, Beheading, Famine, torturing with Boots, Thumikins, etc.'[198] As for the argument that Presbyterianism and monarchy were incompatible, this was simply untrue, Rule insisted: the only reason why the Presbyterians had rebelled on two occasions under Charles II was because they had been driven into rebellion by 'the severity of these Laws, and the Barbarity used in executing them'.[199]

The nature of the dialogue reveals the extent to which the Revolution in Scotland centred around issues that were intrinsically Scottish in the making. Both sides might have sought to appeal to the English to win their support, but what was being addressed was what had gone on in Scotland in the three decades since the Restoration. The dialogue also confirms how polarized this political and religious culture had become, and what little prospect there seemed at this stage of easing existing tensions. Both sides accepted that there had been a 'Revolution in Church Matters',[200] with the Presbyterians positively welcoming the changes, and the Episcopalians regretting them. Inevitably, this was to push the Episcopalians more and more firmly into the Jacobite camp.

10

'This Wofull Revolution' in Ireland[1]

> Ne'er with an Englishman in friendship be;
> Should'st thou be so, 'twill be the worse for thee;
> By treachery he'll destroy thee, if he can;
> Such is th'affection of an Englishman.
>
> Traditional Irish verses (translated from Gaelic)[2]

> Is there no manure for the Land of this Kingdom, but English Blood?
>
> Edward Wetenhall, 23 October 1692[3]

There were two revolutions in Ireland following James's 'abdication' of the English throne in the winter of 1688/9. The first was an attempted Catholic revolution, which sought to restore full political, economic and religious control of the kingdom to the Catholic majority and also to make Ireland more independent from England. The other was a Williamite counterrevolution – a revolution, that is, in the sense of putting the clock back to where things had started. The outcome was decided by war, with the crucial turning point coming with the Williamite victory at the Battle of the Boyne on 1 July 1690, although the war dragged on for another year until the final Jacobite surrender at Limerick on 3 October 1691. The struggle in Ireland has been described in various ways. In Gaelic it is known as *Cogadh an Dá Rí* – 'the war of the two kings'. One contemporary Irish Jacobite styled it simply 'the Irish war . . . undertaken to vindicate the king's [James II's] rights against the rebellion of England'. So far as the inhabitants of Ireland were concerned, Irish historians have argued, 'the war was the climax of a long struggle for supremacy between Protestant settlers . . . and an older, Catholic population'.[4] As the account by Charles O'Kelly, a Gaelic Irish landowner who served in James's army, makes clear, the Catholic majority wanted to promote the interests of their religion, but they also wanted their estates back and to free Ireland from English domination.[5] Protestants have tended to emphasize the religious dimensions of the conflict. Shortly before the Battle of the Boyne, *Mercurius Reformatus*, a Williamite newspaper published in London, asserted that 'It is not now a Civil Interest [i.e., who was the rightful king] properly that animates the two Armies in that Kingdom; In effect 'tis become a Religious War between Papist and Protestant, the one striving to preserve, and the other to propogate [sic] their Religion.'[6] For Protestants in Northern Ireland the victory at the Boyne is still celebrated as the day when William of Orange 'overthrew the Pope and Popery'.[7]

A war of two kings, a struggle for supremacy, for independence, a war of religion – no one description does justice to the complexities of the issues that were at stake in Ireland in 1689–91. The war was, in a sense, a combination of all these, but not all the participants in the struggle, even those who were on the same side, saw things the same way. James II, although a Catholic, was not fighting primarily for religion, but for the crowns of his three kingdoms. He did not want independence for Ireland, since his aim was to get back into a position of power whereby he could rule Ireland as an English dependency, and he was concerned about giving too much ground to the Catholic interest in Ireland for fear of further alienating his English and Scottish Protestant subjects. Within Ireland itself, there was not a straightforward split between Catholics and Protestants. The attempted Catholic revolution of 1689 was carried out in the main by the Old English proprietors, those who had lost their lands during the 1640s and 1650s and had not had them restored at the Restoration. The Gaelic Irish benefited little, while the New Catholic proprietors, those who had reacquired land or purchased new estates after the Restoration, felt they could only lose from a revolution that sought to break the Act of Settlement. Moreover, some Protestants sided with James II, either out of a sense of loyalty to their legitimate king or a desire to offer the path of least resistance. Certainly, there is an important sense in which the struggle was over religion, or between rival confessional groupings. Yet there was always much more at stake than religion: there were the questions of economic and political control, of independence versus colonial dependency, of constitutional propriety, and of the international threat posed by an aggressively expansionist France.

Developments in Ireland between 1689 and 1691, however, served to encourage a simplified perception of the nature of the Irish problem, the essence of which came to be seen as lying in the sectarian divide between Catholics and Protestants. Along with this more starkly polarized view came a hardening of attitudes, especially from the Anglo-Protestant side. In this sense, the author of *Mercurius Reformatus* was correct: the struggle did come to be seen as being basically 'between Papist and Protestant', even though, in reality, the Irish problem had always been much more complicated than this.

THE COLLAPSE OF ORDER IN THE WINTER OF 1688/9

It was in Ireland where support for James II remained strongest over the course of 1688. February saw celebrations in several places for the anniversary of the King's accession (6 February) and at the news that the Queen was pregnant (19 February in Dublin, a week later elsewhere).[8] According to a hostile account, the Irish were universally confident that the Queen 'was with Child of a Son', attributing 'their great assurance to the Prayers of their Infallible Church, which were daily offered to God upon this account'.[9] There was widespread rejoicing when the Queen gave birth to a son that summer, and James was reported to have been greatly satisfied with 'the General Joy . . . the whole Kingdome Conceived upon the happy News'.[10] The recently purged corporation of Dublin spent £50 on claret celebrating the Prince's birth, and the official day of thanksgiving on 1 July was marked throughout the city with bonfires, bells and 'all other outward Marks of Inward Joy and Satisfaction'.[11] The mayor of Limerick, it is said, 'made great rejoicings, and let three hogsheads of wine run among the populace'.[12] Overjoyed Catholics celebrated throughout the night, and forced 'the English out of their

Beds' to drink 'Confusion to the King's Enemies upon their Knees'.[13]

Most Protestants were less enthusiastic, naturally, though their protests were muted. A couple of libels 'reflecting much on the King, Queen, and Queen dowager' were posted on the door of Christ Church and the Temple church in Dublin in January 1688 when news arrived that the Queen was with child.[14] There are hints that the celebrations in Dublin for the Prince's birth were not all they might have been: for example, Tyrconnell's appointee as Lord Mayor had the officers of Christ Church committed to the stocks because 'he fancied they did not make the Bells ring merrily enough'.[15] One clergyman, of Scottish descent, who gave 'a smart Sermon . . . on a publick Occasion' in Dublin that autumn (possibly 23 October), earned himself a rebuke from his cautious prelate. The bold cleric replied: 'My Lord, we have a Scotch proverb, He that is afraid of a fart will never stand thunder.'[16] Some Protestants in County Meath tried to commemorate the anniversary of the Irish rebellion on 23 October, though local Catholics managed to put out their bonfires.[17]

James felt sufficiently secure about his position in Ireland to order Tyrconnell, at the end of September, to send over one battalion of the regiment of guards, two regiments of infantry and one regiment of dragoons – a total of 2,820 men – to help deal with William of Orange's intended invasion of England.[18] The Catholic majority in Ireland remained firmly behind James in the face of William's threat, holding a number of fast days to beseech God for the King's success against his enemies. According to one Dublin Protestant, one of 'the ceremonies they used at the Mass Houses' involved the formal cursing of William's effigy, which they then cut into pieces, cursing and spitting on every bit, before finally burning it.[19] The town of Galway staged a public anti-Williamite demonstration at the beginning of December. A local Protestant had for a number of years kept a statue outside his front door that he had rescued from the stern of an old Dutch ship that had broken up in the harbour, and which had come to be known as the sign of the Prince of Orange. Now a group led by one of the town's sheriffs seized the statue, 'and burnt part of it in one, and part in another of the most publick places of the Town, drinking several times Confusion and Damnation to the Prince of Orange'. Several leading members of the corporation and many local gentry turned up to witness the affair, as did the deputy town sovereign of nearby Tuam, a man by the name of Connor, who proposed to cut off all his hair and burn it 'because it was an Orange Colour'. (His son managed to dissuade him from this drastic course of action.) There was a tar barrel in one of the bonfires, which spilled some of its contents onto the burning statue; when Connor saw this, he 'drew out his Sword, and ran at it, crying, See, I have killed the Son of a Whore, his Heart's Blood runs out of him'.[20]

With well over one-third of his army in England, Tyrconnell set about recruiting and training replacements. Within a short period of time it was reported that he had 9,000 foot and 3,000 horse.[21] Following James's flight in December and subsequent 'abdication' from the English throne, Tyrconnell accelerated the build-up of troops, so that by early February 1689 he had raised an army approaching 45,000 men, made up overwhelmingly of Catholics.[22] Catholic civilians were also encouraged to arm themselves, to protect the country against the Protestants should the army be called away to an engagement elsewhere – these became known as rapparies, or half-pike men, after the weapons they carried. Several reports confirm that the Catholic priests forbade their parishioners from coming to mass unless 'furnished with a Skene of 16 Inches long in the Blade, and a large Half-pike'. By early January it was said that all the Irish were armed, 'not a Cowboy without his Bayonnet, or some such weapon'.[23]

According to Protestant sources, Catholic priests began telling their flock that Tyrconnell would 'free them from the Slavery of their Conquerors', and render Ireland 'free and independent'.[24] Certainly letters began to circulate alleging that the papists were plotting another massacre, along the lines of 1641. One such, dated London, 14 November 1688 (though postmarked Dublin), and purportedly written by one 'Rory McFlynn' to the deputy recorder of Kilkenny, claimed that the Catholics had beaten the 'fanatical army' in England, and would 'ere long cut the throats of all [the] fanatical crew' in Ireland.[25] Another, dated 3 December and addressed to the Earl of Mount-Alexander, warned that 'all Irishmen . . . through Ireland' had sworn that on Sunday 9 December they would fall on all the Protestants and 'murder Man, Wife, and Child', sparing none.

Tyrconnell hastily issued a proclamation promising the Protestants protection and making it an offence to spread false alarms, and urged the Protestant clergy to reassure their parishioners that they would be secured against any acts of violence. This did little to allay anxieties, however.[26] The Mount-Alexander letter reached Dublin on Friday the 7th, and the following day thousands of people abandoned their homes and made their way to the ships in the harbour, 'with Scarce any Cloaths upon their Backs', in the hope of getting out of the country before the atrocity was committed. In several parts of the kingdom the news of the intended massacre arrived on Sunday the 9th, while people were at church, provoking predictable panic: we have reports of people rushing out of church and being trampled under foot, or else jumping out of windows as they scrambled to escape. When a newly raised and not yet properly uniformed Catholic regiment under the command of the Earl of Antrim arrived at Derry on the 7th, to relieve Viscount Mountjoy's largely Protestant regiment, which had been recalled to Dublin, the inhabitants naturally feared the worst. While the civic leaders, reluctant to defy the authority of their king, contemplated what course of action to take, thirteen apprentices took it upon themselves to shut the gates to the troops, draw up the bridge, and seize the magazine. The Protestants of nearby Enniskillen did likewise on the 16th, refusing to admit two companies of foot soldiers.[27]

Many Protestants decided to flee Ireland in the winter months of 1688/9, making their way in vast numbers to Lancashire, Cheshire, Bristol, north and south Wales, Devon and the Isle of Man. Others headed for the Protestant strongholds of the north, particularly Enniskillen and Derry.[28] Those who stayed put found themselves at the mercy of their Catholic neighbours or the Catholic troops. Although the accounts we have need to be treated with caution, there undoubtedly was a serious problem of discipline with the newly raised troops. Tyrconnell did not have the resources to pay for such large numbers of men, despite seizing the rents of Protestant landowners and Trinity College; he expected the officers, in return for their commissions, to subsist the men for the first few months, but their meagre resources soon became exhausted and the army was forced to live at free quarter and from what it could get from the countryside.[29] From a number of towns, including Dublin, Limerick, Galway, Drogheda, Birr and Athlone, came 'heavy Complaints' that the soldiers took 'the very Meat out of the poor Protestants Mouths'. In the countryside the troops seized cattle or grain for their subsistence, and robbed and pillaged the houses of Protestants.[30] On 2 February Tyrconnell issued a proclamation denouncing such depredations, but in reality there was little he could do.[31] Those fleeing Ireland brought news of 'frequent Robberies and Murders' that were 'daily perpetrated in every part of the Country'. Reports from early February claimed that, in the County of Cork alone, 'above 10,000 head of Cattel' had been taken from the Protestants.[32] A few weeks later, one Dublin correspondent reported how 3,000 cows were stolen in Kerry and 'above 4,000 sheep in less than 30 miles circumference in some sheep counties';[33] by the third week of April, we are told, 'not one Englishman in the County of Kerry' had 'the value of one sixpence left'.[34] The Comte d'Avaux, the French ambassador to the Jacobite court in Ireland, estimated that in total some 50,000 cattle and 300,000 sheep were slaughtered over the course of just six weeks.[35]

There may have been a ritualistic element to the attacks on Protestant cattle. One pamphleteer alleged that the Irish 'would not kill a Beef, or a Mutton, before they had called a formal Jury on him, and tried him for Heresie'. In Headford, County Galway, for example, the soldiers who had seized the choice sheep belonging to a local Protestant appointed a judge and jury, and put the sheep, one by one, in the pulpit of the parish church where they were garrisoned, tugging at each poor animal until it started to bleat, whereupon they would cry 'down with the Rogue, he preaches heretical Doctrine'. If the soldiers found 'any small Irish Cattel, that had no Brand' rounded up by mistake, they immediately dismissed them, and indicted and fined those who brought them. But branded beasts, which 'belonged to them that followed the English way of Husbandry' were 'condemned for Hereticks, and immediately slaughtered'.[36]

If the Protestant farmers put up any resistance, reports in the London press claimed, the soldiers simply killed them.[37] Catholic civilians also took advantage of the general breakdown of law and order to join in the attack on Protestants and settle some old scores;

it was even alleged that Catholic priests actively encouraged their parishioners 'to plunder the Protestants'.[38] Accounts from Protestant sources perhaps need to be treated with a degree of scepticism. Nevertheless, the poetry of the Gaelic literatus David Ó Bruadair began to take on a stridently militant tone: 'My friends, we should never forget to thank God in the choir of our Church / That we see their sadness increase since their [the Protestants'] turn to suffer arrived', he wrote on 26 February 1689, adding: 'It is no honest kindness for us to be soft with old fleecers like them . . . / To have suffered such people to live hath brought nought but a nettle-crop forth'.[39] Protestants fleeing Ulster for the Isle of Man in mid-May told how, towards the beginning of that month, the Irish had massacred some 500 Protestants in County Down, sparing neither man, woman nor child. A ship's captain, who had visited the Isle of Man, claimed he 'saw severall Protestants . . . whose noses were cut by the Irish', three of whom had since died, and that he had heard 'that severall weomen's breasts were cut off by the Irish' and that a heavily pregnant English woman had been gang-raped by seven Irish dragoons.[40]

Protestants throughout Ireland naturally tended to look to William of Orange for assistance, especially given that his *Declaration of Reasons* of September 1688 had affirmed his intention to secure 'the Protestant and British Interest there'.[41] Towards the end of November, the nonconformist ministers and gentlemen of note in the Province of Ulster decided to send a delegate to the Prince to represent 'the Dangers and Fears of the Protestants in Ireland' and urge him 'to take some speedy and effectual Care for their preservation and relief'.[42] An address in the name of the Presbyterians of Ireland eventually reached William on 26 December, promising that 'all the Presbyterians in Ireland were at his Highness's service . . . for the perfecting the ends of his Declaration'.[43] In the meantime, the Protestants who stayed in Ireland began to arm in self-defence. Derry and Enniskillen in the north, as we have seen, had been the first to take a stance against Tyrconnell, refusing admission to his troops in December. In early January, Protestants from all the northern counties, numbering over 60,000 men, formed themselves into an armed association to defend their religion, 'Ancient Government' (which they saw 'as depending upon England') and 'Laws and Liberties', against the illegal actions of Tyrconnell and the Catholics; they promised they would protect the Catholics as well, but insisted that only those 'Qualified by the Laws of the Land' should be allowed to bear arms.[44] Within each county there were local centres of resistance. At Hillsborough, County Down, in eastern Ulster, the effort was headed by the Earl of Mount-Alexander; in County Antrim, in the north-east, by Lord Massereene. In the north-west, the Protestants of County Sligo issued a declaration stating they were resolved 'to adhere to the Laws of the Land, and the Protestant Religion', and that they would unite themselves 'with England, and hold to the Government thereof, and a Free Parliament'.[45] Most of this activity was explicitly Williamite. The castle at Ballyshannon in County Donegal declared 'for the Prince of Orange, and Protestant Religion'.[46] When news reached Derry and Enniskillen that the English Convention had voted that King James had abdicated and placed William and Mary on the vacant throne, both places held ceremonies to proclaim the new monarchs, which they conducted 'with such Joy and Solemnity' as their circumstances would allow.[47]

Protestants in the south also began to organize in self-defence. In the second week of December 1688, the Protestants of the town of Bandon, in County Cork, ejected the Catholic dragoons and then shut the town gates.[48] Early in the new year, the Protestant nobility and gentry of the province of Munster issued a declaration justifying their actions. Pointing to the violations to 'Laws of this Kingdom' since James's accession, to the 'almost Subversion of the Protestant Religion' and the 'Thefts and Outrages . . . committed by the Popish Forces of this Kingdom' against Protestants, and how they had been threatened with 'the loss of our Religion, Laws, Lives, Liberties and Properties', they had 'unanimously Resolved', they explained, to repel 'Force with Force', and 'stand by each other in the Suppression of all that shall molest us . . . in our Religion, Laws, Lives, Liberties and Properties'.[49] Towards the end of January, the 180 Protestants of Killmare (now Kenmare), in County Kerry, withdrew to a makeshift garrison at Killowen, an island on the Kenmare River, and declared they had decided to associate in defence of their 'Lives and Religion . . . against the Enemies of the Protestant Church' until they were received into the 'Command of His Highness the Prince of Orange'.[50]

There was also a powerful lobby in London representing Protestant interests in Ireland, comprising both long-time absentee landowners and those who had fled in the face of recent developments. On 21 December, a large contingent of nobility and gentry with 'Estates and Effects in Ireland' addressed the Prince about 'the great danger' facing the Protestants, and imploring his relief.[51] Similar addresses followed at the end of the month and early in the new year, while towards the end of April the Protestant bishops of Ireland petitioned the Lords 'laying open their afflicted condition'.[52]

However, the fate of Ireland was of concern not just to those Protestants with an interest in that kingdom; it was seen as a British concern, in which the Scots and English also had a stake. In the second week of January, the Scottish nobility, worried about the plight of their fellow countrymen in Ulster, drew up an address to William asking him to send forces to Ireland to reduce it 'to the Government of England'.[53] Indeed, at the beginning of February the Scottish council decided to send a considerable supply of muskets and powder from the magazine in Stirling Castle to the Protestants in Derry for their defence.[54] There was pressure from the English as well, and especially those with more Whiggish sympathies, for William to take action on behalf of the Protestant interest in Ireland. Thus on 26 December, the provisional government in London addressed the Prince, pledging their support for his efforts to deliver them 'from the miseries of Popery and slavery' and desiring him 'to take speciall care of Ireland'.[55] In the Commons on 29 January, the Whig lawyers Pollexfen, Maynard, Treby and Somers objected to holding the debate over what conditions should be attached to the offer of the English crown to William and Mary because this 'would necessarily take up much time, whereby Ireland might be destroyed'.[56] The petition presented to the Lords on 2 February from the citizens and inhabitants of London and Westminster, urging that William and Mary might be 'speedily Settled in the Throne', also pleaded 'that Ireland, now in a Bleeding and Deplorable Condition, may be rescued from its Miseries'.[57] For William, too, preserving 'the Protestant religion and the English Interest' in Ireland remained a high priority, as he made clear to both the provisional government in London in late December and again to the Convention Parliament when it convened on 22 January.[58]

However, William was in no position to take speedy military action; that would have to wait until his position within England had been settled and parliament had voted a supply to the army. Tyrconnell himself seemed in two minds: should he try to hold out until James could arrive from France with military reinforcements, or would it be wiser to try to broker a deal with William now, while he still had the chance? William made an attempt to open negotiations with Tyrconnell, sending Richard Hamilton, an Irish Catholic officer in the English army who had been arrested at the time of the Revolution, with an offer of terms. For his part, Tyrconnell dispatched Viscount Mountjoy to France to seek James's permission to treat with William, explaining that he could ruin the kingdom, if that was what his majesty wanted, 'and make it a heap of rubbish', but that 'it was impossible to preserve it and make it of use'. However, this appears to have been a ploy to get Mountjoy out of the country – Tyrconnell also sent Chief Baron Rice to Paris with the secret message that Mountjoy was a traitor and that otherwise Ireland remained loyal to James and would rise on his behalf.[59] Indeed, Tyrconnell was soon making it clear that he would not capitulate. Towards the end of the third week of January, he publicly declared that 'he would raise and arm all the Irish from 16 to 60' if the English invaded, and let them loose upon the Protestants. Many panic-stricken Dubliners hastily took boat for England; at Holyhead, the newly arrived refugees claimed they 'had Certaine advice that all the Papists were ready to Execute their Barbarous designe' whenever they got 'the word of Command'.[60] On 25 January, Tyrconnell issued a proclamation against armed associations, ordering all those so assembled to disperse under pain of treason; a month later he ordered all Protestants in Dublin immediately to hand over their arms and ammunition and called in all serviceable horses (those who refused, he said, 'must run the risk of the ill-consequences which may fall upon them by the disorders of the soldiers'), and on 1 March, he issued orders for the seizure of arms and horses throughout the country.[61] The centres of resistance at Bandon and Killmare caved in; isolated, and with no prospect of immediate relief from William, the Protestants decided to surrender and make the best terms they could with the Catholic forces sent to suppress them.[62] Only the north remained in open defiance to the Jacobite regime. On 22 February, William and Mary, recently designated king and queen of England and Ireland by the English Convention, issued a declaration offering a full indemnity to those in Ireland who laid down their arms and promising Roman Catholics the freedom to exercise their religion in private, but stipulating that those who continued in arms would be deemed traitors.[63] On 7 March Tyrconnell responded with a declaration against the treasonous armed associations in Ulster and Sligo, and sent Richard Hamilton with a force of some 2,500 men to reduce the rebels.[64] It was, in effect, a declaration of war.

THE ATTEMPTED CATHOLIC
REVOLUTION OF 1689

James's supporters in Ireland awaited his arrival with eager anticipation. After several false reports of his landing, prompting bells and bonfires in Dublin and elsewhere,[65] James finally reached Ireland on 12 March, landing at Kinsale, where he was received, we are told, 'with all the demonstrations of Joy imaginable'.[66] James was the first king of England to visit Ireland since Richard II in 1399 – though he did so, of course, only after having lost his English crown. (Ironically, 1399 was also the year that Richard was forced to abdicate the English throne, likewise following a foreign invasion in the face of which he had surrendered without a fight.) From Kinsale James made a slow progress to the Irish capital. 'All along the road', one Irish account states, 'all degrees of people', of both sexes, old and young, came to meet him 'with staunch loyalty, profound respect, and tender love . . . as if he had been an angel from heaven', so that the hundred miles from Kinsale to Dublin were 'like a great fair'.[67] When James arrived at Cork on the 15th, he was greeted by 'the Irish' – after 'their rude and barbarous manner', our Protestant source editorializes – with 'Bagpipes, Dancing, throwing their Mantles under his Horses Feet, making a Garland of a Cabbage Stump, and such like Expressions of Joy'.[68] At Kilkenny, on 22 March, he was presented with an address by one Dr Murphy, the titular Bishop of Ossory, pledging the commitment of 'all Irish heads' for restoring James II to his 'own throne'. Revealingly, the Irish thought of James as king of England, though an English king to whom they professed a particular attachment because he was descended, through his Scottish heritage, from the original line of Irish kings. 'Never was a King of England so kind to this country', the address read; 'never was this country so kind to a British prince'. Whereas 'the other English monarchs' had commanded 'the bare duty of our allegiance . . . our endeavours for your Majesty's interest', Murphy assured James, 'are the effect of a national inclination and the work of a sympathy of blood'.[69] The most magnificent reception was reserved for Dublin, which James reached on the 24th, Palm Sunday. James rode through the town on horseback to the 'lowd and joyfull acclamations' of people 'of all ranks' shouting 'God save the King': the magistrates, nobility, gentry and judges were out in numbers; soldiers lined the streets; tapestries decorated adjacent buildings; there were pageants on specially erected stages; friars sang; 'Oysterwenches, Poultry- and Herb-women', dressed in white, danced and strewed the streets with flowers; pipers played 'The King enjoys his own again'; and the local inhabitants drank toasts with wine paid for out of the town coffers. 'A mad Scots man' apparently 'rushed through the crowd' and flung a hat on James's head, crying out in French, 'Let the King live for ever'.[70]

There were reasons why the Catholic people of Ireland might have thought twice about taking up the cause of restoring their banished king. One retrospective Irish Jacobite account conceded that 'the sad remembrance' of how they 'had been oppressed' by Charles II should have made 'the Irish Catholick nobility' rejoice 'at the misfortune of an ensuing King of England, especially of the immediate successor and brother of their oppressor; which brother at the time of their oppression behaved himself not much better', having 'received into his possession the estates of several Irish Catholicks'. But Catholics, this author continued, regarded loyalty to the 'lawful sovereign' as a religious duty. It was 'the pretended reformed people of England' who were 'prone to rebellion', having dethroned three kings one after another (Charles I in 1649, Charles II on the death of his father, and James II in 1689). It was therefore in the King's interest, the author went on, to make 'Ireland a powerful nation, in order to be a check upon the people of England', and in the process he spelled out what

the Irish Catholics hoped to achieve in return for their loyalty: the
restoration of 'their ancient estates'; an independent Irish Parliament
capable of enacting laws without English approval; judicial independence, so that causes could be determined 'without an appeal to
the tribunals of England'; a 'full liberty' for merchants to export and
import 'without an obligation of touching at any harbour in
England'; Catholic self-governance, meaning 'the principal posts of
state and war' should be conferred 'on the Catholick natives', and
that there should be a Catholic standing army and militia; and the
re-establishment of the Roman Catholic Church in Ireland.[71]

It would be wrong to convey the impression that James had no
Protestant support. Many Protestants, particularly those of the
Established Church, had qualms about renouncing their allegiance to
their legitimate king, even though they had no sympathy for
Tyrconnell's agenda. One anonymous correspondent sent a letter to
Clarendon on 20 November 1688, begging the former Lord
Lieutenant (who was himself to become a Jacobite) to help 'save a
kingdom', in which he stated that there were 'thousands that have
never bowed the knee to Romish Baal, yet who know how to be loyal
to the King'.[72] Although the climate had certainly changed by the
following March, and many Protestants had either fled, been brutal-
ized out of their allegiance, or come to accept the English Convention's judgment that James had abdicated and that William and
Mary were now their lawful sovereigns, there were still some
Protestants in Ireland who welcomed James's arrival, believing that
his presence would help restore law and order. The managers of the
Boyle estate in Munster, for example, provided money for beer and a
bonfire so that the tenants could celebrate James's arrival at Kinsale.[73]
One Protestant broadsheet stated that the late King's arrival in Dublin
on 24 March 'gave us some hopes it would abate the Cruelty of the
inraged Tyr[connel]l';[74] indeed, James did issue a proclamation the
following day forbidding plundering and offering his protection to all
his subjects.[75] Shortly after James's arrival in Dublin, Bishop Dopping
of Meath and the Dublin clergy waited upon James at Dublin Castle
and promised they would 'continue loyal as church principles
oblige'.[76] Quite a few Protestants of the Established Church were to
fight with James against William III; indeed, according to one member

of William's army in Ireland, 5,000 of the 7,000 horse that were to fight with James at the Battle of the Boyne were English Protestants![77] Some of the nonconformists who had benefited from Tyrconnell's assault on the corporations, and most particularly the Quakers, allied themselves with James.[78]

At the same time, the evidence of widespread Catholic support for James should not lead us to assume that the Catholics were in total agreement. Although keen to restore him to the throne because he was a zealous supporter of the Catholic religion, they were all too aware, O'Kelly tells us, that he had showed himself 'as little disposed as his brother . . . to assert the hereditary rights of the natives, or restore their estates'.[79] Many Irish Catholics may have identified more strongly with Tyrconnell, at least at this juncture, since he was known to be eager to challenge the land settlement; indeed, there was some speculation in January among Protestants in Britain that Tyrconnell, who was said to be descended from the old kings of Ireland, might usurp the throne for himself.[80] On the other hand, those Catholics who had either managed to hold on to their estates or else had purchased new ones since the Restoration were reluctant to risk what they had in a war. Their chief spokesman, the Earl of Limerick, had tried to persuade Tyrconnell to come to terms with William before James arrived in Ireland, advising him that 'they had more than they were willing to lose upon this occasion', and thought 'it was not equal to venture the loss of good Estates on the same bottom with those who had none, and who would do anything to get one'.[81] Limerick and the Catholic New Interest did in the end fight for James, though they were to be the first to look for a compromise settlement when things started going against them. James had an incentive to try to build bridges between the Catholic and Protestant populations of Ireland, not least because his aim was to re-establish himself as king in all three of the British kingdoms. There were others close to the King, however, who advised him to throw in his lot totally with the Catholics. In a much publicized coffee-house conversation, Lord Brittas, an Irish noble who had arrived with James from France, allegedly told a local Protestant minister that James could not trust his Protestant subjects, and that it was James's design 'to regain his Thrones by down right force of the Arms of his Catholick Subjects, and by assistance from France', so that coming in as 'an absolute Conqueror', he would 'be free from those Fetters and Chains Wherewith his rebellious Protestants would bind him', and might 'do what he please'.[82]

The tensions that existed within the Jacobite interest in Ireland became evident during the meeting of the Irish parliament, which James summoned to assemble at Dublin on 7 May 1689. With the corporations now dominated by Catholics and the sheriffs hand-picked by Tyrconnell, James and his Lord Deputy were well placed to secure the return of the type of parliament they wanted. Tyrconnell sent out letters with the election writs recommending his choice of candidates; it was also said that the sheriffs were instructed to alert Catholic, but not Protestant freeholders about the election. Not that the Protestants, particularly those in the north, were keen to partici-pate and, by implication, recognize James's right to summon a parlia-ment in Ireland, after the English Convention had conferred the Irish crown on William and Mary. The counties of Donegal, Fermanagh and Londonderry, and a number of boroughs, mainly in Ulster, refused to make returns. The result was a depleted House of Commons, seventy short of its full quota, and one that was over-whelmingly Catholic, there being only six Protestants returned. To judge by the surnames, however, over two-thirds were of Old English stock; the Gaelic Irish were firmly in the minority. The House of Lords should have been a predominantly Protestant body. Yet of the sixty-nine temporal peers who had the right to sit in the upper house, only a handful remained in Ireland, while James set about creating new titles and reversing outlawries in order to boost the Catholic presence. Although Protestant writers criticized James for such practices, it should be pointed out that the Scots allowed forfaulted peers to take their seats in the Scottish Convention of 1689, before their forfault-ures had been overturned. Contemporary accounts disagree over how many sat in the House of Lords. One lists forty-one lay peers as being present on 7 May, but this certainly includes some who were absen-tees and others who left shortly after the opening session; other accounts put the figure at between thirty and thirty-two, which prob-ably reflects the number of those lay peers who were in continual attendance. Of these, only five were Protestants (though it is possible that two or three other Protestant peers might have attended briefly); the rest were Catholic, but again mostly of Old English stock, there being only a few Gaelic Irish peers. Significantly, James insisted that the spiritual peers should be the bishops of the Established Church, not the titular bishops of the Catholic Church. There were only seven left in the kingdom, and three of these had to be excused on the grounds of age or sickness, but four – the bishops of Cork, Limerick, Meath and Ossory – did take their seats.[83]

We might wonder why James chose to call a parliament at this juncture. Would it not have been better to have concentrated on reducing Ulster, rather than get distracted by lengthy parliamentary proceedings? The answer, however, seems straightforward. James had been dethroned in England and Scotland for allegedly promoting popery and arbitrary government; he could not be seen to be doing the same thing in Ireland. This is why James issued a proclamation for the calling of parliament the day after he arrived in Dublin: any initiatives he took in Ireland, even if it was only raising revenues to fight the war, had to be seen to be sanctioned by parliament, and not based solely on royal authority. Hence also why James was careful not to represent himself as promoting the interests of Catholics; instead, he repeatedly emphasized that he was in favour of religious toleration. On the day after his arrival in Dublin he issued another proclamation declaring that henceforth all subjects of his kingdom of Ireland should 'enjoy the free exercise of their religion'.[84] In his opening speech to parliament on 7 May, James again made liberty of conscience his central theme. 'I have always been for Liberty of Conscience', he insisted; 'It was this Liberty of Conscience I gave, which my Enemies both Abroad and at Home dreaded; especially when they saw that I was resolved to have it Established by Law in all my Dominions, and made them set themselves up against me.' He further stressed that he was 'against invading any Man's Property', and promised he would consent to 'such Good and Wholesome Laws as may be for the general Good of the Nation, the Improvement of Trade and the relieving of such as have been injured by the late Acts of Settlement'.[85] On 18 May 1689, James issued a declaration from his court at Dublin in which he pointed out that, since arriving in Ireland, he had made it his 'chiefe concerne to satisfy the minds of our Protestant Subjects, that the defence of their Religion, priviledges and properties, is equally our care with the recovery of our rights'.[86]

The first measure passed by the Dublin parliament was an act recognizing James's 'Just and Most Undoubted Rights' to his 'Imperial Crown', which offered a forthright condemnation of the Glorious Revolution in England. Thus the act began by complaining how James's treasonous subjects in England had 'first forced [him] to withdraw' from Whitehall – no voluntary desertion here then, even with regard to James's first abortive flight – and then placed him 'under a guard of Forreigners' when he had been brought back to London, 'compelling' him 'to go to Rochester', where he 'remained in Restraint' until, through the mercy of God, he was able to escape to France. The 'execrable' usurpation by William of Orange, equalled (as it was) only by 'the barbarous Murder' of Charles I, the act continued, was 'against the Law of God, Nature and Nations'; indeed, most of those who were guilty of helping to bring it about had 'sworn that it was not lawful to take up Arms against [James II] on any pretence whatsoever'. The act then proceeded to rehearse the classic theories of indefeasible hereditary right and divinely ordained, irresistible monarchy. James had succeeded his brother, Charles II, 'by Inherent Birth Right, and Lawful and Undoubted Succession', and James's 'Right' to his 'Imperial Crown' was 'originally by Nature, and descent of Blood, from God alone, by Whom Kings Raign, and not from [his] People, nor by virtue or pretext of any Contract made with them'. Neither the peers, the commons, parliament nor the people had 'any Coercive Power over the Persons of the Kings of this Realm' and subjects' allegiance to the king was 'Indissoluble' and could not 'be renounced by us, or our Posterities'; moreover, this allegiance was due, the act continued, to the king's 'natural Person, from which the Royal Power cannot be separated' – thereby explicitly denouncing the theory (articulated in England at the time of the Revolution) that James II, through his actions, might somehow have unkinged himself. The act of recognition further stressed that the command of all military forces was vested in the king alone, and neither parliament nor the people might 'lawfully . . . raise or levy any War Offensive or Defensive' against the King, his heirs and lawful successors. In short, it was

Utterly unlawful for your Majestie's Subjects of this, or any of your Kingdoms, on any pretence whatsoever, actually to resist your Majesty, or our Lawful, Hereditary King for the time being, by Violence, or Force of Arms; or to withdraw their Allegiance from your Majesty, your Heirs and Lawful Successors; but that the Decision in all Cases of a misused Authority by our Lawful, Hereditary King (if any such should happen) must be left to the sole Judgment of God, the King of Kings, and only Ruler of Princes.

The ideology of royalism offered here was entirely conventional; one might even say it was rather moderate by later Stuart standards, since it did not embrace the language of royal absolutism which figured so prominently in Tory defences of monarchical government during the reign of Charles II. Its rearticulation here points to the radicalism of the act of overthrowing James II in both England and Scotland; no wonder the act accused 'these late Traytors' of having acted upon 'desperate Antimonarchic Principles'.[87]

The legislative programme enacted by the Dublin parliament ended up going much further than James would have liked, while at the same time falling short of what many Irish Catholics hoped for. A generous measure for liberty of conscience was passed. This began by remarking that 'persecuting People upon the account of Religion', far from helping 'advance Christian Faith, or Piety', in fact merely occasioned 'animosities and divisions between his Majestie's Subjects, and discouraged strangers from living amongst them to the great hinderance of Trade, Peace and [the] Welfare of this Kingdom'. It therefore stipulated 'that all and every person and persons whatsoever professing Christianity' should have 'Liberty of Conscience, and full and free Exercise of their respective Religions, Ways and forms of Worship' and should be free to meet and assemble together, with their respective ministers and teachers 'in such Churches, Chapels, private houses, or other places, as they shall have for that purpose', provided that 'nothing be taught, preach'd, or done contrary to their Allegiance, or contrary to his Majestie's peace', and that all such meetings and assemblies 'be always in some open or publick place . . . unto which all persons may have open, free, and uninterrupted access, or passage'. The act also repealed the oath of supremacy and the Jacobean oath of allegiance and all other laws that were inconsistent with liberty of conscience.[88] The Act of Uniformity, however, was left on the statute book: James's intention, as with his agenda in Scotland and England, was to remove the disabilities of the penal laws without undermining the Protestant establishment. Catholics would have liked a full restoration of their Church to the position it was in before the Reformation. The Catholic bishops and clergy, who held a general meeting in Dublin at the time of the parliament, presented the King with an address asking for the repeal of all the penal laws, and particularly the Act of Uniformity, and requesting that the Catholic clergy 'be restored to their Livings, Churches, and full exercise of their Ecclesiasticall Jurisdiction'.[89] The Commons did in fact draft a more radical bill for liberty of conscience, which would have taken away 'the King's Supremacie in Ecclesiasticks' and abrogated 'all Penal Laws against Papists'; lawyers said it would have settled 'Popery as legally as it was in H. 7th's time'. James objected, however, not only because he knew it would further alienate his Protestant subjects in Scotland and England, but also because 'it diminisht his Prerogative' by taking away his position as head of the Church. He insisted he did not wish to destroy the Protestant establishment, but only 'take away the Penalties that were against Liberty'.[90] Nevertheless, the Irish parliament did pass an act stating that in future Catholics should not have to pay tithes to Protestant ministers; the monies should be vested instead in their own clergy.[91]

The most controversial issue in the parliament of 1689 was the land settlement. Most Catholics wanted the Acts of Settlement and Explanation repealed. Lord Chancellor Fitton declared the acts 'Diabolicall and as hatched in Hell', and it was moved that they should be 'burnt by the hands of the Hangman'. The Protestant lords and bishops opposed repeal, as did several Catholics who had purchased land since the Restoration.[92] Lord Chief Justice Keating, one of the remaining Protestant judges, petitioned the King on behalf of the purchasers under the Act of Settlement, arguing that the proposed repeal would ruin 'all the Protestants in the Kingdom', dispossess 'the thriving Catholicks who were Purchasers', destroy 'Trade and Commerce', and 'infallibly destroy your Majestie's Revenue, and sink that of every Subject'. Bishop Dopping of Meath insisted it would be against the King's honour to break his promise not to repeal the acts and 'to consent to the Ruining of so many Innocent Loyal Persons'. Not just Protestants, but also Catholics who had legally acquired land since the Restoration, would suffer. Besides, politically and financially, Dopping continued, repeal made no sense at this juncture. The present possessors would have nothing left to pay taxes, while the old proprietors would come in 'Poor and Hungry' and be unable to pay for some time. Repeal would also ruin the King's 'Interest in the Kingdoms that he has lost', for the Protestants of England and Scotland would not want to see him restored once they discovered how their brethren in Ireland were used; it would 'ruine the Kingdom in point of Trade'; destroy 'the Publick Faith and Credit of the Nation', on which no one would dare to rely, if acts of parliament proved to be no security; and be inconvenient 'when a Civil War is rageing in the Nation, and we are under Apprehensions . . . of Invasions from abroad' – it made no sense to attempt to 'divide the Spoyl before we get it'.[93]

Supporters of repeal emphasized the injustice of the land settlement. Many innocents had never had their claims heard; others had been falsely declared rebels, because they held land in rebel territory; and even those found innocent were seldom repossessed of their estates, since all land that might have been available to compensate existing possessors had been swallowed up by great men such as Ormonde, Anglesey, Orrery and Coote. (James II himself, of course, might have been added to this list.) Although the present purchasers had a right, this was 'posterior to the antient Proprietors', and antiquity took precedence.[94] As for those who had purchased land since the Restoration, they should have realized that the Act of Settlement 'was most unjust, and could by no true Law hold'; the principle of *caveat emptor* obliged the purchaser to buy nothing but what was the true property of the seller. Nevertheless, most acknowledged the need for some sort of compensation for those who had purchased land in good faith.[95]

James unquestionably wanted to preserve the Acts of Settlement and Explanation.[96] It was made clear to him, however, that if he did not consent to repeal 'the whole Nation would abandon him'.[97] He was particularly concerned that parliament would not vote the much needed taxation if he did not capitulate. In the end, he agreed to the passage of an act that gave the landholders of 1641 or their heirs the right to recover their property, and a special court of claims was to be set up to determine individuals' rights. Those who had rebelled against James were also to forfeit their lands, which were to be used to compensate the 'New Interest' purchasers.[98] As one Protestant commentator put it, the act 'unravelled the Act of Settlement all to shreds'.[99] This measure was backed up by an Act of Attainder against Protestants, listing 2,470 individuals who were to be declared traitors, and thus subject to the penalties of execution and the confiscation of their estates, if they did not return to allegiance to James by a certain date.[100] As a result, parliament granted James a much needed subsidy of £20,000 per month for thirteen months, which was in fact some £5,000 higher than the amount James had initially asked for.[101]

The repeal of the land settlement carried with it a rejection of the Protestant interpretation of the Irish Rebellion. Unsurprisingly, therefore, the Dublin parliament repealed the act for the annual commemoration of it on 23 October, on the grounds that it was 'the occasion of great strife, Quarrels, and Animosities between his Majestie's Subjects' of Ireland.[102] It also passed various measures designed to break the Anglo-Protestant ascendancy and secure greater independence for Ireland from England. 'An Act for taking off all Incapacities on the Natives of this Kingdom' stated that 'all and every the ancient Natives of this Realm, of Irish Blood' should be 'capable of all manner of Employments within this Realm, and of Purchasing Land in Plantation Countreys, and elsewhere', and therefore that all laws which placed 'any Incapacities on any natural born Subject of this Realm, either of Irish Blood, or otherwise, by reason of his Names, Blood, or Religion' were 'hereby Repealed, Annulled, and made utterly void'.[103] A Declaratory Act affirmed that 'His Majesty's Realm of Ireland' was and always had been 'a distinct Kingdom from that of His Majesty's Realm of England', and 'as the People of this Kingdom did never send Members to any Parliament ever held in England . . . no Act of Parliament past, or to be past in the Parliament of England' should be 'any way binding in Ireland', unless 'made into Law by the Parliament of Ireland'. It also prohibited appeals from the Irish courts to King's Bench in England.[104] The Bishop of Meath opposed the measure in the Lords, arguing that it was 'prejudicial to the King and Kingdom; robbing the King of his Prerogative, and the Subject of the Liberty of appealing to the King in person'.[105] The Jacobite *Life* later said that James would never have assented to 'such diminutions of his Prerogative', were it not for the realization that he could not afford 'to disgust those who were otherwise affectionate Subjects'.[106] James did, however, manage to prevent the repeal of Poynings' Law, which the Irish saw as 'the greatest Sign and means of their Subjection to England'.[107] The Navigation Acts, on the other hand, were set aside, and acts passed allowing direct trading with the colonies, and prohibiting the import of English, Scottish or Welsh coal. The French hoped to step into the favoured economic position with regard to Ireland previously enjoyed by the English, but James, thinking still as a king of England, blocked a bill that would have allowed the export of raw wool from Ireland to become a French monopoly, and insisted that another bill that allowed for the naturalization of French subjects be modified to apply to all countries.[108]

Taken together, the legislation of 1689, if made effective, would have amounted to a genuine revolution, transferring political, religious and economic power to a new ruling class. The imperial dominance of Ireland by England would have been destroyed and the Anglo-Protestant ascendancy overturned. The repeal of the Act of Settlement would have resulted in a fundamental restructuring of landowning in Ireland; as William King pointed out, with not much exaggeration, 'two thirds of the Protestants of the Kingdom held their Estates' by this Act, while many of the rest would be divested of their estates by virtue of the Act of Attainder.[109] At the same time, however, it was a revolution that would have benefited primarily the Old English. The repeal of the Act of Settlement made no specific provision for those (primarily Gaelic) landowners who had been dispossessed before 1641. In particular, the position of the Ulster Gaels, who had lost their estates in the aftermath of the Earl of Tyrone's rebellion (1593–1603), was never addressed, although they presumably hoped to regain some land at the expense of those Protestants who were holding out for William in the north. Although at one level the legislative initiatives of the Dublin parliament amounted to a bold strike for independence from England, Ireland would still have remained in the hands of its English conquerors, albeit those who had come before the Reformation. For many Irish Catholics, both Old English and Gaelic, the legislation of 1689 did not go far enough. O'Kelly lamented the fact that James could not be persuaded to abrogate the impious laws enacted by Queen Elizabeth against the Roman Catholic faith, for fear it would alienate his English subjects, 'whom he alwaies courted'.[110] As D'Avaux put it, James had 'a heart too English to do anything that might vex the English'.[111] The irony, of course, is that James had already done more than enough to 'vex the English'.

The Catholic revolution in Ireland of 1689, however, was a paper one only. Although liberty of conscience was, in theory, provided for, and some effort made to seize the estates of those Protestants who refused to submit to James, no court of claims was set up for the time being to oversee the transfer of property back to the 1641 proprietors. Whether this revolution could be brought into effect in Ireland would depend on the outcome of the war.

THE WAR OF THE TWO KINGS AND THE TREATY OF LIMERICK

The Jacobite war in Ireland was bloody and long.[112] It was an international war. William employed not just English but also Scottish, Anglo-Irish, Dutch, German, Danish and even French (Huguenot) troops. Although the mainstay of the Jacobite army was Irish Catholics, it did have some British and French officers, and for the campaign of 1690 was supplemented by a sizeable contingent of French, Germans and Walloons.[113] Initial Jacobite successes enabled James to regain control over most of the north, with the exception of Derry and Enniskillen. Derry famously withstood a lengthy siege, lasting 105 days, against the odds and in the face of severe privations. Such was the shortage of food inside the garrison that people were forced to live upon dogs, cats, rats, mice and horseflesh.[114] At the beginning of July 1689 the Jacobite commander General Rosen, in a desperate attempt to induce a surrender, ordered all Protestant men, women and children from within thirty miles to be rounded up and brought before the city walls, where they were to be left without food or shelter. Those inside were faced with the stark choice of either coming to the aid of their Protestant friends and relatives – admitting them into the garrison where they would place an added burden on the dwindling food supplies – or watching them die of starvation at the gates. William King claimed that between 4,000 and 7,000 were brought, naked, before the walls, including 'old decrepit Creatures', 'Nurses with their sucking Children, Women big with Child' and 'some Women in Labour', although his figures were probably an exaggeration. The garrison responded by erecting a gallows on the ramparts and threatening to hang the Jacobite prisoners they had taken if the Protestants outside the gates were not allowed to return home. James was furious with Rosen for violating the terms of the protections he had offered Protestants in Ulster, and ordered his general to back down.[115] The city was finally relieved on 28 July 1689 by Williamite forces under the command of Major-General Percy Kirke; the Jacobite army raised the siege on the 31st and marched away. The depredations caused by the siege were such that when King went to Derry as its newly appointed bishop in March 1691, he 'found the land almost desolate', and nearly all 'country houses and dwellings burnt'; whereas 'before the troubles' there had been 'about 250,000 head of cattle' in the diocese, after the siege there were only about 300 left; out of 460,000 horses, two remained, 'lame and wounded', while there were but seven sheep, two pigs, and no fowl.[116] A Commons' Committee Report of 1705 estimated that '12,000 perished by Sword or Famine' during the siege.[117]

William III came over in person to lead the campaign in June 1690, and on 1 July achieved what proved to be a decisive victory over the Jacobite forces at the Battle of the Boyne, just outside Drogheda. Given that William had an army of 36,000 mainly veteran professionals against James's 25,000, the result might have seemed a foregone conclusion. As always, however, luck and human miscalculation played their part. William himself was nearly killed the day before the battle: as he was reconnoitring the river crossings on 30 June, he was fired upon from enemy lines and struck on the right shoulder by a bullet which 'tore his Coate and shirt, and made his skinn all black'. If William had fallen, it would undoubtedly have been 'a fatal Blow to his Army, and Kingdoms too', as one Protestant eyewitness put it. The actual battle the next day was more conceded by the Jacobites than won by William. When a small contingent of William's troops managed to cross the Boyne at Rosnaree, to the west of the Jacobite camp, James wrongly guessed that the rest of the Williamite army would follow, and so sent the bulk of his forces to cut them off. This opened the way for the major part of William's army to cross the river further east at Oldbridge to face what was a seriously depleted Jacobite right flank. In danger now of being caught in a pincer movement in the bend of the river, the Jacobite troops opted to retreat, throwing down their arms and equipment in a state of confusion. When he saw his men give way, James made haste for Dublin where, at an emergency meeting with his privy council, he announced that since his army was unreliable and had 'basely fled the scene of battle and left the spoil to his enemies' he was 'never more determined to head an Irish army' but was resolved 'to shift for myself, as should they'.[118] The next day James left for Duncannon, in Waterford harbour, and thence took ship for France (via Kinsale), 'leaving his poor Teagues to fight it out, or do what they pleased for him'. The Jacobites withdrew to Limerick and William secured control of Dublin on the 5th.[119]

The actual fighting at the Boyne was limited and the losses slight: perhaps 1,000 on the Jacobite side and half that on William's. Yet although James's flight and the Williamite capture of Dublin were of crucial significance, William failed to cut off the Jacobite army in retreat, thus missing the chance to bring the war to an end there and then. Missed opportunity was followed by a major reverse, when William failed to take Limerick in August. After that William himself returned to England, and although Williamite forces under the command of John Churchill, now Earl of Marlborough, captured Cork and Kinsale in late September and early October, the campaigning season ended without the conflict in Ireland having been brought to a definitive conclusion. Those parts of Ireland back under Protestant control saw a return to the *status quo ante*. Thus, following the withdrawal of the Jacobite government from Dublin in July 1690, eleven aldermen who had been displaced by Tyrconnell in 1687 took it upon themselves 'to revive the magistracy and take up the exercise of it', petitioning William to approve their action and authorize them to elect other members to make the full quota of the city government, which he did accordingly. In October, the restored corporation passed an act disenfranchising Catholic freemen.[120] When Waterford fell, also in July, William simply restored the old corporation 'upon application made . . . by the [displaced] Protestant aldermen'.[121] Likewise Youghall and Kinsale saw the restoration of their old corporations in August and October 1690 respectively.[122]

Following James's flight the Jacobites were divided over the wisdom of continuing the war. Tyrconnell thought the time had come to submit to England and try to get the best terms possible. According to O'Kelly, those Catholics who had bought lands since the Restoration, only to have their purchases jeopardized by the Dublin parliament's repeal of the Act of Settlement, were the most eager to reach an accord with William, knowing that he would not let the repeal stand.[123] The Old Catholic proprietors, together with the Gaelic Irish, tended to want to continue the struggle; the Irish feared that the English intended to extirpate them 'Root and Branch'. There was some discussion about whether the Irish should break completely with England, and 'join themselves to some Catholic crown able to protect them, rather than be subject to the revolutions of the Protestant kingdoms of Great Britain'. Some of the Gaels would have liked to have seen the kingdom put 'into the hands of the antient Irish', a design allegedly promoted by one Balderic O'Donnel, who was trying to build up a popular following among the soldiery with the intention ultimately of making his own peace with the British without James's knowledge or consent.[124] The war therefore dragged on for another year, with Tyrconnell recommitted to the cause, until Jacobite resistance was effectively crushed at the Battle of Aughrim on 12 July 1691, 'the most disastrous battle in Irish history'.[125] As many as 7,000 Irish soldiers were slain and another 450 taken prisoner; the Williamite casualties were about 2,000 killed. A Danish chaplain in the Williamite army described the 'horrible sight' after the battle: 'when many men and horses pierced by wounds could have neither flight nor rest, sometimes trying to rise' only to fall back down suddenly, 'weighed down by the mass of their bodies'; when 'others with mutilated limbs and weighed down by pain' would cry out 'for the sword as their remedy', only to be denied this by their conquerors; and when still 'others spewed forth their breath mixed with blood and threats'. 'From the bodies of all', our source continues, 'blood . . . flowed over the ground, and so inundated the fields that you could hardly take a step without slipping'.[126]

By now William was determined to bring the war in Ireland to an end, so that he could concentrate his efforts and financial resources on the continental campaign. He authorized his commander in the field, Baron de Ginkel, to offer the Jacobites favourable terms if they would surrender. On 21 July the Jacobite enclave at Galway caved in, and in return procured a rather generous treaty of surrender whereby both the garrison and the townsmen were guaranteed their estates. Tyrconnell's death on 14 August following a stroke proved a fatal blow to Irish morale, and the war eventually came to an end when Patrick Sarsfield, Earl of Lucan, now effective ruler of Jacobite Ireland, surrendered Limerick on 3 October. By the time the war was over, some 25,000 men had died in battle. Thousands more had died of disease.[127]

In negotiating their surrender at Limerick, the Jacobites pushed for terms that would have sanctioned the gains they had achieved during James II's reign and, in effect, would return them to the position they were at in 1688. Thus they asked for a full indemnity, the restoration of all Irish Catholics to the estates they had held before the Revolution, complete liberty of worship, and the right of Catholics to be members of corporations, trade freely, and hold military and civil offices.[128] Such proposals were rejected out of hand; the Protestant negotiators wanted a return to the position of Charles II's reign.

The treaty that was finally agreed comprised thirteen civilian and twenty-nine military articles. The first clause of the civilian articles provided that 'The Roman Catholicks of this kingdom' should 'enjoy such privileges in the exercise of their religion' as were 'consistent with the laws of Ireland, or as they did enjoy in the reign of king Charles the second'. Such 'privileges' had, of course, been very limited, and what liberty of conscience the Catholics had enjoyed had been by connivance rather than legally established right. Nevertheless, the same article went on to promise that William and Mary, as soon as their affairs allowed them to call a parliament in Ireland,

would try to procure for the Roman Catholics 'such farther security
. . . as may preserve them from any disturbance upon the account of
their said religion'. Article two promised that all the inhabitants of
Limerick, or any other garrison in the possession of the Irish, and all
soldiers now in arms in the counties of Limerick, Clare, Kerry, Cork
and Mayo (the remaining areas under Jacobite control), 'and all such
as are under their protection',[129] would be restored to 'their estates
. . . and all the rights, titles and interests, privileges and immunities'
they were entitled to 'by the laws and statutes that were in force in the
. . . reign of Charles II' if they submitted to William and Mary and
took the oath of fidelity and allegiance contained in the English
Declaration of Rights. Another article stated that merchants from the
city of Limerick, or any other towns in the counties of Clare or Kerry,
who had absented themselves overseas and not borne arms since
William and Mary were proclaimed in February 1689, would also
have the benefit of the second article if they returned home within
eight months. Subsequent clauses provided an indemnity for any acts
committed during the course of the war and insisted that the only
oath to be administered to Catholics who submitted to the government should be the oath of fidelity and allegiance of 1689; no longer
could they be penalized, in other words, for refusing to acknowledge
the royal supremacy. The military articles allowed 'all persons, without any exceptions', to have 'free liberty' to leave Ireland, if they so
desired, for any country beyond seas, England and Scotland excepted,
with their families and household possessions. The soldiers were to
choose whether to stay behind or go to France, where they would be
transported at English expense.[130]

THE ALLEGIANCE CONTROVERSY

There was no revolution settlement in Ireland in quite the same sense
that there was in England and Scotland. Although there was a peace
treaty following the surrender of Limerick, and a subsequent
Williamite settlement worked out over the years 1692–7, there was
no equivalent of the English Declaration of Rights or the Scottish
Claim of Right nor even any separate constitutional adjudication that

the Irish throne was vacant. James did not need to be separately dethroned in Ireland, because the Irish crown was 'a dependent upon England', as the English House of Lords confirmed on 6 February 1689.[131] The Declaration of Rights of 13 February therefore declared William and Mary to be 'King and Queen of England, France and Ireland', and they were officially crowned with this title at the coronation ceremony of 11 April 1689.[132] Yet there remained the thorny question of how to justify the transfer of allegiance from James to William. In Ireland, James had clearly been overthrown by force; it could hardly be argued that he had deserted the kingdom and left the throne vacant. How were Protestants in Ireland able to rationalize the stance they had taken against James?

In theory, the allegiance of the crown's subjects in Ireland had automatically transferred from James to William and Mary when the English Convention declared William and Mary the new sovereigns. Thus Andrew Hamilton, a Protestant clergyman of the Established Church, in his pamphlet justifying the actions of the Enniskillen men, wrote that when the news came 'That the Convention of Estates in England . . . had Voted the late King James's Desertion to be an Abdication, and placed their present Majesties in the Vacant Throne', we thought ourselves obliged 'from this time on and upon these grounds . . . to behave our selves as their Subjects, our Allegiance being transferr'd and descending from the late King James upon his voluntary Desertion, as if he had been naturally dead'. It was a theory that allowed Protestants who believed in non-resistance and passive obedience to explain, as Hamilton put it in his dedication to William and Mary, 'how we became Subjects to Your Majesties, without breach of our former Loyalty'.[133]

When William came to Ireland in person to lead the war effort, the majority of Protestants in Ireland saw him as their legitimate king who had come to deliver them from Catholic tyranny. Upon entering Belfast on Saturday 14 June 1690, William was met with cries of 'God save the King, God bless our Protestant King, God bless King William'. The Protestants presented him with an address in which they urged him to 'Conquer what is your own, / And add poor Ireland to sweet England's Crown'. That night the streets 'were filled with Bonfires, and Fire-Works', and within three hours, as news of

William's arrival spread, 'all places' that were in Protestant hands 'had made Bonfires so thick, that the whole Country seemed in a Flame'. Those who did not join the celebrations suffered victimization at the hands of Williamite crowds. In Lisburn, when the eminent Quaker preacher George Gregson did not make a bonfire, 'the Soldiers broke all his Windows, pull'd down the Pales round his House', seized his 'Wheel barrows, Shovels, Pick Ax's, Tubs, Pitch and Tar-Barrel's from his back yard, and 'Piled them up before his own Door in a stately Bonfire'.[134] The Presbyterians in the north, however, had their own particular agenda. On Monday 16 June, the Presbyterian ministers of Belfast presented William with a congratulatory address in which they expressed their hope that he would use his influence to get them 'Religious Liberty', which in turn would encourage 'those of our number now in Scotland to return' and 'prove a special Means of more fully planting this Province with such Protestants as will be endeared to your Majesties Government, and a Bulwark against the Irish Papists'.[135]

The gradual 'deliverance' of Ireland from Jacobite control over the course of 1690–91 saw similar celebrating in Protestant quarters. When the Protestants of Dublin learned of the victory at the Boyne, they ran about the streets, shouting with joy, 'saluting and embracing one another, and blessing God for this wonderful Deliverance'.[136] William himself entered Dublin in triumph on 5 July, and 'was received with all possible Demonstrations of Joy', we are told by a Protestant source, 'from a delivered People'.[137] There was more Protestant rejoicing following the victories in the autumn.[138]

Yet it was by no means that simple. Protestants in Ireland had first taken up arms in December 1688, not only long before the English Convention had declared that James had abdicated, but even before James's first attempted flight from England, let alone his second successful escape to France. Moreover, the abdication theory was difficult to sustain when James had come to Ireland in person to defend his right to the crown. As the Jacobite *Life* was later to put it: 'that senceless cant word of Abdication, which was the poor and only excuse for their unnatural rebellion in England, had not the least shaddow of pretext in Ireland, unless the King's comeing into a Country he had never been in before, and governing a Kingdom in person he had hithertoo govern'd by a deputy, must be counted an abandoning of it by the Parliamentary Logick of our days'.[139] The Presbyterians, of course, did not feel constrained by the doctrine of non-resistance and passive obedience as it had come to be articulated during the 1680s; indeed, their clergy openly exhorted their followers to take arms in defence of their religion. But what about Protestants of the Established Church? Were they, as one Presbyterian apologist claimed, 'forc'd to take sanctuary' in the Presbyterian 'sentiments concerning the just measures of Government and Subjection', which they had previously branded as seditious, to defend their own actions 'in this great and happy Revolution'?[140] Or did they manage to artic-ulate an alternative theory to justify their actions, which remained consistent with their Church's teachings on non-resistance?

In the first place, it must be re-emphasized that many Protestants of the Established Church did not engage in armed resistance. Large numbers fled the country. Of those who stayed, many were never actively disloyal to James. One Protestant correspondent in Dublin commented towards the end of January 1689 how 'The Protestants in the Army have all layd down, resolving not to fight against their rel-igion, nor against their King', adding that 'we seem to wish that the Army had done so in England, rather than deserted'.[141] Some contin-ued to serve the man they believed to be their rightful king, either in his administration or even in the army; when the Williamite deliver-ance came, they could justify it in providential terms. This was the stance taken by Anthony Dopping, Bishop of Meath. In July 1683, Dopping had preached in Christ Church, Dublin, asserting that the principles of passive obedience and non-resistance had been the 'con-stant opinion of the Church of England' and endorsed by the Irish Act of Uniformity of 1666, insisting that those who justified resistance to oppose the inundation of popery were not sons of the Church but borrowed their principles from Rome, Scotland or Geneva.[142] At the time of the Revolution Dopping chose to stay in Ireland, and even took his place in the Jacobite parliament of 1689, where, as we have seen, he proceeded to oppose most of the pro-Catholic initiatives. He was quick to go over to William when the latter delivered Dublin in July 1690, leading a delegation of Protestant clergy to thank William on 7 July for rescuing them 'from the Oppressions and Tyranny of

Popery', and delivering a speech in which he praised 'God as the Author of our Deliverance' and William 'as the Happy Instrument raised up by His Providence for the effecting it'.[143] In a sermon preached at St Patrick's, Dublin, on 26 October 1690, Dopping maintained that 'the subjecting of a nation or people to a forrain power is a worke of God almighty and providence' and 'that there is a time, when a people so subdued are bound in duty to submitt to the power of their Conquerors, notwithstanding their allegiance to their former prince'. Even so, Dopping's providentialism was mixed with a prudential view of subjection that allowed subjects to renounce their allegiance to a prince who could not protect them and to choose another master: 'the allegiance of the subject is founded on the protection of his prince, no man being bound to obey a power that either cannot or will not protect him in his life and fortune'.[144]

Providential explanations worked less well, however, for those who had been more active in their resistance. Typically, Protestants of the Established Church maintained that they had acted defensively, and therefore had not actively resisted. Thus Hamilton, after rehearsing the 'miserable Depredations' and 'open Noon-day Robberies' of the armed 'Rabble of the Irish Papists', insisted that the Protestants took arms 'in defence of [their] Laws, against those, who when the King was gone, would govern by Force, tho the Law said they should not be capable of any Employment; and when they declared they would act in contradiction to all the Laws in being'.[145] Another author maintained that it was 'Self-preservation' that motivated the Protestants of Ulster 'to Associate and take up Arms': 'the case of the people of England and Protestants of Ireland differed in several Particulars', for 'those who in England endeavoured the subversion of Religion and laws Established, had no Bloody designs against the Lives of their Country-men . . . neither did they pretend a Title to the generallity of their Estates'.[146] The declarations of the various Associations that formed in the winter of 1688/9 similarly represented the Protestants as acting in self-defence, against an immediate threat to their lives, liberties and religion. The men of Killmare, for example, said that they purposely did not put themselves into regiments, because they had no commission to do so, and they did not want to be the first to draw the sword; they merely put themselves in a 'defensive posture'. Likewise the Protestant nobility and gentry of Antrim declared that 'if we be forced to take up Arms, as it will be contrary to our Inclination, so it shall be only Defensive'.[147]

An extended examination of why the Protestants of Ireland were now free from their oaths of allegiance to James II was offered in a tract of 1691 by Edward Wetenhall, an Englishman educated at Cambridge and Oxford, who moved to Dublin in 1672 and became Bishop of Cork and Ross in 1679. Wetenhall's was a multifaceted argument that acknowledged that different rationales could come into play at different stages of the revolutionary crisis for different types of people. James, he claimed, had made it unlawful for Irish Protestants to keep the oath; God and James had made it impossible for them to do so; and, further, Protestants in Ireland had been formally released from their oaths. James had made it unlawful for Irish Protestants to keep the oath because he had sought 'to subject the Imperial Crown and Dignity of the three Kingdoms . . . to the Power of [a] Foreign Prince or Potentate', which 'for a Subject to do' was treasonous: Irish Protestants could not therefore keep their promise in the oath of allegiance to 'assist and defend such a King . . . because by this assistance . . . we commit Treason against the Crown'. It was also 'unlawful by the Law of God, for a Protestant People to assist and defend in the Exercise and Possession of Regal Power such as James II had made and carried himself', since this would contribute 'not only to the destroying their own, but their Protestant Fellow-Subjects' Estates, Liberties and Lives, and what is more their Common Religion too'. 'Our oaths' could not 'oblige us to be Assistants, and aiding to the cutting off the Heads of innocent Protestant Peers, or hanging up such Commons; and to the disarming, and putting out of Power, all Protestants, and arming and advancing all Papists, and so destroying our selves, Neighbours and Religion'. Wetenhall came close to advocating contract theory when he conceded that rather than say that James had made the oath of allegiance unlawful, it might be more accurate to say he had 'made the Oath as to him void and null', since those who took it were supposed to swear 'to a King who would govern according to Law, and protect his Subjects and their Rights'.[148]

It was also impossible, Wetenhall said, for Protestants to keep their oath of allegiance to James. By the terms of that oath, subjects were supposed to defend and assist the king, but Protestants could not perform this duty because James had disarmed them. Furthermore, God had made it 'morally impossible' for Protestants to keep the oath because He had now 'put us under the power of a second William the Conqueror', who had 'a Right to our Allegiance by conquest'. Moreover, the oath required the crown's subjects to defend all jurisdictions, pre-eminences and authorities granted to the Imperial Crown of the realm, but James had again made it impossible for his subjects in Ireland to do this and at the same time maintain their allegiance to him, because he had assented to an Act (in the Irish parliament of 1689) separating the kingdom of Ireland from the crown of England. Yet if Irish Protestants were freed from obeying James in things unlawful and impossible, 'the Safety of the Persons of the King and Queen, and their Children' were still 'most religiously inviolable'. 'None of us,' Wetenhall insisted, 'would attempt, or consent to any attempt, upon their Sacred Persons.'[149]

Wetenhall then claimed that Irish Protestants had been released from their oaths of allegiance. In the first place the Irish parliament of 1689 had repealed the Jacobean oath of allegiance, the only such oath Irish Protestants had taken, a deed which Wetenhall sarcastically remarked was 'the only Service they did us', which 'we ought not, but with thanks, to acknowledge, and record it to Posterity'. James's forbidding Protestants from keeping arms was also equivalent to discharging them from the oath, given that the oath required them to use such weapons in his defence. And after the Battle of the Boyne, James had told his men 'to shift for themselves', which surely had to be taken as referring to all the people of Ireland – another example of the King releasing Protestants from their allegiance. Turning to the oath in the English and Irish Acts of Uniformity (of 1662 and 1666) against taking up arms against the king or those commissioned by him, Wetenhall protested that commissions to Catholics were against the law and therefore not valid; thus Protestants were justified in rising against Tyrconnell and all Catholics pretending commissions from the king. If James himself chose to head these men, this did not make these officers any more legal, it simply made James 'less a legal King' – not to mention the fact that King James had 'otherwise Un

King'd himself; for certainly a King, which releases his Subjects of their Allegiance . . . is no longer their King'.[150]

So far, Wetenhall's reasoning had been primarily secular. Turning to the question of whether Scripture taught that all oaths were inviolable, however, he shifted to a religious justification for forsaking James, an area where Protestants had to be careful given their insistence that resistance for religious reasons was illegitimate. 'I am not commanded to damn my soul, through fidelity to any Oath,' Wetenhall alleged. Yet 'the Loyalty by this Oath claimed from us,' he went on, 'was not consistent with the common means of our Salvation; namely, not with the Enjoyment and Exercise of true Religion. But without the Publick Exercise of true Religion, People cannot ordinarily and generally attain unto Salvation.' One could not be expected to 'be constant to your Oath of Allegiance to your King, even to the abandoning the means of Salvation, and to virtual renouncing your God and Christian Faith'.[151]

Wetenhall's analysis implied there were a series of different points at which Protestants in Ireland might have ceased to owe allegiance to James II: when James's administration in Ireland under Tyrconnell first began to act illegally (1687–8); when William of Orange successfully completed his conquest of England (and when was that – 11 December; 13 February; 11 April?); when the Irish parliament rescinded the oath of allegiance (summer 1689); after the Battle of the Boyne (1 July 1690); or even perhaps as early as the summer of 1685, when James had first started disarming Irish Protestants, although presumably in this regard Wetenhall was thinking more of Tyrconnell's orders for disarming Irish Protestants of late February and early March 1689. Intriguingly, however, Wetenhall remained adamant that nothing he had said contradicted the doctrine of non-resistance and passive obedience. In the first place, many had indeed suffered passively. Second, this was a doctrine that had 'its Bounds, and Seasons of Practice': on occasions, resistance could be 'necessary and lawful', such as when your adversary has actually declared war on you. To sit back and do nothing at this juncture would have been tantamount to persuading Protestants in the three kingdoms 'to give all their Throats to be cut'. Yet God had delivered them from the hands of those who would destroy them and 'brought us poor oppressed Protestant subjects under a Protestant Prince', and Protestants were free to put themselves under his protection. William and Mary were conquerors; God did not assign Protestants 'any active part in advancing these Princes their Power', or so Wetenhall claimed, 'only a Passive Lot'.[152]

The most extended examination of why Protestants in Ireland were free to renounce their allegiance to James II offered by a Church of Ireland Protestant came from William King, Dean of St Patrick's, Dublin, and subsequently Bishop of Derry and Archbishop of Dublin, in his *State of the Protestants of Ireland Under the Late King James's Government* of 1691. Like Dopping, King had previously upheld the doctrine of non-resistance. In the preface to the published version of a sermon delivered by William Sheridan, Bishop of Kilmore and Ardagh, at King's own church in Dublin in March 1685, King had written that it was 'impossible any one of our Communion should be disloyal without renouncing his Religion'.[153] His experiences over the next few years, including imprisonment by the Jacobite regime in 1689, however, appear to have convinced King that his loyalty to James II could cease without a renunciation of his religion.[154] Nevertheless, like most clergy of the Established Church, his first instinct was to reach for a providentialist explanation. Thus, in a sermon preached at St Patrick's on 16 November 1690 to mark the official day of thanksgiving for the success of the Williamite campaign in Ireland, he insisted that the Revolution was the result of a 'miraculous Concurrence of Providences' – he listed eighteen. We should 'own the whole of our Deliverance', he concluded, 'to be a Work of God'; indeed, 'God in his Providence' had 'so ordered the matter that we in this place have had no hand in it'. Although he acknowledged that James II had faced 'an unexpected Opposition' to his designs in Ireland from the inhabitants of Derry and Enniskillen, once one considered 'the Places and Persons that made this Opposition' and the fact that it was 'a Miracle that they should undertake, much more that they should succeed in it', it became clear that 'God Almighty in his Providence had raised them up for that juncture, and inspired them with Resolution in an extraordinary manner, to show his power in their weakness'.[155]

King's *State of the Protestants* was a detailed attempt, as the tract's subtitle explained, to justify the 'Carriage' of the Protestants of Ireland towards James II, and show 'the absolute Necessity of their endeavouring to be freed from his Government, and of submitting to their present Majesties'. King began by insisting that it was 'granted by some of the highest assertors of Passive Obedience, that if a King design to root out a people, or destroy one main part of his Subjects [in this case, the Protestants] in favour of another whom he loves better [i.e., the Catholics], that they may prevent it even by opposing him with force'. In such a case, King said, the prince 'is to be judged . . . to have Abdicated the Government of those whom he designs to destroy contrary to justice and the Laws', and his 'Subjects may desert their Prince, decline his Government and Service, and seek Protection where they find it'.[156] Resistance was therefore justifiable 'in some cases of extremity': when the mischiefs of submitting to tyranny were more dangerous to the commonwealth than a war, then 'people may lawfully resist and defend themselves', King insisted, 'even by a War, as being the lesser evil'.[157] He also justified William's intervention. 'It may be lawful for one Prince to interpose between another Prince and his Subjects', he said, 'because he may have an Interest in that People and Government, to defend which Interest he may lawfully concern himself, and prevent their Ruin by a War', and 'the same may be lawful, if the Destruction of a People by their Prince, be only a step and degree to the destruction of a Neighbouring People'.[158]

The rest of King's tract sought to document at length that 'King James designed to destroy and utterly ruin the Protestant Religion, the Liberty and Property of the Subjects in general, the English Interest in Ireland in particular, and alter the very Frame and Constitution of the Government', and thereby to justify the Protestants' renouncing their allegiance to James. Discussing the oaths of allegiance and supremacy, King asserted that 'those Oaths were made by us to the King, as Supreme Governor of these Kingdoms', but the King having 'abdicated the Government' by 'endeavouring to destroy us' had absolved the people from them.[159] Implicit in King's thinking was a contract theory of government. He came closest to making this explicit in his discussion of James's use of the dispensing power to promote Catholics to civil and military offices in violation of the law. 'Every Law in these Kingdoms is really a Compact between the King and

People', King alleged, 'wherein by mutual consent they agree on a Rule by which he is to govern, and according to which they oblige themselves to Obedience'. Everyone agreed 'that in Cases of sudden and unforeseen Necessity, there is no law but may be dispensed with', but it was a 'most wicked as well as hazardous thing . . . to pretend a necessity for dispensing with those publick Compacts, when the pretence is not real'. James II's use of the dispensing power could certainly not be justified on the grounds of necessity, since there were plenty of Protestants 'willing enough to serve him in every thing that was for the Interest of the Kingdom'. James, however, knew that the Protestants would not assist him in his plan 'to destroy the Laws, Liberties and Religion of the Kingdom', and so if there was any necessity for James to employ persons not qualified by law, 'it was a criminal Necessity'. 'If he imagined, that such a Necessity would excuse him from his Coronation Oath, of governing according to the Laws, and justifie his dispensing with all the Laws made for the Security of his Subjects, why should he not allow', King asked, 'the same Liberty to his Subjects, and think that an inevitable Necessity of avoiding Ruin, should be a sufficient Reason for them to dispense with their Obedience to him, notwithstanding their Oaths of Allegiance.'[160]

Having gone thus far, however, King ultimately came back to seeing the Revolution in providential terms. The threat to 'our Liberties, Properties, Lives and Religion' was such, he said, that there remained 'no other prospect or possibility for us to avoid this Destruction, but his present Majestie's interposing on our behalf, as he had done for England: A Providence of which we so little dream.' It was clear, then, that William 'was rais'd up by God to be a Deliverer to us and the Protestant Cause'. Indeed, we 'did not make the least step to right our selves by force, till God's Providence appear'd signally for these Kingdoms, in raising them up a Deliverer, and the putting the Crown on their Majesties' Heads'.[161]

Within a purely Irish context, King's account seemed to offer a plausible rationalization, from an Anglo-Protestant perspective, of why it was legitimate for Protestants in Ireland to transfer their allegiance to William and Mary. Viewed from a British perspective, however, King's arguments appeared far less coherent, as the Nonjuring Church of Ireland clergyman and Jacobite polemicist Charles Leslie made clear in his lengthy *Answer* to King. If King's fundamental premise be true, Leslie said, 'That if a King design to destroy one main Part of his People, in favour of another whom he loves better, he does abdicate the Government of those whom he designs to destroy', then it followed that 'the Episcopal Party in Scotland' should be free 'from all Obligation to K. William's Government'. Moreover, although King alleged that it was James's intention in Ireland to overturn the Established Church, in Scotland William actually did overturn the Church 'by law established'. The Scottish Presbyterians might seek to justify their revolution settlement in the Church by saying that this was in accord with what the majority of the people had wanted. Yet by this logic, Leslie pointed out, the Jacobites could argue 'That it was as just to set up Popery in Ireland, as Presbytery in Scotland'.[162] Referring to King's doctrine of abdication, Leslie asserted that 'not only the Papists in England, and Episcopal Party in Scotland, and the present Papists in Ireland, may justifie their taking Arms against the Present Government when they please', but, he continued, in a calculatedly provocative statement, 'the Irish Papists in 41 might have justified their Rebellion against King Charles I by this Author's Principles, which do indeed justifie all the Rebellions that ever were in the World', but which in particular give 'full Liberty to all Dissenters in Religion to take Arms against the Government'.[163] Leslie also challenged the view that William 'had a Title to Ireland, by being King of England, because Ireland is but an Appendix to the Crown of England'. If the government of England was dissolved 'by Abdication, and returned back to the suppos'd Original Contract or first Right of Mankind to erect Government for their own Convenience', it followed that 'the Tye which England had upon Ireland by Conquest was dissolved, and Ireland left as well as England in their suppos'd Original Freedom, to chuse what Government and Governours they pleas'd'.[164] As Leslie's *Answer* brilliantly demonstrated, there was no coherent justification of the British revolutions of 1688–91; William's right to the different crowns of the Stuart three kingdoms could only be justified by different, and at times contradictory, revolution principles.

The Irish rejected the notion that Ireland was obliged to follow England in owning or disowning the kings of England. As one Irish

Jacobite account put it, 'the behaviour herein of the people of England is no rule to Ireland', which was 'a distinct realm' and 'a different nation', with 'discrepant laws' and 'a parliament of her own'. Ireland had 'never acknowledged her king to be chosen by the people, but to succeed by birth; nor her king to be deposable by the people upon any cause of quarrel'. 'When the lawful king of England dies', this author continued, 'Ireland acknowledges immediately the person next in blood, be he Catholic or Protestant, to be the king of England and hers, whether the people of England consent to it or not'. The implications of this argument were that the regal union of the three kingdoms was automatically dissolved as a result of the Revolution in England of 1688–9:

England, separated from the lawful king, has no more right in Ireland than has France or Spain, or hath Ireland in England; so that each nation of the three, viz., English, Scotch, and Irish, is independent of the other two, but all are depending on the king. Hence it is that if the blood royal be extinct, every one of the three nations may choose a distinct government.

As far as the Irish were concerned, therefore, they were conquered by a usurper in 1689–91, who could never have a legitimate claim to the allegiance of the people of Ireland. As the same author put it, writing about the surrender of Limerick, 'the Irish Catholick nation' was brought 'under the heavy yoke of an usurped government'.[165]

THE LEGACY OF THE WAR

The war left a bitter legacy. It led to a hardening of attitudes and an intensification of hatreds, while at the same time encouraging a tendency to see the Irish problem in more starkly polarized terms. We have seen that the Irish problem had never been merely about religion. At its heart lay a cluster of interconnected tensions and resentments, all of which were deeply permeated by the religious question, but which in themselves were not intrinsically religious in nature: resentment at English imperial control over Ireland; concerns over access to political power, economic opportunity, legal rights and privileges; and, most centrally of all, the land question. The war of

1689–91, although it concerned religion, was not a war of religion. James himself was not fighting for religion, but for his kingdoms, and he was prepared to allow liberty of conscience to all religious groups who would be loyal to him. The Catholics were fighting not just for their faith, but to regain control of their country and their land. The Williamites, on the other hand, saw themselves as fighting against the international threat of popery and arbitrary government, and its domestic manifestation within the three kingdoms of England, Scotland and Ireland in the form of James II. Nevertheless, increasingly from 1689, the struggle came to be seen as in essence one between competing faiths – the Protestants and the Catholics, or (which amounted to the same thing) between the English/British and the Irish. That this should have been the case was related to how people, both within Ireland and throughout Britain as a whole, came to experience the war.

Protestant discussions of the war tended not to see the struggle purely in religious terms but identified a broad range of concerns.[166] A major one was national security. Anyone who considered 'the Situation, Ports, Plenty and other Advantages of Ireland', argued the Munster Protestant Sir Richard Cox, in his famous contemporary history of Ireland, would admit that if Ireland should ever 'come into an Enemy's Hands, England would find it impossible to flourish, and perhaps difficult to subsist'. Ireland lay in 'the Line of Trade', and thus English control was essential to guarantee the safety of English shipping, whereas if the Irish were allowed to export their wool themselves, this would 'soon ruine the English-Clothing-Manufacture'. It was for these reasons, Cox insisted, that William needed to reconquer Ireland and keep it 'inseparably united to the Crown of England'.[167] Yet it was not just the security of England, but that of the whole of Europe that was at stake. As William King put it, 'If we consider the State of Europe, the growing Power of France, and how much the late King was in the French Interests', it was clear that the measures of James II 'must have been fatal to all Europe', not just 'to the Protestant Interest' (though admittedly Holland lay nearest to destruction), but also to Catholic Europe, and that was why the international confederation against Louis XIV included both Catholic and Protestant rulers, even the Pope. What had 'been done to King James',

King therefore maintained, should be regarded not 'as the single act of their present Majesties, or of the People of England, but of all Europe'.[168]

Protestant pamphleteers therefore represented the struggle as being against the international pretensions of the major European super-power, France. The French did not seek 'to relieve the poor Irish', one author alleged, 'but to secure the Country for themselves'; indeed, such was the ascendancy that Louis XIV had gained 'over the Fortunes' of James II 'that all his Motions' were now directed by French Ministers, and he stood 'but as a Cypher to . . . justifie the Politicks of the Most Christian King'.[169] Another, writing in May 1689, asserted 'that Ireland is now become a French Province; and he who was lately King of England, Scotland, France, and Ireland, is now but the French King's Deputy of that Kingdom'.[170] Reports from Protestants fleeing Ireland that spring confirmed that 'all things in Ireland [were] Governed by the French Embassador as if Ireland were the French King's and King James under him'.[171] So powerful was this propaganda that Louis XIV found it necessary to deny that he intended 'by Force of Armes to make the Kingdom of Ireland a dependent province of the Realme of France', insisting that his only aim was to restore James II to 'his rightfull Throne'.[172]

Protestant sources repeatedly pointed to the maltreatment of the Protestants within Ireland at the hands of the French. On 14 April 1689, one Dublin diarist recorded how 'Some French', who had landed at Passage on Ireland's south coast, had defaced the local church, burning the seats and tearing the Bible (the leaves of which they wore in their hats) and 'had like to kill the minister'.[173] Other reports complained of various 'insolencies' committed by the French, from intimidation and rape to theft and murder.[174] The behaviour of the French soldiers (there were six regiments of French infantry in Ireland in 1690[175]) was sufficiently bad that a proclamation was issued, in French, on 5 May, forbidding them from taking anything without payment (on pain of death) and from disturbing any Protestant churches or religious meetings (on pain of severe punish-ment).[176] Yet Protestants also sought to represent the Catholic Irish as being unhappy about the French alliance. A letter from Dublin of June 1689 told how 'the Natives look very suspiciously' on the

French, and complained of being 'sold to the French'. 'Putting French Officers in the place of the Irish who raise'd the Men' was a particular cause of discontent, and 'many of the common Souldiers', it was alleged, deserted 'their Colours upon it'.[177] Pamphlets carried accounts of how 'Quarrels often happen between the French or the Irish' and how Irish men of estate and sense began to wish themselves under English government again.[178] In the spring of 1690 some seventeen Irish Catholic officers threatened to resign their commissions when James informed them of his design to use the French troops as his personal guards: 'for they owned', it was reported in England, 'that they had rather submit to the English, then be Slaves to the French'.[179]

Closely related to the fear of France was concern about tyranny. James, it was claimed, by his actions in England and Ireland had made it clear that he aimed at the total subversion of government and the setting up of 'an Arbitrary Tyrannical Power'.[180] There was particular resentment against some of the emergency taxes James found it necessary to levy to finance his war effort, which were seen as 'a Strain of Arbitrary Power' worse than Charles I's levy of ship money.[181] Economic grievances more generally were emphasized. It was not just that the Protestants had lost their estates or that their trade had been ruined, but the whole kingdom had been impoverished as a result of the policies pursued by James and his French allies; the country had been devastated by civil war, and the economy had been further undermined by the debasement of the currency and the introduction of brass money to help finance the Jacobite war effort.[182] One tract, focusing in particular on James's economic exactions, optimistically reported that it was 'generally thought his oppression and tyranny will, in a little time, make the Irish . . . weary of him'.[183]

None of these concerns – over security, over France, tyranny, or the economic well-being of the people of Ireland – were divorced from anxieties over religion. In all these areas, the threat was seen to be coming from a Catholic source, although Protestant polemicists maintained that Irish Catholics had as much reason to be concerned as Protestants. Yet even when Protestant writers did specifically address the issue of Catholicism, they did so in such a way as to make clear that the Catholic menace was not seen in purely religious terms.

Popery was a threat to the political sovereignty of the monarch, even
a Catholic monarch like James II. King recounted how 'The Priests
told us that they would have our Churches, and our Tyths, and that
the King had nothing to do with them'. One Catholic clergyman, in a
sermon preached before James at Christ Church, Dublin, in early
1690, went so far as to assert that 'Kings ought to consult Clergymen
in their temporal affairs, the Clergy having a temporal as well as a
spiritual right in the Kingdom; but Kings had nothing to do with the
managing of spiritual affairs, but were to obey the Orders of the
Church'.[184] When James tried to exempt a Protestant, Sir Thomas
Southwell, from the provisions of the Act of Attainder, he was told by
his Catholic Attorney General, Sir Richard Nagle, that he could not
do it. 'He who in England was flatter'd into a conceit of an absolute
and unlimited Power to dispense with the Establish'd Laws', one
Protestant pamphleteer concluded, 'is not allowed in Ireland the
Priviledge inherent to all Sovereign Powers by the Law of Nations, to
pardon the Offences of a Subject'.[185]

Protestants were therefore well aware that there was much more at
stake in the conflict of 1689–91 than religion. Nevertheless, the experience of a war in which the protagonists were divided overwhelmingly along confessional lines encouraged Protestants to reach the
conclusion that the essence of the Irish problem was the struggle
between Irish Catholics and British Protestants, and that the main
reason why the Irish had proved so vindictive was because of their
religious principles. The main complaint we hear from Protestant
sources during the course and immediate aftermath of the war concerned the treatment of Protestants at the hands of their Catholic
enemies. The promise of liberty of conscience, it was alleged – with
much justification – was not made good. Many Protestants, both lay
and clerical, found themselves thrown into prison, and Catholic
clergy seized possession of several church livings.[186] William King,
who himself was assaulted in the streets by Catholic troops and had
his church services disrupted on a number of occasions, recorded how
'Several of the Inferiour Clergy were beaten and abused' or 'way-laid
as they travelled the High-way', even 'shot at and wounded'. Some
were 'so beaten that they died upon it'; others 'had their Houses set
on fire'.[187] Some Protestant churches were seized by Catholic priests,

others by Catholic troops (under the pretence that the Protestants had hidden arms in them), and still others were defaced by Catholic mobs, who would break the windows, pull up the seats, throw down the pulpit, communion table and rails, and steal whatever they could carry away. In some churches, in order to satirize the Protestant style of worship, 'they hung up a black Sheep in the Pulpit, and put some part of the Bible before it'. Although James issued a proclamation on 13 December 1689 condemning the seizure of Protestant churches as a violation of the Act for Liberty of Conscience, it proved difficult to enforce.[188] When the Dean of St Patrick's in Dublin, Dr Lisbourn, tried to resume preaching following the issuance of this proclamation, he was 'pulled down' from the pulpit 'by the Priests', and had 'his Vestments torn from his Back', while the perpetrators justified their action by telling James that if he gave the least countenance to 'Heresie in the Nation, he could never expect a Blessing on his Army'.[189] James feared such acts of 'indiscreet Zeal' from his Catholic supporters in Ireland, if he did nothing to stop them, would prevent him from returning to England: 'for who will rely on our Royal Word, if they see it publickly broken'.[190] We also have innumerable accounts of alleged wartime atrocities committed on Protestants. Protestants were subjected to free quarter, the plundering of their goods and possessions, imprisonment without trial, economic privation and even starvation. News of such treatment was quick to filter back into England, as the accounts of diarists testify.[191] The most disturbing tales of war atrocities against Protestants in Ireland, of course, were associated with the siege of Derry.

Protestant writers thus tended to blur the distinctions between the different interests among both the Catholics and the Protestants in Ireland, opting instead for a simplified Protestant 'Us' versus Catholic 'Them' dichotomy. Cox, in the introduction to his *Hibernia Anglicana*, fully understood the historical tensions between the native Irish and the Old English, who originally conquered Ireland, and how through to the sixteenth century 'the Old English and the Old Irish' would repeatedly 'split upon the old indelible National Antipathy'. He also recognized that the New English interest that had been established since the Reformation was divided between episcopalians and Protestant dissenters. But these differences among Protestants were now 'very little taken notice of in Ireland', he said. Moreover, the Old English had become assimilated with the native Irish over time: 'they insensibly degenerated not only into Irish Customs, Habit and Manners, but also assumed Irish Names', and since the Reformation the two interests were further tied together by the common bond of their shared Catholic religion. Reflecting on the experiences of the seventeenth century, and posing the question of how these differences stood at the time of the Revolution of 1689, Cox concluded that, 'Whereas the Old English were heretofore on the British side in all National Quarrels, they are now so infatuated and degenerated, that they do not only take part with the Irish, but call themselves Natives, in distinction from the New English; against whom they are (at present) as inveterate as the Original Irish.' He went on to add that the papists were never so enraged against the Protestants as now.[192]

Protestants interpreted what happened in 1689–91 against the backdrop of the Irish Rebellion of 1641. Although the Irish Parliament outlawed the commemoration of 23 October, the day continued to be observed by exiled Protestant communities in England. In 1689, for example, the Archbishop of Tuam, John Vesey, preached a thanksgiving sermon in Bow Church in London, while a number of Protestant dissenting ministers also observed the day 'very solemnly', among them Daniel Williams, a nonconformist divine who had fled Dublin in September 1687 and who preached to an audience comprised heavily of Protestant refugees from Ireland.[193] The following year Richard Tenison, Bishop of Killala, preached to the Protestants of Ireland at St Helen's, London.[194] Once the Protestants regained control of Ireland, sermons on 23 October revived on the Irish mainland – the best known being that delivered by Edward Wetenhall at Christ's Church Cathedral, Dublin, before the members of the newly convened Irish parliament in 1692, which was subsequently printed in amended form.[195]

Although there were differences of emphasis, the sermons tended to rehearse similar themes. All recalled the horrors that the Irish had allegedly committed on the Protestants in 1641, often lifting their examples straight from Sir John Temple's famous *History of the Irish Rebellion* of 1646. Williams claimed that 'Two Hundred thousand Protestants' had been destroyed by the bloody Irish rebels: some butchered, drowned, or burned alive; others stripped naked and left 'to perish by Cold and Famine'.[196] Tenison talked of Irish Catholics 'hewing Christians in pieces' and killing men 'by degrees . . . that they might feel themselves dye'.[197] Vesey spoke of burning, drowning, burying alive, 'ripping up Women big with Child, and giving the Infant to the Dogs; compelling the Wife to kill the Husband, and the Son the Mother, and then murder the Son'.[198] The Irish would have committed similar atrocities again in 1689–91, Wetenhall asserted, had not so many Protestants fled the kingdom. Nevertheless, what was done was bad enough. The Protestants were deprived of 'Defensive Weapons', 'all Manner of Refuge or Security', and 'the very Necessaries of Life'; were imprisoned without cause, even placed under formal sentence of death; while it 'was worse yet with those Forlorn Numbers driven before the Walls of Derry, of whom God alone knows how many perished'. Moreover, the Catholic clergy gave their congregations the same 'Bloody Instructions' as they had in 1641, bidding them to arm themselves 'under pain of Suspension from Mass' and to 'Plunder and Stop all Protestants', to 'spoil and burn' what they could not possess, advising them not to kill the Protestants, 'but starve them with Cold and Hunger'.[199] Likewise, Tenison talked about 'the whole Nation rising again in Arms, seizing our Houses, plundering us of our Goods, and driving us into Exile and Banishment, when we had liv'd Peaceably, Hospitably, and most Obligingly among them'.[200]

The comparison with 1641 enabled these Protestant preachers to delegitimize the grievances of the Irish Catholics. 'All the Favours and Kindness we can shew them, prove ineffectual', Tenison asserted. 'For was not the last Rebellion begun when they enjoy'd their Estates, and had the free Exercise of their Religion? When they were Members of Parliament, and Magistrates of Corporations? When their Lawyers . . . did Practice in our Courts? And when they had all the other Priviledges they could reasonably desire.'[201] Speaking of 1641, Williams claimed that the Catholics of Ireland committed 'all these Villanies . . . when enjoying their Religion, and Civil Immunities in common with the English; and no way provoked by them', while Vesey similarly insisted the Catholics of Ireland were 'a People unprovok'd', who 'enjoy'd equal benefit of the Laws with the Protestants, shar'd equally in the Legislative Power and Administration of Justice; had the Bar fill'd with Lawyers of their own Perswasion' and 'had (by Connivence) the toleration of their Religion and exercise of their Ecclesiastical Jurisdiction'. Nevertheless, such favourable treatment could not 'restrain them from so barbarous a Design'. Why? 'Nothing but their Religion', Vesey concluded, was capable of inspiring them 'to such Cruelty'.[202] Likewise, both Wetenhall and Tenison blamed the Catholic clergy in Ireland for inciting their congregations against the Protestants. Referring to 1641, Tenison charged the Catholic clergy with 'most falsely telling the People, that they were a Free Nation, and had no dependence on England, and should strive to recover their Ancient Rights'; Ireland was not a free nation, since 'it was Conquer'd some hundreds of Years since'. Yet even though 'the Title of England to that Kingdom be so clear, so very ancient and just', Tenison averred, they had 'openly rebell'd five times in less than fourscore years', between 1567 and 1641; and, of course, again now in 1689.[203]

What conclusions, therefore, were Protestants to draw? Given the fact that these were thanksgiving sermons, praising God for deliverance, these preachers naturally urged Protestants to repent their sins. At the same time, it was transparent, they argued, that any concessions granted to Irish Catholics were pointless. 'They have a Natural Aversion and Antipathy to us', Tenison alleged, 'And have resolv'd . . . to be our Enemies for ever . . . undoubtedly, when they have the Power in their hands, we must expect all the Mischief they can do us'.[204] Although the Catholics had been defeated in war, Wetenhall said, only their power, 'not their Malice', was abated, and 'Their very common People' continue to tell us, 'They will yet have a Day for it'. And while he urged the Protestants in Ireland to trust in God for deliverance from the Irish papists, he also warned them to be careful not to contradict that trust, and posited a bleak 'us versus them' dichotomy for future relations between Catholics and Protestants in Ireland: 'Those who mix with them in Sin, must expect to be Sharers in their Vengeance . . . Those who mix with them in Society, will soon mix with them in Sin . . . Those who mix with them in Blood, are thereby most intimately mixt in Society, and consequently cannot avoid mixture in Sin.' Protestants should not trust Irish Catholics: as good Christians, Wetenhall insisted, we should keep faith with them, 'but we ought not to be such Fools . . . as to believe they will ever keep Faith with us'. If anyone were to ask whether 'the Body of the Irish Nation' by the law of the Gospel might qualify for forgiveness, it should be remembered, Wetenhall gloomily concluded, that 'God himself forgives not Impenitents'.[205]

The Protestant clergy were not the only ones to draw such conclusions. One Protestant pamphleteer of 1689 admitted that he 'had once a Charitable and favourable Opinion of many of' the Irish Catholics: although he knew 'that the Church of Rome holds bloody and damnable Principles', he 'was willing to believe, that the poor ordinary Members of it might not be instructed in them'. 'But now', he said, he had 'downright Demonstration, that they . . . cannot be wronged in the worst Character that can be given of them. That they suck in this Romish Poison with their Mother's Milk; and are taught to hate and abhor English Men, and Protestants, as soon as their Pater Noster'. As a result, he would 'never be induced to believe, That true Morality, and Popery; an honest Man, and a thorough-paced Papist can be consistent'.[206]

The extent to which Protestants who lived in or returned to Ireland shared the views articulated by their clergy or by Protestant polemicists is difficult to gauge. The Protestant Jacobite Charles Leslie claimed that in the north of Ireland, where Protestants were more numerous, the Protestants came to style the Irish Catholics 'Bloody Dogs, Inhumane Murtherers, Cut-throats, etc.' during the course of the war, with 'Remember 41' being 'the usual Salutation they gave them'.[207] Many Protestants within Ireland thought the terms of the Treaty of Limerick were too generous. According to Burnet, the concessions in the Treaty were 'no small grief' to 'some of the English, who hoped this war would have ended in the total ruin of the Irish interest'.[208] George Story, a Williamite chaplain, recorded that 'a great many People' in Ireland held that 'Providence seem'd now to have given the Irish up, and that if this occasion was neglected, of putting it out of their power for ever hereafter to endanger the English interest . . . that all the Expense and Blood it had cost England in their Reduction' would 'signifie nothing'. Story himself disagreed, holding that 'the Irish' were still Christians, 'tho' misled and abused in many great Points', and had 'a natural Right to their Countrey', which many of them had 'never forfeited by any Rebellions'. For Story, any policy founded in blood was not 'warrantable by the Law of God', and Protestants should 'be careful not to deface and dissolve the Bonds of Christian Charity; nay of humane Society'; it was 'unreasonable to destroy other People, purely because they cannot think as we do'. Nevertheless, his protests imply that there were many Irish Protestants who held the views that he condemned.[209]

The situation on the ground was always going to be more complicated than Protestant polemicists might like to represent it, however. Wetenhall's own remarks against mixing with Irish Catholics reveals how difficult it was in practice for Protestants who had to live and make a living in Ireland to have no commerce with their Catholic neighbours. Wetenhall bitterly complained how 'Many of us, to this day, much more affect and court the Irish, than our own Countrymen'.[210] There also remained a significant divide within the Protestant community in Ireland between those of the Established Church and the dissenters. During the siege of Derry, an interdenominational truce had been temporarily established, with the episcopalians holding their services in the cathedral in the morning, and the Presbyterians in the afternoon. Yet almost as soon as the war was over, tensions began to resurface. Rival accounts of the siege of Derry reveal the persistence of animosities between English conformists and Scottish Presbyterians. As one Presbyterian writer was to lament, ''Tis pity that distinction of Parties, which was so generously laid aside during the Siege it self, should be soon resum'd in these Discourses it has unhappily occasioned'.[211] On top of this, there remained the question of the nature of the imperial relationship between England and Ireland, which (as we have seen) had been a cause of concern to Protestants in Ireland, as well as to Catholics, in the reigns of Charles II and James II. A return to the *status quo ante*, which was the immediate effect of the Williamite victory, in other words, left many of the problems that had beset Protestants in Restoration Ireland unresolved.

Let us turn finally to a consideration of the plight of the Irish Catholics, which was documented in detail by Leslie in his lengthy

Answer to King's *State of the Protestants*. They too had experienced great suffering during the war. Those in the Protestant-controlled north lived 'in mortal Fear of the Protestants', Leslie asserted, 'and commonly durst not sleep in their Houses, but lay abroad in the Fields least they should fall upon them'.[212] After each victory, the Protestants were quick to take their revenge on the local Catholic population. Leslie wrote of 'the vast Number of poor harmless natives, who were daily Kill'd up and down the Fields, as they were following their Labour, or taken out of their Beds and Hanged, or Shot immediately for Rapparees', which he justly concluded was 'a most Terrible Scandal to the Government'.[213] As the Protestant forces progressively recaptured control of Ireland, many of the local inhabitants fled (or were forced to flee) across the Shannon into those parts that remained under Jacobite control. In reply to King's criticism of the Jacobite tactics at the siege of Derry, which Leslie was at pains to recall that James II had himself opposed, Leslie asked: 'Is not Starving a County, or a Province, as Barbarous as Starving a City? And was not Crowding all the Irish Men, Women, and Children over the River Shannon done on purpose to reduce them to Famine?' It certainly had this effect, since 'many of them' were to die of starvation.[214] One Irish Jacobite account complained how, after the Battle of the Boyne, 'the enemy' plundered the houses of those who had fled, 'took away what cattle they [had] left behind, and seized on their estates and farms'.[215] William's army, which like James's suffered from lack of pay, could be just as brutal towards civilians, and at times was not particularly scrupulous in distinguishing between friend and foe.[216] Thus at the end of November 1690, Roger Morrice heard reports of 'great Complaints of our Army out of Ireland, that they are as burdensome as King James's was, and that they plunder Protestants as well as Papists'.[217] In February 1691, with no end to the war yet in sight, one Dublin Protestant bemoaned the miserable condition of Ireland, complaining how people had been 'reduced to beggary' by a combination of 'our own Army and the Irish Rapparees'.[218]

The sufferings of the Irish Catholics did not end with the conclusion of the war. Under the terms of the Treaty of Limerick, some 16,000 Jacobite soldiers chose to leave Ireland,[219] never to see their homeland again – an exodus known to history as 'the flight of the wild geese'. Some women and children did accompany the soldiers to France. In the process of boarding the ships, however, where the practice was to board the men first, families often got separated. In one gruesome incident, some women, who had seen their husbands already taken on board ship, tried to grab hold of the boat that had returned to pick up the officers, but they were either dragged off, or lost their grip, and drowned, or else 'had their fingers cut off, and so perished in sight of their Husbands, or Relations'.[220] O'Kelly's account confirms that despite the assurance that husbands could transport their wives and children, 'when the ablest Men were once gott on Shipboard, the Women and Children were left on the Shore, exposed to Hunger and Cold, without any Manner of Provision, and without any Shelter in that rigorous Season'. Those who chose to stay behind were no better off, since they had 'Nothing in Prospect but Contempt and Poverty, Chains and Imprisonment, and, in a Word, all the Miserys that a conquered Nation could rationally expect from the Power and Malice of implacable Enemyes'.[221]

Many Irish Catholics felt betrayed by their king, believing (with some justice) that James was more interested in regaining his English throne and appeasing Protestant opinion in Britain than in helping them redress their own grievances. As Leslie put it, 'the Generality of the Irish Papists do . . . lay all their Misfortunes upon K. J., because he would not follow their Measures, and was so inclinable to favour the Protestants'; 'though a Roman Catholic', James was 'too much an English-man to carry on their Business'.[222] James's Irish armies referred to him as '*Séamus an chaca*' – James the beshitten – for the way he fled to France following defeat at the Boyne.[223] Legend has it – though there is no corroboration from contemporary sources – that James said to Lady Tyrconnell after the Boyne, 'Your countrymen, madam, run well', to which she replied, 'Not quite so well as your majesty, for I see you have won the race'.[224] O'Kelly was particularly bitter about the way the Irish had been treated by their military leaders, especially Tyrconnell and Sarsfield, whom he felt had betrayed the cause. The other main Irish Jacobite account of the war was more sympathetic to Tyrconnell, but nevertheless agreed that James had 'spoiled his business in Ireland by his over great indulgence towards' the Protestants, and also blamed the 'want of wisdom' and 'the want of fidelity in some of his counsellors', and 'the ignorance or treachery of some great commanders in the army'.[225]

Yet it would be wrong to exaggerate the degree of disillusionment of Irish Catholics with the Stuart cause. The Irish Jacobites did not see the surrender of 1691 as a permanent settlement, but rather as a local truce in what was a general European conflict. They thus continued to harbour hopes of a French-backed Stuart restoration over the next couple of decades as England remained embroiled in war with France. Irish poets might have accused James II of having 'one English and one Irish shoe' and of 'causing misery all over Ireland'; they also recognized that 'As bad as James was, it [was] worse to be without him'. More generally, the retaliatory legislation enacted against the Catholic population in Ireland following the conclusion of the Jacobite war meant that significant numbers of Irish Catholics remained committed to the Jacobite cause. That Ireland remained quiet during the invasion scare of 1708 and the Jacobite rebellion of 1715 was more to do with a lack of leadership and Ireland's strategic irrelevance than lack of Irish sympathy for the exiled Stuarts.[226]

The above remarks highlight the divisions that existed within the Jacobite cause: James II, the Old English and the Gaelic Irish all had their own agenda. Nevertheless, the struggles of the Restoration period, which came to a head during the reign of James II and the war of 1689–91, had at the same time helped forge a stronger sense of common identity among the Irish Catholics, encouraging the view that the Protestants were the enemy. One Irish Jacobite account, representing the decision in 1689 'to restore the Irish Catholicks their lands' as an attempt 'to render at last that great justice to the nation which had been wanting for forty years', said that he called 'the Irish Catholicks the nation of Ireland, because Protestants therein are deemed but intruders and new comers'. And despite emphasizing the political and economic sources of contention between the Irish Catholics and Anglo-Protestants, the same author nevertheless tended to represent the root of the problem as being religious difference. Thus he wrote of the Protestants of Derry that 'they hate the king for his religion, and love Orange for his contrary persuasion'. 'The people of England, since their fall into heresy', he asserted, 'is a nation prone to rebellion through the depravedness of religion.' England was 'a nation without conscience or fear of God . . . while the Irish Catholics have showed themselves honest men in giving every one his due: to Caesar what is Caesar's; to God, what is God's; to fellow-subjects what is theirs, by not invading their lands or their goods'. Those Irish soldiers who, following the Treaty of Limerick, enlisted to fight in William's army, this author insisted, were 'foes to their country by siding with her enemies', and did 'betray the cause of their religion in strengthening the party of heretics'.[227] In short, the struggle had come to be seen as one between rival religions. As a Dublin diarist put it, as early as January 1689, 'Protestants and Papists' had now become 'the words of contests'.[228] Sir Richard Cox, referring to the religious divide in Irish politics in the introduction to his *Hibernica Anglicana* of 1692, believed that 'This great concern' had 'so silenced all the rest, that at this Day we know no difference of Nation but what is expressed by Papist and Protestant'.[229]

Conclusion: The Revolutions, Their Aftermaths, and the Remaking of Britain, 1691–1720

A MAN TO 'ABHOR AND DETEST'?
JAMES II AND HIS DOWNFALL

James II was not born to be king. He did not die one either. After flee-ing from the Battle of the Boyne in July 1690, he was to spend the rest of his days in exile at St Germain-en-Laye, just outside Paris. Although the exiled court at St Germain became the centre for Jacobite intrigues, James himself appears not to have been that eager to try to reclaim his throne. He dedicated himself to a life of prayer and devotion, believing that his misfortunes were a sign of God's dis-pleasure – not for his promoting Catholicism, of course, but for the sins of his younger days, when he had competed with some of the best rakes at the Restoration court. One of the prayers James wrote in exile opened with the lines, 'I detest and abhor myself when I reflect how oft I have offended so good and mercifull a God, and for having lived so many years in almost a perpetual habit of Sin'. The only way to make atonement, he believed, was through 'corporal mortifi-cation', and in his last years James took to scourging himself and wearing an iron chain around his thigh 'with little sharp points which pierced his skin'. Prone to excess in this, as in many other aspects of his life, his confessor eventually had to intervene in order to mitigate 'his zeal in this particular'. Getting the balance right, it seems, was never one of James's strong points.

James was to live some eleven years in exile. In late February 1701 he suffered a stroke, which left him partially paralysed for a while, although he did then begin to show signs of recovery. He fell ill once more in August, complaining of pains in his stomach and 'spitting of blood now and then', the telltale signs of a stomach ulcer. He collapsed on the 22nd while at mass, and again two days later, this time vomiting 'a great quantity of bloud'. Despite the worst that turn-of-the-century physicians could inflict on him (which included blistering and the dreaded 'kinkinna' or Jesuits' powder, derived from the bark of the quinquina tree), James managed to keep going for a couple more weeks. He grew dramatically worse on 4 September, being 'taken with continual convulsions or shakeing in the hands'. He died on the following day at about three in the afternoon, a little over a month short of his 68th birthday.[1]

It was an ignominious end to an ignominious career. The more we reflect on the fall of James II, the more remarkable it seems. James was both powerful and popular when he came to the throne in 1685. The challenge of the Whigs had been contained and radicalism seemed to be a spent force, as testified by the speed and ease with which the rebellions of Argyll and Monmouth were put down. The vast majority of James's subjects, including those who held power, believed that their king ruled by divine right and was absolute. Yet James ended up being resisted by people who believed in non-resistance, and was held to have done wrong by people who believed that the king could do no wrong. Indeed, it was he who was held accountable while some of his ministers continued to hold on to the reins of power – one thinks here of Sir John Dalrymple and, especially, Tarbat in Scotland, and Sunderland in England (who after a brief period in exile returned to become one of the key political managers under William IIII). This was the wrong way round. As the Quaker Jacobite Charlwood Lawton complained in 1693, 'that admirable Maxim, That the King of England can do no wrong' was supposed to mean that the deeds of the king were 'comprehended in his Ministers' and if those ministers were 'Troublers of our State', then they were 'to be punished'. Yet 'this Revolution', Lawton continued, had resulted in the keeping in employment 'the Men that persuaded King James to, and acted in, what we imputed to him as false steps', when they 'should have been punished, and not [the King] himself dethroned'.[2] For James to have brought this situation about was quite a remarkable achievement.

The jury will doubtless remain out on James for a long time. What exactly was he trying to achieve? Was he an egotistical bigot who wanted to promote Catholicism at all costs and who refused to listen to any who questioned him? Was he a tyrant who rode roughshod over the will of the vast majority of his subjects (at least in England and Scotland) and subverted the rule of law as he took his three kingdoms further down the road of monarchical absolutism? Was he simply naïve, or even perhaps just plain stupid, unable to appreciate the realities of political power in early modern Britain and the fact that there were just some things that a ruler – no matter how absolute in theory – could never get away with? Or was he a well-intentioned and even enlightened ruler – an enlightened despot ahead of his time, perhaps – who was merely trying to do what he thought was best for his subjects?

Opinion will remain divided because it is possible to recognize some attractive traits in James's personality, to identify with some of James's professed goals (or at least the rationalizations he offered for pursuing them), and even, perhaps, to feel sorry for the man. The Jacobite *Life of James II*, a retrospective account based to a large extent on James's own memoirs, inevitably put a positive gloss on what James had sought to achieve. Thus it claimed that James

had given all the markes of love, care and tenderness of his Subjects, that could be expected from a true father of his people: he had . . . encouraged and encreased their trade, preserved them from taxes, supported their credit, [and] made them a rich, happy and a more powerfull people, than they had ever hitherto apear'd in the world.

Indeed, the *Life* elaborated, James was so 'far from affecting an Arbitrary Power', that if only he had been less scrupulous in using that power 'which the Law had put in his hands', he would never have fallen into the hands of his enemies in the first place. Thus James's two major goals were, allegedly, to ensure that his subjects did not suffer, and to enable them to 'encreas their riches whilst others lavished theirs and their blood away' – hence his motive not only for 'granting libertie of Conscience' but also for refusing to enter 'the Confederate League against France', so that by remaining neutral 'he might draw greatest part of the Trade of Europe into the hands of his Subjects'.[3] We might recognize these as admirable ambitions by modern-day standards.

What, then, did the Glorious Revolution save James's subjects from: a Catholic absolutist, bent on augmenting his own power, or a well-intentioned and committed tolerationist, who was prepared to sacrifice his own crown in the pursuit of what he believed was right? It is a question upon which the three-kingdoms perspective helps to shed fresh light.

Let us begin with James's professed commitment to religious toleration. As he sought to promote greater religious freedoms for his co-religionists, James repeatedly protested that he had always been of the opinion that conscience 'ought not to be constrained' or 'people forced in matters of mere religion' (to cite the wording of his English Declaration of Indulgence). The question is whether we can take such boasts at face value. Certainly, as a man who had made life extremely difficult for himself by converting to Catholicism, James must have known as well as anyone that an individual's conscience was not something that could be forced. There is little reason to doubt that James managed to convince himself that he had always been 'against persecuting any for conscience sake', as he put it in a letter to William of Orange on 18 March 1687.[4] Moreover, the government had always claimed that the disabilities had been placed on nonconformists because they were political subversives, not because they were damaging their souls by adhering to a false religion. The penal laws, in other words, had been designed to meet a political threat, not to counter heresy. Many champions of Restoration religious intolerance, therefore, could honestly profess that people were not being forced in matters of mere religion. James's position was that since he, as a Catholic king, could have no reason to doubt the loyalty of the Catholics, they deserved to be immune from the penal laws – as indeed did those Protestant nonconformists of whose loyalty he was convinced. Given that this was how James rationalized the situation to himself, his claim to be 'against persecuting any for conscience sake' was doubtless sincere.

Yet the truth of the matter is that James had in the past shown himself to be a keen advocate of the enforcement of the penal laws against Protestant nonconformists in all three kingdoms; he appears to have believed that most nonconformists were, by definition, political subversives (having a particular dislike of the Presbyterians), and he had backed a policy of ruthless persecution when in Scotland in the early 1680s, and again in England during the years of the Tory Reaction. When the bishops of Rochester and Peterborough scrupled to sign an address of thanks in support of James's first Declaration of Indulgence, they told Sunderland that 'they could not but remember how vehemently the King had declared against toleration, and said he would never by any counsel be tempted to suffer it'. Sunderland replied: 'though they could not choose but remember it, yet they might choose whether they might repeat it or not, for other men as well as the King had altered their minds upon new motives'.[5] Even when James began trying to woo the dissenters in Scotland and England, he showed a hesitancy that seemed to betray a deep uneasiness about the general principle of liberty of conscience. James was somewhat ambivalent in his attitude towards the Huguenot refugees, and he certainly was not as outraged at Louis XIV's efforts to crush the Protestant heresy within France as we might have expected an ardent tolerationist to have been. As James moved towards toleration in England in the second half of 1686, he was nevertheless prepared to allow the continued persecution of those nonconformists who did not petition for relief, making it clear that he wanted dissenters to know that whatever benefits they were going to get they would enjoy by grace of the crown, not because of some natural right to liberty of conscience. Yet it was in Scotland where James really betrayed the limits to his belief in toleration. His initial Scottish Indulgence of February 1687 did not afford the same liberties to Presbyterians as to Catholics or even Quakers, and it was only when the political costs of failing to do so became apparent that James reluctantly agreed to concede more ground. Some might be quick to point out that James's hesitancy was due to the fact that he feared Scottish Presbyterians as political subversives. This would explain the prohibition against field conventicles, which applied equally to Presbyterians and Catholics, and which was retained in the revised Indulgence of July 1687; however, it does not explain why James initially forbade moderate Presbyterians from holding meetings in purpose-built places of worship (an allowance which he granted to the Catholics and Quakers). Besides, the 'political subversives' rationale was the same that Protestants had offered for the penal legislation against Catholics, which James himself was so eager to repeal. The fact that James could free himself of this particular prejudice but found it much more difficult to detach himself from the Stuart monarchy's traditional bias against the Scottish Presbyterians (even of the moderate kind) is revealing. James's professed belief in religious toleration was a rationalization, though one which he undoubtedly came to believe was sincere, of a policy he wanted to pursue for his own political and personal reasons.

Let us now turn to the question of whether James was an absolutist. It has been claimed that James 'did not set out to undermine the English constitution' and that 'his interpretation of the law and of his prerogative was the correct one'.[6] One has to remember, however, that royalist propaganda under Charles II, and particularly during the years of the Tory Reaction, had repeatedly insisted that the king of England was absolute, while north of the border the Scottish parliament had even passed legislation affirming that the king of Scotland was absolute. Saying that James did not set out to undermine the constitution, even if true, hardly frees James from the charge of absolutism therefore. It is probably fair to say that James did not come to the throne with the ambition of establishing a very different type of constitutional set-up in his three kingdoms from that which he understood to have existed under his brother. Thus he appreciated the need to work with parliament, in both England and Scotland, and that permanent relief from the penal laws would require parliamentary sanction. Yet at the same time, James was prepared to use the powers of the monarchy to the full, and he certainly believed the rhetoric of the Tory Reaction that the king was a divine-right ruler who did not share his sovereignty with his people and who could not be resisted. Moreover, he realized that the constitutional position of the monarchy was different in Scotland from what it was in England. Just as Lauderdale had taught Charles II that 'never was [a] King soe absolute as you are in poor old Scotland',[7] so Melfort had taught James that 'Measures need not be too nicely keept with this people' and that the king of Scotland was above the laws.[8] When James failed to induce his Scottish parliament to grant Catholic toleration in 1686 (much to his surprise, since he appears to have believed that the Scottish parliament existed merely to do the crown's bidding), he proceeded by way of his prerogative, insisting that he could have acted in this way all along. His Scottish Indulgence of February 1687 was justified by appeal to the king's absolute authority, which office-holders were now required to swear to obey 'without reserve'. There can surely be no question that James was an absolutist in Scotland; one might go further and suggest that he did, indeed, seek to promote arbitrary monarchy in Scotland, for a monarchy that has to be obeyed without reserve and is thus beyond all control is surely arbitrary. James might have continued to hope for a parliamentary endorsement of his toleration in Scotland, but he was intending to rig the elections before he called another parliament north of the border: hence his attack on burgh liberties, which he pursued by dint of his prerogative alone and without recourse to the legal process of *quo warranto* such as Charles II had undertaken in England in the early 1680s, or as James himself was to undertake in both England and Ireland. Even in Ireland, where the opportunity presented itself, James acted in an arbitrary way. Thus his policy of issuing dispensations for Catholics to hold office was done without the same 'colour or form of Law' as it was in England, as William King observed.[9]

In England, James did invariably act by colour of law. When he wanted to give Catholics dispensations from the penal laws, he made sure the judges approved of what he was doing. When he wanted to establish an ecclesiastical commission (to discipline recalcitrant clergymen) or issue a declaration suspending all the penal laws against Catholics and Protestant dissenters alike, he likewise acted in accordance with the best legal advice he saw fit to take. He did, however, appoint the judges himself, rig the judicial bench, and consult legal experts who would give him the answers he wanted to hear. Thus, of course, he came to believe that his interpretation of the law and his prerogative was the correct one. This is not the same as saying that his interpretation was right, or that James did not act in an arbitrary way. All it suggests is that James appreciated that measures did need to be kept a little more nicely with his English subjects than with his Scottish ones, and that he had to play the system, even if he wanted to subvert it.

We further need to recognize that James attempted to exploit the fact that the constitutional powers of the monarch in Scotland were stronger than in England as a strategy for putting pressure on the English to accede to his demands. In short, James played the British card in the hope of bolstering royal authority throughout his three kingdoms, and was quite conscious about it. He tried to force measures on Scotland first as a means of paving the way for what he wanted to achieve in England. It is hardly surprising then, that as James's English subjects came to see absolutism and arbitrary government promoted ever more aggressively north of the border, they became convinced that the same was intended for England in the near future. Besides, so determined was James to help his co-religionists in all three of his kingdoms that he was prepared to brook no criticism. If people stood in his way, he would circumvent them. He dismissed parliament when it challenged his will; he sacked those who raised scruples about what he was up to; he sought to intrude into political office individuals whom he had reason to believe would support his political and religious agenda. In short, he set out to make the crown independent of any external checks on its authority, whether from parliament, the privy council or the judicial bench at the centre, or lord and deputy lieutenants, JPs and magistrates at the local level – and, of course, even from the ecclesiastical establishment. He sought to suppress the voice of the people in politics; he tried (though he ultimately failed) to stop people from taking to the streets to voice dissident political opinions; and he built up a large standing army that could be used as a police force at home. To all intents and purposes he did seek to establish Catholic absolute monarchy across his three kingdoms. Nor should we be naïve and conclude that James, through the well-intentioned pursuit of noble ideals, became an absolutist by accident. He knew full well, if not that he was playing the system in order to subvert it, that he was pushing the system to its very limits, as evidenced by the speed and extent to which he backtracked in the autumn of 1688 in the face of William's invasion. He knew he had gone too far. He recognized he was guilty of subverting the traditional constitution, as most of his subjects understood it; he had just assumed he would be able to get away with it because of the Church's traditional teachings on non-resistance. He was wrong, and that was to be his undoing. In that sense, the Glorious Revolution undoubtedly did save England, Scotland and Ireland from Catholic absolutism, or, to put it in the contemporary parlance, it saved the three kingdoms from popery and arbitrary government.

James's failure sheds much light on the realities of political power in the three kingdoms. James was forced into an increasingly absolutist position – and to act more and more arbitrarily – because his subjects refused to cooperate with him. Charles II had made the monarchy strong in his final years in part by appealing to public opinion, and by putting into power at the local level those who bought into the Tory-Anglican ideology that the king, although absolute, was obliged to rule by law, and that therefore even a popish successor would uphold the existing legal establishment in Church and state. Indeed, upon acceding to the throne in 1685, James himself repeatedly promised he would protect the existing establishment in Church and state. When he failed to keep that promise, many of those very people who had supported the Stuart monarchy across the three kingdoms in the face of the Whig threat began to desert the crown. They may not have actively resisted, but they refused to comply, dragged their feet, or even continued to enforce laws James had suspended. As a result, James's regime began to collapse from within prior to William of Orange's invasion. It is undoubtedly true that William's invasion was what finally toppled James's monarchy. But it would be misleading to conclude that the Glorious Revolution was therefore brought about from above and outside, or that it was, first and foremost, a foreign invasion. William's invasion was itself predicated upon the fact that James's regime had already begun to collapse from within; indeed, James had already been forced to backtrack by his subjects – that is, a 'revolution' of some sort had already occurred – before William had even set foot on English soil. The Glorious Revolution was thus equally brought about from within and from below.

The roots of the problems that had bedevilled the British polity in the late seventeenth century can be traced back to the restoration of the monarchy in 1660. Despite widespread celebrating at the return of Charles II, there remained deep political, religious and economic tensions that proved impossible to resolve, and which served to foster and perpetuate bitter divisions in all three kingdoms. Such were these tensions that the Restoration regime had been plunged into crisis by the late 1670s, and it seemed to many that '41 was indeed come again. In the final years of his reign, however, Charles II devised an effective way of managing these problems, and was able to emerge not only unscathed but with the power of the monarchy significantly enhanced. James pursued a strategy that brought all the unresolved tensions to the fore once more, adding new sources of discontent in the process, and thereby rapidly propelling the Stuart composite monarchy back into crisis. The Glorious Revolution was thus yet another attempt to address and resolve these problems. The solution was to vary considerably from kingdom to kingdom.

There were three different revolutions in 1688–9. In England, where James had managed to alienate Tories and Whigs, Anglicans and dissenters alike, political consensus was sustained and the revolutionary settlement that was forged in the early months of 1689 was a legally conservative one. The Declaration of Rights purported to be doing no more than vindicating and asserting ancient rights and liberties and, in essence, this was true. More far-sweeping reforms were on the agenda, some of which had been outlined in the twenty-eight Heads of Grievances, although these were not incorporated into the Declaration of Rights and, in the short term, only a few were enacted following the transfer of the crown to William and Mary. This is not to minimize the significance of the Declaration of Rights, however. It provided a final adjudication on a number of issues that had been sources of contention between the crown and parliament under the later Stuarts, and decided firmly in favour of parliament's reading of the law; in that sense, it did limit the powers of the crown and also guaranteed the legal sovereignty of parliament. But the Revolution settlement in England did not seek to remodel the Restoration polity in any fundamental way, beyond a limited measure of religious toleration passed in April 1689 and the proviso that no Catholic could in future inherit the English crown included in the Bill of Rights of December 1689. Moreover, in England it proved possible for most groups to accommodate themselves to the settlement that was achieved in 1689. Not that Tories and Whigs, Anglicans and dissenters, all saw things the same way. Nevertheless, what was achieved in 1689 was sufficiently moderate and ambiguous that the Revolution could be interpreted in different ways by different people depending on one's political and religious outlook. The result was that most people were able to make their peace with the post-Revolution regime and few were driven into Jacobitism.

The situation was very different in Scotland. Here, consensus was not sustained. The Episcopalians were either driven out of, or chose to absent themselves from, the Scottish Convention, which, as a result, came to be dominated by Whigs and Presbyterians who proceeded to forge a highly partisan settlement. Thus the Scots, in their Claim of Right, did declare illegal certain powers that the Scottish crown had undoubtedly possessed under the later Stuarts, powers which had even been confirmed by act of parliament. They also committed the crown to further reforms, in part by calling for the abolition of episcopacy in the Claim of Right, not in their Articles of Grievance (the Scottish equivalent to the English Heads of Grievances), and also by making the offer of the crown conditional upon William and Mary's acceptance of both the Claim of Right and the Articles of Grievances. The result was a more fundamental restructuring of the Restoration polity in Church and state north of the border than anything attempted in England: the Scottish crown was stripped of crucial prerogatives; the Scottish parliament was made more independent of executive interference through the abolition of the Lords of the Articles; and episcopacy was overthrown to be replaced by a Presbyterian system of Church government. There were obvious winners and losers in Scotland, and the losers were the Episcopalians. It thus proved impossible to rebuild consensus after 1689, and many of those who lost out were to be driven into the arms of the Jacobites.

The situation was different yet again in Ireland. Here the majority of the population – the Catholics, of both Old English and Gaelic Irish stock, plus a minority of Protestants – remained loyal to James II, who saw Ireland as a perfect launching pad for a French-backed military effort to regain his Scottish and English crowns. The result was a bloody war between William and James that was to last until 1691. In the spring of 1689 James's Dublin parliament enacted legislation which, if made effective by Jacobite victory in arms, would have amounted to a sweeping revolution, undoing the Restoration land settlement, overturning the Protestant ascendancy, restoring political and economic power to the Catholics, and destroying the imperial dominance of Ireland by England. The Jacobites, of course, were not to win the war, and the attempted Catholic revolution was thwarted by the Williamite victory in arms accompanied by a peace settlement that essentially sought to restore things to the way they had been in Charles II's reign. In Ireland, as in Scotland, there were obvious winners and losers – in Ireland's case it was the Catholic majority who lost out. Yet the upheavals of James II's reign, and the experiences of the war of 1689–91, had the effect of hardening the attitudes of Protestants towards Catholics. Whereas the problems in Ireland had never essentially been about religion, but about a series of interacting political, constitutional and economic issues that tended to break down along confessional lines, after 1689 the essence of the problem came to be increasingly seen (by Protestants in Ireland, in particular) as religious in nature – that is, that the Catholics could not be trusted because they were Catholics. The Revolution in Ireland was thus to have a profound impact on the perception of the nature of the Irish problem which, as we shall see shortly, was to have significant implications for the Williamite victory in Ireland over the course of the next few decades.

Just because the Revolution in England was legally conservative does not mean that it was a tame affair. There was widespread and violent rioting in the latter months of 1688, as crowds across the country attacked mass-houses, local Catholics and the men associated with the implementation of James's unpopular policies. The crowds might have been protesting against men and measures under James II, rather than demanding the installation of a new order, and (in the time-honoured fashion of English crowds) defending what they took to be their rights and liberties against the illegal actions of those in authority. But this did not make them any less frightening. At the same time, armed gangs of noblemen and gentry, together with their tenants, were riding across large parts of the north, the Midlands, East Anglia and Wales, forcibly disarming Catholics, taking over royal garrisons and asserting their own authority over and above that of the royal government. It was clear for all to see that James had lost control of his kingdom. Contemporaries were alarmed and terrified by the levels of crowd violence, as indeed was James himself – hence, in part, his decision to pack his wife and son off to France and to attempt to follow suit himself. This, by itself, should make us wonder whether it is right to see the Glorious Revolution as a tepid, docile affair in comparison to its mid-century counterpart. The assumption that the levels of crowd violence in 1688 were less than in 1641–2 is questionable, at the very least. Sixteen eighty-eight was no mere palace coup, quietly engineered from above. It was a messy, violent affair, which saw the total disintegration of the government and created what to many people at the time must have seemed like a near anarchic situation.

There was also considerable crowd violence in Scotland. Some of this was similar to the type of collective violence that took place in England, with attacks on Catholic chapels and the houses of local Catholic gentry. Yet there was also a more radical form of crowd protest north of the border, as Presbyterian crowds in the south-west took the opportunity presented by the breakdown in royal government to try to enforce their own religious settlement, by forcibly driving local Episcopalian ministers out of their parish livings. And this crowd activity had considerable impact on the eventual Revolution settlement, since the Scottish Convention – the composition of which had been influenced by the intimidatory practices of Presbyterian crowds that had descended upon Edinburgh – actually came to sanction the forcible ejections that had been carried out over the winter of 1688/9. No one, of course, would ever think of calling the Revolution in Ireland a tame affair. Indeed, the popular image of the Revolution of 1688–9 as 'glorious' and 'bloodless' has only been sustained over the years by wilfully leaving Ireland out of the picture (and also by paying insufficient attention to Scotland, one might add). Whatever one makes of the Glorious Revolution – whether one sees it as conservative or radical, restorative or innovative – tame it most certainly was not.

One of the advantages of pursuing a three-kingdoms approach to the political upheavals of the later-Stuart period is the comparative perspective it offers us. We are able to reach a fuller understanding of exactly what was (and what was not) achieved in England in 1688–9, for example, through comparison with what was achieved in Scotland. Despite the efforts of recent historians, studying England in isolation, to invest the Glorious Revolution with more Whiggish and hence more radical credentials, the settlement in England in 1689 appears much less Whiggish or radical when set against what transpired north of the border, and certainly much less revolutionary than what the Catholics in Ireland were trying to achieve through legislation enacted by the Dublin parliament of 1689. Yet the rationale for a three-kingdoms approach is not solely premised on the benefits to be gained from comparative history. There are, it is true, separate national histories that need to be told for the later-Stuart period; and there were separate revolutions, in the three kingdoms, the roots of which lay (in large part) in their own, distinctive national histories. However, there is also a British story to be told; indeed, one cannot fully make sense of the problems and crises that afflicted the later Stuarts – and how the Restoration monarchs could or could not resolve them – without recognizing that these problems and crises were intimately bound up with the fact that the Stuarts ruled over a multiple-kingdom inheritance.

REVOLUTIONARY IMPLICATIONS

So far our account of the dynastic shift and accompanying political and religious settlements brought about by the Glorious Revolution has taken developments up to 1689 in England, 1690 in Scotland, and 1691 in Ireland. We cannot leave the story there, however. The working out of the implications of the separate Revolution settlements was to have significant repercussions, both within each kingdom individually and also for the nature of the relationship between the three kingdoms. Thus the revolutions in turn spawned further dramatic changes in England, Scotland and Ireland, which must be seen as part of the same, respective revolutionary settlements. They also spawned a fourth, 'British' revolution, which not only had implications for the three kingdoms individually but also for the multiple-kingdom inheritance as a whole, transforming that inheritance in the process and resulting in the creation of the British state.

England

Historians have long recognized that further significant changes occurred within the English polity during the reign of William III (1689–1702); indeed, so far reaching were these that one scholar has even claimed that the true English revolution occurred neither in mid-century nor in 1688–9 but in the 1690s.[10] They disagree, however, over whether such changes were the result of the Glorious Revolution itself or of the subsequent war against France (the Nine Years War, or War of the League of Augsburg of 1689–97) in which England became involved. In many respects this is to posit a false dichotomy, since the war was a direct, intended consequence of the Revolution. William invaded intending to bring England into his European alliance against France, and many of those in England who made or supported the Glorious Revolution did so precisely because they wanted such a revolution in English foreign policy.[11]

The war proved incredibly expensive, as contemporaries knew it would, and necessitated a major restructuring of state finances, which in turn carried constitutional implications. Whereas the crown's total yearly income under James II had never exceeded £3 million, annual military expenditure alone had reached £8.1 million by 1696, and spending on war was to peak at £10.2 million in the following decade. In order to help meet some of the cost, a new system of public credit was set up, involving the floating of long-term, funded loans, which in turn resulted in the origin of the National Debt in 1692–3 and the creation of the Bank of England in 1694. Since the interest on these loans had to be guaranteed by parliamentary grants of taxation, the National Debt assured the need for regular parliaments. By 1712 nearly £16 million had been raised on a funded long-term basis. Not all the cost of war, however, could be met by loans; in fact, initially, only a very small percentage of it was. The rest had to be made up by parliamentary grants of taxation – both indirect taxes, such as customs and excise, and England's first, high-yield direct tax, the Land Tax (introduced in 1693). The English state also abandoned the old distinction between ordinary and extraordinary revenue. The financial settlement of 1690 in any case had been deliberately designed to be insufficient for the king to live on in ordinary times, and this immediately became apparent when peace was restored at the end of the Nine Years War in 1697. In 1698, the Civil List Act formally recognized this reality: the king was now given a 'civil list' of revenues – estimated to yield £700,000 a year (any surplus was not to be spent without parliamentary consent) – to meet the expenses of his household and government, while all military and naval expenditure, even in times of peace, were to be the responsibility of parliament.[12] In short, it was the Financial Revolution of the 1690s, rather than the Declaration of Rights, that secured regular meetings of parliament after the Glorious Revolution.

Certain of the fiscal changes of the 1690s were anticipated by some of those who backed the dynastic shift of 1688–9 and welcomed the revolution in foreign policy that occurred as a result. Calls for a national bank had been voiced as early as the 1650s and were to be endorsed again in the second half of the 1680s by opponents of James II's foreign policy and his particular understanding of political economy.[13] There were other consequences of the war which carried with them constitutional implications, however, that could not have been easily foreseen. One was the emergence of the cabinet system of government, to deal with the fact that William was so frequently out of the country in the 1690s leading his armed forces on the Continent. During the second phase of the struggle against France under Queen Anne (1702–14) – the War of Spanish Succession of 1702–13 – the Queen's poor health and limited grasp of public business resulted in the emergence of a prime minister, in the person of the head of the treasury (Robert Walpole's position under George I was in this sense anticipated by the earls of Godolphin and Oxford under Anne), and the establishment of responsibility for the conduct of foreign policy in the secretaries of state.[14] More generally, the wars saw a major transformation in the machinery of executive government: a dramatic expansion of administrative personnel, the creation of new government departments, professionalization and a more scientific approach to government.[15]

Warfare also enabled parliament to secure further political reform. Thus, in 1694, the need for money forced William to agree to a Triennial Act, which provided not only that parliament must meet every three years but also that it should not last more than three years,[16] thereby addressing the demands in the Heads of Grievances both that the 'frequent sitting' of parliament 'be preserved' and that 'the too long continuance of the same Parliament be prevented'. An additional degree of toleration came in 1696 following the abortive assassination plot against William, when Quakers were allowed to affirm rather than swear when giving evidence in court (except in any criminal cases), to accommodate Quaker scruples about taking oaths.[17] Ironically, however, the major issue which the dynastic shift of 1688–9 left unsolved was the problem of the Protestant succession. William's inability to provide an heir, and his sister-in-law's failure to produce a child who could outlive her, necessitated further legislation to settle the succession – the Act of Settlement of 1701 – which, in turn, provided another opportunity to address grievances that had been articulated in 1689. Thus the Act of Settlement stipulated that the succession would pass to Princess Sophia, Electress of Hanover, and her heirs should William and Anne die without issue, paving the way for the eventual succession of George I in 1714. It also required that all future monarchs should be communicating members of the Church of England and provided that judges should hold office on good behaviour (operative 1714), and that royal pardons no longer be pleadable to impeachments in the Commons.[18] To be fair, the Act of Settlement was in part a reaction against political developments under William and not just a belated attempt to enact some of the reforming agenda of 1689: hence the proviso concerning the religion of the monarch (reflecting concerns not just about the Lutheranism of the Hanoverians but also William's Calvinism) and other provisos preventing a future monarch from leaving the British Isles without parliament's consent (repealed 1716) and barring placemen or pensioners being MPs (repealed 1707). Nevertheless, in so far as the Act of Settlement of 1701 was designed to address problems, relating to the succession, that had arisen as a result of the dynastic shift brought about in 1688–9, it has to be seen, at least in part, as a working out of the implications of the Glorious Revolution and therefore as part of that Revolution settlement.

The cumulative effect of the reforms and innovations that occurred during the reigns of William and Anne as a result of the Glorious Revolution, and the revolution in foreign policy which the Glorious Revolution inevitably brought about, went a long way towards creating a new type of monarchy in England. The English monarchy became limited, bureaucratic and parliamentary. It ceased to be a personal monarchy in quite the same way it had been under Charles II or James II. Yet in many respects it became a monarchy with more real power, as a result of the creation of the fiscal military state and the concomitant ability to harness the economic wealth of the country in the service of the sovereign – now the king-(or queen)-in-parliament. It is in this sense that the Glorious Revolution, despite the legal conservatism of the Declaration of Rights, truly brought about a revolutionary transformation of the English state.

Scotland

Let us turn to Scotland. The fact that Scotland and England had two very different revolutions in 1689 transformed the nature of Anglo-Scottish relations. Since the union of the crowns in 1603, the Stuarts had pursued a policy of convergence in ecclesiastical affairs (in order to try to bring the two Churches of the respective kingdoms closer together), and had sought to maintain a tight grip over Scottish affairs through the crown's ability, via the Lords of the Articles, to control legislation enacted by the Scottish parliament. With the Glorious Revolution, however, the policy of convergence in the Church was abandoned, while the abolition of the Articles increased the independence of the Scottish parliament and necessitated the development of new forms of political management to ensure that Scotland backed (or at least accepted) policies initiated in London. The trouble was that the policies decided upon in England – and which were seen as essential to the interests of the crown when viewed from a metropolitan perspective – were not always seen by the Scots as in their best interests. The problem was exacerbated by the fact that the Revolution had transferred sovereignty in England to the king-in-parliament. The Scots had not always taken kindly to being bossed around by an absentee king to whom they at least acknowledged they owed allegiance; they bitterly resented any attempts by the new coordinated sovereign power of king and English Lords and Commons, which in practice meant the king's English ministry, to determine policy for Scotland. The separate revolutions in Scotland and England, in other words, increased tensions between the two kingdoms and made some sort of redefinition of the Anglo-Scottish relationship inevitable.[19]

Tensions between the two kingdoms emerged soon after the Glorious Revolution, as the new regime in England revealed itself to be peculiarly insensitive in its handling of Scottish affairs. William's attempt to pacify the Highlands turned into a disastrous tragedy in 1692, when the dreadful massacre at Glencoe was carried out because MacDonald of Glencoe accidentally missed the deadline for swearing the oath of allegiance to William by five days. Although most of the clan escaped, leaving just thirty-eight to be butchered in the glen, the brutality of the deed was shocking even in this age and did more than anything else to promote Jacobitism in the Highlands.[20] The Episcopalians, of course, who dominated in the north-east coastal plain, had been alienated as a result of the settlement attained in 1689–90. Yet William also managed to upset those lowland Scots who had welcomed or accepted the Revolution through his apparent determination to frustrate Scottish pretensions to greater political independence which they believed they had won in 1689. Thus William kept his Secretary of State for Scotland in London and ignored the demand for frequent parliaments in the Scottish Claim of Right, instead keeping the Convention Parliament in Scotland sitting for nine consecutive sessions. William's foreign policy was determined with English and Dutch interests in mind, but with scant regard for the concerns of the Scots. Scottish trade with France was badly hit by the Nine Years War, at a time when the Scottish economy was suffering in any case, and for all their sacrifices the Scots gained nothing for themselves at the peace treaty of 1697. Furthermore, the English did their best to prevent Scottish merchants from trading illegally with English colonies through a stringent enforcement of the Navigation Acts, and helped frustrate the Scots' attempt to establish their own colony on the Darien peninsula in Panama in the late 1690s, resulting in the capital loss of £153,000 (over £1.8 million Scots), perhaps a quarter of the nation's liquid assets.[21] To be fair, the English were not solely responsible for the failure of the Darien scheme – Spanish opposition and Scottish mismanagement must also be taken into consideration – while the English cannot be blamed for the series of disastrous harvests (caused by a combination of poor weather, poor soil and an outmoded feudal economy) that afflicted Scotland in the 1690s. Nevertheless, many Scots came to feel that the ills which afflicted their country in the last decade of the century were due to William and his ministers and the nature of the political relationship between the two countries fostered by the union of the crowns.

Things seemed merely to go from bad to worse in the new century. Following the King's death in 1702, William's ministers failed to call a new parliament within twenty days (as required by an Act of 1696), waiting ninety days instead in order to give the English privy council time to declare war on France without facing opposition from the Scottish parliament. But the biggest problem in the early eighteenth century centred around the succession. The English Act of Settlement did not apply to Scotland, but it inevitably had enormous consequences for the northern kingdom and the Scots were understandably upset that they were not even consulted. Furthermore, the English tactlessly included in the act clauses which did apply to Scotland, such as that forbidding a future monarch from going 'out of the Dominions of England, Scotland and Ireland without the consent of parliament'. The implication seemed to be that the Scots would be bound by the dynastic settlement reached in England, and even, therefore, that the English parliament had the right to legislate for Scotland. The measure caused a furore in the Scottish parliament of 1703. As Andrew Fletcher of Saltoun asked, when the English nation nominated a successor to their crown, 'Did they ever require our concurrence? Did they ever desire the late King to cause the parliament of Scotland to meet, in order to take our advice and consent? Was not this to tell us plainly that we ought to be concluded by their determinations?'[22] To some it seemed that Scotland was to be reduced to the same state of dependency as Ireland. As an anonymous paper circulated among Scottish MPs enquired, 'I desire to know . . . where lies the difference of our case, from that most deplorable state of Irish parliaments'.[23]

The Scottish response was to raise the stakes: they would go it alone, if need be. Thus on 13 August 1703, the Scottish parliament passed an Act of Security stipulating that if Anne were to die without an heir, the Scottish parliament should nominate the successor to the Scottish crown, who should be both a Protestant and of the royal line of Scotland, but not the same person designated to succeed in England, unless 'there be such conditions of Government settled and enacted as may secure the honour and sovereignity' of Scotland, 'the freedom, frequency and power of Parliaments', and 'the religion, liberty and trade of the Nation from English or any foreigne influence'. At first the English ministers refused to allow the Scottish commissioner to confer the royal assent, but the need for money forced them to back down and in 1704 the measure became law.[24]

The only way out of this impasse, as far as the English were concerned, was a treaty of union between the two kingdoms. It would be wrong to suggest that the Scots were completely opposed to some form of union with England. Political moderates such as Tweeddale and the Dalrymples had, as we have seen, pushed for a political union of the two countries back in 1689, and as the 1690s unfolded more Scots warmed to the idea of a union as the possible answer to Scotland's economic ills. Even some of those who vehemently opposed the incorporating union that eventually came to fruition in 1707 would have been willing to accept some other type of union, such as a federal union. But the proposals for union that were put forth in 1689 and again in 1702–3 came to nothing, essentially because England, at this time, was not interested in pursuing them. The union negotiations of 1706, by contrast, came to fruition because the English were now determined that they should. In 1705 the English parliament responded to the Scottish Act of Security with its provocative Aliens Act, threatening that unless the Hanoverian succession was recognized or a treaty of union set on foot by Christmas Day, the Scots would be treated as aliens in England and Scottish exports to England prohibited.[25] By a combination of political management and bribery – and, it should be said, a willingness to grant concessions on certain issues in an effort to alleviate public anxiety over possible economic and religious implications – the royal administration managed to persuade the Scottish parliament to agree to a treaty of incorporating union with England, which it finally ratified by a vote of 110 to 69 on 16 January 1707.[26] The measure then went rapidly through both houses of the English parliament, passing the

Commons on 1 March 1707 by a vote of 274 to 116, and came into force on 1 May 1707.[27]

By the terms of the treaty, England and Scotland were 'united into one kingdom by the name of Great Britain'. The Scottish parliament was abolished and a new British parliament created, to which the Scots were entitled to send 16 elected peers and 45 MPs. The new body, however, was in essence just an extension of the English parliament: it continued to sit at Westminster, and whereas Scottish constituencies had to be redrawn in order to reduce the number of MPs from 157 to 45, nothing was done to change the English system of representation. Thus England and Wales continued to send 513 MPs to parliament. This disparity was justified on the basis that England and Wales exceeded the taxable capacity of Scotland by a ratio of 38 to 1; on such a logic, Scotland would have merited no more than 14 MPs, so arguably the Scots were getting a good deal. Yet the population ratio was 5 to 1; proportional representation based on demographic criteria would have suggested that Scotland should have had 103 MPs. The treaty also established economic union – free trade between the two countries, one coinage, one fiscal system, and a uniform system of weights and measures – though a sum of money, known as the Equivalent, was to be paid to Scotland to offset future liability towards the rapidly expanding English national debt. Each country, however, was to retain its own system of private law, courts and jurisdictions, and its separate ecclesiastical establishments – in order to alleviate the anxieties of the Presbyterians, an act guaranteeing the security of the Presbyterian establishment passed the Scottish parliament on 12 November 1706 and was declared to be an integral part of the treaty. A similar act for securing the Church of England as by law established was passed by the English parliament, and both acts were appended to the Act of Union and passed in 1707.[28]

The Treaty of Union was far from popular in Scotland. Indeed, most sections of Scottish society had reason to be unhappy with the terms agreed. Jacobites and Episcopalians naturally resented being tied to the Hanoverian succession and a Presbyterian Church establishment. Country party politicians regretted the fact that an opportunity for further political reform had been lost, and indeed that some of the worst features of Scottish life, such as the heritable jurisdictions, had been kept. Radicals bemoaned the loss of Scottish independence and with it the chance to secure the rights and liberties of the Scottish people, which they rightly predicted would hardly be a high priority for the new British parliament. The Presbyterians were worried about a union with a more powerful, episcopalian state, one where their enemies, the bishops, sat in the House of Lords. The mere acceptance of a united parliament seemed to imply a recognition of episcopacy, and thus for hardline Presbyterians a violation of the Covenants. More generally, it was feared that union would bring toleration for episcopacy north of the border, or, worse still, attempts to reintroduce bishops in Scotland.[29] Even the commercial and trading interests of the burghs were far from enthusiastic, being fearful of higher levels of taxation and of competition from England. It was mainly landowners engaged in the export of grain and black cattle, it seems, who anticipated real economic benefits from the union. There were addresses to the Scottish parliament against the proposed union from some 116 localities (15 shires, 22 burghs, 9 towns, 3 presbyteries and 67 parishes), which between them amassed more than 20,000 signatories, in addition to various 'national' addresses from the Commission of the General Assembly, the Convention of the Royal Burghs, and the Cameronians 'in the South and Western Shyres'. There were also riots in Edinburgh, Glasgow and the south-west in the latter months of 1706, not just by Jacobites but also by Cameronians. There was even talk of a concerted uprising of Highland Jacobites and disgruntled Presbyterians, although such plans came to nothing.[30] In the end, the opposition of most mainstream Presbyterians was silenced by the act securing the Presbyterian establishment, though this, in turn, was to cause concern among high church interests in both Ireland and England, who feared that the union might thereby serve to encourage dissent and undermine the ecclesiastical establishment in their respective kingdoms.[31]

On the whole, most Protestants in England and Ireland, it must be said, welcomed the union. In Scotland, however, it left a divided legacy, and enabled the Jacobites and Episcopalians to take over the mantle of Scottish nationalism. Union did at least bring some degree of toleration for Episcopalians. Thus in 1712 a Tory-dominated British Parliament passed an act allowing Episcopalian congregations to meet and worship provided that they used the Scottish liturgy; this did not affect the Nonjurors, however, who continued to use the Scottish prayer book of 1637. Ironically, therefore, the Toleration Act introduced strife among the Episcopalians. That same year, parliament passed an act restoring lay patronage, which had been abolished in 1690, though a majority of the congregations still retained the right to veto a patron's nomination, leaving the matter to be resolved by the presbytery.[32]

Ireland

Let us turn now to Ireland. The Treaty of Limerick of October 1691 was far from being the end of the Revolution settlement in Ireland. There were many Protestants, in both Ireland and England, who felt that the peace terms had been too favourable to the defeated Jacobites and who wanted to make the Irish pay for their rebellion. Yet the war also changed the nature of the relationship between the ascendant Protestant interest in Ireland and the mother country. The crown's need for money to cover the cost of the war gave the parliament in Ireland more political leverage and afforded it the opportunity to challenge the nature of Ireland's subordination to England. It was a challege which the English could not afford to leave unmet, and resulted in a redefinition of the imperial relationship between England and Ireland.[33]

Protestants in England hoped that the cost of putting down the war in Ireland could be met, in time-honoured fashion, by the forfeiture of Irish estates.[34] There was, in fact, to be no general Act of Attainder against Catholics in Ireland, such as the Dublin parliament of 1689 had passed against Protestants. Instead, the Williamite regime chose to pursue individual Jacobites on charges of high treason, with conviction resulting in outlawry and forfeiture of property (though there were no executions). A number of leading Irish Jacobites were indicted in England; then, from the autumn of 1690, following victory at the Battle of the Boyne and the subsequent retreat of the Jacobite forces behind the river Shannon, the treason trials began in Ireland in the counties then under Williamite control. Outlawries were also declared against Irish Jacobites for treason committed abroad. There were nearly 4,000 outlawries in total, although not all of these were Catholic landowners (who numbered about 1,300 in 1688), since many were younger sons, merchants, traders and artisans. In all, 457 landed estates were affected and just over 1 million Irish acres (1.7 million statute acres) of land declared confiscated.

The total number of confiscations, however, was limited by the terms of the articles of Galway and the Treaty of Limerick, which as a bait to induce surrender had allowed not only Jacobite officers but also 'all such as [were] under their protection' in the counties and garrisons then under Jacobite control to keep their lands, provided they swore allegiance to William and Mary. The clause 'all such as are under their protection' was, in fact, omitted from the copy of the articles sent to London for ratification, but William insisted this was merely a clerical error and reinserted it before he signed the treaty in February 1692. Even though the 'omitted clause' was again omitted when the Irish parliament ratified the Treaty of Limerick in 1697,[35] this seems to have had little impact on the way claims under the treaty were dealt with. Thus, many Irish Jacobites were able to escape confiscation by claiming the benefit of the articles. Others were saved by royal pardons issued over the next several years. Little of the land forfeited, however, was set aside to pay for the arrears due to the army. Instead, William sought to use it as a form of patronage to reward royal favourites and loyal servants of the crown, and proceeded to make substantial grants to a number of individuals, several of them foreigners. This drew the wrath of the parliament in England, who used the King's desperate need for money to force him to agree to an Act of Resumption in 1700, which empowered thirteen trustees to hear claims on forfeited estates and to sell whatever property remained. In the process, a small number of persons were able to recover their estates.

The combined effect of the Williamite confiscations was to reduce the proportion of profitable land held by Catholics from 22 per cent in 1688 to 14 per cent in 1703. The percentage loss, in fact, was much smaller than it had been between the Irish Rebellion and the Cromwellian ascendancy, when the proportion had shrunk from 60 per cent to a mere 9 per cent in the late 1650s, or even, in fact, between the Irish Rebellion and the Restoration: under Charles II the

Catholics still possessed only one-third of the amount of land they had held in 1641. However, this was not to be the end of the story. The ability of Catholics in Ireland to own and inherit land was also to be affected by the enactment of new penal laws.

The first article of the Treaty of Limerick had stipulated that Catholics in Ireland should enjoy the same privileges in the exercise of their religion as they had done during the reign of Charles II. However, there were many Protestants, especially in Ireland, but also in England, who had come to believe that the only way to prevent any future rebellions in Ireland was to place further restrictions on the exercise of the Catholic religion. As a result, over the course of the 1690s and early eighteenth century a series of measures dramatically curtailing the rights and religious freedoms of Catholics came to be enacted.[36] The penal laws emerged piecemeal: it would be misleading to portray them as a systematic code. Besides, there was no central decision-making body for Ireland, and because of the workings of Poynings' Law of 1494, which required that any legislation the Irish parliament enacted had to be approved by the English privy council, Irish policy inevitably tended to reflect the interaction of various distinct interests – the members of the Irish parliament, the lord lieutenant in Ireland, the privy council in England, and, of course, the king and his ministers in London – which could pull in different directions.[37] Nevertheless, it would be equally misleading to imply that the penal laws emerged totally haphazardly. They did represent the determination of Protestants on both sides of the Irish Sea, in the aftermath of yet another Catholic rebellion in Ireland, to try to make that kingdom safe for the ruling Protestant elite, and at least some of the measures passed reflected a definite Protestant policy constructed by the King, the English parliament and the Irish parliament acting in concord.[38]

An important preliminary step was taken in 1691, when the English parliament passed an act requiring all office-holders in Ireland and members of the Irish parliament to take the new oaths of allegiance and supremacy stipulated by the English Declaration of Rights, and to subscribe a declaration against transubstantiation.[39] Henceforth, membership of the Irish parliament was to be confined to Protestants. This was crucial because, as a result of William's need to raise revenues in Ireland, the Irish parliament became a much more significant political force after the Glorious Revolution than it ever had been before. No parliament had sat in Ireland since 1666 (not counting James's parliament of 1689); from 1692 it was to meet regularly and was to play a crucial role in shaping what the Revolution settlement was to mean for the people of Ireland.

One of the first things the 1692 parliament did was to pass an Act of Recognition, affirming that William and Mary had 'an undoubted Right to the Crown of Ireland' and that the Kingdom of Ireland was annexed to the imperial crown of England.[40] This simply confirmed the transfer of the crown that had been determined by the English parliament in 1689. Beyond that, however, MPs showed themselves angry over the leniency showed towards Catholics by the Treaty of Limerick and worried by the government's handling of confiscated property. Thus they rejected a number of bills drawn up by the privy council – including a finance bill, on the grounds that it was the sole right of the Commons 'to prepare heads of bills for raising money' – and threatened to censure office-holders suspected of corruption. On this occasion the then Lord Lieutenant, Viscount Sidney, decided to bring the session to a speedy conclusion, rebuking the Commons for its conduct; the parliament was dissolved the following year.[41]

Sidney's successor, however – the virulently anti-Catholic Henry Lord Capel, who served as Lord Deputy in 1695–6 – proved much more willing to appease the prejudices of the Protestant gentry who dominated the Irish Commons. When a new parliament met in 1695 it passed two new penal laws: one imposing a £200 fine on anyone sending their children abroad to be educated in a foreign seminary, abbey, convent or Catholic university or college, the other disarming papists and forbidding them from owning horses worth more than £5 (though a clause was inserted by the English privy council which, in effect, exempted those covered by the Treaty of Limerick). The second act was an understandable security measure, in the aftermath of a Catholic rebellion and at a time of a continued continental war with Catholic France; the Protestants were also alarmed by the increase of rapparee activity in the aftermath of the war, fears of which were heightened by the actions of French pirates off the Irish coast. The first measure was ostensibly motivated by security considerations too:

those educated abroad, the act claimed, abandoned their allegiance 'to the Kings and Queens of this realm, and the affection which they owe to the established religion and laws of their native country', 'engaged themselves in foreign interests', and upon their return invariably became 'the movers and promoters of many dangerous seditions, and oftentimes open rebellion'. The same act also prohibited Catholics in Ireland from teaching or instructing youth in learning: the rationale offered was that conniving at Catholic schools had been a major reason why so many of 'the natives of this kingdom' remained 'ignorant of the principles of true religion', did not 'conform themselves to the laws and statutes of this realm', and failed to use 'the English habit or language'.[42] The measure, therefore, struck not just at the Catholic faith; it also struck at Irishness.

In 1697 the Irish parliament passed an act banishing all Catholic bishops, Jesuits, regular Popish clergy (monks and friars) and all other papists exercising any ecclesiastical jurisdiction, again on the grounds that such persons had been responsible for promoting and carrying on 'the late rebellions in this kingdom'.[43] That same year, when the Irish parliament finally ratified the Treaty of Limerick, it omitted two key articles touching on the religious rights of Catholics – article one, affording Catholics in Ireland the same religious freedoms as they had under Charles II, and article nine, stipulating that no oaths would be required of Irish Catholics other than the oath of allegiance – thereby removing any obstacle to the enactment of any further penal laws.[44] There followed a measure to prevent Protestants from marrying Catholics – on the grounds that such intermarriage led to conversions to popery, to 'the great prejudice of the Protestant interest' – which basically sought to prevent the possibility of Protestant land or wealth passing into Catholic hands as the result of a mixed marriage.[45] In 1698 the Irish parliament passed an act forbidding Catholics from practising the law (which was amended, with stiffer penalties, in 1707).[46] With Catholics already banned from holding office under the crown, the only profession open to them – besides the Church – was now medicine.

The legislation against Catholics was strengthened and extended under Queen Anne. An Act of 1703 forbade Catholic clergy from entering the country after 1 January 1704; with, in theory, no bishops to ordain new clergymen in Ireland and no replacements allowed from abroad, the supply of priests should have effectively dried up. Again, the ostensible motive was security: the act claimed that Catholic bishops, Jesuits and regular clergy had been entering the country (and thus evading the provisions of the Banishment Act of 1697) 'under the disguise or pretence of being Popish secular priests, with intent to stir up her Majesty's Popish subjects to rebellion', and seems to have been designed as a temporary wartime measure, initially being in force for only fourteen years.[47] An act of 1704 to prevent the further growth of popery struck against Catholic landowners: it outlawed primogeniture for Catholics, deeming that estates of Catholics had to be divided amongst all male heirs unless the eldest son turned Protestant; it also prohibited Catholics from buying land or leasing it for more than thirty-one years.[48] The same year an Act for Registering the Popish Clergy required parish priests, on pain of transportation, to take out a bond for their good behaviour – some 1,089 did so – and forbade them from keeping curates and leaving their counties. It also offered pensions of £20 per year to those priests who converted to the Church of Ireland.[49] However an act of 1709, passed in response to a Jacobite invasion scare of the previous year, stipulated that these priests had to take an oath abjuring the Pretender (or face banishment) and made the Act of 1703 banishing popish secular clergy perpetual; at the same time, it increased the pension for priests who converted to £30 per year.[50]

The driving force behind much of the anti-Catholic legislation was, therefore, concern for the security of the Revolution settlement at a time when the British monarchy remained at war with Catholic France. These concerns were heightened in the early eighteenth century as the succession problem again reared its head following the death of Anne's sole surviving child, the Duke of Gloucester (in 1700), the outbreak of renewed warfare with France (from 1702) and Louis XIV's declaration of support for James Francis Edward Stuart (who assumed the title of James III) following the death of James II, and as doubts about the commitment of the English Tories to the Hanoverian succession began to arise during Anne's reign. However, with the accession of George I in 1714 and the failure of the Jacobite intrigues in England and Scotland in 1715, the Catholic question became less of a central issue. In 1719, in response to reports that large numbers of Catholic clergymen were entering the country illegally, the Irish House of Commons introduced a bill proposing that unregistered priests should be branded on the face – the Irish privy council suggested castration as an alternative – and increasing the restrictions on Catholic land transactions, but the measure was rejected by the Irish House of Lords. The only major additional legal disability imposed after the Hanoverian succession was an act of 1728 prohibiting Catholics from voting in parliamentary elections, although since Catholics had already been excluded from corporate office (and hence could only vote in a minority of borough elections in any case), and since there was a declining number of Catholics who met the freehold qualification following the Popery Act of 1704, the impact of this measure was less great than one might expect it to have been.

The cumulative effect of the penal laws could have been dramatic, if strictly enforced. The drive against Catholic clergy did sustain some momentum in the immediate aftermath of the passage of the relevant legislation. Thus some 400 regular clergy were deported following the Banishment Act of 1697; others were forced into hiding.[51] But the Protestant administration in Ireland soon showed that it had neither the ability, desire nor stamina to ensure a rigid enforcement of the penal legislation. A major turning point seems to have come in 1709, with the Act for Abjuring the Pretender: only thirty-three clergy conformed, but the measure proved largely a dead letter, and so long as they were registered and stuck to their own counties Catholic clergy were left unmolested. Moreover, there was no actual prohibition of Catholic religious services, nor a sustained missionary effort by the Protestant establishment to convert the mass of the population. By the time of George II's reign (1727–60), if not earlier, the Protestant minority in Ireland had come to terms with the fact that they would remain a minority. Indeed, Protestant landowners and traders, it was said, preferred to have a servile, underprivileged class to do the sort of menial tasks at low wages which many Protestants thought were beneath them; nor did they want the increased competition for rewarding jobs in the law, civil administration, army or Church that a mass conversion of Catholics to Protestantism would inevitably bring.[52] But the burden of the penal laws did prove particularly heavy for Catholics from the higher rungs of the social hierarchy and many felt under pressure to conform. Between 1703 and 1789, some 5,500 Catholics registered themselves as converts to the Church of Ireland, most of them members of the professional or landed classes. The result of such conversions meant that the total proportion of land held by Catholics fell dramatically: from 14 per cent in 1703 to perhaps as low as 5 per cent by 1779 (if the oft-quoted guestimate by Arthur Young can be treated with any reliability).[53]

The Protestant ascendancy that was being consolidated, however, was to be a Church of Ireland one. The Protestant squirearchy who dominated the Irish parliament were predominantly high churchmen, and they showed themselves almost as concerned about the threat of Protestant dissent, and especially the Scottish Presbyterians in Ulster, as they were about popery. Relations between the Scottish Presbyterians and churchmen in the north of Ireland had never been particularly good, and although differences had been temporarily put to one side in the face of the Jacobite threat in 1689–90, they were soon to re-emerge.[54] Almost as soon as the siege of Derry was over, the two groups started bickering over who deserved the greatest credit. With the conclusion of the war, the Presbyterians expected some form of legal toleration for the sacrifices they had made on behalf of the Protestant cause. Not that the Presbyterians in Ireland had suffered in the way that their brethren in Scotland or even England had. The main laws that affected them were the Elizabethan Act of Supremacy of 1560, which enforced attendance at parish church, and the Act of Uniformity of 1666, which required all ministers to be episcopally ordained and all clerics and schoolteachers to subscribe a declaration against the Covenant, but these measures had seldom been enforced against Presbyterians. Nonconformists did face occasional persecution in some localities; however, the tacit agreement reached after the Restoration seems to have been that the dissenters would be allowed to hold their own religious services unmolested as long as they did not seek to expand their congregations.

The trouble was, in the 1690s the Scottish Presbyterians were expanding in numbers in Ireland – dramatically so – thanks to the arrival of Scots seeking to escape the economic dislocation in their own homeland (most of whom, except for a few Catholic Highlanders, were Presbyterians). We have no accurate statistics for the size of the immigration, though contemporaries estimated that anywhere between 50,000 and 80,000 Scottish families entered Ulster in the reigns of William and Anne. What we do know is that whereas there were 86 Presbyterian ministers in Ulster in 1689, there were over 130 by 1702.[55] Moreover, the act of the English parliament of 1691, stipulating new oaths for Ireland, had repealed the old Elizabethan oath of supremacy, which many Scottish Presbyterians found objectionable because it made the monarch head of the Church, and replaced it with one that omitted this wording, thus opening the door for Presbyterians to hold office. As a result of these developments, in many parts of Ulster (especially counties Antrim and Londonderry), Scottish Presbyterians came heavily to outnumber Protestants of the Established Church; and being engaged mainly in commerce and manufacture, they also came to dominate a number of corporations, such as Belfast, Derry, Carrickfergus and Coleraine, and were thus able to use their power to secure the return of Presbyterians to parliament. With the Revolution in Scotland already having resulted in the overthrow of episcopacy, the Protestant landowners in the Irish parliament and the clergy of the Established Church of Ireland began to fear a similar threat to the ecclesiastical establishment in Ireland, and so refused to grant a formal toleration to Presbyterians unless a test was introduced to exclude them from office. Thus proposals for toleration in 1692 and 1695 were thrown out by the Irish council and the Irish parliament; there were even calls for a stricter enforcement of the laws already on the books. A bitter war of words erupted between the two religious interests and relations between churchmen and Presbyterians at the local level deteriorated dramatically: the churchmen claimed that the Presbyterians withheld tithes and insulted their clergy; the Presbyterians, in turn, suffered harassment, as they were prevented from conducting their own weddings and funerals and compelled to hold office as parish churchwardens without being allowed to hire deputies.

The Williamite regime made no attempt to increase the disabilities on Presbyterians; indeed, it not only continued the *regium donum*, the royal pension given annually to Presbyterian ministers in Ireland, but increased it to £1,200, and resisted pressure from the Irish bishops for government permission to enforce the laws against dissent more strictly. The situation changed under Anne, however, as fears grew among high-church Tories in England, who dominated the royal administrations of the early years of Anne's reign, that the Church was in danger from dissent. Thus in 1704 the English privy council decided to incorporate a clause into the Popery Act of that year requiring all office-holders in Ireland to take the sacramental test, a move that proved very welcome to the Irish parliament, where it was said that the House of Commons was 'made up of two thirds of as High-Churchmen as any in England'.[56] Gradually, the Presbyterians were forced out of the corporations in Ulster.[57] The position for Irish dissenters grew even worse during the final years of Anne's reign, when the high-church Tories were once again ascendant: the *regium donum* was suspended in 1714, and there were even plans to introduce the English Schism Act of that year into Ireland. Things calmed down somewhat following the accession of George I in October 1714. The *regium donum* was restored and augmented, and in 1719, under pressure from the new Whig administration in England, the Irish parliament passed a limited Toleration Act. This exempted Protestant dissenters from the Acts of Uniformity of 1560 and 1666, provided they took the oaths of allegiance and supremacy and abjuring the Pretender, and made a declaration against transubstantiation (Quakers were allowed to affirm). The act recognized their right to hold their own religious meetings if they were licensed and the doors left open. It also exempted nonconformist ministers from serving on juries and in parish or ward offices and allowed dissenters to hire deputies if elected to parish office (though explicitly stating that they were not to be exempt from tithes or other parish dues). It nevertheless left the sacramental test on the books, which was to remain in force until 1780.[58]

The transformed political context after the Glorious Revolution also had an effect on the nature of the relationship between Ireland and England. Ireland had long occupied an ambivalent constitutional position. A country that had been conquered by the English crown, starting in the later twelfth century under Henry II – and arguably reconquered several times following English suppression of various rebellions in Ireland over the centuries – it nevertheless had its own parliament and had been a kingdom in its own right since 1541. Yet Poynings' Law required English approval of any legislation enacted in the Irish parliament, whereas in certain circumstances the English parliament seemed to have the right to legislate for Ireland. Ireland was thus, in some senses, both a kingdom and a colony; not quite a totally independent realm, but neither simply a conquered territory under imperial rule.[59] The Protestant ascendancy in Ireland, however, had tended to resent attempts by the government in England to regulate Irish affairs, especially when such attempts at regulation were designed to ensure that Irish interests were subordinated to English ones; they were less likely to get upset when English interference in Ireland was designed to protect the Protestant interest in Ireland against the threat of popery. Constitutional theorists in Ireland typically chose to represent Ireland as a sister kingdom to England, which owed allegiance to the same sovereign king – a king whose authority extended to all his dominions – but not to the English parliament, since Ireland had its own, autonomous parliament.[60] The trouble for this conception of the constitutional relationship was that the Glorious Revolution in England had involved a shift in the perception of where sovereignty lay: no longer in the crown alone, but in the crown-in-parliament. It followed, at least as far as the English were concerned, that the power that the king once had over his dominions was now vested in the king (or queen), English Lords and English Commons. Increasingly, policy for Ireland came to be determined not by the crown but by the crown's ministers, who came to control the appointment of the lord lieutenant and other offices in the Irish executive and even the membership of the English privy council which oversaw legislation for Ireland. The political elite in Ireland, naturally, were far from happy with such developments.

As we have seen, there had been signs of tension already in the 1692 parliament, when the Irish Commons had refused to sanction bills introduced by the English privy council. But things came to a head towards the end of the decade, when the English parliament pushed for an act (first mooted in 1697, passed in 1699) to prevent the export of Irish woollen goods, in order to protect the interests of the English woollen textiles industry.[61] The proposal created a furore when the Irish parliament met in 1698 and prompted William Molyneux, MP for Trinity College, to publish *The Case of Ireland's being Bound by Acts of Parliament in England Stated* in defence of Irish legislative independence. Molyneux denied a royal title to Ireland based upon conquest, either by Henry II or following any succeeding rebellion; instead, he claimed that 'all the Ecclesiastical and Civil States of Ireland' had made 'an Intire and Voluntary Submission' to Henry II, who in return 'did not only settle the Laws of England in Ireland, and the Jurisdiction Ecclesiastical there . . . but did likewise Allow them the Freedom of Holding Parliaments in Ireland, as a separate and distinct Kingdom from England'. The English parliament was swift to condemn Molyneux's book, and might have taken further action against Molyneux himself had he not died later that year.[62]

Yet although Molyneux is often held up as the intellectual father of Protestant Irish patriotism, which was to come to full fruition in the 1770s and 1780s, Molyneux's main grievance was less the infringement of Irish sovereignty than government without consent. Indeed, far from being a champion of Irish independence, Molyneux even maintained that the Protestants of Ireland would willingly embrace a parliamentary union with England, though he confessed that this was 'an happiness we can hardly hope for'.[63] And as union between England and Scotland came to be placed on the political agenda in the early eighteenth century, many Protestants in Ireland warmed to the idea of a union for themselves – on the grounds that not only would it give them representation in Westminster but would also enhance their prosperity and provide greater security. On three occasions – in 1703, 1707 and 1709 – the Irish parliament made appeals for union, though the English did not see it as being to their advantage and allowed the matter to drop.[64]

Not only did the idea of Irish union come to nothing, but the reality of the Scottish union had a deleterious effect on Ireland. With Scottish independence gone, the tendency for the English to think of Ireland merely as its first colony was considerably reinforced, and the new British administration increasingly tended to appoint Englishmen to civil and ecclesiastical office in Ireland, rather than Protestants born in Ireland. The Irish parliament made one last attempt to assert its political independence in 1719, following a lawsuit concerning the possession of an estate (Sherlock v. Annesley), where, on appeal, the British House of Lords overturned the decision that had first been given by the Irish upper house. The Irish House of Lords made a strong representation to George I, asserting its right of jurisdiction in Ireland and condemning the British Lords for attacking George's sovereignty as king of Ireland. The British parliament responded in 1720 by passing a Declaratory Act, which asserted the right of the British parliament to legislate for Ireland and denied the appellate jurisdiction of the Irish House of Lords.[65] There could henceforth be no doubt of Ireland's subordinate status. It was certainly not a sister kingdom to England. Indeed, some historians have seen the years 1691–1720 as marking Ireland's final descent from kingdom to colony.[66]

BRITISH REVOLUTIONS: SIGNIFICANCE AND HISTORICAL LEGACY

Finally let us turn to a consideration of the larger significance of the revolutions of the later seventeenth century. Historians have long accustomed us to thinking that if there was a revolution in seventeenth-century England, then it occurred in mid-century. Even those revisionist historians who, in the 1970s and 1980s, tried to persuade us that there was no high road to Civil War and that early Stuart England was a most unrevolutionary place, nevertheless still believed that what eventually came to pass in the 1640s and 1650s was not only a revolution but indeed 'the Revolution', a seismic event which had 'profound effects on the subsequent history of the British Isles'.[67] If anything, the recent Britannic shift that the historiography of the early Stuart period has taken has helped to salvage the revolutionary credentials of the mid-century crisis, since if we cease restricting ourselves to England and look at Britain and Ireland as a whole, the train of events set in motion by the Scottish resistance to the imposition of a new prayer book of 1637 appears to have an undoubtedly revolutionary hue. By comparison, as noted in the Introduction, the Glorious Revolution has usually been seen as a mere after tremor, a tidying-up operation, but not the 'major earthquake itself'.[68]

Yet is it right to downplay the significance of the Glorious Revolution in this way? It might help to shape our thinking about this issue by playing a little intellectual game. Imagine that someone – let us make him an Englishman of moderate Whig leanings – who had died towards the end of the 1630s, miraculously returned from the grave fifty years later (before William of Orange's invasion): would he conclude that a major revolution had taken place in the intervening period? He would find in the 1680s, as in the 1630s, Stuart monarchs on the throne who preferred, as much as possible, to rule without parliament, who sought to establish their royal prerogative above the law, and who appealed to notions of divine right and non-resistance to legitimize their rule – if anything, our man would see a more blatant articulation of theories of royal absolutism in the media in the 1680s than he would have been familiar with from his earlier existence. He would see a similar threat to the Protestant religion and English political liberties from popery and arbitrary government in the 1680s as had been complained about in the years before the Civil War, with the difference that after 1685 there was actually a Catholic monarch on the throne in possession of a sizeable standing army, thereby making the threat seem even more real than it would have appeared in the 1630s. Scotland would likewise probably seem in a worse position in the 1680s than it had fifty years earlier. Although episcopacy had been revived under James VI and I (1567–1625), and Presbyterianism was already being undermined (with the 1630s seeing what to many Scots seemed alarming attacks on the traditional style of Scottish worship), there were as yet no penal laws against Presbyterians. Fifty years later, however, our man would see episcopacy in the ascendant and the Presbyterians suffering brutal persecution, with some even being shot in the fields by the king's forces. With regard to Ireland, he would for sure notice significant changes in the proportion of land actually owned by Catholics by the time of his resurrection – a mere third of what it had been fifty years earlier. Yet he would see that the Catholics were beginning to regain some of their lost land, and witness a dramatic Catholicization of the civil and military administration under James II, with Ireland being placed in the hands of a Catholic Lord Deputy and talk of the imminent overturning of the Restoration land settlement. In all three kingdoms, our man

would see a threat to the rule of law and the rights of borough corporations. If there had been a revolution in the intervening fifty years,
he might well be wondering what on earth it had achieved, and how
the political and religious freedoms of Protestants had been secured
as a result.

Imagine now that a man of similar political leanings, who had died
some months prior to William's invasion, returned from the grave just
over thirty years later (let us make it 1720, the concluding date of this
book). He would immediately notice dramatic differences. He would
see a limited monarch, at the head of a British state and the separate
kingdom of Ireland, whose prerogative was beneath the law and who
shared his sovereignty with a parliament which was now assured of
meeting regularly – albeit with general elections every seven years
instead of every three, following the passage of the Septennial Act in
1716. Protestantism would appear safe in all three kingdoms;
Presbyterianism north of the border secured; and the threat of popery
and arbitrary government finally extinguished. It would be immediately apparent that 1720 was a very different world from that of the
1680s. Our man could not help but conclude that something had happened in the meantime which had effected a very fundamental transformation of the British polity.

It is a major conclusion of this study that this fundamental transformation was in large part brought about by the revolutions of the
late seventeenth century. This is not to deny the revolutionary
credentials of the upheavals of the mid-century; indeed, as I have
argued elsewhere, it is important to appreciate what was revolutionary about the mid-century crisis – how it altered the nature of the
British dynamic and changed the structure of politics (particularly
with regard to the growing importance of public opinion as a force in
politics) – in order to understand political developments under the
later Stuarts.[69] Yet this is not the same as saying that there was just
one, long drawn-out revolution that took place over the course of the
Stuart century as a whole. The transformation that was wrought
between the 1680s and 1720s owed little to what had transpired in
the 1640s and 1650s. The mid-century revolution had been defeated,
and although it had left a legacy of problems to be addressed it can
scarcely claim credit for the type of polity that had emerged in the

British Isles by the reign of George I. What transformed the British polity, and what made the political inheritance of the Hanoverians so different from that of the Stuarts, was not the mid-century revolution but the later-seventeenth-century affair that we traditionally refer to as the Glorious Revolution.

Not that this transformation can be attributed entirely to the Glorious Revolution, to be sure. We have to acknowledge that new developments in the 1690s and early eighteenth century also played a vital role in helping to reconfigure the type of political and religious establishments that existed in England, Scotland and Ireland. Nevertheless, this should not lead us to lose sight of the significance of the events of 1688–9. The dynastic shift that was brought about as a result of William's invasion triggered three separate revolutions in all three kingdoms, which, by themselves, were major transformative events in each of those separate kingdoms. These revolutions in turn carried implications – many of which were, in fact, foreseen by those who helped bring about the dynastic shift – that had to be addressed over the next few years and which thus should be seen as part of the working out of the Revolution settlement. These revolutions also affected the nature of the relationship between the three kingdoms, spawning in the process what might be termed a fourth, British revolution, which had fundamental implications for the position of Scotland and Ireland (and their respective relationships with England) within the broader, British polity. One can hardly say that the people who made 1688–9 happen deliberately set out to get to 1707 or 1720. Nevertheless, the fact that the British polity did get to where it was in 1720 had a lot to do, both directly and indirectly, with the revolutions that had happened at the end of the 1680s.

Put like this, the argument may sound unduly Whiggish. Yet it is not my intention to end on a triumphalist note. There were losses as well as gains as a result of the later-seventeenth-century revolutions, as this book has recognized. There would have been hundreds of thousands of people across Britain and Ireland who must have doubted whether the revolutions had done anything to secure the liberties that they particularly cherished: the Catholic majority in Ireland, of course (and the Catholic minorities in England and Scotland, too); the Episcopalians in Scotland (a sizeable minority, to say the least); many of those throughout the three kingdoms who found themselves liable to a much heavier tax burden; even the supposed victors in Scotland and Ireland who found their own political autonomy under threat from the metropolis. The Glorious Revolution might have saved Britain and Ireland from popery and arbitrary government and defeated the trend towards royal absolutism that we see in the 1680s, yet it also accelerated the existing tendencies towards centralization within the British multiple monarchy.[70] Scotland lost its political independence, and although the Scots had representation at Westminster they had limited opportunity to get national issues put on the agenda of the newly created British parliament. In this respect, Ireland fared somewhat better, since it kept its own parliament, and although the Declaratory Act of 1720 confirmed the ability of the Westminster parliament to legislate for Ireland, it only normally exercised this power on matters of private business.[71] Nevertheless, the Protestant ascendancy in Ireland resented the way the English (and now the British) treated them, leading to the emergence over the course of the eighteenth century of a distinctive brand of Irish Protestant nationalism. Besides, the Irish parliament hardly represented the people of Ireland. The Revolution had the effect of making Ireland safe for an ascendant Protestant interest that comprised perhaps only 10 per cent of the population; even Protestant dissenters were to be excluded from holding office in the service of the state. Finally, one cannot fail to point out that many of the problems that were created, bequeathed or exacerbated by the revolutions of 1688–9 have survived with us for well over three centuries. The Scots won back the right to hold their own parliament only in 1999. Sectarian conflict in Northern Ireland still defines itself in terms of the struggles of the later seventeenth century.

The Glorious Revolution was indeed a revolution. More precisely, the dynastic crisis of 1688–9 spawned separate English, Scottish, Irish and British revolutions that wrought major changes across the British Isles which go a long way to explaining why the polity that emerged in the eighteenth century was very different from that which had prevailed (and had survived an earlier attempted revolution) in the seventeenth century. This is merely to recognize a reality rather than to applaud the outcome. It is by historical convention that we describe what took place in 1688–9 as the Glorious Revolution, and it would be churlish to insist that we refrain from using the term altogether, even though we recognize that those contemporaries who coined the term deliberately sought to incorporate a value judgement in the label they affixed to events of which they approved. We can recognize the revolutionary significance of what transpired without necessarily endorsing that value judgement. Glorious for some, not-so-glorious for others, the British revolutions of the later seventeenth century nevertheless had a huge transformative impact. They changed the course of history for the three kingdoms and left a lasting legacy, the implications of which remain with us to this day.

Notes

N.B. All works cited were published in London, unless otherwise stated.

ABBREVIATIONS

APS	*The Acts of the Parliaments of Scotland*, ed. Thomas Thomson and Cosmo Innes (12 vols., Edinburgh, 1814–75)
BIHR	*Bulletin of the Institute of Historical Research*
BL	British Library
Bodl.	Bodleian Library, Oxford
Bulstrode Newsletters	Newsletters of Richard Bulstrode, 1667–89, from the Harry Ransome Humanities Research Center at the University of Texas at Austin (Marlborough, 2002)
Cal. Anc. Rec. Dub.	*Calendar of the Ancient Records of Dublin, in the Possession of the Municipal Corporation of that City*, ed. John T. Gilbert (16 vols., Dublin, 1889–1913)
CClarSP	*Calendar of Clarendon State Papers Preserved in the Bodleian Library*, ed. F. J. Routledge (5 vols., Oxford, 1872–1932)
CJ	*Journals of the House of Commons*
Clar. Corr.	*The Correspondence of Henry Hyde, Earl of Clarendon and of His Brother Laurence Hyde, Earl of Rochester; With the Diary of Lord Clarendon from 1687 to 1690, Containing Minute Particulars of the Events Attending the Revolution*, ed. Samuel Weller Singer (2 vols., 1828)
CLRO	Corporation of London Record Office

Cox, *Hibernia Anglicana* ... *Second Part*	Sir Richard Cox, *Hibernia Anglicana: Or, The History of Ireland from the Conquest thereof by the English, to this Present Time ... In Two Parts* (2nd edn, 1692)
CSPD	*Calendar of State Papers Domestic*
CUL	Cambridge University Library
Dalrymple, *Memoirs*	Sir John Dalrymple, *Memoirs of Great Britain and Ireland; From the Dissolution of the Last Parliament of Charles II till the Capture of the French and Spanish Fleets at Vigo. A New Edition, in Three Volumes; With the Appendices Complete* (1790)
Ellis Corr.	*Letters Written During the Years 1686–88 to John Ellis*, ed. George Agar Ellis (2 vols., 1829)
EUL	Edinburgh University Library
Evelyn, *Diary*	*The Diary of John Evelyn*, ed. E. S. De Beer (6 vols., Oxford, 1955)
Fountainhall, *Decisions*	Sir John Lauder of Fountainhall, *The Decisions of the Lords of Council and Session from June 6th, 1678, to July 30th, 1713* (2 vols., Edinburgh, 1759–61)
Fountainhall, *Hist. Not.*	Sir John Lauder of Fountainhall, *Historical Notices of Scotish [sic] Affairs*, ed. David Laing (2 vols., Edinburgh, 1848)
Fountainhall, *Hist. Obs.*	Sir John Lauder of Fountainhall, *Historical Observes of Memorable Occurrents in Church and State from October 1680 to April 1686*, ed. David Laing and A. Urquhart (Edinburgh, 1840)
FSL	Folger Shakespeare Library, Washington, D.C.
Hatt. Corr.	*Correspondence of the Hatton Family, 1601–1704. Being Chiefly Letters Addressed to Christopher, First Viscount Hatton*, ed. E. M. Thompson (2 vols., 1873)
Henning, *House of Commons*	Basil Duke Henning, ed., *The House of Commons, 1660–1690* (3 vols., 1983)
HMC	*Historical Manuscripts Commission*
Hunt. Lib.	Huntington Library, San Marino, Calif.
LC	Library of Congress, Washington, D.C.
Letters to Sancroft	*A Collection of Letters Addressed by Prelates and Individuals of High Rank in Scotland and by Two Bishops of Sodor and Man to Sancroft Archbishop of Canterbury*, ed. William Nelson Clarke (Edinburgh, 1848)

Leven and Melville Papers	Leven and Melville Papers. Letters and State Papers Chiefly Addressed to George Earl of Melville, Secretary of State for Scotland 1689–1691. From the Originals in the Possession of the Earl of Leven and Melville, ed. William Leslie Melville (Edinburgh, 1843)
Life of James II	The Life of James II, ed. J. S. Clarke (2 vols., 1816)
LJ	Journals of the House of Lords
LMA	London Metropolitan Archives (formerly Greater London Record Office)
Lond. Gaz.	London Gazette
Lond. Int.	The London Intelligence
Lond. Merc.	London Mercury or Moderate Intelligencer
Luttrell	Narcissus Luttrell, A Brief Historical Relation of State Affairs from September, 1678, to April, 1714 (6 vols., Oxford, 1857)
Melvilles and Leslies	The Melvilles Earls of Melville and the Leslies Earls of Leven, ed. Sir William Fraser (3 vols., Edinburgh, 1890)
Merc. Ref.	Mercurius Reformatus
Morrice	Dr Williams's Library, London: Roger Morrice, Entr'ing Books P, Q, R
NA	National Archives (formerly Public Record Office)
NAS	National Archives of Scotland (formerly Scottish Record Office)
NLI	National Library of Ireland
NLS	National Library of Scotland
Orange Gaz.	Orange Gazette
Oxford DNB	Oxford Dictionary of National Biography (Oxford, 2004)
Parl. Hist.	The Parliamentary History of England from the earliest Period to the Year 1803, ed. William Cobbett (36 vols., 1806–20)
Petty–Southwell Corr.	The Petty–Southwell Correspondence 1676–1687, edited from the Bowood Papers by the Marquis of Lansdowne (1928, reprinted New York, 1967)
POAS	Poems on Affairs of State, ed. Geoffrey de Forest Lord, et al. (7 vols., New Haven, Conn., 1963–75)
Pub. Occ.	Publick Occurrences
Reresby, Memoirs	Memoirs of Sir John Reresby, ed. Andrew Browning

	(Glasgow, 1936, 2nd edn with a new preface and notes, Mary K. Geiter and W. A. Speck, 1991)
RO	Record Office
RPCS	*The Register of the Privy Council of Scotland. Third Series, 1661–1691*, ed. P. H. Brown, et al. (16 vols., Edinburgh, 1908–70)
RSCHS	*Records of the Scottish Church History Society*
SR	*The Statutes of the Realm*, ed. A. Luders, T. E. Tomlins and J. France (12 vols., 1810–28)
ST	*State Trials*, ed. T. B. Howell (33 vols., 1809–26)
Steele	Robert Steele, *A Bibliography of Royal Proclamations of the Tudor and Stuart Sovereigns and of others Published under Authority 1485–1714* (3 vols. in 2, New York, 1967)
TCD	Trinity College, Dublin
Univ. Int.	*Universal Intelligence*
Wodrow, *Sufferings*	Robert Wodrow, *History of the Sufferings of the Church of Scotland, from the Restauration to the Revolution* (2 vols., Edinburgh, 1721–2)
Wood, *Life and Times*	Anthony Wood, *Life and Times, 1632–1695*, ed. A. Clark (5 vols., Oxford, 1891–1900)
WYAS	West Yorkshire Archives Service, Sheepscar, Leeds

Introduction

1. Steele, I, no. 3866, II, no. 991, and III, no. 2715.
2. *Ellis Corr.*, II, 52; *HMC, 5th Report*, pp. 378–9.
3. Andrew Barclay, 'Mary [of Modena] (1658–1718)', *Oxford DNB*.
4. *Life of James II*, II, 161.
5. Dalrymple, *Memoirs*, II, 'Part I. Continued. Appendix to Book V', pp. 107–10 (quote on p. 107).
6. Henri and Barbara van der Zee, *1688: Revolution in the Family* (1988), p. 118.
7. [John Whittel], *An Exact Diary of the Late Expedition* (1689), p. 34. Accounts of William's crossing can be found in Thomas Babington Macaulay, *The History of England from the Accession of James the Second*, ed. Sir Charles Firth (6 vols., 1913–15), III, 1118–26; Stephen B. Baxter, *William III* (1966), pp. 237–8; van der Zee, *Revolution in the Family*, ch. 12.
8. 'A Hue and Cry' (1688), in *POAS*, V, 23.
9. Evelyn, *Diary*, IV, 624; Gilbert Burnet, *History of His Own Time: From*

the Restoration of King Charles the Second to the Treaty of Peace at Utrecht, in the Reign of Queen Anne (1850), p. 523; *Clar. Corr.*, II, 249.

10. Burnet, *History of His Own Time*, p. 114.

11. *Painted Ladies; Women at the Court of Charles II*, ed. Catharine MacLeod and Julia Marciari Alexander (2001), p. 203.

12. *HMC, Dartmouth*, I, 36.

13. Cited in van der Zee, *Revolution in the Family*, p. 22.

14. William Bradford Gardner, 'The Later Years of John Maitland, Second Earl and First Duke of Lauderdale', *Journal of Modern History*, 20 (1948), 121–2.

15. Macaulay, *History of England*, II, 663, 670, 781.

16. George Macaulay Trevelyan, *The English Revolution 1688–1689* (1938), pp. 63, 64, 69.

17. F. C. Turner, *James II* (1948), p. 234.

18. J. R. Jones, *The Revolution of 1688 in England* (1972), pp. 17, 53. See also J. R. Jones, 'James II's Revolution: Royal Policies, 1686–92', in Jonathan I. Israel, ed., *The Anglo-Dutch Moment: Essays on the Glorious Revolution and its World Impact* (Cambridge, 1991), pp. 47–71.

19. John Miller, *James II: A Study in Kingship* (Hove, 1978, 3rd edn 2000), pp. 126, 128, 240–1. Cf. John Miller, *The Glorious Revolution* (1983), p. vii.

20. W. A. Speck, *James II: Profiles in Power* (2002), p. 149.

21. Trevelyan, *English Revolution*, p. 64.

22. Jonathan Israel, 'General Introduction' to his *Anglo-Dutch Moment*, p. 5.

23. Cf. Jeremy Black, *A System of Ambition? British Foreign Policy 1660–1793* (1991), p. 135.

24. Geoffrey Holmes, *The Making of a Great Power: Late Stuart and Early Georgian Britain, 1660–1722* (Harlow, 1993), p. 178.

25. *The Diary of Adam de la Pryme*, ed. Charles Jackson, Surtees Society, 54 (1870), p. 14.

26. House of Lords, *Parliamentary Debates (Hansard)*, 5th series, vol. 472 (17 Mar. 1986), p. 796 (speech of Lord Hailsham); Steven Pincus, 'The Making of a Great Power? Universal Monarchy, Political Economy, and the Transformation of English Political Culture', *The European Legacy*, 5 (2000), 541. See also Jonathan Scott, *England's Troubles: Seventeenth-Century English Political Stability in European Context* (Cambridge, 2000).

27. J. C. D. Clark, *English Society 1688–1832* (Cambridge, 1985).

28. Macaulay, *History of England*, III, 1306, 1310, 1312; Trevelyan, *English Revolution*, p. 11.

29. Jennifer Carter, 'The Revolution and the Constitution', in Geoffrey

Holmes, ed., *Britain after the Glorious Revolution, 1689–1714* (1969), pp. 39–58; J. R. Western, *Monarchy and Revolution* (1972); J. P. Kenyon, *Revolution Principles: The Politics of Party 1689–1720* (Cambridge, 1977); Mark Goldie, 'The Roots of True Whiggism 1688–94', *History of Political Thought*, 1 (1980), 195–236; J. R. Jones, 'The Revolution in Context', in J. R. Jones, ed., *Liberty Secured? Britain Before and After 1688* (Stanford, 1992), pp. 11–52; John Miller, 'Crown, Parliament, and People', in Jones, ed., *Liberty Secured?*, pp. 53–87; Tim Harris, *Politics under the Later Stuarts* (1993), ch. 5.

30. Lois G. Schwoerer, *The Declaration of Rights, 1689* (Baltimore, 1981); W. A. Speck, *Reluctant Revolutionaries* (Oxford, 1988).

31. Ian B. Cowan, 'The Reluctant Revolutionaries: Scotland in 1688', in Eveline Cruickshanks, ed., *By Force or By Default? The Revolution of 1688–1689* (Edinburgh, 1989), pp. 65–81; Gordon Donaldson, *Scotland: James V to James VII* (Edinburgh, 1965), p. 383; Rosalind Mitchinson, *Lordship to Patronage: Scotland, 1603–1745* (1983), p. 116.

32. J. G. Simms, *Jacobite Ireland, 1685–91* (1969) is the best study of the Revolution in Ireland.

33. Derek Hirst, *England in Conflict, 1603–1660* (1999), p. 255.

34. Tim Harris, *Restoration: Charles II and His Kingdoms, 1660–85* (2005).

35. Jones, *Revolution of 1688*, p. 13; David H. Hosford, *Nottingham, the Nobles and the North: Aspects of the Revolution of 1688* (Hamden, Conn., 1976).

36. See Harris, *Restoration*, pp. 22–3, 26, for a discussion of the franchise.

37. Mark Goldie, 'The Unacknowledged Republic: Officeholding in Early Modern England', in Tim Harris, ed., *The Politics of the Excluded, c. 1500–1850* (Basingstoke, 2001), pp. 153–94 (esp. pp. 161–2).

38. See Harris, *Restoration*, pp. 67, 194–6.

39. Ibid., pp. 28–9.

40. Ibid., pp. 59, 91, 114.

41. Ibid., p. 29.

42. Ibid., p. 94.

43. Ronald Hutton, *Charles II: King of England, Scotland, and Ireland* (Oxford, 1989), p. 357.

44. J. R. Jones, *Charles II: Royal Politician* (1987), p. 162.

45. Black, *System of Ambition?*, p. 135; Jonathan Israel, 'General Introduction', p. 5; Robert Beddard, ed., *The Revolutions of 1688* (Oxford, 1988), p. 97; Richard Braverman, *Plots and Counterplots: Sexual Politics and the Body Politic in English Literature, 1660–1730* (Cambridge, 1993), pp. 8, 97.

46. Harris, *Restoration*, p. 25.

47. *Parl. Hist.*, IV, cols. 1116, 1118.

48. Harris, *Restoration*, pp. 345–56.

49. Ibid., pp. 390–5, 403–5.

50. Ibid., pp. 242–4.

51. Western, *Monarchy and Revolution*, p. 1; V. F. Snow, 'The Concept of Revolution in Seventeenth-Century England', *Historical Journal*, 5 (1962), pp. 167–74.

52. *The State Prodigal His Returne* [1689], pp. 1, 3.

53. See Harris, *Restoration*, pp. 32–6.

54. W. A. Maguire, ed., *Kings in Conflict: The Revolutionary War in Ireland and its Aftermath 1689–1750* (Belfast, 1990), p. 3.

1 The Accession of the True and Lawful Heir

1. BL, Add. MSS 41,803, fols. 122, 126, 128, 134, 158, 175; F. C. Turner, *James II* (1948), p. 243; George Hilton Jones, *Charles Middleton: The Life and Times of a Restoration Politician* (Chicago, 1967), p. 77.

2. *HMC, Ormonde*, N.S. VII, 331; *Clar. Corr.*, I, 110.

3. *An Account of What His Majesty Said at His First Coming to Council* (1684[/5]); *Lond. Gaz.*, no. 2006 (5–9 Feb. 1684[/5]); *HMC, Egmont*, II, 147–8.

4. *Life of James II*, II, 4; Fountainhall, *Hist. Obs.*, p. 147.

5. Roger L'Estrange, *The Observator in Dialogue* (3 vols., 1684–7), III, no. 1 (11 Feb. 1684[/5]).

6. Benjamin Camfield, *A Sermon Preach'd . . . at Leicester, February the 10th 1684/5* (1685), p. 20.

7. WYAS, MX/R/35/22.

8. Hunt. Lib., STT 2436, Isaac Tyrwhitt to [Sir Richard Temple?], 10 Feb. 1684[/5].

9. BL, MS Stowe 746, fol. 94.

10. Hunt. Lib., STT 728, Bridgwater to Mr Meedon, 7 Feb. 1684[/5]; Steele, I, nos. 3764, 3772.

11. A. F. Havighurst, 'James II and the Twelve Men in Scarlet', *Law Quarterly Review*, 69 (1953), 524.

12. Morrice, Q, 44.

13. *Lond. Gaz.*, nos. 2009 (16–19 Feb. 1684[/5]) and 2010 (19–23 Feb. 1684[/5]); Evelyn, *Diary*, IV, 416–17; Turner, *James II*, pp. 248–52, 366, 384; Steele, III, nos. 2584, 2585.

14. Turner, *James II*, p. 256.

15. *Lond. Gaz.*, 2013 (2–5 Mar. 1684[/5]); Fountainhall, *Hist. Obs.*, p. 157; HMC, *Ormonde*, N. S. VII, 335; Luttrell, I, 335.

16. Fountainhall, *Decisions*, I, 339; James King Hewison, *The Covenanters* (2 vols., Glasgow, 1908), II, 463.

17. *Life of James II*, II, 16; Steele, I, no. 3775.

18. Luttrell, I, 329, 330; Evelyn, *Diary*, IV, 417, 419; HMC, *Ormonde*, N. S. VII, 322, 324; Havighurst, 'James II and the Twelve Men in Scarlet', p. 526.

19. Fountainhall, *Hist. Obs.*, p. 153.

20. Luttrell, I, 332, 337; Fountainhall, *Hist. Obs.*, p. 151; Evelyn, *Diary*, IV, 416, 419; Charles James Fox, *A History of the Early Part of the Reign of James II* (1808), app. pp. lxvi-lxvii; Turner, *James II*, pp. 246–8.

21. HMC, *Ormonde*, N. S. VII, 317, 320; *Letters to Sancroft*, p. 77; Fountainhall, *Hist. Obs.*, p. 149.

22. Camfield, *Sermon Preach'd . . . at Leicester*, p. 20.

23. Erasmus Warren, *Religious Loyalty; Or, Old Allegiance to the New King* (1685), epistle dedicatory.

24. Hunt. Lib., HA 656, Sir Henry Beaumont to Huntingdon, 14 Feb. 1684[/5]; NA, SP 31/1, no. 27. For further examples, see BL, Add. MSS 41,803, fols. 138, 148, 152; Camfield, *Sermon Preach'd . . . at Leicester*, epistle dedicatory.

25. *Lond. Gaz.*, nos. 2009 (16–19 Feb. 1684[/5]) and 2025 (13–16 Apr. 1685); HMC, *Ormonde*, N.S. VII, 318, 325; HMC, *Laing*, I, 427; Luttrell, I, 330; Hunt. Lib., HA 15861, Thomas Stanhope to Sir Arthur Rawdon, 11 Feb. 1684[/5]; Fountainhall, *Decisions*, I, 339; NLI, MS 2993, p. 55; TCD, MS 1178, fol. 18.

26. This insight comes from David Waldstreicher, 'Rites of Rebellion, Rites of Assent: Celebrations, Print Culture and the Origins of American Nationalism', *Journal of American History*, 82 (1995), 37–61.

27. Dorset RO, DC/LR/N23/3, fol. 32. Cf. Berks. RO, H/FAc1, fol. 81 and microfilm T/F41, fol. 261.

28. See, for example, *Lond. Gaz.*, nos. 2008 (12–16 Feb. 1684[/5]), 2012 (26 Feb.–2 Mar. 1684[/5]) and 2028 (23–27 Apr. 1685); BL, Add. MSS 41,803, fol. 138.

29. *Ireland's Lamentation* (1689), p. 7.

30. R. A. Houston, *Social Change in the Age of Enlightenment: Edinburgh, 1660–1760* (Oxford, 1994), p. 52.

31. Fountainhall, *Hist. Obs.*, p. 148.

32. NLI, MS 1793, proclamation no. 40 reverse. Cf. Cox, *Hibernia Anglicana . . . Second Part*, 'Transactions since 1653', p. 16, which retro-

spectively claims that James was proclaimed in Dublin 'with such dismal
Countenances, and so much Concern, as if they had that day foreseen (as
many did) the Infelicity of the following Reign'.

33. Hunt. Lib., HA 15862, Thomas Stanhope to Sir Arthur Rawdon, 21 Feb.
1684[/5]; TCD, MS 1178, fols. 18, 20.

34. *Lond. Gaz.*, no. 2028 (23–27 Apr. 1685); Morrice, P, 458.

35. *Lond. Gaz.*, nos. 2028–2033 (23–27 Apr. to 11–14 May 1685). For addi-
tional celebrations at Leicester, York and Durham, see Hunt. Lib., HA 8417,
Thomas Ludlam to Huntingdon, 25 Apr. 1685; WYAS, MX/R/35/4, George
Butler to Sir John Reresby, 27 Apr. 1685; Margaret Smillie Child, 'Prelude to
Revolution: The Structure of Politics in County Durham, 1678–88', unpub.
Ph.D. thesis, University of Maryland (1972), pp. 98–9.

36. LC, MSS 18,124, IX, fol. 195.

37. *RPCS, 1685–6*, p. 281; *HMC, Ormonde*, N.S. VII, 340; *Council Books
of the Corporation of Waterford 1662–1700*, ed. Seamus Pender (Dublin,
1964), pp. 254–5; *The Council Book of the Corporation of Youghall, from
1610 . . . to 1800*, ed. Richard Caulfield (Guildford, 1878), pp. 366–7.

38. East Sussex RO, Rye 1/17, p. 113; Berks. RO, W/FVc 28 (Mr Jell's
account in the year 1685).

39. *Lond. Gaz.*, nos. 2024 (9–13 Apr. 1685) and 2035 (18–21 May 1685).

40. Ibid., nos. 2014 (5–9 Mar. 1684[/5]) and 2020 (26–30 Mar. 1685).

41. Ibid., no. 2018 (19–23 Mar. 1684[/5]).

42. *HMC, Ormonde*, N.S. VII, 322.

43. *Lond. Gaz.*, no. 2015 (9–12 Mar. 1684[/5]).

44. *The Life of John Sharp, D.D. Lord Archbishop of York*, ed. Thomas
Newsome (2 vols., 1825), I, 63–4.

45. *Lond. Gaz.*, nos. 2016 (12–16 Mar. 1684[/5]) and 2020 (26–30 Mar.
1685).

46. Ibid., no. 2012 (26 Feb.–2 Mar. 1684[/5]).

47. Ibid., nos. 2008 (12–16 Feb. 1684[/5]), 2012 (26 Feb.–2 Mar. 1684[/5]),
2014 (5–9 Mar. 1684[/5]) and 2019 (23–26 Mar. 1685).

48. Ibid., nos. 2016 (12–16 Mar. 1684[/5]), 2019 (23–26 Mar. 1685) and
2022 (2–6 Apr. 1685).

49. Dorset RO, DC/LR/A3/1, Addresses Book, p. 7; *Lond. Gaz.*, no. 2015
(9–12 Mar. 1684[/5]); Henning, *House of Commons*, I, 217.

50. *Lond. Gaz.*, nos. 2020 (26–30 Mar. 1685) and 2027 (20–23 Apr. 1685).

51. Dorset RO, D/FSI, Box 238, bundle 22, Dean of Sarum to Sir Stephen
Fox 'about his Addresse', 12 Aug. 1685. For the address, see *Lond. Gaz.*, no.
2022 (2–6 Apr. 1685).

52. Hunt. Lib., HA 8408, Thomas Ludlam to Huntingdon, 14 Feb. 1684[/5];

Hunt. Lib., HA 656, Sir Henry Beaumont to Huntingdon, 14 Feb. 1684[/5].

53. Reresby, *Memoirs*, pp. 359, 360; *Lond. Gaz.*, no. 2027 (20–23 Apr. 1685).

54. BL, Add. MSS 41,803, fol. 138.

55. *HMC, Ormonde*, N.S., VII, 329–30.

56. *Lond. Gaz.*, nos. 2014 (5–9 Mar. 1684[/5]), 2018 (19–23 Mar. 1684[/5]) and 2025 (13–16 Apr. 1685).

57. Ibid., nos. 2013 (2–5 Mar. 1684[/5]) and 2014 (5–9 Mar. 1684[/5]).

58. Ibid., no. 2018 (19–23 Mar. 1684[/5]); Hunt. Lib., EL 8435, 'The State of the Burrough of Aylesbury' [1685]; Henning, *House of Commons*, I, 139.

59. *Lond. Gaz.*, no. 2013 (2–5 Mar. 1684[/5]).

60. Ibid., nos. 2013 (2–5 Mar. 1684[/5]), 2020 (26–30 Mar. 1685) and 2030 (30 Apr.–4 May 1685).

61. *Cal. Anc. Rec. Dub.*, V, 356–7; *Council Books of Waterford*, p. 252; NLI, MS 2993, p. 56.

62. [William King], *The State of the Protestants of Ireland under the Late King James's Government* (1691), p. 183.

63. BL, MS Lansdowne 1152A, fol. 404.

64. Henning, *House of Commons*, I, 40, 47; Tim Harris, *Politics under the Later Stuarts* (1993), p. 120.

65. Evelyn, *Diary*, IV, 419; *Merc. Ref.*, I, no. 12 (24 July 1689).

66. *CSPD, 1685*, p. 21 (no. 94); R. H. George, 'Parliamentary Elections and Electioneering in 1685', *Transactions of the Royal Historical Society*, 4th series, 29 (1936), pp. 169–72; Victor Stater, *Noble Government: The Stuart Lord Lieutenancy and the Transformation of English Politics* (Athens, Ga., 1994), pp. 156–7; G. W. Keeton, *Lord Chancellor Jeffreys and the Stuart Cause* (1965), pp. 248–51; W. A. Speck, *Reluctant Revolutionaries* (Oxford, 1988), pp. 44–5; J. P. Kenyon, *Robert Spencer, Second Earl of Sunderland 1641–1702* (1958), pp. 114–15.

67. Henning, *House of Commons*, I, 271–2.

68. Luttrell, I, 341.

69. Henning, *House of Commons*, I, 272; George, 'Parliamentary Elections', pp. 176–8.

70. Hunt. Lib., HA 1248, Lawrence Carter to Huntingdon, 14 Mar. 1684[/5]; Hunt. Lib., HA 4, Sir Edward Abney to Huntingdon, 21 Mar. 1684[/5].

71. Hunt. Lib., HA 7744, Gervase Jaquis to Huntingdon, 28 Mar. 1685; Hunt. Lib., HA 1250, Lawrence Carter to Huntingdon, 28 Mar. 1685; Hunt. Lib., HA 8416, Thomas Ludlam to Huntingdon, 30 Mar. 1685.

72. Henning, *House of Commons*, I, 152; *Victoria County History, Chester*, II, 118; L'Estrange, *Observator*, III, no. 25 (4 Apr. 1685).

73. L'Estrange, *Observator*, III, no. 25 (4 Apr. 1685).

74. Henning, *House of Commons*, I, 351, 388; Wood, *Life and Times*, III, 137; Fountainhall, *Hist. Obs.*, p. 157; BL, Add. MSS 34,508, fol. 11 (which reports the demonstration as taking place at Newcastle upon Tyne); BL, MS Althorp C2, 23 Mar. 1684/5, John Wilmington to Halifax.

75. Tim Harris, *Restoration: Charles II and His Kingdoms, 1660–85* (2005), pp. 162, 200.

76. Henning, *House of Commons*, I, 65, 66, 106.

77. Warren, *Religious Loyalty*, quotes on pp. 5, 14–15, 21, 23, 24, 26–7.

78. John Curtois, *A Discourse Shewing That Kings when Dead are Lamented* (1685), quotes from subtitle and pp. 11–12, 19.

79. James Canaries, *A Sermon Preach'd at Selkirk Upon the 29th of May, 1685* (Edinburgh, 1685); [Edward Wetenhall], *Hexapla Jacobaea* (1686); Philp O'Regan, *Archbishop William King of Dublin (1650–1729) and the Constitution in Church and State* (Dublin, 2000), pp. 19–20.

80. Curtois, *Discourse*, p. 10.

81. Canaries, *Sermon . . . Upon the 29th of May, 1685*, pp. 19–22.

82. James Ellesby, *The Doctrine of Passive Obedience* (1685), preface, pp. 2, 19. Ellesby claimed that the sermon had first been preached some years before, and had gone to press before Charles II's death. The preface is dated 9 February 1684[/5].

83. Francis Turner, *A Sermon Preached before their Majesties K. James II and Q. Mary, at their Coronation* (1685), pp. 24, 25–6.

84. Canaries, *Sermon . . . Upon the 29th of May, 1685*, pp. 11–12, 14–15.

85. William Sherlock, *A Sermon Preached . . . Before the Honourable House of Commons* (1685), pp. 26–7, 30, 31–2.

86. BL, Add MSS 41,803, fol. 163.

87. Hunt. Lib., HA 8410, Ludlam to Huntingdon, 18 Feb. 1684[/5]; Hunt. Lib., HA 8411, Ludlam to Lawrence Carter, 21 Feb. 1684[/5]; Hunt. Lib., HA 8412, Ludlam to Huntingdon, 21 Feb. 1684[/5].

88. East Sussex RO, QR/E/225/118, 132.

89. NA, SP 31/1, no. 52A.

90. Centre for Kentish Studies, Q/SB/17/1.

91. WYAS, MX/R/30/2, John Peables to Reresby, 19 Feb. 1684[/5].

92. CLRO, Sessions File, April 1685, indictment of Thomas Smith.

93. Bodl., MS Ballard 12, fol. 9.

94. CLRO, Sessions File, April 1685, indictment of Christopher Smitten.

95. CLRO, Sessions File, July 1685, rec. 99.

96. *Portsmouth Record Series: Borough Sessions Papers, 1653–1688*, ed. M. J. Hoad (Chichester, 1971), p. 129.

97. Curtois, *Discourse*, epistle dedicatory. This sermon was initially preached in his own parish church of Branston on 8 February (the Sunday after Charles II's death), and is discussed on p. 58.

98. CLRO, Sessions File, Feb. 1685, recognizance 4; CLRO, Sessions File, Apr. 1685, indictment of John Paine.

99. NA, SP 31/1, no. 19.

100. NA, SP 31/1, no. 29.

101. *Depositions from the Castle of York*, Surtees Society, 40 (1861), p. 276, note.

102. LMA, MJ/SR/1682, Oyer and Terminer, indictment of Deborah Hawkins.

103. Somerset RO, QR/W/174, nos. 54, 114.

104. Fountainhall, *Hist. Obs.*, p. 157. For other pro-Monmouth sentiment at this time, see Robin Clifton, *The Last Popular Rebellion: The Western Rising of 1685* (1984), p. 157.

105. West Sussex RO, QR/W/174, no. 115.

106. LC, MSS 18,124, IX, fol. 204; *Lyme Letters 1660–1760*, ed. Lady Newton (1925), p. 132; Fountainhall, *Hist. Obs.*, p. 164.

107. Fountainhall, *Decisions*, I, 345.

108. *RPCS, 1685–6*, pp. 50–2, 554–5.

109. Fountainhall, *Decisions*, I, 355.

2 Meeting the Radical Challenge

1. *Melvilles and Leslies*, II, 101.

2. Fountainhall, *Decisions*, I, 342; *Life of James II*, II, 13–14.

3. *APS*, VIII, 455; *Lond. Gaz.*, no. 2031 (4–7 May 1685); *Life of James II*, II, 10.

4. For a discussion of the Lords of the Articles, see Tim Harris, *Restoration: Charles II and His Kingdoms, 1660–85* (2005), pp. 24–5.

5. Fountainhall, *Decisions*, I, 356; *RPCS, 1685–6*, p. 281.

6. *Lond. Gaz.*, no. 2031 (4–7 May 1685).

7. *APS*, VII, 455.

8. *Lond. Gaz.*, no. 2031 (4–7 May 1685).

9. *APS*, VIII, 459–60.

10. Ibid., pp. 463–71.

11. Ibid., pp. 459–61; [Gilbert Rule], *A Vindication of the Church of*

Scotland. Being an Answer To a Paper, Intituled, Some Questions concern-ing Episcopal and Presbyterial Government in Scotland (1691), pp. 26–7.

12. *APS*, VIII, 471, 486–7.

13. [Alexander Shields], *The Hind Let Loose* (Edinburgh, 1687), p. 202.

14. NLS, MS 14,407, fol. 106.

15. *Life of James II*, II, 13.

16. Sir George Mackenzie, *A Vindication of the Government of Scotland, During the Reign of Charles II* (1691), p. 23.

17. *Lond. Gaz*, no. 2036 (21–25 May 1685); *SR*, VI (1819), I; *Parl. Hist.*, IV, cols. 1351–4; *LJ*, XIV, 21; C. D. Chandaman, 'The Financial Settlement in the Parliament of 1685', in Harry Hearder and H. R. Loyn, eds., *British Government and Administration: Studies Presented to S. B. Chrimes* (Cardiff, 1974), pp. 144–54; C. D. Chandaman, *The English Public Revenue 1660–1688* (Oxford, 1975).

18. *SR*, VI, 20; Lois G. Schwoerer, 'Liberty of the Press and Public Opinion: 1660–1695', in J. R. Jones, ed., *Liberty Secured? Britain Before and After 1688* (Stanford, 1992), p. 221.

19. Morrice, P, 468.

20. Cited in F. C. Turner, *James II* (1948), pp. 270–1; Charles James Fox, *A History of the Early Part of the Reign of James II* (1808), Appendix, pp. xc, xciii; Morrice, P, 462; Evelyn, *Diary*, IV, 444.

21. *Parl. Hist.*, IV, cols. 1357–8; Morrice, P, 463–4.

22. Harris, *Restoration*, pp. 312, 351–2, 364–5; David Stevenson, 'Campbell, Archibald, Ninth Earl of Argyll (1629–1685)', *Oxford DNB*.

23. Tim Harris, 'Scott [Crofts], James, Duke of Monmouth and First Duke of Buccleuch (1649–1685)', *Oxford DNB*.

24. *Melvilles and Leslies*, II, 101.

25. Peter Earle, *Monmouth's Rebels* (1977), pp. 97, 195; Richard L. Greaves, *Secrets of the Kingdom: British Radicals from the Popish Plot to the Revolution of 1688–89* (Stanford, 1992), pp. 283, 292.

26. Wodrow, *Sufferings*, II, 530; Greaves, *Secrets*, p. 278; Robin Clifton, *The Last Popular Rebellion: The Western Uprising of 1685* (1984), p. 152.

27. *RPCS, 1685–6*, pp. 307–20; Fountainhall, *Hist. Obs.*, p. 167,

28. Fountainhall, *Hist. Obs.*, pp. 165, 176; *HMC, Athole*, pp. 16, 18, 19, 20; Greaves, *Secrets*, pp. 281–2.

29. Greaves, *Secrets*, p. 65; I. B. Cowan, *The Scottish Covenanters 1660–88* (1976), p. 98.

30. *Letters to Sancroft*, p. 83.

31. *RPCS, 1685–6*, pp. 29–31; Fountainhall, *Hist. Obs.*, pp. 165–7; Fountainhall, *Decisions*, I, 364; Steele, III, nos. 2619, 2624.

32. Fountainhall, *Hist. Obs.*, p. 177.

33. *The Declaration and Apology of the Protestant People . . . now in Arms within the Kingdom of Scotland* (Edinburgh, 1685). This tract also contains *The Declaration of Archibald Earl of Argyle*.

34. EUL, Laing III, 350; [Shields], *The Hind Let Loose*, pp. 149–50; Fountainhall, *Hist. Obs.*, p. 167; Wodrow, *Sufferings*, II, 631; James King Hewison, *The Covenanters* (2 vols., Glasgow, 1908), II, 486.

35. [Thomas Morer], *An Account of the Present Persecution of the Church in Scotland* (1690), p. 8; [Alexander Monro], *The History of Scotch-Presbytery* (1692), p. 45.

36. Clifton, *Last Popular Rebellion*, p. 153; Greaves, *Secrets*, pp. 288–9.

37. Morrice, P, 475, 489. Cf. Fountainhall, *Hist. Obs.*, pp. 202, 203, 223.

38. Clifton, *Last Popular Rebellion*, pp. 193, 246; Robert Dunning, *The Monmouth Rebellion* (Stanbridge, Dorset, 1984), p. 39.

39. R. W. Hoyle, *The Pilgrimage of Grace and the Politics of the 1530s* (Oxford, 2001), p. 293.

40. Morrice, P, 475.

41. This account is based on Morrice, P, 475; Clifton, *Last Popular Rebellion*, ch. 7; Dunning, *Monmouth Rebellion*, pp. 39–46; David G. Chandler, *Sedgemoor, 1685* (1985).

42. Clifton, *Last Popular Rebellion*, ch. 9; Earle, *Monmouth's Rebels*, appendix.

43. Morrice, P, 472, 501.

44. J. G. Muddiman, ed., *The Martyrology. The Bloody Assizes* (Edinburgh, 1929), p. 46; Maurice Ashley, *John Wildman, Plotter and Postmaster* (1947), p. 257; *HMC, 5th Report*, p. 374; Henning, *House of Commons*, III, 598; Earle, *Monmouth's Rebels*, p. 14; Robin Clifton, 'Trenchard, Sir John (1649–1695)' and Richard L. Greaves, 'Wildman, Sir John (1622/3–1693)', both in *Oxford DNB*.

45. *Depositions from the Castle of York*, Surtees Society, 40 (1861), pp. 273–5.

46. *Portsmouth Borough Records: Borough Sessions Papers, 1653–1688*, ed. M. J. Hoad (Chichester, 1971), pp. 124, 130.

47. East Sussex RO, QR/E/227/56.

48. LMA, WJ/SR/1670, gaol calendar.

49. CLRO, Sessions File, July 1685, rec. 51.

50. Melinda S. Zook, *Radical Whigs and Conspiratorial Politics in Late Stuart England* (University Park, Pa., 1999), pp. 130–7.

51. *The Declaration of James, Duke of Monmouth* (1685), pp. 1–4.

52. Ibid., pp. 4–7.

53. East Sussex RO, QR/EW/226/48.

54. 'Monmouth's Proclamation from Taunton on 20 June, 1685', in J. N. P. Watson, *Captain-General and Rebel Chief: The Life of James, Duke of Monmouth* (1979), p. 278; Fountainhall, *Hist. Obs.*, pp. 202–3.

55. East Sussex RO, MS ASH 933, p. 21.

56. Fountainhall, *Hist. Obs.*, p. 201.

57. WYAS, MX/R/41/23, John Thompson, Lord Mayor of York, 11 Jul. 1685. For similar celebrations at Ashby de la Zouch in Leicestershire, see Hunt. Lib., HA 7747, Gervase Jaquis to Huntingdon, 11 Jul. 1685.

58. Roger L'Estrange, *The Observator in Dialogue* (3 vols., 1684–7), III, no. 58 (13 July 1685).

59. BL, Add. MSS, 41,804, fol. 11.

60. A classic example is Thomas Long, *The Unreasonableness of Rebellion* (1685), preached at St Peter's, Exeter, 26 Jul. 1685.

61. Hunt. Lib., HA 7749, Jaquis to Huntingdon, 18 Jul. 1685; Hunt. Lib., HA 7752, same to same, 28 Jul. 1685.

62. *RPCS, 1685–6*, pp. 100–1; Fountainhall, *Decisions*, I, 367.

63. *RPCS, 1685–6*, p. 327; Wodrow, *Sufferings*, II, 540–5; Fountainhall, *Hist. Not.*, II, 652–3.

64. Fountainhall, *Hist. Obs.*, pp. 196–7.

65. *The Last Words of Coll. Richard Rumbold* [1685], pp. 2–3; Fountainhall, *Decisions*, I, 365; Fountainhall, *Hist. Obs.*, p. 223; Wodrow, *Sufferings*, II, 551–2. For Rumbold's trial, see *ST*, XI, cols. 873–88.

66. *RPCS, 1685–6*, pp. 77, 83, 329–31; Fountainhall, *Decisions*, I, 367.

67. Wodrow, *Sufferings*, II, 548–9; John Willcock, *A Scots Earl in Covenanting Times: Being Life and Times of Archibald, 9th Earl of Argyll (1629–1685)* (Edinburgh, 1907), pp. 424–5.

68. Unless otherwise stated, the following account draws on Clifton, *Last Popular Rebellion*, ch. 8; Greaves, *Secrets*, pp. 248–50, 291–5; Zook, *Radical Whigs*, pp. 137–42.

69. Evelyn, *Diary*, IV, 456; *HMC, Egmont*, II, 160–1; Fountainhall, *Hist. Obs.*, pp. 205–6.

70. Morrice, P, 484; BL, MS Althorp C2, Reresby to Halifax, 22 May 1686.

71. Morrice, P, 487; *Mrs Elizabeth Gaunt's Last Speech* [1685]; Melinda Zook, 'Gaunt, Elizabeth (d. 1685)', *Oxford DNB*. For the trials of Lisle, Gaunt, Cornish and Batemen, see *ST*, XI, cols. 297–480.

72. *Depositions from the Castle of York*, p. 276.

73. Luttrell, I, 356; Edmund Calamy, *An Historical Account of My Own Life* (2 vols., 1830), I, 138.

74. Dorset RO, DL/LR/AS/1, p. 20.

75. BL, Add. MS 41,804, fol. 88.

76. *Depositions from the Castle of York*, p. 283.

77. Hunt. Lib., HA 10466, John Reresby to Huntingdon, 19 Mar. 1686[/7].

78. BL, Add. MS 41, 804, fol. 280; *Depositions from the Castle of York*, p. 284.

79. Bodl., MS Tanner 29, fols. 63–4.

80. A. H. Dood, *Studies in Stuart Wales* (Cardiff, 1952), p. 230.

81. *Pub. Occ.*, no. 21 (10 Jul. 1688).

82. BL, Add. MS 41,804, fols. 136–7, 158; *Ellis Corr.*, I, 87–8; Earle, *Monmouth's Rebels*, p. 153.

83. BL, Add. MS 41,804, fols. 168–9, 194, 257–63.

84. Morrice, P, 631–2, 636–7; *Ellis Corr.*, I, 177.

85. Bulstrode Newsletters, Reel 3, 7 Dec. 1685; BL, Add. MSS 72,482, fol. 67; BL, Add. MSS 72,595, fols. 39, 49, 51; Wood, *Life and Times*, III, 173; Steele, I, no. 3828.

86. BL, Add. MS 41,804, fols. 296–307; Somerset RO, Q/SR/169, nos. 1–12; Somerset RO, Q/SP/315, recognizances 49–61; Somerset RO, Q/SI/210, indictments 5, 6.

87. Morrice, P, 478.

88. Charles Allestree, *A Sermon Preach'd at Oxford . . . the 26th of July 1685* (1685), pp. 16, 18.

89. *Lond. Gaz.*, no. 2071 (21–24 Sep. 1685).

90. Luttrell, I, 358; LC, MSS 18,124, IX, fol. 256.

91. Morrice, P, 483; Luttrell, I, 359, 361; Bodl., MS Tanner 31, fols. 215, 217; Wood, *Life and Times*, III, 166; *Lond. Gaz.*, no. 2080 (22–26 Oct. 1685); *The Proceedings on the King's Commission of the Peace . . . at Justice-Hall in the Old-Bayly, The 9th, 10th and 11th of December 1685* (1685?), p. 2; Berks. RO, W/FVc/28 (Mr Jell's account in the year 1685); John T. Evans, *Seventeenth-Century Norwich* (Oxford, 1979), p. 306; Ronald Hutton, *The Rise and Fall of Merry England: The Ritual Year, 1400–1700* (Oxford, 1994), p. 254.

92. Morrice, P, 490, 492; Luttrell, I, 362; Evelyn, *Diary*, IV, 487; LMA, MJ/SR/1678, rec. 34.

93. Hutton, *Merry England*, p. 256.

94. *Lond. Gaz.*, no. 2084 (5–9 Nov. 1685).

95. CLRO, Sessions File, Dec. 1685, indictment of Elizabeth Beard.

96. John Childs, *The Army, James II, and the Glorious Revolution* (Manchester, 1980), pp. 1–2.

97. Berks. RO, A/JQd, informations of Thomas Tomlins and William Middleton.

98. Hunt. Lib., HA 2404, John Eames to Huntingdon, 23 Jul. 1685; Hunt. Lib., HA 2405, the same to the same, 25 Jul. 1685; Hunt. Lib., HA 9378, Charles Morgan to Huntingdon, 27 Jul. 1685.

99. BL, Add. MS 41,804, fols. 48, 99.

100. *Lond. Gaz.*, no. 2063 (24–27 Aug. 1685); Luttrell, I, 356–7; Steele, I, no. 3815.

101. Fountainhall, *Hist. Obs.*, pp. 222–3; Gilbert Burnet, *History of His Own Time: From the Restoration of King Charles the Second to the Treaty of Peace at Utrecht, in the Reign of Queen Anne* (1850), pp. 418, 419; *Clar. Corr.*, I, 149.

102. *LJ*, XIV, 73–4. The debates for this session of parliament can be found in: *Parl. Hist.*, IV, cols. 1367–88; Anchitell Grey, *Debates of the House of Commons from the Year 1667 to the Year 1694* (10 vols., 1763), VIII, 353–72; Bodl., Eng. Hist. d. 210, 'Debates in the House of Commons Relating to the Militia 1685', pp. 1–9; Morrice, P, 492–9; *The Several Debates of the House of Commons Pro and Contra Relating to the Establishment of the Militia* (1689). Both Grey, *Debates* and *Parl. Hist.* misidentify some of the speakers in the debates. The correct names appear in the ms copy of the debates in the Bodleian. Morrice is less complete, but confirms the identifications of the Bodleian manuscript.

103. *Parl. Hist.*, IV, col. 1371; *LJ*, XIV, 74.

104. *Parl. Hist.*, IV, cols. 1373, 1374, 1378–9, 1385–6; Henning, *House of Commons*, II, 100–1.

105. *Parl. Hist.*, IV, cols. 1379–82. For the correct identification of Wyndham and Christie, see Bodl., Eng. Hist. d. 210, pp. 50–3.

106. *Parl. Hist.*, IV, cols. 1386–7; *LJ*, XIV, 88; Fountainhall, *Hist. Obs.*, pp. 228–9, 230; *The Autobiography of Sir John Bramston*, ed. P. Braybrooke, Camden Society, old series, 32 (1845), pp. 216–17; Leics. RO, DG7 P.P. 75; *The Life and Letters of Sir George Savile, Bart., first Marquis of Halifax*, ed. H. C. Foxcroft (2 vols., 1898), I, 458–9; Thomas Babington Macaulay, *The History of England from the Accession of James the Second*, ed. Sir Charles Firth (6 vols., 1913–15), II, 690–4.

107. NLS, MS 1384, fol. 21; Wood, *Life and Times*, III, 172; Morrice, P, 505.

108. Fountainhall, *Hist. Obs.*, p. 232.

109. HMC, *Egmont*, II, 168; Fountainhall, *Hist. Obs.*, p. 229.

3 'That unhappy Island of Ireland'

1. Bodl., MS Clarendon 88, fol. 88.

2. *A Short View of the Methods Made Use of in Ireland for the Subversion*

and Destruction of the Protestant Religion and Interest in that Kingdom (1689), p. 2.

3. *A Faithful History of the Northern Affairs of Ireland* (1690), p. 3.

4. Piers Wauchope, 'Talbot, Richard, First Earl of Tyrconnell and Jacobite Duke of Tyrconnell (1630–1691)', *Oxford DNB*; Thomas Babington Macaulay, *The History of England from the Accession of James the Second*, ed. Sir Charles Firth (6 vols., 1913–15), II, 708; Gilbert Burnet, *History of His Own Time: From the Restoration of King Charles the Second to the Treaty of Peace at Utrecht, in the Reign of Queen Anne* (1850), p. 120; John Miller, 'The Earl of Tyrconnel and James II's Irish Policy, 1685–1688', *Historical Journal*, 20 (1977), 803–25; John Miller, 'Thomas Sheridan (1646–1712) and his Narrative', *Irish History Studies*, 20 (1976–7), 105–28; James Maguire, 'James II and Ireland, 1685–90', in W. A. Maguire, ed., *Kings in Conflict: The Revolutionary War in Ireland and its Aftermath 1689–1750* (Belfast, 1990), pp. 45–57. For the basic narrative of political developments in Ireland under James II between 1685 and 1688, see J. G. Simms, *Jacobite Ireland, 1685–91* (1969), ch. 2.

5. BL, Lansdowne 1152A, fols. 312–17 (quote fol. 314).

6. Ibid., fol. 145.

7. BL, Add. MSS 32,095, fol. 224; *HMC, Stuart*, VI, 4; Simms, *Jacobite Ireland*, pp. 19–22; John Miller, *James II: A Study in Kingship* (Hove, 1978, 3rd edn 2000), pp. 148–9, 216–17.

8. BL, MS Lansdowne 1152A, fol. 396; *Clar. Corr.*, I, 300–1.

9. BL, Add. MSS 21,484, fol. 66.

10. *HMC, Egmont*, II, 155, 157.

11. *CClarSP*, V, 670.

12. Charles O'Kelly, *Macariae Excidium, Or, The Destruction of Cypress; Being a Secret History of the War of the Revolution in Ireland*, ed. John Cornelius O'Callaghan (Dublin, 1850), p. 15.

13. [William King], *The State of the Protestants of Ireland under the Late King James's Government* (1691), p. 18.

14. *Petty–Southwell Corr.*, p. 140.

15. *HMC, Ormonde*, N.S. VII, 368.

16. *Clar. Corr.*, I, 233–7 (quote on p. 236).

17. Tim Harris, *Restoration: Charles II and His Kingdoms, 1660–85* (2005), p. 94.

18. *Clar. Corr.*, I, 188, 197, 211, 224, 231–2, 233–7, 239, 266–7, 272; BL, MS Lansdowne 1152A, fol. 393. See NLI, MS 1453 for 'a petition for the redress of the grievances of the Catholic nobility of Ireland, in particular concerning their lands, after 1685'.

19. *HMC, Ormonde*, N.S. VII, 398; *Petty–Southwell Corr.*, pp. 149–50; *HMC, Egmont*, II, 161–2; *CClarSP*, V, 657.

20. *Clar. Corr.*, I, 308–9.

21. Bodl., MS Clarendon 88, fols. 131, 133v, 135v.

22. BL, Add. MSS 72,881, fols. 58–66.

23. *HMC, Ormonde*, N.S. VII, 372, 376; *HMC, Egmont*, II, 162, 167; [King], *State of the Protestants of Ireland*, p. 144; *Clar. Corr.*, II, 25.

24. *HMC, Ormonde*, N.S. VIII, 343.

25. *Council Books of the Corporation of Waterford 1662–1700*, ed. Seamus Pender (Dublin, 1964), p. 258; *The Council Book of the Corporation of Youghall, from 1610 . . . to 1800*, ed. Richard Caulfield (Guildford, 1878), p. 368; Steele, II, no. 956; Raymond Gillespie, 'James II and the Irish Protestants', *Irish History Studies*, 28 (1992), 127.

26. BL, Lansdowne 1152A, fols. 338–44; Simms, *Jacobite Ireland*, p. 21.

27. *HMC, Ormonde*, N.S. VIII, 343; *HMC, Ormonde*, II, 364; Steele, II, no. 952.

28. *HMC, Ormonde*, N.S. VII, 343, 345, 356, 377, 380, 390, 399, 401–2; Cox, *Hibernia Anglicana . . . Second Part*, 'Letter', pp. 16–17.

29. Bodl., MS Clarendon 88, fol. 186; *Clar. Corr.* I, 222–3; Cox, *Hibernia Anglicana . . . Second Part*, 'Letter', p. 17.

30. *Clar. Corr.*, I, 226–7, 268.

31. *HMC, Egmont*, II, 158.

32. *HMC, Ormonde*, NS, VII, 365–7, 371, 373–4, 378, 380–1, 387, 394, 399.

33. *Clar. Corr.*, I, 189–90.

34. Bodl., MS Clarendon 88, fols. 86–8.

35. *HMC, Ormonde*, II, 364, 365–6, *HMC, Ormonde*, N.S. VII, 391; *HMC, Ormonde*, N.S. VIII, 343; Steele, II, nos. 947, 958; BL, Lansdowne 1152A, fol. 350; *HMC, Egmont*, II, 154.

36. *HMC, Egmont*, II, 157; T. C. Barnard, 'Athlone, 1685; Limerick, 1710: Religious Riots or Charivaris', *Studia Hibernica*, 27 (1993), 66–7.

37. *HMC, Ormonde*, N.S., VII, 349, 391.

38. *Clar. Corr.*, I, 215–16, 217, 230; *HMC, Ormonde*, N.S., VII, 376, 398, 400; *A Full and Impartial Account of all the Secret Consults* (1689), p. 56; *CClarSP*, V, 657, 670–1; *HMC, Egmont*, II, 162, 170, 179; *HMC, Ormonde*, II, 367–8; Steele, II, nos. 959, 963.

39. *Clar. Corr.*, I, 293–4; *HMC, Egmont*, II, 169.

40. Dalrymple, *Memoirs*, I, 'Part I', pp. 62, 130.

41. *HMC, Egmont*, II, 152; *HMC, Ormonde*, N.S. VII, 430, 433, 434–5, 444; *Life of James II*, II, 60; *HMC, Stuart*, VI, 5, 6, 16–17; *Clar. Corr.*, I,

262–3, 264, 281, 339, 393, 433, 470–1, 475, 536; *HMC, Ormonde*, I, 419–35; *Ireland's Lamentation* (1689), pp. 9, 13; 'Sir Paul Rycaut's Memoranda and Letters from Ireland 1686–1687', ed. Patrick Melvin, *Analecta Hibernia*, 27 (1972), 123–83, pp. 144–5, 149, 155; Bodl., MS Clarendon 88, fol. 224; *Short View of the Methods*, p. 3; *Full and Impartial Account of all the Secret Consults*, pp. 56–7; *HMC, Stuart*, VI, 21; Morrice, Q, 248; Miller, 'Tyrconnel', pp. 817–18; John Childs, *The Army, James II, and the Glorious Revolution* (Manchester, 1980), ch. 3 (I have followed Miller's figures rather than those given by Childs on p. 61).

42. *Clar. Corr.*, I, 276–7, 342–3, 346, 356–7, 361–2; 'Rycaut's Memoranda and Letters', pp. 141, 147; Morrice, P, 528; *HMC, Ormonde*, N.S. VII, 416.

43. *Clar. Corr.*, I, 399–400; *HMC, Ormonde*, N.S. VII, 423; *HMC, Ormonde*, N.S. VIII, 345; 'Rycaut's Memoranda and Letters', pp. 147–8.

44. *Clar. Corr.*, I, 246, 284–8, 441–2; *HMC, Egmont*, II, 177–8.

45. *Clar. Corr.*, I, 461–2, 472, II, 20; *Full and Impartial Account of all the Secret Consults*, p. 77; 'Rycaut's Memoranda and Letters', p. 153; Bodl., MS Clarendon 88, fol. 298; *Council Book of Youghall*, p. 372; *The Council Book of the Corporation of Kinsale, from 1652 to 1800*, ed. Richard Caulfield (Guildford, 1879), p. 169; *Council Books of Waterford*, pp. 267, 269, 271.

46. Bodl., MS Clarendon 88, fol. 302v; *HMC, Ormonde*, NS, VII, 460; *HMC, Ormonde*, N.S. VIII, 347.

47. BL, MS Lansdowne 1152A, fols. 335, 365; Childs, *The Army, James II, and the Glorious Revolution*, p. 62; Simms, *Jacobite Ireland*, p. 20.

48. *Clar. Corr.*, I, 300.

49. BL, MS Lansdowne 1152A, fol. 415; *Clar. Corr.*, I, 362.

50. *Clar. Corr.*, I, 462.

51. For example: *Cal. Anc. Rec. Dub.*, V, xliii–xliv, 164, 219, 391–5, 401–6; *Council Book of Youghall*, p. 326; *Council Books of Waterford*, pp. 7, 17–18, 34–5, 174; *Council Book of Kinsale*, p. 157.

52. Morrice, P, 544.

53. *Clar. Corr.*, I, 461–2; *Cal. Anc. Rec. Dub.*, V, 389–91.

54. [King], *State of the Protestants of Ireland*, pp. 70, 71. Cf. *Clar. Corr.*, I, 363, 399.

55. *HMC, Ormonde*, N.S. VII, 434, 443.

56. *A Vindication of the Present Government of Ireland* (1688), p. 6.

57. *Clar. Corr.*, I, 339, 461–2; *Full and Impartial Account of all the Secret Consults*, p. 77.

58. *Clar. Corr.*, I, 313, 335, 355, 395, II, 47; BL, Lansdowne 1152A, fols. 403, 407; O'Kelly, *Macariae Excidium*, p. 308 (note 91); *CSPD, 1686–7*,

pp. 148 (no. 614), 374 (no. 1492); Simms, *Jacobite Ireland*, pp. 27–8.

59. *Clar. Corr.*, I, 365, 387–8; Morrice, P, 544, 564.

60. *Ireland's Lamentation*, p. 8.

61. CUL, Add. 1, fol. 72; [King], *State of the Protestants of Ireland*, pp. 194–5; *Clar. Corr.*, I, 407–8; Andrew Hamilton, *A True Relation of the Actions of the Inniskilling-Men* (1690), p. iii.

62. *Clar. Corr.*, I, 258, 282, II, 61.

63. 'Rycaut's Memoranda and Letters', p. 157.

64. [King], *State of the Protestants of Ireland*, p. 303.

65. *Clar. Corr.*, II, 67, 124–5; O'Kelly, *Macariae Excidium*, passim.

66. *Clar. Corr.*, I, 357; Hamilton, *Inniskilling-Men*, p. ii. Cf. [King], *State of the Protestants of Ireland*, p. 20.

67. *Clar. Corr.*, I, 296; Hunt. Lib., HA 14663, Edmond Ellis to Sir Arthur Rawdon, 13 Mar. 1685[/6].

68. *HMC, Ormonde*, N.S. VII, 428, 435, 471; 'Rycaut's Memoranda and Letters', pp. 155, 157.

69. Bodl., MS Clarendon 89, fol. 12.

70. Luttrell, I, 386; Morrice, P, 529; *HMC, Ormonde*, N.S. VII, 417; Hunt. Lib., HA 15895, Thomas Stanhope to Rawdon, 12 Jul. 1686; Morrice, P, 560.

71. *Clar. Corr.*, I, 415.

72. *Petty–Southwell Corr.*, p. 234.

73. Miller, 'Tyrconnel', p. 815, fn. 40.

74. *Clar. Corr.*, I, 380, 526–7; *HMC, Ormonde*, N.S. VII, 428, 439, 441–2.

75. Bodl., MS Clarendon 88, fols. 188–92; *Clar. Corr.*, I, 190; Barnard, 'Athlone, 1685; Limerick, 1710', pp. 61–71.

76. 'Rycaut's Memoranda and Letters', p. 152.

77. *Clar. Corr.*, I, 479; *HMC, Ormonde*, N.S. VIII, 346; 'Rycaut's Memoranda and Letters', p. 155.

78. Morrice, P, 578.

79. *Clar. Corr.*, II, 53–4, 55, 57–8; *HMC, Ormonde*, N.S. VII, 421, VIII, 346; 'Rycaut's Memoranda and Letters', p. 175.

80. [King], *State of the Protestants of Ireland*, p. 121. See also ibid., p. 55.

81. Morrice, Q, 231.

82. Steele, II, no. 971; *Lond. Gaz.*, no. 2222 (3–7 Mar. 1686[/7]).

83. BL, Add. MSS 72,595, fol. 104; Morrice, Q, 129; BL, Add. MSS 41,804, fol. 279; *HMC, Ormonde*, N.S. VIII, 350.

84. *Clar. Corr.*, II, 73–8, 81–3, 105–6, 145; 'Rycaut's Memoranda and Letters', pp. 175, 178.

85. BL, Add. MS, 72,888, fol. 64v; *Clar. Corr.*, II, 134–5.

86. *Lond. Gaz.*, no. 2216 (10–14 Feb. 1686[/7]); *Clar. Corr.*, II, 150–1; *HMC, Ormonde*, N.S. VIII, 348.

87. *Lond. Gaz.*, no. 2219 (21–24 Feb. 1686[/7]).

88. Albertus Warren, *A Panegyrick to His Excellency Richard Earl of Tirconnell* (Dublin, 1686).

89. *HMC, Ormonde*, N.S. VIII, 348; Morrice, Q, 70; *Clar. Corr.*, II, 146–7.

90. *Lond. Gaz.*, no. 2222 (3–7 Mar. 1686[/7]); *HMC, Ormonde*, II, 371; Steele, II, no. 969; *HMC, Ormonde*, N.S. VII, 484.

91. TCD, MS 1181, p. 7.

92. *POAS*, IV, 309–12.

93. Bulstrode Newsletters, Reel 3, 25 Feb. 1686/7.

94. T. C. Barnard, 'Conclusion. Settling and Unsettling Ireland: The Cromwellian and Williamite Revolutions', in Jane Ohlmeyer, ed., *Ireland from Independence to Occupation 1641–1660* (Cambridge, 1995), p. 279.

95. *The Poems of David Ó Bruadair*, ed. and trans. Rev. John C. Mac Erlean (3 vols., 1910–17), III, 89.

96. *HMC, Stuart*, VI, 18, 20, 22–3; *Ireland's Lamentation*, pp. 11, 14; [King], *State of the Protestants of Ireland*, pp. 75, 313; *Petty Papers. Some Unpublished Writings of Sir William Petty*, ed. Marquis of Lansdowne (2 vols., 1927), I, 70; J. G. Simms, 'The War of the Two Kings, 1685–91', in T. W. Moody, F. X. Martin, F. J. Byrne and Art Cosgrove, eds., *A New History of Ireland* (9 vols., Oxford, 1976–84), III, 480; Simms, *Jacobite Ireland*, p. 33.

97. *Clar. Corr.*, I, 391; *HMC, Egmont*, II, 185.

98. *Full and Impartial Account of all the Secret Consults*, pp. 97–9, 129; *Petty Papers*, I, 71.

99. CUL, Add. 1, fol. 74.

100. [King], *State of the Protestants of Ireland*, p. 118.

101. *Short View of the Methods*, p. 5. See also [King], *State of the Protestants of Ireland*, pp. 119, 146; Bodl., MS Clarendon 89, fol. 175; *Petty–Southwell Corr.*, pp. 257–8, 268–9, 272, 279; *Full and Impartial Account of all the Secret Consults*, pp. 97–9.

102. Bodl., MS Clarendon 89, fol. 102.

103. *HMC, Stuart*, VI, 21.

104. *HMC, Ormonde*, N.S. VIII, 349.

105. *Clar. Corr.*, II, 145–6; *CSPD, 1686–7*, p. 384 (no. 1542); *HMC, Ormonde*, N.S. VIII, 350, 351; *Ireland's Lamentation*, p. 12.

106. *CSPD, 1686–7*, p. 421 (no. 1748); *CSPD, 1687–9*, p. 14 (no. 74).

107. [King], *State of the Protestants of Ireland*, p. 123.

108. *HMC, Stuart*, VI, 26–7; *HMC, Ormonde*, N.S. VIII, 350; *CSPD,*

1686–7, p. 384 (no. 1542); [King], *State of the Protestants of Ireland*, p. 184; Simms, 'The War of the Two Kings', pp. 482–3; Simms, *Jacobite Ireland*, pp. 42–3; *CSPD, 1687–9*, p. 130 (nos. 674–5).

109. Éamonn Ó Ciardha, *Ireland and the Jacobite Cause 1685–1766* (Dublin, 2002), pp. 77–8.

110. *Poems of David Ó Bruadair*, III, 87, 89.

111. *HMC, Ormonde*, N.S. VII, 491; Bodl., MS Clarendon 89, fol. 104.

112. *Short View of the Methods*, p. 6; *Full and Impartial Account of all the Secret Consults*, pp. 130–2; [King], *State of the Protestants of Ireland*, pp. 197–8, 204.

113. Bodl., MS Clarendon 89, fol. 110.

114. Ibid., fol. 148.

115. *Clar. Corr.*, I, 375, 414, 423–4; Bodl., MS Clarendon 88, fols. 284–7.

116. *Clar. Corr.*, I, 447.

117. *HMC, Ormonde*, N.S. VII, 446, 448, 450, 456–7.

118. *HMC, Ormonde*, N.S. VII, 464–70; *A Jacobite Narrative of the War in Ireland*, ed. J. T. Gilbert (Dublin, 1982, rev. edn with an introduction by J. G. Simms, Shannon, 1971), pp. 193–201.

119. *Clar. Corr.*, II, 142.

120. *Petty–Southwell Corr.*, p. 267.

121. NLI, MS 670, quotes on pp. 8, 21; BL, Add. MSS 72,885, fols. 58–72.

122. BL, Add. MSS 72,885, fols. 26–9 (quotes on fols. 26v, 27v, 28).

123. *Petty–Southwell Corr.*, p. 275.

124. *HMC, Stuart*, VI, 14.

125. *CClarSP*, V, 673; *Full and Impartial Account of all the Secret Consults*, pp. 77–8, 80.

126. *Life of James II*, II, 96.

127. *Ireland's Lamentation*, p. 13; *Short View of the Methods*, p. 9.

128. Bodl., MS Clarendon 89, fol. 98.

129. *Cal. Anc. Rec. Dub.*, V, xlv, 406, 422–6, 434–7; *CClarSP*, V, 678; Morrice, Q, 108; BL, Add. MSS 41,804, fol. 278; BL, Add. MSS 72,595, fols. 119, 121; Bulstrode Newsletters, Reel 3, 1 Apr. 1687; Luttrell, I, 420; *Full and Impartial Account of all the Secret Consults*, pp. 79–86; [King], *State of the Protestants of Ireland*, pp. 322–3; *Life of James II*, II, 97; Jacqueline Hill, *From Patriots to Unionists: Dublin Civic Patriots and Irish Protestant Patriotism, 1660–1840* (Oxford, 1997), pp. 59–61.

130. *Full and Impartial Account of all the Secret Consults*, p. 89; [King], *State of the Protestants of Ireland*, p. 81.

131. *Ireland's Lamentation*, pp. 13, 15; *Cal. Anc. Rec. Dub.*, V, xlviii; *HMC, Ormonde*, N.S. VIII, 351; *Council Book of Youghall*, p. 371; [King], *State of*

the Protestants of Ireland, p. 204; Cox, *Hibernia Anglicana . . . Second Part*, 'Letter', p. 18; Simms, *Jacobite Ireland*, pp. 35–6; Phil Kilroy, *Protestant Dissent and Controversy in Ireland, 1660–1714* (Cork, 1994), p. 242; *Full and Impartial Account of all the Secret Consults*, p. 90.

132. [King], *State of the Protestants of Ireland*, p. 81.

133. HMC, *Stuart*, VI, 26.

134. *Life of James II*, II, 98; HMC, *Ormonde*, II, 375–6; Steele, II, nos. 980, 982.

135. HMC, *Stuart*, VI, 27–8.

136. BL, Add. MSS 32,095, fols. 259–60; *Full and Impartial Account of all the Secret Consults*, pp. 114–15, 119–20; HMC, *Stuart*, VI, 31, 42; Simms, *Jacobite Ireland*, pp. 39–42.

137. TCD, MS 1181, p. 7; *An Apology for the Protestants of Ireland* (1689), p. 5; *Faithful History of the Northern Affairs*, p. 5; *Clar. Corr.*, II, 138; Morrice, Q, 58, 61; *Ireland's Lamentation*, p. 10; *Petty–Southwell Corr.*, p. 251.

138. HMC, *Stuart*, VI, 21. Cf. [King], *State of the Protestants of Ireland*, p. 81; Bodl., MS Clarendon 89, fol. 12.

139. Morrice, Q, 61, 70.

140. Gillespie, 'Irish Protestants', pp. 129–30.

141. HMC, *Stuart*, VI, 27.

142. Ibid., p. 21.

143. *Full and Impartial Account of all the Secret Consults*, pp. 91–2.

144. *Petty–Southwell Corr.*, pp. 274, 280; Bodl., MS Clarendon 89, fols. 59–60, 65.

145. Bodl., MS Clarendon 89, fol. 117v; TCD, 888/1, fol. 143. Cf. All Souls' Library, Oxford, MS 257, no. 79: yields from customs and excise for the Michaelmas quarters of 1686 and 1687.

146. *Petty Papers*, I, 71; [King], *State of the Protestants of Ireland*, p. 86.

147. *Faithful History of the Northern Affairs*, p. 5; Bodl., MS Clarendon 89, fol. 65; L. M. Cullen, 'Economic Trends, 1660–91', in Moody, et al., eds., *New History of Ireland*, III, 404–5.

148. TCD, MS 1181, p. 18.

149. Gillespie, 'Irish Protestants', p. 129.

150. Bodl., MS Clarendon 89, fol. 12; Morrice, Q, 70; *Clar. Corr.*, II, 137.

151. HMC, *Ormonde*, N.S. VIII, 351; BL, Add. MSS 28,876, fol. 38; BL, Add. MSS 72,596, fol. 15; Morrice, Q, 207.

152. HMC, *Ormonde*, II, 376; Steele, II, no. 983.

153. *Full and Impartial Account of all the Secret Consults*, p. 69.

154. CUL, Add. MS 1, fols. 77v–78.

155. 'Rycaut's Memoranda and Letters', p. 157.

156. O'Kelly, *Macariae Excidium*, p. 145.

157. *Jacobite Narrative*, p. viii.

158. *Vindication of the Present Government of Ireland*, quotes on pp. 1, 3, 12.

159. *A Letter from a Gentleman in Ireland, To His Friend, in London* (1688), pp. 2–4.

160. Bodl., MS Clarendon 89, fols. 168, 169, 173.

4 Scotland Under James VII

1. NLS, Wod. Oct. XXIX, fol. 309. For the dating, see Fountainhall, *Hist. Not.*, II, 794.

2. Fountainhall, *Hist. Not.*, II, 738; A. I. Macinnes, 'Catholic Recusancy and the Penal Laws, 1603–1707', *RSCHS*, 23 (1987), 27–63.

3. Dalrymple, *Memoirs*, II, 'Part I. Continued. Appendix to Book V', p. 176.

4. The only major scholarly treatment is Kathleen Mary Colquhoun, '"Issue of the Late Civill Wars": James, Duke of York and the Government of Scotland 1679–1689', Ph.D. dissertation, University of Illinois at Urbana-Champaign (1993). For a recent, brief overview, see W. A. Speck, *James II: Profiles in Power* (2002), ch. 5.

5. Ian B. Cowan, 'The Reluctant Revolutionaries: Scotland in 1688', in Eveline Cruickshanks, ed., *By Force or By Default? The Revolution of 1688–1689* (Edinburgh, 1989), p. 65.

6. Michael Lynch, *Scotland: A New History* (1992), p. 297.

7. Fountainhall, *Hist. Obs.*, p. 217.

8. See, for example: *RPCS, 1685–6*, pp. 114, 206–7, 209, 229, 364, 492–6, 501–2, 507–9; *RPCS, 1686*, pp. 367–70, 376–8, 404–8; *RPCS, 1686–9*, p. 101.

9. Wodrow, *Sufferings*, II, 585.

10. *Life of James II*, II, 41.

11. James II, *A Proclamation, For an Anniversary Thanksgiving, in Commemoration of his Majesty's Happy Birthday* (1685); Fountainhall, *Decisions*, I, 369–70; *RPCS, 1685–6*, pp. 166, 183; Steele, III, no. 2658; *Lond. Gaz.*, no. 2080 (22–26 Oct. 1685); Luttrell, I, 361; Keith M. Brown, 'The Vanishing Emperor: British Kingship and its Decline, 1603–1707', in Roger A. Mason, ed., *Scots and Britons: Scottish Political Thought and the Union of 1603* (Cambridge, 1994), p. 69; C. A. Whatley, 'Royal Day, People's Day: The Monarch's Birthday in Scotland, c. 1660–1860', in Norman MacDougall and Roger A. Mason, eds., *People and Power in Scotland* (Edinburgh, 1992), p. 173.

12. Fountainhall, *Hist. Not.*, II, 672.

13. *ST*, XI, col. 1166, note; Fountainhall, *Hist. Not.*, II, 644; *RPCS, 1685–6*, pp. 48–9; Paul Hopkins, *Glencoe and the End of the Highland War* (Edinburgh, 1986), p. 97.

14. F. C. Turner, *James II* (1948), pp. 369–71.

15. Charles W. J. Withers, 'Sibbald, Sir Robert (1641–1722)', *Oxford DNB*.

16. Fountainhall, *Hist. Not.*, II, 688; *HMC, Laing*, I, 444.

17. Fountainhall, *Decisions*, I, 374.

18. Morrice, P, 516; *APS*, II, 535, III, 36; *HMC, Laing*, I, 443; Colquhoun, '"Issue of the Late Civill Wars"', pp. 323–4; Fountainhall, *Hist. Obs.*, pp. 240–1.

19. Fountainhall, *Decisions*, I, 371; *ST*, XI, col. 1167, note.

20. Fountainhall, *Decisions*, I, 398.

21. Ibid., p. 412.

22. James Canaries, *Rome's Additions to Christianity* (Edinburgh, 1686), sig. b1.

23. Ibid., pp. 19–20.

24. Ibid., quotes on sigs. A5, a.

25. Fountainhall, *Decisions*, I, 404; James Canaries, *A Sermon Preached at Edinburgh . . . upon the 30th of January, 1689* (Edinburgh, 1689), p. 70.

26. Fountainhall, *Hist. Obs.*, pp. 243–4; Morrice, P, 525; Fountainhall, *Decisions*, I, 399; *ST*, XI, col. 1013; Luttrell, I, 372; Withers, 'Sibbald'; R. A. Houston, *Social Change in the Age of Enlightenment: Edinburgh, 1660–1760* (Oxford, 1994), p. 305.

27. *ST*, XI, cols. 1013–14; *RPCS, 1686*, p. 7.

28. *ST*, XI, cols. 1020–3; *RPCS, 1686*, p. 12.

29. *ST*, XI, cols. 1014–15; Fountainhall, *Decisions*, I, 399; Fountainhall, *Hist. Obs.*, p. 244.

30. *ST*, XI, cols. 1017–24; Fountainhall, *Decisions*, I, 399, 406, 407; *RPCS, 1685–6*, pp. 544–5; *RPCS, 1686*, pp. 13, 68, 69, 97, 160, 228, 229.

31. Fountainhall, *Decisions*, I, 403–4.

32. Ibid., p. 408; John Miller, *James II: A Study in Kingship* (Hove, 1978, 3rd edn 2000), p. 213.

33. Fountainhall, *Hist. Obs.*, p. 234.

34. Morrice, P, 526.

35. Fountainhall, *Hist. Not.*, II, 712, 736.

36. NLS, Yester MSS 7026, fols. 38, 60; Fountainhall, *Hist. Not.*, II, 715.

37. *HMC, 9th Report*, II, 251; Fountainhall, *Hist. Not.*, II, 714; Bulstrode Newsletters, Reel 3, 9 Apr. 1686; Thomas Babington Macaulay, *The History*

of England from the Accession of James the Second, ed. Sir Charles Firth (6 vols., 1913–15), II, 774–5; Miller, *James II*, p. 215.

38. *HMC, Hamilton*, p. 172.

39. Fountainhall, *Decisions*, I, 413.

40. *HMC, 9th Report*, II, 251.

41. Wodrow, *Sufferings*, II, 594.

42. Thomas Burnet, *Theses Philosophicae* (Aberdeen, 1686); Fountainhall, *Decisions*, I, 415–16.

43. 'Reasons for Abrogating the Penal Statutes', in Wodrow, *Sufferings*, II, app. no. 118, pp. 163–7 (quotes on pp. 164, 166). For the attribution to L'Estrange, see Wodrow, *Sufferings*, II, 595.

44. Fountainhall, *Decisions*, I, 416. These tracts included: Thomas Cartwright, *A Sermon Preached upon the Anniversary . . . of the Happy Inauguration of . . . King James II* (1686); *Popery Anatomis'd* (1686); J. C., *A Net for the Fishers of Men* (1686); [John Gother], *A Papist Misrepresented and Represented* (1685).

45. 'Reasons for Abrogating the Penal Statutes', p. 167.

46. Quoted in Colqhuoun, '"Issue of the Late Civill Wars"', p. 349.

47. Wodrow, *Sufferings*, II, 594.

48. Fountainhall, *Decisions*, I, 413; *RPCS, 1686*, pp. 194, 204.

49. BL, Add. MSS 28,938, fols. 196–202, reprinted in Wodrow, *Sufferings*, II, app. no. 117, pp. 161–3.

50. 'An Answer to a Paper writ for abrogating the penal Statutes', in Wodrow, *Sufferings*, II, app. no. 119, pp. 168–73 (quote on p. 172).

51. 'A Letter from the Heritors of the Shires of . . . to their Commissioners to the Parliament', in Wodrow, *Sufferings*, II, app. no. 120, pp. 173–7 (quotes on pp. 173, 175).

52. Wodrow, *Sufferings*, II, 590; *HMC, Hamilton*, p. 172.

53. *Ellis Corr.*, I, 46–7; T. F. Henderson, 'Stewart, Alexander, Fifth Earl of Moray (*bap.* 1634, *d.* 1701)', revised by A. J. Mann, *Oxford DNB*.

54. James II, *His Majesties Most Gracious Letter to the Parliament of Scotland* (Edinburgh, 1686), quote on p. 2; *APS*, VIII, 579–80.

55. Fountainhall, *Hist. Not.*, II, 719.

56. Morrice, P, 538–9.

57. James II, *Most Gracious Letter to the Parliament of Scotland*, p. 4; *APS*, VIII, 581; Fountainhall, *Hist. Not.*, II, 721; *The Flemings in Oxford, Being Documents Selected from the Rydal Papers in Illustration of the Lives and Ways of Oxford Men 1650–1700*, ed. John Richard Magrath (3 vols., Oxford, 1904–24), II, 158–9.

58. Morrice, P, 546–7; Luttrell, I, 378, 381; *HMC, Hamilton,* p. 173; *HMC, Earl of Mar,* pp. 218–19; *CSPD, 1686–7,* pp. 151–2 (nos. 619, 620).

59. *Life of James II,* II, 68.

60. Bulstrode Newsletters, Reel 3, 11 Apr. 1686.

61. Morrice, P, 536.

62. Fountainhall, *Decisions,* I, 416.

63. Fountainhall, *Decisions,* I, 415; *HMC, Hamilton,* p. 173; Morrice, P, 541, 546.

64. Wodrow, *Sufferings,* II, app. no. 116, pp. 160–1; *HMC, Laing,* I, 446–7.

65. FSL, V. b. 287, no. 18. Cf. BL, Add. MSS 72,595, fol. 85.

66. Morrice, P, 534, 536, 537; *HMC, Hamilton,* p. 173; Fountainhall, *Decisions,* I, 415.

67. Fountainhall, *Hist. Not.,* II, 718.

68. Wodrow, *Sufferings,* II, 593, and app. no. 120, p. 176; Fountainhall, *Decisions,* I, 418–19; Robert S. Rait, *The Parliaments of Scotland* (Glasgow, 1924), pp. 91–2.

69. Fountainhall, *Hist. Not.,* II, 666, 719; *HMC, Laing,* I. 442; *RPCS, 1685–6,* pp. 188, 193–4; Wodrow, *Sufferings,* II, 575–6.

70. Fountainhall, *Hist. Not.,* II, 724, 735.

71. Ibid., pp. 734–5.

72. Ibid., pp. 723, 729; Fountainhall, *Decisions,* I, 416; *RPCS, 1686,* pp. viii, ix, xxi, 221, 228, 237, 238; Wodrow, *Sufferings,* II, 605; Morrice, P, 541, 585, 590.

73. *RPCS, 1686,* pp. ix, xxi, 275; Fountainhall, *Hist. Not.,* II, 737, 740.

74. Dalrymple, *Memoirs,* II, 'Part I. Continued. Appendix to Books III and IV', pp. 109–10.

75. Wodrow, *Sufferings,* II, 598–9; *RPCS, 1686,* p. 435.

76. *RPCS, 1686,* pp. xii, 425, 454; Fountainhall, *Hist. Not.,* II, 740–1, 748, 750; Wodrow, *Sufferings,* II, 598.

77. Hunt. Lib., STT 903; Hunt. Lib., HA 1182; NLS, Yester MSS 7035, fol. 64; *RPCS, 1686,* pp. 454–5; Fountainhall, *Decisions,* I, 424; *Culloden Papers: Comprising an Extensive and Interesting Correspondence from the Year 1625 to 1748* (1815), p. 334.

78. BL, Add. MSS 28,850, fols. 123–4; Fountainhall, *Decisions,* I, 441.

79. Wodrow, *Sufferings,* II, 598; Fountainhall, *Hist. Not.,* II, 759, 762; *RPCS, 1686,* pp. xiii, 511, 524.

80. Fountainhall, *Decisions,* I, 429. For the internal inconsistency of the Test and Episcopalian opposition to it, see Tim Harris, *Restoration: Charles II and His Kingdoms, 1660–85* (2005), pp. 347–56.

81. *RPCS, 1686–9,* p. xxvii; Fountainhall, *Hist. Not.,* II, 768.

82. Fountainhall, *Hist. Not.*, II, 775.

83. Ibid., pp. 772, 783. By the time Sir John was installed in his new position on 17 February, the dispensation was no longer necessary, since James had issued his Indulgence suspending all the penal laws on 12 February.

84. Fountainhall, *Decisions*, I, 432, 451, 466, 502; Fountainhall, *Hist. Not.*, II, 814; *RPCS, 1686–9*, p. xviii; Wodrow, *Sufferings*, II, 643–4, and app. no. 142, p. 200; Matthew Glozier, 'The Earl of Melfort, the Court Catholic Party and the Foundation of the Order of the Thistle, 1687', *Scottish Historical Review*, 69 (2000), 233–8.

85. *RPCS, 1686–9*, p. xxxv; John Miller, *Popery and Politics in England, 1660–1688* (Cambridge, 1973), p. 242.

86. Fountainhall, *Hist. Not.*, II, 772, 773, 794, 823, 856–7, 867; HMC, *Stuart*, I, 30.

87. Wodrow, *Sufferings*, II, app. no. 124, p. 181; Fountainhall, *Decisions*, I, 420, 425.

88. Fountainhall, *Hist. Not.*, II, 773.

89. *RPCS, 1686–9*, p. xvii.

90. Fountainhall, *Decisions*, I, 472–3, 475, 482, 496; *RPCS, 1661–4*, p. 90; *RPCS, 1669–72*, pp. 425, 596, 598; Clare Jackson, *Restoration Scotland, 1660–1690* (Woodbridge, 2003), pp. 41, 43; William Cowan, 'The Holyrood Press, 1686–1688', *Edinburgh Bibliographical Society Transactions*, 6 (1904), 83–100; Alastair J. Mann, *The Scottish Book Trade 1500–1720* (East Linton, 2000), ch. 6.

91. James VII, *By the King. A Proclamation* (Edinburgh, 1687); Steele, III, no. 2684; Wodrow, *Sufferings*, II, app. no. 187.

92. Wodrow, *Sufferings*, II, 616.

93. [Gilbert Burnet], *Some Reflections On His Majestie's Proclamation of the 12th of February 1686/7 for a Toleration in Scotland* [Amsterdam?, 1687], pp. 1, 5.

94. The point was made by [William King], *The State of the Protestants of Ireland under the Late King James's Government* (1691), pp. 20–1.

95. [Robert Ferguson], *A Representation of the Threatning Dangers* [Edinburgh?, 1687], pp. 28–9.

96. *RPCS, 1686–9*, p. 124.

97. Fountainhall, *Decisions*, I, 449–50; Fountainhall, *Hist. Not.*, II, 789; HMC, *Hamilton*, p. 174; HMC, *Earl of Mar*, p. 219; Wodrow, *Sufferings*, II, 616.

98. Luttrell, I, 398, 399; Morrice, Q, 94; HMC, *Earl of Mar*, p. 219; [Thomas Morer], *An Account of the Present Persecution of the Church in Scotland* (1690), pp. 9–10; [Alexander Shields], *The Hind Let Loose* (Edinburgh, 1687), pp. 152–3; Wodrow, *Sufferings*, II, 608, 612.

99. *RPCS, 1686–9*, p. 138; Steele, III, no. 2689.

100. *RPCS, 1686–9*, pp. xvii, 156–8; Steele, III, no. 2693.

101. Wodrow, *Sufferings*, II, 618.

102. Ibid., p. 625; [John Sage], *The Case of the Present Afflicted Clergy in Scotland Truly Represented* (1690), pp. 3–4; [Morer], *Account of the Present Persecution*, p. 11.

103. [Morer], *Account of the Present Persecution*, p. 12.

104. I. B. Cowan, *The Scottish Covenanters 1660–88* (1976), p. 134.

105. Fountainhall, *Decisions*, I, 458, 473, 507, 513; Wodrow, *Sufferings*, II, 614; [Shields], *Hind Let Loose*, pp. 156–7; Steele, III, nos. 2695, 2696.

106. Fountainhall, *Decisions*, I, 495; Wodrow, *Sufferings*, II, 630–8.

107. Wodrow, *Sufferings*, II, 618, and apps. nos. 135 and 136, pp. 195–6; NAS, RH 13/20, pp. 143–4, 150–2; [Sage], *Case of the Present Afflicted Clergy*, pp. 78–80; [Alexander Monro], *The History of Scotch-Presbytery* (1692), pp. 49–50.

108. NAS, RH 13/20, p. 320, 'Presbyterian Loyaltie'.

109. NLS, Wod. Qu. XXXVIII, fol. 112.

110. James Renwick, *The Testimony of Some Persecuted Presbyterian Ministers* (1688), p. 7.

111. [George Mackenzie, Viscount Tarbat, and Sir George Mackenzie of Rosehaugh], *A Memorial for His Highness the Prince of Orange in Relation to the Affairs of Scotland* (1689), pp. 6. Cf. [Alexander Monro], *A Letter to a Friend* (1692), p. 5.

112. Wodrow, *Sufferings*, II, 623.

113. [Gilbert Rule], *A Vindication of the Church of Scotland; Being an Answer to Five Pamphlets* (1691), pp. 5, 16, 19 and Part II, p. 7. Cf. [Gilbert Rule], *A Vindication of the Church of Scotland. Being an Answer To a Paper, Intituled, Some Questions Concerning Episcopal and Presbyterial Government in Scotland* (1691), pp. 31–2; Wodrow, *Sufferings*, II, 620.

114. Fountainhall, *Decisions*, I, 474; *RPCS, 1686–9*, p. xix; Wodrow, *Sufferings*, II, 626–7.

115. Fountainhall, *Decisions*, I, 503; Wodrow, *Sufferings*, II, 638.

116. Wodrow, *Sufferings*, I, 613–14, 620–4; *CSPD, 1687–9*, p. 44 (no. 211); Fountainhall, *Hist. Not.*, II, 819; Gordon Donaldson, *Scotland: James V to James VII* (Edinburgh, 1965), pp. 382–3; Cowan, *Scottish Covenanters*, p. 131.

117. Fountainhall, *Decisions*, I, 453, 456–7.

118. *RPCS, 1686–9*, pp. 227–30 (quote on p. 229); Steele, III, no. 2711.

119. Colin Lindsay, 3rd Earl of Balcarres, *An Account of the Affairs of Scotland, Relating to the Revolution of 1688* (1714), pp. 10–12.

120. Fountainhall, *Decisions*, I, 503; *Letters to Sancroft*, p. 87.

121. Balcarres, *Account*, pp. 7–9.

122. *CSPD, 1687–9*, pp. 35–6, 68 (nos. 181, 333).

123. Morrice, Q, 219.

124. Fountainhall, *Decisions*, I, 513. For the Magdalen College affair, see pp. 226–9.

125. Wodrow, *Sufferings*, II, 638–9; Magnus Linklater and Christian Hesketh, *For King and Conscience: John Graham of Claverhouse, Viscount Dundee (1648–1689)* (1989), p. 142.

126. HMC, *Laing*, I, 447; Fountainhall, *Decisions*, I, 424, 425, 431, 442, 445; *RPCS, 1686*, pp. 454, 491–2, 542–4, 552–3; *RPCS, 1686–9*, pp. xiv, xv, 39, 42–3; Morrice, Q, 39; Donaldson, *Scotland: James V to James VII*, pp. 281–2.

127. *RPCS, 1686–9*, pp. xvii–xxvi; Fountainhall, *Decisions*, I, 473, 486.

128. Rait, *Parliaments of Scotland*, p. 306; Fountainhall, *Hist. Not.*, II, 806.

129. FSL, V.b. 287, no. 54.

130. Dalrymple, *Memoirs*, II, 'Part I. Continued. Appendix to Book V', pp. 90, 99–101; Balcarres, *Account*, p. 15.

131. Macinnes, 'Catholic Recusancy', pp. 35, 56–7.

132. HMC, *Stuart*, I, 30.

133. Cited in Turner, *James II*, pp. 377–8.

134. Fountainhall, *Hist. Not.*, II, 855.

5 Catholic Absolutism in England

1. *Life of James II*, II, 278, 609–10, 612.

2. John Miller, *James II: A Study in Kingship* (Hove, 1978, 3rd edn 2000); J. R. Jones, *The Revolution of 1688 in England* (1972); Jeremy Black, *A System of Ambition? British Foreign Policy 1660–1793* (1991), pp. 24–8; W. A. Speck, *James II: Profiles in Power* (2000).

3. [Gilbert Burnet], *Some Reflections on His Majestie's Proclamation of the 12th of February 1686/7 for a Toleration in Scotland* [Amsterdam?, 1687], p. 5; [Gilbert Burnet], *The Ill Effects of Animosities among Protestants in England Detected* (1688), p. 14.

4. *Clar. Corr.*, I, 198.

5. Morrice, Q, 167.

6. Beinecke Library, Yale University, Osborn MSS 2, box 4, folder 76, p. 69.

7. Black, *System of Ambition*, pp. 25–7; Speck, *James II*, p. 121; Jones, *Revolution of 1688*, pp. 177–9.

8. Luttrell, I, 346, 371; Morrice, P, 540, 587. For public anxiety over James's pro-French leanings more generally, see: Steven Pincus, '"To Protect English Liberties": The English Nationalist Revolution of 1688–1689', in Tony Claydon and Ian McBride, eds., *Protestantism and National Identity: Britain and Ireland c.1650–c.1850* (Cambridge, 1998), pp. 75–104.

9. Morrice, P, 484, 575, Q, 20. Cf. Evelyn, *Diary*, IV, 484–6, 490, 498.

10. BL, MS Althorp C4, Sir William Coventry to Halifax, 4 May 1686; Morrice, P, 537, 546, 588–9.

11. Dalrymple, *Memoirs*, II, 'Part I. Continued. Appendix to Books III and IV', p. 109.

12. Bulstrode Newsletters, Reel 3, 8 Mar. 1685/6; Steele, I, no. 3826 (for the brief).

13. *Lond. Gaz.*, no. 2136 (6–10 May 1686); Morrice, P, 533–5; Evelyn, *Diary*, IV, 510–11, 515; *CSPD, 1686–7*, p. 130 (no. 533); BL, Add. MSS 72,595, fol. 76; Bulstrode Newsletters, Reel 3, 7 May 1686. The book was Jean Claude's *Les Plaintes des Protestants Cruellement Opprimés dans le Royaume de France*, translated and abridged by Mr Rayner, a canon of St Paul's and published as *An Account of the Persecutions and Oppressions of the Protestants in France* (1686).

14. *CSPD, 1686–7*, pp. 149–50 (no. 619).

15. Robin D. Gwynn, 'James II in the Light of his Treatment of Huguenot Refugees in England 1685–1686', *English Historical Review*, 92 (1977), 820–33. See also Matthew Glozier, *The Huguenot Soldiers of William of Orange and the Glorious Revolution of 1688* (Brighton, 2002), ch. 5.

16. *CSPD, 1686–7*, p. 151 (no. 619); Morrice, P, 623, 625; *The Autobiography of Sir John Bramston*, ed. P. Braybrooke, Camden Society, old series, 32 (1845), pp. 245–6, 276; John Childs, *The Army, James II, and the Glorious Revolution* (Manchester, 1980), ch. 4 (esp. pp. 92–4).

17. Luttrell, I, 370; *CSPD, 1686–7*, p. 40 (no. 163).

18. Morrice, Q, 109–10; BL, Add. MSS 72,595, fol. 106.

19. Bulstrode Newsletters, Reel 3, 27 Jun. 1687.

20. Morrice, P, 517.

21. Hunt. Lib., HA 7770, Gervase Jaquis to Huntingdon, 9 Nov. 1686.

22. Morrice, Q, 29.

23. WYAS, MX/R/42/27, 40, 47, 54; WYAS, MX/R/43/29; WYAS, MX/R/44/26, 49, 57; Reresby, *Memoirs*, pp. 409–11, 415–16; *CSPD, 1686–7*, pp. 17 (no. 76), 19 (no. 87); *Depositions from the Castle of York*, Surtees Society, 40 (1861), pp. 278–82; W. A. Speck, *Reluctant Revolutionaries* (Oxford, 1988), p. 155.

24. Samuel Johnson, 'Several Reasons for the Establishment of a Standing

Army, and Dissolving the Militia' and 'A Humble and Hearty Address to all English Protestants in this Present Army' (1686), in [Samuel Johnson], *A Second Five Years' Struggle Against Popery and Tyranny* (1689), pp. 86–7, 110–11; Wood, *Life and Times*, III, 182; Morrice, Q, 9–10, 12–14, 20, 22, 27–8; Hugh Speke, *The Secret History of the Happy Revolution of 1688* (1715), pp. 14–16.

25. Childs, *The Army, James II, and the Glorious Revolution*, pp. 22, 30.

26. *ST*, XI, cols. 1165–1199 (esp. cols. 1193–4, 1196–7, 1199). Sir Edward Herbert elaborated upon his verdict in his *A Short Account of the Authorities in Law, Upon Which Judgement Was Given in Sir Edw. Hales His Case* (1688). For the statute, see *SR*, II, 326–43.

27. Lois G. Schwoerer, *The Declaration of Rights, 1689* (Baltimore, 1981), p. 63; Paul Birdsall, '"Non Obstante": A Study of the Dispensing Power of English Kings', in *Essays in Honor of Charles Howard McIlwain* (Cambridge, Mass., 1936), pp. 37–76; Sir William Searle Holdsworth, *A History of English Law* (17 vols., 1922–72), VI, 225; E. F. Churchill, 'The Dispensing Power and the Defence of the Realm', *Law Quarterly Review*, 37 (1921), 412–41; Carolyn A. Edie, 'Tactics and Strategies: Parliament's Attack upon the Royal Dispensing Power 1597–1689', *American Journal of Legal History*, 29 (1985), 231.

28. Morrice, P, 505, 507, 526, 528, 545, 555; Evelyn, *Diary*, IV, 514; Bulstrode Newsletters, Reel 3, 16 and 26 Apr. 1686; J. R. Tanner, *English Constitutional Conflicts of the Seventeenth Century, 1603–1689* (Cambridge, 1928), p. 291; Lionel K. J. Glassey, *Politics and the Appointment of Justices of the Peace 1675–1720* (Oxford, 1979), p. 69. Milton appears to have qualified himself under the Test Act on this occasion, but required a dispensation when he was transferred to Common Pleas on 16 Apr. 1687: Bulstrode Newsletters, Reel 3, 26 Apr. 1686; Gordon Campbell, 'Milton, Sir Christopher (1615–1693)', *Oxford DNB*; Edward Foss, *The Judges of England* (9 vols., 1848–64), VII, 285–8.

29. *POAS*, IV, 93.

30. Morrice, P, 555, 588, 614; Luttrell, I, 384.

31. Morrice, P, 559, Q, 219.

32. John Miller, *Popery and Politics in England, 1660–1688* (Cambridge, 1973), pp. 198–201.

33. Gilbert Burnet, *History of His Own Time: From the Restoration of King Charles the Second to the Treaty of Peace at Utrecht, in the Reign of Queen Anne* (1850), pp. 429, 464, 465; Miller, *James II*, pp. 148–53; Glassey, *Politics*, pp. 69–70; F. C. Turner, *James II* (1948), p. 323.

34. Luttrell, I, 332, 367; Wood, *Life and Times*, III, 172.

35. *Calendar of Treasury Books, 1660–1718* (32 vols., 1904–57), VIII, 176, 204, 454–6, 610–11.

36. Morrice, Q, 532; Miller, *Popery and Politics*, pp. 242–6.

37. *Ellis Corr.*, I, 23.

38. Luttrell, I, 371; Morrice, P, 527, 529, 562, 589–90; BL, Add. 34,508, fol. 104.

39. *CSPD, 1686–7*, pp. 13 (no. 58), 54 (no. 221), 290 (no. 1084); Evelyn, *Diary*, IV, 489; Wood, *Life and Times*, III, 131; Jones, *Revolution of 1688*, pp. 87–91.

40. Wood, *Life and Times*, III, 214; Miller, *Popery and Politics*, pp. 239–40; J. D. Davies, *Gentlemen and Tarpaulins: The Officers and Men of the Restoration Navy* (Oxford, 1991), pp. 202–3.

41. *Life of James II*, II, 80; Morrice, Q, 71; WYAS, MX/R/49/8; BL, Althorp MS, C2, Sir John Reresby to the Marquis of Halifax [*c.* May 1687].

42. Burnet, *History of His Own Time*, pp. 429–30; Richard Kidder, *Life*, ed. A. E. Robinson (1924), p. 37; *Ellis Corr.*, I, 3; [Robert Ferguson], *A Representation of the Threatning Dangers* [Edinburgh?, 1687], p. 46. Cf. Edmund Calamy, *An Abridgment of Mr Baxter's History of His Life and Times* (2 vols., 1713), I, 373, note; Wood, *Life and Times*, III, 224; Edward Gee, *The Catalogue of All Discourses Published against Popery* (1689).

43. [John Northleigh], *Parliamentum Pacificum* (1688), p. 31.

44. *CSPD, 1686–7*, pp. 56–8 (nos. 227, 228).

45. Morrice, P, 588.

46. BL, Add., 34,508, fols. 110–11; BL, Add. 4182, fol. 66; BL, Add. MSS 72,595, fol. 66; Bulstrode Newsletters, Reel 3, 19 and 26 Apr. 1686; *Ellis Corr.*, I, 83–4, 111, 118; Luttrell, I, 375; Morrice, P, 530–2, 623; Fountainhall, *Hist. Obs.*, pp. 246–7; Tim Harris, 'London Crowds and the Revolution of 1688', in Eveline Cruickshanks, ed., *By Force or By Default? The Revolution of 1688–1689* (Edinburgh, 1989), pp. 47–8.

47. BL, Add. MSS 41,804, fols. 160, 170; BL, Add. MSS 34,508, fol. 116; Bulstrode Newsletters, Reel 3, 31 May 1686; Todd Galitz, 'The Challenge of Stability: Religion, Politics, and Social Order in Worcestershire, 1660 to 1720', unpub. Ph.D. dissertation, Brown University (1997), p. 5.

48. BL, Add. MSS 34,508, fol. 113; Morrice, P, 531, 538, 544, 545, 548, 549, 655; Morrice, Q, 15–16, 51; FSL, Newdigate Newsletters, L.c. 1654, 1 May 1686; Luttrell, I, 379, 380, 389; Bulstrode Newsletters, Reel 3, 30 Apr. 1686.

49. BL, Add. MSS 34,508, fols. 117–18; Bulstrode Newsletters, Reel 3, 17 May 1686.

50. J. R. Western, *Monarchy and Revolution* (1972), p. 198.

51. Morrice, P, 556–7; Luttrell, I, 381; *Life of James II*, II, 91.

52. *CSPD, 1686–7*, p. 202 (no. 788); J. R. Bloxam, ed., *Magdalen College and James II* (Oxford, 1886), pp. 1–2; Wood, *Life and Times*, III, 193–4; Hunt. Lib., Hastings Religious Box 2, no. 5.

53. *SR*, IV, 352.

54. *SR*, V, 315–16.

55. Schwoerer, *Declaration of Rights*, pp. 65–6; Speck, *Reluctant Revolutionaries*, p. 151; David Ogg, *England in the Reigns of James II and William III* (Oxford, 1955), pp. 176–8.

56. Morrice, P, 593–4. Cf. [Henry Care], *The Legality of the Court Held by His Majesties Ecclesiastical Commissioners Defended* (1688), pp. 10–11.

57. *Life of James II*, II, 89.

58. Bulstrode Newsletters, Reel 3, 16 Jul. 1686; *Ellis Corr.*, I, 161; *ST*, XI, col. 1157; [Care], *Legality of the Court . . . Defended*, pp. 10–11.

59. *SR*, V, 113.

60. BL, Egerton MSS 2543, fol. 257; *ST*, XI, col. 1160.

61. East Sussex RO, ASH 931, p. 50.

62. BL, Add. MSS 41,804, fols. 207, 209.

63. Sir Robert Atkyns, 'A Discourse Concerning the Ecclesiastical Jurisdiction in the Realm of England: Occasioned by the Late Commission in Ecclesiastical Causes', in *ST*, XI, cols. 1148–1155. See also: [Edward Stillingfleet], *A Discourse Concerning the Illegality of the Late Ecclesiastical Commission* (1689), which was written during James's reign; EUL, La. I. 333, pp. 1–16, 'A MS treatise on the Court of High Commission'.

64. Steele, I, no. 3828.

65. Michael R. Watts, *The Dissenters: From the Reformation to the French Revolution* (Oxford, 1978), p. 257.

66. Fountainhall, *Hist. Obs.*, p. 246; Luttrell, I, 378; *Calendar of Treasury Books*, VIII, 429–34; W. C. Braithwaite, *The Second Period of Quakerism* (Cambridge, 1961), p. 125; Morrice, P, 529, 530, 536, 543, 554, 563, 568–9, 572, 573–4, 578, 584, 615–18, Q, 15; Wood, *Life and Times*, III, 190–1; Douglas R. Lacey, *Dissent and Parliamentary Politics in England, 1661–1689* (New Brunswick, N.J., 1969), pp. 176–9; Craig W. Horle, *The Quakers and the English Legal System, 1660–1688* (Philadelphia, 1988), p. 93; Miller, *James II*, p. 156; Miller, *Popery and Politics*, pp. 210–11.

67. Hunt. Lib., HA 10141, John Penford et al. to Huntingdon, 18 Oct. 1686.

68. Morrice, Q, 71.

69. Mark Goldie, 'James II and the Dissenters Revenge: The Commission of Enquiry of 1688', *Historical Research*, 66 (1993), 58–9; Luttrell, I, 387.

70. *Lond. Gaz.*, nos. 2167–9 (23–26 Aug. to 30 Aug.–2 Sep. 1686); Berks. RO, R/AC1/1/17, p. 11; *Life of James II*, II, 71.

71. Morrice, P, 618–19.

72. Evelyn, *Diary*, IV, 526; Luttrell, I, 386; *Lond. Gaz.*, nos. 2182–4 (14–18 Oct. to 21–25 Oct. 1686); Morrice, P, 633; Wood, *Life and Times*, III, 198.

73. BL, Add. MSS 34, 508, fol. 136; Morrice, P, 658–9.

74. *The Diary of Adam de la Pryme*, ed. Charles Jackson, Surtees Society, 54 (1870), p. 10; Ronald Hutton, *The Rise and Fall of Merry England: The Ritual Year, 1400–1700* (Oxford, 1994), p. 256.

75. Morrice, Q, 73.

76. CLRO, Shelf 552, MS Box 3, no. 5; Morrice, Q, 9; Luttrell, I, 388; BL, Add. MSS 34,508, fol. 135; *Ellis Corr.*, I, 180–1; LMA, WJ/SR/1696, indictment of Richard Butler.

77. Beinecke Library, Yale University, Osborn MSS 2, box 4, folder 76, p. 69.

78. *Clar. Corr.*, II, 116–17.

79. Miller, *Popery and Politics*, app. III, pp. 269–72; Glassey, *Politics*, pp. 70–5; Victor Stater, *Noble Government: The Stuart Lord Lieutenancy and the Transformation of English Politics* (Athens, Ga., 1994), p. 164.

80. Morrice, Q, 55, 133; Hunt. Lib., HA 14806, G. Gowin to Rawdon, 30 Mar. 1687; Evelyn, *Diary*, IV, 540–1; Miller, *James II*, pp. 163–4; J. P. Kenyon, *Robert Spencer, Second Earl of Sunderland 1641–1702* (1958), pp. 147–8.

81. Morrice, P, 618; Wood, *Life and Times*, III, 246; Roger L'Estrange, *The Observator in Dialogue* (3 vols., 1684–7), III, no. 232 (4 Dec. 1686). Cf. Luttrell, I, 395.

82. *Lond. Gaz.*, no. 2226 (17–21 Mar. 1686[/7]); Morrice, Q, 85–6.

83. J. P. Kenyon, *The Stuart Constitution 1603–1688* (Cambridge, 1966), doc. 115.

84. Speck, *Reluctant Revolutionaries*, pp. 150–1; Schwoerer, *Declaration of Rights*, pp. 62–4; Miller, *James II*, p. 165.

85. Herbert, *Short Account*, pp. 6–7.

86. See Tim Harris, *Restoration: Charles II and His Kingdoms, 1660–85* (2005), pp. 63–4.

87. *An Answer to . . . The Judgement and Doctrine of the Clergy of the Church of England* (1687), pp. 19–20.

88. [Ferguson], *Representation of the Threatning Dangers*, pp. 24–5.

89. [Gilbert Burnet], *A Letter, Containing some Reflections on His Majesties Declaration for Liberty of Conscience* (1687), p. 4; [Burnet], *Ill Effects*, p. 22.

90. Lois G. Schwoerer, *The Ingenious Mr. Henry Care, Restoration Publicist* (Baltimore, 2001), ch. 7; Mary Geiter, *William Penn* (Harlow, 2000), ch. 4.

91. L'Estrange, *Observator*, III, no. 232 (4 Dec. 1686).

92. Morrice, Q, 43; L'Estrange, *Observator*, III, preface p. 8.

93. *The Judgment and Doctrine of the Clergy of the Church of England, Concerning . . . Dispensing with the Penall Laws* (1687), esp. pp. 5, 9–12, 24, 31–3, 41.

94. [William Penn], *A Third Letter From a Gentleman in the Country, To His Friends in London, Upon the Subject of the Penal Laws and Tests* (1687), pp. 4–5.

95. 'A Poem Occasioned by His Majesty's Gracious Resolution Declared . . . For Liberty of Conscience' (1687), in *POAS*, IV, 103–4.

96. *Indulgence to Tender Consciences Shown to be Most Reasonable and Christian* (1687). Cf. A.N., *A Letter from a Gentleman in the City, to a Gentleman in the Country, About the Odiousness of Persecution* (1687), p. 29.

97. [Penn], *A Third Letter . . . Upon the Subject of the Penal Laws and Tests*, pp. 6, 9, 14. Cf. Sir George Pudsey, *The Speech of Sir George Pudsey Kt . . . To the King, Upon His Majesty's Coming to Oxford, Sept. 3 1687* (1687); [Care], *Legality of the Court . . . Defended*, pp. 31–2.

98. E.g. *Judgment and Doctrine*, p. 36.

99. Morrice, Q, 132; H[enry] C[are], *Animadversions on . . . A Letter to a Dissenter* (1687), pp. 21–5.

100. *Lond. Gaz.*, no. 2246 (26–30 May 1687); Morrice, Q, 140; BL, Add. MSS 72,595, fol. 150.

101. BL, Althorp C2, Sir John Reresby to Halifax [ND, *c.* May 1687]. Cf. Reresby, *Memoirs*, p. 452.

102. Hunt. Lib., HA 14806, G. Gowin to Sir Arthur Rawdon, 30 Mar. 1687.

103. Watts, *Dissenters*, p. 258.

104. Bodl., MS Tanner 29, fols. 8, 10.

105. Morrice, Q, 97; *HMC, Egmont*, II, 189.

106. Cited in Geraint H. Jenkins, *The Foundations of Modern Wales: Wales 1642–1780* (Oxford, 1987), p. 145.

107. This calculation is based on the published addresses in the *London Gazette*.

108. *Lond. Gaz.*, no. 2234 (14–18 Aug. 1687).

109. Morrice, Q, 114, 137; *Ellis Corr.*, I, 274; *Petty–Southwell Corr.*, p. 280; *Lond. Gaz.*, nos. 2238 (28 Apr.–2 May 1687) and 2245 (23–26 May 1687).

110. Morrice, Q, 112, 115; *The Works of George Savile Marquis of Halifax*, ed. Mark M. Brown (3 vols., Oxford, 1989), I, 80–1.

111. BL, Add. MSS 34,510, fol. 28v.

112. *Lond. Gaz.*, no. 2304 (15–19 Dec. 1687).

113. Ibid., no. 2254 (23–27 Jun. 1687).

114. Ibid., no. 2242 (12–16 May 1687).

115. Ibid., nos. 2248 (2–6 Jun. 1687) and 2274 (1–5 Sep. 1687).

116. Morrice, Q, 132, 149.

117. *The Diary of Dr Thomas Cartwright, Bishop of Chester*, ed. Rev. Joseph Hunter, Camden Society, old series, 22 (1843), pp. 47–8, 51; Morrice, Q, 107, 114, 118, 127, 138.

118. Bodl. MS Tanner 29, fol. 13; All Souls Library, Oxford, MS 264, fol. 98; [Roger L'Estrange], *A Reply to the Reasons of the Oxford-Clergy against Addressing* (1687); BL, Add. MSS 72,595, fol. 119; Wood, *Life and Times*, III, 220; Morrice, Q, 141–2.

119. Morrice, Q, 137; *Diary of Dr. Thomas Cartwright*, p. 57.

120. *Lond. Gaz.*, no. 2320 (9–13 Feb. 1688).

121. *An Address of Thanks on Behalf of the Church of England to Mris James* (1687), p. 1.

122. *Lond. Gaz.*, no. 2250 (9–13 Jun. 1687).

123. Morrice, Q, 120.

124. Ibid., pp. 101–2.

125. *Lond. Gaz.*, no. 2271 (22–25 Aug. 1688).

126. Ibid., nos. 2252 (16–19 Jun. 1687) and 2254 (23–27 Jun. 1687).

127. WYAS, MS/R/47/41, John Rokesby to Reresby, 4 Jul. 1687; BL, Althorp C2, Sir John Reresby to Halifax, 6 Jul. 1687; Reresby, *Memoirs*, pp. 461–2.

128. Morrice, Q, 138.

129. Luttrell, I, 405.

130. Hunt. Lib., HA 1162, Charles Byerley to Huntingdon, 19 Oct. 1687; Hunt. Lib., HA 13676, Sir Nathan Wright to Huntingdon, 19 Oct. 1687; Paul D. Halliday, *Dismembering the Body Politic: Partisan Politics in England's Towns, 1650–1730* (Cambridge, 1998), p. 242.

131. *Lond. Gaz.*, no. 2285 (10–13 Oct. 1687); *Ellis Corr.*, I, 334–5; Henning, *House of Commons*, I, 314.

132. *Lond. Gaz.*, no. 2313 (16–19 Jan. 1688); Halliday, *Dismembering the Body Politic*, pp. 244–5.

133. *Lond. Gaz.*, no. 2339 (16–19 Apr. 1688).

134. Ibid., no. 2348 (17–21 May 1688).

135. Ibid., nos. 2276 (8–12 Sep. 1687) and 2335 (2–5 Apr. 1688); *Victoria County History, Oxon*, X, 75; Henning, *House of Commons*, I, 358.

136. *Lond. Gaz.*, nos. 2347 (14–17 May 1688) and 2348 (17–21 May 1688); Henning, *House of Commons*, I, 213, 487; Luttrell, I, 405.

137. *Lond. Gaz.*, nos. 2252 (16–20 Jun. 1687) and 2312 (12–16 Jan. 1687[/8]); Henning, *House of Commons*, I, 388.

138. The apothecaries, bakers, barber-surgeons, clothworkers, cooks, cordwainers, cutlers, distillers, glovers, goldsmiths, haberdashers, joiners, mercers, merchant-tailors, painters, plumbers, skinners, stationers and weavers.

139. *Lond. Gaz.*, no. 2284 (6–10 Oct. 1687).

140. Miller, *James II*, p. 169.

141. Morrice, Q, 49.

142. *CSPD, 1686–7*, p. 86 (no. 342).

143. *The Flemings in Oxford, Being Documents Selected from the Rydal Papers in Illustration of the Lives and Ways of Oxford Men 1650–1700*, ed. John Richard Magrath (3 vols., Oxford, 1904–24), II, 176–7, 186; Wood, *Life and Times*, III, 197–8, 200–2; Miller, *James II*, 169.

144. Morrice, Q, 45, 54, 79, 127; Wood, *Life and Times*, III, 214–15; *CSPD, 1686–7*, pp. 333 (no. 1304), 375 (no. 1497); *CSPD, 1687–8*, p. 22 (no. 112).

145. Morrice, Q, 79, 95, 104, 111–12, 122–3, 130; BL, Add. MSS 32,095, fol. 238; Bulstrode Newsletters, Reel 3, 29 Apr. and 9 May 1687; East Sussex RO, ASH 932, p. 75.

146. Bloxam, ed., *Magdalen College*, pp. 12–34; Hunt. Lib., STT 1540 and 1541 (F. Overton to Sir Richard Temple, 23 Jun. and 2 Aug. 1687).

147. Bloxam, ed., *Magdalen College*, pp. 57, 79.

148. Ibid., passim (quotes on pp. 88, 91).

149. [Henry Care], *A Vindication of the Proceedings of His Majestie's Ecclesiastical Commissioners* (1688), pp. 36–58.

150. Herbert, *Short Account*, p. 29. For a recent scholarly treatment of the Magdalen College affair, see R. A. Beddard, 'James II and the Catholic Challenge', in Nicholas Tyacke, ed., *The History of the University of Oxford. Vol. IV. Seventeenth-Century Oxford* (Oxford, 1997), pp. 940–50.

151. Wood, *Life and Times*, III, 196, 213, 254, 257, 261–2, 264, 273–4.

152. Steele, I, no. 3845.

153. *Lond. Gaz.*, nos. 2270–2276 (18–22 Aug. to 8–12 Sep. 1687). See also Luttrell, I, 411–12; *Ellis Corr.*, 336–7; Hunt. Lib., HA 1580, Thomas Condon to Earl of Huntingdon, 6 Aug. 1687; NLS, MS 14407, fol. 111.

154. Coventry City Archives, BA/H/C/17/2, fols. 342–4; BL, Add. MSS 72,596, fol. 1.

155. Wood, *Life and Times*, III, 226–32 (quote on p. 230); BL, Add. MSS 72,595, fols. 150, 152v. Morrice, P, 618–19 tells a similar story about an assault by a mastiff dog on one gentleman on horseback in the King's retinue at Salisbury in August 1686.

156. *Life of James II*, II, 140.

157. Evelyn, *Diary*, IV, 560, n.1. In *The Works of Halifax*, I, 89, fn. 2, Brown puts the figure at 17.

158. *CSPD*, 1687–9, p. 67 (no. 330); Dalrymple, *Memoirs*, II, 'Part I. Continued. Appendix to Book V', p. 84.

159. Miller, *James II*, p. 178; Stater, *Noble Government*, pp. 166–71; Sir George Duckett, ed., *Penal Laws and Test Act* (2 vols., 1872–3).

160. Hunt. Lib., HA 10699, Samuel Sanders to Huntingdon, 19 Dec. 1687.

161. Cited in Turner, *James II*, p. 331.

162. Glassey, *Politics*, pp. 82–7; Miller, *Popery and Politics*, p. 272.

163. Mark Knights, 'A City Revolution: The Remodelling of the London Livery Companies in the 1680s', *English Historical Review*, 112 (1997), 1158–62.

164. This section draws on Halliday, *Dismembering the Body Politic*, ch. 7.

165. Western, *Monarchy and Revolution*, pp. 222–4.

166. *CSPD*, 1687–9, p. 300 (no. 1627).

167. Childs, *The Army, James II, and the Glorious Revolution*, pp. 110–11.

168. West Sussex RO, MF 1145, Chichester City Minute Book, 1685–1737, p. 28.

169. BL, Add. MSS 72,596, fols. 15, 16v; J. R. Jones, 'James II's Whig Collaborators', *Historical Journal*, 3 (1960), 65–73; Goldie, 'James II and the Dissenters' Revenge', pp. 53–4; Knights, 'London Livery Companies', p. 1165.

6 Yielding an Active Obedience Only According to Law

1. Morrice, P, 659.

2. *POAS*, IV, 221.

3. Jeremy Black, *A System of Ambition? British Foreign Policy 1660–1793* (1991), p. 135; Jonathan Israel, 'General Introduction', in Israel, ed., *The Anglo-Dutch Moment: Essays on the Glorious Revolution and its World Impact* (Cambridge, 1991), p. 5; Robert Beddard, 'The Unexpected Whig Revolution of 1688', in Beddard, ed., *The Revolution of 1688* (Oxford, 1988), p. 97; Geoffrey Holmes, *The Making of a Great Power: Late Stuart and Early Georgian Britain, 1660–1722* (Harlow, 1993), p. 178.

4. Elinor James, *My Lord, I Thought it My Bound Duty* (1687).

5. See, for example, J[onathan] C[lapham], *Obedience to Magistrates Recommended* (1683), p. 13.

6. *An Answer to a late Pamphlet, Intituled The Judgment and Doctrine of the Clergy* (1687), pp. 14, 29–30. Sherlock's tract is *The Case of Resistance* (1684).

7. *An Address of Thanks On Behalf of the Church of England to Mris James* (1687), p. 2.

8. *A New Test of Church of England's Loyalty* (1687), pp. 3, 5, 8.

9. [Thomas Cartwright], *An Answer of a Minister of the Church of England* (1687), pp. 31–2.

10. *The New Test of the Church of England's Loyalty, Examined* (1687), pp. 1–2.

11. Gilbert Burnet, 'An Answer to a Paper Printed with Allowance, Entitled, A New Test of the Church of England's Loyalty', in his *Six Papers* (1687), pp. 31–2, 35, 38–9.

12. [Samuel Johnson], *The Tryal and Examination of a Late Libel, intituled, A New Test of the Church of England's Loyalty* (1687), quotes on pp. 2, 3, 6.

13. [William Penn], *A Letter from a Gentleman in the Country, To His Friend in London, Upon the Subject of the Penal Laws and Tests* (1687), pp. 5–6. See also [William Penn], *A Second Letter from a Gentleman in the Country, To his Friends in London, Upon the Subject of the Penal Laws and Tests* (1687), pp. 6, 9.

14. *A Letter in Answer to a City Friend Shewing How Agreeable Liberty of Conscience Is to the Church of England* (1687), pp. 1–2. Cf. *Address of Thanks . . . to Mris James*, pp. 1–2.

15. Bodl., MS Tanner 29, fol. 9.

16. Morrice, Q, 120.

17. Ibid., p. 116.

18. *Pub. Occ.*, nos. 4 (13 Mar. 1687[/8]), 6 (27 Mar. 1688), 7 (3 Apr. 1688), and 9 (17 Apr. 1688).

19. Morrice, Q, 116.

20. [Gilbert Burnet], *The Ill Effects of Animosities among Protestants in England Detected* (1688), quotes on pp. 19, 20, 22.

21. Ibid., pp. 10–11, 16–17.

22. Ibid., p. 20.

23. [Gilbert Burnet], *A Letter, Containing some Reflections on His Majesties Declaration for Liberty of Conscience* (1687), p. 6; Burnet, 'An Answer to . . . a New Test', p. 33.

24. *Some Reflections on a Discourse, Called, Good Advice to the Church of England* (1687?), in *State Tracts – Farther Collection* (1692), p. 366.

25. [Robert Ferguson], *A Representation of the Threatning Dangers* [Edinburgh?, 1687], pp. 32, 36, 37, 44, 47.

26. Ibid., p. 13.

27. Ibid., pp. 29–30.

28. FSL, V. b. 287, fol. 32, Sir James Fraser to Sir Robert Southall, 8 Sep. 1687; Mark M. Brown, 'Introduction', *The Works of George Savile Marquis*

of Halifax, ed. Mark M. Brown (3 vols., Oxford, 1989), I, 81.

29. H[enry] C[are], *Animadversions on . . . A Letter to a Dissenter* (1687), p. 7.

30. Halifax, *A Letter to a Dissenter, Upon Occasion of His Majesties Late Gracious Declaration of Indulgence* (1687), in *The Works of Halifax*, I, 250–64 (quotes on pp. 251–2, 256–7).

31. Ibid., pp. 259, 262–4.

32. Mark Goldie, 'The Revolution of 1689 and the Structure of Political Argument', *Bulletin of Research in the Humanities*, 83 (1980), 480.

33. John Miller, *The Glorious Revolution* (1983), p. 103.

34. *A Letter to a Friend. In Answer to a Letter to a Dissenter* (1687), p. 1.

35. T[homas] G[odden], *A Letter in Answer to Two Main Questions of the First Letter to a Dissenter* (1687), pp. 18–19.

36. [William Penn], *Remarks upon a Pamphlet Stiled, a Letter to a Dissenter, etc. In another Letter to the same Dissenter* (1687), p. 7.

37. C[are], *Animadversions*, pp. 7, 10, 17, 31–3.

38. The debate over the 'equivalent' is discussed in *The Works of Halifax*, I, 90–111.

39. C[are], *Animadversions*, pp. 36–7.

40. J. R. Western, *Monarchy and Revolution* (1972), p. 228; *The Works of Halifax*, I, 92.

41. C[are], *Animadversions*, p. 6.

42. Morrice, Q, 227, 232.

43. John Miller, *James II: A Study in Kingship* (Hove, 1978, 3rd edn 2000), p. 177; J. R. Jones, *The Revolution of 1688 in England* (1972), p. 227; Morrice, Q, 234.

44. Gaspar Fagel, *A Letter . . . Giving an Account of the Prince and Princess of Orange's Thoughts Concerning the Repeal of the Test and the Penal Laws* (Amsterdam, 1688).

45. BL, Add. MSS 72,596, fol. 32v.

46. BL, Add. MSS 34,502, fol. 96.

47. Steele, I, no. 3855.

48. E.g. Berks. RO, N/AC1/1, fol. 99; Hunt. Lib., HA 12521, Arthur Stanhope to Huntingdon, 30 Jan. 1687[/8].

49. *Clar. Corr.*, II, 156.

50. Dalrymple, *Memoirs*, II, 'Part I. Continued. Appendix to Book V', p. 92.

51. Wood, *Life and Times*, III, 254–5.

52. BL, Add. MSS 72,596, fol. 32.

53. Hunt. Lib., HA 7783, Gervase Jaquis to Huntingdon, 7 Feb. 1687[/8]; Wood, *Life and Times*, III, 256.

54. *Clar. Corr.*, II, 160.

55. Steele, I, nos. 3864, 3865.

56. Morrice, Q, 255–7. Cf. *Life of James II*, II, 152–3.

57. *ST*, XII, col. 239; Bulstrode Newsletters, Reel 4, 22 and 27 May 1688; Morrice, Q, 259–60.

58. Morrice, Q, 261.

59. Gilbert Burnet, *History of His Own Time: From the Restoration of King Charles the Second to the Treaty of Peace at Utrecht, in the Reign of Queen Anne* (1850), p. 468.

60. BL, Add. MS 34,512, fol. 82; *Clar. Corr.*, II, 172–3; [William Sherlock], *A Letter from a Clergy-Man in the City, To his Friend in the Country, Containing his Reasons For not Reading the Declaration* (1688), p. 8; Burnet, *History of His Own Time*, p. 468; *ST*, XII, cols. 432–3, note; Bulstrode Newsletters, Reel 4, 21 and 28 May 1688.

61. Morrice, Q, 261.

62. Wood, *Life and Times*, III, 267.

63. Luttrell, I, 440; Bulstrode Newsletters, Reel 4, 18 Jun. 1688.

64. Luttrell, I, 451; Bulstrode Newsletters, Reel 4, 16 Jul. 1688; *Lond. Gaz.*, no. 2374 (16–20 Aug. 1688); *Life of James II*, II, 167.

65. Herbert Croft, *A Short Discourse Concerning the Reading of His Majesties Late Declaration in the Churches* (1688), quotes on pp. 6–7.

66. [Poulton], *An Answer to a Letter From a Clergyman in the City, to his Friend in the Country, Containing his Reason for not Reading the Declaration* (1688), p. 3.

67. BL Add. 11,268, fols. 89–93, 'A Country-Clergie-Man's Answer to the Reasons of the City Clergie-man for not Reading the Declaration'.

68. 'The Clerical Cabal' (1688), in *POAS*, IV, 220–1.

69. *An Answer to the City Minister's Letter, from a Country Friend* (Oxford?, 1688), pp. 2, 3.

70. [Sherlock], *Letter from a Clergy-Man in the City*, pp. 2–3, 5, 6.

71. BL, Add. MS 34,512, fol. 83; Bulstrode Newsletters, Reel 4, 27 May 1688.

72. Morrice, Q, 269; Douglas R. Lacey, *Dissent and Parliamentary Politics in England, 1661–1689* (New Brunswick, N.J., 1969), pp. 210–12.

73. West Sussex RO, MF 1145, Chichester City Minute Book 1685–1735, pp. 33, 36.

74. The addresses can be traced in the *London Gazette*. This total excludes those addresses from Totnes and Scarborough, which were drawn up on 28 April but were clearly belated responses (by recently purged corporations) to the Indulgence of the previous year.

75. Morrice, Q, 267–8; FSL, V.b.287, fol. 70, Sir James Fraser to Sir Robert Southwell, 9 Jun. 1688; *Lond. Gaz.*, no. 2354, (7–11 Jun. 1688); Burnet, *History of His Own Time*, pp. 468–9; *Clar. Corr.*, II, 175; *HMC, Portland*, III, 410; *Hatt. Corr.*, II, 81; *Memoirs of Thomas Earl of Ailesbury*, ed. W. E. Buckley (1890), p. 170.

76. FSL, V.b.287, fol. 72, Fraser to Southwell, 16 Jun. 1688; Bulstrode Newsletters, Reel 4, 15 Jun. 1688; *ST*, XII, cols. 189–277; Morrice, Q, 271–3.

77. *Clar. Corr.*, II, 177; Morrice, Q, 280; Luttrell, I, 445; *The Autobiography of Sir John Bramston*, ed. P. Braybrooke, Camden Society, old series, 32 (1845), p. 390; BL, Add. MS 34,487, fol. 7; BL, Add. MSS, 34,510, fols. 126v, 129v–30, 133–5; BL, Add. MSS, 34,515, fol. 82v; Burnet, *History of His Own Time*, p. 469; CLRO, Sessions Papers, 1688; *Pub. Occ.*, no. 19 (26 Jun. 1688).

78. Bulstrode Newsletters, Reel 4, 18 Jun. 1688.

79. BL, Add. MSS 34,510, fol. 138; BL, Add. MSS 34,512, fol. 89; Morrice, Q, 280.

80. *ST*, XII, cols. 277–431 (quotes on cols. 279, 339, 357, 361, 363–4, 367–9, 370–1, 397, 425–6).

81. *ST*, XII, col. 399.

82. *ST*, XII, cols. 426–7; FSL, V.b.287, fol. 76, Fraser to Southwell, 3 Jul. 1688.

83. BL, Add. MSS 34,487, fol. 9; BL, Add. MSS 34,510, fols. 138–9; BL, Add. MSS 34,515, fol. 88; *HMC, Portland*, III, 414; *Ellis Corr.*, II, 5, 11–12; Bramston, *Autobiography*, pp. 310–11; *Clar. Corr.*, II, 179; Bulstrode Newsletters, Reel 4, 29 Jun. 1688; Reresby, *Memoirs*, p. 501; *Pub. Occ.*, no. 20 (3 Jul. 1688); Burnet, *History of His Own Time*, pp. 469–70; Ailesbury, *Memoirs*, p. 170; *The Rawdon Papers*, ed. Rev. Edward Berwick (1819), p. 291; A. C. Edwards, ed., *English History from Essex Sources, 1550–1750* (Chelmsford, 1952), pp. 106–7.

84. Hunt. Lib., HA 3992, John Gery to the Earl of Huntingdon, 5 Jul. 1688; Hunt. Lib., STT 391, W[illiam] C[haplyn] to Sir Richard Temple, 5 Jul. 1688; Luttrell, I, 449; Thomas Babington Macaulay, *The History of England from the Accession of James the Second*, ed. Sir Charles Firth (6 vols., 1913–15), II, 1035; Laurence Echard, *The History of England* (3 vols., 1707–18), III, 874; Wood, *Life and Times*, III, 271–2; D. R. Hainsworth, *Stewards, Lords and People: The Estate Steward and his World in Later Stuart England* (Cambridge, 1992), p. 150.

85. BL, Add. MSS 34,487, fol. 9; Burnet, *History of His Own Time*, p. 470.

86. Reresby, *Memoirs*, p. 500; Luttrell, I, 452.

87. Dalrymple, *Memoirs*, II, 'Part I. Continued. Appendix to Book V', p. 116.

88. Edwards, *Essex Sources*, p. 107; BL, Add. MSS 34,487, fol. 9.

89. Bodl., MS Tanner 28, fol. 113; Macaulay, *History*, II, 1018.

90. *Catalogue of Prints and Drawings in the British Museum*, ed. F. G. Stephens and M. Dorothy George (11 vols., 1870–1954), I, no. 1169.

91. *Life of James II*, II, 168.

92. Bulstrode Newsletters, Reel 3, 13 and 16 Jul. 1688; CLRO, Sessions File, July 1688.

93. BL, Add. MSS 34,487, fol. 11; *Ellis Corr.*, II, 108–9.

94. Bulstrode Newsletters, Reel 4, 2, 6, 9, 13 and 30 Jul. 1688; *Lond. Gaz.*, nos. 2364 (12–16 Jul. 1688) and 2375 (20–23 Aug. 1688); Morrice, Q, 281–2; *ST*, XII, col. 434.

95. Hunt. Lib., STT 1843, Thomas Sprat, Bishop of Rochester, to the Ecclesiastical Commissioners, 16 Aug. 1688; BL, Add. MSS 28,876, fol. 146; All Souls Library, Oxford, MSS 257, no. 65; *Ellis Corr.*, II, 137.

96. Steele, I, no. 3866.

97. BL, Add. MSS 27,448, fols. 342, 344, 349; *Lond. Gaz.*, nos. 2355 (11–14 Jun. 1688), 2356 (14–18 Jun. 1688) and 2357 (18–21 Jun. 1688).

98. Bulstrode Newsletters, Reel 4, 11 Jun. 1688.

99. Wood, *Life and Times*, III, 268, 270–2.

100. Luttrell, I, 443, 445–6; *Pub. Occ.*, no. 17 (19 Jun. 1688); BL, Add. MSS 34,515, fol. 82v; Hunt. Lib., HA 666, Sir Henry Beaumont to Huntingdon, 13 Jun. 1688; Hunt. Lib., HA 665, Beaumont to Huntingdon, 1 Jul. 1688; Hunt. Lib., HA 12979, George Vernon to Huntingdon, 1 Jul. 1688; Hunt. Lib., HA 33, J. Adderley to Huntingdon, 2 Jul. 1688; Hunt. Lib., HA 3992, John Gery to Huntingdon, 5 Jul. 1688; Echard, *History of England*, III, 862, 868. The addresses were published in the *London Gazette*.

101. *Pub. Occ.*, no. 22 (17 Jul. 1688); Morrice, Q, 284; *HMC, 5th Report*, p. 378–9; *Ellis Corr.*, II, 52; Luttrell, I, 451.

102. Dalrymple, *Memoirs*, II, 'Part I. Continued. Appendix to Book V', p. 175.

103. *The Sham Prince Expos'd* (1688).

104. For the warming-pan scandal, see J. P. Kenyon, 'The Birth of the Old Pretender', *History Today*, 13 (1963), 418–26; Rachel Weil, *Political Passions: Gender, the Family and Political Argument in England 1680–1714* (Manchester, 1999), ch. 3. In an attempt to refute the warming-pan myth, James published the depositions from over 70 witnesses to the birth: *Depositions taken the 22d of October, 1688, Before the Privy-Council and Peers of England, Relating to the Birth of the (Then) Prince of Wales*

[Edinburgh, 1688]; FSL, Newdigate Newsletters, L.c. 1932 (23 Oct. 1688).
105. Dalrymple, *Memoirs*, II, 'Part I. Continued. Appendix to Book V',
pp. 107–10.

7 The Desertion

1. Morrice, Q, 207.
2. Jonathan I. Israel, 'The Dutch Role in the Glorious Revolution', in Israel,
ed., *The Anglo-Dutch Moment: Essays on the Glorious Revolution and its
World Impact* (Cambridge, 1991), pp. 105–62; Jonathan Scott, *England's
Troubles: Seventeenth-Century English Political Stability in European
Context* (Cambridge, 2000), chs. 9, 20; Simon Groenveld, '"J'équippe une
flotte trés considérable": The Dutch Side of the Glorious Revolution', in
Robert Beddard, ed., *The Revolutions of 1688* (Oxford, 1988), pp. 213–45.
3. Israel, 'Dutch Role', p. 106; Jonathan Israel and Geoffrey Parker, 'Of
Providence and Protestant Winds', in Israel, ed., *Anglo-Dutch Moment*, p.
337; John Childs, *The Army, James II, and the Glorious Revolution*
(Manchester, 1980), pp. 174–6, 184; Stephen Saunders Webb, *Lord
Churchill's Coup: The Anglo-American Empire and the Glorious Revolution
Considered* (New York, 1998), pp. 141, 337 (note 43); W. A. Speck, *James
II: Profiles in Power* (2002), p. 76.
4. *CSPD, 1687–9*, p. 270 (no. 1472).
5. *Lond. Gaz.*, nos. 2376 (23–27 Aug. 1688) and 2384 (20–24 Sep. 1688);
Luttrell, I, 462; John Miller, *James II: A Study in Kingship* (Hove, 1978, 3rd
edn 2000), pp. 196–7; J. R. Jones, *The Revolution of 1688 in England*
(1972), pp. 150–1.
6. *Lond. Gaz.*, no. 2386 (27 Sep.–1 Oct. 1688); *RPCS, 1686–9*, p. xxv;
Morrice, Q, 296; Childs, *The Army, James II, and the Glorious Revolution*,
p. 180; Steele, I, no. 3876; Hunt. Lib., HA 7164, James II to Huntingdon, 22
Sep. 1688; *CSPD, 1687–9*, pp. 279–86; *The Earl of Sunderland's Letter to a
Friend* (1689); J. P. Kenyon, *Robert Spencer, Second Earl of Sunderland
1641–1702* (1958), p. 215; *Ellis Corr.*, II, 209–10, 219; Steele, I, no. 3873.
7. *Lond. Gaz.*, no. 2386 (27 Sep.–1 Oct. 1688); *Ellis Corr.*, II, 226–7;
Morrice, Q, 298.
8. *Lond. Gaz.*, no. 2387 (1–4 Oct. 1688).
9. Bodl., MS Tanner 28, fol. 187v; EUL, La. II. 89, fols. 304–6 (no. 192).
10. Morrice, Q, 303.
11. *CSPD, 1687–9*, pp. 309 (no. 1677), 320 (no. 1732), 321 (no. 1740);
Lond. Gaz., nos. 2388 (4–8 Oct. 1688) and 2391 (15–18 Oct. 1688);
Luttrell, I, 465; NLS, MS 7011, fol. 74; J. R. Bloxam, ed., *Magdalen College*

and James II (Oxford, 1886), pp. 252–65; Wood, *Life and Times*, III, 279–80; Steele, I, no. 3881; Paul D. Halliday, *Dismembering the Body Politic: Partisan Politics in England's Towns, 1650–1730* (Cambridge, 1998), pp. 257–9; Lionel K. J. Glassey, *Politics and the Appointment of Justices of the Peace 1675–1720* (Oxford, 1979), pp. 94–7.

12. BL, Add. MS 63,057B, fol. 130; Gilbert Burnet, *History of His Own Time: From the Restoration of King Charles the Second to the Treaty of the Peace at Utrecht, in the Reign of Queen Anne* (1850), p. 495; Lois G. Schwoerer, *The Declaration of Rights, 1689* (Baltimore, 1981), pp. 109–11.

13. *The Declaration of His Highnes William Henry . . . Prince of Orange, etc. Of the Reasons Inducing him to Appear in Armes in the Kingdome of England* (The Hague, 1688).

14. Morrice, Q, 324.

15. *Lond. Gaz.*, nos. 2387 (1–4 Oct. 1688), 2389 (8–11 Oct. 1688) and 2390 (11–15 Oct. 1688); Luttrell, I, 467–8; *Ellis Corr.*, II, 233.

16. Somerset RO, DD/SAS/C/795, 'Pr. Of Orange, 1688'; Matthew Prior, 'The Orange', in *POAS*, IV, 308.

17. Steven Pincus, 'The Making of a Great Power? Universal Monarchy, Political Economy, and the Transformation of English Political Culture', *The European Legacy*, 5 (2000), 539.

18. J. D. Davies, *Gentlemen and Tarpaulins: The Officers and Men of the Restoration Navy* (Oxford, 1991), pp. 205–17.

19. David H. Hosford, *Nottingham, the Nobles and the North: Aspects of the Revolution of 1688* (Hamden, Conn., 1976), pp. 30–43.

20. Robert Beddard, *A Kingdom Without a King: The Journal of the Provisional Government in the Revolution of 1688* (Oxford, 1988), p. 21.

21. Jeremy Black, *A System of Ambition? British Foreign Policy 1660–1793* (1991), p. 135.

22. *Lond. Gaz.*, nos. 2398 (8–12 Nov. 1688) and 2399 (12–15 Nov. 1688); [John Whittel], *An Exact Diary of the Late Expedition* (1689), p. 46; *A True and Exact Relation of the Prince of Orange His Publick Entrance into Exeter* [1688]; Eveline Cruickshanks, 'The Revolution and the Localities: Examples of Loyalty to James II', in Cruickshanks, ed., *By Force or By Default? The Revolution of 1688–1689* (Edinburgh, 1989), p. 30; Jones, *Revolution of 1688*, p. 294.

23. [Whittel], *Exact Diary*, p. 48.

24. Burnet, *History of His Own Time*, p. 502; Beddard, *Kingdom Without a King*, pp. 21–2.

25. *Ellis Corr.*, II, 294–6; *Lond. Gaz.*, no. 2399 (12–15 Nov. 1688); Morrice,

Q, 317, 321; David Hosford, 'Lovelace, John, Third Baron of Lovelace (*c.* 1640–1693)', *Oxford DNB*.

26. Morrice, Q, 322; [Whittel], *Exact Diary*, p. 51; Childs, *The Army, James II, and the Glorious Revolution*, p. 186.

27. *Lond. Gaz.*, no. 2402 (19–22 Nov. 1688).

28. Ibid., no. 2400 (15–17 Nov. 1688); Hunt. Lib., HA 12452, J. Smithsby to Huntingdon, 27 Nov. 1688; Morrice, Q, 317–18, 327; Childs, *The Army, James II, and the Glorious Revolution*, chs. 6 and 7 (esp. pp. 159, 186–7, 190).

29. *POAS*, IV, 309–14; Burnet, *History of His Own Time*, p.502; Mrs Manley, *A True Relation of the Several Facts and Circumstances of the Intended Riot and Tumult on Queen Elizabeth's Birthday* (3rd edn, 1712), p. 5.

30. Wood, *Life and Times*, III, 284; Hosford, *Nottingham, Nobles and the North*, ch. 6; Morrice, Q, 326, 331, 337; Laurence Echard, *The History of England* (3 vols., 1707–18), III, 928; W. A. Speck, *Reluctant Revolutionaries* (Oxford, 1988), pp. 226–30; Reresby, *Memoirs*, p. 536; *Great News from Salisbury, The Sixth of December, 1688* [1688].

31. *To the King's Most Excellent Majesty, the Humble Petition of the Lords Spiritual and Temporal* (1688); Luttrell, I, 476; Steele, I, no. 3901.

32. Speck, *Reluctant Revolutionaries*, p. 232; Luttrell, I, 475, 480; *Ellis Corr.*, II, 333.

33. Hunt. Lib., HA 4801, Countess of Huntingdon to Huntingdon, 3 Dec. 1688. Cf. Hunt. Lib., HA 4808, same to the same, 7 Dec. 1688.

34. *Lord Del_r's Speech* [1688?].

35. *The Declaration of the Nobility, Gentry, and Commonalty at the Rendezvous at Nottingham, Nov. 22 1688* [1688].

36. Martin Greig, 'Burnet, Gilbert (1643–1715)', *Oxford DNB*.

37. [Gilbert Burnet], *An Enquiry into the Measures of Submission to the Supream Authority* (1688, Wing B5808 edn), pp. 1, 2, 4.

38. Ibid., pp. 5, 6.

39. Tim Harris, *Restoration: Charles II and His Kingdoms, 1660–85* (2005), pp. 58, 72, 75–6, 78, 175–9; Mark Goldie, 'Danby, the Bishops and the Whigs', in Tim Harris, Paul Seaward and Mark Goldie, eds., *The Politics of Religion in Restoration England* (1990), pp. 75–105.

40. [Thomas Osborne, Earl of Danby], *The Thoughts of a Private Person; About the Justice of the Gentlemen's Undertaking at York. Nov. 1688* (1689), pp. 1–2, 3, 4, 5, 7.

41. Ibid., pp. 8, 9, 10, 11, 12, 17, 22.

42. Reresby, *Memoirs*, pp. 497–8; WYAS, MX/R/50/84–5, MX/R/53/1, 4, 6,

MX/R/54/1–5; Luttrell, I, 434; Wood, *Life and Times*, III, 257; *Pub. Occ.*, no. 4 (13 Mar. 1687[/8]).

43. BL, Add. MSS 34,512, fol. 108v; BL, Add. MSS, 38,175, fol. 140; Evelyn, *Diary*, IV, 599; Luttrell, I, 465. For general studies of the anti-Catholic violence of the latter part of 1688, see William L. Sachse, 'The Mob and the Revolution of 1688', *Journal of British Studies*, 4 (1964), 23–40; Robert Beddard, 'Anti-Popery and the London Mob of 1688', *History Today*, 38, no. 7 (July 1988), 36–9; Tim Harris, 'London Crowds and the Revolution of 1688', in Cruickshanks, ed., *By Force or By Default?*, pp. 44–64; John Miller, 'The Militia and the Army in the Reign of James II', *Historical Journal*, 16 (1973), 659–79.

44. Luttrell, I, 467; *Ellis Corr.*, II, 240; *Hatt. Corr.*, II, 95.

45. *HMC, Le Fleming*, pp. 216–17; *HMC, 5th Report*, p. 379.

46. Morrice, Q, 310; Luttrell, I, 472; *HMC, 14th Report*, IX, 448; *Ellis Corr.*, II, 269; Evelyn, *Diary*, IV, 602.

47. Morrice, Q, 311; *HMC, Le Fleming*, p. 218.

48. Luttrell, I, 474, 475; *Ellis Corr.*, II, 291–2; BL, Add. MSS 34,487, fol. 35; Morrice, Q, 317; Evelyn, *Diary*, IV, 607; *Hatt. Corr.*, II, 99–100; CLRO, Lieutenancy Court Minute Books 1685–88, 13 Nov. 1688; *The Autobiography of Sir John Bramston*, ed. P. Braybrooke, Camden Society, old series, 32 (1845), p. 332; FSL, Newdigate Newsletters, L.c. 1934 (13 Nov. 1688).

49. BL, Add. MSS 34,510, fols. 177v, 179v–80; Luttrell, I, 477.

50. Luttrell, I, 468.

51. *CSPD, 1687–9*, p. 348 (no. 1915).

52. BL, Add. MSS 34,510, fol. 159v; *CSPD, 1687–9*, p. 316 (no. 1715).

53. Hunt. Lib., STT 48, Mr Andrews and others to Dear Sir, 1 Nov. 1688; Wood, *Life and Times*, III, 281.

54. Wood, *Life and Times*, III, 285; Morrice, Q, 337; Reresby, *Memoirs*, p. 531; FSL, Newdigate Newsletters, L.c. 1944 (6 Dec. 1688).

55. *HMC, Le Fleming*, p. 226; Bodl., MS Ballard 45, fol. 20.

56. Wood, *Life and Times*, III, 286–7.

57. Morrice, Q, 338; Luttrell, I, 482–4; Bodl., MS Tanner 28, fol. 283; *Univ. Int.*, no. 1 (11 Dec. 1688); *Great News from Nottingham, The Fifth of December, 1688* [1688]; FSL, Newdigate Newsletters, L.c. 1944 (6 Dec. 1688).

58. [Hugh Speke], *By His Highness William Henry, Prince of Orange, a Third Declaration* (1688); Hugh Speke, *The Secret History of the Happy Revolution, in 1688* (1715), pp. 32, 34–40; Edmund Bohun, *The History of the Desertion* (1689), pp. 87–8; John Oldmixon, *The History of England*

during the Reign of the Royal House of Stuart (1730), p. 759.

59. Burnet, *History of His Own Time*, p. 503; Morrice, Q, 341.

60. Evelyn, *Diary*, IV, 609.

61. Speke, *Secret History*, pp. 43–4.

62. BL, Add. MSS 72,596, fol. 45; Hunt. Lib., HA 12452, Smithsby to Huntingdon, 27 Nov. 1688; Morrice, Q, 329; *Lond. Gaz.*, no. 2406 (29 Nov.–3 Dec. 1688); Steele, I, no. 3909; *CSPD, 1687–9*, p. 361 (no. 1987).

63. Morrice, Q, 325, 345; FSL, Newdigate Newsletters, L.c. 1939 (24 Nov. 1688) and 1946 (11 Dec. 1688); [Whittel], *Exact Diary*, p. 69; *An Account of Last Sunday's Engagement Between His Majesty's, and the Prince of Orange's Forces, in the Road between Reading and Maidenhead* (1688); Henri and Barbara van der Zee, *1688: Revolution in the Family* (1988), pp. 179, 187–8.

64. [Whittel], *Exact Diary*, pp. 64–6; Beddard, *Kingdom Without a King*, pp. 25–9.

65. Andrew Barclay, 'Mary [of Modena] (1658–1718)', *Oxford DNB*.

66. *HMC, 14th Report*, IX, 451; *HMC, Dartmouth*, I, 226; Luttrell, I, 485; BL, Add. MSS 32,095, fol. 297; Reresby, *Memoirs*, pp. 536–7; Jones, *Revolution of 1688*, p. 305.

67. *Lond. Gaz.*, no. 2409 (10–13 Dec. 1688); *Univ. Int.*, no. 1 (11 Dec. 1688).

68. BL, Add. MSS 34,487, fols. 50–1; BL, Add. MSS 34,510, fols. 197–9; *Ellis Corr.*, II, 345–52; Bramston, *Autobiography*, pp. 339–40; Reresby, *Memoirs*, 537; *HMC, 5th Report*, p. 379; *HMC, Dartmouth*, I, 229–33; *HMC, Le Fleming*, p. 228; *HMC, 14th Report*, IX, 452; *HMC, Portland*, III, 420; Luttrell, I, 486; *Univ. Int.*, nos. 1 (11 Dec. 1688) and 2 (11–15 Dec. 1688); *English Currant*, no. 2 (12–14 Dec. 1688); *London Courant*, no. 2 (12–15 Dec. 1688); *Lond. Gaz.*, no. 2409 (10–13 Dec. 1688); *Lond. Merc.*, nos. 1 (15 Dec. 1688) and 2 (15–18 Dec. 1688); Morrice, Q, 350–2; FSL, Newdigate Newsletters, L.c. 1947 (13 Dec. 1688); Evelyn, *Diary*, IV, 610; Hunt. Lib., HA 1226, Thomas Carleton to Huntingdon, 13 Dec. 1688; Hunt. Lib., HA 4806, Countess of Huntingdon to Huntingdon, 15 Dec. 1688; A. C. Edwards, ed., *English History from Essex Sources, 1550–1750* (Chelmsford, 1952), pp. 110–11; *A Full Account of the Apprehending of the Lord Chancellor in Wapping* (1688); Echard, *History*, III, 932.

69. *Univ. Int.*, nos. 3 (15–18 Dec. 1688), 4 (18–22 Dec. 1688), 5 (22–26 Dec. 1688) and 7 (31 Dec.–3 Jan. 1688[/9]); *Lond. Merc.*, nos. 4 (22–24 Dec. 1688) and 5 (24–27 Dec. 1688); Morrice, Q, 389; FSL, Newdigate Newsletters, L.c. 1955 (1 Jan. 1688[/9]) Geraint H. Jenkins, *The Foundations of Modern Wales: Wales 1642–1780* (Oxford, 1987), p. 147.

70. *Lond. Merc.*, no. 1 (15 Dec. 1688); *Univ. Int.*, no. 3 (15–18 Dec. 1688); Morrice, Q, 362; *HMC, 5th Report*, p. 324; *Memoirs of Thomas Earl of Ailesbury*, ed. W. E. Buckley (1890), pp. 200, 203, 205, 206; Luttrell, I, 487; *Ellis Corr.*, II, 356–7; Bohun, *History of the Desertion*, pp. 99, 103; Oldmixon, *History*, p. 761. For a general account, see G. H. Jones, 'The Irish Fright of 1688: Real Violence and Imagined Massacre', *BIHR*, 55 (1982), 148–52; P. G. Melvin, 'The Irish Army and the Revolution of 1688', *The Irish Sword*, 9 (1969–70), 298–9, 302–7.

71. *Lond. Merc.*, nos. 2 (15–18 Dec. 1688), 3 (18–22 Dec. 1688), 5 (24–27 Dec. 1688) and 7 (31 Dec. 1688–3 Jan. 1688[/9]); *Univ. Int.*, no. 5 (22–26 Dec. 1688); Hunt. Lib., HA 1043, [Theophilus Brookes] to Huntingdon, 19 Dec. 1688; Morrice, Q, 359, 389; *HMC, Portland*, III, 421; BL, Add. MSS 34,487, fol. 50; Echard, *History*, III, 933; Jenkins, *Foundations of Modern Wales*, p. 147.

72. Bramston, *Autobiography*, p. 340; *A Dialogue between Dick and Tom* (1689), p. 8.

73. Beddard, 'Anti-Popery and the London Mob', quote on p. 36; Sachse, 'Mob and the Revolution', esp. pp. 26, 35.

74. Morrice, Q, 310; *Ellis Corr.*, II, 351; *Univ. Int.*, no. 2 (11–15 Dec. 1688).

75. Oldmixon, *History*, p. 757; Burnet, *History of His Own Time*, pp. 503, 505.

76. Luttrell, I, 477; Morrice, Q, 323.

77. Bodl., MS Ballard 45, fol. 20.

78. Thomas Babington Macaulay, *The History of England from the Accession of James the Second*, ed. Sir Charles Firth (6 vols., 1913–15), III, 1178. Cf. [Charles Leslie], *An Answer to a Book, Intituled, The State of the Protestants in Ireland* (1692), sig. b 2v.

79. BL, Add. MSS 32,095, fols. 302–11; Hunt. Lib., HA 1226, Thomas Carleton to Huntingdon, 13 Dec. 1688; Wood, *Life and Times*, III, 288; *Hatt. Corr.*, II, 123; Ailesbury, *Memoirs*, p. 208; Bramston, *Autobiography*, p. 338; Reresby, *Memoirs*, p. 539; Burnet, *History of His Own Time*, p. 505; 'Récit du Départ du Roi Jacques II D'Angleterre, Ecrit de sa main', in Sir James Mackintosh, *History of the Revolution in England in 1688* (1834), p. 706.

80. BL, Add. MSS 4182, fol. 71; *Clar. Corr.*, II, 230; Ailesbury, *Memoirs*, pp. 214–15; Reresby, *Memoirs*, p. 540; Wood, *Life and Times*, III, 289; *Life of James II*, II, 262; Burnet, *History of His Own Time*, p. 506; 'Récit du Départ du Roi Jacques II', p. 707; *HMC, Dartmouth*, I, 236; *HMC, Le Fleming*, p. 230; *Ellis Corr.*, II, 362–3; *Univ. Int.*, no. 3 (15–18 Dec. 1688); *Lond. Merc.*, no. 2 (15–18 Dec. 1688); *London Courant*, no. 3 (15–18 Dec. 1688); Echard, *History*, III, 934–5.

81. Bramston, *Autobiography*, p. 340; FSL, Newdigate Newsletters, L.c. 1949 (18 Dec. 1688); Oldmixon, *History*, p. 762; Bohun, *History of the Desertion*, p. 100; Edmund Bohun, *Diary and Autobiography*, ed. S. Wilton Rix (Beccles, 1853), p. 82; *A Poem on His Majesties Return to Whitehall* (1688); *Lond. Gaz.*, no. 2410 (13–17 Dec. 1688).

82. *Life of James II*, II, 263–78 (quotes on pp. 263, 267, 274); James II, *His Majestie's Reasons for Withdrawing Himself from Rochester* (1688); Ailesbury, *Memoirs*, p. 218; *Univ. Int.*, nos. 4 (18–22 Dec. 1688) and 5 (22–26 Dec. 1688); *Lond. Merc.*, no. 7 (31 Dec. 1688–7 Jan. 1688[/9]); *HMC, Hamilton*, p. 175; *Ellis Corr.*, II, 372–3; Wood, *Life and Times*, III, 289–91; Beddard, *Kingdom Without a King*, pp. 63–4.

83. Hunt. Lib., HA 1227, Thomas Carleton to Huntingdon, 18 Dec. 1688; Hunt. Lib., HA 4807, Countess of Huntingdon to Huntingdon, 18 Dec. 1688; BL, Add. MSS 20,716, fol. 5; FSL, Newdigate Newsletters, L.c. 1950 (20 Dec. 1688); *Clar. Corr.*, II, 231; Luttrell, I, 489; *Lond. Merc.*, no. 3 (18–22 Dec. 1688); *English Currant*, no. 3 (14–19 Dec. 1688); *Univ. Int.*, no. 4 (18–22 Dec. 1688); Morrice, Q, 378; [Whittel], *Exact Diary*, p. 71; Burnet, *History of His Own Time*, p. 508; *Ellis Corr.*, II, 369; Reresby, *Memoirs*, p. 541; *The Rawdon Papers*, ed. Rev. Edward Berwick (1819), p. 292; Oldmixon, *History*, p. 763; Echard, *History*, III, 938–40; BL, Evelyn Papers, JE A2, fol. 54.

84. Morrice, Q, 383; *Lond. Merc.*, no. 4 (22–24 Dec. 1688).

85. BL, Evelyn Papers, JE A2, fols. 54v–5v.

8 'The Greatest Revolution that was Ever Known'

1. Lucille Pinkham, *William III and the Respectable Revolution* (Cambridge, Mass., 1954); Stuart E. Prall, *The Bloodless Revolution: England, 1688* (Garden City, N.Y., 1972); Jennifer Carter, 'The Revolution and the Constitution', in Geoffrey Holmes, ed., *Britain after the Glorious Revolution, 1689–1714* (1969), pp. 39–58; J. R. Western, *Monarchy and Revolution* (1972); J. P. Kenyon, *Revolution Principles: The Politics of Party, 1689–1720* (Cambridge, 1977); Howard Nenner, 'Constitutional Uncertainty and the Declaration of Rights', in Barbara Malament, ed., *After the Reformation: Essays in Honor of J. H. Hexter* (Philadelphia, 1980), pp. 291–308; Robert J. Frankle, 'The Formulation of the Declaration of Rights', *Historical Journal*, 17 (1974), 265–79.

2. John Morrill, 'The Sensible Revolution', in Jonathan I. Israel, ed., *The Anglo-Dutch Moment: Essays on the Glorious Revolution and its World Impact* (Cambridge, 1991), p. 103.

3. R. A. Beddard, 'The Unexpected Whig Revolution of 1688', Beddard, ed., *The Revolutions of 1688* (Oxford, 1988), esp. pp. 94–7.

4. Lois G. Schwoerer, *The Declaration of Rights, 1689* (Baltimore, 1981), quote on p. 248.

5. W. A. Speck, *Reluctant Revolutionaries* (Oxford, 1988), pp. 141, 162. Cf. Geoffrey Holmes, *The Making of a Great Power: Late Stuart and Early Georgian Britain, 1660–1722* (Harlow, 1993), p. 217.

6. Steven Pincus, 'The Making of a Great Power? Universal Monarchy, Political Economy, and the Transformation of English Political Culture', *The European Legacy*, 5 (2000), 532. See also Steven Pincus, *The First Modern Revolution* (forthcoming).

7. Robert Beddard, *A Kingdom Without a King: The Journal of the Provisional Government in the Revolution of 1688* (Oxford, 1988), pp. 36–41, 49–51, 57–60.

8. *Lond. Gaz.*, no. 2414 (27–31 Dec. 1688); Morrice, Q, 378, 382; Gilbert Burnet, *History of His Own Time: From the Restoration of King Charles the Second to the Treaty of Peace at Utrecht, in the Reign of Queen Anne* (1850), p. 509; *Clar. Corr.*, II, 225; Henry Horwitz, *Revolution Politicks: The Career of Daniel Finch, Second Earl of Nottingham* (Cambridge, 1968), pp. 68–9; Schwoerer, *Declaration of Rights*, pp. 133–4; Beddard, *Kingdom Without a King*, pp. 63–5; Beddard, 'Unexpected Whig Revolution', pp. 38–40.

9. J. H. Plumb, 'The Elections to the Convention Parliament of 1689', *Cambridge Historical Journal*, 5 (1937), 235–54; Henry Horwitz, 'Parliament and the Glorious Revolution', *BIHR*, 47 (1974), 36–52; Schwoerer, *Declaration of Rights*, pp. 150–2; Speck, *Reluctant Revolutionaries*, pp. 92–4; Henning, *House of Commons*, I, 106–7.

10. Morrice, Q, 436; Anchitell Grey, *Debates of the House of Commons from the Year 1667 to the Year 1694* (10 vols., 1763), IX, 2; *CJ*, X, 9; *LJ*, XIV, 101.

11. *Life of James II*, II, 292.

12. Schwoerer, *Declaration of Rights*, p. 156; Mark Goldie, 'The Revolution of 1689 and the Structure of Political Argument', *Bulletin of Research in the Humanities*, 83 (1980), 478.

13. *Life of James II*, II, 292–3; Luttrell, I, 497. Cf. Burnet, *History of His Own Time*, pp. 512–13.

14. *The Anatomy of an Arbitrary Prince* (1689).

15. [Gilbert Burnet], *An Enquiry into the Measures of Submission to the Supream Authority* (1688, Wing B5808 edn), p. 6.

16. [Robert Ferguson], *A Brief Justification of the Prince of Orange's*

Descent into England, and of the Kingdom's Late Recourse to Arms (1689), quotes on pp. 9, 15, 17–18, 19.

17. *Four Questions Debated* (1689). Cf. *Reasons Humbly Offer'd, For Placing His Highness the Prince of Orange, Singly in the Throne During his Life*, in *The Eighth Collection of Papers Relating to the Present Juncture of Affairs in England* [1689], pp. 17–18.

18. [Ferguson], *Brief Justification of the Prince of Orange's Descent into England*, quotes on pp. 23–4, 31–2, 34, 37.

19. Mark Goldie, 'The Roots of True Whiggism 1688–94', *History of Political Thought*, 1 (1980), 195–236; Schwoerer, *Declaration of Rights*, ch. 8. Schwoerer mistakenly includes Robert Ferguson in this group, who in early 1689 was decrying against a commonwealth and saw no need for further limitations on the crown.

20. [John Humfrey], *Advice Before it be too Late: Or, A Breviate for the Convention* [1689].

21. [John Wildman], *Some Remarks upon Government, and Particularly upon the Establishment of the English Monarchy Relating to this Present Juncture* (1689), p. 27.

22. *A Plain and Familiar Discourse concerning Government* [1688], p. 2.

23. *Now Is the Time* (1689). Also published as *A Modest Proposal to the Present Convention*, in *The Sixth Collection of Papers Relating to the Present Juncture of Affairs in England* (1689), pp. 17–18.

24. [Wildman], *Some Remarks upon Government*, quotes on pp. 5, 19, 21–3, 27–8.

25. [Humfrey], *Advice*, p. 4.

26. *A Letter to a Friend, Advising in this Extraordinary Juncture, How to Free the Nation from Slavery for Ever* (1689), p. 1.

27. Morrice, Q, 400, 406, 422, 424, 427, 430–1, 433.

28. *A Speech to His Royal Highness the Prince of Orange, by a True Protestant of the Church of England* (1689).

29. William Sherlock, *A Letter to a Member of the Convention* (1689), pp. 1–3.

30. *LJ*, XIV, 101; *CJ*, X, 11; Grey, *Debates*, IX, 3–5; *Parl. Hist.*, V, cols. 31–5; Steele, I, no. 3953.

31. All Souls, Oxford, MS 251, fol. 154.

32. For various accounts of the debate, see: Grey, *Debates*, IX, 6–25; *Parl. Hist.*, V, cols. 36–50 (which follows Grey); Lois G. Schwoerer, 'A Jornall of the Convention at Westminster begun the 22 of January 1688/9', *BIHR*, 49 (1976), 242–63; John Somers, 'Notes of what passed in the Convention upon the Day the question was moved in the House of Commons concerning the

Abdication of King James II, the 28th January 1688–9', in *Miscellaneous State Papers, from 1501 to 1726*, ed. P. Yorke, 2nd Earl of Hardwicke (2 vols., 1778), II, 401–12. The debate is best reconstructed by combining Schwoerer, 'Jornall' with Grey, *Debates*. Grey's account lists the speeches in the wrong order. 'A Jornall' provides what seems to be the right order, and gives a much fuller account of some of the speeches, though for other speeches the compiler merely summarizes what was said, and for these it is better to follow Grey.

33. Grey, *Debates*, IX, 7–9, 21.

34. Schwoerer, 'Jornall', pp. 250–1. Cf. Grey, *Debates*, IX, 19–20.

35. Schwoerer, 'Jornall', p. 255. Cf. Grey, *Debates*, IX, 24.

36. Schwoerer, 'Jornall', pp. 256, 259; Grey, *Debates*, IX, 12, 17.

37. Schwoerer, 'Jornall', pp. 252–3. Cf. Grey, *Debates*, IX, 21–3.

38. Grey, *Debates*, IX, 18, 24; Schwoerer, 'Jornall', pp. 257, 259.

39. Grey, *Debates*, IX, 11; Schwoerer, 'Jornall', p. 258

40. Grey, *Debates*, IX, 12, 15, 23; Schwoerer, 'Jornall', pp. 255, 256, 258.

41. Grey, *Debates*, IX, 25; Schwoerer, 'Jornall', p. 261; *CJ*, X, 14, 15. The three who voted against were Lord Fanshaw (who wanted to delay the vote), Viscount Cornbury, and Sir Edward Seymour.

42. Morrice, Q, 446–7, 450; *LJ*, XIV, 110; *Parl. Hist.*, V, cols. 58–9; Eveline Cruickshanks, David Hayton and Clyve Jones, 'Divisions in the House of Lords on the Transfer of the Crown and Other Issues, 1689–94', in Clyve Jones and David Lewis Jones, eds., *Peers, Politics and Power: The House of Lords, 1603–1911* (1986), p. 82.

43. Morrice, Q, 445, 451–2; *LJ*, 111–12.

44. BL, Add. MSS 15,949, fol. 13; Morrice, Q, 445.

45. Reresby, *Memoirs*, p. 547; Luttrell, I, 499; Morrice, Q, 450.

46. Morrice, Q, 453–4; Reresby, *Memoirs*, pp. 548–9; Luttrell, I, 499–500; John Oldmixon, *The History of England during the Reign of the Royal House of Stuart* (1730), p. 771; *Clar. Corr.*, II, 258; *Lond. Int.*, no. 7 (2–5 Feb. 1688[/9]); *Lond. Merc.*, no. 10 (10 Jan.–6 Feb. 1688[/9]); Grey, *Debates*, IX, 45; Schwoerer, *Declaration of Rights*, p. 211.

47. *CJ*, X, 18–19; *LJ*, XIV, 115–17; BL, Add. MSS 15,949, fol. 16; Morrice, Q, 456; Grey, *Debates*, IX, 49–50.

48. *CJ*, X, 20; Grey, *Debates*, IX, 53–65 (quotes on pp. 55, 56).

49. *Parl. Hist.*, V, cols. 66–108 (quotes on cols. 68, 69, 70, 72); *LJ*, XIV, 118–19; Morrice, Q, 459–60, 462; West Sussex RO, Shillinglee Archives, no. 482, Robert Chaplin to Sir Edward Turner, 9 Feb. 1684[/5]; Burnet, *History of His Own Time*, pp. 518–19.

50. Grey, *Debates*, IX, 29–30.

51. Schwoerer, *Declaration of Rights*, p. 186.

52. Grey, *Debates*, IX, 30–4; Morrice, Q, 447–8.

53. *CJ*, X, 15; Grey, *Debates*, IX, 33, 35, 37, 48.

54. *The Publick Grievances of the Nation, Adjudged Necessary, by the Honorable House of Commons, To be Redressed* (1689); Schwoerer, *Declaration of Rights*, Appendix 2, pp. 299–300.

55. Grey, *Debates*, IX, 33, 51; *CJ*, X, 19; Schwoerer, *Declaration of Rights*, pp. 220–1.

56. Morrice, Q, 459–61; Speck, *Reluctant Revolutionaries*, p. 110.

57. *CJ*, X, 21–9; Grey, *Debates*, IX, 70–83.

58. Steele, I, nos. 3957–61

59. Schwoerer, *Declaration of Rights*, Appendix 1, pp. 295–8.

60. *HMC, 7th Report*, p. 759; *HMC, House of Lords, 1689–1690*, p. 29; *CJ*, X, 25.

61. William Cavendish, Duke of Devonshire, *Reasons for His Majestie's Passing the Bill of Exclusion* (1681), p. 5.

62. Tim Harris, *Politics under the Later Stuarts* (1993), pp. 69–70.

63. See Tim Harris, *Restoration: Charles II and His Kingdoms, 1660–85* (2005), pp. 63–4.

64. *CJ*, X, 26; *HMC, 7th Report*, p. 759; *HMC, House of Lords, 1689–1690*, p. 29.

65. Sir Edward Herbert, *A Short Account of the Authorities in Law, Upon Which Judgement Was Given in Sir Edw. Hales His Case* (1688), quotes on pp. 13, 16, 27, 28, 34.

66. Ibid., p. 29. See p. 228.

67. *A Letter to a Gentleman at Brussels, Containing an Account of the Causes of the People's Revolt from the Crown* (1689), p. 15.

68. W[illiam] A[twood], *The Lord Chief Justice Herbert's Account Examin'd* (1689), esp. pp. 9, 11–13, 26–8, 31, 50–1, 62, 67, 70–2. Cf. Sir Robert Atkyns, 'Enquiry into the Power of Dispensing with Penal Statutes' [1688], in *ST*, XI, cols. 1200–51.

69. Herbert, *Short Account*, pp. 4, 35, 37.

70. *Ellis Corr.*, II, 227. James said this at a meeting with the bishops on 28 September.

71. BL, Egerton MSS 2543, fol. 257. See pp. 202–5.

72. Joyce Lee Malcolm, *To Keep and Bear Arms: The Origins of an Anglo-American Right* (Cambridge, Mass., 1994), p. 40.

73. *CJ*, X, 25; *LJ*, XIV, 122.

74. See John Miller, 'Crown, Parliament and People', in J. R. Jones, ed., *Liberty Secured? Britain Before and After 1688* (Stanford, 1992), pp. 81–2.

75. Malcolm, *To Keep and Bear Arms*, pp. 121–2.

76. Lois G. Schwoerer, 'To Hold and Bear Arms: The English Perspective', *Chicago-Kent Law Review*, 76 (2000), 27–60.

77. Morrice, P, 385, 430, 472, 477, 501, 526, 543. See Harris, *Restoration*, pp. 179, 314, and above p. 82.

78. Harris, *Restoration*, pp. 142, 179, 185, 296, 315, 316.

79. *ST*, IX, cols. 585–94; J. M. Beattie, *Crime and the Courts in England 1660–1800* (Princeton, 1986), p. 378.

80. Speck, *Reluctant Revolutionaries*, p. 148; Schwoerer, *Declaration of Rights*, pp. 96–7; David Ogg, *England in the Reign of Charles II* (Oxford, 1934), p. 431; John Miller, *James II: A Study in Kingship* (Hove, 1978, 3rd edn 2000), p. 142.

81. Schwoerer, *Declaration of Rights*, ch. 15; Speck, *Reluctant Revolutionaries*, pp. 113–14.

82. *CJ*, X, 29–30; *LJ*, XIV, 127; Grey, *Debates*, IX, 83–4.

83. *LJ*, XIV, 132; *CJ*, X, 34; Grey, *Debates*, IX, 84–106, *SR*, VI, 23–4.

84. *SR*, VI, 61–2; Morrice, Q, 489; *HMC, Athole*, p. 36; Grey, *Debates*, IX, 128–9; *CJ*, X, 42.

85. *SR*, VI, 56–7; Lois G. Schwoerer, 'The Coronation of William and Mary, April 11, 1689', in Schwoerer, ed., *The Revolution of 1688–1689: Changing Perspectives* (Cambridge, 1992), pp. 107–30 (esp. pp. 123–5, 128–9).

86. *LJ*, XIV, 191; *SR*, VI, 57–60.

87. *CJ*, X, 42.

88. *SR*, VI, 142–5; Schwoerer, *Declaration of Rights*, ch. 16.

89. NLS, MS 7011, fol. 149.

90. *SR*, VI, 74–6; Horwitz, *Revolution Politicks*, pp. 87–93.

91. BL, Add. MSS 4236, fols. 19–20.

92. *The State Prodigal His Returne* [1689], p. 3.

93. CUL, Sel 3, 237, no. 143.

94. *LJ*, XIV, 148; Morrice, Q, 507; Tony Claydon, *William III and the Godly Revolution* (Cambridge, 1996), p. 152; Henry Horwitz, *Parliament, Policy and Politics in the Reign of William III* (Manchester, 1977), p. 22.

95. W. C. Braithwaite, *The Second Period of Quakerism* (Cambridge, 1961), pp. 155, 181.

96. Western, *Monarchy and Revolution*, pp. 334–44, 352–3; Paul D. Halliday, *Dismembering the Body Politic: Partisan Politics in England's Towns, 1650–1730* (Cambridge, 1998), pp. 268–76.

97. *Parl. Hist.*, V, cols. 560, 561; Clayton Roberts, 'The Constitutional Significance of the Financial Settlement of 1690', *Historical Journal*, 20 (1977), 59–76 (figures on p. 63); E. A. Reitan, 'From Revenue to Civil List,

1689–1702: The Revolution Settlement and the "Mixed and Balanced" Constitution', *Historical Journal*, 13 (1970), 571–88.

98. [John Somers], *In Vindication of the Proceedings of the Late Parliament of England* (1689), pp. 13–14.

99. *Lond. Gaz.*, no. 2427 (11–14 Feb. 1688[/9]); Morrice, Q, 467; Luttrell, I, 501; Reresby, *Memoirs*, p. 554; Laurence Echard, *The History of England* (3 vols., 1707–18), III, 978, 981.

100. HMC, *Portland*, III, 429; D. R. Hainsworth, *Stewards, Lords and People: The Estate Steward and his World in Later Stuart England* (Cambridge, 1992), p. 124; Hunt. Lib., STT, 413, W[illiam] C[haplyn] to Sir Richard Temple, 17 Feb. 1688[/9]; Luttrell, I, 503, 505, 507, 514; Berks. RO, N/AC1/1/1/fol. 103; *Lond. Gaz.*, nos. 2429–34 (18–21 Feb. to 7–11 Mar. 1688[/9]).

101. Luttrell, I, 520–1, 522.

102. *News from Bath* (1689); *The Loyalty and Glory of the City of Bath* (1689).

103. HMC, *Portland*, III, 429.

104. See, for example, Berks. RO, H/Fac1, fols. 95–6 (Abingdon?), N/AC1/1/1/, fol. 112 (Newbury), W/FVc/28 (Wallingford).

105. Grey, *Debates*, IX, 110, 112.

106. Ibid., IX, 131.

107. Morrice, Q, 476.

108. Luttrell, I, 540.

109. Echard, *History*, III, 981.

110. Morrice, Q, 487.

111. CLRO, Sessions File, Jul. 1689, inds. of George Smith and Joseph Sheere, and gaol calendar.

112. Luttrell, I, 606–7.

113. *The Proceedings on the King and Queens Commissions of the Peace, and Oyer and Terminer, and Gaol Delivery of Newgate, held for the City of London, and County of Middlesex, at Justice-Hall in the Old Baily* (15–16 Jan. 1690[/1]).

114. Goldie, 'Revolution of 1689'.

115. Ibid., pp. 489–90.

116. BL, Add. MSS 32,095, fol. 325.

117. William E. Burns, 'Sherlock, William (1639/40–1707)', *Oxford DNB*.

118. [Charles Leslie], *An Answer to a Book, Intituled, The State of the Protestants in Ireland* (1692), p. 123.

119. Goldie, 'Revolution of 1689', p. 490.

120. Samuel Jeake, *An Astrological Diary of the Seventeenth Century*, ed.

Michael Hunter and Annabel Gregory (Oxford, 1988), p. 195.

121. Hunt. Lib., STT, Literature (9), [Sir Richard Temple], 'The False Patriot Unmasked; Or, A Short History of the Whigs' [c. 1690], quote on p. 10.

122. *Four Questions Debated*, quote on p. 10. The tract was published before 6 Feb. 1689, and so is not in Goldie's list.

123. Goldie, 'Revolution of 1689', p. 490.

124. Goldie, 'Revolution of 1689', pp. 488–9, 490; Mark Goldie, 'Edmund Bohun and *Ius Gentium* in the Revolution Debate, 1689–1693', *Historical Journal*, 20 (1977), 569–86. For Burnet's justification of the Revolution, see Claydon, *William III and the Godly Revolution*.

125. *Merc. Ref.*, I, no. 11 (17 Jul. 1689).

126. *Life of James II*, II, 317; Gilbert Burnet, *A Pastoral Letter Writ by the . . . Bishop of Sarum, to the Clergy of his Diocess* (1689).

127. Mark Goldie, 'Edmund Bohun'.

128. Harris, *Politics under the Later Stuarts*, ch. 8.

9 The Glorious Revolution in Scotland

1. NLS, Wod. MSS Qu. XXXVIII, fol. 115.

2. Ian B. Cowan, 'The Reluctant Revolutionaries: Scotland in 1688', in Eveline Cruickshanks, ed., *By Force or By Default? The Revolution of 1688–1689* (Edinburgh, 1989), pp. 65–81.

3. Gordon Donaldson, *Scotland: James V to James VII* (Edinburgh, 1965), p. 383.

4. Rosalind Mitchinson, *Lordship to Patronage: Scotland, 1603–1745* (1983), p. 116.

5. Bruce Lenman, 'The Poverty of Political Theory in the Scottish Revolution of 1688–1690', in Lois G. Schwoerer, ed., *The Revolution of 1688–1689: Changing Perspectives* (Cambridge, 1992), pp. 244–5, 249; Kathleen Mary Colquhoun, '"Issue of the Late Civill Wars": James, Duke of York and the Government of Scotland 1679–1689', Ph.D. dissertation, University of Illinios at Urbana-Champaign (1993), p. 21.

6. *Lond. Gaz.*, nos. 2358 (21–25 Jun. 1688) and 2366 (19–23 Jul. 1688).

7. *CSPD, 1687–9*, p. 389 (no. 2128); Fountainhall, *Hist. Not.*, II, 869–70.

8. Colin Lindsay, 3rd Earl of Balcarres, *An Account of the Affairs of Scotland, Relating to the Revolution of 1688* (1714), pp. 12–13.

9. *Leven and Melville Papers*, pp. xvi–xvii; Morrice, Q, 367; Fountainhall, *Decisions*, I, 511; Maurice Ashley, *The Glorious Revolution of 1688* [1966], p. 212; Dalrymple, *Memoirs*, II, 'Part I. Continued. Book V', pp. 21–2; Richard L. Greaves, *Secrets of the Kingdom: British Radicals from the*

Popish Plot to the Revolution of 1688–89 (Stanford, 1992), pp. 323–4; Magnus Linklater and Christian Hesketh, *For King and Conscience: John Graham of Claverhouse, Viscount Dundee (1648–1689)* (1989), pp. 147–8; Robert Beddard, *A Kingdom Without a King: The Journal of the Provisional Government in the Revolution of 1688* (Oxford, 1988), p. 21.

10. William III, *The Declaration of His Highnes William Henry . . . Prince of Orange, etc. Of the Reasons Inducing him to Appear in Armes in the Kingdome of England* (The Hague, 1688), pp. 5, 8.

11. [Thomas Morer], *An Account of the Present Persecution of the Church in Scotland* (1690), p. 14.

12. William III, *The Declaration of His Highness William . . . Prince of Orange, etc. of the Reasons Inducing Him, To Appear in Armes for Preserving of the Protestant Religion, and for Restoring the Laws and Liberties of the Ancient Kingdome of Scotland* (The Hague, 1688).

13. Luttrell, I, 466, 474; Wodrow, *Sufferings*, II, 646; *A Letter from the Archbishops and Bishops* (Edinburgh, 1688).

14. *RPCS, 1686–9*, pp. xxv, li, 328; *Lond. Gaz.*, nos. 2388 (4–8 Oct. 1688) and 2392 (18–22 Oct. 1688); *Melvilles and Leslies*, III, 192.

15. *Lond. Gaz.*, no. 2401 (17–19 Nov. 1688).

16. *RPCS, 1686–9*, p. 346.

17. *CSPD, 1687–9*, pp. 388–9 (no. 2128).

18. NLS, Wod. MSS Qu. XXXVIII, fols. 112v–114v.

19. Balcarres, *Account*, pp. 30–1; Andrew Lang, *Sir George Mackenzie, King's Advocate, of Rosehaugh, His Life and Times 1636(?)–1691* (1909), p. 296.

20. Balcarres, *Account*, pp. 36–7; *RPCS, 1686–9*, p. liv; *Life of James II*, II, 336, 338.

21. *Five Letters from a Gentleman in Scotland to His Friend in London* (1689), p. 2.

22. *Melvilles and Leslies*, III, 193.

23. Dalrymple, *Memoirs*, II, Part I, Book V, p. 21, and Book VI, p. 210; Reresby, *Memoirs*, p. 536; Morrice, Q, 368–9, 395.

24. Luttrell, I, 469.

25. Wodrow, *Sufferings*, II, 649.

26. *Five Letters*, p. 1; R. A. Houston, *Social Change in the Age of Enlightenment: Edinburgh, 1660–1760* (Oxford, 1994), p. 306.

27. Balcarres, *Account*, pp. 34–5, 38–9; NLS, MS 7026, fol. 81; *Five Letters*, p. 1; Wodrow, *Sufferings*, II, 650; *Melvilles and Leslies*, II, 102.

28. NLS, MS 7026, fol. 89; *Five Letters*, p. 3; *Lond. Merc.*, no. 6 (27–31 Dec. 1688); Morrice, Q, 403, 417; Balcarres, *Account*, pp. 44–7; *Melvilles and*

Leslies, III, 193.

29. NLS, MS 7026, fols. 81v–2, 87; Balcarres, *Account*, pp. 39–43; Luttrell, I, 488; BL, Add. MSS 28,850, fol. 93; *Lond. Merc.*, no. 3 (18–22 Dec. 1688); *Univ. Int.*, no. 4 (18–22 Dec. 1688); *Melvilles and Leslies*, II, 102–3; Robert Chambers, *Domestic Annals of Scotland. Volume III: From the Revolution to the Rebellion of 1745* (Edinburgh, 1861), p. 12; L.L., *Scotland Against Popery* (1689); *Five Letters*, pp. 1–4; [Morer], *Account of the Present Persecution*, p. 15; [Alexander Monro], *An Apology for the Clergy of Scotland* (1693), p. 8; Wodrow, *Sufferings*, II, 650–1; *Life of James II*, II, 338; [Charles Leslie], *An Answer to a Book, Intituled, The State of the Protestants in Ireland* (1692), sig. b 2; Gilbert Burnet, *History of His Own Time: From the Restoration of King Charles the Second to the Treaty of Peace at Utrecht, in the Reign of Queen Anne* (1850), p. 510; Houston, *Social Change*, pp. 306–8.

30. Robert Chambers, *Domestic Annals of Scotland. Volume II: From the Reformation to the Revolution* (2nd edn, Edinburgh, 1849), pp. 499–501; *HMC, Laing*, I, 460–2.

31. NLS, Wod. MSS Qu. XXXVIII, fol. 119v.

32. *Five Letters*, p. 4; [Monro], *Apology for the Clergy of Scotland*, p. 8.

33. NLS, Wod. MSS Qu. XXXVIII, fol. 115; *Lond. Merc.*, no. 6 (27–31 Dec. 1688); *Five Letters*, p. 4; NLS, MS 7026, fols. 89, 90; Morrice, Q, 403; [Morer], *Account of the Present Persecution*, p. 15; [Leslie], *Answer*, sig. b 2.

34. [Robert Reid], *The Account of the Popes Procession at Aberdeene, The 11th of January, 1689* ([Aberdeen], 1689).

35. Morrice, Q, 432.

36. NLS, Wod. MSS Qu. XXVIII, fol. 115; Chambers, *Domestic Annals, Volume II*, p. 499.

37. *Five Letters*, pp. 1–2.

38. *Univ. Int.*, no. 4 (18–22 Dec. 1688); Luttrell, I, 488.

39. NLS, Wod. MSS Qu. XXXVIII, fol. 119; NLS, MS 7026, fol. 98; *Five Letters*, p. 4; Wodrow, *Sufferings*, II, 649. Some of the Society People, however, later complained about Boyd's initiative before their General Assembly, because William's Declaration had made no mention 'of the Covenanted work of Reformatione'.

40. [Reid], *Account of the Popes Procession*, pp. 2, 4.

41. [John Sage], *The Case of the Present Afflicted Clergy in Scotland Truly Represented* (1690), pp. 5–6; [George Mackenzie, Viscount Tarbat, and Sir George Mackenzie of Rosehaugh], *A Memorial for His Highness the Prince of Orange in Relation to the Affairs of Scotland* (1689), p. 20; *The Present*

State and Condition of the Clergy, and Church of Scotland (1689), pp. 1–2; [Leslie], *Answer*, sig. b 2; Burnet, *History of His Own Time*, p. 510.

42. [Sage], *Case of the Present Afflicted Clergy*, 'First Collection', pp. 4, 39–40, 42.

43. BL, Add. MSS 28,850, fol. 124.

44. NLS, Wod. MSS Qu. XXXVIII, fols. 116–17, 119r–v, 121v. Cf. [Sage], *Case of the Present Afflicted Clergy*, p. 5.

45. NLS, MS 7035, fol. 86; [Sage], *Case of the Present Afflicted Clergy*, 'First Collection', pp. 45–6.

46. *APS*, VIII, 486–7.

47. [Sage], *Case of the Present Afflicted Clergy*, 'First Collection', p. 1.

48. NLS, MS 7026, fol. 119.

49. [Gilbert Rule], *A Vindication of the Church of Scotland; Being an Answer to Five Pamphlets* (1691), p. 22. Cf. [Monro], *Apology for the Clergy of Scotland*, p. 10, who denies the logic of Rule's argument, asserting that an interregnum 'cannot properly fall out in an Hereditary Monarchy; for the King never dies'.

50. [Sage], *Case of the Present Afflicted Clergy*, 'First Collection', pp. 33–4.

51. NLS, Wod. MSS Oct. XXX, fol. 62v.

52. *HMC, Laing*, I, 468; [Sage], *Case of the Present Afflicted Clergy*, p. 6; [Morer], *Account of the Present Persecution*, p. 41; [Leslie]. *Answer*, sig. c.

53. William III, *His Highness the Prince of Orange his Speech to the Scots Lords and Gentlemen, with their Address and His Highness his Answer* (1689); Earl of Arran, *A Speech made . . . to the Scotch Nobility and Gentry . . . , on the Eight of January 1689* ([Edinburgh?], 1689); *CSPD, 1687–89*, p. 392 (no. 2141); Dalrymple, *Memoirs*, II, 'Part I. Continued. Book VII', pp. 265–7.

54. P. W. J. Riley, *King William and the Scottish Politicians* (Edinburgh, 1979), esp. ch. 1.

55. *Five Letters*, p. 4.

56. Morrice, Q, 491.

57. Bruce P. Lenman, 'The Scottish Nobility and the Revolution of 1688–1690', in Robert Beddard, ed., *The Revolutions of 1688* (Oxford, 1988).

58. NAS, RH 13/20, pp. 146–50; Wodrow, *Sufferings*, II, 651–2 and apps. nos. 152 and 153, pp. 207–12; NLS, MS 7026, fol. 95; NLS, MS 7035, fol. 167; [Tarbat and Mackenzie], *Memorial*, pp. 17, 19; Morrice, Q, 440, 471–2, 492; Luttrell, I, 503.

59. *Great News from the Convention in Scotland, Giving a Further Account of Their Proceedings and Occurrences* (1689).

60. EUL, La. III. 350, no. 245; NLS, Wod. MSS Qu. XXXVIII, fols. 124v, 128.

61. *Letters to Sancroft*, pp. 91–5, 102–3, 105.

62. Ian B. Cowan, 'Church and State Reformed? The Revolution of 1688–9 in Scotland', in Jonathan I. Israel, ed., *The Anglo-Dutch Moment: Essays on the Glorious Revolution and its World Impact* (Cambridge, 1991), p. 175; Clare Jackson, *Restoration Scotland, 1660–1690* (Woodbridge, 2003), p. 212.

63. Morrice, Q, 486, 492.

64. [Tarbat and Mackenzie], *Memorial*, p. 5.

65. Morrice, Q, 426.

66. *Leven and Melville Papers*, pp. 12, 125–7.

67. Lenman, 'Scottish Nobility and the Revolution', p. 146.

68. James Canaries, *A Sermon Preached at Edinburgh . . . upon the 30th of January, 1689* (Edinburgh 1689), pp. 1, 6–16.

69. Ibid., pp. 22, 38, 39, 40.

70. Ibid., pp. 55, 60, 61.

71. Ibid., pp. 70, 79.

72. Ibid., p. 66.

73. *Melvilles and Leslies*, III, 193.

74. Lionel K. J. Glassey, 'William II and the Settlement of Religion in Scotland, 1688–90', *RSCHS*, 23 (1989), 317–29.

75. NLS, MS 7026, fols. 77, 115–16, 134. Cf. NLS, MS 7011, fols. 151, 171. For a general discussion of Tweeddale and the scheme for union, see: Riley, *King William*, pp. 49–53.

76. NLS, MS 7026, fol. 94a.

77. NLS, MS 7026, fol. 95. Cf. ibid., fol. 134.

78. Riley, *King William*, p. 53.

79. [Tarbat and Mackenzie], *Memorial*, pp. 7–8.

80. William III, *A Letter . . . to the Estates of the Kingdom of Scotland, at their Meeting at Edinburgh* (Edinburgh, 1689).

81. William III, *Speech to the Scots Lords and Gentlemen*, p. 2.

82. NLS, Wod. MSS Qu. XXXVIII, fols. 122v–123v.

83. [William Strachan], *Some Remarks upon . . . An Answer to the Scots Presbyterian Eloquence* (1694), p. 33; [Morer], *Account of the Present Persecution*, p. 23.

84. NLS, Wod. MSS Oct. XXX, fol. 59v.

85. NAS, PA 7/12, p. 228 (no. 50[1]); Balcarres, *Account*, pp. 60–2; Morrice, Q, 509; *An Account of the Proceedings of the Estates of Scotland* (1689), p. 1; [Morer], *Account of the Present Persecution*, p. 3; Dalrymple, *Memoirs*,

II, 'Part I. Continued. Book VIII', pp. 301–2; Robert S. Rait, *The Parliaments of Scotland* (Glasgow, 1924), p. 95.

86. *APS*, IX, 8–10; NAS, PA 7/12, p. 232 (no. 50³); *Lond. Gaz.*, no. 2438 (21–25 Mar. 1689).

87. NLS, Wod. MSS Qu. XXXVIII, fol. 127; NLS, MS 7026, fol. 158; Morrice, Q, 509, 510; *APS*, IX, 11–12, 23, 33–4; *Account of the Proceedings of the Estates*, pp. 18, 21; [Sage], *Case of the Present Afflicted Clergy*, 'Fourth Collection', pp. 90–1; Balcarres, *Account*, pp. 24, 31; [Leslie], *Answer*, sig b v; Dalrymple, *Memoirs*, II, Part 1. Continued. Book VIII', p. 306; Lang, *Mackenzie*, pp. 298–9; Chambers, *Domestic Annals, Volume III*, pp. 5–6.

88. *APS*, IX, 3–5.

89. *Leven and Melville Papers*, p. 125; Rait, *Parliaments of Scotland*, pp. 95–6.

90. *APS*, IX, 6–22.

91. *Account of the Proceedings of the Estates*, pp. 14, 16.

92. *Culloden Papers: Comprising an Extensive and Interesting Correspondence from the Year 1625 to 1748* (1815), pp. 317–18; NLS, MS 7035, fol. 157; NLS, MS 7026, fol. 209; Balcarres, *Account*, pp. 76–7; *APS*, IX, 60; *Account of the Proceedings of the Estates*, pp. 46, 51, 52; Riley, *King William*, p. 53.

93. Arran, *Speech . . . to the Scots Nobility*; *Life of James II*, II, 345–6.

94. *A Short Historical Account Concerning the Succession to the Crown of Scotland* (1689). Cf. *Salus Populi Suprema Lex* ([Edinburgh?], 1689), pp. 4–5.

95. *APS*, IX, 33–4.

96. Lenman, 'Poverty of Political Theory', p. 255.

97. Balcarres, *Account*, p. 82.

98. Dalrymple, *Memoirs*, II, 'Part I. Continued, Book VIII', p. 308.

99. *Leven and Melville Papers*, p. 9.

100. Balcarres, *Account*, p. 82.

101. [Robert Ferguson], *The Late Proceedings and Votes of the Parliament of Scotland* (Glasgow, 1689), p. 25.

102. NLS, Wod. MSS Oct. XXX, fol. 68.

103. NLS, Wod. MSS Qu. XXXVIII, fol. 131v.

104. *Account of the Proceedings of the Estates*, p. 26; *Lond. Gaz.*, no. 2443 (8–11 Apr. 1689). Most historians have erroneously followed Balcarres, *Account*, p. 83, in giving the figure of five dissentient voices. NAS, PA 7/12, p. 251, the contemporary minutes of the proceedings of the Convention, simply states that the vote was 'approven be the plurality'.

105. Balcarres, *Account*, p. 83. Interestingly, however, Atholl had been a member of the grand committee of 24 that on 1 April had approved, *nemine contradicente*, the reasons for declaring the throne vacant: *Account of the Proceedings of the Estates*, pp. 19, 24.

106. *APS*, IX, 34; *Lond. Gaz.*, no. 2443 (8–11 Apr. 1689).

107. All citations from the Claim of Right are taken from *APS*, IX, 37–40.

108. John R. Young, 'The Scottish Parliament and the Covenanting Heritage of Constitutional Reform', in Allan I. Macinnes and Jane Ohlmeyer, eds., *The Stuart Kingdoms in the Seventeenth Century* (Dublin, 2002), pp. 226–50.

109. *APS*, III, 23; *APS*, VIII, 238.

110. Sir George Mackenzie, *Jus Regium* (2nd edn, 1684), pp. 184–6.

111. Fountainhall, *Decisions*, I, 339.

112. *APS*, II, 535, III, 36, 545; *APS*, VII, 26.

113. Ibid., VII, 554.

114. *APS*, VIII, 243–5; *HMC, Laing*, I, 443.

115. [Robert Ferguson], *A Representation of the Threatning Dangers* [Edinburgh?, 1687], p. 28.

116. See Tim Harris, *Restoration: Charles II and His Kingdoms, 1660–85* (2005), pp. 125–7.

117. *APS*, VII, 13, 480.

118. Harris, *Restoration*, pp. 350, 365–7.

119. Ibid., p. 347.

120. *APS*, VIII, 461.

121. BL, Add. MSS 63,057B, fol. 64v.

122. [Alexander Shields], *The Hind Let Loose* (Edinburgh, 1687), p. 97; *To His Grace, His Majesties High Commissioner, and to the Right Honourable the Estates of Parliament. The Humble Address of the Presbyterian Ministers, and Professors of the Church of Scotland* (Edinburgh, 1689), p. 1.

123. Rait, *Parliaments of Scotland*, pp. 98, 302.

124. Harris, *Restoration*, p. 346.

125. I owe this point to Lionel Glassey.

126. *APS*, V, 303.

127. *APS*, V, 298–9.

128. Burnet, *History of His Own Time*, p. 538; NLS, MS 7026, fols. 173, 190.

129. *APS*, IX, 45; *An Account of the Affairs of Scotland* (1690), esp. pp. 12, 14, 16, 18.

130. *APS*, IX, 48–9.

131. *APS*, IX, 40–1, 43–4; *Lond. Gaz.*, no. 2445 (15–18 Apr. 1689); Luttrell,

I, 522.

132. *Account of the Affairs of Scotland*, p. 29.

133. NLS, Wod. MSS Oct. XXX, fol. 60; *Account of the Proceedings of the Estates*, pp. 85–9; *Lond. Gaz.*, no. 2453 (13–16 May 1689); *HMC, Hamilton*, pp. 181–2; Luttrell, I, 533; *Culloden Papers*, pp. 320–1; *APS*, IX, app. p. 133; Morrice, Q, 555; *Account of the Affairs of Scotland*, p. 2. The request that the Convention be turned into a Parliament was agreed to on 24 April: *APS*, IX, 61.

134. *Leven and Melville Papers*, pp. xvii, 23–4, 29, 81; *Melvilles and Leslies*, II, 32.

135. William III, *His Majestie's Gracious Letter To the Meeting of the Estates of His Ancient Kingdom of Scotland* (1689); *Account of the Affairs of Scotland*, pp. 1–27. Cf. *HMC, Hamilton*, p. 176.

136. *APS*, IX, 98.

137. *APS*, IX, 104, and app. pp. 129, 130, 135.

138. *Account of the Affairs of Scotland*, pp. 6, 29.

139. Glassey, 'William II and the Settlement of Religion'.

140. *APS*, IX, app. pp. 128, 130–1, 137, 138; *Leven and Melville Papers*, pp. xviii, 143; *Melvilles and Leslies*, II, 108–11.

141. *Leven and Melville Papers*, pp. 414–15; *Melvilles and Leslies*, III, 201–5; *The Speech Of His Grace the Earl of Melvill, His Majesties High-Commissioner to the Parliament of Scotland, Edinburgh, April 15, 1690* (1690); *APS*, IX, app. p. 38.

142. *APS*, IX, 111, 113, 133–4, 196–7; Young, 'Scottish Parliament and Constitutional Reform', pp. 234–9.

143. *Account of the Affairs of Scotland*, p. 3; Colin Kidd, *Subverting Scotland's Past: Scottish Whig Historians and the Creation of an Anglo-British Identity, 1689–c.1830* (Cambridge, 1993), p. 52; Young, 'Scottish Parliament and Constitutional Reform'.

144. *Leven and Melville Papers*, p. 32.

145. Jackson, *Restoration Scotland*, ch. 8.

146. *RPCS, 1686–9*, p. 431; NLS, MS 14407, fol. 131; *Leven and Melville Papers*, pp. 57–8; *An Account of the Besieging the Castle of Edinburgh* (1689).

147. For the rebellion, see Andrew Murray Scott, *Bonnie Dundee: John Graham of Claverhouse* (Edinburgh, 2000), chs. 5–8.

148. *RPCS, 1686–9*, p. 441.

149. *Life of James II*, II, 431.

150. *Leven and Melville Papers*, pp. 27, 32, 52, 92; Dalrymple, *Memoirs*, II, 'Part II. Book II', p. 71; Colin Kidd, 'Mackenzie, George, First Earl of

Cromarty (1630–1714)', *Oxford DNB*.

151. NLS, MS 14407, fol. 142.

152. Chambers, *Domestic Annals, Volume III*, pp. 8–9; NLS, Wod. MSS Qu. XXXVIII, fols. 132–45.

153. *RPCS, 1686–9*, pp. 471, 486–7.

154. Paul Hopkins, *Glencoe and the End of the Highland War* (Edinburgh, 1986), chs. 4–6; Keith M. Brown, *Kingdom or Province? Scotland and the Regal Union, 1603–1715* (1992), pp. 170–1.

155. Burnet, *History of His Own Time*, p. 538.

156. For Montgomery's Jacobite intrigues, see: James Halliday, 'The Club and the Revolution in Scotland 1689–90', *Scottish Historical Review*, 45 (1966), 143–59; Riley, *King William*, pp. 30–1, 39–41; Mark Goldie, 'The Roots of True Whiggism 1688–94', *History of Political Thought*, 1 (1980), 228–9; Hopkins, *Glencoe*, pp. 208–9, 211, 219–21, 273–4, 312, 367.

157. [Alexander Monro], *A Letter to a Friend* (1692), p. 27.

158. HMC, *Athole*, p. 38; Balcarres, *Account*, pp. 116–50, passim; *Life of James II*, II, 425–8; *Leven and Melville Papers*, pp. xx–xxi; *Melvilles and Leslies*, III, 220–2.

159. [James Montgomerie], *Great Britain's Just Complaint* (1692), quote on p. 30.

160. APS, IX, 43, 134; *Lond. Gaz.*, no. 2446 (18–22 Apr. 1689).

161. *RPCS, 1689*, pp. xvii–xxi, 19–20, 77–8; Luttrell, I, 574; *Leven and Melville Papers*, pp. 239–40; Cowan, 'Church and State Reformed?', p. 176.

162. *RPCS, 1689*, pp. 31, 369–70, 425; *Leven and Melville Papers*, p. 319.

163. *RPCS, 1689*, p. 305.

164. Ibid., pp. 447–9.

165. Ibid., pp. 372–7.

166. Tristram Clarke, 'Williamite Episcopalians and the Glorious Revolution', *RSCHS*, 24 (1990), 33–51; Tristram Clarke, 'The Scottish Episcopalians 1688–1720', unpub. Ph.D. thesis, University of Edinburgh (1987).

167. HMC, *Hamilton*, p. 194; HMC, *Laing*, I, 468–9; [Sage], *Case of the Present Afflicted Clergy*, pp. 10–12, 15; Clarke, 'Williamite Episcopalians', p. 40; R. Buick Knox, 'Establishment and Toleration during the Reigns of William, Mary and Anne', *RSCHS*, 23 (1989), 343.

168. *RPCS, 1689*, pp. 294–7.

169. *Melvilles and Leslies*, II, 46.

170. Clarke, 'Williamite Episcopalians'; Buick Knox, 'Establishment and Toleration', p. 347; Brown, *Kingdom or Province?*, pp. 174–5.

171. Chambers, *Domestic Annals, Volume III*, p. 7.

172. J. A. Inglis, 'The Last Episcopalian Minister of Moneydie', *Scottish Historical Review*, 13 (1916), 232–3; Glassey, 'William II and the Settlement of Religion', p. 329.

173. *Leven and Melville Papers*, p. xxx; Buick Knox, 'Establishment and Toleration', p. 347; Clarke, 'Williamite Episcopalians', p. 36.

174. BL, MS Egerton 2651, fol. 203.

175. [Morer], *Account of the Present Persecution*, 'To the Reader'.

176. [Leslie], *Answer*, sig. c 2.

177. See in particular: *Present State and Condition of the Clergy and Church of Scotland*; [Morer], *Account of the Present Persecution*; [Sage], *Case of the Present Afflicted Clergy*; [Strachan], *Some Remarks*; [Monro], *Letter to a Friend*.

178. *Present State and Condition of the Clergy, and Church of Scotland*, p. 2; *A Brief and True Account of the Sufferings of the Church of Scotland* (1690), p. 23.

179. [Morer], *Account of the Present Persecution*, pp. 2, 58; [Strachan], *Some Remarks*, p. 34.

180. [Tarbat and Mackenzie], *Memorial*, p. 22. See also Sir George Mackenzie, *A Vindication of the Government of Scotland, During the Reign of Charles II* (1691).

181. [Morer], *Account of the Present Persecution*, p. 49. Cf. [Monro], *Apology for the Clergy of Scotland*, esp. pp. 11, 85; [Strachan], *Some Remarks*, pp. 23–5.

182. [Alexander Monro], *The History of Scotch-Presbytery* (1692), sig. A4.

183. [Morer], *Account of the Present Persecution*, p. 9.

184. [Tarbat and Mackenzie], *Memorial*, pp. 26, 30.

185. [Strachan], *Some Remarks*, pp. 54–5.

186. Ibid., p. 62. See also: [Monro], *Apology for the Clergy of Scotland*, p. 28; [Alexander Monro], *The Spirit of Calumny and Slander* (1693), pp. 61–3.

187. [Gilbert Crockatt and John Munro], *The Scotch Presbyterian Eloquence; Or, The Foolishness of their Teaching Discovered* (1692, 2nd edn 1693), quotes on pp. 4, 5, 15.

188. *Leven and Melville Papers*, p. 337.

189. [Monro], *Letter to a Friend*, pp. 8–9; [Crockatt and Munro], *Scotch Presbyterian Eloquence*, p. 101.

190. [Morer], *Account of the Present Persecution*, p. 61.

191. [Sage], *Case of the Present Afflicted Clergy*, p. 106.

192. NLS, Wod. MSS Oct. XXX, fol. 62.

193. *Leven and Melville Papers*, p. 336.

194. [Strachan], *Some Remarks*, pp. 48–9.

195. [Gilbert Rule], *A Vindication of the Church of Scotland. Being an Answer To a Paper, Intituled, Some Questions concerning Episcopal and Presbyterial Government in Scotland* (1691), p. 35.

196. [Gilbert Rule], *A Vindication of the Church of Scotland; Being an Answer to Five Pamphlets* (1691), p. 5.

197. *Leven and Melville Papers*, pp. 376–7.

198. *Brief and True Account of the Sufferings of the Church of Scotland*, p. 24. Cf. *Merc. Ref.*, II, no. 13 (5 Mar. 1690).

199. [Rule], *Vindication . . . Being an Answer To . . . Some Questions*, pp. 21, 32–5.

200. [Monro], *Letter to a Friend*, p. 26.

10 'This Wofull Revolution' in Ireland

1. Charles O'Kelly, *Macariae Excidium, Or, The Destruction of Cypress; Being a Secret History of the War of the Revolution in Ireland*, ed. John Cornelius O'Callaghan (Dublin, 1850), p. 158.

2. Ibid., p. 364 (note 144).

3. Edward Wetenhall, *A Sermon Setting Forth the Duties of the Irish Protestants* (Dublin, 1692), p. 21.

4. *A Jacobite Narrative of the War in Ireland*, ed. J. T. Gilbert (Dublin, 1892, revised edn, with an introduction by J. G. Simms, Shannon, 1971), p. 127; Harman Murtagh, 'The War in Ireland, 1689–91', in W. A. Maguire, ed., *Kings in Conflict: The Revolutionary War in Ireland and its Aftermath 1689–1750* (Belfast, 1990), p. 61.

5. O'Kelly, *Macariae Excidium*, passim.

6. *Merc. Ref.*, II, no. 29 (25 Jun. 1690).

7. Peter Berresford Ellis, *The Boyne Water: The Battle of the Boyne, 1690* (Belfast and St Paul, Minn., 1989), p. xi; Ian McBride, *The Siege of Derry in Ulster Protestant Mythology* (Dublin, 1997).

8. HMC, *Ormonde*, II, 377; Steele, II, no. 986; *Council Books of the Corporation of Waterford 1662–1700*, ed. Seamus Pender (Dublin, 1964), p. 281; *The Council Book of the Corporation of Youghall, from 1610 . . . to 1800*, ed. Richard Caulfield (Guildford, 1878), p. 378; *Cal. Anc. Rec. Dub.*, V, 475.

9. *A Full and Impartial Account of all the Secret Consults* (1689), pp. 127–8.

10. NLI, MS 37, pp. 39–41.

11. *Cal. Anc. Rec. Dub.*, V, 482–3; *Lond. Gaz.*, no. 2363 (9–12 Jul. 1688).

12. *The Poems of David Ó Bruadair*, ed. and trans. Rev. John C. Mac Erlean

(3 vols., 1910–17), III, 113.

13. *Full and Impartial Account of all the Secret Consults*, p. 44.

14. Wood, *Life and Times*, III, 255.

15. [William King], *The State of the Protestants of Ireland under the Late King James's Government* (1691), p. 91.

16. BL, MS Stowe 746, fol. 106.

17. *HMC, Ormonde*, N.S. VIII, 354.

18. *CSPD, 1687–9*, p. 283 (no. 1552).

19. *HMC, Ormonde*, N.S. VIII, 355; John Childs, *The Army, James II, and the Glorious Revolution* (Manchester, 1980), p. 4.

20. *A Short View of the Methods Made Use of in Ireland for the Subversion and Destruction of the Protestant Religion and Interest in that Kingdom* (1689), pp. 9–10.

21. Morrice, Q, 386–7, 394.

22. Murtagh, 'War in Ireland', p. 62. Cf. BL, Egerton 917, fol. 91; *Lond. Merc.*, no. 10 (10 Jan.–6 Feb. 1688[/9]); *Orange Gaz.*, no. 14 (19–22 Feb. 1688[/9]); *Jacobite Narrative*, p. 38; *Journal of the Proceedings of the Parliament in Ireland* (1689), p. 11.

23. *HMC, Ormonde*, N.S. VIII, 359; *Short View of the Methods*, p. 16; BL, Egerton 917, fol. 91; BL, Add. MSS 28,876, fol. 186; *Orange Gaz.*, no. 14 (19–22 Feb. 1688[/9]); Wetenhall, *Sermon Setting Forth the Duties*, p. 15. For a general discussion of the rapparees, see Éamonn Ó Ciardha, *Ireland and the Jacobite Cause 1685–1766* (Dublin, 2002), pp. 68–76.

24. *An Account of a Late Horrid and Bloody Massacre in Ireland* (1689), pp. 1–2.

25. *HMC, Ormonde*, N.S. VIII, 355.

26. *HMC, Ormonde*, II, 388–9; Steele, II, no. 1004; TCD, 1995–2008/61; Hunt. Lib., HA 15788, Order to all High and Petty Constables and Other Subjects, 7 Dec. 1688.

27. *HMC, Ormonde*, N.S. VIII, 355–7; *Jacobite Narrative*, pp. 40–1; [King], *State of the Protestants of Ireland*, pp. 102–3, 345, 348; *Full and Impartial Account of the Secret Consults*, pp. 137–8, 140; [George Philips], *An Apology for the Protestants of Ireland* (1689), pp. 10–13; Andrew Hamilton, *A True Relation of the Actions of the Inniskilling-Men* (1690), pp. 1–3; Cox, *Hibernica Anglicana . . . Second Part*, p. 19; G[eorge] P[hilips], *The Second Apology for the Protestants of Ireland* (1690), p. 5; *The Rawdon Papers*, ed. Rev. Edward Berwick (1819), p. 294; George Walker, *A True Account of the Siege of London-Derry* (2nd edn, 1689), pp. 11–12; John Mackenzie, *A Narrative of the Siege of London-Derry* (1690), pp. 1–5.

28. Morrice, Q, 362, 467; *An Account of the Present, Miserable, State of*

Affairs in Ireland (1689); *Full and Impartial Account of all the Secret Consults*, p. 143; *Lond. Merc.*, no. 3 (18–22 Dec. 1688); *Orange Gaz.*, no. 11 (8–12 Feb. 1688[/9]).

29. *Lond. Merc.*, no. 4 (22–24 Dec. 1688); *Lond. Int.*, no. 4 (22–24 Jan. 1688[/9]); *Orange Gaz.*, no. 7 (21–26 Jan. 1688[/9]); Morrice, Q, 423; Diarmuid Murtagh and Harman Murtagh, 'The Irish Jacobite Army 1689–91', *The Irish Sword*, 18, no. 70 (Winter, 1990), 33.

30. *Short View of the Methods*, p. 21; HMC, *Ormonde*, N.S. VIII, 359; Luttrell, I, 504; *The Present Dangerous Condition of the Protestants in Ireland* (1689); *Full and Impartial Account of all the Secret Consults*, pp. 144–5; [King], *State of the Protestants of Ireland*, p. 91.

31. Steele, II, no. 1010; HMC, *Ormonde*, II, 392.

32. *Orange Gaz.*, no. 14 (19–22 Feb. 1688[/9]); BL, Add. MSS 34,773, fol. 6.

33. BL, Egerton 917, fol. 100.

34. HMC, *Egmont*, II, 190. Cf. Cox, *Hibernica Anglicana . . . Second Part*, 'Transactions since 1653', pp. 19–20.

35. Richard Doherty, *The Williamite War in Ireland 1688–1691* (Dublin, 1998), p. 37.

36. *Short View of the Methods*, pp. 18–19. M. Perceval-Maxwell, *The Outbreak of the Irish Rebellion of 1641* (Montreal, 1994), pp. 232–3, notes the occurrence of trials of English cattle during the Irish Rebellion of 1641.

37. *Lond. Merc.*, no. 11 (6–11 Feb. 1688[/9]).

38. *Full And Impartial Account of all the Secret Consults*, pp. 140–2; *Short View of the Methods*, p. 16.

39. *Poems of David Ó Bruadair*, III, 117, 119.

40. Leics. RO, DG7, HMC Vol. II, p. 209/2.

41. William III, *The Declaration of his Highnes William Henry . . . Prince of Orange, etc. Of the Reasons Inducing him to Appear in Armes in the Kingdome of England* (The Hague, 1688), p. 8.

42. J[oseph] Boyse, *A Vindication of the Reverend Mr Alexander Osborn* (1690), p. 11.

43. Morrice, Q, 403.

44. *Orange Gaz.*, nos. 6 (17–21 Jan. 1688[/9]) and 7 (21–26 Jan. 1688[/9]); Luttrell, I, 498. Cf. Hamilton, *Inniskilling-Men*, pp. vi–vii.

45. *A Faithful History of the Northern Affairs of Ireland* (1690); *Lond. Int.*, no. 5 (24–29 Jan. 1688[/9]); Mícheál Ó Duígeannáin, ed., 'Three Seventeenth-Century Connacht Documents', *Journal of the Galway Archaeological and Historical Society*, 17 (1936–7), 147–61; J. G. Simms, *War and Politics in Ireland, 1649–1730*, ed. D. W. Hayton and Gerard

O'Brien (1986), p. 169.

46. *Orange Gaz.*, no. 3 (3–7 Jan. 1688[/9]).

47. Hamilton, *Inniskilling-Men*, p. 8; *Orange Gaz.*, no. 17 (1–5 Mar. 1688[/9]); *Jacobite Narrative*, p. 41.

48. *HMC, Ormonde*, N.S. VIII, 357; *Jacobite Narrative*, p. 42.

49. *The Declaration of the Protestant Nobility and Gentry of . . . Munster* (1689).

50. [Richard Orpen], *An Exact Relation of the Persecution, Roberies and Losses, Sustained by the Protestants of Killmare* (1689), p. 11.

51. *Lond. Merc.*, no. 4 (22–24 Dec. 1688); Luttrell, I, 490.

52. Luttrell, I, 493, 495; Morrice, Q, 472, 544.

53. Morrice, Q, 420.

54. NLS, MS 7026, fols. 127, 129; *Orange Gaz.*, no. 14 (19–22 Feb. 1688[/9]).

55. Robert Beddard, *A Kingdom Without a King: The Journal of the Provisional Government in the Revolution of 1688* (Oxford, 1988), p. 166.

56. Morrice, Q, 447.

57. *Lond. Int.*, no. 7 (2–5 Feb. 1688[/9]); *Lond. Merc.*, no. 10 (10 Jan.–6 Feb. 1688[/9]); Morrice, Q, 454.

58. Beddard, *Kingdom Without a King*, p. 168; *Parl. Hist.*, V, col. 32.

59. TCD 1995–2008/65; BL, Add. MSS 28,876, fol. 164; J. G. Simms, *Jacobite Ireland, 1685–91* (1969), pp. 50–2; Doherty, *Williamite War*, pp. 35–6.

60. [Philips], *Apology for the Protestants of Ireland*, p. 9; BL, Add. MSS 28,876, fols. 172, 180; CUL, Add. 1, fol. 82.

61. *HMC, Ormonde*, II, 390–5; Steele, II, nos. 1009, 1017, 1018.

62. [Orpen], *Exact Relation*, pp. 19–23; *Jacobite Narrative*, p. 42.

63. Steele, II, no. 1013.

64. *HMC, Ormonde*, II, 395–6; Steele, II, no. 1020; Doherty, *Williamite War*, p. 37.

65. *HMC, Ormonde*, N.S. VIII, 360; *Orange Gaz.*, no. 18 (5–9 Mar. 1688[/9]); *Short View of the Methods*, p. 26; *Full and Impartial Account of all the Secret Consults*, p. 148.

66. *Life of James II*, II, 327; *Ireland's Lamentation* (1689), p. 26.

67. *Jacobite Narrative*, p. 46.

68. *A Full and True Account of the Landing and Reception of the Late King James at Kinsale* (1689), p. 2.

69. *HMC, Ormonde*, N.S. VIII, 362, 389–91.

70. *Life of James II*, II, 330; *Ireland's Lamentation*, pp. 26–7; *Cal. Anc. Rec. Dub.*, V, 497; *Jacobite Narrative*, p. 47.

71. *Jacobite Narrative*, pp. 36–7, 39–40.

72. *CClarSP*, V, 684.

73. Raymond Gillespie, 'James II and the Irish Protestants', *Irish History Studies*, 28 (1992), 131.

74. *Account of the Present, Miserable, State of Affairs* (1689). Cf. *The Anatomy of an Arbitrary Prince* (1689), p. 2.

75. Steele, II, no. 1023.

76. [Charles Leslie], *An Answer to a Book, Intituled, The State of the Protestants in Ireland* (1692), app. no. 8, pp. 28–9.

77. Morrice, R, 194.

78. BL, Egerton 917, fol. 107.

79. O'Kelly, *Macariae Excidium*, p. 18.

80. NLS, MS 7026, fol. 108.

81. *Orange Gaz.*, no. 17 (1–5 Mar. 1688[/9]); *Short View of the Methods*, pp. 12–13.

82. *Two Letters Discovering the Designs of the Late King James in Ireland* (1689), pp. 1–2; *Anatomy of an Arbitrary Prince*, p. 2; *Short View of the Methods*, p. 27.

83. [King], *State of the Protestants of Ireland*, pp. 149–53, and apps. 20 and 21, pp. 369–77; *A Journal of the Proceedings of the Pretended Parliament in Dublin* (1689); J. G. Simms, 'The Jacobite Parliament of 1689', in Simms, *War and Politics*, pp. 66–9 and app. A, pp. 83–8; Simms, *Jacobite Ireland*, pp. 74–5; Francis G. James, *Lords of the Ascendancy: The Irish House of Lords and its Members, 1600–1800* (Dublin, 1995), pp. 48–50, 193 (note 35). For forfaulted peers taking their seats in the Scottish Convention, see above p. 388.

84. *HMC, Ormonde*, II, 396–8; Steele, II, nos. 1026, 1029.

85. Thomas Davis, *The Patriot Parliament of 1689: With its Statutes, Votes and Proceedings*, ed. Sir Charles Gavan Duffy (3rd edn, 1893), pp. 40–2; Hunt. Lib., EL 9882; *HMC, Ormonde*, N.S. VIII, 391–2; *Life of James II*, II, 355; [Leslie], *Answer*, app. no. 1, pp. 1–2.

86. *Life of James II*, II, 363.

87. *Anno V. Jacobi II Regis. A Collection of Acts Passed by the Irish Parliament of the 7th May 1689* (1689), pp. 1–5.

88. Ibid., pp. 6–8.

89. Patrick Russell, *An Address Given in to the Late King by the Titular Archbishop of Dublin* (1690), quotes on pp. 6, 8.

90. *Journal of the Proceedings of the Pretended Parliament*, p. 2; *The Journal of the Proceedings of the Parliament in Ireland* (1689), p. 19; *A True Account of the Whole Proceedings of the Parliament in Ireland* (1689), p. 4.

91. *Collection of Acts Passed by the Irish Parliament*, pp. 47–8; Davis, *Patriot Parliament*, p. 51.

92. BL, MS Egerton 917, fol. 108; *Journal of the Proceedings of the Pretended Parliament*, p. 2.

93. [King], *State of the Protestants of Ireland*, apps. nos. 22 and 23, pp. 377–98 (quotes on pp. 383, 387, 392, 393, 394, 395, 396); *HMC, Ormonde*, N.S. VIII, 392–401; *Life of James II*, II, 356–8.

94. *Life of James II*, II, 359–60.

95. [King], *State of the Protestants of Ireland*, app. no. 17, p. 370; *Jacobite Narrative*, pp. 60–1.

96. [Leslie], *Answer*, p. 102.

97. *Life of James II*, II, 360.

98. *Collection of Acts Passed by the Irish Parliament*, pp. 9–36; Davis, *Patriot Parliament*, pp. 73–124.

99. BL, MS Egerton 917, fol. 105.

100. [King], *State of the Protestants of Ireland*, app. pp. 241–98; Davis, *Patriot Parliament*, pp. 125–36.

101. *At the Parliament begun at Dublin the seventh Day of May, Anno Domini 1689 . . . An Act of Supply for His Majesty for The Support of His Army* [Dublin, 1689]; Davis, *Patriot Parliament*, pp. 49–50; Morrice, Q, 561.

102. *Collection of Acts Passed by the Irish Parliament*, p. 40; Davis, *Patriot Parliament*, p. 51.

103. *Collection of Acts Passed by the Irish Parliament*, pp. 37–8.

104. Ibid., pp. 41–5; Davis, *Patriot Parliament*, pp. 43–8.

105. *Journal of the Proceedings of the Parliament in Ireland*, p. 5.

106. *Life of James II*, II, 361.

107. [King], *State of the Protestants of Ireland*, p. 153.

108. *Négociations de M. le Comte d'Avaux en Irelande*, with an introduction by James Hogan (Dublin, 1934), p. 226; Davis, *Patriot Parliament*, pp. 52–4, 55–62; Simms, *Jacobite Ireland*, pp. 92–3.

109. [King], *State of the Protestants of Ireland*, pp. 154–7.

110. O'Kelly, *Macariae Excidium*, p. 34.

111. D'Avaux, *Négociations*, p. 255.

112. Useful general accounts of the war are found in: Simms, *Jacobite Ireland*; Doherty, *Williamite War*; Murtagh, 'War in Ireland'.

113. Murtagh and Murtagh, 'Irish Jacobite Army', pp. 32–48; Kenneth Ferguson, 'The Organisation of William's Army in Ireland, 1689–92', *The Irish Sword*, 18, no. 70 (Winter, 1990), 62–79.

114. *HMC, Hamilton*, p. 189; *Melvilles and Leslies*, II, 143; Walker, *True*

Account, p. 34.

115. [King], *State of the Protestants*, p. 173 and app. no. 28, pp. 399–400; *HMC, Hamilton*, p. 185; *Jacobite Narrative*, pp. 79–80; Walker, *True Account*, pp. 34–7; Mackenzie, *Narrative*, pp. 42–3; Simms, *Jacobite Ireland*, pp. 107–8.

116. C. S. King, *A Great Archbishop of Dublin: William King, His Autobiography . . . and . . . Correspondence* (1906), p. 32.

117. O'Kelly, *Macariae Excidium*, p. 320 (note 105).

118. *HMC, Ormonde*, N. S. VIII, 401–2.

119. *Mémoires du Maréchal de Berwick* (2 vols., Paris, 1780), I, 69–73; Morrice, R, 167–8; George Story, *A Continuation of the Impartial History of the Wars of Ireland* (1693), pp. 20–6.

120. *Cal. Anc. Rec. Dub.*, V, lviii–lix, 509, 634–5; *To The King's . . . Humble Address of Mayor of Dublin* (1690); Jacqueline Hill, *From Patriots to Unionists: Dublin Civic Patriots and Irish Protestant Patriotism, 1660–1840* (Oxford, 1997), pp. 62, 68.

121. *Council Books of Waterford*, pp. 282–3.

122. *Council Book of Youghall*, p. 379; *The Council Book of the Corporation of Kinsale, from 1652 to 1800*, ed. Richard Caulfield (Guildford, 1879), pp. 190–1.

123. O'Kelly, *Macariae Excidium*, pp. 71, 106–7, 114, 145–6; *Jacobite Narrative*, pp. 110–11.

124. O'Kelly, *Macariae Excidium*, pp. 92, 385–6 (note 170).

125. Simms, *Jacobite Ireland*, p. 227.

126. Murtagh, 'War in Ireland', pp. 88–9; John Jordan, 'The Battle of Aughrim: Two Danish Sources', *Journal of the Galway Archaeological and Historical Society*, 26 (1954–5), 6–7.

127. W. A. Maguire, ed., *Kings in Conflict: The Revolutionary War in Ireland and its Aftermath 1689–1750* (Belfast, 1990), p. 3.

128. Story, *Continuation of the Impartial History*, pp. 230–1.

129. 'And all such as are under their protection in the said counties' is the famous missing clause which was omitted from the official version of the Treaty sent back for William to ratify in 1692. See p. 501.

130. The Treaty of Limerick can be found in *Jacobite Narrative*, pp. 298–308.

131. Morrice, Q, 461.

132. Lois G. Schwoerer, *The Declaration of Rights, 1689* (Baltimore, 1981), p. 297.

133. Hamilton, *Inniskilling-Men*, pp. viii, 8.

134. *An Exact Account of His Majesty's Progress from His First Landing in*

Ireland (1690); Leics. RO, DG7 HMC II, p. 298/1.

135. *The Address Presented to the King at Belfast* (1690).

136. O'Kelly, *Macariae Excidium*, p. 365 (note 145).

137. *A Journal of the King's March from Hilsburgh to . . . Dublin* (1690).

138. *A Full and True Relation of the Taking of Cork* (1690).

139. *Life of James II*, II, 466.

140. Boyse, *Vindication of the Reverend Mr Alexander Osborn*, pp. 8–9.

141. CUL, Add. 1, fol. 82v.

142. TCD, MS 1688/1, pp. 61–93 (quotes on pp. 70, 76–7).

143. Anthony Dopping, *Speech . . . When the Clergy Waited Upon His Majesty at His Camp nigh Dublin, July 7 1690* (1690).

144. TCD, MS 1688/1, pp. 414, 422–3.

145. Hamilton, *Inniskilling-Men*, pp. v–vi.

146. *Some Reflections on a Pamphlet Entituled, A Faithful History of the Northern-Affairs of Ireland* (Dublin, 1691), pp. 8, 10.

147. [Orpen], *Exact Relation*, pp. 18–19; Mackenzie, *Narrative*, p. 51.

148. [Edward Wetenhall], *The Case of the Irish Protestants* (1691), pp. 3–5.

149. Ibid., pp 6, 8–9, 10.

150. Ibid., pp. 11–14.

151. Ibid., pp. 17–18.

152. Ibid., pp. 18, 22–5.

153. William Sheridan, *Catholick Religion Asserted by St. Paul, and Maintained in the Church of England* (1686), preface, sig. A4; [Leslie], *Answer*, p. 117.

154. Patrick Kelly, 'Ireland and the Glorious Revolution: From Kingdom to Colony', in Robert Beddard, ed., *The Revolutions of 1688* (Oxford, 1988), p. 178; King, *Great Archbishop*, pp. 21–7.

155. William King, *Europe's Deliverance from France and Slavery* (Dublin, 1691), pp. 13, 18–19, 21.

156. [King], *State of the Protestants of Ireland*, pp. 1–2, 3.

157. Ibid., pp. 4–5.

158. Ibid., p. 6.

159. Ibid., pp. 9–10.

160. Ibid., pp. 67, 69–71.

161. Ibid., pp. 225–6.

162. [Leslie], *Answer*, 'To the Reader', sigs. d–d^v.

163. Ibid., p. 46.

164. Ibid., p. 47.

165. *Jacobite Narrative*, pp. 171, 183–4.

166. Tony Claydon, *William III and the Godly Revolution* (Cambridge,

1996), pp. 140–2.

167. Cox, *Hibernia Anglicana . . . Second Part*, sig. A3v.

168. [King], *State of the Protestants of Ireland*, p. 7.

169. *A True Relation of a Horrid and Barbarous Murder* (1689), pp. 1–2.

170. *The Present Condition of London-Derry* (1689), p. 2.

171. NLI, MS 8651, Charles Thompson to Henry Gascoigne, Chester, 9 Apr. 1689.

172. EUL, La. III. 350, no. 289.

173. *HMC, Ormonde*, N.S. VIII, 363.

174. BL, MS Egerton 917, fol. 105; *An Account of the Transactions of the Late King James* (1690), p. 62; *A Full and Particular Account of the Seizing and Imprisonment of the Duke of Tyrconnel* (1690), p. 2.

175. Murtagh and Murtagh, 'Irish Jacobite Army', p. 33.

176. *HMC, Ormonde*, N.S. VIII, 381–2.

177. *Journal of the Proceedings of the Parliament in Ireland*, p. 17. Cf. *HMC, Ormonde*, N.S. VIII, 366.

178. *A List of All the Irish Army in Ireland under the Late King James* (1690); *Present Condition of London-Derry*, p. 2.

179. *A Letter to a Friend, Concerning the Present State of the Army in Ireland* (1690).

180. *Four Questions Debated* (1689), pp. 4–5.

181. *Account of the Transactions of the Late King James*, p. 22.

182. Ibid., pp. 10–13, 16–19; *Merc. Ref.*, II, no. 8 (29 Jan. 1690); *The Present State of Affairs in Ireland* (1690), p. 2; *The Last Paper of Advice from Ireland* (1690); [King], *State of the Protestants of Ireland*, pp. 133–41; Morrice, Q, 589. For Jacobite discussions of economic problems in Ireland, and the pros and cons of brass money, see: O'Kelly, *Macariae Excidium*, pp. 98–101; *Jacobite Narrative*, p. 54; *Life of James II*, II, 370, 386–7. For a modern discussion, see Robert Heslip, 'Brass Money', in Maguire, ed., *Kings in Conflict*, pp. 122–35.

183. *Full and Particular Account of the Seizing . . . of Tyrconnel*.

184. [King], *State of the Protestants of Ireland*, p. 16.

185. *Account of the Transactions of the Late King James*, p. 4.

186. Luttrell, I. 566.

187. [King], *State of the Protestants of Ireland*, pp. 217–19; *Last Paper of Advice from Ireland*, p. 2; TCD, 1995–2008/70.

188. [King], *State of the Protestants of Ireland*, pp. 208–13 (quote on p. 208); *HMC, Ormonde*, N.S. VIII, 369, 374–5; Steele, II, no. 1084; *HMC, Ormonde*, II, 418–19.

189. *An Account of the Late Action and Defeat* (1690).

190. NLI, MS Joly 27, p. 15.

191. Luttrell, I, 592, 609; Morrice, R, 19; *HMC, Ormonde*, N.S. VIII, 373.

192. Cox, *Hibernia Anglicana . . . Second Part*, sigs. c–c2.

193. Morrice, Q, 626; John Vesey, *A Sermon Preach'd to the Protestants of Ireland in and about the City of London* (1689); Daniel Williams, *The Protestants' Deliverance from the Irish Rebellion* (1690).

194. Richard Tenison, *A Sermon Preach'd to the Protestants of Ireland* (1691).

195. Wetenhall, *Sermon Setting Forth the Duties*.

196. Williams, *Protestants' Deliverance*, pp. 9–10.

197. Tenison, *Sermon Preach'd to the Protestants of Ireland*, p. 20.

198. Vesey, *Sermon Preach'd to the Protestants of Ireland*, p. 29.

199. Wetenhall, *Sermon Setting Forth the Duties*, pp. 13, 15–16.

200. Tenison, *Sermon Preach'd to the Protestants of Ireland*, p. 25.

201. Ibid., pp. 24–5.

202. Williams, *Protestants' Deliverance*, p.10; Vesey, *Sermon Preach'd to the Protestants of Ireland*, pp. 28–30.

203. Tenison, *Sermon Preach'd to the Protestants of Ireland*, pp. 14, 16.

204. Ibid., p. 25.

205. Wetenhall, *Sermon Setting Forth the Duties*, pp. 16, 18–19.

206. *Short View of the Methods*, pp. 19–20.

207. [Leslie], *Answer*, p. 85.

208. Gilbert Burnet, *History of His Own Time: From the Restoration of King Charles the Second to the Treaty of Peace at Utrecht, in the Reign of Queen Anne* (1850), p. 572.

209. Story, *Continuation of the Impartial History*, pp. 273–5.

210. Wetenhall, *Sermon Setting Forth the Duties*, p. 18.

211. Boyse, *Vindication of the Reverend Mr Alexander Osborn*, p. 27; Simms, *Jacobite Ireland*, pp. 100–1; McBride, *Siege of Derry*, pp. 20–32.

212. [Leslie], *Answer*, p. 84.

213. Ibid., p. 164.

214. Ibid., p. 185.

215. *Jacobite Narrative*, p. 104.

216. TCD, MS 1180, p. 131.

217. Morrice, R, 221.

218. CUL, Add. 1, fol. 87v.

219. Murtagh and Murtagh, 'Irish Jacobite Army', p. 32.

220. Story, *Continuation of the Impartial History*, p. 292.

221. O'Kelly, *Macariae Excidium*, pp. 156–7.

222. Ibid., p. 311 (note 93).

223. Ó Ciardha, *Ireland and the Jacobite Cause*, p. 83.

224. Simms, *Jacobite Ireland*, p. 153 (note 69).

225. O'Kelly, *Macariae Excidium*, pp. 96–7; *Jacobite Narrative*, pp. 50, 63. Cf. John Gerard Barry, 'The Groans of Ireland', *The Irish Sword*, 2, no. 6 (Summer, 1955), 133.

226. Ó Ciardha, *Ireland and the Jacobite Cause*, pp. 83, 86; S. J. Connolly, *Religion, Law and Power: The Making of Protestant Ireland, 1660–1760* (Oxford, 1992), pp. 233–45. For the retaliatory legislation, see below pp. 502–6.

227. *Jacobite Narrative*, pp. 54–5, 80, 184, 188–9.

228. HMC, *Ormonde*, N.S. VIII, 359.

229. Cox, *Hibernica Anglicana . . . Second Part*, sig. c2.

Conclusion

1. *Life of James II*, II, 585–6, 591–9; John Miller, *James II: A Study in Kingship* (Hove, 1978, 3rd edn 2000), pp. 234, 239–40. For a recent reassessment of James's Catholic piety, see Geoffrey Scott, 'The Court as a Centre of Catholicism', in Edward Corp (with contributions by Edward Gregg, Howard Erskine-Hill and Geoffrey Scott), *A Court in Exile: The Stuarts in France, 1689–1718* (Cambridge, 2004), pp. 235–56.

2. [Charlwood Lawton], *The Jacobite Principles Vindicated* (1693), pp. 8–9.

3. *Life of James II*, II, 278, 608–9.

4. Dalrymple, *Memoirs*, II, 'Part I. Continued. Appendix to Book V', p. 53.

5. *The Diary of Dr. Thomas Cartwright, Bishop of Chester*, ed. Rev. Joseph Hunter, Camden Society, old series, 22 (1843), p. 48.

6. Miller, *James II*, p. 240.

7. APS, VII, 554–5; NLS, Wod. MSS Qu. XXXVIII, fol. 2; Gilbert Burnet, *History of His Own Time: From the Restoration of King Charles the Second to the Treaty of Peace at Utrecht, in the Reign of Queen Anne* (1850), p. 192; *Lauderdale Papers*, ed. Osmund Airy, Camden Society, new series (3 vols., 1884–5), II, 164.

8. HMC, *Laing*, I, 443.

9. [William King], *The State of the Protestants of Ireland under the Late King James's Government* (1691), p. 71.

10. Angus McInnes, 'When was the English Revolution?', *History*, 117 (1982), 377–92.

11. Steven Pincus, 'The Making of a Great Power? Universal Monarchy, Political Economy, and the Transformation of English Political Culture', *The European Legacy*, 5 (2000), pp. 533–4; Steven Pincus, '"To Protect English

Liberties": The English Nationalist Revolution of 1688–1689', in Tony Claydon and Ian McBride, eds., *Protestantism and National Identity: Britain and Ireland, c.1650–c.1850* (Cambridge, 1998), pp. 75–104.

12. D. W. Jones, *War and Economy in the Age of William III and Marlborough* (1988), pp. 29, 70–1; E. A. Reitan, 'From Revenue to Civil List, 1689–1702: The Revolution Settlement and the "Mixed and Balanced" Constitution', *Historical Journal*, 13 (1970), 571–88; Wilfrid Prest, *Albion Ascendant: English History 1660–1815* (Oxford, 1998), pp. 83–5; Geoffrey Holmes, *The Making of a Great Power: Late Stuart and Early Georgian Britain, 1660–1722* (Harlow, 1993), ch. 17; P. G. M. Dickson, *The Financial Revolution in England: A Study in the Development of Public Credit, 1688–1756* (1967); John Brewer, *The Sinews of Power: War, Money and the English State, 1688–1787* (New York, 1989), ch. 4.

13. Pincus, 'The Making of a Great Power?', pp. 535–41.

14. Holmes, *The Making of a Great Power*, p. 224.

15. Ibid., ch. 16.

16. *SR*, VI, 510.

17. *SR*, VII, 152; W. C. Braithwaite, *The Second Period of Quakerism* (Cambridge, 1961), pp. 183–4.

18. *SR*, VII, 636–8.

19. Useful surveys, to which the following account is heavily indebted, are: William Ferguson, *Scotland 1689 to the Present* (1968), chs. 1–2; William Ferguson, *Scotland's Relations with England: A Survey to 1707* (Edinburgh, 1977), chs. 9–14; Jim Smyth, *The Making of the United Kingdom, 1660–1800* (Harlow, 2001), ch. 5; P. W. J. Riley, *The Union of England and Scotland: A Study in Anglo-Scottish Politics of the Eighteenth Century* (Manchester, 1978); Christopher A. Whatley, *Bought and Sold for English Gold? Explaining the Union of 1707* (2nd edn, East Linton, 2001). For the broader context, see Brian P. Levack, *The Formation of the British State: England, Scotland, and the Union of 1603–1707* (Oxford, 1987).

20. Paul Hopkins, *Glencoe and the End of the Highland War* (Edinburgh, 1986), esp. ch. 10.

21. Christopher A. Whatley, *Scottish Society, 1707–1830* (Manchester, 2000), p. 38.

22. Andrew Fletcher, 'Speech by a Member of the Parliament Which Began at Edinburgh the 6th of May, 1703', in *Political Works*, ed. John Robertson (Cambridge, 1997), p. 147.

23. George Ridpath, *Proceedings of the Scottish Parliament* (Edinburgh, 1704), pp. 304–6.

24. *APS*, XI, 74, 136–7.

25. *SR*, VIII, 349–50.

26. *APS*, XI, 404–6.

27. From Ferguson, *Scotland 1689 to the Present*, pp. 52–3; Riley, *Union of England and Scotland*, p. 303.

28. *APS*, XI, 406–14; *SR*, VIII, 566–77.

29. Riley, *Union of England and Scotland*, pp. 224–5.

30. Karin Bowie, 'Public Opinion, Popular Politics and the Union of 1707', *Scottish Historical Review*, 82 (2003), 226–60 (figs. on pp. 229 (and note 13), 251); John R. Young, 'The Parliamentary Incorporating Union of 1707: Political Management, Anti-Unionism and Foreign Policy', in T. M. Devine and J. R. Young, eds., *Eighteenth-Century Scotland: New Perspectives* (East Linton, 1999), pp. 24–52; Whatley, *Bought and Sold for English Gold?*, pp. 59–60, 75–8; Ferguson, *Scotland's Relations with England*, pp. 267–9; David Hayton, 'Constitutional Experiments and Political Expediency, 1689–1725', in Steven G. Ellis and Sarah Barber, eds., *Conquest and Union: Fashioning a British State, 1485–1725* (1995), pp. 288–9.

31. Smyth, *The Making of the United Kingdom*, p. 99; Tim Harris, *Politics under the Later Stuarts* (1993), pp. 153–4; Jeffrey Stephen, 'The Kirk and the Union, 1706–07: A Reappraisal', *RSCHS*, 31 (2002), 68–96.

32. Ferguson, *Scotland 1689 to the Present*, pp. 110–11.

33. Patrick Kelly, 'Ireland and the Glorious Revolution: From Kingdom to Colony', in Robert Beddard, ed., *The Revolutions of 1688* (Oxford, 1988), p. 189.

34. This section draws on J. G. Simms, *Williamite Confiscation in Ireland 1690–1703* [1956]; W. A. Maguire, 'The Land Settlement', in Maguire, ed., *Kings in Conflict: The Revolutionary War in Ireland and its Aftermath 1689–1750* (Belfast, 1990), pp. 139–56.

35. *The Statutes at Large, Passed in the Parliaments held in Ireland . . . A.D. 1310 to . . . A.D. 1800* (21 vols., Dublin, 1786–1804), III, 343–8.

36. The definitive study is S. J. Connolly, *Religion, Law and Power: The Making of Protestant Ireland, 1660–1760* (Oxford, 1992). General surveys are also provided by S. J. Connolly, 'The Penal Laws', in Maguire, ed., *Kings in Conflict*, pp. 157–72; Thomas Bartlett, *The Fall and Rise of the Irish Nation: The Catholic Question 1690–1830* (Savage, Md., 1992), ch. 2; J. C. Beckett, *The Making of Modern Ireland 1603–1923* (1966), ch. 8; R. F. Foster, *Modern Ireland, 1600–1972* (1988), pp. 153–8; J. G. Simms, 'The Establishment of Protestant Ascendancy, 1691–1714', in T. W. Moody, F. X. Martin, F. J. Byrne and Art Cosgrove, eds., *A New History of Ireland* (9 vols., Oxford, 1976–84), V, ch. 1; Marcus Tanner, *Ireland's Holy Wars: The*

Struggle for a Nation's Soul, 1500–2000 (New Haven, Conn. and London, 2001), pp. 162–5. My account draws heavily on these sources.

37. Bartlett, *Fall and Rise*, pp. 20–1; Connolly, 'Penal Laws', p. 166; J. G. Simms, 'The Making of a Penal Law (2 Anne c. 6) 1703–4' and 'The Bishops' Banishment Act of 1697', both in Simms, *War and Politics in Ireland, 1649–1730*, ed. D. W. Hayton and Gerard O'Brien (1986), pp. 235–49, 263–76.

38. Charles Ivar McGrath, 'Securing the Protestant Interest: The Origins and Purpose of the Penal Laws of 1695', *Irish History Studies*, 30 (1996), 25–46. For a more extreme view, that the penal laws were designed, through social engineering, to transform Ireland into a Protestant country in one or two generations, see R. E. Burns, 'The Irish Popery Laws: A Study in Eighteenth-Century Legislation and Behaviour', *Review of Politics*, 24 (1962), 485–508. A useful discussion of the contours of the historiographical debate can be found in S. J. Connolly, 'Religion and Liberty', *Irish Economic and Social History*, 10 (1983), 73–9.

39. *SR*, VI, 254–7.

40. *Statutes at Large . . . Ireland*, III, 241–3.

41. James I. McGuire, 'The Irish Parliament of 1692', in Thomas Bartlett and D. W. Hayton, eds., *Penal Era and Golden Age: Essays in Irish History, 1690–1800* (1979), pp. 1–31; Simms, 'Establishment of Protestant Ascendancy', p. 2.

42. *Statutes at Large . . . Ireland*, III, 254–67 (quotes on pp. 254, 259).

43. Ibid., pp. 339–43 (quote on p. 339).

44. Ibid., pp. 343–8.

45. Ibid., pp. 349–53.

46. Ibid., pp. 512–14, IV, 121–5.

47. Ibid., IV, 5–6 (quote on p. 5).

48. Ibid., pp. 12–31.

49. Ibid., pp. 31–7.

50. Ibid., pp. 190–216.

51. Connolly, 'Religion and Liberty', p. 77.

52. Bartlett, *Fall and Rise*, pp. 28–9.

53. Connolly, 'Penal Laws', pp. 169–71, 193 (note 15).

54. The following account draws on: J. C. Beckett, *Protestant Dissent in Ireland, 1687–1780* (1948), chs. 1–7; David Hayton, ed., *Ireland after the Glorious Revolution* (Belfast, 1986), pp. 6–10, 17–25; Phil Kilroy, *Protestant Dissent and Controversy in Ireland, 1660–1714* (Cork, 1994), pp. 188–98.

55. Simms, 'Protestant Ascendancy', in Moody et al., eds., *New History of Ireland*, IV, 23; J. L. McCracken, 'The Social Structure and Social Life,

1714–60', in Moody et al., eds., *New History of Ireland*, IV, 39; L. M. Cullen, 'Economic Development, 1691–1750', in Moody et al., eds., *New History of Ireland*, IV, 134; Hayton, *Ireland after the Glorious Revolution*, p. 7.

56. Beckett, *Protestant Dissent*, p. 46; J. S. Reid, *A History of the Presbyterian Church in Ireland*, ed. W. D. Killen (3 vols., Belfast, 1867), II, 527.

57. Beckett, *Protestant Dissent*, pp. 48–9.

58. *Statutes at Large . . . Ireland*, IV, 508–16.

59. Tim Harris, *Restoration: Charles II and His Kingdoms, 1660–85* (2005), pp. 25–6.

60. Smyth, *The Making of the United Kingdom*, p. 88; Aiden Clarke, 'Colonial Attitudes in Ireland, 1640–1660', *Proceedings of the Royal Irish Academy*, 90 C, no. 11 (1990), 357–75.

61. H. F. Kearney, 'The Political Background to English Mercantilism, 1695–1700', *Economic History Review*, 2nd ser. 11 (1959), 484–96; Patrick Kelly, 'The Irish Woollen Export Prohibition Act of 1699: Kearney revisited', *Irish Economic and Social History*, 7 (1980), 22–44.

62. William Molyneux, *The Case of Ireland's Being Bound by Acts of Parliament in England Stated* (Dublin, 1698), pp. 12–13, 29; Kelly, 'Ireland and the Glorious Revolution', pp. 186–7; Patrick Kelly, 'Recasting a Tradition: William Molyneux and the Sources of *The Case of Ireland . . . Stated* (1698)', in Jane H. Ohlmeyer, ed., *Political Thought in Seventeenth-Century Ireland* (Cambridge, 2000), pp. 83–106; Jim Smyth, '"Like Amphibious Animals": Irish Protestants, Ancient Britons, 1691–1707', *Historical Journal*, 36 (1993), 785–97: J.G. Simms, *William Molyneux of Dublin 1656–1698*, ed. P. H. Kelly (Naas, 1982), pp. 111–13; Jacqueline Hill, 'Ireland without Union: Molyneux and his Legacy', in John Robertson, ed., *A Union for Empire: Political Thought and the British Union of 1707* (Cambridge, 1995), pp. 271–96.

63. Molyneux, *Case*, pp. 97–8.

64. Jacqueline Hill, *From Patriots to Unionists: Dublin Civic Patriots and Irish Protestant Patriotism, 1660–1840* (Oxford, 1997), p. 11; *English Historical Documents 1660–1714*, ed. Andrew Browning (1953), pp. 780–1; Smyth, '"Amphibious Animals"', pp. 792–7; Smyth, *The Making of the United Kingdom*, pp. 99–102; James Kelly, 'The Origins of the Act of Union: An Examination of Unionist Opinion in Britain and Ireland, 1650–1800', *Irish History Studies*, 25 (1986–7), 236–63. See also [Henry Maxwell], *An Essay upon an Union with England* (Dublin, 1704).

65. SR, XIV, 204–5; Kelly, 'Ireland and the Glorious Revolution', pp. 188–9;

J.L. McCracken, 'The Rise of Colonial Nationalism, 1714–60', in Moody et al., eds., *New History of Ireland*, V, 110–11.

66. Kelly, 'Ireland and the Glorious Revolution'. Cf. Connolly, *Religion, Law and Power*, pp. 105–14, who challenges the helpfulness of labelling Ireland a colony.

67. J. S. Morrill, *The Nature of the English Revolution* (1993), pp. 1, 17.

68. Lawrence Stone, 'The Results of the English Revolutions of the Seventeenth Century', in J. G. A. Pocock, ed., *Three British Revolutions: 1641, 1688, 1776* (Princeton, N.J., 1980), p. 24.

69. Tim Harris, 'The Legacy of the English Civil War: Rethinking the Revolution', *The European Legacy*, 5 (2000), 501–14.

70. A point made by Ian McBride in his '"The Common Name of Irishman": Protestantism and Patriotism in Eighteenth-Century Ireland', in Tony Claydon and Ian McBride, eds., *Protestantism and National Identity: Britain and Ireland c.1650–c.1850* (Cambridge, 1998), pp. 242–3.

71. Hayton, 'Constitutional Experiments', p. 303; Connolly, *Religion, Law and Power*, pp. 108–9; Hill, 'Ireland without Union', pp. 289–90; J. C. Beckett, *Confrontations: Studies in Irish History* (1972), pp. 124–5.

Index

uprisings 124, 125
Clarges, Sir Thomas 97, 98, 321, 327–8
Claridge, Samuel 135
Clarke, Robert 111
Claverhouse, Earl of 178, 380, 381
see also Dundee, Viscount
Cleland, William 368
'Clerical Cabal, The' 239
Clonmel 111
Cochrane, Sir John 66, 75, 78
Cogadh an Dá Rí 422
Coke, Sir Edward 193, 194, 338, 345
Coke, John 98
Colchester, Lord 283
Coleraine 508
Collins, Dr John 217–18
commonwealthmen 316–19
Compton, Henry, Bishop of London
  Catholic toleration 96–7, 99, 100
  Ecclesiastical Commission 202, 204,
    206, 341
  Glorious Revolution 285, 306
  letter to William of Orange 3, 271–2
  pledge to restore 277
  Revolution settlement 319
Confession of Faith 1643 (Scotland) 407
Congregationalists 218, 219
Connor, Mr 426
contract theory 314–15, 358–9, 408, 455
Conventicle Act 1670 (England) 207, 248
Conventicle Act 1670 (Scotland) 21–2
Convention (England) 313–20
  Declaration of Rights 329–48
  James's abdication 320–28
  post-Declaration of Rights settlement
    348–54
Convention (Scotland) 364, 380, 386–91,
  487, 489
  Revolution settlement 391–409
Convention of Royal Burghs 178
Cork (city) 138, 433, 447
Cork (county) 124
Cork, Bishop of 438
Cornbury, Viscount 284
Cornish, Henry 89
Cornwall 49
coronation
  James II 44, 48, 59–60, 69
  William and Mary 349, 355
coronation oath
  England 395–6
  Scotland 404, 405–6
Corporation Act 1661 (England) 84
corporations 55, 206
  England 189, 277; Declaration of
    Indulgence 221–3; James's accession

50–51, 52; Monmouth's rebellion
  84; purge 232–4; Revolution
  settlement 352
  Ireland 116, 118, 134–6, 137, 447–8;
    under William and Anne 508, 509
county commissions of the peace 231–2,
  276–7
Court of High Commission 203
Coventry 201, 219, 222, 229, 230, 355
Coventry Letter 132–3
Cox, Sir Richard 463, 467–8, 476
Cranston, Alexander 90
Craven, Earl of 302
Crawford, Earl of 371, 372, 381, 382,
  406, 418, 421
Crockatt, Gilbert 418
Croft, Bishop of Hereford 261
Cromdale 411
Cromwell, Oliver 23, 102, 337
crowd, *see* out-of-doors politics
Cumberland 51, 281, 286
Cumnock, Ayrshire 378
Curtois, John 58, 59, 63
customs and excise
  England 44–5, 49–50, 71–2, 188, 491
  Ireland 102, 121–2, 139
  Scotland 411

d'Adda, Ferdinando 196
Daes, James 167
Dalrymple, Sir James, *see* Stair, Sir James
  Dalrymple of
Dalrymple, Sir John 478
  appointment by James 167, 181
  committee of elections 388
  political union 390–91, 497
  and William of Orange 368, 371, 381,
    405, 406
Dalzeell, Sir John 162
Danby, Earl of 281
  bail 344
  bishops' trial 264
  Catholic toleration 211, 224
  letter to William of Orange 3, 271
  Mary of Modena's pregnancy 258–9
  pardon 332
  Revolution settlement 328
  Williamite resistance movement 4, 285,
    288–90
  William's draft manifesto 279
Dangerfield, Thomas 234
Dare, Thomas 344
Darien scheme 495–6
Dartford 299
Dartmouth, Lord 296
d'Avaux, Comte 428, 445

and Argyll's rebellion 77–8, 87
Ireland 102
and Monmouth's rebellion 74–5, 79,
    84, 89–90
parliament 346
plotters 62, 82, 251, 368
punishments 344, 345
torture 399–400

Sacheverell, William 56, 330
Saffron Walden 233
Sage, John 419
St Albans 55, 56
St David's 219
St Germain-en-Laye 362, 477
Salisbury, Dean of 51
Salisbury, Earl of 198, 267, 294, 297
Salisbury Plain 275, 284, 294–5
Saltash 48
Sancroft, Archbishop of Canterbury 217,
    224, 277, 285, 319
    Ecclesiastical Commission 202
    letters from Scottish bishops 383
    Revolution settlement 362
    second Declaration of Indulgence 259,
        260, 264–9
Sandwich, Kent 248
Sanquhar, Dumfriesshire 78
Sarsfield, Patrick, Earl of Lucan 295, 449,
    474
Savoy, Duke of 186
Sawyer, Sir Robert 266, 323
Scarborough 53, 223
Schomberg, Duke of 295
schools 130, 224
Scotland 30–31, 101–2, 144–7, 179–81,
    236, 408
    absolutism 482–4
    Argyll's rebellion 73–4, 75–8, 86, 87–8
    black rainy Parliament 153–65
    Charles II 24
    and England 184–5
    Exclusion Crisis 32–3
    Glorious Revolution 12, 13, 15, 35,
        36, 364–78, 487, 489, 512,
        515–16; balance of forces 379–86;
        Convention 386–91; implications
        494–500; settlement 391–409
    growth of discontent 147–53
    and Ireland 23, 431
    James II 33–4
    James's accession 40, 43, 44, 46, 47,
        48–9, 53–4, 65
    loyalist sermons 58–9, 60
    Monmouth's rebellion 86
    parliament 55, 67, 68–71

prerogative, indulgence and the rap-
    prochement with dissent 165–79,
    211
religious toleration 481–2
Restoration settlement 20–22
Revolution settlement 321, 328, 333,
    347, 351; battle over 409–21
standing army 275, 277, 411
Tory Reaction 28
William of Orange's *Declaration* 280
Scott, James, *see* Monmouth, Duke of
Scottish Presbyterians, *see* Ulster
Presbyterians
Seaforth, Earl of 166
*Second Apology for the Protestants of
Ireland, The* (Philips) 273
Sedgemoor 75, 79, 80–81, 88
seditious rhymes 61–2
Sedley, Catherine 9
Selkirk 410
Selkirk, Mr 418
Seymour, Sir Edward 72, 97–8, 283, 313,
    326, 330
Shaftesbury, Earl of 31, 56, 251, 336
Sharp, Anthony 135
Sharp, James, Archbishop of St Andrews
    22, 77
Sharp, John, Dean of Norwich 50, 202,
    325
Shaw, Lord, of Greenock 371
Sheere, Joseph 357
Sheffield 217
Sheldon, Ralph 296
Sheridan, Thomas 127–8, 137, 138
Sheridan, William 458
sheriffs 116, 117, 128
Sherlock, Dr William 60–61, 199, 215,
    239, 243, 259, 262–3, 326
    Revolution settlement 319, 320, 359,
        361
Sherlock v. Annesley 512
Shields, Alexander 173, 364, 370, 374,
    417
Shiell, George 149
Shorter, Sir John 223, 232, 235
Shrewsbury 48, 229, 230, 294
Shrewsbury, Earl of 3, 179, 271, 282, 283
Sibbald, Dr Robert 148, 151
Sidney, Henry 3, 271, 282
Sidney Sussex College, Cambridge 225,
    293
Sittingbourne 299
Sligo, County 430, 433
Smith, George 357
Smith, Stephen 122
Smith, Stephen the younger 122

Smith, Tabitha 91
Smith, Thomas 63
Smitten, Christopher 63
Smyth, William 415
Society People, see Cameronians
Solemn League and Covenant (Scotland)
    21, 408
Somers, Sir John 266, 328, 330, 334, 354
Somerset 92–3, 219, 283
Somerset, Duke of 208
Sophia, Princess, Electress of Hanover 493
Southampton 52
Southwell, Sir Thomas 466
Spalding 91
Speke, Hugh 294
Spence, William 77–8, 399–400
Spencer, Lord 184
Sprat, Thomas, Bishop of Rochester 202,
    219, 261, 269, 277, 481
Stafford 294
Staffordshire 223
Stair, Sir James Dalrymple of 167, 382
    appointment by William 406
    Convention 394
    political union 390–91, 497
    Williamite conspiracy 268, 279, 282,
        381
Stamford 357
Stamford, James 200
standing army
    England 95–100, 183, 187–91, 205,
        233, 267; Declaration of Rights
        336, 337, 341–3; dispensing power
        191–5; Revolution settlement 331
    Scotland 399
State of the Protestants of Ireland Under
    the Late King James's Government
    (King) 458–60, 473
Stephens, Edward 316
Stern, Peter 123
Stewart, James 257
Stillingfleet, Edward 199, 259
Story, George 471–2
Strachan, William 417, 418, 420
Strafford, Countess 190
Street, Justice 194
Strickland, Sir Roger 198, 282
Stroud-Water, Gloucestershire 223
Stuart, James Francis Edward, Prince of
    Wales 296, 505
    birth 2–3, 239, 242, 258, 269–71,
        367–8, 424–5
    exclusion from succession 393
    William of Orange's Declaration 280
Subjection for Conscience Sake Asserted
    (Burnet) 287

succession 493, 496–7, 505
    see also Exclusion Crisis
Succession Act 1681 (Scotland) 32, 44, 54,
    73, 396
Sunderland, Earl of 43, 96, 195, 256, 276,
    294, 478
    1685 elections 55
    bishops' trial 265
    conversion to Catholicism 198
    Declaration of Indulgence 219, 220,
        481
    Ecclesiastical Commission 202
    Ireland 105, 132
    Monmouth 63–4
suspending power 212–13, 241, 301, 483
    Declaration of Rights 336, 337
    Revolution settlement 331
Sutherland, Earl of 381, 382
Swinton, Alexander 167

Talbot, Richard, see Tyrconnell, Earl of
Tamworth 267
Tarbat, Viscount 148, 179, 478
    Catholic toleration 154, 159
    Convention 390
    Dundee's rebellion 410
    Glorious Revolution 371, 381, 383–4,
        386
    Memorial 175, 417, 419
    political union 390–91
Taunton 85, 92, 224, 300
tax farming 402
Teddington, Middlesex 190
Temple, Sir John 468
Temple, Sir Richard 45, 360
Tenison, Richard, Bishop of Killala 468,
    469, 470
Tenison, Thomas 199
Test Act 1673 (England) 28, 117, 351
    army 96, 97, 98, 99
    dispensations 192–5, 235, 338, 339–40
Test Act 1678 (England) 28, 351
Test Act 1681 (Scotland) 28, 33, 68, 70,
    145, 398
    Argyll 73–4
    dispensations 167, 176–7
    repeal 153, 157–8
Tests, William of Orange 256–7
Thanet, Earl of 97
Tillotson, John 199, 259, 351
Toleration Act 1689 (England) 350–52,
    354
Toleration Act 1712 (Great Britain)
    499–500
Toleration Act 1719 (Ireland) 509
Tor Bay 4–5, 274